INTERPRETATIVE REPORTING

INTERPRETATIVE

SEVENTH EDITION

REPORTING

CURTIS D. MACDOUGALL, PH.D., LITT.D.

Professor Emeritus of Journalism, Northwestern University

MACMILLAN PUBLISHING CO., INC.

NEW YORK

COLLIER MACMILLAN PUBLISHERS

LONDON

Earlier edition entitled *Reporting for Beginners* copyright 1932 by
Macmillan Publishing Co., Inc. Earlier editions entitled *Interpretative Reporting*
copyright 1938 and 1948 and © 1957 and 1963 by Macmillan Publishing Co., Inc.,
copyright © 1968 and 1972 by Curtis D. MacDougall.
Copyright renewed 1960, 1966, and 1976 by Curtis D. MacDougall.

Macmillan Publishing Co., Inc.
866 Third Ave., New York, N.Y. 10022

Collier Macmillan Canada, Ltd.

Library of Congress Cataloging in Publication Data

MacDougall, Curtis Daniel, (date)
  Interpretative reporting.

  Includes index.
1. Journalism.   2. Reporters and reporting.
1. Title.
PN4781.M153   1977   070.4'3   75-30864
ISBN 0-02-373110-9

Printing: 1 2 3 4 5 6 7 8   Year: 7 8 9 0 1 2 3

This book is dedicated to my wife,
Genevieve Rockwood MacDougall

PREFACE

This book now has endured for almost a half century. It first appeared in 1932 entitled *Reporting for Beginners.* When it was revised in 1938 the title was changed to the present one and, for copyright purposes, the count had to begin again. So this is really the eighth edition. It contains some of the material and examples that appeared in the 1932 edition, which suggests the reason for its longevity: it has stressed fundamentals, which don't change. It has remained a " how to do it " book for reporters, newsgatherers, journalistic fact finders whose task remains the same despite any changes in media production and/or distribution.

" Real live journalists " have helped to keep this book timely and fresh. I have solicited and valued the advice and assistance of professional practitioners above that of behavioral scientists, communicologists, McLuhanites and other theorists who'd have a difficult time figuring out how to cover a fire. The perspective never has been that of the trade school advocate. I stirred up a storm merely by changing the title at a time when interpretation was still a dirty word in most editorial offices. The book's objective always has been to demonstrate how mastery of the fundamentals leads to their socially constructive use.

Throughout the book's lifetime journalistic fads have come and gone. In the '40s publishers went overboard for Rudolf Flesch and readability testing. They spent millions in the futile effort to discover the proper word and sentence lengths to increase circulation. Finally, rebelling writers convinced them of the impossibility of writing by formula. However, for several editions of this book I had to devote considerable space to the phenomenon, as some journalism teachers were taken in also. A few post mortem remarks on readability tests and on semantics, another onetime fad, appear in Chapter 6.

More recently it has been New Journalism, a term used to include a great many supposedly innovative techniques about which a quantity of articles have been written. The sixth edition of this book appeared two years earlier than was originally planned to take cognizance of the situation. Today fortunately a state of comparative sanity has been restored but alarm is now sounded because of the technological revolution in newspaper production methods. Oldtimers scream, young staff members catch on easily and soon everyone gets used to having clean newsroom floors rather than overflowing wastebaskets. Editors continue to think up assignments and reporters continue to cover them.

Today's biggest excitement is over Investigative Reporting, inspired by the feats of Bob Woodward and Carl Bernstein, Jack Anderson, Seymour Hersh and other contemporary counterparts of a long list of journalistic crusaders and/or muckrakers of the past. See the new Chapter 10 on modern trends for details.

The major problem in revising a book is deciding what to eliminate to make room for new material so as not to increase the size of the volume. Dated examples naming former presidents or mentioning streetcars and the like obviously must be replaced, but I have learned that teachers who have used the book for a long time do not like wholesale changes. They become fond of certain examples which they have learned to use effectively in the classroom. My rule is: don't replace unless there's something better. In early editions there were examples of foreign correspondence and national news. In recent editions there have been only examples with immediate educational value for the cub reporter. They illustrate assignments he might expect to receive comparatively early in his career or to which he might aspire before long. I wish there were room for many more examples, but teachers and students can find good ones in the daily press.

Ideally *Interpretative Reporting* should be the basic text for three semesters of a journalism curriculum. Thereafter it should be a valuable reference work. It should not be skipped over lightly. There has been too much shortcutting of education within the past generation. In our field editors are beginning to complain even about the poor spelling and grammatical ignorance of recent graduates, as well as the low quality of their reporting and writing. Professional journalism organizations are becoming aroused as never before. They are forming committees, holding seminars and making studies. One committee of the Associated Press Managing Editors already has deplored the downplaying of reporting in many journalism schools once considered the best. The APME report recommends that students be informed that they are not being prepared adequately and that nobody is likely to employ them.

All the behavioral scientific gobbledegook does not change the fact that the fundamental purpose of journalism is reporting which means newsgathering and fact finding. All journalism is really reporting. New theories and methodologies are not going to change the basic responsibility of the journalistic media to serve the cause of democracy which is why the free press exists.

This book continues to be dedicated to the purpose of providing a guide to the training of the kind of journalists that the contemporary world needs.

Curtis D. MacDougall

ACKNOWLEDGMENTS

It would take at least five pages to list the names of all who have rendered assistance to me during the 45 years of this book's existence. A fairly complete list appeared in the sixth edition. Most of their contributions and suggestions are still reflected in this edition. The following list, however, is restricted to those who contributed new material or ideas specifically for this edition. To all, my deepest gratitude.

Baden, Leon, copy desk chief, Harrisburg (Pa.) *Evening News*
Bernays, Edward L., Cambridge, Mass., " father " of public relations
Black, Creed, editor, Philadelphia *Inquirer*
Block, Mervin, assistant professor of journalism, University of Illinois
Botts, Jack C., professor of journalism, University of Nebraska
Brier, Warren C., journalism dean, University of Montana
Brown, Fred, Denver *Post*
Bukro, Casey, environment editor, Chicago *Tribune*
Cade, Dr. Dozier, journalism director, University of Tennessee
Carty, James W., professor of journalism, Bethany College
Cento, W. F., public relations editor, St. Paul *Dispatch* and *Pioneer Press*
Childs, Richard, National Municipal League
Driscoll, Thomas, managing editor, Peoria *Journal-Star*
Edelstein, Alex S., director, School of Communications, University of Washington
Finnegan, John R., executive editor, St. Paul *Dispatch* and *Pioneer Press*
Foster, Creston J., director of communications, American Farm Bureau Federation
Fulks, J. R., formerly Chicago office, United States Weather Service
Full, Jerome, New York tourist trade public relations counsel
Graham, Patrick, assistant city editor, Milwaukee *Journal*
Halbe, James, assistant professor of journalism, University of South Florida
Howey, Jack E., managing editor, Peru (Ind.) *Daily Tribune*
Jinks, Larry, executive editor, Miami *Herald*
Kendrick, Richard, Waukegan *News-Sun*
Krieghbaum, Hillier, professor emeritus of journalism, New York University
Linford, Ernest, professor of journalism, University of Wyoming
Lund, Eric, assistant managing editor, news, Chicago *Daily News*
MacDougall, A. Kent, associate professor of journalism, American University
McDonald, Stewart, executive director, American Newspaper Publishers Association
Nenno, Mary K., director, Policy and Research Division, National Association of Housing and Redevelopment Officials

Nofziger, Fred, assistant city editor, Toledo *Blade*
Peeks, Edward, Charleston (W. Va.) *Gazette*
Perlik, Charles, president, The Newspaper Guild
Pride, William, executive news editor, Denver *Post*
Roberts, Charles, director of information, National Wildlife Federation
Spencer, Frank, Chicago bureau, United Press International
Stark, Julia M., director of inter-religious affairs, National Conference
  of Christians and Jews.
Thomas, William, editor, Los Angeles *Times*
Towers, Kenneth, assistant managing editor, Chicago *Sun-Times*
Van Cranebrock, Allen, Reuter Midwest senior financial correspondent
Witwer, Stan, columnist, St. Petersburg *Times*
Wright, Del, editor, Waukegan *News-Sun*
Wylie, William, business editor, Pittsburgh *Press*

CONTENTS

PART ONE

PRINCIPLES
OF NEWS
WRITING

A NEWSPAPERMAN'S CREDO

By Max Lerner

1. I believe in the integrity of the newspaperman to the facts and events with which he is dealing. He must give the event as it actually happened, the facts as they actually are, to the best of his descriptive power. His obligation to what actually happened is as exacting as the obligation of a historian, and his regard for evidence must be as scrupulous.

2. He has also the obligation, whenever the facts or events do not speak for themselves, to give the frame within which their meaning becomes clear. This may be a frame of history, or a broader interpretative frame of fact. In doing this he must make clear the distinction between fact and event on the one hand and his own opinion on the other.

3. In deciding what to include or omit he must use to the best of his ability the test of what is newsworthy in the minds of his readers, and what is of importance in the flow of events. He must resist the temptation of including or excluding on the basis of what will help or harm whatever team he is on and whatever crowd he runs with.

4. This means that he must give a hearing even to unpopular causes, including those which he may himself detest. He has the obligation to keep the channels of the press open for a competition of ideas, since only through such a competition will the people be able to arrive at their own decisions of what is right and good.

5. In any contest of opinion he has the obligation to state, as fairly as he knows how, the opposing viewpoints. At the same time, if he is presenting opinion in an editorial or a column, he has the obligation to set forth his own position honestly and forthrightly as his own, regardless of the consequences.

6. Beset as he inevitably will be by favor-seekers, special interests, press agents, public relations men, and operators of all kinds, he must keep himself scrupulously independent of their favors and pressures. This means that he must be strong enough to make himself unpopular with those who can smooth his path or make life pleasant for him.

7. He must resist all pressures from outside, whether they be from advertisers, government officials, businessmen, labor organizations, churches, ethnic groups, or any other source which has an effect on the circulation or revenue of his paper. This applies whether the newspaperman is a publisher, editor, reporter, reviewer, or columnist. Since the danger in many cases is that he will anticipate the pressures before they are exerted, and censor, a news story, review, or opinion which may hurt circulation or revenue, he has the obligation to resist the voice from within himself which tells him to play it safe.

8. His responsibility is to his craft and to the integrity of his mind.

Editor & Publisher

1

THE MODERN NEWSGATHERER

Journalism is newsgathering, fact finding, reporting. It is important anywhere at any time. It is indispensable in a democracy. People cannot govern themselves without information. No matter what changes—social, economic, political or other—occur in the future, it is inconceivable that there ever will come a time when there will not be those whose full-time function it is to find out what is going on and to transmit that information to others, together with a proper explanation of its significance.

JOURNALISM, TODAY AND TOMORROW

As the world's population zooms and it becomes possible to visit all parts of the globe in a few hours, possibly even minutes, the problems and areas of interest with which the editor of the future must be concerned will multiply many times. The complexity and interdependence of all aspects of human living, furthermore, continue to enlarge both the opportunities and responsibilities of the newsgatherers and disseminators. And it will make no difference what the future medium of distribution is: slave runners, town criers, news-letters, carrier pigeons, telegraphs, telephones, printing presses, motion pictures, radio, television—or thought waves. Nor will it matter whether reporters use pencil or pen, typewriter or some electronic machinery.

This also seems certain: It is going to take better men and women to report and edit the news of the world in the future than it has in the past. The qualifications required of those who enter journalism will continue to broaden as they have been doing steadily during the past quarter century. More and better education will be required and there will be an augmented need for those capable, after adequate preparation as general practitioners, to become specialists in a multitude of fields.

The improvement in the quality of the personnel engaged in journalism will continue to be both a business necessity and an essential to future existence of democratic society. Only a competent and responsible jour-nalism can provide the knowledge and understanding the masses of man-kind need in order to maintain government of the people, by the people and for the people. From the standpoint of the young person choosing a career, this means that there is no other field of endeavor more likely to provide challenges and opportunities for personal development and service to mankind.

This book is for the benefit of beginners in this field who aspire some day to be newspaper publishers, magazine editors, radio or television com-mentators, foreign correspondents, editorial writers, syndicated columnists or authoritative journalistic experts on specialized subjects for any or all of the media. Just as the youngster who dreams of growing up to be a concert pianist begins with scales, finger exercises and Bach two-part inventions, so must the journalistic neophyte acquire the basic skills which he later can use regardless of the specific activity in which he is engaged.

No matter what electronic devices are developed for the use of the com-municator, the need for a permanent record will persist. This means that there always is going to be something akin to the newspaper. This is so despite the fact that the huge expenditures involved in contemporary pub-lishing have reduced the number of daily newspapers in the United States from approximately 2,600 to about 1,750 in a half century during which the population has more than doubled. Despite the decline in the number of newspapers, their total circulation reached an all-time high of over 63 million at the end of the same period. About 100 million Americans read some newspaper every day.

Anyway, whatever the future may bring, as of today the daily news-paper still provides the best basic training for beginners in journalism, no matter what their lifetime ambitions may be. No other medium comes anywhere close to duplicating its efforts at speedy, accurate and thorough coverage of the news of the world. Acquiring the skills necessary for success as a newspaper reporter, therefore, is the smartest "first step" that anyone can take in the field of journalism. News magazines, television stations and other media prefer employees who have such experience.

Understandably, the young person considering a newspaper reportorial career asks himself

1. How do I know I would like it?
2. How do I know I am qualified?
3. How should I prepare myself?
4. What about the ethics or morality of journalism?

THE NATURE OF NEWSPAPER WORK

Old-time movies notwithstanding, newspaper reporters do not often emulate detectives in exposing murderers, kidnapers and subversives, nor do they shout "stop the presses" and compose headlines over the telephone after profanely "telling off" unreasonable superiors. Rather, they put in a regular full day's work in and out of remarkably quiet and orderly newsrooms, where they remove their hats.

In large cities, some reporters spend their entire working days on "beats" in the pressrooms at police headquarters, city hall, the county buildings, the federal building and other places where it is certain important news will originate. They telephone their information to rewrite men in note form or they dictate it, composing as they go along. Many now send copy via facsimile machines from pressrooms in outlying offices to the city room. On smaller newspapers, beat men visit their news sources once or twice daily, returning to their offices to compose their own accounts. They also may double as "general assignment" reporters, covering news which occurs at places other than the familiar spots. In all instances they are under the careful direction and scrutiny of the city editor who in turn is responsible to the managing editor who has general charge of the entire news-editorial operation. How departmentalized a newspaper operation is and how split up the managerial and operational functions are depend upon its size. On even small papers the sports and society (or women's) departments usually are separate. Someone is in charge of handling news that reaches the office via the teletypesetters or leased wires of the press associations (Associated Press and United Press International), so there may be a telegraph or wire desk or, on larger papers, a foreign news department with a cable desk as a part of it. Some large newspapers also have a central copy desk where most stories from whatever source are checked for style, accuracy, etc., and given headlines. Makeup (deciding where stories and other, mostly illustrative, material are to appear) may be handled by a separate makeup editor, by a news editor or by someone else performing multiple duties.

The growing complexity of the news is augmenting the trend toward a multiplicity of semiautonomous departments: business and finance, real estate, travel, environment, science, literary and artistic news and criticism and others. Specialized reporters often constitute one-man departments and have considerable leeway in assignments. They cannot "stay put" in any one press room because usually there are several agencies, public and private, with an interest in the same newsworthy situation. The roving beat reporter becomes a specialist in some field of public concern.

Although the reporter may consider himself haunted constantly by deadlines (the last minutes at which copy can be submitted to make editions), there is generally less monotony and consequently danger of "getting into a rut" in newspaper work than there is in almost anything else he could do today. This is the age of the Organization Man in which white-collar as well as blue-collar workers increasingly are becoming comparatively smaller and smaller cogs in huge industrial machines whose total operations (or even purposes) it is difficult for them to understand. Many recent authors have deplored the extent to which the contemporary economy puts a premium on conformity, stifles imagination and originality and, consequently, destroys initiative and even self-respect. They see youthful unrest, on and off college campuses, as owing in considerable part to these factors.

There is, of course, considerable similarity in the news from the same source day after day. Nevertheless, no two stories ever are exactly alike. The principals at least are different and so are their reactions to whatever befalls them: arrest, accident, honor, etc. And, even though the swashbuckling days of Richard Harding Davis are long since past, there is still a thrill, or at least a satisfied feeling, with every assignment successfully concluded. There is a greater pride of workmanship and sense of accomplishment than is possible for workers in most industries and offices in late-twentieth century.

Even though he may consider himself low man on the press' totem pole, the cub reporter carries more prestige with the public than do apprentices in most other fields. At the scene of a fire or riot he flashes his press pass and is allowed across police lines. On the routine beat he is courted by those who want to get something in or to keep something out of the paper. From the very start of his journalistic career, by the very nature of his work, he "is somebody," and this fact cannot help but be gratifying to the human ego.

His is not a dream world or fool's paradise. The reporter actually *is* a responsible person. Several other persons will have a part in determining how whatever news he handles appears in the paper. Nevertheless, he has "first crack" at it. The original judgment which he exercises in determining whether and/or how something is to be reported is of the utmost importance. He, in other words, is the backbone of the newsgathering and disseminating operation. Truly, every reporter is also an editor and, conversely, the best editors continue throughout their future careers to maintain the attitudes of reporters.

The occupational disease that newspapermen must guard against is cynicism. Whereas skepticism is a journalistic asset, a hard-boiled or flippant attitude toward the so-called realities of life can lead not only to a flagrant disregard of the public interest but also to personal deterioration. Many of the public figures with whom he comes into diurnal contact, the reporter knows, do not deserve public adulation but are, to use the vernacular, stuffed shirts or phonies. Disillusionment comes also with discovery that the "rules of the game"—as the game actually is "played" in politics, business and many other aspects of life—are often crass, mercenary and hypocritical. Overcoming gullibility and learning the "facts of life" can be valuable, provided they lead to intelligent sophistication.

Much superfluous effort has gone into the attempt to determine whether journalism is a profession, business or trade. What really counts is the attitude of the individual toward his work. Professionalism can be present or absent among carpenters, hotel clerks, nurses, doctors, lawyers, taxi drivers, newspapermen and anybody or everybody else. As for journalism, there is no field which offers greater opportunities for the development of a professional point of view, idealism, public service and the like. It is the place for the starry-eyed youngster who wants to help "save the world." There is no better way for one who wants to help make democracy work more effectively to devote his talents. As in every other worthwhile endeavor, the road to the top is long and strewn with obstacles. At the summit, however, are the prestige and power which make the struggle worthwhile.

REPORTORIAL QUALIFICATIONS

As regards the myth that newspapermen are born and not made, Joseph Pulitzer, patriarch of the old New York *World*, and founder of the Pulitzer School of Journalism at Columbia University, said years ago

> The only position that occurs to me that a man in our Republic can successfully fill by the simple fact of birth is that of an idiot. Is there any position for which a man does not demand and receive training—training at home, training in schools and colleges, training by master craftsmen, or training through bitter experience—through the burns that make the child dread the fire, through blunders costly to the aspirant?
>
> The "born editor" who has succeeded greatly without special preparation is simply a man with unusual ability and aptitude for his chosen profession, with great power of concentration and sustained effort. . . . Even in his case might it not be an advantage to have a system of instruction that would give him the same results at a saving of much time and labor?

A few years ago a committee on schools of journalism of the American Society of Newspaper Editors reported

> We want the departments of journalism to turn out men . . . capable of appraising the changed and new world which will be theirs tomorrow. We want these boys—of course, they will start at the bottom—capable of rising to the posts of great newspaper power, equipped to wield that power intelligently. In other words, we wish them, while they are collecting police news and reporting banquets, to carry the mental equipment which, rightly directed, will one day invest them with editorial control. Each graduate ought to have in the knapsack of his mind the baton of the editor and publisher. . . . This society knows it is

far more vital to the welfare of mankind that the men who make its journals of public opinion be culturally superior than it is that the surgeon or corporation lawyer be a man of manifold intellectual attainments.

Altogether too many college freshmen think training for journalism consists primarily in learning how to write. They are mostly students who did well in high school English and were inspired with literary ambitions by teachers who were surprised and grateful to find fewer than the average number of grammatical errors in their themes. Unfortunately, there is no such thing as "just writing," in journalism or any other field. William Shakespeare is immortal not because of vocabulary or style but because of greatness of thought. He had an incomparable knowledge of history, psychology, geography, philosophy and many other fields. He and other masters of past centuries are read today because they had something extraordinarily worthwhile to say.

Because great ideas rather than beautiful words and phrases make for superior writing, everything that a journalism student studies is of potential value to him. The subject matter of journalism includes all that is taught in courses in political science, history, economics, sociology, chemistry, physics and other subjects too numerous to mention. The student who recognizes this fact in his freshman year has a big advantage. By the time he takes his first journalism course in his sophomore, junior or senior year, he will have more than the average liberal arts student's superficial interest in and knowledge of the contents of the innumerable textbooks he will have studied. He should have his head and files full of information on which to rely when he starts wandering on and off the campus in quest of news. It is the purpose of his journalism courses to make his textbook knowledge come alive, to show him how to utilize it in understanding and interpreting the contemporary scene. Through experience in hiring both liberal arts and journalism school graduates, editors have learned that a so-called broad background of general courses is not in itself adequate preparation for newspaper reporting. Since, however, the journalist deals mostly with news related to the subject matter of courses in the different social sciences, the student who discovers he has little or no interest in political science, economics and sociology should take stock to determine whether he really is wise to aspire to a career in journalism.

Valuable Traits

The young person who should be encouraged to go into journalism, therefore, is the one who wants very badly to spend his adulthood saying or writing worthwhile things about contemporary problems. His chances of success may be judged by the extent to which at an early age he becomes interested in the world of affairs. There is no sense aspiring to a newspaper career unless one finds newspaper reading pleasurable as a youth. The more cosmopolitan the interests the better.

Among the courses which relate to the kind of news the future journalist will cover are ones in criminology, urban sociology, labor problems, public finance, taxation, political parties, population problems, state and local government and others in the fields of sociology, political science and economics. Taking them is the comparatively "easy" way to learn what any successful journalist must know; the "hard" way is on the job. A student supposedly goes to college to get a head start.

Most of the personality traits usually listed as valuable for the journalist are ones which would be equally essential for success in most other professional fields: intelligence, friendliness, reliability, imagination, ingenuity, nerve, speed, accuracy, courage, endurance, ability to organize one's activities, perseverance, mental alertness, honesty, punctuality, cheerfulness, the power of observation, shrewdness, enterprise, optimism, humor, adaptability, initiative and the like.

If there is any clue to be discovered in childhood by which to estimate journalistic capacity, it probably would be in the extent to which the boy or girl demonstrates curiosity and skepticism. A newsgatherer's stock in trade is his ability to keep on asking questions until he has exhausted all angles of an assignment. The youngster who wears out his parents by his querulousness may be worth encouraging as a potential journalistic great.

Nose for News

Usually listed first among the special qualifications which a newsgatherer needs is a "nose for news," which means the ability to recognize the news possibilities of an item of information and involves

1. The ability to recognize that the information can be made of interest to readers.
2. The ability to recognize clues which may be very casual but which may lead to the discovery of important news.
3. The ability to recognize the relative importance of a number of facts concerning the same general subject.
4. The ability to recognize the possibility of other news related to the particular information at hand.

The following anecdote, possibly apocryphal, is told of Deems Taylor when he first became music critic for the New York *Times*. He is said to have arrived at the premiere of an opera only to learn that the prima donna had taken poison in her hotel room and the program had been canceled. Taylor, it is hard to believe in view of the eminence he later attained, went home and to bed. He was awakened in the middle of the night by an outraged editor who told him every other paper in town had the suicide story on Page One. Taylor murmured, "Well, there was no opera performance to write about, so what else could I do but go home?"

Another, possibly fictitious, reporter was assigned to cover a speech which an important man was to deliver. He was instructed to follow the speech with the advanced copy in his hands to see if the speaker deviated at all from the manuscript. The speech, in the meantime, had been written up and its publication awaited only the actual delivery. The reporter strolled back to his editor's presence and reported that the speaker had cast aside his prepared manuscript and had talked extemporaneously. He said that it had been impossible to follow the speaker by means of the copy which he had. The reporter, however, had failed to take a single note on the speaker's impromptu remarks.

From these "classic" examples it is clear that common sense is indispensable for the reporter. Especially in these days of public relations counsel and press releases, making news sources often difficult to see, the reporter must ask question after question to draw out whomever he does get to interview to learn about less obvious but important phases of the subject at hand. He must, in other words, be inquisitive, perceptive and healthfully skeptical.

The reporter with a cultivated nose for news realizes that, although the same elements may be present in similar stories, they invariably are there in different proportions as to importance. For instance, in an automobile accident story the reporter always must find out the names of all persons concerned, the extent of the injuries details, of the collision, etc. In Story A, however, the name of a person injured may be most important. In Story B the most important element may be the name of a prominent person who escaped injury. No two accidents ever result from exactly the same cause. In one case it may be a defective brake; in another, a drunken driver; and in a third, a billboard obstructing the view. Often the cause of an accident is very unusual —as when a bee makes a driver lose control of his machine.

In the same accident story there may be other important features which the reporter could not know without considerable questioning of the persons concerned. Perhaps the same two persons had been in accidents together before. Perhaps one of them recently left a hospital where he was recuperating from a previous accident. Perhaps one of them was on his way to an important engagement, a sick bed or the scene of another accident.

The possibilities of a feature in a simple accident story have by no means been exhausted. Enough has been said, however, to indicate that to report a story "in depth" a reporter must be constantly "on his toes," as the expression goes. He has to think and think and think, and he has to ask and ask and ask. Good reporting consists in getting all the pertinent facts and then some more. Otherwise the story will not be complete and may be misleading because some of the important elements are left out. The reporter who learns to do a thorough job of delving into all of the potential angles of a simple "straight" news story is obtaining valuable training for interpretative reporting.

"Smelling a rat" is also an attribute of the straight news reporter and, especially, the interpretative reporter. For example, a reporter learned that a certain congressman was going to deliver a public address. He was sharp. enough to inquire whether this meant that an important hearing over which the representative was to preside had been called off or postponed. Another reporter, unable to buy a certain game at several stores, investigated and learned that there was a new recreational fad in existence. Still another, noting that average school attendance in the elementary grades had gone up, investigated and came up with an article on the successful use of cold shots and other sickness preventatives.

This "smelling a rat" attitude should be the most valuable attribute of any kind of researcher, journalistic or academic. The truth-seeking reporter explores every possible avenue for information. If he is operating correctly he has no predetermined ends to seek, no hypothesis to prove—just the truth to be determined. The manner in which his information is transmitted is an important subject for scholarly research, and it is to gasp to conjecture what changes the development of electronics may bring. Nevertheless, the first essential step always will be the same: to seek and to obtain the facts. They cannot be transmitted until they have been gathered, and that task will continue to be performed by human beings, not by robots.

What Is News?

Scholarly attempts to define news, for which the reporter is supposed to have a nose, correctly emphasize the fact that it is the account of an event not the event itself. At any given moment billions of simultaneous events occur throughout the world. Someone dies, is born, gives a speech, attends a meeting, takes a trip, commits a crime and so on ad infinitum. All of these occurrences are potentially news. They do not become so until some purveyor of news gives an account of them. The news, in other words, is the account of the event, not something intrinsic in the event itself.

Professional newsgatherers judge the potential interest and/or importance of an event before deciding whether to render an account of it, thus making it news. These newsgatherers are men, not deities. They possess no absolutistic yardstick by which to judge what to report and what to ignore. There is nothing that cannot be made interesting in the skillful telling; and only a supernatural power could say what is important.

Understanding of the nature of news is not improved by adding such words as "timely," "concise," "accurate" or the like to definitions, as all such adjectives require explanations which differ with the editors or the circumstances. Nothing is news until it is reported, no matter when it occurred. Nor is its nature changed by analysis of its effect on those who learn of it, regardless of whether the response is immediate or delayed. Valuable as the study of such factors as audience reaction may be for total understanding of social behavior, the first-rate newsgatherer acting as such persists in his search for truth. He does not ask himself what the potential use or effect of his information will be or how many "gatekeepers" will handle it; rather, his sole duty is to concentrate on discovering the truth.

The Need for Interpretation

The successful journalist of the future is going to have to be more than a thoroughly trained journeyman if he is to climb the ladder of success. He must be capable of more than routine coverage and to interpret as well as report what is going on.

To interpret the news it is necessary to understand it, and understanding means more than just the ability to define the jargon used by persons in different walks of life. It involves recognizing the particular event as one of a series with both a cause and an effect. With their perspective the historians of the future may be better able to depict the trends and currents of the present, but if the gatherer of information is well informed, through his reading of history, his study of economics, sociology, political science and other academic subjects, and has acquaintance with the attempts of other observers to interpret the modern scene in books and magazine articles, he will at least be aware of the fact that an item of news is not an isolated incident but one inevitably linked to a chain of important events.

The interpretative reporter of the future should be as shock proof as a psychoanalyst and a practical philosopher in his general outlook on life. He cannot succeed if he is hampered by prejudices and stereotyped attitudes which would bias his perception of human affairs. Modern psychiatry has proved that the first step in ridding a person of complexes is to make him aware of their bases. Hence, the newsgatherer should have a firm understanding of how men think and why, both to avoid pitfalls in his own search for so-called truth and to understand the behavior of those whose actions it is his responsibility to report.

Can the journalist avoid being influenced by his personal biases? Possibly not entirely. However, as is true of no other profession, his entire training is devoted to overcoming or sidestepping his prejudices. He is encouraged to be as openminded and objective as it is humanly possible to be and to be aware of any emotional obstacles that he may have to overcome. By contrast most other people go through life unaware of their inhibitions.

What is this thing called public opinion which the newspaperman may think he is influencing? How explain a new political movement in terms of economic tendencies which give rise to such symptoms? What about the power which the demagogue of the moment seems to be able to exert? The interpreter of the news must see reasons where ordinary individuals observe only overt happenings. And he must study them as the scientist scrutinizes the specimen in his microscope, scientifically. Ordinarily he cannot be a participant in the events of which he writes or his viewpoint will be decidedly warped. To convey meaning, or feeling, to readers, however, it may become necessary to "role-play" to learn what makes others "tick." That means joining the action as stunt reporters do when they get themselves committed to jails or take employment of one sort or another. Feature stories or exposes which result from such reporting still are valuable, but the complexity of contemporary problems demands more than skeptical journalistic detective work; rather, it demands sympathetic participation if feeling is to be conveyed to others. Unless a reporter can make readers understand what an event means to its principals, he may have failed in his effort to interpret it. Doing his best, he will err constantly; scientific method is nothing but being as approximately correct as possible. His mistakes, however, will be honest ones of an expert and not the blunders of an ignoramus.

HOW TO PREPARE

Informational Background

The rule to follow in preparing for a career in journalism is: learn as much about as many things as possible and stay intellectually alert. The ignorant reporter is at a tremendous disadvantage. He annoys news sources, doesn't obtain all of the essential facts, and may make gross errors of fact as well as emphasis when he writes his story.

To cover intelligently a police station, criminal court, city hall, county, state or federal office, or political headquarters, one must understand the setups of government, the nature and functions of various offices. The reporter must be able to read and quickly digest the contents of legal documents. He must know the meanings of such terms as "corpus delicti," "habeas corpus," "injunction" and "certiorari." He cannot say "divorce" when he means "separate maintenance," or "parole" when he means "probation." He must be able to read a bank-balance sheet, know when a financial market is bullish and when bearish and what it means to sell short, hedge and stockpile. He must understand what it means to refinance a bond issue or liquidate the assets of a corporation. He doesn't confuse craft unions with industrial unions.

It is impossible for an interpretative reporter to write that the last obstacle to beginning a slum-clearance program has been removed unless he knows the procedure by which such projects are developed. He can't explain the status of a pending city ordinance unless he understands what the rules provide for future consideration of it. It is impossible for him to interview a prosecuting attorney regarding the course of action he may take in a particular case unless he knows what the alternatives are.

Although most editorial offices today are equipped with good libraries, or morgues as they often still are called, the reporter has to know which reference books and clipping files to consult to obtain historical and other explanatory information to "round out" a story. As he gathers experience he becomes a veritable storehouse of knowledge himself. Aware of the nature of different organizations, public and private, he knows which ones to consult on which occasion and what each group's slant or interest is likely to be.

Without background knowledge in a field a reporter cannot fill out an account by declaring that the home run was the longest ever hit in the park; that this was the first time a certain ward gave a voting majority to the candidates of a particular party; that a fatal accident occurred at an intersection where the city council once refused to permit the erection of stop signs; that what seems to be a new proposal for civic reform really was resurrected from a decade-old report by an elder statesman.

At a recent Associated Press Managing Editors meeting, Robert Paine of the Memphis *Commerial Appeal* cited the following story:

> Grand Junction, Tenn., Feb. 19.—(AP)—A smooth-working hound flushed seven bevies of quail in a three-hour trial yesterday for the top performance of the national championship.

Commented Paine:

> I imagine that every bird-dog owner in the country shuddered in horror at the word HOUND. That would be about the same as saying a cow won the Kentucky derby. There are strictly different kinds of dogs and bird-dog fanciers have a habit of shooting from the hip when one of their dogs is called a hound.
>
> Secondly, the word FLUSH is the exact opposite of the word that should have been used. That would be about like saying Babe Ruth won the game by striking out. Flush means to frighten the birds into flying away. The correct word is point.

It was not too many years ago that a journalistic ignoramous asked the Nobel prize-winning physicist Dr. Robert Millikan what cosmic rays were "good for." Those were the days when science was treated more or less as a joke in editorial offices and reporters assigned to science news stories were capable of little more than asking when the scholars expected to fly to Mars, find the missing link or take the smell out of the onion. No wonder that many scientists still are reluctant to talk to reporters.

The interpretative reporter "reads the fine print" of a news story in order to answer the reader's query, "What does it mean?" To keep a particular news event "in focus," the interpretative reporter shows its comparative importance. Darrell Huff began his *How to Lie with Statistics*, a book every journalist of whatever kind would find valuable reading, with a warning that widespread reporting of a particular type of news, such as crime, easily can create a distorted impression as regards a social situation.

Mere figures showing total numbers of different types of crime committed in two or more areas only suggest the real story. Explanations of why styles in lawbreaking differ in different places at the same time, and at the same place at different times, are to be found in such variable factors as size and complexion of population, police policies and activities and many others.

To present anywhere near a true picture of the housing situation in any community, a reporter must consider the age of the community and of the dwelling units; the adequacy of zoning and building codes and their enforcement; the influx of newcomers and the effect, including that caused by prejudice against certain types of persons because of race, national origin, religion or other reasons; the extent of overpopulation; transportation and parking facilities; educational, cultural and recreational advantages; the income and cost of living indices; nearby urban and suburban growth and similar factors. With such data he can provide readers with an understanding of the situation and enable them properly to evaluate proposals for change.

Mere announcement that consumer credit outstanding at any given time is such-and-such means little or nothing unless the reader knows how the figures given compare with similar ones for comparable periods in other months or years. Tables, graphs and charts help show trends; the news magazine *U.S. News & World Report* makes very effective use of them. For a broader picture of the state of the economy as a whole, more than comparative figures in any one economic category is necessary. In addition to installment buying, price indices, extent and kind (savings or checking) of bank deposits and withdrawals, a breakdown of the types of depositors (by size of deposits), purchase and cancellation of government securities (with comparable breakdown) bank loans, mortgages, new businesses, business failures, growth of chains and monopolies and other similar factors must be considered.

Often the motives of persons in the news must be known to make their actions understandable. The more a spectator knows about the strategy involved in an athletic contest, for instance, the more enjoyment he derives from it and the better able he is to second-guess the manager or be a Monday morning quarterback. If, on the other hand, he knows little or nothing about such strategy, he won't understand why a weak hitter was given an intentional base on balls in order to pitch to a weaker one, possibly one batting from the same side as that from which the pitcher throws and supposedly more likely to hit into a double play. Or he will not understand why a quarterback called for a play which could not help but lose ground on the third down in order to put the ball in better position to try for a field goal on fourth down.

Just as sports writers explain the strategy of coaches, managers and contestants, so could reporters dealing with political affairs explain that precinct captains who rival the positions of ward committeemen often are made candidates for judgeships in order to remove them from active politics. The interpretative reporter knows that cornerstone layings, dedications of buildings, openings of parks and other public facilities and similar acts are timed so as to have the maximum beneficial effect for the officeholders in charge. After he has "been around" long enough the interpretative reporter knows the "tricks of the trade" and can at least suggest probable causes for the behavior of many newsworthy persons. If he fails to do so, readers are in the position of just not knowing "what's going on."

To write with the perspective of the cultural anthropologist or historian of a century means to be aware of "schools of thought," "climates of opinion" and social, economic and political trends. A journalistic scholar should know when the views of an educator are consistent with those of an outstanding scholar or organization or with what has been attempted elsewhere. He should know what "progressive versus traditional" in pedagogical methods means. If he covers social welfare he should know the difference between the missionary (settlement house or boys club) and the self-help (area or community project) approaches.

There is a correlation between the extent of a feeling of insecurity and attacks upon civil liberties. Quite naturally the "curves" fluctuate with periods of war and depression, although it always is dangerous to draw historical parallels without thorough consideration of all possible factors.

Of this the studious interpretative reporter is certain: nothing just happens. A wave of intolerance has a cause. So has a revival movement, excessive hero worship, a bullish stock market, an increase in superstition, or any fad, fashion, craze or mass movement. Sometimes what seem to be isolated phenomena in several different fields really stem from the same causal roots. At any rate, there always is an explanation for how we "got that way." For instance, when violence erupts and persists simultaneously in many parts of the world, it is shortsighted to treat a local incident as an isolated phenomenon.

Academic Preparation

Although there probably always will be exceptions, present trends indicate that future journalists will be college trained. Such, in fact, is already the case on most metropolitan newspapers and, except for old-timers, most of the degree holders went to schools of journalism. The proportion of those with master's and other higher degrees also is increasing.

Modern journalism schools are not trade schools. From two-thirds to four-fifths of a student's classwork is taken in the liberal arts or other divisions. Anything and everything that a future journalist studies has potential future value for him and it is frustrating not to be able to take the entire curriculum in the humanities and the natural and physical sciences. Those who are ambitious to specialize ultimately in particular fields should do so, but the majority should strive for a thorough and well-rounded background in the social sciences: political science, sociology and economics in particular The student should try to get in courses in public finance, criminology and labor problems among others. History courses give him perspective and psychology enables him to come closer to understanding both individual and crowd behavior.

In his advanced journalism courses the student should expect to be taught how to utilize the background and theoretical knowledge acquired all over the rest of the campus in reporting and intepreting the contemporary scene. On assignments, he observes "theory becoming action," and if he takes some philosophy he will be better able to comprehend and evaluate the immediate incident in terms of the general and eternal.

A strict journalism instructor, simulating the exactness of a hard-boiled city editor, can teach sound methods of research. The journalistic fact finder does not begin with a hypothesis for which he seeks factual proof. Rather, he is an open-minded seeker after truth who explores every possible avenue of investigation; and only after he has exhausted every chance to obtain additional information does he attempt to draw conclusions regarding the accumulated data. This objective approach to knowledge is much sounder than that practiced by many researchers in other academic fields. In the process, the student-reporter becomes familiar with the nature of reference or source material; he may learn how to read and understand a county board's budget or the complicated declaration filed to begin a civil law action.

Since World War II, a number of social scientists have become interested in quantitative analysis of various aspects of social behavior and in communication theory. They use the tools of the statistician and the language of the sociologist to examine the effects of various ways to influence human thought and behavior. Many of their findings are of value to the propagandist, advertiser, public relations counsel and others who have ideas or products to sell. Knowledge of what they are up to is important for the true journalist who is a protector of their potential victims. He should, however, be wary of academic fads and should examine the so-called behavioral sciences and communications theory courses to determine whether they have relevance to anything journalistic and whether the teachers of them have any practical knowledge of the profession of newsgathering. *Social Science As Sorcery* by Stanislav Andreski (St. Martin's Press, 1972) is an edifying critique by a Reading University scholar.

Cub Reporting

Fortunate is the school of journalism graduate whose first job enables him to write as well as report. He should avoid being "buried" in a pressroom on a beat where he merely phones in the news, or on a copy desk or in a radio or television newsroom where press association and newspaper leads are rewritten so as to be suitable for broadcast.

There is no better vantage point from which to observe a cross section of life "in the raw" than police headquarters or courts. There the reporter will meet novelists, playwrights and magazine-article writers as well as sociology, law and other scholars and students observing and gathering authentic information for their own understanding and usage. It is the place to "get your nose rubbed in it," meaning to come face to face with the squalid side of life, social problems, human frailties and personality types. Few would care to remain on the police beat indefinitely but anyone who skips the experience is shortchanged.

Thorough preliminary journalistic training also should include some contact with politics and government as well as the mine run of general assignments: meetings, speeches, obituaries, accidents, interviews, routine business, society and similar news. After a few years of such varied experience the beginner is able to start thinking about settling down to specialize. Thereafter, however, he will be wise to arrange for "change-of-pace" interludes such as those which discerning publishers and editors provide editorial writers, columnists, foreign news editors and others when they send them on trips of observation and fact-finding and encourage them to stay out of the rut or ivory tower.

Occupational Aids

Until recently, few reporters felt the need of shorthand since the task of translating notes, of which there was temptation to take too many, slowed rather than hastened the process of reporting and writing. Today, however, when it often is necessary to interview news sources in the company of other reporters or to attend news conferences at which only a few get to ask questions, a verbatim record of what happened often is valuable. Testimony in court or at committee hearings also can best be taken down in shorthand; thus more and more newsgatherers who specialize in such kind of work are learning it.

Those who have not done so usually develop their own system of short longhand, and may know some of the commercialized systems which are based primarily upon abbreviations for common syllables and combinations of letters. The reporter who develops his own system uses abbreviations for frequently used words and phrases. For instance, "2" is used for "to," "too" and "two," and "c" for "see," "u" for "you," "r" for "are." The reporter can use simplified spelling in note taking if not in actual copy and can make use of such common abbreviations as "rr" for "railroad" and "inc" for "incomplete." He may even use foreign words which are shorter than English, as the French "selon" instead of "according to." Instead of "capital punishment" he may jot down "cp" and instead of "labor union" he may write "lu." Still used by some old-timers is the Phillips Telegraphic Code patented in the late 19th century by an Associated Press official. Typical code abbreviations are xgr for "legislature," bd for "board," sap for "soon as possible," xn for "constitution," and itxd for "intoxicated." There are several similar systems all using abbreviations, including Zinman Rapid Writing and Streamline.

Tape recorders today are in widespread use by magazine and free-lance writers and by newspaper reporters gathering material for feature or other articles for which the deadline is not immediate. Under all conditions the recorder is valuable at news conferences and public functions and even during some interviews as a means of protecting both interviewer and interviewee as to the accuracy of subsequent quotation. There is the danger, however, that such interviews can become too formal and stilted and that the presence of the electronic device cause the interviewee to become overly cautious in his remarks. The same is true if motion pictures or television recordings are made. In such case, of course, the reporter does not have to know how to operate the gadgets. On some small- and medium-sized papers, however, he may be expected, on occasion at least, to be able to use a camera when a staff photographer is unable to accompany him on assignment. Labor union contracts may forbid his doing so in other places. In any case, it is unlikely that he will have to know more than how to take the pictures; the development and printing will be the task of others.

The greatest drawback to using the tape recorder is the time necessary to replay and make notes of the points of use in the story at hand. Obviously, it must be necessary to take even more time for such translation as that consumed by the interview itself. Therefore, the tape recorder is of limited value to the daily newspaper reporter with immediate deadlines to make. It is of great value to a feature writer for newspaper or magazine.

Within the past decade much that before seemed like science fiction to newsroom old-timers has become reality. Because several manufacturers are engaged frantically in research and experimentation, some newspapers are delaying reorganizing their operations. Many others, however, have made drastic technological changes. Much greater skill than two-fingered hunt-and-peck reporters possess is required to use IBM Selectric typewriters, essential to produce copy for a "scanner" or OCR (optical character reader) which transfers the contents of the typewritten sheet or its equivalent onto computer tape which is fed into a phototypesetter.

Another new method of getting stories into cold type is by VDTs (visual display terminals), also known as CRTs (cathode ray tubes). Reporters compose as on a typewriter and watch the stories appear on a screen. Editing is by push buttons. Most old-timers have been surprised and relieved to discover how easy it is to adjust. They say that the only important new skill is to be able to use an electric typewriter effectively. They feel that the mechanical revolution will increase the control of the newsroom over content and presentation of the news. Because so much competitive experimentation is underway it would be folly to describe in detail any process, especially so since to date the reporting function continues without much change. The same doubtless will remain true even if some of the fantastic predictions come true regarding facsimile, ultrafax, communication satellites, computers that can translate languages, read handwriting or typewriting and change spoken words into written words on perforated tape. Future reporters of the news may dictate their stories into microphone-like gadgets for transmission to "voice setting" machines, which in turn will correct the words into "type" ready for the page form. Other machines may "think" their words and transfer them to their assigned space in newspaper pages, together with pictures and headlines, electronically and photographically. The words may go into international newspapers, facsmilies produced in the homes of readers automatically translated into languages indigenous to the various countries in which they are circulated.

Before these or any other Jules Verne or Buck Rogers types of inventions can be used, however, the news still will have to be gathered by human beings. And the most important "machine" will continue to be the human reporter whose training cannot be neglected while he becomes enamored with the mechanical possibilities of tomorrow.

THE ETHICS OF JOURNALISM

In considering a possible life work, any young person with an adequate social conscience asks himself, "How much of my soul would I have to sell?" As regards journalism he wants clarification of the accusations he has heard that the media are owned and run by conservative or reactionary businessmen whose interest is profit-making rather than public service, that new sand editorial policy are influenced too much by advertisers and powerful pressure groups and that the individual reporter, to survive, must suppress, exaggerate, sensationalize and distort the news which he often gathers by means of dishonest practices, unjustly invading the privacy and betraying the confidences of those with whom he deals.

The Reporter's Prerogatives

Flat denial of these and similar charges is impossible. Bad journalistic practices *do* exist in some places and it may not be much solace to know that a review of history reveals that the worst offenders ultimately succumb. There is a decided limit, however, to which the rank-and-file journalist deserves sympathy when he rationalizes his own sins and shortcomings by blaming his superiors. No editor worth working for requires any member of his staff to violate his moral standards or conscience. Any "dirty" assignments go to those who give evidence early in their careers that they are easy or perhaps eager to be pushed around. In few other occupations is it possible for hirelings to "talk up" to their bosses as much as in journalism. A careful fact gatherer has a better-than-even chance on most publications if he undertakes to persuade his superiors to publish what he has found to be true. No matter how money-minded his publisher may be, the reporter on assignment is not so motivated. By contrast, a clerk or salesman is constantly aware of his responsibility to make a sale and even the smiles and courtesies with which he greets customers may be feigned. Lawyers cynically "cut corners" in the interest of clients. It is difficult to find the person who is qualified to "cast the first stone" at the working journalist.

Newspaper Policy

It is true that newspapers and other journalistic media are big business enterprises, which means they are owned and operated by wealthy persons whose natural and sincere outlook is generally what is called conservative. Many of these publishers deserve more credit than they receive for their efforts to prevent their personal biases from distorting the fairness of basic news coverage. It is not true that on larger publications the advertisers dictate news and editorial policies. Especially as regards larger publications, the advertisers need the good will of the publication more than the publication needs them. Granting favors in the form of publicity stories for "sacred cows" or soft-pedaling unfavorable news is a decidedly shortsighted policy. The press' conservatism, which reflects itself mostly in endorsement of presidential candidates and attitudes toward national political issues, is derived honestly, no matter how unwisely, from the sincere beliefs of owners and publishers. They also are sensitive to reader and other criticisms, as witness the fact that research into the handling of recent political campaigns indicates extraordinary fairness following some bitter charges of bias in 1952 and 1956.

The American press is a patriotic one, which means that often it is duped itself and misleads readers by rushing into print with statements by prominent public officials which later have to be modified or counteracted. Since the end of World War II, the overwhelming majority of American newspapers, magazines, radio and television networks and stations and other journalistic media have been strong supporters of United States cold war foreign policy in principle. However, the increasing disillusionment among readers as the Indo-Chinese conflict dragged on gradually influenced editorial writers, so that it became as unpopular to be hawkish as it previously had been to be dovish. More important, editors revolted against the secrecy exercised by the executive branch of the federal government, with the result that the press often misinformed readers.

Journalists shared the nationwide shocks which resulted when congressional hearings and court trials revealed corruption and led to the resignations of a vice president, a president and others and the convictions of many prominent political figures. Subsequently, in lectures, magazine articles and books, many principals revealed or confirmed unsavory facts concerning the Central Intelligence Agency, Federal Bureau of Investigation and other prestigious agencies of government. All developments were reported by newspapers about 95 per cent of which endorsed Richard Nixon in 1972.

Certainly, at the beginners' level, newsgatherers are not instructed to fake or commit hoaxes. One beneficial by-product of the decline of competition, perhaps, has been the reduction of temptation to use unethical practices to obtain scoops. Few reporters any longer engage in picture stealing or misrepresent themselves as policemen or coroners' deputies. However, law enforcement officers have masqueraded as journalists, sometimes using forged press cards and other credentials. If reporters fail to give their readers more "inside dope" it usually is because they don't possess it themselves. A reporter is the last person to whom someone wishing to conceal facts unburdens himself. On the other hand, newspapers have expended huge sums of money, involving great expenditures of time and energy, to expose corruption or to verify or discover facts in the public interest.

Reportorial Decision-Making

The same is true as regards many other ethical or policy matters as whether to play up or down an outbreak of interracial violence, sensationalism in the handling of news of sex or crime, the details or even the facts of suicide, identification as to race, nationality or religion and the like. The reporter can "pass the buck" to his superior when he knows he has operated in accordance with publication policy.

A troublesome decision which the reporter sometimes has to make for himself is whether to listen to "off-the-record" statements; that is, whether to receive information in confidence. Sometimes, by promising not to quote a news source, he can obtain facts which the public has a right to know, or he may get tips which he can follow up without implicating the tipster. At other times, however, he may find that he has allowed himself to be "conned" into suppressing something. It is difficult to set a rule which applies to all situations. One thing is certain, however: once given, a promise must be kept. Almost half the states have laws giving newsmen the absolute or conditional right to refuse to reveal the identity of a news source. Many of these were passed after the United States Supreme Court in June 1972, by a 5 to 4 decision, ruled against Earl Caldwell, a New York *Times* reporter who refused to testify before a federal grand jury regarding the source of information given him about the Black Panthers. Faith in the protection offered by the First Amendment thus shattered after almost two centuries, the Reporters Committee for Freedom of the Press was organized with headquarters in Room 1310 at 1750 Pennsylvania Ave. NW, Washington, D.C. 20006. In its bimonthly *Press Censorship Newsletter* it has cited hundreds of attempts to compel journalists to disclose confidential information and scores of cases of reporters who went to jail for refusing to do so.

Reporter Power

In the spirit of the times newspaper reporters today are emulating minority groups in asserting their rights. Although some crusty representatives of management panicked, most made concessions intended to give rank-and-filers who do most of the hard spadework in the newsrooms an opportunity to complain and advise and participate to a greater extent in determining news and editorial policies. The model Newspaper Guild contract now contains a "voice" clause. In practice this means regular, generally monthly discussions between representatives of management and of the reportorial staff, and possibly also delegate attendance at regular editorial board and similar high-level meetings. In several cities editorial employees have been granted the right to approve appointments of subeditors. The managing editor of the Burlington (Ia.) *Hawk-Eye*, an out-of-towner, was elected by the staff over two local applicants.

Some reportorial groups have won "integrity" clauses, meaning the right to refuse orders to write anything contrary to their consciences or to refuse to permit their by-lines to be used. Another frequent demand is that reporters be informed of any letters to the editors complaining about their work. The Philadelphia *Bulletin* and some other papers hold seminars for young staff members. The annual A. J. Leibling counterconvention sponsored by (*More*) has given impetus to working journalists' demands. The examples of *Le Monde* and some other European publications are cited to support the contention that reporter power is democratically workable.

In January 1975 a National Labor Relations Board administrative law judge upheld the Guild unit of the Madison (Wis.) *Capital-Times* that any code of ethics was a matter for negotiation and could not be decreed arbitrarily by management. Such matters as free tickets, travel and gifts from news sources are working conditions about which newsmen have a right to bargain collectively.

Freedom of the Press

Properly to evaluate any journalistic performance, the original purpose of the freedom of the press clause in the First Amendment to the Constitution must be borne in mind. On one hand, the founding fathers wanted to prevent any governmental interference with or censorship prior to publication of news in the public interest, as they recalled the centuries of struggle which it took in England to obtain such rights. On the other hand, freedom of the press also was intended as a positive instrument to bolster the chances of success for an experimental government of, by and for the people. It really was the "right to be informed" that was being protected. If the founding fathers had thought some form of governmental regulation would best serve that purpose, undoubtedly they would have prescribed it. However, they felt the opposite: that wide-open freedom for any and all to publish or speak as they chose, even untruthfully and unfairly, would, in the long run, serve the public interest best. Thus, freedom of the press is a means to an end, not primarily an end in itself.

In the light of this purpose, it is discouraging to read the results of Gallup and the other public opinion polls which show gross and widespread ignorance regarding names and events in the news. The blame, however, is hardly primarily that of the journalistic media, which are there for the public to use. Rather, superficiality of interest in public affairs must be traced to failures in the homes, schools, churches and other places. Perhaps it is caused by the complexities and insecurities of our contemporary society. If the increasingly monopolistic press furthermore gives only one point of view on major issues, there nevertheless exist a quantity of liberal and iconoclastic magazines, newsletters and other periodicals to which it is possible to subscribe. There exist scores of anti-Establishment publications formerly known by the inappropriate label of Underground Press but now generally called the Alternative Press. Thus, it is not necessary to be uninformed or befuddled in the United States, the most literate nation in the world; and it is unfair to scapegoat the press, despite its shortcomings, for any public apathy. Doubtless, a more enlightened and vigorous defense of civil liberties and civil rights by journalistic media would help, but it would go only so far in combating undemocratic forces. Anything that the idealistic newcomer to the ranks of journalism can contribute to the improvement of the role of the news media in this respect is in the public interest. The opportunities for such service are greater than the young person would find in most other places. The Credo of the Chicago *Tribune* suggests what the profession involves:

> The newspaper is an institution developed by modern civilization to present the news of the day, to foster commerce and industry, to inform and lead public opinion, and to furnish that check upon government which no constitution has ever been able to provide.

The American Society of Newspaper Editors is in the process of adopting a Statement of Principles to supersede its Code of Ethics which dates from 1923. No newsman can do better than to attempt to live up to the code of ethics adopted in 1973 by the Society of Professional Journalists, Sigma Delta Chi. It follows:

The Society of Professional Journalists, Sigma Delta Chi, believes the duty of journalists is to serve the truth.

We believe the agencies of mass communication are carriers of public discussion and information, acting on their Constitutional mandate and freedom to learn and report the facts.

We believe in public enlightenment as the forerunner of justice, and in our Constitutional role to seek the truth as part of the public's right to know the truth.

We believe those responsibilities carry obligations that require journalists to perform with intelligence, objectivity, accuracy, and fairness.

To these ends, we declare acceptance of the standards of practice here set forth:

● **Responsibility:** The public's right to know of events of public importance and interest is the overriding mission of the mass media. The purpose of distributing news and enlightened opinion is to serve the general welfare. Journalists who use their professional status as representatives of the public for selfish or other unworthy motives violate a high trust.

● **Freedom of the Press:** Freedom of the press is to be guarded as an inalienable right of people in a free society. It carries with it the freedom and the responsibility to discuss, question, and challenge actions and utterances of our government and of our public and private institutions. Journalists uphold the right to speak unpopular opinions and the privilege to agree with the majority.

Ethics: Journalists must be free of obligation to any interest other than the public's right to know the truth.

1. Gifts, favors, free travel, special treatment or privileges can compromise the integrity of journalists and their employers. Nothing of value should be accepted.

2. Secondary employment, political involvement, holding public office, and service in community organizations should be avoided if it compromises the integrity of journalists and their employers. Journalists and their employers should conduct their personal lives in a manner which protects them from conflict of interest, real or apparent. Their responsibilities to the public are paramount. That is the nature of their profession.

3. So-called news communications from private sources should not be published or broadcast without substantiation of their claims to news value.

4. Journalists will seek news that serves the public interest, despite the obstacles. They will make constant efforts to assure that the public's business is conducted in public and that public records are open to public inspection.

5. Journalists acknowledge the newsman's ethic of protecting confidential sources of information.

● **Accuracy and Objectivity:** Good faith with the public is the foundation of all worthy journalism.

1. Truth is our ultimate goal.

2. Objectivity in reporting the news is another goal, which serves as the mark of an experienced professional. It is a standard of performance toward which we strive. We honor those who achieve it.

3. There is no excuse for inaccuracies or lack of thoroughness.

4. Newspaper headlines should be fully warranted by the contents of the articles they accompany. Photographs and telecasts should give an accurate picture of an event and not highlight a minor incident out of context.

5. Sound practice makes clear distinction between news reports and expressions of opinion. News reports should be free of opinion or bias and represent all sides of an issue.

6. Partisanship in editorial comment which knowingly departs from the truth violates the spirit of American journalism.

7. Journalists recognize their responsibility for offering informed analysis, comment, and editorial opinion on public events and issues. They accept the obligation to present such material by individuals whose competence, experience, and judgment qualify them for it.

8. Special articles or presentations devoted to advocacy or the writer's own conclusions and interpretations should be labeled as such.

• **Fair Play:** Journalists at all times will show respect for the dignity, privacy, rights, and well-being of people encountered in the course of gathering and presenting the news.

1. The news media should not communicate unofficial charges affecting reputation or moral character without giving the accused a chance to reply.

2. The news media must guard against invading a person's right of privacy.

3. The media should not pander to morbid curiosity about details of vice and crime.

4. It is the duty of news media to make prompt and complete correction of their errors.

5. Journalists should be accountable to the public for their reports and the public should be encouraged to voice its grievances against the media. Open dialogue with our readers, viewers, and listeners should be fostered.

• **Pledge:** Journalists should actively censure and try to prevent violations of these standards, and they should encourage their observance by all newspeople. Adherence to this code of ethics is intended to preserve the bond of mutual trust and respect between American journalists and the American people.

2

PROBLEMS OF NEWSGATHERING

Sometimes a reporter is present at a news event of which he writes, as a meeting, speech, court trial or athletic contest. More often he obtains his information secondhand, through interviewing eyewitnesses, authorities and others, or from press releases, reports and documents. Even when the newsgatherer is at the scene he has to check facts and details with firemen, policemen, convention chairmen and the like.

INTERVIEWING

Resourcefulness

Newspaper reporters not only have risked and lost their lives in the front lines during warfare, but they also have braved danger in peacetime to cover floods, hurricanes, fires, strikes, riots, crimes and many other kinds of stories. No editor expects a reporter to place himself in unreasonable jeopardy, but he does drill into every cub the fact that there always is more than one way to get any story. Resourcefulness by the reporter is imperative; the editor miles away cannot do his most importamt thinking for him.

Consider an experience with which the beginning reporter in a small city is likely to meet: arrival at the scene of an automobile accident after the crowd has disappeared, the injured persons have been removed and the wreckage has been cleared away. The unresourceful reporter probably would phone his office that he is unable to get the story. The resourceful reporter, however, makes inquiries at the stores and residences nearby. He tries to find the policeman on the beat who probably has the names of the persons who were involved. Unsuccessful in these attempts, he hastens to the nearest garages to find the damaged automobiles. Succeeding in that, he makes a notation of the license numbers in case the garage proprietor is unable to give him names. He phones police headquarters to discover the owners' names and addresses. He also phones the nearest hospitals. From one of these sources surely he learns the identity and whereabouts of the individuals whom he wishes to see. If he knows that someone was killed, he investigates at the morgue or calls the coroner.

Actually, today on this type of story the reporter's task is easier because police departments are motorized and radio equipped. Large newspapers furthermore have room for only the barest facts, probably obtained by telephone from police headquarters. Major or unusual accidents, however, in small and large cities alike, still are reported and old-fashioned ingenuity remains a journalistic asset.

The experienced reporter possesses the knowledge of all the possible channels through which he can obtain the information that he desires. Unidentified persons can be traced by means of laundry and other marks on their clothing, by dental work, even by bodily scars and deformities. In these days of numbers—social security, driver's license, credit card and the like—it is newsworthy when there is difficulty in making identification rather than the opposite. A suicide may be explained by friends of the dead person who recall conversations which at the time seemed unimportant to them but which later cast light on the deceased's motive in taking his own life. Often the reporter may recall some news story printed in his paper weeks or months previously which suggests a solution to the mystery at hand. The wise reporter makes a practice of reading his own and rival newspapers daily, and he preserves news items which may be of value to him later. When in doubt whether to clip a certain article, he follows the safer policy and clips.

Perseverance

When he has established contact with someone able to give him information, the reporter may be chagrined to discover that the news source is reluctant to cooperate to the desired extent. Maybe he just doesn't want to become involved in some matter, for fear of being summoned as a witness in court or of arousing the displeasure of public officials, gangsters and others whom he fears. Possibly he does not want to reveal his ignorance or to tip his hand regarding business or personal plans. The reasons why a news source slams the telephone or door or "clams up" may be many and diverse, but the obligation of the reporter is the same. It is his duty to discover any facts that it is in the public interest be made known.

In many situations perseverance usually is rewarded. If a person deliberately evades the press by refusing to answer the telephone or by locking himself in his office or home, he plays a losing game. If he is a person whose information or opinion the newspaper has a right to request, his refusal to grant an interview does not make him appear in a very favorable light to readers. The reporter must be careful in stating that a man has disappeared to avoid being interviewed or facing charges, but he can say that a person could not be reached. In fact, he should include such a statement in his story to let his readers know that he has made the effort. If a person grants an interview but still refuses to talk, his silence may be even more important news than any statement would have been. Once the reporter has questioned a person and has received a noncommittal answer or no answer at all, he can say that Mr. So-and-So refused to make any comment. Then readers can draw their own conclusions as to why Mr. So-and-So would not talk.

Mayor Alvin R. Potter had nothing to say today regarding the accusation that city employees, including himself, obtain free gasoline from the city yards.

The charge was made yesterday by Ald. Leonard Ball, chairman of the streets committee. The chief executive's only reply to inquiring reporters was: "I have no statement to make at this time."

Sometimes the reporter may be able to convince his subject that it is to his advantage to make some statement. If a person knows that the paper will run a story of his refusal to comment, he may be frightened into speaking against his previous resolution not to do so.

In his *Inside Story* (Doubleday, 1974), Brit Hume, assistant to Jack Anderson, says it is a "common technique" to persuade a person that you have been told a truly lurid story to inspire him to reveal the truth. Hume often was sly in identifying himself with the syndicate that distributed the Anderson column rather than with his employer. And he recommends the two-questioner technique popular with police whereby one interrogator assumes a belligerent attitude while the other seems protective. The Washington *Post* reporters Carl Bernstein and Bob Woodward, Pulitzer prize winners for the Watergate scandal expose, reveal in their book *All the President's Men* (Simon and Schuster, 1974) that they inspired confidence when Bob said he was a registered Republican and Carl argued a sincere antipathy for both parties. When an interviewer asked who gave the reporters his name, they could explain the necessity of protecting their sources, thus inspiring confidence from a jittery interviewee. They often called at interviewees' homes unannounced and always created the impression of seeking the truth regarding partial information they possessed. The confessions of these and several other topflight reporters inspired a great deal of soul searching throughout the entire journalistic world. The ethical beginner who is studying this textbook should acquaint himself with the memoirs of many contemporary reporters.

A person who becomes involved in the news in a way distasteful to him may hesitate to speak for publication for fear of being misquoted or misrepresented. The personality and sincerity of a reporter may suffice to cause such a person to talk. Everything depends upon the approach which the reporter makes and upon his own attitude during the interview. His purpose should be to convince his subject that he bears no malice, and that he is seeking an accurate and fair quotation. If the reporter can convince his subject of this fact, he may find the person grateful for the opportunity of at last being able to talk to someone who is sympathetic and who affords him the chance of making his version of a story understood.

Fortunate is the reporter who possesses some bit of information which his subject does not expect him to know. Skillful interjection into the interview of this information may bring to an end any attempt at bluffing or fabrication. If he does not possess knowledge with which to initimidate his subject, the reporter may himself start bluffing. If often is necessary to put on a bold front and to challenge statement with statement.

The reporter should realize at all times that he has a powerful organization, his newspaper, in back of him. If he "curls up" and permits himself to be browbeaten, he fails in his duty to his editor, which means his readers. If he is treading on ground where he has a perfect right to tread, he never should be humble. Men who have been in public life for any length of time realize the power of the press and respect it. This does not mean that the reporter should be overbearing or that he should resort to threats, except in extreme cases where such measures are justified. The reporter must be guided by his common sense and his understanding of what constitutes public interest in determining when to threaten and when to cajole.

The best kind of interview is that which proceeds in a natural, friendly, informal way. The reporter may inspire confidence and make himself attractive by not coming to the point of his visit at once, but by beginning the conversation with some general comment. If he can get his subject chatting about another matter, he may be able to lead the interview easily into the channel that he wishes it to take.

It is wise to take as few notes as possible during an interview of this kind. Often it is disastrous to take a single note. If the reporter can get his subject to forget that he is speaking for publication, he will obtain much more than if the person is constantly reminded that the interviewer is taking down verbatim what he is saying.

Sometimes the interviewee requests that the reporter take verbatim notes. Or the reporter at the end of an interview may remark, "By the way, would you mind spelling that name for me?" Or he may ask for exact figures, addresses, etc., which the interviewee will be glad to have him get correctly. The reporter must be careful in asking for such information, however, that he does not suggest to the interviewee that he had better start designating which of his remarks were for publication and which not.

The reporter must train his memory to recall, an hour or so afterward, all the important remarks of the interviewee. He should make immediate mental note of any startling statement which he will want to use verbatim, and should keep turning it over in his mind during the rest of the interview.

He should seize the first opportunity after leaving the scene of the interview to write down such a statement and to make any other necessary notes. If he has an hour or so before he must write his story, he will be surprised to find that, bit by bit, virtually the entire interview will come back to him.

In writing an opinion interview, it often is wise, for the sake of authority, to mention that the statements were made during an interview. If so, "Mr. White stated in an interview today" is better than "Mr. White told a News reporter today." The newspaper should not boast of an exclusive interview unless it has shown ingenuity in outwitting opponents.

Friendships on Beats

Because nobody is as grammatically correct while speaking as while writing, it is common practice to "fix up" unprepared oral statements of persons in the news so as not to embarrass them or create a wrong impression. The sense of any quotation must, of course, be retained. On occasion, it may not be in the public interest to protect a source. If, for instance, despite overwhelming evidence to the contrary, a public official declares that he "knows nothing" of a scandalous situation with which he should be familiar, it is not unfair to quote him verbatim. When such necessity arises, the beat reporter who has daily contact with the news source would be pleased to have a "special" or general assignment reporter sent over to handle that particular story. Often the beat man finds it wise to warn someone with whom he has made friendly contact that an unfavorable story is going to appear. In other words, a reporter cannot be effective if he makes enemies of those on whom he must depend for information. How to maintain personal relationships of friendship and at the same time fulfill his newsgathering obligations is one of the most vexatious problems with which the beat reporter has to contend. As one of them put it:

> A newspaper reporter, especially if he is assigned to a particular beat, enters into a very personal relationship with his news sources after a while.
> It can't be avoided, for these are the people you are talking with every day. In contrast, the public for which a reporter is writing, and to which he is responsible, is always a very impersonal and nebulous thing. There is a constant danger of giving the human being the benefit of the doubt at the expense of some quite abstract body of readers. For example, the superintendent of schools gets himself into a bad situation. Knowing him, you understand that he had the best motives in the world, but simply made a mistake of judgment. You know he recognizes it is your duty to advise the public of his action. Or, a situation I actually ran into: a cop had been suspended for striking a prisoner. I found out about it. The cop was a guy I had talked with every day for nearly a year. He'd told me all about himself, his family and his ambitions. The suspension had been ordered promptly and there was no doubt that he was being properly punished for his action. I wondered at the time what possible good it would do the public to know of the suspension. Who was the public, anyway? Of course, I wrote the story and spent much time trying to explain to the cop and to his superior why it was necessary that the public be advised. But the point is that

the reporter is called upon often to make that kind of decision, and unless he is very careful, he will unconsciously find himself giving in to the very human appeal of his news sources. I think I've found this the toughest temptation to guard against in the business.

One of the greatest pitfalls the cub reporter must avoid is naivete. No matter how pleasing the personality of the interviewee, or how logical whatever he has to say, the reporter must realize that it is necessary to check, corroborate, diligently seek the other side and in general not be gullible. With complete sincerity a news source usually presents a one-sided version of whatever is at issue. A callow reporter may be tremendously impressed with the account given him of how a business, governmental unit or social agency operates if he relies entirely on what an interested party tells him. Omissions, misplaced emphases and distortions may become apparent only by interviewing other persons known to be critical. Otherwise the reporter may become only a messenger boy for press releases or one-sided "good" news. Probing, both by intensive interviewing of original news sources and of others, will not always end in complete reversal of original impressions, but it is a necessary precaution against error through excessive exuberance.

Publicity Seekers

By no means are all persons reticent about granting interviews. The person who attempts to cajole or bulldoze reporters or to "hand out" statements promoting himself or a cause is ubiquitous. The reporter must be constantly on guard to spot the phony.

Entertainers and authors advertising their books are eager to be interviewed, especially on television. They have secretaries or press agents who may have typewritten or mimeographed answers to stock questions. The enterprising reporter, of course, wants much more. If the primary purpose of the interview is to obtain information or opinion on some public matter, he may encounter the unhappily growing tendency on the part of celebrities to expect monetary reward. Magazines, radio and television offer huge sums for memoirs, life stories and personality sketches or profiles. Those who have such to sell are reluctant to give them away free to newspaper reporters.

When a public official or other prominent person returns from abroad, especially if he has been on a public mission or involved in a newsworthy experience, he hardly can avoid granting some kind of interview to the press. It is obtaining an exclusive audience with the celebrity that challenges the reporter's ingenuity. Sometimes a letter of introduction from some other prominent person helps. Accosting an interviewee in a hotel lobby generally achieves little more than laconic replies to quick questions—at best an appointment for a future time.

A musician, scientist, writer, politician or any other person who has become prominent despises the reporter who betrays ignorance of his activities and reputation. Anyone with a speciality, furthermore, is bored to have to talk to another who is utterly uninformed concerning his field of interest.

There are numerous biographical reference books which the reporter can consult to learn something about a person's life and achievements. The newspaper's reference department, probably computerized or about to be, should be able to supply information as to what the interviewee actually has done.

The importance of being prepared was impressed upon an Atlanta reporter who asked Vivien Leigh what part she played in the motion picture version of *Gone With the Wind* when the actress attended the premiere of the reissue of the 1939 Academy Award winner. Miss Leigh simply informed the reporter that she did not care to be interviewed by such an ignorant person.

Not only national celebrities but also local persons who have won honors, taken new positions of importance, or been in the news prominently are the frequent subjects of reportorial inquiry. Reporters follow candidates for public office around during a day of campaigning to make a full report on their activities. Articles written after interviews with newly appointed school superintendents, bank presidents, chairmen of civic organizations and the like may resemble the profiles (combined biography, character sketch and description) originally made popular by *The New Yorker*. The object is to give readers the "feel" of the person, not just statistical facts regarding him and his activities.

When a person is being written up primarily because of his information or opinions regarding a matter, personality traits and description should be kept to a minimum or ignored. If a man shouts, bangs on the table, hesitates before giving an answer or in some other way behaves so that proper understanding of his comments requires mention of such circumstances, they may be included. Unless such is the case, references to "the balding professor" or "the slight soft-spoken man" may be inconsistent and out of place.

Entirely the opposite is true when the object is to make readers thoroughly acquainted with the subject of the interview as a person. In such cases, the subject's opinions are secondary and are used to help build a total word picture. How a person appears, talks and behaves during the interview may be pertinent, especially if the reporter elects to write in the first person.

These rules are applicable to all kinds of subjects including the off-the-beaten-path "characters" who may be the subjects of feature articles: retiring lifeguards, octogenarians, persons with unusual hobbies or reminiscences and the like. Pictures supplement and confirm written accounts in such cases, not the contrary.

High school reporters may be excused for referring to notes while asking questions. The professional, however, memorizes his questions. These should be related to the interviewee's field of interest and yet should not be too elementary or questions which it is reasonable to suppose the person has been asked time and time again. The reporter should try to find some new angle of approach, some fresh subject upon which the person interviewed will be able to speak. He should not try to cover his subject's entire field of interest. To do so would mean failure to cover any aspect with any degree of thoroughness. The best stories following interviews with celebrities are on specific points about which the interviewer has questioned his subject thoroughly.

Formal Interviews

Persons who know that they are to be interviewed by the press often arrange for formal interviews at which representatives of all the newspapers and perhaps electronic and other media in the community are present. From the standpoint of the reporter, such an interview is undesirable because none of the information he obtains is exclusive.

An advantage of the formal interview, however, lies in the fact that there are several minds thinking up questions to ask. Frequently the person to be interviewed announces in advance that these questions must be prepared in writing and submitted some time before the hour of the interview. This procedure permits the reporter to know exactly what the subject matter of the interview is to be, but it also allows the interviewee to prepare guarded answers to questions which, if presented spontaneously, might bring forth answers more to the reporter's liking.

Even when interviewing a person in the company of other reporters, it is possible to obtain material on which to write a different story from those which the others will write. The keenest listener and the sharpest wit present writes the best story. Comparison of several writeups based on a joint interview often discloses several different methods of handling the subject. One reporter plays up one statement and another reporter picks an entirely different one for his feature. Still a third writer concentrates on the personality of the interviewee rather than upon his remarks.

Denials

Sometimes a person quoted in an interview as having made a certain statement issues a denial. He may even aver that he never saw the reporter who wrote the story. This happens when a reporter plays up some extemporaneous remark of an interviewee's which the person would not have made in a formal interview.

A denial of the facts of an interview, of course, can be avoided by presenting the copy of the writeup to the subject, but few newspapers favor such a practice. To do so means that the interviewee will delete everything the least bit unfavorable to himself. It also means delay which a newspaper may not be able to afford, and a surrender of the newspaper's privilege to gather its information and write up its stories as it sees fit.

If the reporter is not guilty of misquotation he may "stick to his guns" and, if his newspaper stands back of him, defy the interviewee who has denied making a statement. In another story he reaffirms that his original story was correct. Then the public can believe whomever it pleases. Too often it chooses to believe the person interviewed when the reporter really was right.

Reporters frequently do not use remarks which they suspect the interviewee would deny. If he wishes to make sure that the interview will not be denied, the reporter can phone or call upon the interviewee again to obtain verification of whatever he wishes to write. When he does so, or even when he obtains his original interview, he may take a third person with him as a witness to the interview. This, however, seldom is feasible as the presence of a third person may prevent informality.

A tape recording is the best defense that any interviewer can have of his accuracy. Most of the problems considered so far in this chapter would be reduced or eliminated if it were possible to use electronic recording devices on all occasions. Such is, of course, impossible. Unless there is surreptitious use of the devices, which would raise legal as well as moral questions, most interviewing for spot news stories will continue to be of the old-fashioned pencil and notebook kind. At present effective use of tape recorders must be limited to feature interviews with the time element not so pressing as daily press deadlines.

THE INTERVIEWER

The scientist in his laboratory and the author in his den can be as shy as a mouse in the presence of a cat, uncommunicative, embarrassed by the company of others, incapable of either social conversation or formal speech-making—can be, in fact, an anthrophobe (one who fears people) and still be considered a personal success and a benefactor of mankind; the newspaper reporter must be an entirely different kind of person.

It is conceivable that the newsgatherer secretly may dislike most of those with whom his work brings him into contact, but he is forced to learn how to conceal any such feeling and to be able to meet people, all sorts of people, and to get them to feel so easy in his presence that he can obtain what he wants from them.

Because they are unaccustomed to dealing with them, many persons are suspicious of newspapermen, regarding them almost as some strange species of animal life not to be trusted or treated with the courtesy customarily shown those with other ways of earning a livelihood. Says Henry F. Pringle, veteran reporter: "The novice about to be interviewed for the first time assumes that all reporters are ghouls waiting for the emergence of the family skeleton." Such people think nothing of using methods of evasion and prevarication to hinder a reporter in his legitimate quest for information which they condemn in obstreperous terms if he himself tries.

What this amounts to is that the newspaperman must be an expert salesman. Good salesmanship is the basis of all good reporting, and fundamental to successful salesmanship are personality and tact. Although the timid, awkward cub may get what he wants by creating pity, it is the person who gives the impression of self-confidence, self-assurance and self-respect whose success is enduring. It is in the presence of such persons that others feel most at ease.

It is impossible to lay down general rules on how to develop personality and tact. There are many types of newspapermen, all equally successful. On the whole, however, newspapermen are extroverts or compensated introverts with poise, self-assurance and self-respect. Caspar Milquetoasts don't succeed in newspaper or any other kind of work calling for daily contact with the public.

A few specific suggestions to beginners are the following:

1. Don't conceal your identity. Begin an interview with a frank acknowledgment of who you are and of the purpose of your visit. Give the impression that you have an absolute right to obtain the information wanted and have no doubt of your ability to get it. Thus, it is wise to avoid negative questions, as "You wouldn't care to say anything on this matter, would you?"

2. Inspire confidence and even awe by directness in speech. Don't "beat around the bush" by informing a person "We'd like to know if you will give us a statement—" Rather, ask "What do you think about it?"

3. Have something worth asking. Know exactly what you want of the interviewee. Prepare specific questions which merit specific answers. Do not imitate the stupid television reporter who shoves a microphone into a woman's face to ask "How does it feel to be wife of a newly elected mayor?" or "What do you have to say about your son's being found guilty of murder?" In other words, be tactful and avoid boorishness and banality. Know what you're doing.

4. Be particularly careful in telephone conversations when the other party has the power to end the interview simply by hanging up the receiver. Don't say, "I wonder if—" "I'd like to ask you—" A good beginning is "This is —— of the *Daily News*. I'm calling to ask your opinion about—" and don't end a telephone conversation with "All righty" or "Okey doke" or some similar moronic expression.

5. Always give the impression of knowing more about a story than you really do or that you have other ways of obtaining information if the immediate source fails to cooperate. At the same time, don't make threats except as a last resort in special cases. Often a person can be induced to give facts by questions which make him believe the reporter has wrong information which he'll use if not corrected. From fear of having a wrong impression broadcast, he may open up and tell the truth.

6. Often, if a person is reluctant to talk, it is advisable to engage him in conversation about some unrelated subject, as an object in the room, his wife's picture or an extraneous bit of gossip. After the ice has been broken and an attitude of friendship has been created, it is possible cautiously to bring up the real subject occasioning the visit.

7. Don't stop questioning until you have all the facts you want or flat refusals on the part of the news source to give them. Often a person's refusal to make a statement is better news than if he were to become voluble.

There is no succinct set of simple rules for a beginning interviewer to master. It is impossible to advise a cub: always do this, generally avoid doing that, etc. No two situations are the same, but it is essential that the reporter (1) know about the interviewee, (2) know the subject matter and (3) be sharp, which means flexible, perceptive, penetrating and possessed of common sense and, in the public interest, a strong ethical sense.

PUBLIC RELATIONS

Most persons who quit newspapers or other journalistic media go into public relations work. Often this is because of the lure of a fatter paycheck, in which case the more basic reportorial experience the better. Others have been cynical failures in their attempt to find adequate means of self-expression where they were. Still others seek opportunities to promote causes in which they believe.

Their most recent attempt to improve their public image is to call themselves directors or vice presidents in charge of public affairs. Over half of the nation's largest corporations now use the terms "public affairs" or "corporate relations" instead of "public relations." The trend is also for governmental agencies at all levels to do the same.

To Edward L. Bernays, who coined the term "public relations" in 1919, the phenomenon is partly the result of "the operatives in the White House who called themselves public relations experts and who were not." Bernays is dubious about the value of name change, saying that "a group of highbinders" could commit some "kind of professional mayhem" and then "another name would have to be sought." As he has since 1923 in *Crystallizing Public Opinion*, the first book ever written on the subject, Bernays advocates state licensing of public relations counsel to safeguard the public from quacks.

Adverse Criticism

Until recently, practicing journalists were almost unanimous in condemning public relations men as brazen if not unscrupulous space-grabbers and fakers. Today, this harsh judgment has been considerably modified, partly because of the impossibility of covering the wide range of potential news without assistance, and partly because of the considerable elevation of standards within the public relations field. Once they were mostly press agents, whose forte was the manufacturing of stunts, and, more recently, they were mere publicity men whose success was determined largely by the amount of space their clients got in the legitimate news columns of the media. Now the best of them are skillful participants in top-level policy making who have the total "image" of their clients in mind. Instead of courting publicity they may, in fact, advise against seeking any journalistic mention. They concern themselves with internal problems of personnel and morale, advertising, product, salesmanship and total behavior. In their exalted positions they may be considered by some to be even more "dangerous" as hidden persuaders, pressure boys, masters of the invisible sell, space-grabbers, ballyhoo boys, hucksters or malicious engineers of public consent, to use some of the titles by which they are known to their detractors.

In Defense

In their own defense, the hundreds of thousands, if not millions, of persons who perform public relations functions contend that their activities are of great social benefit. They take credit for having converted business and industry completely away from the "public-be-damned" attitude and say that they have humanized business, helped give it good manners and, most important, a conscience; and that they have taught it that he profits most who serves best. They define public relations or its synonym as simply doing the right thing and letting people know about it, applying the Golden Rule in everyday activities while not letting one's light shine unnoticed under a basket. To them, sound public relations means the daily application of common sense, common courtesy and common decency in accordance with a continuous program of enlightened self-interest through good works which not only earn one a good reputation but also cause him to deserve it as a good neighbor.

In further defense of public relations as it relates to news media, it is indisputable that almost every legitimate news item which appears in public print has publicity value for someone. Even unfavorable mention or scandal doesn't seem to be fatal to national heroes, especially in the entertainment world. Readers' memories are short and inaccurate and when they go to the polls the familiar name has advantage, no matter how unsavory the situation in connection with which it was publicized. Organized baseball and other professional sports are commercial enterprises which have thrived on free publicity, through good-sized sports sections, for generations. The same is true of the theater, book publishing, concert stage and other artistic enterprises which are not entirely philanthropies.

Since John D. Rockefeller I hired Ivy Lee early in the century, the policy of the public relations profession has been increasingly toward more co-operation with the newsgathering media rather than agencies to suppress unfavorable news or retard newsgatherers in their efforts to obtain it. Public relations departments of railroads, airlines and industries today are a great asset to reporters at times of fires, accidents and other disasters, whereas a generation ago exactly the opposite was the case.

The news or publicity or information division of a public relations department provides a quantity of legitimate news handouts, full texts of speeches by important people, notices of meetings and conventions, plans for changes in policies and operations of both private and public institutions, and other services which no newspaper or magazine could afford to obtain by means of its own paid employees. To some extent, the media are today at the mercy of the public relations people to keep them informed of what is going on in large segments of society.

Dangers

The great danger is the extent to which public relations men erect a barrier between the reporter and original news sources. If all news is obtained through carefully prepared news releases, the reporter becomes little more than a glorified messenger boy. Good newspapers and magazines consist of more than such handouts with proper headlines and picture captions added by the editors. No matter how cooperative and sensible, the public relations man never can lose sight of the fact that his primary obligation is to his employer. The reporter, on the other hand, is a public servant in a democracy. There are bound to be at least occasional clashes of interest. News releases today are usually well written and reliable but often there are omissions and obscurities which can be corrected only by personal contact between newsgatherer and news source.

Large news conferences, especially with the president and other prominent public figures, can be extremely frustrating as no reporter present has the opportunity to probe deeply into any matter. Too often a reporter is limited to a single question so that as many as possible can have a turn. Planted questions are asked by friendly newsmen who have been advised by press agents. It's impossible under such circumstances to be thorough in one's fact finding. Even if better conditions prevail, a public relations man may hover over the shoulder of the interviewee to advise, augment and correct his statements. Reporters often are infuriated and feel that their dignity has been injured. Serving one's editor and the public is extremely difficult under such circumstances.

If the interview is broadcast live, the nonelectronic media newsgatherers may be at great disadvantage to follow up misconceptions that already have become familiar to millions of watchers. It is possible for public figures to misuse television to the detriment of all. The task of the print media to correct errors and to supplement incomplete details is becoming tremendous.

From their standpoint, public relations men recognize the value of good will on the part of reporters. Hence, they not only try to create the impression at least of the best cooperation possible, but they also make life easier in other ways. At meetings and conventions there are usually press tables and press-rooms with ample refreshments, desks, telephones and other equipment. Publications differ in the extent to which they allow staff members to accept favors from public relations men, public officials and others. Some even forbid the acceptance of free books to review, of passes to athletic, dramatic, and other performances or of gifts on Christmas or other holidays. Others, however, allow and even welcome large favors such as trips and tours, even to foreign lands. The beginning reporter does well to learn what his superiors' attitude happens to be regarding all forms of what is opprobriously called "payola" which is widespread despite the Code of Ethics of the Public Relations Society which forbids it.

A more subtle way of influencing news judgment is the awards which are given in recognition of stellar performance in a particular field. The decision in such a case as to what constitutes good journalism is that of the donor of the prize. Some newspapers are eager to wallpaper their offices with plaques and certificates, and some keep a careful tab on announcements of such honors in the offing. *Editor & Publisher* issues an annual *Directory of Journalism Awards.* In 1975 it listed 178 competitions, most of them annual contests, with prizes totaling more than $990,000. Too much ambition may develop into exaggerated emphasis on news of a certain character rather than unprejudiced evaluations of the happenings of the day. In other words, conscious efforts to please the donors of prizes can badly warp good editorial performance.

LEGAL OBSTACLES

Unless he is forewarned, one of the first big surprises that the young reporter may experience is the discovery that he can invoke the freedom of the press clause in the Constitution from morn to night and still be denied access to some documents which his naivete might lead him to believe are public records open to all. Should he be able to break down certain barriers, he still might run the risk of being cited for contempt of court or sued for libel were he to use information thereby obtained.

It is regrettable that there is no place to which the reporter, or the editor either, can be directed for a clearcut statement of what his rights and privileges in particular instances are. Not only are the laws of different states different, but also the same law is likely to have been interpreted differently by two or more courts of law in what would seem to be cases involving identical issues. As regards a number of important legal problems involving newspapers, there is little or no law, either statute or common. For this, newspapers themselves are partly if not largely to blame because they prefer to settle law suits out of court.

The principle generally observed, regardless of the clarity of state or municipal law, is that the public—which includes the press—has the right to inspect public documents except when the public interest thereby would be harmed. The frequent clashes between newspapers and public officials result from differences of opinion as to what constitutes a public record and what constitutes public interest. Some states have been careful to define public documents; others haven't. In either case, and regardless of the fact that there have been few tests in court, newspapers do not expect to be allowed to cover grand jury proceedings, executive sessions of law-making bodies, or to be shown records of unsolved cases in the police detective bureau, the report of an autopsy before it is presented to a coroner's jury, the report of an examiner to either a fire marshal or public banking official or a number of other similar documents. In fact, public officials probably would be sustained by most courts were they to refuse the press access to many records now available to it.

Pleading "public interest," the county clerk who refuses to disclose the names of applicants for marriage licenses, so as to protect them from commercial salesmen, probably is on sound legal ground.

The cub reporter should learn what both the law and general practice are in the community where he is to work, and the policy of his paper as to defiance or circumvention of public officials seeking to conceal news. Some editors encourage reporters to search for "leaks" whereby grand jury and executive session news may be obtained and they have defied judges' orders with resultant citations for contempt. Many years ago, the United Press forced the United States Senate to modify its rule regarding secret sessions after Paul Mallon obtained a secret roll call on the confirmation of a presidential nominee for a cabinet position. Despite resolutions to the contrary, however, congressional committees still hold closed sessions when legislation is being drafted.

Over half of the states have passed "open record" and "open meeting" laws, many of them based on Sigma Delta Chi's "model" laws. Nevertheless, reporters continue to be frustrated by the evasive practices of some governmental bodies, such as city councils and school boards, which go into executive session and hold informal meetings in private places. Often important matters are decided at such clandestine rendezvous so that what transpires in public legally is merely a confirmation and leaves the newsgatherer ignorant of the factors which went into the decision-making.

Only one state, Tennessee, obeys all 11 criteria for an ideal open meeting, or "sunshine," law according to a study conducted for the Freedom of Information Foundation of the University of Missouri by Dr. John B. Adams of the University of North Carolina. The criteria are (1) a statement of public policy in support of openness, (2) an open legislature, (3) open legislative committees, (4) open meetings of state agencies or bodies (5) open meetings of agencies and bodies of political subdivisions of the state, (6) open county boards, (7) open city councils, (8) no closed executive sessions, (9) legal recourse to halt secrecy, (10) actions taken in meeting which violate the law are null and void and (11) penalties for violation of the law.

United States Supreme Court decisions affecting freedom of the press rights have increased in recent years and probably will continue to do so. The court has upheld the right to publish names of rape victims that are included in official documents. In the case at issue the victim was murdered. The court also ruled that the press has no right to general access to lists of welfare recipients. The United States Bureau of Prisons was upheld when it forbade prison inmates to hold press interviews.

GOVERNMENT SECRECY

The ghastly extent to which the American people were uninformed and misinformed about many matters, especially the conduct of foreign affairs, was revealed during the congressional hearings into the Watergate scandals and by subsequent exposes of the censorship and propaganda activities of earlier administrations. Revelations of infringements of the Bill of Rights by the CIA, FBI, IRS, military branches and other agencies were shocking. Some charged the press with overplaying the news but most came to realize that American democracy was saved by the so-called fourth estate which accelerated its activities when the official three branches floundered.

Systematic post-World War II infringement of the people's right to know began Sept. 24, 1951, when President Harry S Truman ordered all federal departments and agencies to classify and withhold news as the State and Defense departments already were doing, the categories being "classified," "top secret," "secret," "confidential" and "restricted." Under pressure from all of the journalistic organizations, President Eisenhower eliminated the "restricted" category which proved meaningless as "classified" became the catchall.

With the support of the ANPA, ASNE, SDX and other journalistic groups, a House committee chaired by Rep. John Moss of California embarrassed a number of bureaucrats who tried to justify their censorship actions, using a 1789 "housekeeping" statute intended to help George Washington get his administration started. Congress passed an amendment to the 1789 law to state it "does not authorize withholding information from the public or limiting the availability of records to the public." Joy died when President Eisenhower, on signing the bill, declared it did not "alter the existing power of the head of an executive agency to keep appropriate information or papers confidential in the public interest."

In 1966 President Lyndon B. Johnson used virtually the same language when he signed the Freedom of Information act which established the right of the public, including the press, to inspect the *Federal Register* descriptions of the operations of federal agencies, their rules and records. Several kinds of information, mostly allegedly related to national security or privacy, were excepted and the measure was of little help to journalists. Whereas private law firms and businesses utilized the law 640 times, the press used it only 90 times. In 1975 passage of 17 amendments over President Ford's veto supposedly simplified and accelerated use of the privilege. However, bureaucratic stalling and exorbitant service charges still were obstacles.

In July 1971 the United States Supreme Court ruled, 6 to 3, that the New York *Times* and Washington *Post* could publish articles based on the so-called Pentagon Papers, documents detailing much of the behind-the-scenes diplomacy which led to American military involvement in Southeast Asia. The papers were leaked to the press by a former Rand Corporation researcher, Dr. Daniel Ellsberg, whose trial for conspiracy and other offenses ended with the revelation of the attempted burglary of his psychiatrist's office by members of the White House Plumbers group which also burglarized the National Democratic headquarters in the Watergate. Some of the Plumbers' leaders had been prominent in the fiasco of the Bay of Pigs invasion of Cuba a few years earlier.

In permitting publication of the Pentagon Papers the Supreme Court did not invalidate the classification system which remains intact. Perhaps 20,000,000 documents remain inaccessible because of the actions of about 30,000 federal governmental bureaucrats with censorship powers.

A sizable library exists of books by frustrated journalistic scholars who tried to "set the record straight" as regards such events as the U-2 incident, the Bay of Pigs, the Cuban missiles crisis, the invasion of the Dominican Republic, the Vietnam War, America's attitude during the Indo-Pakistani War, the role of the CIA in insurrections, including assassinations in several countries such as the Congo, Guatemala, Iran, Indonesia and Chile. Fresh facts regarding these and other incidents are still emerging, in congressional investigations, from confessions of repentent principals, and, not the least, from journalistic activity. In the meantime the American public has had to wait to know the truth about important historical events. The so-called adversary role of the press toward government is decidedly in the best interests of democracy.

3
ORGANIZING THE FACTS

Even before he has completed the task of gathering the facts concerning a particular news event, the reporter starts thinking of how he will organize them into a news story. The more experienced he is, the more automatic or unconscious this habit becomes. As new information is obtained he may modify earlier ideas regarding the theme or central idea coming out of the assignment.

CONTEMPORARY TRENDS

Since World War II, there have been numerous studies of the traditional methods of organizing a news story. At several annual conventions the Associated Press Managing Editors devoted considerable attention to ways of making news writing more readable. In part, they were motivated by the success of news magazines in presenting the news in brighter and livelier ways. Also, and perhaps more important, radio and television newscasters demonstrated how the gist of a story often could be presented in fewer words than were contained in the usual traditional newspaper story lead.

    The press associations and some large newspapers employed experts in readability to analyze their practices. A few journalistic higher-ups became so enthusiastic over some readability formulas that they blamed widespread reader ignorance and indifference upon traditional styles of journalistic composition. Some others thought the answer was to be found in greater understanding by journalists of the philosophical and statistical aspects of the communication process. More recently critics within the newsroom have joined some laymen in insisting that the press must assume greater leadership in investigating and crusading in the public interest.

Because they have been taught to journalistic novitiates for several generations, the five *w*'s often seem to be trite and academic. Nevertheless, no matter what writing or speaking style is used, and regardless of whether the contents are objectively descriptive or subjectively analytical, the reader or listener's curiosity has to be satisfied as regards the *who, what, when, where* and *why*, as well as the *how* of a newsworthy occurrence. What has happened, largely as a result of the blandishments of the readability conscious and statistically conscious communications researchers and the socially conscious rank-and-file, is a considerable loosening of the rigid rules regarding the structure of a news story. Whereas a generation ago it was virtually mandatory that as many as possible of the five *w*'s and *h* be mentioned in the first paragraph of a news story, today considerably greater freedom is permitted in presenting them. Now that radio and television have taken the edge off the spot news lead, stories may be written in seeming disregard of the old principle. Nevertheless, though delayed, the old *w*'s are included somewhere in the full account of a timely news event.

THE INVERTED PYRAMID FORM

Despite the extensive experimentation that has taken place, the great majority of news stories still are written in accordance with the traditional rule that the first part—whether it be a conventionally written single paragraph or a half-dozen or more one-sentence paragraphs—contain a succinct resume of the story as a whole. The beginner ambitious to eventually achieve stylistic originality does well to master the rules first in order to break them intelligently later.

The striking difference between news writing in the United States and other forms of written composition, such as the essay, poetry, drama, novel and short story, continues to be this: whereas the authors of these other forms of composition usually begin with minor or incidental details and work to a climax near or at the end of their compositions, the news writer reverses this plan of organization. That is, he begins with the climax or end of the story. Given a schedule of facts to arrange in the form of a newspaper article, he selects the most important fact or climax of the story he has to tell and puts it at the beginning. The second most important fact comes second, the third most important fact third and so on.

The traditional form of news writing is called the *inverted pyramid form*. It is said to have originated in Civil War days when correspondents used the telegraph for the first time. From fear that their accounts would not be transmitted all at one time, the war correspondents crowded as much information as possible into their first paragraphs.

Throughout the decades since that time, press associations, which transmit stories by telegraph, have perfected the system. Before the teletypesetter was introduced about mid-century, few leading stories ever were transmitted in one piece. Instead, a few paragraphs of several important stories were sent first and then the later paragraphs. Throughout a day's sending, there were numerous new or substitute first paragraphs (leads), inserts and additions.

Locally written news followed the press association pattern. The inverted pyramid form of organization was defended in several different ways:

1. *To facilitate reading.* The reading matter of the average newspaper, if printed in book form, would fill a large volume. The American newspaper reader hasn't time to read that much daily. Neither is he interested in all the articles appearing in any newspaper. If the climax of every story is at the beginning, the reader can learn the gist of the news quickly and, if interested, can continue to the details of stories which interest him. He should not have to read any article to its conclusion to learn what it is about.

2. *To satisfy curiosity.* This is the natural way of telling an important item of news. If someone drowns while swimming, the average person would not begin telling of the incident by narrating the dead person's preparations for a visit to the beach with a group of friends. Rather, he would tell the important news first—John was drowned while swimming. Then he would relate the supplementary details of how, when and where it happened.

3. *To facilitate makeup.* In rectifying a page, the makeup editor often finds it necessary to cut the length of some articles. If the least important details are at the end of a story, he can do this without harming the story. The makeup editor should feel free to cut ordinary articles without consulting other editors.

4. *To facilitate headline writing.* The headline consists of the key words or their synonyms necessary to give an idea of what a story contains. If the story is well written, the headline writer should not have to look beyond the first paragraph or two to find these words.

A few years ago the Writing committee of the Associated Press Managing Editors cited the story in the right-hand column below as one of the best examples of news writing of the year. It was written in the traditional inverted pyramid style. In the left-hand column below, the same facts, using the identical phraseology as much as possible, are rearranged in chronological order.

Chronological Style

About 1 A.M. today, Mrs. Harry Rosenberg was awakened by the sound of a car roaring out of the driveway of her home. She rushed to the living room where she discovered that her granddaughter, Judith Ann Roberts, 7, no longer was sleeping on the studio couch

Newspaper Style

Judith Ann Roberts, blue-eyed, 7-year-old daughter of a Baltimore attorney and labor leader, was kidnaped from the home of her grandparents here today, raped and beaten to death.

Police found the child's nude and brutally battered body in a clump of

Chronological Style	**Newspaper Style**

and that the front door was standing open.

Mrs. Rosenberg called her daughter, Mrs. Shirley Roberts, wife of a Baltimore attorney and labor leader, who was visiting her parents. Mrs. Roberts, the missing child's mother, notified police of her daughter's kidnaping at 1:10 A.M.

Police said the kidnaper sneaked into the home of the grandparents, stole the keys to the Rosenberg's car from the grandfather's trousers pocket and took the child away.

Four hours and ten minutes after they were called, police found the Rosenberg car abandoned in the strip of sandy land between Bayshore drive and the shore of Biscayne Bay. Its wheels were mired in the sand and the tire marks showed the driver tried frantically to get it out.

Judith Ann's nude and brutally battered body was found a block from the car in a clump of bushes off fashionable Bayshore drive. It was caked with blood and dirt, indicating she put up a brave fight for her life. The blue-eyed child had been raped and beaten on the head with a heavy instrument and a piece of gauze was knotted about her throat. Her flimsy seersucker nightgown, white with red polka dots, lay eight feet from her body.

bushes off fashionable Bayshore drive five hours after her mother, Mrs. Shirley Roberts, reported her missing.

She had been beaten on the head with a heavy instrument and a piece of gauze was knotted about her throat. Her flimsy seersucker nightgown, white with red polka dots, lay eight feet from the body.

Judith Ann's little body was caked with blood and dirt, indicating she put up a brave fight for her life.

Police said the killer sneaked into the home of the grandparents, Mr. and Mrs. Harry Rosenberg, about 1 A.M., stole the keys to Rosenberg's car from his trousers pocket and took the child from the studio couch in the living room where she was sleeping.

Mrs. Rosenberg was awakened by the sound of the car roaring out of the driveway. She found the child missing and the front door standing open.

Police were called at 1:10 A.M. Four hours and ten minutes later, they found the Rosenberg car abandoned in the strip of sandy land between Bayshore drive and the shore of Biscayne Bay. Its wheels were mired in the sand and the tire marks showed the driver tried frantically to get it out.

Judith's body was found a block from the car.

"Note, please," the APME Writing committee asked, "the many fine points . . . 'the seersucker nightgown, white and red polka dots, lay eight feet from the body.'

"How many little nightgowns like that are all over this land? And *eight feet* . . . no guess-work there; the reporter was seeing it for you. Too, the killer sneaked in about 1 A.M. and 'police were called at 1:10 A.M.' The car was found *four hours and ten minutes later* . . . not simply later in the day."

Although few would argue with an unnamed telegraph editor with more than forty years' experience, whom the committee quoted as saying, "That Miami story is one of the finest writing jobs I've ever seen," the points cited by the committee indicate that the story's strength derived primarily from the fact that an extraordinary job of reporting, involving keen observation, had preceded its composition. In other words, *the most important step in communication is obtaining something worthwhile to communicate.* Stated still another way, the basis of all good journalism is thorough reporting. Shorter words, sentences and paragraphs, desirable as they may be for clarity, cannot add important details to a journalistic account. *There is no substitute for good reporting no matter what writing style is used.* It is the message and not the medium that counts, and journalists should not be misled by crackpot theories to the contrary.

THE LEAD

The Miami story was written in traditional inverted pyramid style. That is, the first paragraph contained the gist or skeleton outline of the entire story in a minimum of words. Subsequent paragraphs elaborated upon various aspects of the lead, making them more definite; or they supplied additional details in the order of their importance as the reporter judged them.

Since, for more than a half-century, this has been the orthodox form of news writing, the *lead* of a straight news story came to be defined as the first paragraph which contained all of the elements (five *w*'s and *h*) necessary for the complete telling of the essential facts.

This practice often led to long and crowded first paragraphs. The lead of the Miami story, for instance, might have read something like this:

> The nude and brutally beaten body of Judith Ann Roberts, blue-eyed, 7-year-old daughter of a Baltimore attorney and labor leader, was found by police in a clump of bushes off fashionable Bayshore drive here at 1 A.M. today after she had been kidnaped from the home of her grandparents, Mr. and Mrs. Harry Rosenberg, and raped.

In the effort to avoid such cumbersome lead paragraphs, and to increase readability, some newspapers have gone to the opposite extreme of invoking the "one-fact sentence" rule which would lead to something like the following:

> A 7-year-old girl has been kidnaped, raped and beaten to death.
> She was blue-eyed Judith Ann Roberts of Baltimore. Her father is a lawyer and labor leader.
> Police found the child's body in a clump of bushes off fashionable Bayshore drive.
> The body was nude and brutally battered.
> The child's mother, Mrs. Shirley Roberts, reported her daughter missing at 1:10 A.M.
> That was four hours and ten minutes before the body was found by police.

It is difficult to determine exactly how many of the one- or two-sentence paragraphs of a story written in this manner constitute the lead, or first unit of the story. Every sentence relates to some word or fact in a preceding sentence, and it takes a half-dozen or more of them to present all of the information which once would have been crowded into half the space or less. This form of writing says less in more words but is scored as more readable. The original version of the Miami story was a compromise between the new and old extremes.

Since the inverted pyramid form still is adhered to, even in the staccato type of paragraphing illustrated above, in that facts are arranged in the order of their supposed importance, the traditional definition of a news story lead holds: the first unit of the story which performs the function of telling the entire story in epitomized form.

A good lead, no matter how much it is strung out, has the following qualities:

1. Answers all of the questions that a reader wants to have answered when hearing of a particular incident. These include the cause and result (the *how* or *why* and the *what*), the *who* and often the *where* and the *when*. These elements are called the five *w*'s and the *h*. Not all of these must be present in every lead, but no important one should be omitted. (See Chapter 4.)
2. Plays up the feature of the story if there is one. (See Chapter 5.)
3. Is attractive and induces the reader to continue with the rest of the story, observing the canons of good news writing. (See Chapter 6.)
4. Suggests or gives the authority on which the news is printed. (See Chapter 7.)
5. Identifies the individuals mentioned in the story (or the story itself) by relating them (or it) to previous or contemporaneous news. (See Chapter 8.)

The Miami story fulfilled these requirements in this way:

Who—Judith Ann Roberts.
What—Killed.
When—July 7; time of day (1 A.M.) given later.
Where—Miami, Fla.
How—Kidnaped, raped and beaten to death.
Authority—Police and relatives obvious sources of information.
Identification—Seven-year-old daughter of a Baltimore lawyer and labor leader.
Feature—Kidnaped from home of grandparents.

THE BODY

In view of the tendency to reduce the first sentence of a news story to the fewest possible words, the function of the sentences and paragraphs which immediately follow is clearly to restate the facts of the first sentence so as to make them more definite. Loosening of the rule that the lead contain all of the five *w*'s and the *h* means that succeeding paragraphs often must supply some additional pertinent facts crowded out of the lead in the interest of brevity.

It doesn't make any difference what academic labels are placed on units of a news story, and it is difficult or impossible to chart news stories so that units do not overlap. If you wish, you can consider the extreme attempt at epitomized writing ("A 7-year-old girl has been kidnaped, raped and beaten to death") as the lead and call all the rest of the story by its traditional name, *body*. Or you can insist that the lead proper include as many sentences as are necessary to make the basic elements (five *w*'s and *h*) definite.

In either case, there often remain a number of additional paragraphs which can be labeled either "body" or "second part of body." If new details are added in the same sentences or paragraphs in which there is further amplification of the lead, telling exactly where the last unit of the story begins isn't easy.

Spiraling

Perhaps a spiral with the broad part at the top would be a better metaphor than inverted pyramid to describe how a well-constructed news story today may unfold. Either by definite grammatical reference or linkage of thought, every well-written succeeding paragraph flows from the preceding one.

In the following example observe how every succeeding paragraph makes more definite an element of the preceding paragraph (words in italics) and in addition contains some new information.

Aaron L. Engstrand, who recently completed a study of previously made civil service surveys for the city administration, will get a full-time city *job* July 1.

He will become consultant to the city Civil Service commission, empowered to put into effect *recommendations* he submitted.

They include "more realistic examinations" in the *selection of city employees*, and improvements in personnel relations.

John S. Christopher, commission president, announced the appointment Friday. He said that one of Engstrand's first jobs will be to hire a *director of personnel* for the city.

Engstrand, a veteran in public administration and social-service work, refused the personnel director job when it was offered him recently.

Unity

A method of obtaining rhetorical unity as one short paragraph follows another is by use of *linkage* words. Note in the following example how their skillful use creates a flow and, at the same time, enables the writer to introduce new facts. This story could be cut at the end of almost any paragraph and there still would be a rhetorically complete account.

By Associated Press

Mighty rivers on a late winter rampage surged through south central sections of Alabama, Georgia and Mississippi Wednesday, leaving wide trails of muddy ruin amounting to millions.

Except around Jackson, Miss., the highest levels of the flooding rivers were spread largely across rural areas as they continued toward their common draining point, the Gulf of Mexico.

However, more flood menace lies ahead for downstate residents, and even in ravaged mid-state sections where the worst is over, it will be days before the rampant rivers fall within their banks.

ALABAMA AT CREST

At Selma in central Alabama, *for example*, the Alabama River reached its crest of 58.3 feet Tuesday night, but the muddy waters are not expected to creep back to the 45-foot flood level until March 9.

In hard-hit Selma and Montgomery and Demopolis, Ala., *as well as* Jackson, Miss., and West Point and Columbus, Ga., thousands in evacuation centers looked to more days of waiting for water to seep out of their homes.

To relieve the tension of Montgomery refugees, many facing their fifth night in shelters, the Red Cross put on recreation programs.

Damage to Alabama's public facilities *has already topped* $10 million in pre-liminary estimates. That includes only roads and bridges and county and municipal places—not homes, businesses, farmland and livestock.

CATTLE DROWNED

In central Alabama's Montgomery and Elmore Counties alone, a livestock broker estimates that about 2,500 head of cattle worth $500,000 have drowned *during the current flood.*

As the swollen Pearl River swirled around the Jackson, Miss., area Tuesday night and Wednesday, cutting a three-mile swath in some places, about 850 residents left their low-lying homes and most flocked to refuge centers.

[Tampa *Tribune*]

Block Paragraphing

In longer stories, regardless of whether the lead was one or several para-graphs long, or "straight" or spiraling, paragraphs are so written as to include a single subtopic each.

This type of paragraphing differs from the type which English com-position students are taught is best. Because newspaper paragraphs of neces-sity (appearance) must be short, they do not follow the orthodox rule of rhetoric that every paragraph should include a complete thought or topic. Rather, in newspaper paragraphing the idea-unit is broken up into sub-topics. In other words, news writers paragraph their paragraphs.

This type of paragraphing, called *block paragraphing*, is distinctly ad-vantageous for news writing. It permits the insertion or deletion of paragraphs without disarranging a story. Frequently it is necessary, in the light of new information, to recast certain paragraphs, to add additional paragraphs and to remove others. For example, note in the following story how additional information might be added without serious trouble. The paragraphs in italics quite conceivably could have been added after the story was written. Furthermore, several of them could have been inserted at other places in the story. Quite a few of the paragraphs, italicized or not, could be shifted around without destroying the effectiveness of the story. Often, different inserts are written by different reporters.

A five-alarm fire last night wrecked a big grain elevator in the 700 block West Jerome avenue, just west of Fort Alston.

Thirty-five pieces of fire equipment fought the blaze for three hours at the Northern Manufacturing company.

Damage was estimated at $225,000.

Flames and thick billows of smoke leaped high above the burning building as the blaze lighted the western sky. Periodically, a galaxy of sparks would burst from the roof, illuminating the entire area.

The wood-and-sheet metal building was still standing shortly before 1 A.M. *but Patrick L. O'Hara, chief engineer of the Fire department, said the structure was a total loss.*

One fireman was slightly injured when he ran a nail through his boot, but he was treated at the scene and returned to duty. No one else was reported hurt.

The blaze was discovered at 9:50 P.M. by Waldo Wozniak of the 2700 block Hazel avenue who was driving his children along Jerome avenue after showing them where he worked—the Key highway yards of the Keystone Steel company.

Mr. Wozniak said he saw flames through one of the elevator's windows.

He hurried west on Jerome avenue to Hurlburd street, the location of the No. 16 Engine company an the No. 18 Truck company. Mr. Wozniak told Firefighter Emerson Hudnutt what he had seen and led the first pieces of equipment to the scene.

The Police department sent sixteen motorcycle men and two radio cars to handle the traffic.

The fireboats *Mayo* and *Stirrup* quickly pulled into one of the Marble Point piers on the opposite side of Jerome avenue to supply additional water pressure for the land equipment's hoses.

Chief Mott had his men surround the burning elevator, which is about five stories high, and ordered them to direct their high pressure hoses against the building to keep the flames confined to as small an area as possible.

Three nearby tanks were scorched by the flames but received no further damage. Fire fighters watered down adjacent buildings to prevent them catching fire.

Themes

Some stories can be written around a central theme which is perceivable although not bluntly stated or restated throughout. The following story was written to explain the importance to the community of the news it concerns. This purpose is achieved in successive paragraphs which introduce and elaborate upon various aspects of the story as a whole.

J. R. MacDonald, president and chairman of the board of General Cable Corp., announced yesterday that the Tampa plant will manufacture a $4.8 million order of telephone cable to be shipped to Israel.

The order was believed by MacDonald to be the largest manufacturing order destined for export trade ever to be handled in Florida.

He saw it as a "harbinger" of Florida becoming a state doing an extensive manufacturing business in export trade.

Fulfilling the order will mean the hiring of about 120 additional persons who will be kept busy for a year at the plant on E. Hanna St. Additional equipment is being installed in the Tampa plant and the hiring and training of the added personnel is underway.

All material going into the order will come to Tampa through its port and the finished product will be shipped from the port.

MacDonald said the quality of workmanship available at the Tampa plant and lower manufacturing costs here were reasons for Tampa facility making up the order.

Enough wire will be produced for the order that, if wrapped around the world, it would circle the globe 10 times.

The order was negotiated jointly by General Cable and Automatic Electric International Inc., a wholly owned subsidiary of the General Telephone and Electronics Corp. [Tampa *Tribune*]

Chronological

Still another widely used method of organizing the material after the lead is chronological, at least for a number of paragraphs, after which new facts can be added in block paragraph style. This type of organization is effective in stories in which action is described, as in the following example:

A gunman yesterday robbed the Eastwood Federal Savings and Loan association of about $7,000 while scores of noonday shoppers walked past the building at 118 S. Jeffrey street.

The bandit walked in at 12:45 P.M., normally the busiest time of day, and found the office empty of customers. A teller, Miss Virginia Kole, one of four employees present, asked the man if she could help him.

"Yeah. There's a lot you can do to help me," the man answered as he leaped up on the 4-foot high counter and pulled out an old rusty revolver.

"Get back, get back," he ordered from his perch. "I'm not fooling. I'll shoot the lady first. Don't step on the alarm."

Joseph L. Dierks, vice-president, said he was sitting in the back of the office and did not move, waiting to see what the man would do next.

The bandit jumped down on the floor behind the counter and ordered the four to a rest room in the rear. The other two workers were Howard K. Jacobs, secretary-treasurer of the association, and Robertson Evans, a teller.

As the holdup man was directing the group to the rear room, a customer came in. He was Walter Mather, 2130 W. Otis avenue, who also was ordered to the back room.

The robber closed the door on the five and went back to the front of the office where he rifled three cash drawers and the open safe.

When Mr. Evans heard the front door close, he hurried from the back room and ran to the front door hoping to see which way the bandit fled. The man apparently became quickly lost in the crowd and Mr. Evans could not see him.

Mr. Dierks said an early count indicated the stolen money totaled $6,829.15, but he thought the final tally would be higher, perhaps as much as $8,500.

The vice-president considered the holdup man an extremely lucky amateur. He pointed out that an experienced robber probably would have looked over the office several days in advance and would have realized that the association usually was busiest between 12:15 and 1:15 P.M. when many customers come in on their lunch hours.

Mr. Dierks said the gunman was probably a very athletic person, judging from the way he hopped about the office. He appeared to be in his early twenties, about 5 feet 6 inches tall, and weighed about 140 pounds. He wore a blue cap, green shirt, and khaki trousers.

What must be avoided is making the lead sentence merely a "peg line." For example, "Alderman John F. Gates today called Mayor Henry R. Penrose a liar" is superior to "An alderman today called the mayor a liar." It is inferior to "Alderman John R. Gates today charged that Mayor Henry R. Penrose lied when he said he never owned any west-side real estate." If by some grotesque error the former lead sentence were to appear alone, there would be considerable embarrassment if not worse. There is, in other words, a limit beyond which it is wise to be brief. Too often brevity necessitates being vague or indefinite, which requires more rather than less effort on the part of the reader who seeks the facts of a news story.

THE REPORTER'S NOTES

Prerequisite to a well-organized news story is a careful rearrangement of the reporter's notes. For the experienced reporter, the task of dictating a story over the telephone to a rewrite man from a handful of notes scribbled on copy paper while standing in a stuffy booth is an everyday matter. The reporter who uses an electric typewriter in an electronically equipped newsroom does not jerk "false start" leads from his mill to help litter the newsroom floor with crumpled copy paper. It is to his interest to make as few false starts as possible, thus avoiding the push-buttoning involved in making corrections. While he's learning the cub reporter profits by an outline of the facts he has gathered. He has, first of all, to pick the feature to go into his lead; next, to be certain he has answered all of the essential questions which need to be answered and has sufficient identification and authority; then, to decide which phases of the lead need amplification in the first part of the body of the story and how it is to be provided and, finally, to arrange the other facts which he wishes to include.

Seldom, if ever, does the reporter jot down facts in the order in which he will use them in his story. As he learns more and more about the incident he is reporting, one or more lead possibilities strike his attention. There are few if any reporters, regardless of experience, who fail to profit by a study of all notes taken and an outlining of them, if only in the head, before beginning to write or dictate. The young reporter frequently finds it profitable to number the facts included in his notes in the order of importance.

The necessity for rearranging and discarding notes can be seen by imagining how the reporter who covered the Judith Ann Roberts case gathered his facts. If he were stationed at police headquarters, the first imformation he obtained was: Mrs. Shirley Roberts called to report that her child had been kidnaped from the home of her parents whose address was given. Either then or when policemen, accompanied by reporters, arrived at the residence, the mother gave a complete description of the child's appearance and habits. She and her parents told how the child's disappearance was discovered and the condition of the room, including the empty couch and open door. Mr. or Mrs. Rosenberg provided a description of their automobile: its make, model, color, license number, mileage and distinguishing features.

In the search for clues, police and reporters asked the three adults and other residents about the visit of the mother and child to Miami. They wanted to know how the family and child spent the preceding day, especially what they did during the evening. They asked about Mr. Roberts and whether either he or any of the others had any enemies who might wish them ill. They wanted to know whom Judith had met, talked with, played with, where she had gone and so on.

Before the body was found, reporters made notes on the activities of the police: how many and who were assigned to the search, where they went and whom they questioned, what alarms were sent out, what clues, if any, they considered important and the like. They inquired carefully into how discovery of the body was made—whether as part of a careful plan of investigation or by accident.

Bear in mind that the example given was written for a press association, which means it was intended for publication in cities other than Miami. In that city the story received much longer treatment with many additional details of interest to local readers.

To summarize: The first step in good news writing is good reporting. No story writes itself. The factual material must be gathered first. The person who doesn't know how to observe and gather facts never will be able to write a good news account.

4
PLAYING UP THE FEATURE

There is no exact "one way" to write any news story. Given the same schedule of facts, equally competent writers will compose accounts which read differently, and an impartial judge might find it impossible to choose the best.

The first and most important step in news writing is selection of the lead. That requires the exercise of editorial judgment to determine what angle or phase of the total information available is to receive emphasis. It is not enough that the first part of a story answer as many of the questions Who? What? When? Where? Why? and How? as the story demands be answered. These elements must be so arranged as to give proper emphasis to those which are most important.

The entire tone of a news story is determined by the feature which is emphasized in the lead, often in the first sentence or even the first clause or phrase of the first sentence. Giving proper emphasis to the different ingredients of a news story is a simple, standard *method of interpretation* which was practiced long before words were used to describe it. The reporter who develops facility in this regard is training himself well for the future.

NEWS VALUES

Disregarding considerations of policy as a determinant of news judgment, newspapers and other media of communication, despite their differences, have similar criteria by which to determine the potential newsworthiness of the thousands or millions of occurrences from which they make their selection daily. Psychologically these criteria may be superficial or erroneous, but they have been tested by years of experience and, rightly or wrongly, are in vogue in all but a negligible number of news rooms.

Differing in arrangement, nomenclature and emphasis, the main determinants of news values, textbook writers and editors in the main agree, are these:

1. Timeliness.
2. Proximity.
3. Prominence.
4. Consequence.
5. Human interest.

Timeliness

Familiar to every newsman of the past half century is the axiom that "nothing is so dead as yesterday's newspaper." Today, possibly, should be added "or the radio or television newscast of an hour ago." Certainly the increased speed by which news is transmitted has increased the zeal of all who are engaged in the communications business to obtain and stress "latest developments first." The rule is always to bring a story up-to-date as much as possible before going to press or on the air and, if at all possible, to avoid using "yesterday" except in early morning reports.

This "last minute" effect often can be obtained by omitting the "when" from the lead, as in the following:

> A Circuit court judge has given the owners of a slum tenement 60 days to repair their building or face losing the property to the city.
> The action was taken Thursday by Judge Ernest L. Eberholtz in a case involving the five-story brick building at 2122 W. Ashberry street.

In reporting speeches, announcements and the like, this form can be used:

> Elimination of all overnight street parking is necessary to reduce Milltown's traffic accident rate in the opinion of Traffic Engineer L. Scott Updike.
> "Many pedestrians are being injured at night because parked cars obstruct the vision of drivers," Updike told the Milltown Executive club last night.

Proximity

Wars and revolutions, political, economic and other crises no matter where they occur have expanded the home-town newspaper reader's interests. As a consequence, within a generation the old newsroom rule "It takes a very important foreign story to crowd out a fairly important local story" no longer holds true.

Nevertheless, most events occurring within the territory of a newspaper's circulation are still of greater interest than similar events outside that area. A $50,000 fire in Keokuk will get a bigger play in a Keokuk paper than a $100,000 fire in Baton Rouge. People still want to know what is going on in their communities. As metropolitan newspapers have felt the necessity to print more national and international news, there has been an increase in the number of community and suburban papers devoted primarily to local coverage and to special pages and supplements in the big city press.

Not only do people like to read of happenings in their vicinity of which they have no previous knowledge, but also, perhaps especially, do they look for accounts of events with which they are familiar. They like to see their own names in print and to read what the paper has to say concerning situations about which they already know something. When a person expects that his name, or the name of someone whom he knows well, is to appear in the newspaper, he looks first of all for the item containing it. He is eager to read the newspaper's account of a meeting that he has attended, an accident that he has seen or an athletic contest at which he has been present. Logically, the contrary should be true: he should read first that which he already does not know. But he doesn't, and editors know that he doesn't. This being so, newspapers try to please as many readers as possible. If they feel that there is any chance of an appreciable number of readers being interested in an item, no matter how trivial it may be, they print the item, space permitting.

This statement contradicts the supercilious attitude that it is only rural folk who delight in gossip. Just the opposite is true. We do not read in a New York paper that Mary Taylor is spending the weekend with relatives in New Haven merely because not enough people are acquainted with Miss Taylor. Those who do know her are interested in the item of her visit; if the name happens to be Elizabeth Taylor there is a strong possibility that the item will be published. There is no gossip about celebrities too trivial for publication in a metropolitan newspaper. No city reader has any right to laugh at readers of country weeklies who are interested to learn that Henry Jones has painted his barn red.

Writers are enjoined to play up the local as well as the latest angles of stories. For instance,

> Robert A. Brown Post No. 89 of the American Legion will be represented at the tenth annual convention of the state American Legion Monday, Tuesday and Wednesday at Neillsville, by a delegation of approximately 50 members, including 35 members of the fife and drum corps.

This is better than

> The tenth annual convention of American Legion posts of the state will be held Monday, Tuesday and Wednesday at Neillsville. The local post. . . .

Newspapers rewrite or supplement the stories of press associations, correspondents and press releases, which carry general leads, such as the second, in order to meet the interests of local readers. They localize national stories, as illustrated by the following:

> The nationwide airline strike is having little or no effect on air mail service in Lincoln, Postmaster Kenneth Lewis said.
>
> He said that sufficient flights are available on nonstruck lines to ship air mail cargo from Lincoln.
>
> Problems, however, are occurring at the national transportation centers such as Denver, Kansas City and Omaha. National air mail deliveries are being delayed as much as 24 hours.
>
> Mail has been moving on airlines not affected by the strike and most of them have put on extra flights. But, William J. Hartigan, assistant U.S. postmaster general, reported that the emergency scheduling cannot be maintained and some of the extra flights will be canceled.
>
> Military mail for servicemen in Southeast Asia and in Europe has been proceeding on an almost normal basis because all airlines have maintained their military contracts. [Lincoln (Neb.) *Journal*]

Prominence

All men may be created equal, but some grow up to be more newsworthy than others. This may be because of the positions they hold, because of their entertainment value or because they have behaved so unusually in the past that they have created interest in whatever else they may do.

What is true of persons also is true of places and organizations. All other elements being equal, a newsworthy event, such as a fire or crime, is more important if it occurs in one's home town. The reader, however, does not have the same interest in all other places. Such large population centers as New York, Chicago and Los Angeles rate ahead of most small cities and towns. Among the latter, however, there are some considered more newsworthy than others, often because they have become associated with a particular kind of news. Among such places are Reno, Las Vegas, Hollywood, Tia Juana and Monte Carlo.

To the home-town editor, news of all potential subscribers is important, and he tries to use the names of as many of them as space permits. Newspapers often print long lists of delegates to conventions, guests at weddings and social events, committee memberships and so forth. Reporters are instructed to obtain as many names as possible and are cautioned to get complete names and their correct spellings. Last names seldom are enough. News media should use a person's name as he himself uses it in business and society generally. Sometimes a telephone book or city directory may give a full name whereas the person uses one or more initials or even a nickname. The only safe way is to ask the person.

If a widely known person figures in a news event, that fact may become the feature of a story, as in the following:

> State Sen. Lyle G. Fitzhugh and six other persons were injured last night when a row of temporary bleacher seats collapsed during the Milltown-Rushville basketball game.

Consequence

Not only the prominence of persons, places and things mentioned in news stories originating outside the community which a newspaper serves causes them to be published in place of local news; an equal or perhaps more vital factor is the importance of the item.

To illustrate: News from Washington, D.C. is front-page copy in Chicago and San Francisco not primarily because it contains the widely known names of a senator or cabinet member, but because the problem with which those figures are connected vitally concerns the best interests of readers all over the country. Every American citizen is directly affected by an important piece of legislation before Congress. National or state political news often is more important than local political news. In a nuclear age one-world-mindedness is a necessity.

Stories concerning changes in the weather or fashions, and stories of epidemics and pestilences, are important because the immediate community may be affected indirectly if not directly. A coal strike in a distant state may lead to a local shortage of fuel; a new model of automobile will be on sale locally within a short space of time: an important scientific discovery may change a reader's way of thinking on a metaphysical problem. The interest in such stories is very personal and very real.

In addition to localizing nationally important stories, newspapers emphasize the consequence of news by seeking the *tomorrow* angle on strictly local stories. This device serves to make the item seem timely and to point up significance. Emphasis is on results rather than causes, on explaining what the present continuing or probable future effect will be.

> Policemen, firemen and other city service employees would be allowed to live in the suburbs under an ordinance introduced Wednesday in the City Council.

> The cost of riding city busses in Lincoln is about to increase.

> The Nebraska State Railway Commission reported Thursday it has approved the application of Lincoln City Lines for a 5-cent-per-fare rate hike, effective Aug. 1.

> The change will boost the adult fare from 15 to 20 cents, and the fare for children under 12 from 10 to 15 cents. [Lincoln (Neb.) *Journal*]

Human Interest

Interest in human beings as such, and in events because they concern men and women in situations which might confront anyone else, is called *human interest*.

It is human interest, interest in the lives and welfare of others and in the well-being and progress of mankind as a whole, that causes us to read, with interest and sympathy, of loss of life and property in communities far removed from our own. When an earthquake destroys homes and takes lives in southern Italy or in Japan, there is little likelihood of our being affected directly, except perhaps as we are asked to contribute to the Red Cross relief fund; but we are interested in learning of such "acts of God" because other human beings like ourselves are involved.

It is this personal appeal which editors mean when they say that an item of news has reader interest even though it may not possess any of the other elements of news value: timeliness, proximity, prominence and consequence.

Strictly speaking, all reader interest is human interest. Because readers differ in their occupational, recreational and other interests, some news which has a *personal appeal* to one reader fails to interest another. Any reader, however, no matter how cynical or self-centered, has some *sympathetic interest* in the lives and well-being of other humans. This interest includes both extremes of the pathetic and humorous in everyday life, whatever causes a reader to feel sorry for or to laugh with or at some other fellow being.

Interest in accounts of disasters involving loss of life and property is sympathetic. There may be other elements of interest in stories of fires, wrecks, accidents and other catastrophes; but when individuals are mentioned in unfortunate situations, there also is sympathetic interest. Sickness, near death, suffering of any kind, loss of wealth and the like create attitudes of sympathy in readers.

At the other extreme, ludicrous accounts of typical men and women touch a sympathetic vein also. Americans like to laugh and are amused at almost anything in any way incongruous. In most humorous stories there is someone who suffers some inconvenience, but this does not detract from the humor of the situation any more than does knowledge of possible injury to a person who has slipped on a banana peel and fallen suffice to suppress the smile which comes to one's lips.

Such incidents also involve *unusualness*. People everywhere, and perhaps Americans in particular, love thrills and anything with an "-est" to it. Unusual people, quaint and picturesque places, exciting adventures, all appeal to us. And when we cannot meet those individuals, see those places, experience romance ourselves, we like to read of them all the more. We take vicarious pleasure from stories of adventure and romance.

Once news of new theories and discoveries in the field of science was considered unusual. In the present nuclear age the element of surprise has disappeared, but the interest in *progress* continues. Likewise, unfortunately, the element of reader interest which probably outweighs all others—that in *combat*—also continues. Critical examination of the lists of "biggest" news stories of any year indicates that there is no other single element of reader interest which is present more frequently. Americans, it must be, like a good fight and consider life as a whole to be a struggle. The element of combat is found most prominently in stories of athletic contests, crime, politics, adventure, disaster and heroism. Man against man or man against nature always draws a big crowd, which usually roots for the underdog.

If there is *suspense* in the story of combat, or in any other story for that matter, the interest is heightened. Frequently, the attention of an entire nation is centered upon a single news event, as in the case of a mine disaster when rescuers work frantically to save human lives. Illness, especially of a prominent person or from an unusual cause, may be reported so as to emphasize the element of suspense. There is suspense in political campaigns, in law cases and in athletic contests.

The so-called human interest in any kind of story is enhanced if the principals include a child, an animal or a woman, preferably a good-looking young woman. Hieroglyphic warnings against the increasing immorality of youth have been discovered by excavators, proving that adolescence always has been a problem. Furthermore, since before the days of chivalry, the female sex has caused more worry than the male.

Times haven't changed much and "flaming youth" still is having its inning, with debutantes, coeds, waitresses and heiresses flaming perhaps a bit more brightly than ever before. The growth of newspapers and of newspaper photography has helped satisfy the desire for accurate information of just what our allegedly wayward sons and daughters are doing and how they look.

So-called middle age is, from the news standpoint, the drabbest of man's several stages. Precocious infancy and childhood and virile old age vie with hilarious adolescence in front-page importance: the little girl who calls on the mayor to let her doggie out of the pound, and the grandma who takes her first ride in an airplane. The thirties, forties and fifties are the trying years if one is a publicity seeker. At those ages he really has to do something to get by the copy desk; or else he must employ an adroit public relations counsel.

Interest in animals is similar to interest in children and old age. Sometimes the reader is sympathetic, as in the case of a dog who refuses to leave his master's grave; sometimes he is resentful, as when a tame animal turns on someone and hurts him.

Stories of unusual intelligence in animals always are good copy, especially if the well-being of humans thereby is fostered. Also, anecdotes of admirable qualities, as faithfulness, have an appeal. Any freak from the animal kingdom attracts attention, as Barnum knew, and there is plentiful interest remaining in the disappearing sport of hunting, especially of big game.

The beginning reporter must learn to recognize the human interest possibilities of stories and to brighten up what he writes by giving it the twist which turns a drab yarn into a bright one without, of course, exaggeration or distortion.

The following are sprightly leads to factual news stories made so by adroitness on the part of their authors in picking and playing up phases lending themselves to human interest treatment or emphasis:

> Toronto—(UP)—John Brock, 32, began serving a two-year penitentiary term Tuesday because he hates women.
>
> He was convicted of assault for breaking into the ladies room of a downtown tavern and mussing up a young housewife who was fixing her makeup. The housewife told police that Brock crashed in and shouted, "I hate women and you're one."   [Duluth *News-Tribune*]

> Roars and snarls of protest raged around the Denver zoo Friday, but the noise was emanating from the city and county building, not City park.
>
> The hubbub concerns the plans of Mayor Nicholson's administration to sign over management of the zoo to the Denver Zoological Foundation, a group of citizens long interested in the zoo's problems who believe they can operate it better than the city.   [Denver *Post*]

These examples illustrate that it is possible to adhere to the rules regarding the news story form and at the same time avoid "wooden" leads.

THE FIVE *W*'S AND THE *H*

The *who* or the *what* usually is the feature of a short one-incident (simple) news story. It often is difficult to determine which is more important, as most news concerns people and what they do. For instance, in the following short item many readers will be interested primarily in the young man mentioned as a friend or acquaintance. Others, however, will be interested chiefly because of the extent to which the local schools will be affected by the news. When the news is about a definite person the name usually comes first, as

> Peter L. Clay has resigned his position as instructor in history in the local high school to accept a teaching fellowship in history at Booster college.

The *Who*

The *who* is unmistakably the feature in the following story:

> George L. Rose has been elected ninth vice-president of the American Council of Civil Service Employees.

Often the interest in the *who* comes from the kind of person involved (judged by his occupation, religion, sex, age and so on, or by the circumstances in which he figures in the particular story), or from the number of persons involved, as

A private watchman shot a safecracker Tuesday when he and his accomplice resisted arrest.

The indefinite *who* is used increasingly as cities become larger and persons in the news are known to fewer other persons in proportion to the population as a whole.

The *What*

The *what* is more important than the *who* when the circumstance would be significant no matter who the persons involved, as

One man was shot and another was beaten today in an outbreak of violence as strikers tried to prevent operation of the Johnson-Smith corporation.

A youth who went beserk with a butcher knife was captured and held by police tonight as a suspect in two recent murders in Milltown.

Press associations usually write their stories in this way, as names may not mean anything outside the immediate vicinity in which the event occurred. The writer of a news story always must decide which is more important, the name or the event.

Often a *what* lead begins with the *who* as an easier rhetorical method or to emphasize authority. Note in the following example that, although the *who* comes first, the *what* is more important:

President Joseph E. Jennings today announced that the county board is able to pay off current expenditures as they arise, despite the fact that it has retired $568,910 in outstanding debts since he assumed office three years ago.

In the following example the *what* is unmistakably predominant:

Vandalism against cars was reported in Southside Milltown Friday.
Vice squad detectives began an investigation after auto windshields and windows were reported smashed on Haberkorn road, Lakeside drive, Alcott drive and Norton road, SW.

In action stories readers usually are interested in results rather than causes, as

Two infant brothers perished and three firemen attempting a dramatic rescue of them were injured Monday in a blaze at 3142 N. Patzin St.

The *Why*

Sometimes, however, it is the cause rather than the result that is the feature of the story, as

Trying to pass another car while travelling at high speed brought serious injury to two men last night when their automobile overturned twice on Washington boulevard at Potter avenue.

Taxpayers want to know the reasons for the actions of public officials.

> In order to save money and to allow men to spend New Year's Day with their families, the Sanitation Department, in its early planning, has decided to cut back sharply on its force for tonight's midnight-to-8 A.M. shift, leaving only a thin force of 188 men on duty.

The *Where*

In advance stories of meetings, speeches, athletic events, accidents, etc., the *where* must be very definite. Room numbers, street addresses, etc., should be given. In local stories, it is not always necessary to mention the name of the city or a street address. The immediate community is understood, as

> Eight testing lanes on which motorists must submit their automobiles and trucks to examination for safe driving qualifications will be opened tomorrow.

The *where* may be the featurized element:

> In her 400-year-old ancestral home, the only daughter of an English general recently became the wife of a gypsy, who worked as a handyman on the estate.

In each of the following examples, the *where* definitely was the feature, although, in the second example, the *when* rhetorically came first:

> A tract of approximately 30 acres at Forest boulevard and Kerwood avenue, assessed at $90,000, has been sold by Herschel Steel, represented by the Wray-Graw Co., to John L. Finch.

> Beginning today, parking will be permitted in the Underground Lakeside Exhibition hall of Citizen's hall by patrons of events at the hall and the Civic auditorium, at a rate of 40 cents per car.

When a place is more familiar than the names of those associated with it, the following style may be used:

> The operator of a candy store at 717 S. Ninth street pleaded guilty Monday in U.S. District court of the purchase, possession, and sale of 5 ounces of heroin.
> He is Andrew Solberg, 41, of 141 Oak street, who was arrested by narcotics agents last month.

The *When*

About the same may be said of the *when* as of the *where*. It ordinarily is included inconspicuously in the lead, as

> Fur thieves hit two Milltown stores early Wednesday and got away with a total loot estimated at $230,000.

Frequently the *when* may be left until the second paragraph, as

> Commissioner William Wheat has appointed a seven-man hospital committee to look into the situation surrounding construction of a county-wide hospital for pay patients.
>
> The members were appointed at a Monday afternoon session with the commissioner.

Such omission of the *when* from the first paragraph is common practice with press associations, especially when preparing news of one day for use in the morning newspapers the following day.

The *when* may be a matter of "continuous action," as

> A couple of perky oldsters who defied the wilderness for ten days on a can of beans, a bit of jelly and a small packet of powdered milk are recovering from exhaustion and hunger in Milltown hospital.

The *when* may be the featured element, as

> Midnight tonight is the deadline for 1976 automobile license plates and vehicles in use after 12:01 A.M. tomorrow must carry 1977 plates, the Bureau of Motor Vehicles reminded automobile owners yesterday.

A type of *when* lead is the "duration of time" lead, as

> After deliberating five hours last night, a Superior court jury returned a verdict of guilty in the steel purchase fraud trial of four Gruner county highway employees.

A similar type of *when* lead is the "since when" lead, as

> After being gone for two weeks, Duke, a wistful looking Collie-Spitz hybrid, decided he liked his old home better and trudged 40 miles to return to the residence of his former owner, Humane Officer Thompson Meredith.

The *How*

By definition the *how* means details to explain how something occurred. Consequently, when the feature unmistakably consists in such details, care must be exercised to avoid wordiness:

> Mrs. Frederick Bascom managed to drive off an Alberto Expressway ramp yesterday in Evergreen, tear a tree completely out of the ground, knock a corner off a garage two blocks away, bounce off a car and come out of the whole incident without a scratch and with only one traffic charge.

Sports stories frequently are given *how* leads:

> Fritz Tech used seven pass interceptions to throttle the Ironton Academy attack and converted one of them into a one-yard scoring plunge by Peter Baldwin for the winning touchdown Saturday in a 38–27 win over the Eagles.

RHETORICAL DEVICES

Skillful use of the ordinary rhetorical devices enables the news writer to play up a feature.

The Summary Statement

Most news leads are mere summary statements consisting of simple sentences or of compound or complex sentences with the principal clauses first. Many examples given so far in this chapter illustrate how the feature of a story can be emphasized by means of such simple straightforward writing. Observe, in addition, the following example:

> A woman cashier escaped unharmed through a recently installed emergency door when a man ignited gasoline in a holdup attempt Saturday in the Gross Pointe Currency Exchange, 4112 W. Leonard St.

Conditional Clauses

Often, however, it is difficult to get the feature into a main clause. This is so when the feature is present in addition to the main news idea which the writer must include in his lead. Features to be found in accompanying circumstances, conditions, coincidences in the *when* and *where* and so on often can best be played up by beginning the lead with a complex or complex-compound sentence with the conditional clause first.

In the following examples note how the conditional clause contains the feature, whereas the main idea, which is the excuse for the story, still is in the main clause.

> Because Paul Gregg, 17-year-old high school boy, was caught as a stowaway and locked in the infirmary of the liner *Justice*, he started to burn the ship to seek his freedom, he admitted to steamship authorities here today.

This emphasizes the feature much more than would inversion of the clause order, as

> Paul Gregg, 17-year-old high school boy, today admitted to steamship authorities here that he set fire to the liner *Justice* to obtain his freedom after being caught as a stowaway and locked in the infirmary.

The Substantive Clause

The substantive clause usually takes the form of a "that" clause which has been much overworked by news writers because it is easy to write and is consequently taboo in many offices. Occasionally the substantive is forceful, as

That the present legislative appropriation must be doubled if minimum essentials are to be provided relief clients, is the warning contained in the monthly report made today by Harold G. Todd, local relief administrator, to the State Department of Public Welfare.

Return to the pioneer days, when youths in their early teens could assemble a muzzle-loader and pick off game 50 yards away, was sought in a bill before the state legislature today.

Phrases

Infinitive, participial, prepositional and gerund phrases and absolute constructions also may be used to emphasize a feature when it happens to be one of the minor *w*'s or *h*. In such constructions, the main clause contains the *who* and *what*, one of which is modified by the phrase.

Inverted sentence structure may be used to identify (tie-back) the news with previous news (see Chapter 8) and to identify persons, places and events. Use of phrases and of the absolute construction for different purposes is illustrated in the following examples:

WHEN

After a three-hour search by police and relatives, James Fillmore, 30, his wife and four children who had been missing since Saturday, were found early yesterday in a friend's home.

WHERE

Beside the Ring river, which he made famous in song and verse, the body of Feodor Vladik today was buried with only a handful of close relatives present.

WHY

Delayed somewhat by recent hurricane alerts, work to complete Harris Civil Defense Headquarters in the basement of the Carnegie Free Library was pressed anew last week.

HOW

Citing a permissive 1867 ordinance which never has been repealed, Henry Bucher today won the right to raise geese in his backyard at 10 Cherry Lane.

TIE-BACK

Disregarding three previous failures, Grace Slawson, 21-year-old grocery clerk, tomorrow will attempt to set a new record for swimming across Lake Malthusia.

Care must be taken to avoid what Roy Copperud calls "linguistic smog," illustrated by the following example by Howard C. Heyn in an article, "A Newsman's View: Writing With Precision," in the 1970 *Montana Journalism Review:*

Two firemen fought their way into the smoke-filled building where a boy was trapped on the second floor and died of asphyxiation.

To make it clear who died the phrasing had to be converted to a direct approach in this manner:

> Two firemen were asphyxiated while trying to rescue a boy trapped on the second floor of the smoke-filled building.

The Cartridge Lead

When war is declared or ends, when a president or some other widely known figure dies and on similarly important occasions, it is customary to tell the gist of the news in the fewest possible words, as

> Galvania has declared war on Powry.
> Mayor Charles A. Brinshaw is dead.
> The Maroons are conference champions.

Stories written entirely in such staccato fashion have a breathtaking quality. Consequently, the style should not be used too extensively but reserved for occasions of particular importance.

The Punch Lead

What has traditionally been called a *punch lead* performs a function similar to that of the cartridge lead, but it is not so short, abrupt or definite. Since World War II, it has grown in popularity and on some newspapers is used for almost any kind of story, not just stories of presumed extra newsworthiness. It has been called the "blind" lead because of its emphasis on situations rather than specific persons and details. It is a form of writing easily open to misuse (1) in stories whose importance is thereby exaggerated and (2) by being excessively indefinite or "empty." An example of the latter is "Politics has a different look in Congress today," a sentence which tells exactly nothing. Paragraphs two and three of a well-written story with a punch lead should supply definite details:

> A policeman has been suspended on charges that he deserted his school-crossing post.
> Placed on indefinite suspension by Police Chief Patrick C. O'Brien Tuesday was Albert Murchison, 27, of 885 W. Strong avenue, attached to the Vickers station, 1412 E. Vickers avenue.
> Lieut. Ira Walters of the Vickers district said a routine check at noon Monday disclosed that Murchison was absent from his post at Bristol and Sacramento roads.

The Astonisher Lead

Beginning writers are discouraged in the use of superlatives and expressions of opinion. When deserved, however, superlatives should be used, as

> For the first time in its history, the bottled water industry hit the $80 million mark in sales in 1976 and estimates by experts in the field are that it will be in excess of $100 million this year.

MORE THAN ONE FEATURE

So far, only stories containing simple features relatively easy to pick even though related to important events have been considered. Not infrequently, an item of news presents so many angles that the rhetorical devices described in this chapter are inadequate. There are several ways out of this difficulty.

Separate Stories

The easiest way is to write more than one story. When there are sidelights or interviews of opinion or features connected with a news event, the assignment usually is divided between two or more reporters. Some repetition usually occurs but is not discouraged; in fact, in some cases it is encouraged, and a paper may run several stories of the same event written by different reporters.

The Crowded Lead

When the various elements of interest are of nearly equal value, a number of facts may be crowded into a single lead, as

> Standing committees were appointed, the street-lighting contract was continued for one year and a proposed new ordinance regulating business licenses was referred to the Finance committee last night at the weekly meeeting of the Board of Aldermen.

Succeeding paragraphs naturally would take up each item mentioned in the lead, providing full details.

The "Shirttail" Method

To avoid crowded and vague leads, one item deemed the most important can be played up. Paragraphs containing mention of other items then can be introduced by such expressions as "In other actions the City Council . . ." or "In a similar accident . . ." and so forth.

> Ald. Val G. Grauer (17th Ward) has been elected chairman of the powerful Finance committee of the Board of Aldermen.
> Other standing committee chairmen, named at last night's board meeting, follow . . . .
> The board also voted to continue for one year its contract with the Republic Light company for street lighting . . . .
> In other actions, the board referred a proposed new ordinance regulating business licenses to the Finance committee and rejected a request by Front street property owners that all-night parking be permitted in the 400 block.

Boxes

Often, statements, tabulations, data, side features and the like can best be presented by means of a box set either ahead of the lead, within the main article or in an adjoining column. There are many other uses for the box, most of them connected with makeup. Material most frequently boxed includes the following:

1. Lists of dead and injured in accidents.
2. Telling statements from speeches, reports, testimony and so on.
3. Statistics.
4. Summaries of facts included in the story itself or in two or more related stories.
5. Brief histories of events connected with the story.
6. Local angles on press association stories.

After requiring 12 employees and six customers to lie face downward on the floor, three armed and masked bandits shortly after 8 A.M. today removed approximately $75,000 in currency from the cashiers' cages of the First National bank, 109 N. Main street, and escaped in a waiting automobile driven by a fourth man.

FOURTH IN TWO YEARS

Today's burglary of the First National bank was the fourth in two years in Milltown. Others, together with losses and outcomes, were:

March 3, 1975—First National bank, $17,451 cash, recovered upon arrest of Abe Mason, now serving a ten-year term in the state penitentiary.

Sept. 21, 1975—Milltown State bank, $41,150 cash and bonds, recovered when sheriff's posse killed John "Gunman" Hays three miles south of town the same day.

July 15, 1976—Citizen's National bank, $50,000 removed by blowing open safe at night. Still unsolved.

The men were described by Wilmer Asher, head cashier, as all apparently under 25 years of age. They wore blue overalls and caps which were drawn down just above the eyes.

The 1–2–3–4 Lead

After a short summary statement of the situation constituting the news, the different features can be emphasized by tabulation and numbering, as

The wishes of Mayor Louis T. Tupper were ignored by the new Board of Aldermen in several votes at its organizing meeting last night. Most importantly the board did the following:

1. Elected Ald. Val G. Grauer (17th ward), political rival of the mayor's, chairman of the powerful Finance committee.

2. Referred a proposed new ordinance regulating business licenses to Ald. Grauer's committee. The mayor has called the new ordinance unnecessary.

3. Continued for one year the contract with the Republic Light Company for street lighting. The mayor opposed the renewal in campaign speeches last month.

4. Rejected a property owners' petition for all-night parking in the 400 block on Front street which the mayor had approved.

The preceding lead, of course, is interpretative. It plays up the significance of the board's actions rather than merely reporting them deadpan. It does not editorialize for or against the board's insurgency, and the treatment probably could be adversely criticized only if it could be shown that every board action was taken despite rather than because of any attitude toward Mayor Tupper.

The article as written does not say the four actions indicated hostility by the board toward the mayor. Nevertheless, there is no mistaking the fact that such an impression is given. If, at a subsequent meeting, the board were to vote in favor of a number of measures sponsored by the mayor, the facts as they existed after the earlier meeting would have to be reexamined. If, however, the facts as stated in the first story are accurate, the reporter could not be accused of coloring his account. Certainly he provided his readers with background information whereby it would be possible for them to draw conclusions, whereas a strictly factual account of the actions of the Board of Aldermen, without attempt at any perspective, might have created a wrong impression.

It cannot be pointed out too often that essential for this kind of interpretative reporting is knowledge. Without it, the newsgatherer will consider as new something that is very old and will have news sources "revealing" and "disclosing" information that is common knowledge among a wide circle of readers.

In other words, you can't play up a feature unless you have brains enough to pick it.

5

MAKING IT ATTRACTIVE

A. The News Peg
B. The Contrast Lead
C. The Question Lead
D. The Descriptive Lead
E. The Staccato Lead
F. The Explosive Lead
G. The Figurative Lead
H. The Epigram Lead

I. The Literary Allusion Lead
J. The Parody Lead
K. The Quotation Lead
L. The Dialogue Lead
M. Cumulative Interest
N. Suspended Interest
O. Sequence
P. Direct Address

If the first part of a news story answers as many of the five *w*'s and *h* as necessary (see Chapter 3) and gives the proper emphasis to the one which constitutes the feature (see Chapter 4), it is a good lead. If, in addition, the beginning of the news story is so interestingly written that the reader continues for that reason alone, it is a superior lead. No one reader is interested in a majority of the news items contained in any single newspaper edition; it is the purpose of headlines to direct him to those stories in which he does have an interest. The lead of a story authenticates and supplements its headline and is sufficient for a large proportion of readers who get that far.

Every news story, however, is composed for the minority of readers who peruse it to its very end. Both its content and the way it is written determine its interest value. In Part Two, the emphasis is on how to obtain completeness of detail in gathering information regarding a number of different kinds of events. The purpose of this chapter is to offer assistance to the beginning writer in how to attain rhetorical excellence without sacrificing news interest. The examples also illustrate how to give emphasis or perspective— elementary forms of interpretation—to otherwise routine stories.

THE NEWS PEG

When a lead is written in feature or semifeature style, either to play up a feature angle or for rhetorical attractiveness, the part that contains the kernel or more of news regarding the event which is the story's excuse for being is called the *news peg*. The extent to which it can be made secondary to featured fact or language depends upon its importance. If it is of vital public interest, it must be given emphasis. If, on the other hand, the feature interest of the story outweighs its importance as public information, the news peg can be played down. In the following examples however, despite the feature treatment, the news pegs are present in the leads:

> After dressing her three small daughters in their Easter finery and taking them to church where they were baptized, Mrs. Nora MacMahon returned yesterday to her Pineville home and strangled them.

> Indianapolis (AP)—About 1,000 men and women, many elderly, walked through a snow-covered Indianapolis cemetery Wednesday to attend graveside rites for a door-to-door peddler who feared no one would come to his funeral. Herbert A. Wirth, 73, had no known relatives. He had prepaid his funeral expenses.

THE CONTRAST LEAD

Sometimes the feature of a news story consists in the contrast between the immediate and a former situation or between the event at hand and another of which, for any of a number of reasons, it is a reminder. Note that the news peg is retained in the following lead, though not so definitely, the emphasis being upon the unusual situation:

> Behind the same walnut desk which he used to dust 25 years ago as an office boy, Virgil F. Stimson yesterday received congratulations upon becoming president of Andalia Trucking company.

THE QUESTION LEAD

Ordinarily the reporter should answer, not ask, questions in his news stories. To do otherwise merely delays telling the news, as in the case of a lead beginning. "What causes delinquency?" followed by a summary of a new idea advanced by some authority. It would be much better to start: "Failure of teenagers to obtain jobs causes them to become delinquent in the opinion of . . ."

When the story concerns a problem of public interest or a matter likely to provoke debate among readers, however, it may be possible to obtain interest by means of a question lead, as

> Baltimore, Aug. 7 (AP)—Could one man in one night at one bar on The Block, Baltimore's strip-tease row, run up a bill of $1,900? Or $1,349.50? Or $1,722.11 at three clubs?
> The Baltimore Liquor Board investigating complaints from credit card holders about the bills they found on their vouchers, had its doubts. . . .

> **By Norman Mlachak**
> **Labor Writer**
> Can a labor union shut down an industrial plant even though the union isn't the officially elected bargaining agent for the workers?
> Teamsters Local 507 is proving that it can.
> It struck the American Screw Products Co. in Bedford Heights five weeks ago today.
> Is it legal?... [Cleveland *Press*]

THE DESCRIPTIVE LEAD

The feature or key to the spirit of a story may be in its setting, in the physical appearance of some person or object involved or in an unusual phase of the action with which it deals. In such cases, a graphic or descriptive lead may be the most effective to give the tone or feeling necessary to proper understanding and appreciation. Before he can describe, the reporter must know how to observe; the best descriptive leads are written by eyewitnesses. To be avoided are superfluous and inapplicable adjectives, extraneous matter serving no purpose except, perhaps, to prove the writer's possession of an extensive vocabulary of trite and hackneyed expressions—cliches. The following leads to important stories avoid these hazards:

> A fusillade of gunfire shattered the quiet of a Milltown street shortly before midnight, and when it was over a young man lay dead.

> For more than a minute today the sun hung over central Minnesota like a twinkling, slate-blue Christmas ornament as the moon moved between it and the earth.
> In the awesome half-light that covered the area, hundreds of scientists and thousands of other persons had a perfect view of the total solar eclipse.
> [New York *Times*]

THE STACCATO LEAD

When the time element—either fast action or the intervals separating a series of related events—is to be emphasized, the staccato lead occasionally suffices. It consists in a series of phrases, punctuated either by periods or dashes and usually is a form of descriptive lead. The style suggests the tone of the story, its feeling.

Hanover, June 23—An ear-wracking roar followed by a series of cloudburst demonstrations. A serpent's tongue of flame. Dense billows of black smoke thinning gradually into white. Movement made almost invisible by velocity.

Thus the observer's brain recorded the spectacle of Fritz von Opel's rocket car blazing along the railroad tracks in the environs of this city today at a speed of 254 kilometers an hour—39 faster than has ever been achieved before by a vehicle running on rails.

Thirty years ago—back in 1946—in a different era, in a different life, after 40 years of happiness in her simple home, the light went out for Mrs. Hattie Downs, of Gregoryville and she became blind—stone blind.

Years passed—thirty of them—long and torturous—and suddenly her prayers were answered, and Mrs. Hattie Downs could see.

THE EXPLOSIVE LEAD

Similar to the staccato lead but consisting of grammatically complete sentences, the explosive lead is especially useful for feature articles. It can, however, be used for straight news stories as well.

A fellowship wooded retreat, freeing the human mind, communal living, Renaissance songs, sensitivity training—they're all there in the next six weeks of the Near North Unitarian Univeralist Fellowship.   [Chicago *Daily News*]

By Paul McGrath
Cloudy, lazy afternoon on Thanksgiving Day, no school, nothing to do.
On the North Side, two boys jump on the back of a bus to hitch a ride. One of the trolleys snaps and hits one of the lads on the head and he dies of a fractured skull.
On the South Side, four boys are playing cards in an apartment. One of them is horsing around with a gun he bought on the street earlier in the week. The gun goes off and a 16-year-old youth dies. . . .   [Chicago *Sun-Times*]

THE FIGURATIVE LEAD

Triteness must be avoided in the use of metaphors, similes and other figures of speech, either in the lead or in any other part of a news story. Many expressions have become so common through usage that they are hardly noticed by casual readers as figurative. Among them are "ax to grind," "shoe on the wrong foot," "hitch his wagon to a star," "put all its eggs in one basket" and many more. If the writer uses such expressions naturally, without strain, possibly even without awareness that they are figurative, the result is more likely to be good than if he deliberately tries for effect:

Knocked on the ropes by a wet and windy one-two punch, Milltown's July heat wave refused to call it quits Friday.

May and December joined hands in reverse of usual style when Mrs. Susanne Drew, 50, teacher, became the bride of Lawrence Eli Walker, 21, student, yesterday at Crown Point, Ind.

THE EPIGRAM LEAD

The tone or moral of a story also may be emphasized by means of an epigram lead, in the writing of which bromides and platitudes must be avoided. The epigram is a concise and pointed expression, usually witty. The epigram lead may be either a familiar saying or a moral applicable to the story at hand, as

Silence can be golden in more ways than one, Shortstop Tommy Jacobs of the Maroons has discovered.

After striking out three times against Bristol Aug. 12, Jacobs complained to his manager, Bucky Johnson, that he had been the victim of several debatable strike decisions.

"The trouble with you," said Johnson, "is that you spend so much time turning around to squawk that you're not ready to hit the ball. Just for the fun of it, forget to turn around and look at the umpire for any reason and concentrate on hitting the ball."

Tommy followed the advice and compiled the following record . . . .

THE LITERARY ALLUSION LEAD

The writer with a normal background of knowledge in literature or history will have frequent chances to use it to advantage. Care must be taken to limit references to fictional or historical characters and to literary passages familiar to the average reader. The following examples illustrate how it is possible effectively to make use of one's general knowledge to improve his writing:

By Ralph Blumenthal
A desire named streetcars is growing—a desire for the return of one of America's oldest forms of urban public transportation.   [New York *Times*]

By Mary Jane Gustafson
Brooklyn Center's winter skating program has grown like Topsy!

From seven warming houses in 1970, the program included 16 warming houses this winter plus additional hockey rinks at seven of the parks or 23 skating rinks to maintain.   [North Hennepin (Minn.) *Post*]

THE PARODY LEAD

Popular song hits, bons mots by famous persons, titles of best-selling books or of motion pictures or new-coined phrases or expressions of any sort may be used while still fresh, usually in parodied form, to brighten an occasional news story lead. Well-established expressions may be used similarly. The following leads avoid the ever-lurking danger of triteness in such writing:

Sheridan, Wyo., Jan. 29.—Maybe it's a case of absence of water makes the heart grow fonder, but citizens of this northern Wyoming city have risen nobly to the call to help the flood-stricken dwellers along the Ohio River Valley.

Actor Charles Keller says you can't take it with you because the government takes it first.

The 77-year-old stage-and-screen star Tuesday urged outright repeal of the federal income tax, which he called an "economic cancer."

THE QUOTATION LEAD

In reporting speeches, public statements and the like, it almost always is better to epitomize the feature in the reporter's own words rather than by means of a direct quotation.

Weak	Strong
"A sharp decrease in maternal mortality, medical progress, and greater economic prosperity have enabled welfare agencies to solve most of their problems except that of the emotionally disturbed child," Horace V. Updike, Council of Social Welfare director, said yesterday.	The emotionally disturbed child is the "No. 1 problem" facing welfare agencies today, Horace V. Updike, Council of Social Welfare director, said yesterday.

In news stories which are not accounts of speeches or documents, however, it sometimes is effective to begin with a direct quotation, as in the following examples:

"In this country, as in yours, we take a rather dim view of serious infractions of this kind," Provincial Judge P. J. Bolsby said yesterday to a 22-year-old New York City man charged with assaulting a police officer while trying to gatecrash Saturday's rock festival at the Canadian National Exhibition.

[Toronto *Globe-Mail*]

"Don't be an old grouch on the road!"

This advice for those who wish to stay alive although they drive in Labor Day weekend traffic comes from Francis Carroway, 18, judged Milltown's best teenage driver.

The following was the lead to a story judged best by 37 journalism professors and 32 city editors to whom nine writeups of an interview with an Ohio State university campus editor were submitted:

"To get ahead in journalism, you have to do a little more than people expect of you."

This is the advice Lantern Spring Quarter editor-in-chief Ron Shafer gave freshmen journalism students today.

"You may not think that anybody notices that extra work, but they do," Shafer continued.

The partial or broken quote often can be used to add authenticity without making the lead unwieldly, as

> The city manager of Cresswood refused today to "commit myself" on revoking the liquor license of a saloon raided five times by sheriff's police in a year.

THE DIALOGUE LEAD

It is difficult, if not impossible, to begin a serious news story of an important event with dialogue. Minor court stories, with strong human interest, and occasionally stories of a more significant nature, however, can be handled effectively by means of a dialogue lead, as

> "Wouldn't it be terrible," asked Hazel Muller, 22, of 1864 E. Payne avenue, "if I got locked in that record vault and couldn't get out?"
>
> "Ho, ho," replied Thomas Keyes, production manager of the Majestic Foundry company at 146 E. Belmont avenue, where Miss Muller is a secretary, "It couldn't happen."
>
> But it DID happen Tuesday and it WAS terrible.
>
> Here's a play-by-play account . . . .

CUMULATIVE INTEREST

Most of the examples given so far have been leads to news stories which otherwise conform to the standard rule that they be written to make possible the cutting of at least a few paragraphs from the bottom up, without sacrificing completeness.

There are three principal types, rhetorically speaking, of news feature stories which must be printed in their entirety to preserve the news interest. One is the cumulative interest story, the lead of which differs from those of the other two types because it contains some sort of news peg. In addition to emphasizing the tone or situation of the story as it progresses, this kind of story incites reader interest which cumulates as each succeeding sentence and paragraph makes for greater definiteness:

> Long Beach, Calif. (AP)—The young woman said a friend had given a bottle to her with instructions to throw it at anyone who tried to mug her.
>
> Police officials said Miss Jackie Lynn Samay, 22 years old, had telephoned to ask them what to do with the bottle in her refrigerator, "a pint of nitroglycerine."
>
> Bomb-squad officers rushed to her residence, ordered a four-block downtown area evacuated, packed the bottle in ice from a nearby liquor store and had Army experts transport it carefully in a thick metal box to nearby Fort MacArthur. Traffic was cleared from all streets along the route.
>
> The next day the Army reported the liquid was glue.   [New York *Times*]

SUSPENDED INTEREST

A suspended interest feature is one in which the writer "strings along" the reader to the very end before giving him the news peg on which the item is based. Such stories resemble magazine short stories in that they must be read in their entirety. Frequently, the climax may be a surprise; in any case, it satisfies the reader's interest which has been suspended because of the indefiniteness of early details. The lead of a suspended interest story is not so definite as that of a cumulative interest story:

> An ice-cream cone failed to have a cooling effect Saturday night on Patrolman Harry O'Brien.
> O'Brien, assigned to the burglary detail, was parking his car on Auburn street near Wilson avenue, when a man approached the car, mumbling incoherently.
> "What did you say?" O'Brien asked.
> Without another word, the man suddenly jammed an ice-cream cone into the policeman's face.
> O'Brien alighted, drew his gun, seized the man and was told, "You'll have to fight to take me in."
> With that, the prisoner slugged O'Brien in the mouth with his fist, O'Brien countered with an uppercut which knocked the man flat.
> At the Kenton Avenue Station the arrested man identified himself as Willis C. Solano of 1768 W. Tree street and said he thought policemen were "too hot" and he wanted to "cool one off."

SEQUENCE

The sequence story differs from both the cumulative and suspended interest stories only in arrangement of material, the object in all three cases being to postpone the climax or satisfaction of the reader's curiosity until near the end. The distinguishing feature of a story written in sequence style is that the facts are arranged in strictly chronological order, as

> Three-year-old Byron Halpert, being an inquisitive little fellow, opened a second-story window Tuesday a few minutes after his mother had left to take her daughter to school.
> Byron leaned out to see what he could see. But he leaned so far that he lost his balance, fell through the opening and wound up hanging from the window sill by his finger tips, 20 feet above a concrete walk.
> Just then a police car came by. Officer William Watson, sizing up the situation, ran to the spot below the window just as little Byron let go. The boy landed squarely in the policeman's arms, unhurt but tearfully scared.

DIRECT ADDRESS

Beginning reporters are admonished to keep out of their own stories, only an occasional reference to the fact that a reporter asked a certain question or made an unsuccessful effort to obtain an important fact being permitted. Use of either the first or second person is discouraged. Columnists, special writers who sign their articles and writers of feature stories are exempt from this rule when effectiveness cannot be obtained otherwise. The following are examples to show how the first or second person occasionally may be used in an ordinary news or news feature story such as a beginning reporter might write

> Kids, when Ma and Pa take a look at your report card then start the sermon about how smart they were in high school, do you see red? Do you want to chew nails?
> Relax, kids, you've got a friend.
> He is Dr. F. H. Finch of the University of Illinois, and he takes your side today in a monograph of the American Psychological Association.
> [Chicago *Daily News*]

> If you haven't heard of it, and wouldn't believe it if you had, it probably will be on display today at the National Inventors' Congress in the Hotel LaSalle.
> Window glass that can't be seen through, lamps that give invisible light and solid water pipes that have no hollow space for the water—those are some of the things you may expect to find.

6

JOURNALISTIC STYLE

A. Conciseness
   1. Superfluous Details
   2. Superfluous Words
   3. Superfluous Phrases
   4. Superfluous Clauses
   5. Simplicity
   6. Passive and Active Voice
   7. Proper Emphasis
B. Avoiding Banality
   1. Figures of Speech
   2. Bromides
   3. Shopworn Personifications
   4. Journalese
   5. Gobbledegook

C. Readability Formulas
D. Semantics
   1. Unfamiliar Words
   2. Connotations
   3. Puffs and Boosts
   4. Evaluative Words
E. Correct Usage
   1. Grammatical Faults
   2. Parts of Speech
   3. Troublesome Words

Of eight eminent American novelists studied, "the style of four with journalistic backgrounds displayed a tendency toward the elimination of semantic noise, characterized by compressed syntax, clear and active word choice and concrete, objective detail," according to Donald A. Sears and Margaret Bourland, whose article "Journalism Makes the Style" appeared in the Autumn 1970 *Journalism Quarterly*.

The journalist-novelists and their periods of creativity were Stephen Crane (1880–1900), Theodore Dreiser (1900–1920), Ernest Hemingway (1920–1940) and John Hersey (1940–1960). The nonjournalists were Henry James (1880–1900), Edith Wharton (1900–1920), Thomas Wolfe (1920–1940) and Truman Capote (1940–1960).

Today's recognizable journalistic style evolved during the past century and is economical and suited to the needs of the medium. Its characteristics include the following:

1. Compact, usually short, sentences, each word selected and placed for maximum effect.

2. Short, terse paragraphs, each complete in itself and generally capable of being removed without destroying the sense of a story.
3. Conciseness, directness and simplicity, through elimination of superfluous words, phrases and clauses and through proper emphasis.
4. Factualness, without editorial opinion, puffs and boosts, unwise superlatives, adjectives, nouns or other dogmatic words.
5. Avoidance of "fine" writing, strong verbs and nouns being preferred to trite, hackneyed and obsolete words and expressions.
6. Observance of the rules of good grammatical and word usage.

CONCISENESS

The objective of effective journalistic writing should be to avoid cumbersomeness without becoming choppy or repetitious through the excessive use of referents.

Superfluous Details

Relaxing of the rule that all of the five *w*'s and *h* must be included in the first paragraph of a news story generally achieves the objective of uncluttering the lead.

Cluttered	Uncluttered
Clifford Britt, 38, 1459 Grove street, and another passenger on an eastbound Mitchell boulevard street car were injured about 8 A.M. today when the car jumped the track and collided with a westbound car at Mitchell boulevard and Perkins street.	Two men were injured and scores shaken when two street cars collided at Mitchell boulevard and Perkins street about 8 A.M. today.
Scores of other passengers en route to work who filled both cars were heavily jostled and shaken up as the two cars came together, according to Mitchell boulevard police who also said another man was injured but disappeared from the scene of the accident.	One car was going west and the other east on Mitchell boulevard.
	Hitting an open electric switch, the eastbound car jumped the tracks, struck the other, and derailed it.
	One of the injured men was Clifford Britt, 38, 1459 Grove street. Police said another man was injured but disappeared from the scene of the accident.
Britt was taken to Municipal hospital with cuts and bruises on the head and hands.	Britt received cuts and bruises on the head and hands. He was taken to Municipal hospital.
	Both cars were filled with passengers en route to work. They were heavily jostled as the two cars came together.

General wordiness is "a famous barrier" to effective news writing according to Howard C. Heyn in "A Newsman's View: Writing With Precision," in the *Montana Journalism Review* for 1970. Typical of the many examples in this valuable article is this loose sentence:

The police officer accompanied the two to Utah last week inasmuch as it was felt that the young Marvin could be of use in helping to locate or identify the killer.

Heyn suggests that the "message" of this 31-word sentence really was this:

The policeman took them to Utah last week, hoping Marvin could locate the killer.

Superfluous Words

The articles *the*, *a* and *an* often can be eliminated, as

WEAK: The Booster students who heard the talk—
BETTER: Booster students who heard the—
WEAK: It is for the men who make good.
BETTER: It is for men who make good.

Erling H. Erlandson warns against excess in adherence to this rule. Otherwise the result might be "nonsensical writing," as "Cause of the dispute was the overtime clause. Union had demanded time and a half for work after 5 P.M." Says Erlandson: "Two words saved at the expense of communication."

Sentences may be shortened and made more forceful by making verbs more direct, as

WEAK: The committee arrived at a conclusion.
BETTER: The committee concluded.
WEAK: The society held a discussion on the matter.
BETTER: The society discussed the matter.
WEAK: They did away with the old building.
BETTER: They razed the old building.

In their *The Art of Editing* (Macmillan, 1972) Floyd Baskette and Jack Sissors list 48 "pet" circumlocutions which can be reduced to save 100 words:

A good part of (much)
A little less than (almost)
Accidentally stumbled (stumbled)
As a general rule (usually)
At the present time (now)
At the rear of (behind)
Bouquet of flowers (bouquet)
Basic fundamentals (fundamentals)
Commuted back and forth (commuted)
Concentrated his efforts on (concentrated on)
Continued on (continued)
Disclosed for the first time (disclosed)
Drew to a close (ended)
Due to the fact that (because)
Easter Sunday (Easter)
Entered a bid of (bid)
Estimated at about (estimated at)
Filled to capacity (filled)
Gave its approval (approved)
Grand total (total)
Hot water heater (water heater)

In the not too distant future (eventually)
In the immediate vicinity (near)
Invited guests (guests)
Jewish rabbi (rabbi)
Kept under surveillance (watched)
Long chronic illness (chronic illness)
Made arrangements (arranged)
Made an arrest (arrested)
Mental telepathy (telepathy)
Officiated at the ceremony (officiated)
New recruit (recruit)
Soothing balm (balm)
Once in a great while (rarely)
Paid a visit (visited)
Personal friendship (friendship)
Present incumbent (incumbent)
Private industry (industry)
Promoted to the rank of (promoted to)
Put in his appearance (appeared)
Reached an agreement (agreed)
Referred back (referred)
Rough estimate (estimate)
Strangled to death (strangled)
Tendered his resignation (resigned)
Voiced objections (objected)
Went up in flames (burned)
With the exception of (except)

It is not necessary to include the state with the names of large cities, or to mention the state with the name of a city in the same state as the place where the newspaper is published.

WEAK: He lives in Los Angeles, Calif.
BETTER: He lives in Los Angeles.

But:

VAGUE: He lives in Springfield.
CLEAR: He lives in Springfield, Mass.

Don't waste words in giving dates, as

WEAK: The Chemical society will meet on Saturday.
BETTER: The Chemical society will meet Saturday.
WEAK: The meeting will be held this coming Friday.
BETTER: The meeting will be held Friday.
WEAK: The meeting was held at 12 o'clock noon.
BETTER: The meeting was held at noon.

Sometimes a series of related facts can be presented in *series* form, in chronological order, as a word saver. Robert G. Martin cites the following example:

He was born in Russia, reared in Austria, graduated in 1914 from the University of Vienna, and then served throughout World War I as an Austrain artillery officer on the Italian and Russian fronts.

Erlandson, on the other hand, correctly warns against misuse of this style, as "Born in Tennessee, he served on the Los Angeles Board of Education from 1935 to 1941." Wrote Erlandson: "When two unrelated facts are jammed together, it may be bright writing but it's also faulty subordination."

Superfluous Phrases

WEAK: The meeting was held for the purpose of discussing the matter.
BETTER: The meeting was held to discuss the matter.
WEAK: We met at the corner of Spring and High streets.
BETTER: We met at Spring and High streets.

What someone who makes this mistake means is "intersection," where there are four corners, not just one.

WEAK: We reached him by the use of telephone.
BETTER: We reached him by telephone.
WEAK: The color of the cart was red.
BETTER: The cart was red.
WEAK: He will be here for a period of three weeks.
BETTER: He will be here for three weeks.

Often a strong verb, adjective, adverb or possessive form can be substituted for a phrase.

WEAK: A baby with brown eyes.
BETTER: A brown-eyed baby.
WEAK: The arguments of Brown.
BETTER: Brown's arguments.
WEAK: They assembled with little commotion.
BETTER: They assembled quietly.
WEAK: The howitzer went off with a boom.
BETTER: The howitzer boomed.

Before emulating the last preceding example, the writer must be certain that he has not distorted meaning. There is great temptation to use shorter action verbs which create a feeling of excitement not justified by the facts of the story. Some newspapers have been accused of offending considerably in this respect through frequent use of such words as *hits, slaps, traps, raps, rips, flays, slays, breaks, looms, dooms, lashes, kills, fires, cracks, nabs, grabs, quizzes, grills, curbs, blocks* and *foils,* to use a list compiled by Sydney J. Harris.

Superfluous Clauses

WEAK: All citizens who are interested should come.
BETTER: All interested citizens should come.
WEAK: He will speak at the meeting which will be held Monday.
BETTER: He will speak at the meeting Monday.
WEAK: John Farrell, who is secretary of the Engineers' club, will be there.
BETTER: John Farrell, secretary of the Engineers' club, will be there.

On the other hand, clauses can be used effectively for word-preserving interpolations.

Even though he lost them both, 8–6 and 9–7, he outscored Sedgman in earned points, 46–43, and his passing shots, often executed while he was running full tilt, were beautiful to watch.

Simplicity

Simplicity is obtained in large part by avoiding "elegant" words when simple ones would do better. Usually

about is better than *with reference to*

agreement is better than *concordance*

although is better than *despite the fact that*

before is better than *prior to*

body is better than *remains*

buried is better than *interred*

burned is better than *destroyed by fire*

city people is better than *urban people*

clear is better than *obvious*

coffin is better than *casket*

danger is better than *precariousness*

died is better than *passed away* or *succumbed*

dog is better than *canine*

farming is better than *agriculture*

fear is better than *apprehension*

fire is better than *conflagration*

forced is better than *compelled*

funeral is better than *obsequies*

horse is better than *domesticated quadruped*

if is better than *in the event of*

leg is better than *limb*

man is better than *gentleman*

marriage is better than *nuptials*

meeting is better than *rendezvous*

money is better than *lucre*

nearness is better than *contiguity*

normal is better than *traditional*

since is better than *inasmuch as*

theft is better than *larceny*

truth is better than *veracity*

understand is better than *comprehend*

well paying is better than *lucrative*

woman is better than *lady*

When two words are synonyms, brevity can be obtained by using the shorter, as

after for *following*

ask for *request*

buy for *purchase*

car for *automobile*

expect for *anticipate*

get for *obtain*

try for *attempt*

use for *utilize*

Passive and Active Voice

The active voice usually is more emphatic than the passive. The passive should be used, however, when warranted by the importance of the grammatical object of a sentence. In the following sentences, for example, the passive voice is preferable to the active:

Henry Binger has been appointed chairman of the County Republican campaign committee.

Earl Kromer, prominent local merchant, was killed instantly early today when a bolt of lightning struck his home, 34 E. Wilson street.

Increased rates for the Middletown municipal water works were ordered by the public service commission in an order issued Thursday.

In other cases the feature can better be played up by use of the active voice, as

WEAK: The accident was witnessed by ten boys.
BETTER: Ten boys witnessed the accident.
WEAK: The report was received by the mayor.
BETTER: The mayor received the report.
WEAK: The keynote address was delivered by Governor Furman.
BETTER: Governor Furman delivered the keynote address.

Proper Emphasis

Vagueness and indefiniteness are avoided, and clarity is obtained, by placing important ideas at the beginnings of sentences. Also by playing up the action, significance, result or feature of the paragraph or story, by avoiding vague and indefinite words and by eliminating superfluous details, words, phrases and clauses.

VAGUE: Some 50 persons were present.
BETTER: About 50 were present.
WORDY: People of Chester will be asked to contribute $4,000 to the National Red Cross campaign to relieve suffering in the drought area of the United States, according to announcements made yesterday by John Doe, local chairman.
CONCISE: Chester's quota in the National Red Cross campaign for drought relief is $4,000, John Doe, local chairman, said yesterday.
WEAK: When asked what he thought of the compromise plan of unemployment relief, Senator Sapo today said that—
DEFINITE: Senator Sapo today condemned the compromise plan for unemployment relief as demagogic, unconstitutional and inadequate.
WEAK: The purpose of the Student Council meeting at 7 P.M. Monday in Swift hall is to discuss the proposal to limit student activities.
BETTER: The Student Council will discuss limitation of student activities at 7 P.M. Monday in Swift hall.
WEAK: It was decided by the Men's club at its meeting last evening to hold a smoker next Monday evening in the club room.
BETTER: The Men's club will hold a smoker Monday evening in the club room, it was decided at last evening's meeting.

Newspaper style books and journalism texts once admonished reporters never to begin a story with an article or indefinite pronoun. Like every other rule, this one could and should be broken on occasion. Such a lead as "There will be a meeting, etc." ordinarily should be avoided. Such effective writing as the following, however, should be encouraged.

There was to have been a birthday party Saturday in the Ken Rose Rest Home, 6255 N. Kenmore. But instead there was quiet sadness.

The party was to have celebrated the 102d birthday of Miss Frances Benson, a resident of the home.

Miss Benson, a retired Chicago schoolteacher, died Friday after suffering a sudden stroke.

[Chicago *Daily News*]

AVOIDING BANALITY

The day of the grammatical purist is gone. Contemporary authorities recognize that language makes dictionaries and not vice versa. Many words in common use today were once frowned upon as slang or vulgarisms. Every year prominent writers coin new words or resurrect archaic ones which meet with popular acceptance. The fault of young writers as regards word choice is not so much selection of what might be called undignified words but tactless use of bromides, platitudes and cliches. What constitutes tactfulness in using slang, trite and hackneyed expressions is for the English department, not the school of journalism, to teach. Nevertheless, the journalism teacher and certainly the newspaper copyreader can spot a threadbare word or phrase used in a threadbare way.

There isn't a word listed below, as one to be used cautiously, which can't be used effectively on occasion. This is decidedly not a don't section, merely one of precaution.

Figures of Speech

The following figures of speech generally should be avoided because they are likely to be misused. They are whiskered with age and mark their innocent user as callow.

a checkered career	flow like water
acid test	hail of bullets
alike as peas in a pod	hangs in the balance
ax to grind	heart of the business district
blessing in disguise	honest as the day is long
busy as a bee	in the limelight
busy as a one-armed paperhanger	innocent as a newborn babe
clutches of the law	long hours of the night
cool as a cucumber	loomed like sentinels
departed this vale of tears	met his Waterloo
dull as dishwater	never rains but it pours
eyes bigger than his stomach	nipped in the bud

old as Methusaleh
picture of health
pillar of the church
police combing the city
pretty as a picture
rains cats and dogs
round into shape
sea of upturned faces
silver lining
since Hector was a pup
slow as molasses in January
smell a rat
sober as a judge

something the cat dragged in
spread like a house afire
stormy session
the crying need
the great beyond
the wings of disaster
threw a monkey wrench into
to swing the pendulum
watery grave
went by the boards
white as a sheet
won his spurs
worked like Trojans

Bromides

Generally considered too trite or hackneyed for effective use are the following:

all-out effort
almost fatally injured
any way, shape or form
as luck would have it
augurs well
bated breath
beaming smile
better half
bids fair
bigger and better
blushing bride
bright and shiny
broad daylight
burly Negro
crisp bill
dances divinely
departed this life
doing as well as can be expected
doomed to disappointment
dull thud
each and every
easy prey
fair maidens

favor with a selection
feature
few and far between
green-eyed monster
hale and hearty
head over heels
hectic
he-man
host of friends
in the offing
internal fury
laid to rest
last but not least
last sad rites
leering ghost
light fantastic toe
loomed on the horizon
making it a whole new ball game
many and various
method in his madness
music hath charms, etc.
no uncertain terms
order out of chaos

point with pride
powder keg
present day and generation
received an ovation
red-blooded
resting comfortably
scintillating
sigh of relief
signs of the times
smashed to smithereens
sparkling eyes
take a hard look
thick and fast
threw his hat into the ring
trend of public sentiment
variety is the spice of life
view with alarm
vital stake
weather permitting
wild and woolly

Shopworn Personifications

The following mythical characters have been introduced into all kinds of writing so often that they have lost their ability to impress or amuse:

Betty Coed	G.I. Joe	Lady Luck
Dame Fashion	Grim Reaper	Man in the Street
Dame Rumor	Jack Frost	Mother Earth
Dan Cupid	Joe College	Mother Nature
Father Neptune	John Q. Public	Mr. Average Citizen
Father Time	Jupiter Pluvius	Old Sol

Journalese

Newspapers have not contributed so much as one might expect to the coinage of new words, but they have helped exhaust the effectiveness of a large number through indiscriminate repetition. Among these are the following:

blunt instrument	grilled by police	rush
bolt from a clear sky	gruesome find	sleuths
brutal crime	gumshoes	smoke-filled room
brutally murdered	hot seat	smoking revolver
cannon fodder	infuriated mob	solon
cheered to the echo	man hunt	speculation is rife
clubber	moron	swoop down
crime wave	mystery surrounds	thug
cynosure of all eyes	news leaked out	usual reliable sources
death car	police drag nets	war clouds
fatal noose	political pot boiling	while thousands cheer
feeling ran high	probe	whirlwind tour
focus attention	quiz	will be staged

Lazy journalistic habits include use of such meaningless descriptive phrases as "a policeman's policeman," "a lawyer's lawyer" and the like and overuse of the word "controversial" presumably to heighten interest in a person, event or thing.

Gobbledegook

Heyn warns against "pretentious phrasing, guaranteed to scare the reader away from the story." He cites this example:

National Association for Advancement of Colored People attorneys told the Supreme Court today that overt public resistance is insufficient cause to nullify federal court desegregation orders.

He also warns against governmentese and other gobbledegook and cites some clauses and phrases that "should have a familiar ring," as follows:

Since over-all policy was brought into focus . . .
. . . under mandate to achieve conformity.
Suspension of the principle is all the more important . . .
. . . finalize a program for federally impacted school areas.

Wallace Carroll, editor and publisher of the Winston-Salem *Journal* and *Sentinel*, laments the extent to which Emerson's law has become Nosreme's law. In his article "Ralph Waldo Emerson, Thou Shouldst Be Living at This Hour," in the June 1970 *Nieman Reports*, Carroll refreshes his readers' memory of Emerson's aphorism: "If a man can write a better book, preach a better sermon, or make a better mousetrap than his neighbor, though he builds his house in the woods, the world will make a beaten path to his door."

Carroll laments the decline in quality in many areas of life, both material and immaterial. Specifically, as regards "the realm of words and images," he comments:

Here, too, Emerson is in full retreat. All of us know that if an obscure man can take two clear, simple words like "hot" and "cool" (words that cannot be misunderstood even by a retarded four-year-old), and if that man can so twist and mangle those words that everybody in his right mind will wonder what in the name of McLuhan he means by them—if a man can do this he will be hailed as a genius in "communications"; foundations will be richly endowed for him so that he can perpetuate his befuddlement among succeeding generations.

The McLuhan whose activities Carroll deplores is Prof. Marshall Mc-Luhan for whom "the medium is the message." In *Understanding Media* and other books, McLuhan cites the growing importance of television and other electronic media and comes close to predicting the disappearance of the printed word. To Carroll and others, however, it does not necessarily follow that the contents of a message are unimportant. Rather, the essence of good journalism remains good reporting, which means having something to say—the contents rather than the medium is the message. It just is not so that what you don't know won't hurt you. In a democracy widespread knowledge is essential. Carroll strongly warns against adoption of Nosreme's law, which he defines as follows:

If a man can write muddier prose than his neighbor, if he can arrange words in ways that befuddle the brain and grate on the ear, he will never have to monkey with a better mousetrap.

Carroll describes the difficulty the newsgatherer today encounters:

Do you want to be recognized as an authority on reading in the public schools? Then you have only to write like this:
"Perhaps the task of developing proper motivation is best seen, at least in a nutshell, as limiting the manipulation of extrinsic factors to that of keeping

homeostatic need and exteroceptive drive low, in favor of facilitating basic information processing to maximize accurate anticipation of reality."

Do you want to become a professor of the behavioral sciences in a great university? Then you simply need to express yourself in this way:

"If the correlation of intrinsic competency to actual numerical representation is definitely high, then the thoroughly objective conclusion may inexpugnably be reached that the scholastic derivations and outgrowths will attain a pattern of unified superiority."

Do you want to become the chief of a government bureau? Then learn to write and talk like this:

"The Board's new regulatory goal is to create a supervisory environment conducive and stimulative to industry adaptation to its fundamentally altered markets. We will give you the options to restructure both sides of your statement of condition, but the decision-making and the long-range planning function is management's . . . We will look to you for input of information which we shall rely on in making our decisions."

Or do you want to become an expert on business management and go around lecturing to leaders of industry? You can if you will learn to talk like this:

"The focus of concentration rests upon objectives which are, in turn, centered around the knowledge and customer areas, so that a sophisticated awareness of those areas can serve as an entrepreneurial filter to screen what is relevant from what is irrelevant to future commitments."

This bastardization of our mother tongue is really a disaster for all of us in the news business. The English language is our bread and butter, but when ground glass is mixed with the flour and grit with the butter, our customers are likely to lose their appetite for what we serve them.

The popularity of fuzzy writing indicates the widespread existence of fuzzy thinking by pseudo-intellectuals who, in their frustration, accept what they don't understand as probably profound and who then struggle to interpret. As a result shallow books such as *The Greening of America* by Charles Reich and Thomas A. Harris' *I'm O.K.— You're O.K.* become bestsellers. The best exposure of the superficiality of this sort of thing is *Social Sciences As Sorcery* by Stanislav Andreski (St. Martin's Press, 1972).

READABILITY FORMULAS

Shortly after World War II the two major press associations and several magazines and newspapers experimented with readability formulas which stressed brevity—shorter words, shorter sentences and shorter paragraphs—in the belief that thereby the average American, who has only a ninth grade education, would find the result easier to read and comprehend.

The formulas grew out of studies of several researchers, most important of whom were Rudolf Flesch of New York University and Robert Gunning, director of Readable News Reports of Columbus, Ohio. Following the recommendations of the former, the Associated Press reduced its average lead sentence length from 27 to 23 words and its average word sentence length from 1.74 to 1.55 syllables. Upon the advice of the latter, the United

Press simplified its writing style so as to be suitable for readers with 11.7 years of education, whereas formerly it presumably was writing for those who had gone to school 16.7 years.

Flesch's formula allegedly estimated "reading ease" and "human interest." The former was measured by the average length of words and sentences—the shorter, the easier to read, 1.5 syllables and an average sentence length of 19 words being considered best for newspapers. Human interest was measured by the percentage of "personal words" and "personal sentences" Flesch said 6 per cent of the former and 12 per cent of the latter made for good newspaper reading.

Gunning considered three factors: (1) sentence pattern, difficulty beginning when the average number of words per sentence exceeded twenty; (2) Fog Index, a measure of complex or abstract words as "rendezvous" for "meeting," "undoubtedly" for "no doubt," etc.; (3) human interest—the frequent use of names of people, referents to those names and other human interest words.

As an APME Readability committee once reported: "The virtue of the Flesch experiment is that it *has* made writers think more of their writing."

The same, of course, could be said of the Gunning and several other formulas.

That these and other techniques to obtain brevity can be overdone, however, is obvious. After what they considered fair trial, some newspapermen concluded that a new rigid formula merely was being substituted for another. One of the most outspoken of rewrite men who considered the new "strait jacket" worse than the old was Robert Faherty of the Chicago *Daily News* who wrote

> The formula wastes writer-time, which costs money. It wastes writer-skill. It wastes writer-strength, cutting efficiency. It kills writer-creativeness, which some editors regard as desirable.

Stephen E. Fitzgerald pointed out that many of the classics had a high Fog Index but managed to communicate. Of the "readability boys," this author wrote, "They threaten to put our words in a literary strait jacket, leaving us only the solace of an illusion ... that by shortening our sentences, we have somehow clarified our thought."

Brevity, this and other critics contend, does not necessarily equate with clarity. A short word can be as vague as a long one, and a short sentence can be as misleading as a book. Using the syllable-length criterion advanced by Flesch, such words as *beautiful, patriotism, vacation, prearrange, improbable, candlestick, bracelet, watermelon* and other familiar ones would be considered difficult whereas use of *ohm, joule, watt, erg, baize, arn, tweak, volt* and *tort* would contribute to a high readability score.

Different from either the Flesch or Gunning system, in that it takes account of the reader's probable familiarity with words, is the system devised by Prof. Edger Dale and Mrs. Jeanne S. Chall of the Bureau of Education Research of Ohio State University. The Dale-Chall system takes into account average sentence length but also uses a list of 3,000 words familiar to fourth graders.

Dr. Dale discounts the value of counting affixes, suffixes and prefixes, as advocated by Flesch, by declaring that no two skilled judges ever get the same count. He also rejects Flesch's personal referent principle and is fond of citing a quotation from Koffka's *Principles of Gestalt Psychology* which contains personal pronouns equal to 5.8 per cent as follows:

> In the first case, real moving objects present in the field, the shift of the retinal pattern leads to behavioral motion of objects, whether I fixate a nonmoving object or follow a moving one with my regard; in the second case, when my eyes roam stationary objects, such a shift will not have this result. . . .

That would be considered very readable by both the Flesch and Gunning systems.

Proper names, other critics of these formulas have pointed out, do not necessarily lead to greater understanding unless the reader knows the persons mentioned and understands the references to them. "He was as mad as Hamlet," for instance, is about as readable as you can get; but if the reader never has heard of Hamlet, its meaning is lost on him.

SEMANTICS

Despite its length, the following sentence probably would be considered readable by the readability experts:

> Many boys and girls are working at too young an age, for too long hours, too late at night, in dangerous and other undesirable conditions.

A great semanticist, however, would be quick to point out that no matter how clear the sentence may be, the information it conveys is vague and biased. How many is "many"? When you say "boys and girls" do you mean little children, such as used to work in sweatshops, or do you mean teenagers? What determines when one is too young to deliver newspapers, set pins in a bowling alley, run errands for a grocer, sew buttons or work on a lathe? How long is "too long" and how late is "too late"? What is a "dangerous" condition? Especially, what are "other undesirable" conditions?

No experienced newsgatherer would fail to ask these questions if such a statement were made during the course of an interview. Often, however, such "glittering generalities," as the Institute for Propaganda Analysis (1937–1942) would have called them, appear in publicity releases and in public addresses, especially by politicians. They need amplification to convey important meaning to others, and it will be a happy day when editors toss them into the wastebasket unless it is possible to obtain such amplification.

On assignment, the interpretative reporter must be sharp enough to ask the proper questions to clarify vague statements and define "virtue" or "smear" words. Often, if not always, this requires more than the usual amount of knowledge on the reporter's part regarding the field of interest. In other words, the more one knows about a subject, the better able he is to interview someone regarding it. All the readability formulas and other aids to good writing cannot substitute for thorough fact gathering.

"Pin the man down" should be the newsgatherer's first rule. If his subject talks about "progress," the reporter should ask him what he means by the term and for the facts and figures that justify its use. If the person being interviewed mentions "special circumstances," he should be asked what he means by "circumstances" and what makes them "special" and to give specific examples of what he's talking about.

Unfamiliar Words

If the words an interviewee uses are specific but nevertheless unfamiliar, the reporter had best overcome any sheepishness and ask for a little elementary shop talk from his subject. Otherwise, he might neglect to inquire deeply enough into the potential facts of the story at hand. Lacking such an opportunity for "depth" reporting, the reporter should consult dictionaries, encyclopedias and other reference works to fill the gaps in his own knowledge.

If a reporter has to ask or look up the meaning of an expression, he can be fairly certain that a goodly number of his readers will need explanation of it. Perhaps he can even avoid use of the unfamiliar word in his story. He can, for instance, say, "Union A is attempting to persuade members of Union B to change their membership from B to A." Then he can explain, "This is called 'raiding' in labor circles." Or, if he uses "raiding" in his principal statement, he can define it, perhaps in an italicized parenthetical insert.

"Jurisdictional strike," "mass picketing" and "secondary boycott" are among the other terms in a story of a labor dispute which may need explanation. In weather stories, it probably is wise to make clear the difference between hurricanes, tornadoes, cyclones and just plain gales or wind storms. Few readers probably remember what a nautical knot is or a French kilometer or an English mile. With the world becoming more complex daily and the areas of specialization growing, the need for such explanatory journalism is increasing. Thorough reporting is the best safeguard against the misuse of words.

Connotations

"The workers *won* a wage boost" has one connotation. "The workers *were given* a wage boost" has quite another. Only painstaking reporting can determine which is correct in any particular case. There can be no laziness or carelessness when the public interest is involved, as it usually is in stories pertaining to labor relations, governmental activities and the like.

Perhaps a news source condemns government "interference" when he really means he opposes government "regulation" in a particular area. Such words are loaded. Reportorial questioning should lead to specific details rather than vague charges or mere name calling. If loaded words are used from some necessity, they probably should be included in quotation marks or some explanatory matter should be added to indicate the alternative words for the same thought.

Newspapers propagandize if they use the labels of those with whom they agree editorially to describe pending legislation or situations. Examples of such editorializing would be "slave labor bill" for a measure regulating the mobility of the labor force in time of emergency, "dictator bill" for a proposal to increase the power of an executive, "goon" for labor union pickets and the like. It makes a great deal of difference whether you write

> crop relief *or* farm dictatorship
> foreign *or* alien
> labor organizer *or* labor agitator
> nonstriker *or* loyal worker
> picketing *or* mass picketing
> a company's earnings declined 36 per cent *or* they plunged to that extent
> regulation *or* regimentation
> UAW chieftain *or* UAW dictator
> open shop *or* right to work

Sydney J. Harris, whose column originates with and is syndicated by the Chicago *Daily News*, is a fervid semanticist. The following, entitled "More Antics With Semantics," is typical of his writings:

> Why is it that Our secret agents are "patriots," while Their secret agents are nothing but "spies"?
>
> When I have one over the limit, I become "the life of the party"; when you have one over the limit, you become a "loudmouth."
>
> I am "strongminded," but you are "opinionated."
>
> My candidate's plan for the future shows he has "vision," but your candidate's plan for the future makes him a "wild-eyed dreamer."
>
> I am about the only capable and careful driver on the road; all other motorists are either "stick-in-the-muds" or "reckless maniacs."
>
> My failure to laugh at your dirty jokes shows my "good breeding," but your failure to laugh at my dirty jokes shows "stuffiness."
>
> * * *
>
> The British are too "reserved," and the French are too "effusive"; the Italians are too "impulsive," and the Scandinavians are too "cold"; the Germans are too "arrogant," and the Japanese are too "diffident"—surely God must be an American.
>
> My new two-tone car is "gay," but your new two-tone car is just "loud."
>
> I give an inexpensive present because "it's the spirit behind it that counts," but you give an inexpensive present because you're cheap.
>
> My son hit yours over the head with a block because he is "playful," but yours hit mine over the head because he is "vicious."

A "sound" man is a man who sounds like me.

When I spread gossip, it is always a "harmless tidbit," but when you spread gossip, it is "malicious rumor-mongering."

A "realistic" novel is a novel that agrees with the idea of reality I held before I even opened the book.

*　　*　　*

My family, which is poor, lost its tremendous fortune during the Depression; but your family, which is rich, made all its money profiteering during the War.

Why is it that "modern" is an approving adjective for plumbing, but a disapproving adjective for art?

My wife's dress is "simple," but your wife's dress is "dowdy."

Likewise, my summer wardrobe is "casual," but yours is "sloppy."

Our relatives may "get into trouble," but your relatives have illegitimate babies, go to jail and take up dope. (ours, are, of course, "unfortunate," but yours are "bad.")

Puffs and Boosts

Against one type of editorializing most newspapers are sufficiently on the alert. That is the practice of making gratuitous complimentary remarks regarding a person or event rather than stating the facts and allowing them to speak for themselves. Some such expressions, obsolete in most newsrooms, are the following:

a big success	happy pair
a good time was had by all	in a very entertaining manner
a stellar performance	it beggars description
an enjoyable occasion	it bids fair
an impressive sight	likeable personality
an interesting program was offered	prospects are bright
	proud possessor
attractive decorations	replete with interest
charming hostess	talented young man
everything went along nicely	the trip was the most popular ever
fills a long-felt need	taken

Such expressions are taboo if for no other reason than that they have been overworked.

Evaluative Words

In quite a different category are attempts to improve the reader's understanding by the use of qualifying adjectives, other parts of speech and expressions. Even some editors who have been outspoken in adverse criticism of interpretative reporting have for years allowed and encouraged their reporters to write "One of America's *leading composers* will play his own compositions," "The two *top contenders* for the championship will meet in the first round," "An *unusual* workshop class in creative writing for talented children will be organized," "The court will hear arguments on the *complex, controversial and crucial questions*" and the like.

There is no denying that such expressions involve judgment and, to be socially responsible, the judgment must be based on adequate information. When a sports writer, for instance, writes that the outcome of a contest was "a stunning upset," he must know that leaders in the sports world and fans expected it to be different. No competent reporter uses superlatives without investigating to determine whether they are justified: "most devastating fire," "largest audience," "longest report," "rare appearance." Nor does he call every gruesome murder "the crime of the century."

NOUNS

When, however, can you call a disturbance a "panic" or "riot"? When can you use such words as "catastrophe," "fiasco," "disaster," "climax," "zenith" or "debacle"? All you can say is that such terms should be used judiciously. To make common use of them would be to devitalize them. It would be like crying "wolf" when there was no wolf.

What, therefore, is judicious use? The experienced reporter who has covered many similar stories has a basis for comparison, and his own experience usually is better than that of most everyone else, especially axgrinders with motives for hoping he uses this word instead of that. Competent reporting and integrity are more likely to give readers correct information than writing formulas and communication theories are.

ADJECTIVES

When is a girl pretty or beautiful? Not every time she gets into a newsworthy situation certainly. Since the development of photography, reporters have become more cautious over indiscriminate use of such descriptive adjectives. Since there is no similar restraining influence in other areas the best that can be done is to advise caution in the use of such words as the following:

brave	ferocious	popular
brilliant	gigantic	remarkable
clever	happy-go-lucky	successful
cowardly	huge	tasteful
eloquent	illimitable	unpatriotic
enjoyable	impressive	valiant
exciting	nice	widely known

VERBS

Verbs must be exact. If a news source answers "yes" to a reporter's question, it is not always proper to say he "admitted" something. When he makes an announcement, he cannot be said to have "revealed" or "disclosed" something unless the matter previously had been kept secret intentionally. "Charge" is a strong word implying an accusation which the news source might have had no intention of making. "Claim" suggests that some one is trying to correct a wrong impression or obtain possession of something which he considers rightfully his. "Probe" implies detectives of some sort are afoot.

Since very few words are exact synonyms for each other, a good dictionary or thesaurus is a better companion for the writer seeking to impart correct information than Gunning's formula to determine the Fog Index. The practice of intentionally using a strong synonym for maximum visceral effect on readers instead of the word which comes closer to stating the situation correctly cannot be condoned.

Here is a list of verbs which the reporter should be hesitant about using:

allege	laugh	sneer
beg	object	squeak
confess	plead	threaten
flee	prowl	urge
grimace	roar	whine
implore	shout	whisper
insult	sneak	yell

ADVERBS

A properly placed adverb can change the entire meaning of a news story. Consider the potential power of the following:

accidentally	facetiously	jokingly
angrily	grimly	laughingly
boastfully	immodestly	mockingly
calmly	inadvertently	seriously
carelessly	intentionally	stupidly
casually	ironically	viciously

PHRASES

Evaluational phrases can "make or break" a news story and also, perhaps, some of the principals mentioned in it. Consider the potency of the following:

angry response	pale with anger
in an arrogant manner	shaking with grief
in an unprecedented personal state- ment	showing great dignity
	under duress
in top oratorical form	with profound feeling

CORRECT USAGE

It is presumed that the student has completed a course in English grammar and composition and, therefore, that he knows the rudiments of good English. Although some reputable writers still split their infinitives without losing effect, few misuse "lay" and "lie," use "none" as a plural, get "don't" and "doesn't" twisted, misplace "only" or use "like" when they mean "as if" or become confused over the difference between "its" and "it's." If the student of this book is deficient in his knowledge of grammar, he had better concentrate on it constantly. Cubs who cannot make their subjects and predicates agree and who can't spell ordinary words don't last long.

In every newspaper office some rules of grammar, word usage and punctuation are emphasized more than others. Most newspapers issue style sheets for the guidance of new staff members as to what kind of writing is preferred.

Grammatical Faults

Several years of correcting journalism students' papers have convinced the writer that the following are among the most common grammatical errors about which aspiring reporters need caution.

> WRONG: Neither the mayor nor the city clerk are willing to talk.
> RIGHT: Neither the mayor nor the city clerk is willing to talk.
> WRONG: The Chamber of Commerce will begin their annual membership drive Monday.
> RIGHT: The Chamber of Commerce will begin its annual membership drive Monday.
> WRONG: Howard is not as tall as Harold.
> RIGHT: Howard is not so tall as Harold.
> WRONG: He gave it to John and I.
> RIGHT: He gave it to John and me.
> WRONG: Less than 35% of the group favor the idea.
> RIGHT: Fewer than 35% of the group favor the idea.

The next two examples do not illustrate infallible rules; in other cases, the constructions listed as weak may be better:

> WEAK: He has always wanted to go.
> BETTER: He always has wanted to go.
> WEAK: He was ordered to immediately arrest Jones.
> BETTER: He was ordered to arrest Jones immediately.
> WRONG: Having arrived an hour late, the audience had begun to disperse before Smith began to speak.
> RIGHT: Having arrived an hour late, Smith found his audience had begun to disperse.
> WRONG: After Graham and Mitchell had shaken hands he turned to greet the senator.
> RIGHT: After Graham and Mitchell had shaken hands the former turned to greet the senator.
> STRONGER: After Graham shook hands with Mitchell he greeted the senator.

Parts of Speech

To obtain originality of expression, writers (not all of them journalists) sometimes change the part of speech of a word. In many cases the dictionaries have caught up with popular usage. For instance, it is proper to say "chair a meeting," "jail a prisoner," "hospitalize a sick person" or "table a resolution." Even such words as "alibi," "probe," "host" and "torpedo," to whose use as verbs objection often is heard, are listed as such. President Kennedy used "finalize" as a verb and the practice of inventing verb forms of nouns is widespread; thus we say "victimize," "contact," and the like indiscriminately.

In view of the dynamic character of the language, one hesitates to become crotchety when a newspaper columnist says someone "week-ended" or "house-guested" another or that a dowager "lorgnetted" a stranger. In recent years such words as "babysit" and "moonlight" have come into common usage as verbs. Use of "-wise" as a suffix (businesswise, timewise, bookwise, saleswise) still is regarded as somewhat flippant, however expressive.

The congressional hearings of 1974 popularized many expressions and new usages that dictionaries probably will take note of. For example, "Watergate" may become a synonym for political intrigue and "stonewall it" may be defined as maintaining silence on a matter. Comedians and others are understood when they make clever use of such expressions as "at this point in time," "inoperative," "hardnose it" and "expletive deleted." An Associated Press poll revealed that 30 per cent of the papers surveyed did not censor Nixon's profane and vulgar language as revealed by the tapes. However, a year later Charles T. Alexander was fired because he permitted a four-letter word to appear in the Dayton *Journal-Herald* of which he was editor.

Usually it is left to special writers who sign their stories, sports writers and feature writers to invent unusual word usages. Authors of formal stories are more conservative and wait until the dictionaries have sanctioned an innovation before using it casually. When Webster's *Third New International Dictionary* appeared, however, it created a storm for allegedly going too far in legitimatizing new usages. Among the leading liberal authorities in this field are Roy Copperud, who conducts a column for *Editor & Publisher*, and Prof. Bergen Evans of Northwestern University, who coauthored *A Dictionary of Contemporary American Usage* with Cornelia Evans. Defenders of the Webster dictionary pointed out that in 1800 such words as "banjo," "hominy" and "possum" were considered too slangy for its edition that year. On the other hand there is Edwin Newman who argues powerfully in *Strictly Speaking* (Bobbs-Merrill, 1974) against too much license, especially by journalists.

Troublesome Words

No matter what the viewpoint regarding definitions, there can be no disagreement that words should be used to convey the meaning intended by their employers. Caution, therefore, is advisable in deviating from standard usages.

The following are some words and expressions which often cause difficulty:

Above. Should not be used for *over* or *more than.*

Accord. Do not use in the sense of *award. Give* is better.

Act. A single incident. An *action* consists of several acts.

Actual facts. All facts are actual.

Administer. Used with reference to medicine, governments or oaths. Blows are not *administered,* but *dealt.*

Adopt. Not synonymous with *decide* or *assume.*

Affect; effect. Affect means to have an influence on; *effect* means to cause, to produce, to result in.

Aggravate. Means to *increase;* not synonymous with *irritate.*

Aggregate. Not synonymous with *total.*

Allege. Not synonymous with *assert.* Say the *alleged* crime, but "He *said* he is innocent."

Allow; permit. The former means *not to forbid;* the latter means *to grant leave.*

Allude. Do not confuse with *refer* or *elude.*

Almost; nearly. Almost regards the ending of an act, *nearly* the beginning.

Alternative. Indicates a choice of two things. Incorrect to speak of *two alternatives* or *one alternative.*

Among. Use when more than two is meant; for two only, use *between.*

Annual. Don't write *first annual.* It's not annual yet.

Antecedents. Do not use in the sense of *ancestors, forefathers, history* or *origin.*

A number of. Indefinite. Specify.

Anxious. Implies worry. Not synonymous with *eager* which implies anticipation or desire.

Anyone or *none.* Use in speaking of more than two. *Either* and *neither* are used when speaking of only two. All take singular verbs.

Appears, looks, smells, seems, etc. Take an adjective complement.

As the result of an operation. Avoid this expression. Usually incorrect and libelous.

At. Use *in* before the names of large cities: He is *in* New York, but the meeting was held *at* Greenville.

Audience. An *audience* hears, *spectators* see.

Autopsy. An *autopsy* is *performed,* not *held.*

Averse; adverse. The former is an adjective meaning *opposed to;* the latter is an adjective meaning *bad.*

Avocation. A man's pleasure, while *vocation* is his business or profession.

Awful. Means to *fill with awe;* not synonymous with *very* or *extremely.*

Balance. Not synonymous with *rest* or *remainder.*

Banquet. Only a few dinners are worth the name. Use *dinner* or *supper.*

Because. Better than *due* in "They fought because of a misunderstanding."

Beside; besides. The first means *by the side of;* the second, *in addition to.*

Bloc. Don't confuse with *block.*

By. Use instead of *with* in such sentences as "The effect was gained by colored lights."

Call attention. Do not use it for *direct attention.*

Canon; cannon. The former is a *law;* the latter is a large *gun.*

Canvas; canvass. The former is a *cloth;* the latter means to *solicit.*

Capitol. The building is the *capitol;* the city is the *capital.*

Casualty. Should not be confused with *disaster, accident, mishap.*

Childish. Not synonymous with *childlike.*

Chinese. Don't use *Chinaman.*

Claim. A transitive verb. One may "claim a dog" but not that "Boston is larger than Portland."

Cold facts (or statistics). When is a fact hot?

Collide. To collide both objects must be in motion.

Commence. Usually *begin* or *start* is better.

Compared with. Use *compared with* in speaking of two things coming under the same classification; use *compared to* if the classes are different.

Completely destroyed. Redundant.

Comprise. Do not use for *compose.*

Confess. A man confesses a crime to the police, but he does not confess to a crime.

Conscious. Not synonymous with *aware.*

Consensus. Don't say *consensus of opinion;* simply say *consensus.*

Consequence. Sometimes misused in the sense of "importance" and "of moment," as "They are all persons of consequence" (importance); "A matter of no consequence" (moment).

Consist in. Distinguish between *consists in* and *consists of.*

Consummation. Look up in the dictionary. Do not use in reference to marriage.

Continual; continuous. That is *–al* which either is always going on or recurs at short intervals and never comes (or is regarded as never coming) to an end. That is *–ous* in which no break occurs between the beginning and the end.

Convene. Delegates, not a convention, *convene.*

Correspondent; co-respondent. The former *communicates in writing;* the latter *answer jointly* with another.

Council; counsel. The former is a *meeting for deliberation.* The latter is *advice* or *one who gives advice.*

Couple. Used only when two things are joined, not of separate things. Use *of* with it.

Crime. Do not confuse with *sin* or *vice. Crime* is a violation of the law of the state; *vice* refers to a violation of moral law; *sin* is a violation of religious law.

Cultured. Don't use for *cultivated.*

Cyclone. Distinguish from *hurricane, typhoon, tornado, gale* and *storm.*

Dangerously. Not *dangerously* but *critically* or *alarmingly* ill.

Data. Plural. *Datum* is singular.

Date from. Not *date back to.*

Depot. Don't use for *station.* A *depot* is a storehouse for freight or supplies; railway passengers arrive at a *station.*

Die of. Not *die from.*

Different from. Not *different than.*

Dimensions; proportions. The former pertains to *magnitude;* the latter to *form.*

Divide. Don't say, "The money was divided between Smith, Jones and Brown." Use *among* when more than two are concerned.

Dove. Should not be used for *dived.*

Drops dead. Falls dead is what is meant.

Drown. Don't say *was drowned* unless it was murder; just say *drowned.*

During. Do not confuse with *in. During* answers the question "How long?" *in* answers the question "When? At what time?" as "We were in Princeton *during* the winter"; "We received the letter *in* the morning."

Each other; one another. The former pertains to *two;* the latter to *three* or *more.*

Either; neither. Use when speaking of two only.

Elicit. Means to "draw out against the will."

Emigrant. Do not confuse with *immigrant.* An *emigrant* leaves, and an *immigrant* comes in.

Envelop; envelope. The former means *to surround;* the latter is a *covering* or *wrapper.*

Event. Do not confuse with *incident, affair, occurrence* or *happening.*

Experiment. Don't say *try* an experiment. Experiments are *made.*

Fail. To *fail* one must try. Usually what is meant is *did not.*

Fakir; faker. The former is an Oriental ascetic; the latter is a street peddler.

Farther. Denotes distance; *further* denotes time.

Final; finale. The former means *last;* the latter is a *concluding act* or *number.*

Fliers; flyers. The former are *aviators;* the latter are *handbills.*

Flout; flaunt. The former means *to scoff* or *mock;* the latter means *to make ostentatious display.*

Frankenstein. He was the monster's maker, not the monster itself.

From. A person dies *of*, not *from*, a disease.

Graduate, as a verb. Colleges *graduate;* students *are graduated.*

Gun. Don't confuse with *revolver* and *pistol.*

Had. Implies volition. Don't say, "Had his arm cut off."

Head up. The *up* is superfluous.

Healthy. A person is *healthy*, but climate is *healthful* and food *wholesome.*

Heart failure. Everyone dies of heart failure. There are several *heart diseases.*

Hectic. "Hectic flush" is the feverish blush of consumption. Not to be used in the sense of *excited, impassioned, intense, rapturous, uncontrolled* or *wild*, except when a jocosity is intended.

High. Distinguish from *large.*

Hoi polloi. "The many." Do not use "the" before it.

Hold. Use advisedly. The Supreme Court *holds* a law constitutional, but one *asserts* that one man is a better boxer than another.

Hung. A criminal is *hanged.* Clothes are *hung* on a line.

Inaugurate. Does not mean *begin.*

Incumbent. It is redundant to write *present incumbent.*

Indorse. Not synonymous with *approve.*

Infer; imply. The former means *to deduce;* the latter *to signify.*

Initial. A man may sign his initial, but he does not make an *initial payment.* He makes the *first payment.*

Innumerable. Not synonymous with *endless.*

Invited guests. Most guests are invited; omit the adjective.

Last. Not synonymous with *latest* or *past.*

Leave. Don't confuse with *let.*

Leaves a widow. Impossible. He leaves a *wife.*

Less. Use *less* money for *fewer* coins.

Like. The slogan "Winstons taste good like a cigaret should" has helped make the use of "like" legitimate as a substitute for "as."

Literally. Often the exact opposite, *figuratively,* is meant.

Locate. A building is *located* when its site is picked; thereafter it is *situated.* A person is *found,* not located.

Majority. The lead over *all* others; a plurality is a lead over *one* other.

Marshal; Marshall. The former is a title; the latter a proper name.

Mathematics. Singular.

Memorandum. Singular. *Memoranda,* plural.

Mend. You *mend* a dress but *repair* a street.

Minister. Distinguish between *minister,* a term used in Protestant churches, and *priest,* used in Catholic churches. Every *preacher* is not a *pastor;* a *pastor* has a church, a *minister* may not.

Musical; musicale. The former means *rhythmic;* the latter is a *recital* or *concert.*

Name after. The correct form is *name for.*

Near accident. There is no such thing.

Nee. Give only last name, "Mrs. Helen Kuenzel, nee Bauman."

Nice. Means *exact,* not *agreeable* or *pleasant.*

Notorious. Different from *famous.*

Occur. Accidents *occur* rather than *happen,* but weddings *take place.*

Old adages. There are no *new adages.*

Oral; verbal. The former emphasises use of the mouth; the latter applies to either spoken or written words.

Over. Means *above; more than* means *in excess of.*

Partly completed. Has no meaning. The words are contradictory.

Past. Not synonymous with *last.*

People. Refers to population. Do not confuse with *persons.*

Per cent. Do not say "large per cent" when you mean "large proportion."

Politics. Singular.

Practically. Not synonymous with *virtually.* Different from *almost.*

Principle. Always a noun. *Principal* is generally an adjective.

Prone on the back. Impossible. The word means "lying on the face." *Supine* is "lying on the back."

Provided. Not *providing* he will go.

Public. Singular.

Put in. You *occupy, devote* or *spend* time, never *put in* time.

Quite. Means *fully* or *wholly.* Do not, for example, write "He is *quite* wealthy," but "He is *rather* wealthy."

Raised. Animals are *raised;* children are *reared.*

Render. You *render* lard or a judgment, but you *sing* a song.

Rumor. It is redundant to write *unverified rumor.*

Secure. Means *to make fast.* Don't use it for *obtain, procure* or *acquire.*

Sensation; emotion. The former is *physical;* the latter is *mental.*

Ship. Cattle are *shipped* but corpses are *sent.*

So. Use in a negative comparison instead of *as.*

Someone, somebody, etc. Take singular verbs.

Suicide. Do not use as a verb.

Sustain. Injuries are not *sustained* but *received.*

To the nth. An unspecified number, not necessarily infinite or large. Do not use for *to the utmost possible extent.*

Transpire. Means *to emerge from secrecy into knowledge, to become gradually known.* Not to be used in the senses of *happen, occur,* etc.; must not be followed by an infinitive.

Treble; triple. The former means *three times;* the later means *three kinds.*

True facts. Facts never are false.

Try and. Use *try to.*

Unique. Its adverbs are *absolutely, almost, in some respects, nearly, perhaps, quite, really* and *surely.* It does not admit of comparison. There are no degrees of uniqueness. It means *alone of its kind. Different* means *out of the ordinary.*

Unknown; unidentified. The former means *not recognizable by* anyone; the latter means *not yet recognized.*

Various. Not synonymous with *different.*

Vender; vendor. The former is a *seller;* the latter is a legal term.

Want; wish. The former means *need* and *desire;* the latter means only *desire.*

We. Don't use the editorial *we.* Name the paper.

Well-known. Usually *widely known* is meant.

Whether. Do not use for *if.* Don't add *or not.*

Widow. Never use *widow woman.*

Yacht. Do not say *private yacht.* There are no *public* ones.

A clever warning against misuse of the language was contained in the following informative feature article:

By Dennis Montgomery

CENTRALIA, Ill. (AP)—Inflation is devaluing the language as well as the dollar.

For instance, when you want to point out a ridiculously low price you might say, "It's dirt cheap." But dirt's not so cheap anymore.

Illinois highway officials building Interstate 64 say they paid 72 cents a cubic yard for dirt fill in 1972, $1.30 last year and $1.55 this month.

Chicken feed has been another synonym for cheapness, but it has doubled in price in two years. A 100-pound sack, about as much as a chicken eats in its life, now costs $9.50. That's $7 more than the purchase price of a chicken.

Then there's the American expression: "Not worth a continental."

Inflation spawned that one when the Continental Congress issued so much unsecured currency it wasn't worth the paper it was printed on. But inflation has pushed the worth of a 1776 vintage continental in good condition to $40, compared to about $15 two years ago.

The paper it's printed on? Well, the paper you have in your hand, standard grade newsprint, costs about $11 a hundredweight. Fifteen months ago it was about $8.50.

If you're angry at something you might say: "It's not worth the powder it takes to blow it up." Gunpowder prices have shot up 22 to 40 per cent, depending on grade, since last year. A pound will cost you $2.03, or 68 cents more than a year ago.

Finally, there is a phrase the colonists brought with them: "Not worth a tinker's damn." It's hard to find a tinker anymore, but there does happen to be one here in Centralia—and he gets $8 an hour.

Now, if the tinker gave you a particularly soulful curse, say a 15-second ear-bender for hitting his thumb with a hammer, it would be worth 2.5 cents.

7

WINNING READER CONFIDENCE

The chief complaint of a newspaper's critics—that is, everybody who reads it—is not bias through distortion and suppression. Nor is it sensationalism with its by-product, violation of the right to privacy. On the contrary, the American reader prefers the newspaper which gives him a point of view coinciding with his own and complains of prejudice only when he disagrees. His patronage of newspapers which specialize in lurid details discounts any feigned distaste for them.

What the average American newspaper reader considers the cardinal journalistic sin is inaccuracy. Suppress news favorable to the other fellow and play up news favorable to your side but score the point through use of facts. It is a terrible letdown to be faced with irrefragable proof that something one wants to believe is false. Likewise, if the juicy sex story or other sensational yarn is shown to be untrue it ceases to entertain.

Readers don't mean it when they say they don't believe anything they read in the newspapers; actually most of what they know is learned in that way. They apply the opprobrious term "just newspaper talk" to a story unpleasant to believe, regardless of its truth.

Because editors are aware of these aspects of man's social behavior, and because there is no reason why a newspaper should be anything but one hundred per cent accurate in a vast majority of the stories it publishes, one of the first lessons the beginning reporter must learn is how to avoid making mistakes. There are some newsrooms even in large cities where a certain amount of carelessness is condoned, but not many. A standard of accuracy way beyond anything to which the recent college graduate has been accustomed in his English composition classes is maintained by a large majority of those newspapers worthy of being called first-rate. Lucky is the cub who starts his reporting career under an editor or desk man who "raises the roof" whenever he detects a misspelled word or incorrect middle initial in a piece of copy.

HOW TO BE ACCURATE

Several research studies have been conducted to determine news story accuracy by questioning persons involved in the news or in positions to recognize errors in the reporting. The first study, conducted in 1936 by Prof. Mitchell Charnley of the University of Minnesota, revealed that of 591 straight news stories in three Minneapolis dailies only 319, or 54 per cent, contained no errors of any kind. In 1965 Charles Brown found a 59.5 per cent accuracy score for 143 stories in 42 small weeklies. In 1966 Fred C. Berry Jr. reported 270 stories in two metropolitan and one suburban dailies were 47.3 per cent accurate and in 1967–68 Prof. William B. Blankenburg of the University of Wisconsin got a 40.1 per cent accuracy score for 332 stories in one suburban and one rural daily. A summary of these and other studies appeared in an article by Blankenburg, "News Accuracy: Some Findings on the Meaning of Error," in the *Journal of Communication* for December 1970.

Why this situation? Probably for several reasons which will be discussed in connection with suggestions of remedies.

Secondhand Information

Most news is gathered by reporters secondhand. News sources unquestionably are responsible for at least as many news story errors as are reporters. Mistakes made by those giving out news may be intentional or unintentional. If intentional, the news source has reasons for wanting a half-truth or untruth to appear in print. If unintentional, the source was a faulty witness or has a poor memory. The errancy of testimony and the influences, including suggestion and what is popularly called wishful thinking, which make for errors in observation and recall have been examined by psychologists and proved in the experimental laboratory so often as to leave no element of doubt regarding the really small chance the reporter has to get accurate answers during interviews for facts.

The reporter's weapons against inaccuracy, as a result of a news source's inability or unwillingness to give reliable information, are verification and honesty of purpose. If he does not rely on one person's say-so but interviews as many as possible, he invariably is able to correct many mistakes made in the first stages of gathering material about a news event. If he approaches the task of both reporting and writing his story without prejudice, whatever errors he does make will be at least unintentional. Fairness and caution both require that, when two persons interviewed differ greatly as to what is the truth, the statements of both be included in the news story. To achieve this objective, newspapers go to extremes of which the general public hardly dreams. The sentence saying that Mr. Smith could not be reached for a statement may have been added to a story after hours of futile effort to attain eithei accuracy or fairness or both.

Newsgatherers increasingly are up against what has been called "handoutitis," which means the refusal of many news sources to provide any more information than is contained in carefully prepared publicity releases. Between the reporter and a principal in the news is the public relations or public affairs counsel, as publicity men and press agents like to call themselves today. On the whole, these intermediaries perform a useful function, as no newspaper could possibly employ a staff large enough to cover all a community's activities. They also can be helpful to the reporter who wants additional information not included in a press release or who is seeking an original story. It must not be lost sight of, however, that public relations or public affairs men are employed to advance the best interests of their employer, which means that often ways to circumvent them must be sought. The reporter who is content with what is included in a mimeographed press release may become little more than a messenger boy.

Verification

Verifying a story means more than checking the statements of different news sources against each other. It also means making use of the standard books of reference to check spellings, addresses, middle initials and many similar details. In many newsrooms, reporters are required to write "All names verified" on their copy, and woe be it to them if such is not true. In many police and court stories more than the newspaper's reputation for accuracy may be at stake; innocence or carelessness is no defense against libel.

The newspaper takes a chance whenever it prints an unverified story. Mere rumor it generally can detect, but when a story contains something which seems improbable it is safer to miss an edition than use the story before checking. Often men in public life say things to reporters which they later regret. It may seem to the layman that the newspaper should quote them regarding what they have let slip and then stand by its guns and insist upon its own accuracy. It is the same layman, however, who with few exceptions believes an important personage's denial even though it be a gross lie. For this reason many an editor has held up a story until he has had a chance to check on even a reliable reporter's work.

Telephone books, city directories, clippings in the newspaper's library and books of reference are available to the newspaper reporter for a purpose —so that they will be used. In interviews, it is possible to repeat information to be sure it has been heard correctly. Over the telephone, difficult words can be spelled in code: A as in Adam, B as in Boston, etc. A humorous incident once occurred on the Dayton *Journal-Herald* that emphasizes the need for great care in taking news by telephone. A reporter, doing a late phone check of police/fire, wrote a story that 2,003 pigs had been killed in a barn fire. A check by a skeptical desk man revealed that the accurate casualty list was two sows and three pigs. How the error occurred as the result of a telephone interview can easily be imagined.

If the reporter has profited by his high school and college education, he should avoid many errors which the uneducated might commit, such as giving a ship's speed as "knots per hour," the office as chief justice of the Supreme Court instead of chief justice of the United States, the Court of St. James instead of the Court of St. James's, Noble instead of Nobel prizes, half-mast instead of half-staff, John Hopkins University instead of Johns Hopkins University, and many other "teasers," mastery of which is a journalistic prerequisite.

Qualification

When certain about the main facts of a story but doubtful about others, a way to make the earliest edition before complete verification is possible is to qualify what is written, as

> A man believed to be Hillyer Swanson, 30, of Salt Lake City, was found by police today wandering in Forest Park, apparently an amnesia victim. Partial identification was made by means of a billfold and checkbook found in his possession.

> Fire thought to have resulted from faulty electric wiring in the coal cellar caused approximately $500 damage early today to the dwelling at 1514 Murphy place occupied by Mr. and Mrs. O. B. Ryan and their three small children.

Stories such as the following inspire confidence in readers that newspapers attempt to give the truth as far as possible.

> Mayor Ezra Hawkins today intimated that he will not be a candidate for reelection, but Corporation Counsel Fred Bacon, who managed the mayor's last campaign, declared that "when the time comes the proper announcement will be made" and that "friends of His Honor will be pleased by the announcement."

It is when the reporter guesses or takes a chance that he is most likely to err. Such careless habits not only are bad practice from the newspaper's selfish standpoint, but reprehensible ethically as well. The speed with which newspapers are produced and the other obstacles to accuracy in reporting make a minimum number of errors seem almost inevitable. If the newspaper is generous in publishing corrections of the most serious errors and if it gives evidence of striving to attain the ideal of absolute accuracy, the supercilious reader should not be "off" a newspaper for life because on one occasion it made a mistake in the middle initial of his great-aunt's brother-in-law.

Systematic Checking

The practice is growing among newspapers of soliciting the comments of readers much in the same way the scientific researchers do. Increasingly also readers are urged to take the initiative in pointing out errors and many newspapers have institutionalized their handling. In addition to "The Public View," a letters-to-the-editor column, the St. Petersburg *Times* has "Hotlines," edited by Stan Witwer to handle criticisms of the paper's policies and performance. During 1974 the paper received 8,603 letters and 3,401 calls. In addition, 20,384 responded to coupon polls on public issues. Some months letters calling the paper to account for "misdeeds" outnumbered those on public issues.

The practice also is growing of soliciting the comments of readers through questionnaires. Among the earliest attempts was that of the Minneapolis *Star* and *Tribune*, whose Bureau of Accuracy and Fair Play was founded in 1945 "to deal courteously with any person who feels that he or she has not been justly treated in any news story or business dealing involving the newspapers." Since the news and editorial staffs of the papers were separated in 1967, the *Tribune* retained the bureau and the *Star* established a similar Reader's Referee. Every day stories are selected at random, clipped and mailed to persons mentioned in them with a request that the recipients answer the following questions: (1) Are names of persons and/or organizations spelled correctly? (2) Are addresses, ages, titles or other identifying information accurate? (3) Does the story present a factual and unbiased report of events? (4) Is all essential information included? (5) Is the headline accurate? Space is provided for both corrections and comments.

During one six-week period, 29 of 49 persons receiving the questionnaires responded. Most had no adverse criticism and complimented the paper.

At the nearby St. Paul *Dispatch* and *Pioneer Press*, W. F. Cento, public contact editor, every week selects six to twelve articles in which inaccuracies or unfairness might be most likely to occur, such as any meeting report in which two sides are presented, articles on controversial topics, reports of public hearings, trials or court rulings, labor disputes and spot news stories written under pressure of deadlines. During one six-week period questionnaires were mailed to 33 newsmakers; the paper was caught in three errors. One involved the title of a police officer involved in a supermarket siege; another involved the accuracy of a percentage used in an inmate suicide article; the third involved the quote of a citizen in a report of an open meeting conducted by the mayor of St. Paul. Says Cento in summary: "Ninety per cent or more of the respondents told us our facts were correct; more than 90 per cent indicated such things as names and addresses were correct; nearly 85 per cent said the stories were complete and nearly 90 per cent considered the headlines accurate and fair."

During the first six months the Chicago *Sun-Times'* Bureau of Fairness and Accuracy received about three letters a day in response to an invitation to submit complaints and comments which appear in the paper every day. About ten corrections were made, mostly in the anchored position up front, others where the mistakes occurred. The mail can be classified in seven categories according to Kenneth D. Towers, assistant managing editor:

1. Letters pointing out actual errors which require printed corrections.
2. Letters that dispute an interpretation or presentation of facts. In such cases, we contact the reporter to obtain his reaction and respond to the complaining individual with an explanation of how and why we presented our information as we did.
3. Letters taking issue with opinion or commentary articles. The better ones go into the Letters column; several have run as Commentary articles.
4. Letters that report minor errors which, in our opinion do not change the understanding of a story or a portion of a story.
5. Letters that complain of a lack of coverage in certain areas. These can be helpful alerts.
6. Letters that complain of poor printing, home delivery snafus and other problems better handled by other departments.
7. Letters that raise "Action-Time"-type issues, which we route to that department.

The Twin Cities papers are under the constant surveillance of the Minnesota Press Council, on which the newspapers and general public have equal representation. Its manager, Robert A. Shaw, calls it "a bold challenge to our critics to 'put up or shut up' and a force to make the papers take a sharper look at their ethics." Similar local press councils exist in Riverside, Calif. and several other places. All are in their experimental infancy and there has not yet been any "big issue" or "best case" to determine their value. The same is true of the National News Council, founded in 1973 by the Twentieth Century Fund to investigate complaints against the major television and radio networks, major wire services and a few prestigious newspapers. In 1974 the council adjudicated 36 complaints of which four were upheld. There also is AIM which means Accuracy in Media. It is a strongly conservative critic of press performance. It writes letters and inserts advertisements to correct errors in interpretation and editorial opinion. It watches Jack Anderson carefully and goes after radio and television commentators, contending that the networks never criticize each other.

Total Effect

An account can be devoid of errors in facts, spellings and the like and still be inaccurate if the impression it gives as a whole is wrong. This, as has been pointed out several times in earlier chapters, can happen when pertinent facts are omitted, when motivations are disregarded, when cause and effect relationships are not made clear and in many other similar ways.

Thorough reporting is the best protection against unintentional distortion. For example, a story telling of an arrest for reckless driving could be error free, but would it be accurate unless it were explained that the apparently careless motorist was trying to get to his injured child's side? Without the part after the "but" the following lead would have given an erroneous impression. The reporter obviously asked, "Why?"

> Chicago—The number of persons drawing unemployment compensation declined by 5,154 during the second week of this month, but indications are that more than 3,000 of them were off the rolls because their eligibility expired.
>
> [Peoria *Transcript*]

Prof. David Manning White of Virginia Commonwealth University has warned the press against becoming "unwitting or unwilling accomplices in creating an atmosphere in which prejudice, half-truths and misinformation bloom with a noisome stench." He had in mind so-called deadpan reporting of unsupported charges by United States senators and others without attempt to allow simultaneous reply by persons affected by the charges.

The simple first step in avoidance of inaccuracy through total impression is to try to get the other side of every story that is in any way controversial. To print inaccurate statements merely because they were made by some newsworthy person is not accurate reporting. It can be irresponsible journalism.

The following example indicates a common method of presenting both sides, even when the original story comes from a press association:

> Cairo, Ill., July 14.—(AP)—William P. McCauley of Olney, American Legion rehabilitation commission chairman for Illinois, charged in a speech here today that the removal of cancer patients from the Veterans Administration Hospital at Hines, to the Chicago Loop Medical Clinic was "for no other reason than to make guinea pigs of war-veteran cancer victims."
>
> McCauley told the 5th Division American Legion convention that the clinic at Hines had resulted from many years of Legion effort, that the Legion had spent $7,000 for the first radium used there and that its work was responsible for the recent addition of 500 beds there.
>
> (Informed of McCauley's charges, Charles G. Beck, Veterans Administration deputy director for the Midwest region, declared in Chicago:
>
> ("I think the statement that we're going to make guinea pigs of these cancer patients is, to say the least, ridiculous. The removal of which McCauley speaks has not yet taken place. It will not take place for at least a year.
>
> ("When we move our cancer center, the men will receive treatment at least as good as they have received at Hines. The entire clinic, its doctors, nurses, and equipment will be moved. How can that mean any change for the worse?"
>
> IDEA CREDITED TO BRADLEY
>
> ("It was the idea of Gen. Omar Bradley, head of the V.A., that these unfortunate veterans would be better served if they were located in the city, instead of 12 miles away from it.")
>
> In another speech, Omar J. Mackin, Salem, State Legion commander, asked the state's 1,029 Legion posts to pass resolutions against the Ku Klux Klan, which he termed "un-American and contrary to the principles and the rights guaranteed under the Constitution."   [Chicago *Sun*]

AUTHORITY IN THE NEWS

Everything that has been said so far in this chapter goes to prove that the most convincing authority a newspaper can give to a particular story is its own general reputation for authenticity. If it has established itself as a publication ambitious to be accurate and fair, it doesn't have to resort to elaborate means to quote authority in every paragraph of every news story.

As a matter of fact, however, newspapers which are the most careful to relate every important fact in every story to someone enjoy reputations for coming closest to the truth. "Who said this?" bawls out the city editor of such a paper to the cub. "Why, Mr. Smith, whose name is in the lead as having given the speech," is no defense but merely provocation for a further remark such as, "You don't say he said this unquoted part down in the fifth paragraph. I know he made the statement in the lead, but the rest of your story reads like an editorial."

Direct Quotation

To avoid such reprimands, the smart reporter "documents" his stories. How to attain accuracy and authority in different types of news stories will be considered more fully in the chapters devoted to them in Part Two. Including authority in the lead adds emphasis, satisfies the reader's curiosity and partially protects the newspaper against criticism.

> Promotion of W. C. Fairchild, 2308 S. 10th street, lieutenant of the Superior Railroad police in the Milltown division, to captain of police of the Logan division, was announced today by Ronal Weber, superintendent of the Milltown division.

When the news consists in the fact that an announcement or statement has been made, especially if it is one which has been expected for some time, authority should be given the greatest emphasis possible by beginning the lead with it, as

> Mayor Herbert G. Van Duesen announced today charges of irregularities in the collection of business licenses made by the Chamber of Commerce will be referred to the Board of Aldermen Friday evening.

When someone in public life makes an attack on another, the lead should begin with that person's name, as

> State Sen. Rollin A. Bishop today called Gov. Joseph B. Dilling a "crackpot" and described his plan to consolidate seven state departments as "the wild idea of a neophyte in public life."

This type of lead is much better than the following:

Gov. Joseph B. Dilling is a "crackpot" and his plan to consolidate seven state departments is "the wild idea of a neophyte in public life," State Sen. Rollin A. Bishop said today.

It is the fact that Senator Bishop attacked the governor that is news; what he said is opinion unless he was much more definite than either lead would indicate. If he did make specific charges, then what has been said regarding efforts to obtain "the other side" applies.

In stories growing out of public reports, statements or announcements, mention of the authority may be delayed until the second paragraph but seldom should be any later than that:

> Milltown users of natural gas pay a higher rate than consumers in any other American city of comparable size, but local rates for electricity are among the lowest in the United States.
> These facts were revealed by a Federal Power commission report released today. . . .

Care, however, must be exercised to avoid a "tag line" type of lead which, standing alone, is misleading, as

> Rep. Y. S. Owen could defeat Mayor L. L. Wood.
> That is the opinion of Judge K. K. Wendell who spoke at noon today.

Caution must be exercised so as not to declare as certain something which still is a matter of debate or further official action. For instance, a reporter erred when he wrote

> Baxterville will have a new 20-story office building by next spring.
> Plans for it will be presented tonight to the City Planning commission.

In this instance the Planning commission disapproved the project, which the reporter might have anticipated if he had interviewed more than its enthusiastic proponents. The hoary adage which applies is never to count your chickens before they hatch.

The extent to which a careful newspaper goes to give adequate authority throughout a controversial story is indicated in the following example:

> All ships of the North German Lloyd and Hamburg-American lines may be placed on the strike list of the International Longshoremen's association along with the Cunard White Star and Furness-Withy lines, *it was announced today* by Joseph P. Ryan, president of the longshoremen, when he learned a North German liner was scheduled to arrive at Montreal today.
> If the ship is unloaded at Montreal by members of a union not affiliated with the I.L.A., *Mr. Ryan said*, his union will strike all German ships on the Atlantic coast from Portland to Newport News.
> Although peace efforts continued in a three-way conference among I.L.A. officers, steamship officials, and representatives of the Montreal independent unions, plans were made for a protracted flight if necessary, *Mr. Ryan said*.
> Threats of delay failed to halt the sailing of the Furness-Withy liner, Queen of Bermuda, which left her pier at 55th street and the North river promptly at

3 P.M. without tugs. The ship left behind more than a hundred tons of freight, but officers arranged to have crew members carry aboard the baggage of passengers.

The presence of 700 travelers in Bermuda awaiting return to New York caused the company officials to proceed without waiting for freight. Before the Queen of Bermuda sailed *Mr. Ryan declared* that if crew members carried aboard the baggage "they can continue doing it from now on." *He also said* that if tugs were used it would be "a long time" before the tugs would again take any ships out of New York. Two tugs were ready, but were not required because of the favorable tide.

A peace conference between Mr. Ryan and his associates and officers of the National Independent Longshoremen's Union apparently made some headway. *Mr. Ryan said* that he "told them what terms they (the Canadians) could have."

There are 700 passengers awaiting return from Bermuda, *it was said*.

The steamship officials regard the trouble as largely out of their jurisdiction because it revolves about an inter-union dispute. *They expressed* the hope that a quick adjustment could be made, and offered to sit in at the union meetings as "observers."

That efforts of the C.I.O. to organize waterfront workers is behind the I.L.A. move to assert its claims was indicated by *Mr. Ryan in a statement* protesting against C.I.O. inroads.   [New York *World-Telegram*]

Indirect Reference

Even the parts of the example just given which are not attached definitely to an authority imply that they were verified by a careful reporter. Note in paragraph 4, for instance, that the writer knew of "threats to delay" and that "officers arranged" to meet the situation. Possibly this paragraph and the first sentence of paragraph 5 were guesswork, but the careful inclusion of both cause and effect regarding each incident, plus the adequate authority given in other parts of the story, gives the reader confidence in the correctness of the story as a whole.

No reporter should write a story supplied by an anonymous source, which means that practical jokers and persons with grievances who telephone and write to newspapers in the hope of giving news without disclosing their identity seldom are successful. When taking, over the telephone, information about which any question may arise, the reporter should obtain the informant's number, hang up and call him back. This practice often will expose impersonators, provided the reporter also checks the telephone numbers in the directory. Sometimes, at the request of high public officials, newspapers thinly veil sources of information by referring to "sources close to," "a source known to be reliable," "an official spokesman," "a high official" and the like.

It is irritating to any reputable reporter to have to write this way, and protests against the refusals of public officials to permit their names to be used as authorities are frequent. Such vagueness weakens the confidence of readers in any newspaper which practices it on its own volition.

Sen. Joseph R. McCarthy once gave reporters a statement regarding monitored telephone calls, but insisted that it be used as emanating from "a person who declined to let his name be used publicly." Commented Russell Wiggins, Washington *Post* managing editor, "The press associations and the publishing newspapers allowed him to put out a transcript under conditions that it originated from an unprejudiced source." To this, Claude Ramsey of the Asheville *Citizen & Times* added: "Senatorial immunity is bad enough without being compounded with senatorial anonymity."

High government officials, including the president, may designate into which of four classes what they say at a press conference falls: (1) quotable directly, (2) quotable as from a reliable source, (3) not quotable but valuable as background information or (4) completely off the record. Reporters begrudgingly acquiece unless they defiantly boycott the session and then try to learn what happened secondhand from someone who did attend. Such an informant might be another journalist. Most leaks of all kinds, however, originate with disgruntled or public-spirited underlings.

When Unnecessary

In the average run of police, legislative and many other types of news it is possible to omit specific mention of the source of information. In such stories it is presumed that a reliable authority was interviewed, and the newspaper's general reputation for accuracy is the reader's safeguard, as in the following examples:

> The Keeler polygraph gave the lie today to Henry (Hank) Munson's denial that he shot and killed his nephew, Arnold Munson, Sunday in the rooming house at 717 Victoria place where they both live.

> The 95 boys and girls who came to Milltown to participate in the state spelling bee finals Friday will attend a banquet at 6:15 P.M. today at the Hotel Bedford.

One way excessive attribution can be avoided is by being careful not to cite authority for old, especially widely known facts. You wouldn't, for instance, write: "The capital of Wyoming is Cheyenne, according to Senator Blimp." Neither, unless there was uncertainty regarding it, would you give authority when mentioning the capital of Tibet, Afghanistan or any other place. Such facts, though probably unfamiliar to most people, are easily obtained from standard reference books.

To cite authority for old facts can be misleading. It is likely to create the impression that the information is new. For example,

> To be eligible for low-cost public housing a person must not earn more than $3,600 annually, Theodore McCoughna, economist for the Public Housing administration, said today.

The statement would be bad if the $3,600 ceiling had been in effect for some time. It would be worse if "revealed," "announced," "admitted," or some similar verb had been used. When a statement of fact is inserted in a story as part of the background to enable readers properly to evaluate some item of news, it should not be attributed to any authority unless, in the newsman's judgment, it might not be accepted as true otherwise. Then dictionaries, encyclopedias, public laws and other authoritative reference works can be mentioned. Never use such vague expression as "statistics prove" or "authorities agree."

A lead which must be handled with caution is the "opinion here today" type. Seldom is such a lead based on an exhaustive survey of the "trend of public sentiment." The danger, from the standpoint of ethics, is the creation of what social psychologists call the "illusion of universality." It may be a gross exaggeration to write that "the entire city today mourned the death of Mayor Bull," or that "the world of music lovers was turned topsy-turvy," or that "business leaders today feared . . . ."

In sports stories, which are written with a recognized good nature and prejudice for the home club, such leads may be condoned, but when used in political writing they generally are misleading. If it actually can be established that a majority of public officials or of any other group believe a certain way, there should be some indication not too long delayed that the news writer knows what he's talking about.

OBEYING THE LAW

Further legislation and judicial decisions to clarify First Amendment rights mentioned in Chapter 2 (see pages 39–42) must be forthcoming soon. Otherwise reporters will continue to be subpoenaed in the attempt to get them to betray confidential news sources, and they will be arrested, fined, jailed and cited for contempt for attempting to use public records, attend public meetings and report legal proceedings.

Debates on a free press vs. a fair trial and on the right of an individual to privacy vs. the public's right to know are being waged. Until the lawmakers and judges act, journalists will continue to operate diligently in what they consider the public interest.

INVASION OF PRIVACY

No legal or judicial clarification ever has been made of the extent to which any person possesses a right to privacy. Generally accepted is the fact that anyone who courts public attention, as the politician or entertainer, sacrifices much or most of his privacy. Others, such as witnesses to accidents, crimes and the like, lose it temporarily through no fault of their own. Few persons like gossip about themselves but fewer still fail to enjoy it when it involves someone else. Many newspapers suppress the names of juvenile first offenders, relatives of persons unfavorably in the news, innocent victims of rape and other offenses and the like. Such policies are determined at the journalistic summit and should be made clear to all newsgatherers who then know they will be supported by their superiors in their grass-roots decision making.

Editors deplore, as do all others, insensitivity and stupidity by newsgatherers. An example cited to show lack of common sense by television reporters was the question "How did you feel?" asked of a father who had just seen a jet plane with his daughter aboard break into flames and crash.

Passage of the Family Education Rights and Privacy Act in 1974 is bound to make business for many lawyers. Known as the Buckley amendment for its sponsor, Sen. James Buckley, Con., N.Y., it gives parents the right to inspect, challenge and protest records of their children and denies federal funds to any school that releases such records to others without written parental permission. It was not long before some literal-minded school authorities were refusing to allow news photographers to take pictures of graduates or reporters to report on any student activities.

The law was passed shortly after the United States Supreme Court ruled that no child can be suspended from public school without notice of charges and a hearing. Several other United States Supreme Court decisions are important. The court struck down Florida's "right to reply" law which compelled newspapers to print responses from persons attacked in their columns. It also ruled that Georgia's law forbidding publication of the identity of rape victims was not applicable after the information became part of a public record. In the case at issue the woman had been murdered. The court made further litigation inevitable when it confined its ruling to "the narrower interface between press and privacy" rather than "the broader question whether truthful publication may ever be subjected to civil or criminal liability."

A feature story about the family of a man killed when a bridge collapsed contained "calculated falsehoods" and portrayed the family "in a false light through knowing or reckless untruths," according to the highest court in upholding an Ohio jury verdict of $60,000 against the Cleveland *Plain Dealer*. Mrs. Margaret Mae Cantrell testified that the story created the false impression that the reporter had interviewed her whereas he spoke only to the children in their mother's absence.

HOW TO AVOID LIBEL

Appealing for financial support for Dr. Martin Luther King's Southern Christian Leadership Conference, 64 persons inserted a full-page advertisement in the New York *Times* for March 29, 1960. It was headed "Heed Their Rising Voices" and charged that a reign of terror against Negro students prevailed in Alabama. L. B. Sullivan, Alabama commissioner of public affairs, sued the newspaper for libel and won in the lower courts. The United States Supreme Court, however, declared that a public official may not receive damages for defamatory statements relating to his official conduct unless he proves that the statements were made with "actual malice" with knowledge that they were false or in "reckless disregard" of truth or falsity.

That was in 1964. Five years later, in *Curtis Publishing Company vs. Butts*, the court extended the "public official" rule to cover "public figure," who in this case was a university football coach libeled by a national magazine. And in June 1971 it came close to making state libel extinct, when, in a Pennsylvania case, it extended the "actual malice" requirement to a private individual who has been projected into the public interest area.

Virtually every journalistic publication ran an article to the effect that for all practical purposes the law of libel was dead. Many newspapers canceled their libel insurance.

And then came *Gertz vs. Robert Welch, Inc.*, publisher of the John Birch Society magazine, *American Opinion*. In 1974 Elmer Gertz, a Chicago lawyer, successfully sued the magazine for falsely accusing him of having "framed" a policeman who was convicted of murdering a 19-year-old boy. The judge, however, set aside the $50,000 judgment on grounds that the publisher had not shown reckless disregard for the truth. The United States Supreme Court decided that Gertz was not a public figure and so needed only to prove that the publisher acted negligently. Abandoned was the principle that a private citizen speaking on public issues had to prove actual malice and so, as journalistic publications now declared, there were "new ground rules for the old ball game." In every journalist's mind is the question "What next from the court?" In the meantime it behooves reporters to be overly cautious, and newspapers are reinstating their libel insurance.

What is Libel?

According to the *American and English Encyclopedia of Law*

A libel is a malicious defamation expressed either by writing or printing or by signs, pictures, effigies or the like; tending to blacken the memory of one who is dead, or to impeach the honesty, integrity, virtue or reputation, or to publish the natural or alleged defects of one who is alive and thereby expose him to public hatred, contempt, ridicule or obloquy; or to cause him to be shunned or avoided, or to injure him in his office, business or occupation.

It will be seen from this definition that cartoons, photographs and other illustrations are included.

Commission of a libel is a graver offense than slander because the written statement appearing in a publication with a wide circulation has greater possibilities of injury. In conversation, one may call another an opprobrious name and the effect be short-lived and restricted to a small circle of bystanders. Such statements made in print, however, have a far-reaching and more important effect.

There is no reliable criterion by which to anticipate how either judge or jury will decide. In their *Hold Your Tongue!* Morris L. Ernst and Alexander Lindey reveal the following situation: It has been held libelous to call a man an "arch hypocrite" but not libelous to call him a "political hypocrite." In Tennessee one may, with impunity, call a woman a "hermaphrodite" but may not make the charge in Ohio. California holds "son of a bitch" not libelous and New York has legalized "God damn." On the other hand, however, while it is not libelous to say of a man that "he caught the pox," it is libelous to say that he "got the pox from a yellow-haired wench." In Minnesota, the statement "You did rob the town of St. Cloud, you are a public robber" was held not libelous because the crime of robbery cannot be committed against a town; similarly, there was no redress for a church warden who was accused of stealing the bell ropes, because the warden is custodian of the ropes and cannot steal his own property. On the other hand, when it was said of a woman, "She did have pups," and when the accused sought to defend herself by alleging the inherent improbability of the accusation, an Indiana judge held that though the people are bound to know the law, they are not bound to know scientific facts and might therefore believe the charge a possible one. In New York, a similar statement, "She had a litter of pups," was held not libelous for exactly the reason that it could not be true.

These few examples should be sufficient to impress the young reporter as to the care he must exercise to avoid committing libel. While many of the cases to which reference has been made involved editorial comment rather than news stories, exactly the same inconsistencies are to be found in judicial decisions regarding other kinds of libel actions. It has been held that the dead both can and cannot be libeled, that a newspaper is and is not responsible for libelous statements in press association stories and that a libelous headline alone is sufficient cause for action and that an article must be judged as a whole.

Dangerous Words

Despite the confusion, to be on the safe side, especially in view of the uncertainty regarding what the courts will decide next, the reporter may expect that these acts will be considered defamatory:

To

1. Charge that a person has committed or has attempted to commit a crime, or that he has been arrested for the commission of a crime, has been indicted for a crime, has confessed to committing a crime or has served a penitentiary sentence.
2. Impute that a person has committed an infamous offense, even though the words do not designate the particular offense.
3. Tend to diminish the respectability of a person and to expose him to disgrace and obloquy, even though they do not impute commission of a crime.
4. Tend to disgrace, degrade or injure the character of a person, or to bring him into contempt, hatred or ridicule.
5. Tend to reduce the character or reputation of a person in the estimation of his friends or acquaintances or the public from a higher to a lower grade, or tend to deprive him of the favor and esteem of his friends or acquaintances or the public.

6. Impute that one has a perverted sense of moral virtue, duty or obligation, or that he has been guilty of immoral conduct or has committed immoral acts.
7. Impute commission of fraud, breach of trust, want of chastity, drunkenness, gambling, cheating at play, violation of duties imposed by domestic relations, swindling, etc.
8. Impute weakness of understanding or insanity.
9. Impute a loathsome pestilential disease, as leprosy, plague or venereal disorders.
10. Tend to expose a person in his office, trade, profession, business or means of getting a livelihood to the hazards of losing his office, or charge him with fraud, indirect dealings or incapacity and thereby tend to injure him in his trade, business or profession.

A libel may be committed by mere insinuation. It is necessary only that the insinuation contain the elements of libel and that the readers of the paper understand it in its derogatory sense.

Likewise, allegory and irony may be libelous, as imputing to a person the qualities of a "frozen snake in the fable" or heading an article in regard to a lawyer's sharp practices "An Honest Lawyer."

Damages

Damages resulting from libel suits may be of three kinds: (1) general, (2) special and (3) punitive or exemplary.

General damages are awarded in cases of proof of libel when injury is recognized as the natural consequence of such publication. No proof of actual injury need be submitted.

A plaintiff may receive special damages when he can prove particular loss. When special damages are asked, proof of specific injury must be established by the plaintiff. Special damages may, however, be awarded in addition to general damages.

Punitive damages are inflicted as punishment for malice on the part of the offending publication. Proof of malice must be established by the plaintiff. Punitive damages may be awarded upon proof of gross negligence or if a newspaper reiterates its libelous statement after being warned that it is untrue.

Defenses

There are five possible defenses against libel:

1. Truth. In civil actions the truth of a publication is a complete defense, even though natural inferences of a defamatory character might be drawn which would be untrue. If malicious intent can be proved, however, truth may not be a defense. In criminal prosecutions, unless the publication was made for the public benefit or with good motives and for justifiable ends, truth is not a defense. The law in this respect differs in different states.

A publication must not only know the truth of what it has printed, but it must be able to submit legal proof. It is not a defense to claim that the libelous matter was printed upon the authority of another person. For example, publication of libelous statements made in a public address is not privileged, and the injured party can sue both the individual making the statement and all publications which reported it.

2. Privilege. Publication of the contents or of extracts of public records and documents for justifiable purposes and without malice, even though they contain libelous matter, is privileged by law. Publication of the contents of complaints or petitions before a public hearing has been held on them is not privileged; neither is publication of the proceedings of a private hearing, the contents of a warrant before it is served, confessions to police, news of arrests unless by warrant and many other exceptions.

3. Fair comment. Authors, playwrights, actors, officeholders and other public characters who invite the attention of the public to their work are liable to fair comment and criticism. This privilege, however, extends only to an individual's work and not to his private life, and there must be no malice.

In the case of officeholders, comment or criticism must be confined to official acts or actual qualifications, and there must be an honest purpose to enlighten the community upon the matter under discussion.

The language of such criticism cannot be so severe as to imply malice, and the statement or comment must, in fact, be comment and not an allegation of fact. It, furthermore, must be on a matter of public interest, such as comment on public affairs, the church, the administration of justice, pictures, moving pictures, architecture, public institutions of all kinds, other publications and the like.

4. Absence of malice. As indicated, malice is an important element of all libel suits. Its presence leads to larger damages than its absence. Malice is either *in fact*, which means that it springs from ill will, intent, hatred and so on, or *in law*, which is disregard for the rights of the person without legal justification.

Sylvan Meyer, eminent Southern editor, has written

> More than error is required to commit libel. Libel suits grow out of the atmosphere of a story or a campaign, out of the running relationship between the newspaper and the supposed victim of the libel. And, according to several astute editors, the gee whiz, slam bang stories usually aren't the ones that generate fear of libel, but the innocent-appearing, potentially treacherous minor yarns from police courts and traffic cases, from routine meetings and from business reports.

Absence of intent to libel is no defense, but proof of unintentional libel helps to mitigate damages. In proving absence of malice the defendant in a libel suit may show

    a. That the general conduct of the plaintiff gave the defendant "probable cause" for believing the charges to be true.

    b. That rumors to the same effect as the libelous publication had long been prevalent and generally believed in the community and never contradicted by the accused or his friends.

c. That the libelous article was copied from another newspaper and believed to be true.
d. That the complainant's general character is bad.
e. That the publication was made in heat and passion, provoked by the acts of the plaintiff.
f. That the charge published had been made orally in the presence of the plaintiff before publication, and he had not denied it.
g. That the publication was made of a political antagonist in the heat of a political campaign.
h. That as soon as the defendant discovered that he was in error he published a retraction, correction or apology.
i. That the defamatory publication had reference not to the plaintiff, but to another person of a similar name, concerning whom the charges were true, and that readers understood this other person to be meant.

5. *Retraction*. Often a newspaper can avoid a suit by prompt publication of a retraction. If a suit does result, such retraction serves to mitigate damages, especially if it is given a position in the paper equally prominent to that given the previously published libelous statement. A few states have passed laws making complete retraction and apology a complete defense in libel cases.

COPYRIGHT

Facts (news) cannot be copyrighted. The actual wording of an account of those facts, however, can be. A Conference of Press Experts called by the League of Nations in 1927 at Geneva stated the principle as follows:

> The Conterence of Press Experts lays down a fundamental principle that the publication of a piece of news is legitimate, subject to the condition that the news in question has reached the person who publishes it by regular and unobjectionable means, and not by an act of unfair competition. No one may acquire the right of suppressing news of public interest.
>
> The Conference affirms the principle that newspapers, news agencies, and other news organizations are entitled after publication as well as before publication to the reward of their labor, enterprise and financial expenditure upon the production of news reports, but holds that this principle shall not be so interpreted as to result in the creation or the encouragement of any monopoly in news.

Although facts cannot be copyrighted, newspapers can seek redress for pirating of news as a violation of fair business practices. In the case of *Associated Press vs. International News Service*, the United States Supreme Court declared Dec. 23, 1918:

> . . . Except for matters improperly disclosed, or published in breach of trust or confidence, or in violation of law, none of which is involved in this branch of the case, the news of current events may be regarded as common property. . . . Regarding the news, therefore . . . it must be regarded as quasi-property, irrespective of the rights of either as against the public.

A newspaper which wishes to rewrite or quote a copyrighted article appearing in another publication either buys the copyright privilege or requests permission to quote. In either case, credit must be given to the publication which originally printed the material. If the copyright privilege is purchased, this credit line appears at the top of the article, as

By Larry Green and Rob Warden
© 1975, Chicago Daily News

A Chicago undercover policeman operated as a double agent, spying on antiwar groups and at the same time selling those groups information on police intelligence operations, a Daily News investigation has found.

Otherwise, if permission to quote is given, the newspaper which copyrighted the article is given credit in the story itself. Unless permission is received, the paper using material in this manner is in danger of being sued for violation of copyright laws.

Detroit, Aug. 3.—(AP)—The Detroit *Times*, in a copyright story, said today that a Wyandotte, Mich., grandmother has identified "Little Miss 1565," hitherto unidentified victim of a Hartford, Conn., circus fire, as her granddaughter. . . .

Magazine articles and books usually are copyrighted but a newspaper seldom cares to quote enough of such material to run the risk of violating copyright privileges. Often a magazine article or book contains an important fact which a newspaper wants to quote. Credit always is given to the original publication, as

How lobbyists for the National Federation of Soothsayers defeated a bill which would have licensed their activities is told in the May issue of Revelation, the organization's official publication.

A copyright runs for 28 years and can be renewed for a second 28 years. After that the previously copyrighted material passes into the public domain and can be quoted with impunity. For years the Authors League of America has lobbied for a bill to revise this law, which dates from 1909, to provide protection for "life plus 50 years" and to liberalize the "fair use" section to allow educators greater latitude in reproducing parts of copyrighted works. To date the bill has made little progress in Congress.

8

KEEPING UP-TO-DATE

There is nothing so short as a newspaper reader's memory. No matter how carefully he reads a news story—and most newspaper purchasers read newspaper stories hurriedly if at all—when the next day's issue appears with news of later developments about any event, he finds that he has forgotten many if not most details of the first account.

As with events, so also with persons in the news, no matter how prominent they may be. Results of current-events quizzes in which college students and other supposedly well-informed persons make bad "boners" are amusing, but instructions for such tests usually indicate that a very low score is "average." Names, like faces, may be familiar, but try to identify them! It is part of the interpretative reporter's responsibility to refresh readers' memories so that the immediate news account is more meaningful.

IDENTIFICATION

The obligation of the newspaper adequately to identify persons, groups, places and events in straight news stories is recognized in any efficient newsroom. The rule is never to presume that the reader has seen yesterday's story.

It is seldom that the name of a person is mentioned in a news story without some identification. Even the occupant of the White House is given his title, and other persons mentioned frequently in the news are identified by their news past or importance. Ordinary persons may be identified in several ways. The most common methods of identification include the following:

1. Address	9. Achievement
2. Occupation	10. Life span
3. Age	11. Reputation
4. Title	12. Relationship
5. Nicknames	13. Marital status
6. Race, nationality	14. Description
7. War record	15. Occasion
8. News past	

Address. "Where do you live?" is one of the first questions asked anyone who is supplying information about himself. A man's address in a news story locates him, and the reader does not have to ask himself, "I wonder if that is the Newton Blue who lives in the next block?" Readers are interested in news pertaining to persons residing in their own or in a familiar neighborhood, even though not personally acquainted with them.

Great care must be taken to get correct addresses. Libel suits have been started by persons with names similar to those of others mentioned in news stories. Rare cases have been reported of two persons by the same name living at the same address. It is important to ascertain whether it is "street," "avenue," "place," "boulevard," "terrace" and so on, as there may be both a Ridge avenue and a Ridge terrace. Whether it is East, North, West or South also must be mentioned.

> Peter R. Farrel, 159 E. Trembly place, was taken to Municipal hospital today after he had accidently cut his right foot while chopping wood.

Emmett Dedmon, executive editor of the Chicago *Sun-Times*, modified what he called "a journalistic shibboleth of long standing" with the following memorandum:

> The Sun-Times does not wish , as a matter of policy, to cause undue hardship or to invade the personal privacy of persons who are in the news through no fault of their own.
>
> While it is usually necessary to identify persons with their home address in a city as large as Chicago, The Sun-Times will refrain from doing so when good judgment would indicate such identification unnecessary or undesirable.
>
> In general the rule is: Don't use the address if it is secondary to the main point in the story, or if the address does not add to the identification of the individual.
>
> In all instances good judgment and clarity will be the criteria.
>
> Following are a few examples of situations where an address is not necessary:
> —John Smith is held up in his drug store. Use the address of the drug store but not his home address.
> —Mary Smith is posed in a weather picture.

—Richard Rowe is a witness in a crime trial. His connection with the case is sufficient identification.

—Five girls are arrested for prostitution at 1976 N. Dearborn. The Dearborn street address is sufficient.

—John Doe, a printer, found the body, called police, gave the alarm, identified the suspect etc. As long as he is identified in some way the home address is not necessary.

—A police officer captures a bandit. His station or section is sufficient identification.

These examples are not meant to be a complete list but should give enough of an idea to explain the general rule. There are of course countless other situations which will have to be evaluated as they arise.

Occupation. "What do you do?" also is high up in the list of questions asked when data are being sought about a person. The reader wonders if Harry Snow, 1516 Chestnut street, is the carpenter by that name who worked on his new garage.

> Donald C. Sorenson, 51, Edwardstown, district representative for the Common Laborers Union, Monday was sentenced to a two-year jail term and fined $1,500 for income tax evasion.

The occupation of a person mentioned in the news may be the feature, as

> A butcher today used his knowledge of animal anatomy to save the life of his hunting dog, Romeo, accidentally caught in a bear trap.

Sometimes the feature is in the fact that a person in a particular position has done a certain thing, whereas the same thing done by another would not be so newsworthy.

> An assistant postmaster general charged here today that Sen. Edwin F. Dietz has been talking out of both sides of his mouth in critizicing the Post Office department.

Age. It is customary to give the age of a person who is involved in a law suit or the victim of an accident. Otherwise, unless age has importance in the story, it may be omitted. Many persons do not like to have their ages known but readers are eager to find out how old popular heroes and heroines are.

> William Murphy, 16-year-old Greenwich high school junior, today identified John Pratt, 21-year-old bootblack, as the armed bandit who robbed him of his clothing and $15 in cash Sunday night on W. Totze avenue.

Age frequently is the feature, as

> An 18-year-old girl will marry a 73-year-old man on Saturday because "our common religious beliefs are of far more importance than the disparity in our ages."

Title. When a person has a title by which he is known, the news writer should use it. A short title is better placed before a name; a long title should be placed after a name, as

> City Clerk George Johannsen will deliver the commencement address at 10 A.M. tomorrow at Craven Junior High School.

> James R. Wesley, commissioner of public works, will represent the city tonight at . . . .

Nicknames. Nicknames seldom are used without first names; rather, they are inserted between the first name or initials and the surname. In sports stories and in feature articles, nicknames may be used alone. Often persons prominent in the news are better known by their nicknames than by their real names, as "Ike" Eisenhower, "Bing" Crosby, "Babe" Ruth etc. When such nicknames become widely familiar, the quotation marks usually are omitted. It is a common practice with some newspapers to invent nicknames for persons mentioned in the news, frequently in crime stories. In doing so, care must be exercised so that the connotation given the nickname is not prejudicial to the proper administration of justice or otherwise socially harmful.

> William "Wee Willie" Doody, pint-sized killer-bandit of the 1920s, died Wednesday evening in the Stateville prison hospital. Death was attributed to a liver infection.
> The baby-faced killer, who got his nickname because he was only 5 feet 3 inches tall, was serving a life sentence for the slaying in 1929 of Berwyn's police chief. [Chicago *Daily News*]

Race, nationality. Deciding when to pass copy containing "Negro," "Puerto Rican," "Polish-born," "of German descent," and similar identifications has caused many an editor many a headache. Members of racial and nationality minority groups understandably object to persistent use of such identifications in crime stories, especially in headlines: "Negro Rapist Sought," "Italian Gangster Shot." There is a slow but steady drift away from such practices, but the rule remains that race or nationality shall be used when pertinent. Determining just when that is often is not easy. When someone is in the limelight—a politician, athlete or entertainer, for instance—his fans are eager to learn every picayunish fact regarding him, including his ancestry; certainly no injustice is intended when such details are given. For some people, as musicians and artists, a foreign background may be considered an asset.

It is only since World War II that a majority of newspapers have capitalized *Negro.* For a period in the '60s most Negro leaders preferred to be called "colored," to emphasize the idea that differences were only skin-deep. Most recently militant Negroes have promoted the slogan "black is beautiful" to stress pride in color; they resent being called anything but black. A minority of others, however, prefer Afro-American. The term *Negro,* which biracial human relations groups advocated for years, thus becomes the "neutral" term and the safest for journalistic purposes.

Alfred M. Bowler yesterday became the first Negro to be elected to public office in Calhoun county since Reconstruction Days.

War record. Under pressure from veterans' organizations, most newspapers have ceased identifying veterans as such in crime stories. Often, however, veteran status is a legitimate, even necessary, identification. It may, in fact, be the feature.

> Thomas Thomas, a former paratrooper, just couldn't get his training out of his head. He was sleeping in the apartment of a friend when he awoke and jumped out of a third floor window. He landed on a roof a few feet below the window sill. He was not hurt, and he explained that he had dreamed he was back in the army and had been given an order to jump.

News past. After having once appeared in the news in connection with an important event, a person continues to be potentially more newsworthy than others. Should he become "copy" again his former exploits are a means of identification.

> Miss Jane Boynton, 22, winner of a "most beautiful baby" contest 20 years ago, today filed suit against Dr. N. O. Holten, for $15,000, charging that his plastic surgery "disfigured her for life."

> Leon L. Desmond, star witness in the Fox-Delaney murder case four years ago, today was appointed chief deputy inspector of Raymond county by Sheriff L. L. Tyler.

Achievement. More than 40 years later, the late Charles A. Lindbergh still was being identified as "the first person to make a non-stop solo flight from New York to Paris." The achievement of one's early life may be his identification in later life or after death, as

> Dr. Hal Foster, first Kansas City physician and surgeon to specialize in the treatment of eye, ear, nose and throat, died at 6 o'clock this morning at his home at the Brookside hotel, Fifty-fourth street and Brookside boulevard. He was 88 years old.

Life span. Sometimes it is pertinent to identify a person in relation to the historical events or changes that have occurred during his lifetime, especially as they relate to the news at hand.

> Julius C. Jacobsen, who joined the internal revenue staff 38 years ago, when relatively few persons paid income taxes, and stayed long enough to see virtually everyone pay, will retire Saturday.   [Milwaukee *Journal*]

> Mrs. Eliza Addis, who was born in Philadelphia when City Council met in Independence Hall and City Hall was just a blueprint, is celebrating her 100th birthday today.   [Philadelphia *Bulletin*]

Reputation. When identifying a person by means of his reputation, it is necessary to be careful that the reputation is deserved. It is possible for a newspaper to make or break a person by referring to him constantly as the foremost authority on a certain subject, or as a mere pretender or charlatan.

> James (Jimmy) Eder, reputedly the wealthiest and most successful jockey in the history of the Latin American turf, yesterday was named defendant in a suit for divorce or separate maintenance filed in Superior court by Mrs. Ruth Eder.

Relationship. A person's news importance may depend upon the prominence of a relative or friend. How much the families of persons important in public life or in the news of the day should be written up and photographed is another problem for debate by a class in newspaper ethics. Relationship may be used as identification even when the members of the family referred to are not of particular importance. Minors often are identified by parentage.

Legitimate use of relationship in identification is illustrated in the following examples:

> Maj. James R. Garfield, II, training officer of the 107th Armored Cavalry Regiment, Ohio National Guard, and great-grandson of James Abram Garfield, 20th President of the United States, is taking summer training at Fort Knox.
> [Louisville *Courier-Journal*]

> Robert Campbell MacCombie Auld, 80, a descendant of Robert Burns and an authority on the Scottish poet's life and Scottish history, died yesterday after a five weeks' illness.

A different kind of identification by relationship is illustrated by the following example:

> A 30-year-old father of five was stabbed to death Saturday night in a dispute on the street near his home in the Porterfield section of Avon. The victim was identified as . . . .

Marital status. Under pressure from feminist groups, some newspapers use Ms. for a woman regardless of marital status. The argument that Mr. fails to indicate marital status so Ms. is needed to indicate equality is, however, counteracted by the fact that a large majority of married women continue to take their husband's name and prefer to be known as Mrs. John Smith. A compromise style is Miss for unmarried women, Mrs. for women using their husband's name and Ms. for a woman who retains her former name. This does not satisfy some feminists and it is recommended that some way be devised to indicate masculine bachelorhood, possibly M as distinguished from Mr.

Description. Sometimes the writer brightens up his identification by a bit of personal description, without which it often would be impossible to obtain a true impression of the story's importance. In the following example, note the use of descriptive identification throughout:

> Their shoes didn't squeak. They didn't talk out of the sides of their mouths. They showed no inclination to clip anyone on the jaw.

Yet the dozen plain-looking fellows who gathered at the Hotel Sherman last night were honest-to-goodness private detectives. They were holding their first postwar meeting of International Investigators, Inc.

Head man is Ray Schindler, world-famed New York detective. Other members include Leonarde Keeler, inventor of the lie detector, Dr. Le Moyne Snyder of Lansing, medical-legal director of the Michigan State Police, and Clark Sellers, Los Angeles handwriting expert and document ace who worked on the Lindbergh kidnaping case.

Most of the men, unlike such movie detectives as Alan Ladd, Humphrey Bogart and Dick Powell, are in the 50s and 60s and are quite calm about their work.

But one, at least, was not without a kind word for their movie counterparts. Said Harry Lewis of Sioux City, Iowa: "Those boys talk pretty tough and seem to run into an awful lot of trouble. But they get their job done and that's what counts." [Chicago *Sun*]

Occasion. A person's part in a news story must be explained no matter how else he is identified.

Prince Albert of Belgium, who is on a two-month study tour of the United States, will visit Chicago Oct. 12–13.

A mother, burned in a street car-gasoline trailer crash which killed 31 persons Aug. 14, 1967, won a $30,000 out-of-court settlement Monday.

Picking the Identification

The proper method by which to identify a person must be decided in every case. The appropriate identification should be sought in the case of a person with a number of achievements or a considerable news past, as

Harold Bank, president of the senior class, today announced committees for class day.

Harold "Bud" Bank, football captain, will not be a candidate for the basketball team this winter.

The Associated Press Managing Editors once debated the propriety of identifying former New York Governor Thomas E. Dewey as "a two-time failure as a Republican presidential candidate" years after his candidacies and in stories which did not deal with national politics. The consensus was that in many instances recalling that part of Dewey's "news past" was poor journalism. The same arguments applied to Adlai Stevenson II.

Often the occasion calls for special identifications for prominent persons, identifications which would be inappropriate at most other times.

Cleveland, July 25—(AP)—Federal Judge Paul Jones, once a football player himself, will hear injunction suits against Bobby Freeman and Jack Locklear, who jumped contracts with a Canadian pro team to join the Cleveland Browns.
[Baltimore *Sun*]

DOUBLE IDENTIFICATION

Sometimes, especially in obituary stories, more than one identification may be crowded into the lead, as

> Wiliam Jay Schieffelin, retired chairman of the board of Schieffelin & Co., wholesale drug concern, and a crusader for government reform, education for Negroes and many other humanitarian causes, died Friday night at his home, 620 Park Avenue, after a long illness. He was 89 years old on April 14.
>
> [New York *Times*]

SYNONYMS

It is impossible, however, to use more than two or three identifications without making the lead awkward. One way out of this difficulty is to use the points of identification as synonyms for the person's name after the name itself has been used once. In this way, nicknames, reputation, news past, various titles and so on can be brought in and repetition of the name or of personal pronouns avoided, as

> Former Alderman Guy L. Millard today charged that the local Fair Employment Practices commission is failing to perform its functions.
> Chief backer of the commission when he was a member of the City Council, Millard now believes the agency's work is being sabotaged. The 78-year-old president of the Royal Dye Works said he has personally interviewed 20 local workers who had sought the commission's help in vain.

IDENTIFICATION AS THE FEATURE

When the achievement, reputation, occasion or news past by which a person may be identified seems more important or better known than the person's name, the identification should precede the name, as

> Murray, Ky., July 28—(AP)—The man who wrote the official history of General Dwight Eisenhower's unified European command will deliver the commencement address at Murray State college's summer exercises next Friday.
> He is Dr. Forrest C. Pogue, commissioned by President Eisenhower to write a history of his World War II record, "Supreme Command."

INDEFINITE "WHO"

When the *what* of the story is more important than the *who*, the identification may be featured, names being delayed until the second paragraph, as

> A 32-year-old Congregational minister has been named director of Youth Inc., a new nondenominational religious research agency.
> The Rev. Ernest S. Ernst, minister of the Westchester Community Church since 1963, will take over direction of the agency in January at Boone, Iowa.

DELAYED IDENTIFICATION

Similarly, overcrowding a lead already packed with important facts can be avoided by postponing identification until the second paragraph, as

The eloquence of Reginald Burnett held a crowd of 1,200 farm delegates and their wives spellbound for an hour and 20 minutes here.

The sandy-haired president of the United Plastic Workers amused and delighted his National Farmers Union audience Tuesday night with raps at big business, Wall Street and the Department of Agriculture.

WHEN UNFAIR

Experts in the field object to use of "former mental patient" even when accurate. They contend its use is as unfair as it would have been to refer to St. Paul as "a former persecutor of Christians" or to Gandhi as "a former convict" or to Thomas Jefferson as "a former slaveholder."

To be avoided is any attempt to correlate appearance with personality or character. Fads and fashions change. From the Revolutionary War to the Civil War, all American presidents (Washington through Buchanan) were clean shaven. From the Civil War to World War I every president (Lincoln through Taft with the exception of McKinley) had a beard and/or mustache. From World War I to the present all of the presidents (Wilson through Ford) again have been clean shaven. This should be sobering evidence when it is attempted to classify hairy hippies or others. No personality traits scale, including ones based on bodily characteristics, ever has stood the test of scientific scrutiny.

Organizations

Organizations as well as persons must be identified adequately:

BY TYPE

Directors of the Monument Builders of America, Inc., a national association of the retail monument dealers, today condemned as "a national disgrace" the unkempt condition of the Statue of Liberty.

BY PURPOSE

Milltown's Transit Authority, set up to bring order out of the city's long existent transportation muddle, has ended a year of operation with a record of substantial accomplishments although difficulties still lie ahead.

The eight-man board held its first meeting Jan. 29, 1976 in offices at 35 Elm street, beginning operations with the backing of a $200,000 fund made up of two equal contributions from the city and state, joint sponsors of the enterprise.

As a municipal authority, it has the power, fixed by state law, to acquire and operate transportation lines in and around Milltown.

BY ACHIEVEMENT

The Alameda County Fair, which has been America's "jockey incubator" since the close of World War II, has a record crop of apprentices on hand for its 12-day race meeting opening here Friday.

BY REPUTATION

The Milltown Associates, which for 23 years was the leader in promoting city beautification, will disband Jan. 1.

In stories related to important public issues—controversial matters—brief identification of an organization usually is not enough. The interpretative reporter may have to write a parenthetical paragraph, sidebar or full-length feature to provide proper understanding of what is involved. Readers cannot judge the true nature of a group by a high-sounding title. Typical situations in which full-length identification of an organization may be necessary include the following:

1. When the name resembles closely that of another group whose outlook is different. Example: the National Council of the Churches of Christ in the United States of America and the American Council of Christian Churches.
2. When a powerful group takes a stand on a public issue or a pending piece of legislation. In such cases it may be wise to point out whether the immediate action is consistent with previous activities by the same group. It may be possible to throw light on any selfish motives by revealing the business or other connections of the group's leadership or the general nature of its membership.
3. When a new group is organized, especially when its aims are expressed in semantically vague terms or it seems interested in only a single measure or matter of public interest. In such cases it may be a "front" organization for some other older interest group. Identification of the leadership may cast more light on the organization's real purposes than a quotation from its charter or constitution.
4. When an organization is involved in an act of force or violence. In such cases it may be necessary to seek reasons for the group's very existence in the social, economic or political conditions that brought it into being. Care must be taken not to place the blame for any disturbance on the victims of it rather than on its perpetrators, regardless of the prestige factor involved.

Places

Places must be identified when they are not widely known or when significant or the feature of the story, as

> Purchase of the 1600 block on Palmer road for a new junior high school was announced today by the Board of Education. Twenty-three private dwellings, almost all of them condemned by the Department of Health, now occupy the site.

A place's news past or its proximity to another place previously in the news may be the best identification; often it is the feature:

> Within a few feet of the spot where once grew the elm under which George Washington accepted command of the Continental Army, 25 Boston University students yesterday organized the Army of American Liberation. Its purpose is to "wage incessant warfare against forces which are destroying American democracy."

Places, as individuals, have reputations which may be used to identify them, as

> Sauk City, Minn., the "Gopher Prairie" of native son Sinclair Lewis' "Main Street" . . .
>
> Reno, Nev., divorce capital of the United States . . .
>
> Tarrytown, near which Rip Van Winkle allegedly took his long nap . . .

Events

Events may be identified and explained

1. By their significance (the occasion).
2. By their importance in relation to other events (comprehensive leads and stories).
3. By relating them to the "atmosphere" in the light of which they must be understood (the situation).
4. By their probable consequence (prediction).
5. By definite reference to preceding events to which they are related (tie-backs).
6. By the coincidence between them and other events.

OCCASIONS

Circumstances of a news event—purpose, importance, significance and so forth—must be made clear, as

> The most crippling airline strike in the nation's history entered its 16th day Saturday and continued to strand travelers, disrupt tours and snag air freight service.   [Lincoln (Neb.) *Journal*]

Often the feature of the story may be found in the purpose or importance of the occasion which is the subject of the story, as

> Fort Washakie, Wyo.—(UP)—An age-old tradition was broken here when an Indian woman with white blood in her veins became a "chief" of the Arapahoe tribe.

The comparison between the immediate event and preceding similar events may be pointed out, either in the lead paragraph or shortly thereafter, as

> For the first time in memory, neither political party has a contest for any office in Crow county in the April 8 primary election.

COMPREHENSIVE LEADS AND STORIES

The comprehensive lead is correlative and explanatory. Used in straight news writing, it is not opinionated, however, because it deals with the incontrovertible.

One kind of comprehensive lead attempts to interpret the immediate news in the light of previous events, as

> Six more witnesses Friday were called before the federal grand jury investigating the distribution of juke boxes in Farwell township.

> Further evidence that the voters of this city really elected a "reform" administration last month was provided by today's order by Mayor L. O. Oliver closing all amusement places in violation of municipal health ordinances.

A comprehensive lead emphasizes situations. When several stories related to the same general news event are received, they may be combined into one story and a general roundup or comprehensive lead be written. This type of lead is suitable particularly for election stories, stories of wrecks and other disasters, accidents, weather stories, etc. Facts on which a comprehensive lead and story of this sort are wirtten usually are gathered by more than one reporter or correspondent.

PREDICTIONS

The significance of an event may be explained by pointing out the probable consequences or likely "next steps."

> The City Council's Big 10 crime commission starts five days of public hearings Wednesday—probably the last hearings the committee will hold.

> Drastic revision of the curriculum of Serena Junior High School will result if the Board of Education approves the unanimous recommendation of its Educational Policies committee.
> Among the changes which Mrs. Rose Blakely's committee says should be made are the following . . . .

THE TIE-BACK

The tie-back is the part of the lead of a story which shows the relation between the immediate news and some previous news event. In the following examples, the tie-backs are in italics:

> Miss Colista Connor, 20, reputed heiress to a $500,000 fortune, *who disappeared mysteriously a week ago and returned Wednesday night to explain she was "on vacation,"* was gone again yesterday.

> Five hundred and fifty-two *additional* influenza cases were quarantined in Will county today, *a slight increase over yesterday's figures*, while six deaths were recorded from flu and 14 *more* from pneumonia.

COINCIDENCES

The tie-back to a previous story may be made by emphasizing coincidence In many cases, the immediate incident may be newsworthy primarily or solely because of the coincidence, and the prior event may have received no publicity.

A second tragedy within two months today deepened the sorrow of Mrs. Mary McKinley, 26.

On June 1, her husband, Thomas, 35, a tuckpointer, was killed in a 12-foot fall. Yesterday her son, Robert, 4, was crushed to death by a truck.

Words

Parenthetical sentences or paragraphs sometimes are necessary to define or explain the context in which unusual words or expressions appear. Rep. Clarence Brown of Ohio, for instance, sent reporters to the thesaurus when he accused the president of "ingannation." At that time, the Louisville *Courier-Journal* interjected the following in a United Press account:

(The word is not in *Webster's New International Dictionary*. The United Press said it meant to confuse or bewilder, and the Associated Press reported solemnly "On consulting a thesaurus, reporters found the word ingannation listed as a synonym for deception.")

When President Truman accused a senator of raising many "Macedonian cries or yells," the Chicago *Daily News* used the following italicized parenthetical paragraph:

(A Macedonian cry is a cry for help, so called from Acts XVI, 9, "Come over into Macedonia and help us.")

When the President told the nation that it could achieve a production goal of $500 billion a year within ten years, the same newspaper explained as follows:

(Five hundred billion dollars is half a trillion. A trillion is a 1 with 12 zeros behind it.)

Sometimes it is a legal term that needs explaining or a diplomatic proceeding, as the following which was once used when the United Nations received a plea for the application of sanctions:

(Sanctions are positive measures that may be taken against aggressor governments under the U.N. charter, such as cutting off trade, communications, etc.)

THE FOLLOW-UP

Most of the news in any edition of a newspaper is related in some way to other news. It usually takes more than a single article to tell any story. After the first account has appeared, there usually are new developments.

Ability to sense phases of a news story which must be investigated further (followed up) is a valuable asset to a reporter or editor. Newspapers are read carefully for stories which in their original form are incomplete or which should be watched for further development.

The Second-Day Story

The second-day story of any event may include (1) new information not available when the first story was written, (2) causes and motives not included in the first story, (3) more recent developments, results and consequences since the first story and (4) opinions regarding the event.

Latest developments always are emphasized in follow-up stories, and the use of a tie-back is a rigid rule. Never should the writer of a news story presume that a reader has seen the previous story or stories. Just as each installment of a serial story is prefaced by a brief summary of what has gone before, so each news story related to a single event has a short reference to previous news stories.

The tie-back usually is inserted in the lead in the form of a phrase or dependent clause, but any grammatical device may be used; sometimes the tie-back is delayed until the second paragraph.

NEW INFORMATION

A 44-year-old Ardmore woman who was found unconscious on Coulter street near Sibley avenue, a block from her home, is in serious condition at Bryn Mawr hospital today while police searched for an unidentified man believed to have attacked her without motive.   [Philadelphia *Daily News*]

CAUSE—MOTIVE

Four firemen who perished in a flaming back-draft that surged through the Backstage night club early Tuesday morning died while fighting a fire which was deliberately, criminally set.

That flat charge came yesterday from Fire Marshal Frank Kelly, chief of the San Francisco fire prevention and investigation bureau.

"The fire was not accidental," Chief Kelly declared following more than 24 hours of investigation. . . .   [San Francisco *Chronicle*]

NEW DEVELOPMENT

Hartford Conn.—(AP)—John T. Emmanuel, trapped six days in the wreckage of a small plane, died Wednesday in Hartford Hospital.

Emmanuel, who had been rescued Sunday from the slopes of Mt. Higby in nearby Middletown, was transferred Tuesday to Hartford Hospital from Meriden Hospital.

OPINION

Angry parents today charged the "L" system with neglect in the crossing death of an 8-year-old boy.

A system whereby one man controls two crossings at Flournoy and Lexington at Long endangers the lives of children in three schools, the parents declared.

Donald Kieft, 5227 Lexington, was crushed to death Monday when he attempted to cross the tracks at Flournoy on a bicycle.

The crossings are protected by gates. So many trains traveling at a high rate of speed pass the intersections in the residential district that the lone gateman keeps the gates lowered even when trains are not approaching. . . .

Metropolitan morning newspapers frequently use the follow-up technique on stories which broke for the afternoon papers the day before; afternoon papers do the same for stories the first news of which appeared in the morning papers.

Featurizing the Follow-up

An important news story breaks too fast to permit investigation of its feature possibilities. By a later edition or the next day, however, the features are developed either in a rewritten story, or in supplementary stories (sidebars). If the reporter finds himself stuck with few new facts, he may simply retell the story in feature style:

Laramie Boomerang

A freak accident was investigated early this morning when an automobile belonging to Ralph Conwell, 803 Flint, crashed into a parked pickup belonging to C. H. Melvin, 657 North Eighth, and then crashed into the front of the Melvin home.

Police said apparently the Conwells were starting on a trip and after taking the car out of his garage, Mr. Conwell got out of the car to check if the garage was locked and the lights were out inside.

The car started creeping forward headed west on Flint, Mrs. Conwell, who was in the car and had on a safety belt, attempted to halt the car by applying the foot brake and inadvertently applied pressure to the accelerator.

The car surged forward hitting the curb and climbing it at the corner of Flint and Eighth and then headed north, striking glancingly on the outside of the Melvin pickup, also headed north, which was parked next to the curb, knocking the pickup upon the parking.

The Conwell car continued and jumped the curb to the right and came to a stop after uprooting a large lilac bush and smashing into the front of the Melvin home.

The impact of the car was just beneath the window of the bedroom where Mr. and Mrs. Melvin were sleeping. Although the wall was driven in about ten inches from the impact, the window pane remained intact.

Police said there were no injuries reported to them.

Laramie Bulletin

It was 4 A.M. Tuesday.

Mr. and Mrs. Ralph Conwell were parked in front of their home ready to leave for a vacation at their ranch near Daniel, Wyo.

Conwell started the car. Mrs. Conwell was secure in a new safety belt next to the driver's seat.

Conwell remembered he left the garage door open and left the car to close it.

The car began rolling.

Mrs. Conwell struggled to get out of her "secure" position, gave up the idea and reached for the steering wheel and the brake.

She got the wheel, but hit the accelerator with her foot.

Around the corner she went, her husband running after her, the horn honking.

The car struck a parked ton truck, threw it 40 feet, jumped the curb, hit a 25-year-old lilac bush, threw it several feet, and smashed into the bedroom of Conwell's next door neighbors—Mr. and Mrs. C. H. Melvin.

Said Mrs. Conwell:

"It was the safety belt that saved me. You can never tell when an accident is going to happen."

Said Mrs. Melvin: "I thought it was a drunken driver."

Said Mr. Melvin: "My mother-in-law planted that bush here 25 years ago. I never thought it'd save our lives."

Mr. Conwell wasn't available for comment—he went back to the ranch, leaving his wife behind.

Second-Day Comment

Whenever the president delivers an important message, the Supreme Court hands down a significant decision, a new scientific discovery is announced or any one of a number of unusual events occurs, newspapers and press associations scour the country to obtain opinions from persons qualified to comment cogently. In such stories exaggeration must be avoided, as in the following piece in which generalizations were limited to the principals who are mentioned specifically.

By Brian Sullivan
AP Science Writer

Linus Pauling's claims for Vitamin C as a powerful weapon against the common cold have resulted in a spurt of sales at many of the nation's drugstores. But in the scientific community, with a notable exception, the response has been more subdued.

At Herzog's Drugstore in Buffalo, N.Y., pharmacist Howard Carpenter said sales had at least quadrupled. He said the store has put bottles of Vitamin C into a basket adorned with Pauling's picture.

Many scientists remain generally skeptical, however. Some refused to be drawn into the matter at all, and others were cautious: A Baylor University Medical School virus-cold researcher said Pauling's ideas are based on an uncontrolled experiment.

PROBE FIRST

Another warned against continued, mass dosage without investigating it first.

The exception is Dr. Albert Szent-Gyorgyi of the Marine Biological Laboratory at Falmouth, Mass., who won the 1937 Nobel Prize in medicine for isolating Vitamin C in 1928.

Localization

A news item originating in a faraway place may have a local "angle," or it may cause readers to ask, "Could it happen here?"

Local parents need have no fear that babies in local hospitals will become confused and cause another Pittman-Garner baby mix-up a generation or so hence.

So thorough is the identification system employed in this community's three hospitals that their authorities consider mix-ups like Madeline Louise Garner-Pittman's in Georgia last month an impossibility.

Although many hospitals throughout the country supplement foot and palm printing as an added precaution, adequate supervision is the only real safeguard, in the opinion of H. James Baxter, superintendent of General Hospital since 1971. . . .

Reminiscences

Similarly, readers may ask, "Has anything like that ever happened before?" Old timers draw parallels between the present and the past and relate anecdotes brought to mind by the immediate news item.

By AP

The Easter Sunday slaying of 11 members of the Ruppert family in Hamilton, Ohio, is believed to be the largest involving members of one family in such a short time.

But it was far from being the largest mass murder in the nation's history.

That statistic is held by a homosexual torture ring in Texas, where the bodies of 27 young men were found in 1973. Teen aged boys disappeared without a trace for months, but the case did not come to light until 33-year-old Dean Corll was shot to death.

Elmer Wayne Henley, now 18, admitted killing Corll and told police a tale of horror which led them to the graves of 27 youths. Corll was identified as the ringleader. Henley and David Owen Brooks, now 20, were convicted in some of the slayings. Henley is now serving a 594-year prison term, and Brooks recently received a life sentence.

In the nation's second-largest mass murder case, the bodies of 25 itinerant farm workers were discovered in shallow graves along the Feather River in California.

Juan Corona, a farm labor contractor, was convicted in the case and sentenced to serve 25 consecutive life terms. In 1973, Corona was attacked in his cell by fellow inmates. He was stabbed 32 times and lost his left eye.

Other mass slayings in the United States include:

—The Manson Family. Actress Sharon Tate and four other persons were butchered in her California home in 1969. Charles Manson, whose followers thought he was Christ, and three women are serving life sentences for the slayings.

—The Speck Case. Eight student nurses were strangled in their apartment in Chicago in 1966. A drifter named Richard Speck was convicted of the murders and is now in prison in Illinois.

—The Whitman case. Two weeks after the student nurse murders, Charles Whitman climbed an observation tower at the University of Texas in Austin and opened fire with a rifle. In 90 minutes before police shot him dead, Whitman killed 16 persons and wounded 31.

—The Boston Strangler. Thirteen women were strangled in the Boston area in the early 1960s. No one was ever brought to trial for the slayings. Albert DeSalvo once confessed to being the strangler, but authorities were unable to find any evidence to support his statement. In 1973, while serving a life sentence for unrelated assaults, DeSalvo was stabbed to death in his cell.

—In Cold Blood. Herbert Clutter, his wife and two teenaged children were executed in their Kansas farmhouse in 1959. Six years later, Perry Smith and Richard Hickock were hanged for the murders. Author Truman Capote chronicled the case in a best-selling book which later became a movie.

—The Starkweather Case. In 1958, 19-year-old Charles Starkweather and his 14-year-old girlfriend, Caril Fugate, set off across Nebraska and Wyoming, leaving a trail of bodies. Starkweather was electrocuted. Miss Fugate was sentenced to life imprisonment. She was turned down for parole in 1973 but may get another chance for freedom in 1976.

—The Camden Killings. In 1949, Bible-reading World War II veteran Howard Unruh, took a 12-minute walk down a street in Camden, N.J., and killed 13 persons with a Luger pistol. Unruh was found unfit to stand trial. Twenty-five years later, he is still in a New Jersey hospital for the criminally insane and is appealing to get out. If he does, he will face criminal charges in the 1949 slayings.

—The St. Valentine's Day Massacre. Seven members of George "Bugs" Moran's gang were lined up against a garage wall and machine-gunned to death in Chicago on Feb. 14, 1929. No one was ever charged in the slayings.

[Mexico City *News*]

The Running Story

Newspapers continue to follow up stories as long as there are new angles or developments to investigate or until reader interest lags. Each succeeding story is written to bring the situation up to date.

In case of a flood, war, important court trial or political contest (to mention only a few of the possibilities), daily, almost hourly, stories are written to give the latest developments. A murder story frequently occupies the front page for weeks.

Note how the following story developed day by day, as shown by three successive leads from the Kansas City *Star:*

> About 124,000 women here today are being given the opportunity to state whether they desire to serve as jurors. The ballots should be returned to the Jackson County courthouse by June 10.

> Eighty-six ballots on jury service for women had been received this afternoon at the jury commission office in the Jackson County courthouse. Twenty-nine indicated a desire to serve on juries here. Fifty-seven declined to serve.

> The number of women desiring jury service was increasing this afternoon when 314 of the 1,440 ballots received by the jury commission indicated that more than one in four women responding to the poll were willing to be jurors. The remaining 1,136 do not desire to serve on Jackson County juries other than federal.

The Revived Story

Days, weeks or months later a reporter may be assigned to find out "what ever happened to so-and-so" or regarding "such-and-such."

By B. J. McFarland
Portland, Ore. (UPI)—

What happened to D. B. Cooper, history's first and only successful para-chuting sky bandit?

Where is he and where did he stash the cash?

Three years ago on Thanksgiving Eve Cooper boarded a Northwest Orient Airlines flight in Portland for a short hop to Seattle.

The plane wasn't off the ground five minutes when it all started.

Cooper, threatening to set off an explosive, demanded and got $200,000 in $20 bills delivered, along with three parachutes, to the plane in Seattle.

After allowing the passengers to get off, he ordered the crew to fly the 727 to Reno, following a course down western Washington and Oregon before cutting across the mountains. Somewhere en route he bailed out the tail exit.

NO TRACE OF COOPER OR THE MONEY EVER WAS FOUND

It set off a chain of similar skyjackings that changed the face of air travel.

But only Cooper beat the law at taking the money and jumping. The law still is looking for him.

"The case is an active one, not only here but throughout the United States," said Julius Mattson, agent in charge of the Portland FBI office.

"We're still getting leads," he said, "but not quite as heavy as we were. The case still is in the public mind and when the public thinks of it, it also thinks of us.

"There really has been no substantive development. The work now is mostly eliminating possibilities, proving or disproving tips.

"Not one of the $20 bills has turned up."

Cooper apparently strapped the money to his body for the jump. A theory that he may have fallen into Lake Merwin east of Woodland in southwest Washington about 30 miles north of Portland could not be proved following an exhaustive search by the FBI and Army troops from Ft. Lewis, Wash.

[Pittsburgh *Press*]

Some newspapers, notably the New York *Times* and the Chicago *Sun-Times*, have a weekly follow-up feature column to bring readers up to date on stories which were once in the news and have disappeared from the headlines. Typical items from one *Times*' column were the following:

BETTY HUTTON

Back in June, after it was disclosed that Betty Hutton, the one-time Hollywood star, was working as a cook at a Roman Catholic church in Rhode Island, a benefit was given in her honor at the Riverboat, with the proceeds to go to the parish.

Arthur Riback, the publicity man who was an organizer of the benefit, said last week that "in excess of $10,000" would go to the church, St. Anthony's in Portsmouth, and that two-thirds of the amount had already been turned over.

The Rev. Peter McGuire, pastor of the parish, indicated that no firm decision had been made on what to do with the money, but he said it would probably be used either to repair the 100-year-old rectory or build a new one.

Miss Hutton, incidentally, is still there.

LOVE'S LABOR'S LOST

Hopes ran high at the Bronx Zoo last winter that an elderly (55-year-old) male condor, Long John Silver, would breed with a fertile young female, Miss MacNasty, to produce the first condor born in captivity here.

Alas, Long John Silver is not up to the task.

"I'm afraid that he's somewhat beyond the pale as a Romeo," said Joseph L.

Bell, the zoo's curator of ornithology. "They are cohabiting, but that's about it."

Dr. Bell noted that not many of the giant birds were in captivity in the first place, and said that zoos that had males like to keep them for their own females. "I don't see much hope for Miss MacNasty," he said.

Investigations

Often follow-up assignments are for policy purposes, but the disclosures from the resultant investigations may be definitely in the public interest. Newspapers frequently keep after someone, particularly a public official, to correct an evil brought to light by some news event.

By Curtis Fuller

Doors still swing inward at Niles Center and Morton Grove taverns a year after seven persons, two of them Northwestern university students, burned to death in the Club Rendezvous. Doors still swing inward for bodies to pile up against, and do not even have exit signs to mark them.

Last year a week after the Rendezvous tragedy, two Daily News-Index reporters visited more than 15 taverns in the Howard street, Morton Grove, and Niles Center districts to discover if conditions existed which might cause other Rendezvous tragedies some day. They found fire hazards frequent. Sunday night the reporters visited the same taverns again, found the same conditions.

In three of a dozen Morton Grove and Niles Center taverns, doors comply with county fire regulations by opening out. In two of the three, exit signs direct customers to the doors.

The Cook county board April 4 passed a new fire ordinance to take effect April 30, ordering all taverns to have at least two exit doors that open outward, progress through which is unimpeded. Electrically operated catches for exit doors are prohibited by the ordinance. Other provisions included use of fire-proof or slow-burning construction.

These regulations are not enforced. They are violated by more than half the taverns visited Sunday night.

Nowhere did we see fire extinguishers in plain sight. One of the ironies of the evening came as we sat in the Paris Gardens talking to the bartender. A man dashed in yelling that his car was on fire. There was no fire extinguisher handy, and the bartender handed him a seltzer bottle which the man took and dashed out.   [Evanston (Ill.) *News-Index*]

The Resurrected Story

Sometimes a mystery is years in the solving, or a new fact is discovered which casts new light on some historical event or personage. In writing such a story the "tie-back" rule must be observed, although the lead seldom is adequate to supply all of the "resurrected" facts which must be told. For instance, if a criminal who has long evaded capture is arrested, the story may include a recapitulation of his crime and may even be accompanied by pictures and diagrams taken or made at the time of its commission. Later, when the person is brought to trial, the story may be repeated, and again if the criminal is put to death legally.

In every news office there are notations of stories which are said to be "hanging fire," and which may break at any time. Verdicts are withheld, a committee delays its report, there is a postponement in the filing of a suit, or an important person does not make an announcement of which he has hinted.

North Manchester, July 4.—Midnight lights burned by a Dr. Elies Ohmart prior to 1885 were explained here when Tom Richardson came across an ancient, handwritten record book in the attic of the John W. Ulrey home which he recently purchased.

The book contained notes of scientific inventions including a telephone patented by Bell in 1876, an electric arc lamp, the separation of aluminum from clay, a mechanical table of logarithms and an electric sign board.

[Fort Wayne (Ind.) *News-Sentinel*]

REWRITE

The day of the major newspaper scoop is gone. In the first place, except in a small and dwindling number of large cities, there is no competitor for the one surviving daily newspaper to scoop. Furthermore, the important day-by-day news of the world is gathered mostly by two press associations (Associated Press and United Press International) and transmitted simultaneously to all subscribers. Most important, radio and television have made it impossible for any periodical to be first with such news.

Newspapers and magazines amplify, explain and interpret the news sometimes shortly after its occurrence, but, often, weeks, months or years later when new information becomes available or the passage of time gives new perspective. Newspapers today often are competitors of magazines in the attempt to obtain first rights to the memoirs of persons able to cast new light on old events.

The Nature of Rewrite

Within newspaper offices the title rewrite man now is used to designate a person who spends his time in the office taking news over the telephone, mostly from the paper's own reporters. There persists, however, a considerable amount of rewriting in the old sense; "borrowed," with little or no attempt to obtain additional facts, from other printed sources.

Such sources include press releases, community newspapers, trade journals, house organs, public and private reports and announcements, newsletters intended for special interest groups and out-of-town newspapers (exchanges). Some papers run a column of news briefs or oddities from the exchanges or the day's wire report. Stories in the earlier editions of one's own newspaper may be rewritten for later editions, when new facts are obtained or for reasons of space, clarity, etc.

Usually, the rewirite man attempts to compose an item which will read as though it had been written up on original information. In his attempt to play up a new fresh angle he must avoid killing a good lead and burying an undoubted feature. Awareness of the extent to which radio and television have taken the edge off some of the news may lead to this error unless there is conscious effort to avoid it.

Picking the Feature

The rewrite man must obey the rules of good news writing which, among other things, means that the lead of his story must play up the feature of the item. The difficulty of the rewrite man is obvious when it is realized that this feature probably already was played up in the original story. The poorer the first story, the easier the task of the rewrite man who must do more than merely restate or reword the original lead.

The rewrite man, with no facts in addition to those of the original story, therefore, asks himself several questions, including these:

1. Did the writer play up the real feature of the story or is it buried some place in the article?
2. Is there another feature of equal or almost equal importance as the one which the writer used that might be played up?
3. Can I make my story read like a follow-up story by emphasizing the latest developments mentioned in the first story, or by suggesting the next probable consequence?
4. Can I write a comprehensive lead which will interpret this item of news in the light of other news?
5. Is there any other news today with which I can combine this story?
6. In the case of stories appearing in publications outside of the immediate community, is there a local angle that can be played up?

BURIED FEATURE

If the writer of the original story has missed the feature, the task of the rewrite man is simple, as

Original Story	Rewritten Story
The question of submitting to the voters of Milltown at a special election Mayor A. L. Hunter's proposal to issue $400,000 worth of street improvement bonds again was the major "bone of contention" at last night's City Council meeting.	Milltown voters will decide Sept. 14 at a special election whether the city's bonded indebtedness shall be increased $400,000 to finance Mayor A. L. Hunter's street improvement program.
Ald. Joel Oldberg, 15th ward, presented a list of streets which he said are badly in need of repair and urged the holding of the special election. Opposing him was Ald. Arthur West, 21st ward, who said the city already has too large a bonded indebtedness.	Decision to submit the matter to voters was made by the City Council last night after three hours' debate. The vote was 21 to 17.
After three hours of debate the Council voted 21 to 17 in favor of Alderman Oldberg's motion to call a special election Sept. 14.	The motion was passed over the opposition of Ad. Arthur West, 21st ward, who argued that the city already is heavily indebted. Maker and chief supporter of the motion was Ald. Joel Oldberg, 15th ward, who presented a list of streets which he says need repairs.

Note in the following example how the rewrite man found a second feature equally as important as the one played up on the original story:

Original Story

Loss of between $75,000 and $100,000 resulted from a fire which raged for three hours early today in the Central Chemical company plant at Calumet City. The plant, which manufactured nitric acid, was a subsidiary of Wilson & Co., packing firm.

Spontaneous combustion is believed to have been the cause of the fire which was noticed about 2:30 A.M. by two workmen, only occupants of the building at the time. In the attempt to save acid valued at about $50,000 in storage tanks, the two men, Abel Puffer and Jared Bean, shut off safety valves to the tanks.

Exact loss cannot be determined until the tanks are opened today and tests made as to whether water reached their contents. Because nitric acid is highly inflammable, Hammond and Calumet City firemen were in constant danger as they fought the fire.

Rewritten Story

Firemen of Hammond and Calumet City braved the dangers of huge stores of highly inflammable nitric acid yesterday to battle a fire which destroyed the Central Chemical company plant at Calumet City. The loss was estimated at $75,000 to $100,000.

The plant, a subsidiary of the packing firm of Wilson & Co., is devoted entirely to the manufacture of the acid. Quantities of acid valued at $50,000 were in storage tanks.

The blaze raged for three hours. The acid tanks will be opened today to determine whether water seeped into them and spoiled the stores.

Two workmen, the only persons in the plant, shut off safety valves to the tanks when the fire began, apparently from spontaneous combustion.

FOLLOW-UP FEATURE

In rewriting the following story, the writer certainly was safe in assuming the next probable consequence. Note how this story contains a tie-back and reads as a follow-up story, although no new information is included:

Original Story

After strangling her three baby daughters with a clothesline, Mrs. Gilda Heyda last night hanged herself in her home at 423 S. Reba street.

The bodies of the three girls, Roberta, 4, Ruth, 2, and Hazel, four months, were discovered by Mrs. Sylvia Priem, mother of Mrs. Heyda, when she arrived about 8 P.M. for a visit. The children were lying on a bed with the body of their mother nearby.

The father and husband is Wilfred A. Heyda, unemployed carpenter, believed to be somewhere in the middle west on his way to Texas to seek employment.

Chief piece of evidence at the inquest which was to open this morning

Rewritten Story

Somewhere in the middle west today tragic news followed a father who is in pursuit of employment to support his wife and three small daughters.

The young husband and father, Wilfred Heyda, unemployed carpenter, was sought by authorities who were to inform him his wife, Mrs. Gilda Heyda, strangled their three baby girls and then committed suicide last night in their home at 423 S. Reba street.

As an inquest opened into the deaths this morning, police expressed the belief that Mrs. Heyda had become despondent from loneliness. She left a note to her mother, Mrs. Sylvia Priem, saying:

"It's pretty good! Wilfred has kids

Original Story

will be a note to her mother left by Mrs. Heyda, reading:

"It's pretty good! Wilfred has kids and can't even send them a card while on a trip."

Heyda left three weeks ago and was last heard from in Cincinnati from where he expected to go to Indianapolis, Chicago, Spingfield, Ill., and St. Louis before heading for the southwest.

Police believe Mrs. Heyda's act resulted from loneliness because of her husband's absence and failure to write more frequently.

Rewritten Story

and can't even send them a card while on a trip."

The last word from the father, who left home three weeks ago, was from Cincinnati. From there he wrote he was on his way to Texas by way of Indianapolis, Springfield, Ill., Chicago, and St. Louis.

The slain children were Roberta, 4, Ruth, 2, and Hazel, four months. Their bodies were discovered by Mrs. Priem lying on a bed when she came to visit. Nearby was the body of Mrs. Heyda who apparently had used a clothesline to strangle her daughters and then take her own life.

COMPREHENSIVE LEAD

The rewrite man's knowledge of recent news events is valuable. In the following example, the writer was able to supply additional information out of his memory. If time permits and the story merits the trouble, the rewrite man may consult the newspaper's library and reference department to obtain information of this kind.

Original Story

Virgil Miner, 17, son of Mr. and Mrs. Charlton Miner, 386 Coates street, last night won first place in the annual state high school extemporaneous speaking contest. Speakers from 11 other high schools competed at Beardstown Municipal auditorium.

Representing the local high school, Virgil drew "Neutrality" as his subject. All contestants were given 30 minutes in which to prepare and each spoke ten minutes. Judges were . . .

Rewritten Story

For the second time in five years, the Milltown high school entry won first honors in the annual state high school extemporaneous speaking contest when Virgil Miner last night was declared the winner at Beardstown Municipal auditorium.

Three years ago, Leland West, now a student at Booster college, won the contest which was held at Lincoln. By an odd coincidence, both boys drew the same topic, "Neutrality."

Virgil is the 17-year-old son of Mr. and Mrs. Charlton Miner, 386 Coates street, and a senior at the high school.

Rules of the contest give each entrant 30 minutes in which to prepare to give a ten minute speech. Twelve students competed last night. Judges were . . .

COMBINED STORIES

The following example shows how one rewrite man combined two items into a single story:

Original Stories

Losing control of his automobile when a butterfly flew against his face, Edgar Lewis, 33, 1301 Sherman street, crashed into a fire hydrant about 6:30 P.M. yesterday at the northwest corner of Simpson and Michigan streets. He was taken to Municipal hospital with only minor bruises.

Sylvester Finger, 28, 1428 Grove street, is in Municipal hospital today with two fractured ribs as the result of an automobile accident about 7 P.M. yesterday. Finger's car struck a telephone pole at the southeast corner of Michigan and Central streets after he took his hands off the steering wheel to drive away ants which were crawling on his ankles.

Combined Story

Insects were responsible for two odd automobile mishaps in Milltown early last evening.

Ants crawling on the ankles of one driver led to a smashup which sent him to Municipal hospital with two fractured ribs. In the other accident, a butterfly flew against the driver's face and caused him to lose control of his machine.

The injured man is . . ..

LOCAL ANGLE

The rewrite man who reads newspapers from other cities, official reports and documents, press agent material and the like, should look for a local angle to feature, as

Original Story
Peoria Newspaper

A state-wide membership drive of the Fraternal Order of Leopards will be planned here next Thursday at a meeting of representatives of the eight original chapters in as many cities.

Goal of the campaign will be 25 chapters and 2,000 members before July 1, according to J. S. Kienlen, Peoria, state commander, who called the meeting.

Cities to be represented at Thursday's meeting and delegates are: Wayne Lueck, Danville; R. S. Kirschten, Cairo; Lowell Watson, Freeport; S. O. McNeil, Aurora; Silas Layman, Springfield; Richard Yates, Elgin; O. L. Moss, Bloomington; and Mr. Kienlen.

Rewritten Story
Freeport Newspaper

Lowell Watson, 34 W. Bushnell place, commander of the local chapter of the Fraternal Order of Leopards, will attend an organization meeting next Thursday at Peoria to help plan a state-wide membership campaign for the order.

Representatives from all eight original Leopards chapters in the state will take part in the meeting called by J. S. Kienlen, Peoria, state commander.

Objectives of the proposed campaign are a membership of 2,000 and 25 Illinois chapters. To attend Thursday's meeting, in addition to Watson and Kienlen, are . . ..

9

GIVING IT SUBSTANCE

A. Completing the Account
1. Factual Background
2. Eyewitness Accounts
3. Sidebars
4. Localization
5. The "Other Side"
B. Interpretations
1. The Growth of Interpretation
2. The Interpretative Viewpoint

3. Causes and Motives
4. Significance
5. Analysis
6. Comparisons
7. Forecasts
C. Providing Perspective
1. Resumes
2. Surveys
3. Situations and Trends

Experienced reporters who develop specialties often become recognized experts. They write not only authoritative newspaper articles but magazine pieces and books as well. Their vast amount of background knowledge enables them to give meaning to current happenings. More than that, they become critics in their fields and can warn and forecast and even give advice to policy leaders, including heads of state. They may have a powerful effect upon public opinion.

Later journalistic success is determined by early experience. Nobody, that is, is catapulted into a top position of prestige and influence without having served a long apprenticeship during which he learned correct work habits and attitudes. Local reporting provides the first and best opportunity for the development of such essential traits as thoroughness, accuracy, resourcefulness and the like. The aspirant for future fame and fortune as an interpretative reporter and writer begins by becoming a superior gatherer of so-called straight news which he writes objectively. He "gets around" more than his competitors do and he digs deeper in his fact-finding. In other words, he does whatever is required and then a bit more, the key to success in most any area of endeavor.

The reporter who deals firsthand with the events which make news lays the foundation for a future as interpreter as well as chronicler of current affairs by conditioning himself to inquire regarding each assignment:

1. What happened? That is, what *really* happened—the complete story, not just the end results of a series of incidents.
2. Why (or how) did it happen? That is, what is the explanation?
3. What does it mean? That is, how interpret it?
4. What next? In the light of today's news, what may be expected to happen tomorrow?
5. What's beneath the surface? What are the trends, ideologies, situations and so on, of which one should be aware so that an overt news incident will make sense?

COMPLETING THE ACCOUNT

Factual Background

When an event of major significance occurs, because of the mass of detailed information involved and from lack of time and space, first news stories may be in the straight news-writing tradition, leaving the interpretation for another edition or day. If, however, the reporter has an adequate knowledge and understanding of preceding events related to the one at hand, even his first story, prepared in haste, will have greater substance.

If there are both a morning and an afternoon newspaper, any news story inevitably breaks to the comparative advantage of one over the other. The publication with the earlier deadline will be able to print the story first, but the other paper should be able to prepare a more detailed account. For instance, the Peoria (Ill.) *Journal-Star*, a morning newspaper, once reported that an attempt by an alderman to have a painting contract awarded to the second lowest bidder was defeated when the mayor cast the deciding vote. The Peoria *Transcript*, that afternoon, with more time, cast new light on the incident by revealing that the alderman and contractor were brothers-in-law, that the alderman was atttending his first meeting following election and that the mayor's vote brought about a tie, not a majority.

The knowledgeable reporter will recall the history of a bill or ordinance and of previous attempts to promote similar legislation. He knows whether lawmakers are behaving consistently, the identity of individuals and groups in support or opposition and other facts of the same sort which enable readers to come to a better understanding of the immediate occurrence.

Eyewitness Accounts

To supplement the formal stories, it is common practice to ask victims of disasters (train wrecks, floods, fires) to relate their personal experiences. Often, such accounts are ghostwritten or are printed under the by-lines of the principals "as told to" some staff writer. Reporters themselves write eyewitness accounts of important scenes they have witnessed. Such stories are more informal than straight news accounts and usually provide graphic word pictures of what happened.

Photography, including motion pictures and television, has not yet made written description obsolete, nor is it likely to do so for some time, if for no other reason than that cameramen are not always present at news events about which it is necessary to answer "What did it look like?" in order to present a complete account. Before he can describe well, a reporter must be able to observe. Careful observation means noting features which escape the untrained spectator. A bizarre vocabulary containing innumerable adjectives is not essential. The reader, in fact, will "see" best what the writer is describing if the words are familiar; ambiguous qualitative adjectives such as "handsome" or "delicate" are omitted and figures of speech, historical and literary allusions and other rhetorical devices must be easily understood.

In selecting anecdotes to relate and persons to describe, caution must be exercised so that they are either important in their own right or typical of a general situation. Otherwise a distorted impression can be created. A typical situation in which this might occur is a mine cave-in or flood or similar disaster. At the scene, probably accompanying rescue workers, the reporter is attempting to describe the reaction of victims and others so the reader can get the "feel" of the story. He must realize that one sobbing woman does not constitute an hysterical mob. The reader must be able to depend upon the integrity of the reporter.

That the best-intentioned newsgatherers will differ in their observations and impressions is inevitable. Carl Lindstrom, who quit the executive editorship of the Hartford (Conn.) *Times,* after a quarter-century, and wrote *The Fading American Newspaper,* and others point up the danger of permitting reporters to attempt to be interpretative. They cite the example of widespread differences in reports of a press conference with Dr. Otto John after he fled from West to East Germany. According to the Associated Press,

> He spoke nervously at first. Then he got over his first mild stage fright and was completely at ease. Pink-cheeked, he was the picture of German health. His low modulated voice was pleasing to hear, regardless of how one would react to the sentiments involved. He made many wisecracks that brought laughter, wisecracks appreciated only in his native German tongue which lost much of their salt in translation. Not all of the laughs came from the Communist press either.

What the United Press reporter saw was as follows:

> His press conference statement today was recited grimly and hurriedly, much in the manner of confessions made by the victims of numerous Red Purge trials.
> He gave the tell-tale evidence of Communist brainwashing tactics; he was wooden-faced and nervous at the conference. He never smiled, although some of his comments brought laughter from newsmen.

An International News Service writer in Washington, using material purported to be supplied by Allied counterintelligence sources, wrote

> These sources are convinced that, through use of a highly developed combination of hypnosis and hypodermic needles, Dr. John became a virtual "zom-

bie" without a will of his own, capable of acting and speaking only at the dictates of his Communist masters.

Over the National Broadcasting company airways, Robert McCormick commented as follows:

> John handled himself with self-confidence and assurance. He definitely showed no signs of being drugged, beaten or tortured and, in fact, seemed quite happy. If anything, he looked more content than he looked in Bonn.

It is impossible to argue with the importance of attempting to describe Dr. John's attitude after his sensational act. No deadpan recording of whatever words he spoke would have sufficed to give readers a hint of the motive for his act. Equally obvious is the fact that at least one (which?) of those who attended the press conference was a thoroughly incompetent reporter. The example does not disprove the value or necessity of interpretative reporting. Rather, it provides argument for the fact that journalists, whether they report and write objectively or interpretatively, must be highly ethical.

Sidebars

When an important news event occurs, reporters often use sidebars to round out the complete account. A sidebar deals with phases of a story as a whole which conceivably could be included in the main account but not without either lengthening it too much or sacrificing some details. When an office building in Chicago's Loop exploded, among the anecdotal sidebars were the following: (1) 105,000 square feet of new glass being rushed to city to replace show-window glass broken; (2) analysis of city ordinances covering gas leakage which allegedly caused the blast; (3) description of army of glaziers at work in area; (4) police pass system to admit workers employed in area; (5) refusal of pass to a window washer, obviously because there were no windows left to wash; (6) symposium of eyewitness accounts; (7) narrow escape of nearby elevated tower operator; (8) instructions on how to enter area; (9) Red Cross activities; (10) list of buildings whose windows were blown out.

The page 1 streamer headline of the Los Angeles *Times* for Feb. 10, 1971, was DAY OF DISASTER and the two-line head read "Quake Leaves 42 Dead, 1,000 Hurt; Periled Dam Forces 40,000 to Flee." A picture and an area map occupied about one-third of the page. There were two inside pages devoted entirely to pictures and enough other scattered pictures to total the equivalent of a third page. The main account began in the right-hand column on page 1 and jumped for about the equivalent of a full page on inside pages. The headlines of 26 other stories related to the disaster suggest their contents and consequently the extent of the coverage which William Thomas, since then promoted from metropolitan editor to editor, who directed the operation, says was perhaps "the closest we have come to accomplishing" the objective of bringing "some of our interpretative and analytical techniques to the spot news story."

Virtually all of the stories were finished within six hours of the actual quake. The headlines: (1) 39 Still Missing in Hospital Ruins; (2) Reservoir Dwarfs Old One in Baldwin Hills [there was fear that it might give way]; (3) First a Rumble, Then Houses Catch Fire, Glass Shatters [an eyewitness impressionist account]; (4) Reagan Favors Gas Tax Rise to Repair Streets; (5) Antelope Valley Cut Off as Bridge Collapses; (6) Shock Stronger Than One That Hit Long Beach; (7) New Skyscrapers Ride It Out, Damage Slight; (8) Disaster Planning Brings Quick Aid; (9) Olive View Hospital Termed Total Loss; (10) City Schools Will Stay Closed Today; (11) Some Guard Units Activated for Duty; (12) Partial Death List Gives Scant Details; (13) Beagle Was the Alarm for Sleeper [terrified dog jumped on bed]; (14) Sea Bubbles Off Malibu Most of Day; (15) Phone, Water, Electric, Gas Services Disrupted; (16) It Was A-Test to Las Vegas; (17) Little Quake Insurance in Effect, Broker Says; (18) Quake Talks Delayed by the Quake [relates to meeting of Structural Engineering Association on subject of laws on earthquake safety]; (9) 7 Emergency Shelters Open to Quake Victims; (20) Special Loans to Be Offered; (21) Homeless Offered Vacant VA Houses; (22) Expert Tells What to Do in a Quake; (23) Care Urged in Drinking Water Use; (24) Quake Interferes with Apollo Lines [Apollo 14 was homeward bound]; (25) Eclipse Lineup Linked to Quake by Scientist; (26) Hundreds of Aftershocks.

Thomas reminisces concerning the experience,

One editor was in charge: I, along with considerable help from two assistants. Any complex coverage has to be directed by one person or it becomes incoherent.

From there, you play it by ear. You send out to cover all conceivable action, which really is not difficult, and everything stems from this. A guy at the shattered hospital comments that it seemed a long time before help came, and that gets you to thinking about the disaster warning setup. Did it work and how well and exactly how? A report comes in that the injured are going to such a place, and as you send a team there you wonder how the evacuation process was planned and did it do the job, etc. A reporter wonders how much of the damage is covered by insurance, and you say, "That's a good idea" and you assign a man to that aspect.

As you're doing all this, you are listing your areas of coverage and deciding how to break them into dovetailing stories. Here is where our earthquake coverage differed from, say, our Watts riot coverage. The same thing was done during Watts but, instead of interpretative pieces, as we did on the riots, we assigned them for immediate publication.

Several things made this possible. First and most important is a staff who can do it. You could never do this under the old rewrite setup, where there are eight guys suitable mainly for leg work for every one who is a competent writer. We did away with the rewrite concept almost entirely some time ago, and for some years I have hired only writers. So everybody can communicate his own findings, which gives us several desirable things; greater authenticity, greater speed, better and more believable stories all around, a happier staff.

Was it organized, you asked, or random? You'd have to say it was organized in a random manner, or random in an organized manner, whichever you like best. In other words, the story was unfolding as the interpretative package was being put together so it certainly was random to that extent.

But there are certain procedures which experience dictates will bring the best results in such situations (i.e., keeping a number of the best writers in the office to handle the complex interpretative stories you know will develop, even though the temptation is to fire them out into the general area; putting the guys strongest on action reporting into those situations, the guys best on reflective stories into those, etc.). This isn't very clear, but to this extent—and to the extent that you retain a very clear idea where everybody is and what he can be expected to contribute—it is an organized procedure.

I guess you try to be organized to deal effectively with random happenings.

When the news relates to a scheduled event, several reporters may be assigned to cover different angles. A woman reporter, for instance, may stay close to the wife of a visiting celebrity; at the same time, another reporter may concentrate his attention on the crowd, noting its size and nature, ever watchful for unusual personalities and incidents. Still another may observe the behavior of the police, marshals, secret-service men and the like, or he may interview members of the party of either the guest or the host or both. Someone else, who might not even need to be present, can compare the occasion with similar ones in the past, here and/or elsewhere. Some of the information obtained by members of a reportorial team may be used by whoever writes the main story of the event but each probably will have enough left for a separate piece.

Localization

The effects of some news events are felt at considerable distances. Without mention of some of the repercussions, the original story is not complete. For instance, whenever the president of the United States or some other leader of government makes an important announcement, there are reverberations on Capitol Hill, where congressional leaders abandon or alter old tactics or institute new ones. The stock market may be influenced by mere rumor. A Supreme Court decision may affect governmental practices and legal procedures in the states and cities.

In all such and similar cases, the reader wants to know, "How will this affect me?" That is the perspective from which the interpretative reporter should approach his task. In that spirit, the Evanston (Ill.) *Review* figured out the average cost for every man, woman, and child in Illinois of a newly announced federal budget. Similarly, when the United States Supreme Court upheld the blue laws of some Eastern states, the United Press International bureau in Topeka compiled a list of laws still on the books in Kansas regulating behavior on the Sabbath. The Baltimore *Sun* used a similar story to explain how a Supreme Court decision regarding motion-picture censorship would affect Baltimore and Maryland. When Sen. George McGovern revealed in March 1971 that the Vietnam War had caused 920,028 deaths, the Chicago *Daily News* figured out that "If all those killed in the Vietnam war had lived in the same U.S. city, only seven other American cities would be larger."

Many a newspaper has investigated to determine how long the local supply of coal or steel or some other commodity would last in the event a strike continued affecting the faraway source of supply. How a new federal or state law will affect the community specifically, probably always should be explained by the public-spirited local press.

By Robert M. Lewin
Daily News Labor Writer

What will the new steel price increases do to the cost of things you buy?

The price of steel used in a 30-gallon water heater will go up 21 cents, according to the arithmetic of Armco Steel Corp., the first to follow Inland Steel Co. in increasing steel prices.

Armco's estimates also showed:

The cost of steel in a home gas furnace will go up 32 cents; 23 cents in a washing machine; 16 cents in an automatic dishwasher; 28 cents in a refrigerator; 15 cents in an automatic clothes dryer, and $3 in an automobile.

Armco contends that the increases of $2 and $3 a ton on the price of hot-rolled steel sheets and strip and cold-rolled sheets "are so modest they cannot be consequential."

The auto and appliance industries are chief users of those products. The increases are scheduled to go into effect Wednesday. . . .

[Chicago *Daily News*]

The "Other Side"

Deadpan reporting of the contents of a report, speech or the like, even when the source is reputable, may be misleading in that it does not give readers the "whole" or "essential" truth. When the news source is irresponsible, grave disservice may be done the reading public. It certainly is newsworthy when someone important in public life attacks another person. Such news often cannot be ignored. It can, however, be put in better perspective if there is simultaneous opportunity for reply by the otherwise injured party. Readers want to know how those most affected by any news event react to it. Unless their curiosity is satisfied, the account is incomplete.

"Real objectivity" was attained by an interpretative reporter for the Memphis *Press-Scimitar* who merely filled in background and, without drawing conclusions, gave readers additional information by which to judge a current news story. The incident occurred during the campaign of B. Carroll Reece, Republican candidate for United States senator from Tennesseee.

In a Memphis speech, Reece lambasted the "motley crowd" of Democrats in charge of the federal government for speaking "with such a variety of accents, all of them un-American, that they sound like the tongues of Babel." Continued Reece:

These mixed tongues are chanting many themes that are utterly offensive to our American instincts. None is more offensive than their chant that "States' Rights might give way to human rights." Under this sweetsounding slogan is a snake in the grass as vicious as any reptile we have ever encountered. Herein lie the efforts of men who are either recent immigrants to our shore or whose ideas of government are immigrant to our shore—to move in on our system of States' Rights for the kill. . . . We of the South shall throw the pretty phrases back in their teeth. We say to them that the South has always preserved human rights. . . .

Straight-faced reporting of this speech would have appeared under some such headlines as, "ALIENS CONTROL U.S. GOVERNMENT, WARNS REECE." However, the Memphis reporter included in his interpretative article the fact that in an earlier speech in Buffalo (N.Y.) Reece said

This element (the Southern Democrats) which of course stemmed from the slave-holding oligarchy which once plunged this nation into a bloody war to preserve the institution of slavery, is the group which still maintains itself in power in a large section of this country by the practice of outrageous racial discrimination, preventing millions of American citizens from exercising the right to vote. It is the element of the party which inaugurated Jim Crow laws; the element which had pushed discrimination into the North. . . .

The interpretative article was headed, "REECE VERSUS REECE."

Many American editors came to wish they had accorded the late Sen. Joseph McCarthy of Wisconsin similar treatment.

There are, of course, a pro and a con regarding every public issue. The ethical newspaper considers itself a public forum for the airing of diverse opinions. The obligation, however, is not just to the person who wishes to express himself, but primarily to readers so that they can be fully informed. When a new curfew law for adolescents is under consideration, for instance, the paper should seek out persons who are in positions to have intelligent opinions on the subject. This is not the inquiring-reporter technique which often results in obtaining uninformed and unrepresentative viewpoints. Rather, it is a search for the best opinion available.

INTERPRETATIONS

It decidedly is not true that "what you don't know won't hurt you." On the contrary, in a democracy it is essential that everyone have access to as many facts as possible so that he can form proper judgments and influence public affairs. For almost a century, however, there has been increasing recognition that mere reporting of objective facts is not sufficient to serve the informational needs of a self-governing people. The result: interpretative reporting.

The Growth of Interpretation

The first important impetus to interpretative handling of the news was provided by World War I. When it broke out most Americans were surprised—dumfounded in fact—and utterly unable to explain its causes. In his doctoral dissertation at the University of Wisconsin in the mid-'30s, the late Maynard Brown suggested the extent to which the newsgathering agencies were responsible for this phenomenon. Brown wrote in part

> Where the Associated Press failed most was in preventing its reporters from sending background and informative articles based on politics and trends. It smugly adopted the attitude of permitting correspondents to report only what had definitely transpired. It wanted no interpretation of events but the mere factual reporting of the obvious. Some of its correspondents were trained in foreign affairs, but too few were able to interpret or discern significant events and tendencies.

Not only the Associated Press but other press associations and newspapers as well learned a great lesson from the experience of being totally unprepared either to understand the final steps which plunged the world into war or adequately to report the war once it started. During the '20s and '30s they peopled the capitals and other important news centers of the world with trained experts qualified not only to report but also to explain and interpret factual occurrences. Among the best of these journalistic scholars were Walter Duranty, John Gunther, Vincent Sheean, Edgar Ansel Mowrer, Edgar Snow, Quentin Reynolds, William Shirer and W. M. Fodor. In newspaper stories, magazine articles, authoritative books and radio commentaries, they and others did such a thoroughly competent job that, by contrast with 1914, for years before World War II began in 1939, an overwhelming majority of Americans expected it or at least knew it was possible if not probable.

Reader demand for more than mere drab objective reporting of domestic news grew tremendously after the stock-market crash of 1929 and during the depression years of the '30s and the period of New Deal experimentation which brought with it nationwide awareness of the increased importance in the life of every citizen of the federal government. Readership of the recently created weekly news magazines, *Time*, *Newsweek* and others, skyrocketed; so did the circulation of *Reader's Digest* and a multitude of other monthly digest magazines. So did the number and readership of how-to-do-it and other easily read books, allegedly compendious accounts of how to understand what was happening in a variety of fields of human interest and activity. So also did newsletters for general and specialized audiences.

Slow to modify their basic news formula, newspapers nevertheless expanded their contents to include signed columns by political analysts, most of which were syndicated at reasonable cost so as to be available for moderate- and small-sized newspapers. In the mid-'30s newspapers also experimented with weekly news reviews, some of which (notably that of the New York *Times*) have survived. They also tried out various forms of daily reviews, expanded Sunday magazine or feature sections and increased the number of supplemental articles to provide historical, geographical, biographical and other background information to help make current news more understandable and meaningful. A whole new vocabulary developed to categorize these writings. Instead of lumping them all under the general heading of "think pieces" as in the past, newsmen talked of sidebars, explainers, situationers, wrap-ups, button-ups, blockbusters and other types of explanatory, enterprise, offbeat, background, subsurface, creative, speculative or interpretative reporting and writing.

Today, the debate is virtually over, with only a few still arguing against the necessity for interpretative reporting. This means that to become more than a humdrum journeyman the future reporter must prepare himself to help meet the increasing need and demand for "subsurface" or "depth" reporting, to "take the reader behind the scenes of the day's action," "relate the news to the reader's own framework and experience," "make sense out of the facts," "put factual news in perspective," "put meaning into the news," "point up the significance of current events," and so on, to use the expressions of various authorities.

Foremost defender of interpretative reporting against its critics has been Lester Markel, longtime associate editor of the New York *Times*, who wrote

> Those who object to interpretation say that a story should be confined to the "facts." I ask, "What facts?" And I discover that there is in reality no such thing as an "objective" article in the sense these objectors use it—or in any sense, for that matter.
>
> Take the most "objective" of reporters. He collects fifty facts; out of these fifty he selects twelve which he considers important enough to include in his piece, leaving out thirty-eight. This is the first exercise of judgment.
>
> Then the reporter decides which of these twelve facts shall constitute the lead of the story. The particular fact he chooses gets the emphasis—which is important because often the reader does not go beyond the first paragraph. This is the second exercise of judgment.
>
> Then the editor reads the so-called objective story and makes a decision as to whether it is to be played on page 1 or on page 29. If it is played on page 1 it may have considerable impact on opinion. If it is put on page 29 it has no such emphasis. The most important editorial decision on any paper, I believe, is what goes on page 1. This is the third exercise of judgment.
>
> In brief, this "objective" news is, in its exponents' own terms, very unobjective and the kind of judgment required for interpretation is no different from the kind of judgment involved in the selection of the facts for a so-called factual story and in the display of that story.

In other words, just as the Constitution is said to mean what the Supreme Court says it means, so is news what newspapers and other media of communication decide it is to be.

The Interpretative Viewpoint

In gathering information about a news event, the reporter seeks answers to the *who, what, where, when, why* and *how* of whatever happened. Of these, the first four are basic to virtually any account. The emphasis that they should receive under different circumstances was discussed in Chapter 3. Offhand, it might be held that not all stories have a *why* or *how* element important enough to engage much of the newsgatherer's attention. Actually, exactly the contrary is the case. In delving into the *what* of most stories, the reporter really is asking "why?" even though the answers he receives may become part of the *what*. The beginning journalist should be aware that whenever he does a thorough job of interviewing for what may seem to be a minor or simple story, he is training himself for more penetrating assignments in the future. He is developing an attitude or frame of mind toward newsgathering. To illustrate,

> Police arrested Carter Davis, 14, son of Mr. and Mrs. George Davis, 4513 W. Coral street.

Why?

> Because he used a knife to stab his eighth-grade teacher at Tyler Junior high school, 1216 N. Marshall street. She is Mrs. Vivian Heller, 48, 5141 W. Falconer avenue.

Why did he do it?

> The assault occurred just after she had told the boy that he would fail his course in English.

But other teenagers fail in their school work without committing violence against their teachers. *Why is this boy different?* The Behavior Clinic psychiatrist is examining him now in an attempt to find out. While waiting for the report, further facts can be obtained: the circumstances and sequences of the events, the victim's condition, police activities and so forth. Questioning of school authorities reveals Carter's academic and deportment records. Classmates tell of his behavior toward and reputation with his peers, expressing either surprise or the opposite as regards the immediate situation.

Further clues as to the answer to the *why* are obtained by a visit to Carter's home and neighborhood, by talks with parents and other relatives, neighbors and friends and recreational and other workers with whom the boy has had contact.

The reporter is able to ask penetrating questions to a considerable extent because of his knowledge of modern thinking in the fields of psychology, social psychology, psychiatry and sociology. Not too many decades ago he would presume, with most everyone else, that there is a dichotomy of good boys and bad boys, determined largely by the individual's exercise of free will. A more lenient attitude would be to consider the social misfit a victim of some sort of demoniacal possession. In any case, harshness of punishment was the only known corrective. Police operated on the "catch 'em and kill 'em" philosophy and were goaded on by journalists who reflected the indignation of most of their readers whenever a particularly heinous example of misbehavior occurred.

Within a generation, the attitude of a majority of enforcement officers, judges, educators, journalists and others has changed. Today it is recognized that there is "something wrong" with a boy who commits an act like Carter's. Psychiatrists still are reluctant to discuss cases with newsgatherers until they have made their formal reports to whatever public authorities are involved. In the meantime, reporters must refrain from making medical diagnoses on the basis of their own investigations. They can, however, publicize such pertinent facts as that a misbehaving child comes from an underprivileged, broken slum home, or from a wealthy family where everything was lavished upon him except the most important ingredient of all—parental attention.

Why do some youngsters reared in the same neighborhood "go bad" whereas others do not? The answer concerns the behavior clinician who may conclude that the boy who does not act in accordance with group standards is the problem child rather than others who "go along" with the gang in committing antisocial acts. Human motivation is an extremely complex subject for scientific research, with multitudinous influences in and out of the home and other primary institutions affecting different children differently. The journalist should be warned against acceptance of "panacea" explanations such as broken homes, poverty, slum environments and especially television, comic books, the movies and so forth as providing easy answers to explain intricate situations. Especially must all journalists not panic when "law and order" advocates seek a return to the philosophers of the Middle Ages.

Even if a reasonably clear picture emerges as regards an individual case, the probing reporter can continue to ask "why?" at several different levels of inquiry. If social statistics indicate that there are correlations between various factors, as slum conditions, racial, religious or nationality backgrounds, economic status and so forth, for understanding it is necessary to ask "why?" as regards each item. What are the cause-and-effect relationships? And how explain the type of behavior which results? Why violence instead of suicide or something else? Because of the extreme frustration or sense of insecurity in the individual from whatever cause—an organic or biological reflex? Or because violence is an accepted or admired form of behavior in a group whose respect is desired? Or because there is violence in other aspects of the environment, including the international scene? These are matters which concern many different specialists in the social sciences whose erudition and research the newsgatherer cannot hope to duplicate. He can, however, solicit their information, assistance and advice. Most important, he can get more out of his assignments, both for immediate journalistic usage and for promotion of his general understanding, if he recognizes that the isolated news event is not really isolated.

It would be impossible and superfluous to attempt extensive probing into the broader aspects of every incident such as the hypothetical one of Carter Davis. Space will not permit usage of exhaustive analyses of every vagrant, jack roller, tough juvenile, prostitute or others of society's "problem children." There is no beat to compare with police, however, to provide an opportunity to begin cultivation of a querying attitude toward life. When he later attempts to fathom the causes of a depression, war or major issue of any kind, the experienced newsgatherer utilizes the habits of mind that he cultivated back in his cubhood. If he doesn't take advantage of the opportunities provided to him at the beginning of his journalistic career, his grandchildren will still be visiting him in the same pressroom where he got his start.

A typical defense of interpretative reporting by Lester Markel follows:

> Interpretation, as I see it, is the deeper sense of the news. It places a particular event in the larger flow of events. It is the color, the atmosphere, the human element that give meaning to a fact. It is, in short, setting, sequence, and, above all, significance.
>
> There is a vast difference between interpretation and opinion. And the distinction is of the utmost importance. Three elements, not two, are involved in this debate; first, news; second, interpretation; third, opinion. To take a primitive example:
>
> To say that Senator McThing is investigating the teaching of Patagonian in the schools is news.
>
> To explain why Senator McThing is carrying on this investigation is interpretation.
>
> To remark that Senator McThing should be ashamed of himself is opinion.
>
> Interpretation is an objective judgment based on background knowledge of a situation, appraisal of an event. Editorial judgment, on the other hand, is a subjective judgment; it may include an appraisal of the facts but there is an additional and distinctive element, namely, emotional impact.
>
> Opinion should be confined, almost religiously, to the editorial page; interpretation is an essential part of the news. This is vital and it cannot have too much emphasis.
>
> I see no difference between "interpretation" and "background." Of course, part of interpretation may be the setting out of some antecedent facts—and this many editors consider "background" as distinguished from "interpretation." But interpretation is much more than shirttail material; it is in addition to the presentation of the pertinent facts, present and past, an effort to assay the meaning of those facts.

Causes and Motives

The probing reporter keeps on asking "why?" as he seeks the news behind the news. He knows that official proclamations and carefully prepared press releases may conceal causes and motives which preceded the spot or "end result" news of the moment. So he digs beneath the surface.

Sometimes it is possible to conjecture. For instance, if a mayor and corporation counsel have disagreed frequently in public, the reasons for the latter's impending resignation would seem to be obvious. Too often, however, newspaper columnists and others, acting on rumors and tips from "persons close to" or "usually reliable sources," may be wrong. If, for instance, the mayor and corporation counsel announce after a conference that they have settled their differences and, in fact, now "see eye to eye," only a naive journalist would accept the announcement on its face value. To obtain the "real lowdown," however, may be difficult or impossible. Perhaps the counsel threatened to make a public statement which would be embarrassing to the mayor. Perhaps he agreed to "go along" on some current matter in exchange for a promise of political support at some future date. Perhaps the mayor indicated he would withdraw some patronage from the counsel's followers. The possibilities are many and the responsible journalist must be careful not to give currency to gossip, rumor and surmise.

Once a large company with plants in several cities announced it intended to close its factory in City A and shift operations to City B. The announcement included a strong statement of regret by management, praise for City A and the like but explained that it had become necessary to retrench, operate closer to its supply of raw materials and avoid the necessity of investing in costly new machinery. This sounded reasonable but an experienced reporter "smelled a rat" and started snooping. Before long he learned that months earlier the company had negotiated a contract with a union local in City B at a wage rate much lower than that which prevailed in City A. The City B union accepted the deal as it would mean jobs for several thousand unemployed members. Further probing revealed that this act was considered by City A unionists to be a "sellout" and was part of the campaign of a certain national labor leader to increase his strength. The City B union consisted mainly of his followers whereas those in City A belonged to a rival faction within the national organization. Facts such as these are necessary for a proper understanding of the news. The free press has been called a watchdog on government. It can perform no more worthwhile function than to scrutinize carefully everything which affects the public interest.

Significance

Referring a proposal to a committee may mean either that its enactment into law is being accelerated or that it is being killed. The perspicacious newsgatherer should know which and should so inform his readers. The same for all other acts of all branches of government. Readers are able to understand the significance of parliamentary and diplomatic maneuvering, but it must be pointed out to them by someone who keeps close check.

When a convicted person is sentenced to a long term of imprisonment, it is customary to point out the minimum time that he would have to serve before being eligible for release on parole. When a deadline passes for filing or withdrawing a petition, it should be pointed out what thereby becomes possible or impossible. If a diplomat attends one function and boycotts another, there may or may not be significant repercussions. In some cases, in other words, it is not difficult to explain consequences objectively. In others, a certain amount of guesswork may be necessary, in which case the rule of caution must be invoked.

Analysis

Long and/or complicated documents, including ordinances and statutes, must be analyzed so that they can be understood. This often is merely a job of tedious objective reporting to explain what now is forbidden, allowed or required and who will be affected in what way. Often the analyst will discover ramifications and repercussions which escaped even the lawmakers.

Speeches by important persons are analyzed almost immediately by journalists and later by scholars. What the speaker emphasizes, the number of times he mentions a particular matter and what he omits are noted. Qualitative judgment enters into evaluating the importance of gestures, facial expressions, tone of voice, pauses in delivery and the like and also in estimating the reaction of a visible audience. It is not difficult to note the amount and duration of applause, of course, but the intangibles are so many that great restraint is needed by the reporter. The audience, for instance, may be easily identifiable as partisan to begin with. Nevertheless, how it reacts is part of the complete coverage. Sometimes explanation is needed for proper analysis. This is often true of crime records. Changes in the frequency of certain types of offenses may be seasonal. The population complexion of areas may change during a reporting period. Police departments have been known to alter their methods of reporting, even with the intention of making the results seem better than they should. An example would be to list automobiles as missing instead of stolen.

Comparisons

As with crime statistics, so with the budgets of public and private bodies, achievements of athletes, votes received by candidates and numerous other matters, the reader wants to know how the present compares with the past. Is something more or less, higher or lower, better or worse? Answers to such questions must be given with all possible influencing factors considered so as not to be deceptive. It would, for instance, be misleading to cite an expenditure as twice that for a comparable item some time in the past without taking into consideration changes in the value of the dollar, population increases, changing needs and demands and so forth.

Political party platforms can be compared with each other and with those of previous years. Faced with a vexatious local problem, public officials and newspapers may send representatives to other communities to study what steps were taken there by way of solution. Whenever a disaster of importance occurs, it is common journalistic practice to prepare sidebars, often in the form of charts or tabulations, to show how the immediate catastrophe compares in intensity with others of the past.

Old-timers are prone to draw historical parallels, to feel that some contemporary event is "just like" one they recall from years before; they feel they have "lived through this before," possibly when they observe a widespread practice which they consider undesirable, as excessive installment buying, stock market speculation, real estate booms and the like. There is no gainsaying the fact that history teaches many valuable lessons, but what may seem to be history repeating itself may not be that at all. Numerous cities previously tried and abandoned services which today are orthodox, as parking meters, traffic signals, one-way streets and off-street parking, to mention only examples in one area. Increasing populations and automobile ownership created new conditions for which new remedies no longer were premature.

Reform movements come and go in many communities. One reason for their failure to last often is the tendency of many supporters to become lackadaisical after the immediate first objective has been attained. History does prove that eternal vigilance is a prerequisite for a properly functioning democracy.

Forecasts

Giving a news story a "tomorrow" angle often is a form of interpretation. Based on his analysis of an action by the city council, a reporter can predict new employment, building, police activities and the like. He can see "trouble ahead" for certain groups as the result of a sweeping court decision and business advantages to others. A drastic price cut by one retail establishment usually results in a price war among competitors. Tightening child labor laws may have the immediate effect of throwing a certain number of minors out of work.

When it comes to predicting beyond the immediate effect, as that unemployed juveniles will become delinquent, the reporter may be merely speculating. He should draw on expert opinion and historical example and still be slow about making deductions. The death of a prominent figure may or may not clear the way toward a reconciliation between disputing factions, lead to a struggle for succession to a position of power or destroy the chances for achieving a certain goal. The expert can point out the possibilities but he should not forget that some pundits have lost the confidence of their audiences by excessive smugness which the future exposed as such.

PROVIDING PERSPECTIVE

News does not consist only in specific incidents which can be written up with clearcut inclusion of all of the five *w*'s. Ideas are news. So are ideologies, trends of thought, psychological situations and similar intangibles. It is not highbrow to believe that it would be a better world if more newspaper readers were aware of social, political, economic and other stresses and strains which often must be written about without definite news pegs. The "think piece" is a comparatively old journalistic device, but its use constantly is being broadened to include areas previously reserved for research scholars.

As Robert E. Garst, then assistant managing editor of the New York *Times*, wrote in *Nieman Reports:*

> Too much of past reporting has dealt only with the surface facts—the spot news—and too rarely has dug into reasons for them.
>
> A race riot, a prison outbreak, a bad slum condition—even a murder—has a social background, deeply rooted perhaps in the customs, traditions, and economic conditions of a region or community; but it is there and discoverable. It's the newspaper's job, it seems to me, to discover it. Only with that knowledge can a remedy be found for many of the ills that affect us.

Resumes

News weeklies, monthly digest magazines and weekly newspaper news reviews got their start during the depression years and appealed to persons in all walks of life who sought understanding in the midst of confusion. They have continued as an adjunct to quick spot-news reporting to provide recapitulations or resumes of series of fast-happening events. Few occurrences are treated as isolated happenings but as related to other events preceding and following them.

In addition to weekly news reviews, newspapers use "wrap-up" articles on running stories such as legislative assemblies, court trials, political campaigns and the like. In such stories, the expert reporter treats the events of a number of days, usually a week, as constituting material for a single story. Readers' memories are refreshed and relationships are pointed out. Often a condensed chronological recapitulation of the news is sufficient. In other cases, interpretation is added. This week, the observant reviewer may write, a certain objective came closer to realization because of this or that train of events. Defense strategy, another may explain, became clearer as cross-examination of prosecution witnesses continued in a court trial. A public official took two steps forward and one backward under observation by a knowledgeable journalist. And so on, all in the attempt to round up the events of a period into a comprehensive single story with proper perspective.

At the end of any session of the state legislature, a resume of its activities is a journalistic must. Annual or semiannual appraisals of the handling of his official acts by a public official are in the same category. The news reviewer often takes a second look at the cumulative record about every part of which he previously has composed separate accounts.

Surveys

When similar news occurs in a number of places, a journalistic medium may conduct a survey to find out what the overall situation happens to be.

Perhaps attempts to enact similar legislation were made in a number of states, in which case a compilation of the results is significant. Let disaster of any kind occur in one place and a follow-up survey reveals how widespread are conditions believed to have been its cause.

Newspapers have conducted surveys to determine the death rates on transcontinental highways, the outcomes of referenda on school bond issues, the use of prison labor on private projects, the attitude of condemned prisoners toward capital punishment, the extent of racial and religious discrimination in housing, schooling and job opportunities, the increase in the ownership of yachts, and on many and many other matters. Some of the material, though not quite so up-to-the-minute, might have been obtained from public and private research agencies.

In drawing conclusions from any kind of data, the press must avoid the error which professional researchers and pollsters also must avoid, that of inadequacy or lack of representativeness of the sample. It is incorrect to write, "Public opinion today here is this or that" unless one has exhaustively questioned persons in all walks of life, something it is rarely possible for a newspaperman to do. Even an impressive group of interviewees within a given area may not be typical. There is no field in which unanimity exists among experts. Quoting leaders is good journalism but minorities also should be contacted and exaggeration always avoided.

Situations and Trends

Getting his idea from an article on the subject in a national magazine, a city editor assigned a reporter to "find out how much moonlighting there is in this community." Other editors have sought the answers to such questions as "What do we do for the mentally retarded in our town?" "What about juvenile delinquency among girls?" "Are there any independent grocers left?" "What's happening to our wildlife?"

Often such assignments result in feature articles concerning little-known or off-the-beaten-path persons or groups. In other cases, there may be forthcoming broader expositions of current situations to which the journalistic limelight is applied. The net result is a better acquaintance with all aspects of the life of the community and possibly an arousal of civic interest in improvement where needed.

No reporter should start on an assignment of this sort without adequate preparation which should include not merely examination of the publication's own clipping files but also the reading of books, magazine articles and other material to acquaint himself with the aspects of the situation which he should bear in mind during his fact finding. When the reporter encounters someone with views contrary to those which he believes to be orthodox, he should avoid altercation. Instead, he should tactfully request his news source to comment on the viewpoint of the "other side" as he understands it.

Fortified with information from a number of other places, the perceptive reporter may conclude that what he is studying is not just a local phenomenon but part of a widespread trend. Farmers on the fringes of suburban areas, for instance, may be keeping land out of cultivation in expectation of selling their property to urban developers. Redlining by moneylending institutions, sit-in demonstrations, sympathetic picketing, streaking by college students, fads in games, dress, music and the like may be national or international in extent. The locally written feature can stress home-town manifestations but would be inadequate if it did not mention the broader aspects.

Ora Spaid did a colossally successful job for the Louisville *Courier-Journal* when he investigated post-basketball game fights between rival gangs of high school boys. The following extracts, approximately the middle third of the first of three articles, indicate how Spaid tackled the assignment writing as the careful reporter and specialist-expert that he is, having been a social worker before he turned to journalism:

ATHLETICS

One of those not-new conditions is overemphasis of athletics.

A high-school basketball game has become an orgy of emotionalism closely resembling a voodoo ritual. Big crowds pack into small gyms. Drums pound a savage throb, and pretty little girls whip up frenzied partisan spirit that doesn't let up even when play begins.

Sportsmanhip is usually evident—as in the exchange of "Hello" yells at the beginning. But it breaks down easily, as when a player from the other team steps to the line for a crucial free throw and the crowd jeers and shouts to distract him.

Coaches talk of the "home-court advantage"—the fact that the crowd is so partisan you can't expect a fair contest.

EMOTIONS STIRRED

Emotional pitch is built before the game in school-wide "pep assemblies," a practice that teachers consider "a necessary evil." A psychology teacher says pointedly that pep assemblies "are a real study in mass psychology sometimes."

The question is: Where does school spirit leave off and hysteria begin?

The concept of high-school sports for participation long ago lost out to the necessity of winning. Coaches build the equivalent of farm systems to produce material for winning teams. A coach becomes as much a victim of "ratings" as a television show; there's a tendency to enlarge the point spread over a defeated opponent to gain a higher rating.

Utterly lost is the grace of losing. High-school girls weep as if death had descended when their teams lose. Fathers grumble about ineffective coaches.

But gainsaying overemphasis of athletics is not enough. Why are athletics overemphasized?

It's a result, some say, of "urbanization." The exodus of people from the cities of recent decades and attendant flight to the suburbs produces a lonely-in-the-crowd society.

It also produces the big school, a factor that men like Richard Van Hoose, superintendent of Jefferson County schools, and Sam V. Noe, his counterpart in Louisville schools, hold as the root cause of many problems.

THE BIG SCHOOL

Today's suburban high school of 2,500 or more students is almost what yesterday's college was.

Let Earl Duncan, principal of the 2,600-student Waggener High School, tell of some of the prolems.

"In a school of 2,600, only 12 boys can play basketball, but certainly a lot more would like to," he said. "Only five youngsters can be elected to offices in a graduating class of 350. Think how many that leaves out."

It's a case of being lost in a big school.

A bright boy in a big suburban school came home last week with failing grades. He told his mother, "I'm not good at sports; I'm not in the band; I can't get on the school paper. I've just lost all interest in school."

Most young people don't lose interest—they plunge. If they can't find something they can participate in actively, they participate vicariously. The school is something they can belong to, something to "give them identity," as the psychologists say. So they become rabid fans, fanatic followers.

MAY BOIL OVER

But nonparticipation isn't too satisfying; there's not much opportunity to blow off steam, unless in violent rooting. And it's always possible that this pent-up steam may boil over into violence, particularly if there is some way to rationalize it, like defending the school's honor or avenging a lost game.

Big schools build up tension in ways other than pep assemblies—subtler ways, often overlooked.

Principal Duncan points out that when you have only one gymnasium and it is given over to varsity teams, there is no place for other youngsters to play. To "make the best use of facilities," in gym periods or after school, the play must be scheduled and organized. Regimentation is another word for it— constant supervision, no opportunity to just horse around.

Drop in at one of these big schools at noon hour and you will see long lines of students in the cafeteria. The sheer impossibility of feeding all students at once means they eat in shifts. And mark this: lunch hour usually lasts only 20 minutes. Not only that, but by the time a student gets his food, he may have only 10 minutes to eat it. Of necessity, he must "bolt his food" or miss his next class.

DIFFERENCE IS GREAT

Compare this with the paper-sack days when pupils brought their lunches, ate leisurely and spent the rest of a long lunch hour dozing under a tree or breaking the tension of long hours at a desk in a make-up ball game.

This means that today's school children put in a 7-hour day with little let-up, seldom released from supervision. Even recess is now a matter of "supervised play," and in some schools, children are given a grade for lunchroom conduct.

Then there is homework. There always has been homework, but it seems to a lot of students that teachers are trying to close up the missile gap with Russia by the sheer bulk of homework they assign. The youngsters respond, not by learning from homework, but merely by "getting it done."

Getting it done means more hours under supervision, this time from a Mom or Dad anxious to see a good report card.

All this adds up to this: youngsters today are under greater tension than ever before but have less opportunity to dissipate it.

The foregoing was written by an expert, which many journalists become after considerable experience in covering a specialized type of news. They deserve and receive respect and their prestige is bound to grow as social scientists and others become so engrossed with their Theory and Methodology that they become unreliable witnesses to anything real. Spaid obviously wrote with a liberal slant. The liberalism of journalists is not the result, unfortunately, of what they learn in school but results from their practical experience as they come in firsthand contact with life. Members of the Establishment, including many newspaper owners and publishers, become alarmed at what they read in newspapers. But, as they are fond of telling fellow luncheon clubbers, the newspaper is merely a mirror and should not be scapegoated. The interpretative reporter today holds the mirror the highest.

10
MODERN TRENDS

A. The New Journalism   F. Humanistic Reporting
B. Activism and Advocacy   G. Investigative Reporting
C. Origins   H. Stunts
D. Impressionistic Reporting   I. Crusading; Muckraking
E. Saturation Reporting

In the early '70s a widespread ambition among journalism students was to practice the New Journalism. Then came Watergate and they yearned to do Investigative Reporting. It detracts none from the importance of youthful zest to reveal that the New Journalism is neither new nor journalism, and that Investigative Reporting is only what people always have called crusading if they approved or muckraking if they didn't.

Complicating the scholar's effort to identify and analyze what was "new" about New Journalism was the plethora of presumed synonyms—advocacy, activist, participatory, tell-it-as-you-see-it, reformist, saturation, humanistic and others. As used by authors of an avalanche of magazine articles in general circulation as well as professional journalism periodicals, these terms all had a pejorative connotation. Furthermore, they referred to not one but two matters.

THE NEW JOURNALISM

The term "New Journalism" grew out of the practice of some magazine writers and novelists to use the literary devices of the fiction writer to retell factual journalistic accounts. Thus, Truman Capote's *In Cold Blood* and Gerold Frank's *The Boston Strangler* read like novels but are only recapitulations of facts familiar to any careful newspaper reader. Some critics pointed out that John Bartlow Martin did it better a generation ago in *Why Did They*

Kill? an account of multiple murders in southern Michigan. All these authors and others, of course, did additional research, as would any reporter assigned to do a weekend roundup.

There is nothing new about writers drawing on newspaper stories for plot material. Many a great novel has been a thinly disguised account of real people and real events, and some libel suits have resulted as a consequence. Robert Penn Warren's *All the King's Men* was a fairly accurate biography of Huey Long. Theodore Dreiser's *An American Tragedy* was a byproduct of his reportorial coverage of a murder trial; he changed the name of the murderer from Chester Gillette to Clyde Griffiths and similarly camouflaged others. Orson Welles "did" William Randolph Hearst in *Citizen Kane*. The testimony in *Inherit the Wind* is verbatim from the Scopes trial where the rival attorneys were William Jennings Bryan and Clarence Darrow, not Matthew Harrison Brady and Henry Drummond as in the play.

So, even though not new, the term "New Journalism" meant a system of fact gathering and a style of writing suitable for certain magazines and novels but hardly applicable to everyday newspaper reporting. Furthermore, Tom Wolfe, Jimmy Breslin, Gay Talese and the other modern self-styled new journalists had plenty of counterparts in the past among newspaper feature and special writers and columnists. Youngsters impressed by their writings will be dumfounded if they dig into the files and read many masterly descriptive and detailed, accounts—eyewitness and imaginative both—by past masters such as Meyer Levin, Meyer Berger, James O'Donnell Bennett, Bob Casey, Ben Hecht, Howard Vincent O'Brien, Irvin S. Cobb, Heywood Broun, Simeon Strunsky and scores and scores of others. They practiced New Journalism a generation or more before the name was invented and mostly they did it better.

ACTIVISM AND ADVOCACY

Because of the furor over New Journalism, the sixth edition of this book appeared two years earlier than originally planned. Most prestigious of the reports and articles warning against contemporary trends in journalism, or at least the rebelliousness of young staff members, was a 17-page report, *Activism and Advocacy*, prepared for the Associated Press Managing Editors by Malcolm F. Mallette of the American Press Institute. It defines activism and advocacy as a philosophy but unfortunately includes no examples of news writing which have been affected by it. Nor does it mention any newspaper or newspaperman converted to it. Nevertheless, the report views with strong alarm what Paul A. Poorman of the Detroit *News* says is "an articulate trend," what Ed Heins of the Des Moines *Register* and *Tribune* believes is "becoming a strong tendency," what Joseph W. Shoquist of the Milwaukee *Journal* thinks is a "fairly strong trend" and what Robert H. Hollingsworth of the Dallas *Times-Herald* "does not like" but which he feels "is growing and growing rapidly."

This book's author wrote to all of the contributors to the APME symposium and to authors of all the most important magazine articles. Typical responses included: "I do have a problem finding examples," "Are they real? I hear too much evidence to think otherwise" and "It is highly subjective. I cannot document this statement." Not one of the alleged authorities sent an example or even named a newspaper or newspaperman as the cause of his rage.

What these and many others fear is not any revolt against traditional techniques of news reporting and writing which would upset the validity of any of the contents of this book. Rather, what disturbs the journalistic administrative status quo is a developing demand on the part of rank-and-file editorial workers that they be given at least a consultative share in policy-making. As such, the reporters' revolt is definitely "in tune with the times," and cannot be evaluated or completely understood without relating it to worldwide demands that the Establishment relent and allow minority opinions to be heard. In every field the old order is being challenged (see section on Reporter Power, pages 22–23).

Impetus to development of militancy among journalists was provided by the attitude of some newspaper managements at the time of the Democratic National Convention in Chicago in August 1968. Conservatively estimated, 100 reporters and photographers were victims of physical violence during what the report *Rights in Conflict*, submitted by Daniel Walker to the National Commission on the Causes and Prevention of Violence, called a "police riot." Belief that their superiors had failed to support them led to the organization by Chicago reporters of the Association for Working Press and the publication of a monthly, *Chicago Journalism Review*, which performed a watchdog function and presented continuous critical analysis of the performance of the journalistic media in Chicago until its demise in late 1975. Several similar publications in other cities have had to struggle to exist and few have lasted long. In several cities, reporters formed committees of one sort or another to make demands on management on matters not related to working conditions with which The Newspaper Guild is concerned. Rather, the rank-and-file discontent is almost entirely in opposition to what is considered excessive conservatism in news and editorial policies.

Although the leadership in these new ventures comes from veterans, enthusiastic support is provided by cub reporters fresh out of college. They are socially conscious and believe that most newspapers are too conservative and lackadaisical in promoting the public interest. In other words, they disagree with Spiro Agnew, who said the press is too liberal-radical; rather, they think Adlai Stevenson II was closer to the truth when he condemned the One Party Press as too conservative-reactionary. These young idealists want more investigations, not merely to uncover political and governmental crookedness but also to ferret out weaknesses in the social and economic environment.

Those who believe in the existence of a New Journalism, are referred to an address which Newbold Noyes Jr. of the Washington *Evening Star* delivered May 1, 1953, at the University of Missouri. In it Mr. Noyes advocated "impressionistic reporting," by which he meant attempts by skilled and impartial reporters to create in the reader the same feeling about an important event as the reporter had as an eyewitness of it.

Further evidence of the early origin of what passes as advanced thought today was an article, "War, Peace and Journalism," in the April 16, 1949, *Nation*. In it Thomas Sancton pleaded for "gestalt journalism," which he defined as "journalism which seeks the whole truth in any given field of politics, deeming the whole truth, or even the mere effort to discover it, greater and qualitatively different than piecemeal, selective reporting of the parts—gestalt journalism in this sense describes only what serious reporters have tried to do since writing began."

Sancton cited several news situations when "my on-the-scene notes contained, as a reporter's notes invariably do, more of the total mood and meaning . . . came closer to its 'gestalt' than their ultimate rewriting would ever have done."

Some advocates of what they call new today claim spiritual descent from the great English pamphleteers, including Daniel Defoe, Joseph Addison and Richard Steele; from the American Tom Paine; the early 20th century muckrakers such as Upton Sinclair and Lincoln Steffens, the irascible H. L. Mencken and other journalistic all-time greats and, there is no doubt, none typical of the journalists of their times. Certainly they were heretical as regards what came to be regarded as journalistically orthodox in the early part of the 20th century. None has described that development better than Newbold Noyes Jr. in the lecture already cited.

> In 1900, when my grandfather, Frank Noyes, helped found the modern Associated Press and embarked on 38 years of service as first president of that news agency, he and his associates were pretty sure they knew the answer to our question, how to tell the truth. Their answer was a thing called "objectivity." It was a very good answer, too.
>
> Up to then, newspapers had been quite personal in their approach to the news. Most reporters fancied themselves as so many 19th century Westbrook Peglers. What they wrote was vastly entertaining, but they were not nearly so concerned with telling people the truth as with telling people off. They faithfully promoted their own ends, and cudgelled their enemies with gusto, and a good time was had by all. But the truth, somehow, tended to get lost in the shuffle.
>
> The Associated Press realized at the start that it couldn't possibly cater to the opinion whims of all the different publishers receiving its service. It set out to correct the situation by instituting the principle and practice of "objective" news coverage. Gradually, as time went by, this revolutionary principle became accepted as the Number 1 item in the creed of the responsible press all over the country. It wholly changed the face of the newspaper world, and it set the pattern for a full half-century of journalistic growth and progress.
>
> The idea of objective reporting is second nature to all of us today—so much so that we have to stop and think when it comes to defining it. Fundamentally, however, to the men who first preached it, objectivity meant that the only safe thing in a newspaper—outside of the editorial page—was a fact. The reporter's

duty was to supply his readers with the cold, hard barren details of what had happened—and with nothing more. If he *did* try to give them something more, he was moving into dangerous ground—for he was interfering with the reader's right to make up his mind on the basis of the facts alone.

In the early decades of this century, in short, our responsible press operated under the theory that it was better to take a chance on *not* informing its readers than it was to take a chance on misinforming them. It tried, as we try today, to tell the public the truth. But it was afraid of trying to tell the *whole* truth. Its overriding concern was making sure that what it dispensed was *nothing* but the truth. It operated on the assumption that it simply was not feasible for a newspaper to attempt to tell the truth, the whole truth and nothing but the truth—all three at the same time.

The principle of strictly objective reporting was eminently sound. It provided an atmosphere in which the newspaper of this country could grow up out of its lusty and carefree youth into something like responsible maturity. The cult of objectivity, in other words, supplied the ground rules of a safe adolescence for American journalism.

But the day inevitably comes when an ex-adolescent must test for himself the forbidden fruits he has been taught are so dangerous. That time is hard upon us now.

The internecine debate over Objectivity vs. Interpretation ended with the recognition that the late Sen. Joseph R. McCarthy of Wisconsin was misusing the objective press to the injury of many. At that time one of those who had some eloquent last words was Elmer Davis, one of the first great radio commentators and wartime director of the Office of War Information. In an article, "News and the Whole Truth," in the August 1952 *Atlantic*, later reprinted in his book *But We Were Born Free*, Davis wrote as follows:

> But objectivity often leans over backward so far that it makes the news business merely a transmission belt for pretentious phonies. . . .
>
> There was not much objectivity in the American press through most of the nineteenth century; if a story touched on the political or economic interest for the editor or owner, it was usually written so as to make his side look good. Some papers still follow that practice, but most of them, for some decades past, have accepted the principle that they ought to try to be objective in the news columns, leaving arguments to the editorial page. Publish everything that is said on both sides of a controversial issue, and let the reader make up his mind. A noble theory; but suppose that men who talk on one side (or on both) are known to be lying to serve their own personal interest; or suppose they don't know what they are talking about. To call attention to these facts, except on the editorial page, would not, according to most newspaper practice, be objective. Yet in the complex news of today, how many readers have enough personal knowledge to distinguish fact from fiction, ignorance from knowledge, interest from partiality?
>
> This practice is perhaps not quite so prevalent now as it was twenty-five years or so ago—in the golden age of Calvin Coolidge, when it was the general opinion that things are what they seem. In those days, if the Honorable John P. Hoozis was an important person, you were likely to see him quoted at length in the newspapers, on almost any subject, with no indication that he had a

strong personal interest in getting people to believe what he said—even if the editor who printed the story happened to know it. He was an important man; he had made a statement; and it would not have been objective not to print it. We have been getting away from that dead-pan objectivity of late years—or were, till the rise of Senator McCarthy.

IMPRESSIONISTIC REPORTING

To use the terms employed by Noyes and Sancton, to be impressionistic or to achieve a gestalt or to give correctly the atmosphere or essential reality concerning a news situation is primarily a task of fact gathering. What the actual words shall be is dependent upon what needs to be written. After he cross-examined Senator Joseph R. McCarthy during the Army-McCarthy hearings, Chief Council Joseph N. Welch "went outside into the hallway where he broke down and wept," the Associated Press reported. Some managing editors objected to inclusion of this fact in the AP report. Others didn't like the statements "Stevens bowed to the demands of McCarthy," and "Many spectators in the jam-packed steaming hearing room broke into loud unchecked applause after Welch denounced McCarthy." Still others thought it was bad to report during the subsequent Senate committee hearing that Sen. Francis Case slammed down a report "with a force that scattered papers." A majority of those who expressed opinions, however, favored inclusion of such details in the interest of completeness and accuracy.

In the same edition of the APME *Red Book* in which appears the report of the discussion of the service's handling of the McCarthy hearings, there is also included a resume of other parts of the Managing Editors' conference. The first few paragraphs of one section were as follows:

> Mary Margaret McBride, AP Newsfeature columnist, stole the show and the hearts of many of the editors when she matched them quip for quip in an hour of verbal sparring touched off by her contention that it is wrong to depart-mentalize all women's news under a "woman's page" label.
>
> This widely known writer, wearing a mink stole and a colorful orchid, beamed beneath an upswept hair-do as she prodded, argued, baited and cajoled while appearing at the two-part session on Newsfeatures, directed by Roderick J. Watts, of the Houston *Chronicle*, chairman of the News-feature committee.
>
> On one occasion, Miss McBride even shouted. And the editors loved it. Some were seen to wipe tears of laughter from their eyes as their colleagues sought to match wits with Miss McBride in an unsuccessful attempt to beat her at her own game—the art of interviewing.

This obviously violated the Associated Press' own rules for proper sentence length, but everyone who read it probably caught the spirit of the occasion.

That the account includes "value" judgments there can be no doubt. The writer thought Miss McBride "prodded, argued, baited and cajoled," for instance. Quite possibly another observer might have thought she was becoming histrionic in the attempt to conceal inadequacy in the face of a barrage of questions.

The clever writer who attempts to convey his impressions of an occasion substantiates such statements as "And the editors loved it," by reporting that "Some were seen to wipe tears of laughter from their eyes." Not always, of course, is there such tangible reportable evidence available. In such cases the reporter's experience, informational background, record of past achievement and, most of all, integrity are his weapons and his readers' protection.

Warren J. Brier gives scores of examples of good impressionistic journalism in an article, "The Lively Language of the Pros: A Glimpse at their Technique," in the 1963 *Montana Journalism Review*. Typical is the following from a UPI story about the Adolph Eichmann trial:

> Hausner, a small, hawk-faced, baldheaded man in a black legal gown, faced the defendant with both hands on his hips. An angry flush appeared on Eichmann's ashen-grey cheeks as the prosecutor pressed his attack.
>
> A nerve in Eichmann's jaw twitched and he licked his lips nervously between questions. His voice rose angrily as he answered some of the more pointed questions.

In his *Nieman Reports* article (see page 91), Wallace Carroll recalled a complaint the New York *Times* received after it included the following in its account of a United States Supreme Court decision: "In a passionate and despairing dissent, Justice Hugo Black rejected the majority opinion." According to a dissatisfied reader, who identified himself as a former newspaperman, "passionate" and "despairing" are "editorial words and you can't use them in a news story." According to Carroll, who was responsible, his "betters" on the *Times* commented, "We agree." Nevertheless, Carroll responded as follows:

> It is possible that this alumnus of the A.P. in Seattle has a better "feel" for the story than we had in Washington. But before I cleared the offending passage, I read Justice Black's dissent—all 18,000 words of it. And what impressed me from beginning to end was the passionate and despairing tone. And because passion and despair are seldom encountered in a judicial opinion, I thought this was news and worthy of noting in the *Times*.

In the cases cited, typical of what happens almost daily in any newsroom, the reporters were present as eyewitnesses, with no preconceived opinions, no causes to promote, intent on subduing their personal prejudices. So they acted as impartial critical experts. Admittedly there never will exist the completely emotionless reporter, editor or reader, but in the instances cited any bias was unconscious and deliberate efforts were made to avoid it. All anybody can do is his best to be scientifically neutral.

In an article in the February 1970 *Quill*, "The Reporter as Artist: A Fourth Revolution," Dr. J. K. Hvistendahl described "truth-as-I-see-it reporting" in this way: "It is an honest attempt on the part of the reporter to bring together all the material that he can on a subject on which he has strong feelings. The article may be one sided or it may be balanced." Thus, a great deal of what up to now has been called expert investigative reporting would be classifiable under this new terminology. For example, William Braden, an expert on the subject he had investigated exhaustively, began the first of two articles for the Chicago *Sun-Times* as follows:

Cook County Jail is not so bad as recent publicity has made it out to be. It is much, much worse.

Even now, only a few people know how bad it really is.

It is evil. It is unjust. It is dangerous.

Those who know describe it as a cultural sink, a breeding ground for next summer's riots—and a deadly weapon aimed at the heart of the community.

After several more paragraphs of editorial conclusions, Braden began to produce his painstakingly gathered evidence:

There are two essential factors relating to the jail and its inmates.

1. The jail (as a building) was designed for the short-term incarceration of the most vicious and dangerous sort of criminals.

2. The vast majority of inmates do not fit that classification.

It is in the public interest to have scholarly minded journalists like Braden on the job, protecting the public interest by investigating such places as the jail. It would be utterly absurd to insist that a man of his caliber should not state his opinions after he has done his prowling in the public interest.

A type of impressionistic reporting more within the realm of the possible for the ordinary small city reporter is represented by the following example:

By Cal Turner
Evening News Staff Writer

Elizabethtown—Dick Gregory is still at it. Swift, sharp and close to the bone, he cuts the U.S. into little pieces, tidies up its heart and puts it back together. and his listeners love it.

Appearing at Elizabethtown College yesterday, he held a press conference before taking the podium. In a style ranging from instant indignation to a beguiling placidity, he shot down questions from the old and weary, the young at heart and those with no cause but to sit and listen. The acid sometimes dripped.

Coming off a long fast which had as target the nation's anemic attempt to snuff out the narcotics traffic, he stroked a bearded jaw, rolled his eyes, gestured extravagantly and pictured doomsday just around the corner.

"The country is sick," he said. "Nothing will change it until its people learn how to deal with human problems on a human level. Why today, the automobile is more important than the youth."

If the tune sounded antique, the mood he wrought wore long after the conference ended. Calling himself, a "social doctor," he looks at America's ills with a venomous glee.

"I don't like to go into my predictions of the past," he said. "And I don't like to place myself as a prophet." Lacing his thin fingers together, it was here that he ripped into the CIA (Central Intelligence Agency).

"There's a good chance of this country being overthrown by the CIA within the next 18 months," he snapped, his eyes riding to the edge of their sockets.

"And if they don't do it, you may see one of the damnedest blood baths the world has ever seen within the next five years."

Digging deeper, he emphasized this was possible because the American people just don't believe it can happen.

"The CIA doesn't have to answer to nobody," he said. "Not even the President. We just don't believe it can happen, yet the CIA goes all around the world, creating incidents, toppling governments. Why, they called off those trials about Vietnam (the massacres). They tap our phones. If America doesn't awaken, then you're going to see what this all will lead to."

Just back from Tokyo, the final lap on a world trip, Gregory said he had looked long and hard at the problems of poverty on a global scale.

[Harrisburg (Pa.) *Evening News*]

Not many, if any of the so-called straight news stories about the Yuba City mass murders came so close to giving the reader the feeling of the tragedy as the following story by Douglas E. Kneeland in the June 1, 1971, New York *Times*, especially paragraphs 3, 4 and 5.

By Douglas E. Kneeland
Special to The New York Times

Marysville, Calif., May 31—Nobody much missed the faceless men who disappeared from Lower D. and nobody much mourns them now as their hacked up bodies are dug from the soft loam of peach orchards in the outskirts of Yuba City across the Feather River from here.

More than 20 of them dropped out of sight in the last two months from the four- or five-block Skid Row here that is anchored by the lower end of D. Street. Hardly anybody noticed. Perhaps because if the men existed at all in the minds of Marysville and Yuba City, they were already lost, already dead.

They were the men New Yorkers stare hard not to see on the side streets off Times Square. The men Chicagoans brush by on Division Street. The men San Franciscans avoid in the Mission district.

The weaving, tattered men with the red eyes and the stubbly beards. The ageless men, all old beyond their years. The thousands and thousands—nobody knows how many—who drift endlessly, aimlessly across the underside of America. The men who are as invisible in the small towns and cities as they are in the big ones.

Every day they turn up dead in the dank doorways of the cities, behind a shabby village saloon, beside a lonely railroad track.

It took a lot of them dead in one place to make anyone notice much at all. But 23 bodies have been dug from the orchard graves during an investigation led by Sheriff Roy D. Whiteaker, and Juan V. Corona, a 37-year-old farm labor contractor with a history of mental illness, is being held on murder charges.

Now the nation is watching and asking how so many could have been so forgotten. . . .

This is great writing, and it certainly is not in accordance with the objectivity rules of the Associated Press of bygone days. To repeat, however, it is not new. Rather, it is reminiscent of much of what came 25 to 50 years ago from the newspaper reportorial pens of such journalistic greats as Ben Hecht, Theodore Dreiser, Stephen Crane, Meyer Berger, Vincent Sheean, Ernest

Hemingway, Heywood Broun and many others. Much of the complaint against the so-called new or activist or whatever-you-want-to-call-it journalism today is, as always, from those who fear exposure of the facts which the probing and sensitive newsgatherers describe.

Definitely in the old tradition was the following column by Robert T. Smith in the Minneapolis *Tribune*.

A scene at a Minneapolis Red Owl supermarket. . . .

The small slightly-built boy of about 7 was doing the shopping for his mother and little sister. The Red Owl check-out clerk said the boy doesn't have a father and his mother works.

He had put several items in his cart, but he couldn't read part of the note his mother had given him. He got to the check-out counter and there was a long line behind him.

"Could you read this for me?" he asked the young girl clerk.

There were some grumbles from those waiting behind the boy. But the clerk studied the note a minute and said the only thing the boy didn't have were three small turkey pot pies.

The boy looked a little bewildered.

"C'mon," said the clerk and she took him to the aisle and found the pies.

The lineup became more disgruntled. Some left and got into other lines. Their places were taken by other shoppers.

"Well, for heaven's sakes," said one middle-aged woman.

"You'd think we had nothing to do but stand in lines all day," said an irritated man.

An elderly woman wearing a blue stocking cap waited patiently. She had what you often see in the carts of the elderly; a half pound of hamburger, not ground beef; a small loaf of day-old bread, a small can of applesauce and a bag of the kind of coffee you grind yourself.

There were bare leather streaks on the fur collar of her coat. There was a hole in the finger of one of her mittens.

When the clerk and the auburn-haired boy returned, a thin, nervous woman in line said: "Maybe now we can get some service here." She pushed her cart up against the man in front of her.

The clerk totaled the boy's groceries and presented him with the bill. He reached into his jacket pocket and came up with nothing.

"What now?" asked a man.

The boy blushed and he searched other pockets. Others left the line. But with newcomers the line remained about the same.

From his right rear pants pocket the boy found the food stamps. He smiled and handed them to the clerk.

"I'm sorry," said the clerk, "but you're a dollar seventy-three cents short."

"This could go on forever," said the middle-aged woman. The boy blushed again and was frightened. He wouldn't look at anybody.

"That's all I've got," he said. "And my mother's not home yet from work."

A further exodus from the line. A man and woman tangled their carts as they moved to another check-out counter.

The elderly woman with the blue stocking cap left her cart and went forward to the young clerk and the boy.

"Give him his groceries and I'll take care of it," she said.

The boy smiled and in a few minutes was out of the door. At 7, you don't always remember to say thank you. Especially when you want to hurry away from something.

When it was the elderly woman's turn to check out, she also paid the $1.73 for the boy. With her food stamps.

An example of what those who believe in the existence of New Journalism and/or the recency of activism and advocacy in newspapering would find in the files of yesteryear is this story from the St. Louis *Post-Dispatch* for July 21, 1925, under the by-line of Paul Y. Anderson:

A memorable scene was enacted yesterday afternoon beneath the great maples that canopy the yard of the Rhea County Courthouse. On a platform, where was convened the trial of John T. Scopes, Clarence Darrow placed William Jennings Bryan on the witness stand, and what followed was an event in the intellectual history of the world. It was magnificent and tragic, stirring and pathetic, and above all it was pervaded by the atmosphere of grandeur which befitted the death grapple between two great ideas.

Two old men, one eloquent, magnetic and passionate, the other cold, impassive and philosophical, met as the champions of these ideas and as remorselessly as the jaws of a rock crusher under the crumbling mass of limestone, one of these old men caught and ground the other between his massive erudition and his ruthless logic. Let there be no doubt about that. Bryan was broken, if ever a man was broken. Darrow never spared him. It was masterly, but it was pitiful.

It was profoundly moving. To see this wonderful man, for after all, he was wonderful, this man whose silver voice and majestic mien had stirred millions, to see him humbled and humiliated before the vast crowd which had come to adore him was sheer tragedy, nothing less.

SATURATION REPORTING

Saturation reporting is the name coined by Tom Wolfe to designate the type of fact finding engaged in by a number of magazine article and book authors who use the literary techniques of fiction writers in producing nonfiction. *The New Yorker*, *Esquire* and *New York* magazines were pioneers in encouraging such writers as Jimmy Breslin, Gay Talese, Norman Mailer, Truman Capote and, of course, Tom Wolfe.

According to Wolfe, saturation reporting is much harder than traditional journalistic interviewing. He writes:

You are not after just facts. The basic units of reporting are no longer who-what-when-where-how and why but whole scenes and stretches of dialogue. The New Journalism involves a depth of reporting and an attention to the most minute facts and details that most newspapermen, even the most experienced, have never dreamed of. To pull it off you casually have to stay with the people you are writing about for long stretches. You may have to stay with them days, weeks, even months—long enough so that you are actually there when revealing scenes take place in their lives. You have to constantly be on the alert for chance remarks, odd details, quirks, curios, anything that may serve to bring a scene alive when you're writing. There is no formula for it. It never gets easier just because you've done it before.

Capote did a prodigious amount of journalistic-type research as he was not an eyewitness to the incidents described in *In Cold Blood*. Nor was Norman Mailer's *Of a Fire on the Moon*, about the Apollo XI flight, written from firsthand observation. On the other hand, *Miami and the Siege of Chicago* was based on Mailer's personal experiences during the 1968 conventions.

The popularity of so-called New Journalism received a jolt with exposes that some or the character or personality sketches were composites, including the supposed true life story of a prostitute, Redpants, in *New York* and an article about two burglars in *Philadelphia Magazine*.

Today several columnists and roving reporters are objects of envy by journalism students and young reporters. Among the most prominent are Nicholas von Hoffman, Washington *Post*, Tom Fitzpatrick, Chicago *Sun-Times*, and Mike Royko, Chicago *Daily News*. The following piece by Bob Greens of the Chicago *Sun-Times*, his favorite, illustrates the freedom that the experienced journalistic expert enjoys in "giving feeling" regarding an important assignment.

Five in the family, dead. It happened up there, in that red-brick, ranch-style house. The neighbors are starting to come around. Ropes in the neighborhood, blocking off the lawns. Strange afternoon in Park Ridge. The chat is of multiple murders.

"Is Lynda one of them?" The questioner is Gayle Kreft. Gayle is 15, a freshman at Maine Twp. East High School. Gayle has just walked over from her own house, and she is wearing faded jeans and a denim jacket with a silver star design on the back. "Lynda's a weird one,'" Gayle says present tense. "She's not like the rest of us, you know? We like to party every night. She just sits at home. She's a tomboy. She dresses real straight."

There is a gas-powered air pump clattering outside the front door of the death house, part of the firemen's equipment. The visitors automatically raise their voices to talk above the machine sound. They are waiting to see some bodies.

". . . Arms tied behind her," the coroner's man is saying, standing in the driveway of the death house. He is giving out the early details of the death of the Raymond A. Fuchs family, and his voice heightens and then disappears, leaving grotesque phrases in the air. ". . . tied to a sink in the basement," the coroner's man says, ". . . knife found floating in the water." The children of the neighborhood press close, trying to get some of this for themselves. ". . . An animal found dead, too," the coroner's man says.

No tears for the Fuchs family. Not this afternoon, outside the death house. It is growing chilly, and the drizzle is turning into a hard rain, but the crowd does not diminish. Not mourners, not yet. Five dead in Park Ridge, and it provides an eerie fascination to break the quiet of the last days of spring. The dark green trees in front of the house sag with the weight of the droplets, and the curious visitors stare, dry-eyed.

"I hardly ever saw him, except when he was walking their dog," Debi Gustafson says. Debi is 18, wearing a halter top, and standing in the garage of her house, just down the block from the death house. "I'm talking about Jeff," she says. "He was the one who was my age. He was real smart. He never did anything. No class in the way he dressed, you know what I mean? I don't even hang out around Park Ridge, myself. My friends are in the city."

The bodies are still inside the house, the four of them that are left. One—the one they found upstairs—was taken away hours ago. But the final four—the four that were wrapped in blankets, down in the basement, with the heads and faces covered with towels—they still have to be carried out. An ambulance is waiting in the driveway. In the yard, against the trunk of one of the Fuchs' trees, an empty Dunkin' Donuts carton brims over with coffee and Coca-Cola cups and tissue-paper doughnut wrappers, the flotsam of the people come to call on the afternoon of death.

"Remember how Jeff always carried a briefcase in school?" says a boy pressing against the police ropes.

"Weird," says a friend.

The bodies are coming through the garage, carried by firemen and policemen, moving with deliberation, a slow-motion movie. The first body is in a long, heavy, shiny green bag. The men in uniform turn sideways so that they can edge between the cars in the garage, a gray Oldsmobile and a gold Dodge, consecutive license plates, NH2527 and NH2528. The bag is shoved into the back of the red and white ambulance. Now the second body, in a second green bag. The ambulance pulls noiselessly away. Two bodies still left.

"Help me, I think I'm fallin', in love with you. . . ," Joni Mitchell sings, her voice lifting tinnily out of a transistor radio carried by a boy on a bicycle with raised handlebars.

". . . And I don't know why they can't tell us how long the bodies have been dead," a reporter complains mildly. "They should know just by the odor. I know plenty of firemen who can come close to getting it exactly, just from their experience."

The men from the board-up company have arrived, and they are banging big plywood sheets over the front windows, where the firemen had knocked out the panes to clear the smoke. As the workmen construct the temporary closure, the ambulance returns. Time for the final bodies.

These two are brought out in a hurry, this time in bags of black vinyl-like material. They are placed in the ambulance one immediately after the other, and then they are gone, the last of the Fuchs family taken from their home.

Gayle Kreft is still watching. "It's kind of a neat day," she says. "Nothing like this ever happens around here. Another block and it could have been us." Next fall she will be a sophomore. Quiet horror on a strange suburban afternoon. . . .

The so-called underground or alternative press presumably encourages this sort of writing, but study of the contents of a representative sample hardly indicates that it thrives on literary excellence. Rather, it investigates and exposes and gives coverage to situations and activities which the standard press minimizes or ignores. Writers enjoy almost complete latitude to categorize any of it as related to the medium in which it appears. The only certain characterization of it is that it is richly experimental.

HUMANISTIC REPORTING

Since the fall of 1968 the School of Communications at the University of Washington has been conducting a program in humanistic newswriting for both students and professional newspapermen, According to Prof. Alex S. Edelstein, program director, humanistic reporting "is that which is concerned with the impact of news on the individual. It is individualized and personalized, in the hope that the reader will see common threads of experience between his own life and that of another individual."

Sue Hutchison, an environmental reporter for the Seattle *Post-Intelligencer*, who participated, devised the following examples to illustrate the difference between conventional reporting and humanistic writing. These are three possible leads to the same story:

> The City Planning Commission yesterday recommended addition of an RM 1600 zoning classification to the Seattle Zoning Ordinance.

> Additional land will be opened up for apartment house and townhouse development if the city adopts a recommendation made yesterday by its planning committee.

> It may soon be possible for a poor family to slowly buy an apartment with enough room to seem like a home.

The third lead is obviously humanistic and, as the reader can determine by referring to the section "Consequence" (page 99) in Chapter 4, Playing Up the Feature, of this book, it is good old-fashioned orthodox interpretative reporting. Writes Dr. William Ames, Professor Edelstein's colleague: "I think I would agree with you that what we are really talking about is a kind of depth interpretation."

What distinguishes humanistic reporting and writing is the viewpoint of the reporter. As Professor Edelstein puts it: "It is not the objectively determined nor the qualitatively assessed elements of anything that make it humanistic but—speaking now in terms of the reporter—what the reporter can see in it as being meaningful to others. . . . We are not concerned with titillating people. We are concerned with giving people insight into their own lives."

INVESTIGATIVE REPORTING

All reporting is investigative as the newsgatherer seeks facts. Prof. Jay Jensen of the University of Illinois says it's "just old fashioned, traditional expose stuff, uncovering what is being covered up, revealing what is being hidden, nailing down lies that have been told, etc.," but *Newsday* came closer to what those who use the term mean: "uncovering something somebody wants to keep secret."

Any newspaper with standing in its community is constantly being importuned to "look into" this or that, which usually means to uncover facts which it allegedly is in the public interest be known but which someone is attempting to conceal. Annoying and time consuming as it may become to observe the rule, it is unsafe to ignore tipsters, no matter how unreliable or crackpot they may seem to be. Maybe the policeman whose neighbor cannot understand how he is able to afford an expensive car *did* inherit a large sum of money. On the other hand, his affluence may be the clue to scandal involving others as well as himself.

No special attributes are required of the investigative reporter except a sharp inquisitive mind and familiarity with the area of his investigation. The investigative reporter seldom plays detective in the sense of shadowing persons. Rather, his quest more often takes him to public records where he uncovers information about which to query interviewees. In print, these facts usually speak for themselves.

Brit Hume, one of Jack Anderson's investigative reporters, wrote in *Inside Story:* "Investigative reporting is, much of the time, tedious and discouraging work. An investigative reporter's job is to establish the facts that those in power want most to keep hidden. There is no way to compel answers to embarrassing questions, no subpoena power. Countless stories which a reporter may suspect strongly are true must be abandoned because there is no way to verify them."

Rule No. 1 for the investigative reporter: try to find yourself a Deep Throat as did Bernstein and Woodward.

Stunts

Often the best, perhaps the only, way to investigate a situation is from the inside. Edgar May of the Buffalo *Evening News* won a Pulitzer prize for his series of articles after working for three months as a caseworker for the Eric County Department of Social Welfare. Ted Smart of the Chicago *Daily News* won several citations for his expose of conditions in the Chicago Bridewell to which he got himself committed as a common drunk. Several official investigations resulted after Edward Williams, Milwaukee *Journal* reporter, spent ten days in the House of Correction posing as a vagrant. By becoming an applicant himself, Sam Washington of the Chicago *Sun-Times* exposed an examiner who was soliciting bribes from students taking a General Educational Development Test.

When William Jones, Chicago *Tribune* reporter, since then promoted to managing editor for news, heard unconfirmed reports alleging that Chicago police were bribed to steer hospital call cases to private ambulance companies, he thought it worthwhile following up. So he trained as a first-aid man and got a job as an ambulance driver. The results: a six-part expose of official collusion; a grand jury that handed up 16 indictments; and a Pulitzer prize for special local reporting for Jones.

For journalism students Jones has this advice: "If you really want to make your time count in this business, then set your sights on becoming an investigative reporter" who, he explains, does more than just report the news. "Thousands of press agents in the public and private sector are now doing that for us. It is up to the investigative reporter and his editors to double back frequently and find out which of the glorious predictions have failed through corruption, bungling or influence peddling. To do it you must know your target. If you plan to zero in on the failure of a city building department to enforce housing codes, for example, you must know as much or more about the agency as those who claim they run it. Be prepared to push, push, push because anybody of any influence can erect barriers or slam a door at a moment's notice.

"Consider the fact that some of the best investigative reporting began with a single complaint from a single voiceless citizen who sought help from a newspaper that was willing to dig out the facts. This kind of reporting is what newspapering is all about."

Other reporters have obtained employment as guards or attendants in prisons, mental hospitals and other public institutions. The existence of illegal gambling has been exposed by investigative reporters who were supplied with money and told to find bookmakers with whom to place bets. Because of the growing complaint by teachers that students are unruly, reporters with the proper credentials have obtained teaching positions or have acted as substitutes in the classroom to observe firsthand.

The opportunities for such "undercover" journalism are boundless. Usually, some properly qualified official, as a judge or social worker, is "in" on the stunt, often to legalize it and, in any case, to soften adverse criticisms of entrapment or other unethical conduct. Certainly the responsibility is great not to yield to the temptation to merely "make a case" in the interest of a sensational story. It is easy to find that for which one earnestly is looking. The reporter and newspaper are vulnerable unless the highest principles of ethical journalism are observed.

Crusading; Muckraking

Probably no book since Lincoln Steffens' *Autobiography* inspired more cub reporters than did *All the President's Men* in which Carl Bernstein and Bob Woodward revealed how they painstakingly unraveled the Watergate scandals to win a Pulitzer prize.

Many other post-World War II reportorial exploits have proved inspiring. Seymour Hersh, then with the Dispatch News Service, won a Pulitzer prize for uncovering the facts about the Mylai massacre; Neil Sheehan of the New York *Times* was similarly honored for his articles based on the Pentagon Papers which it took a United States Supreme Court decision to publish. Jack Anderson won his Pulitzer for exposing official Washington hypocrisy during the Pakistani-Indian war. With many other exposes to his credit, Anderson ranks with Ralph Nader as the outstanding contemporary crusader. Nader won a $425,000 court judgment against General Motors which hired private investigators to harass him after his iconoclastic *Unsafe at Any Speed* was published. Nader is the only muckraker ever to institutionalize himself. His organizations include Center for the Study of Responsive Law, Public Interest Research Group, Corporate Accountability Research Study, Public Citizen Inc. and many others.

Activist-minded reporters, young and old, favor more newspaper initiative in emulation of Anderson and Nader, the late Rachel Carson whose *Silent Spring* inspired much of the interest in threats to the environment and Vance Packard whose *Hidden Persuaders* put advertisers on guard.

Together with many books by foreign correspondents who have set the record straight concerning episodes in recent American foreign policy, these and similar crusading efforts make the present outshine the Era of the Muckrakers, when a small coterie of magazine article writers exposed corruption in business and government. Outstanding examples of their work were *The Shame of the Cities*, by Lincoln Steffens; *The Jungle*, a novel about Chicago's stockyards by Upton Sinclair which led to the first pure food and drug act; Ida Tarbell's history of the Standard Oil Co. and many magazine series and books by Ray Stannard Baker, David Graham Phillips, Charles Edward Russell and others.

Although President Theodore Roosevelt considered muckraking as opprobrious term when he adapted it from John Bunyan's *Pilgrim's Progress* to apply to enterprising journalists, the first decade of the 20th century is today regarded as a "golden period" of public service journalism. Unquestionably the achievements of the press in exposing the Watergate and related scandals and American atrocities in Vietnam will be remembered similarly.

Many newspapers and magazines organized special staffs to engage in investigative reporting during the '60s and '70s. In 1966 the newly created Special Assignment Team of the Washington Associated Press was called "the most significant innovation in news coverage ever undertaken by the association." A decade later the original team of eleven had been cut more than in half but the investigative viewpoint had permeated the entire staff. Freed of everyday duties Brooks Jacobson became an expert on campaign finance corruption. He broke stories on illegal contributions to Wilbur Mills' bid for the presidency in 1972, on illegal dairy contributions before 1972 and on devices for concealing the origin of contributions by "laundering" the money through special committees.

One participant in the AP effort explained how investigative reporting works:

> Our assignment is to dig out, one way or another, the wealth of important, significant information that your readers must have if they are to comprehend the incredible complexity that is the federal government. . . . What we're talking about, investigative reporting, is both the basis and the only justification for the constitutional guarantee of a free press.

A September 1969 letter to members summarized some of the stories up to that time.

—A five-part series on the nation's nursing homes. The recipients of a billion-dollar bonanza through the federal medicaid and medicare programs. The series reported that most nursing homes have made vast improvements in the past decade, but that problems linger. Many of the nation's million nursing home patients haven't seen a doctor in months; restraining straps and drugs often are substituted for psychiatric care; and fraud feeds on the federal dollar. The series prompted a Senate committee chairman to call hearings on the subject.

—Government records so secret that even Congress hasn't seen them list plush medicare payments to doctors across the nation. Two famed Houston heart surgeons receive $200,000 apiece, and turn the money over to a medical school fund. One Florida osteopath, who received a quarter-million-dollars in payments, explains: "I work hard."

—Key officials of the Civil Aeronautics Board accept free trips to Europe, Africa and the Bahamas. The tab for their air fare is picked up by an airline company—one of those which the CAB regulates.

And many more of the same sort.

It's nice work if you can get it, an exciting and self-satisfying way to earn a living.

PART TWO

HANDLING IMPORTANT ASSIGNMENTS

THE REWARDS OF A REPORTER

By Philip Kinsley, Chicago *Daily Tribune*

The last fifty years have brought so much of invention, discovery, and knowledge regarding man and his universe that we have not had time to assimilate the new ideas. Here lies a unique opportunity for the reporter, one which emphasizes the need of all the so-called education that he can muster. Where human activities tend to become more and more specialized, it needs someone to look over the fence and see what is going on in the next yard and tell his neighbors about it. In scientific conventions, I have noticed, the terminology of specialists becomes so abstruse that one group does not know what the other is talking about. The reporter should have just enough education to understand and appreciate these groups, and yet not too much to become warped.

It would be impossible to draw a line here. People never know when they are insane or their judgment is bad. It is safe to say that we can never know enough. Our blind sides correspond with those of this insect and lower animal world.

In the course of thirty years I have probably written five million words about human affairs, living men and living problems. It may be mere rationalization for not having gone into something more important, but I cannot think of a greater responsibility than that of historian of current events. The words may be leaden or winged, but they certainly carry their reactions into future events of some sort. The ripples widen and touch far shores. I think that if I should meet de Lawd walking in some green pastures here that he would ask: "Did you tell the truth?" I might say, "Yes, Lawd, as I saw it," and he would say, "Go and learn some more."

Out of all this medley of good, bad and indifferent, I must conclude with John Burroughs in his Sundowm Papers that the only fruit I can see is in fairer flowers, or a higher type of mind and life that follows in this world and to which our lives may contribute. This valley with its rocks and streams and trees seems eternal, but we know that it is constantly changing and shifting its component parts under major laws of cause and effect. The same is true of the human scene but where the mind enters this change may have a measure of direction. Beyond this we need not know.

The foregoing was extracted from the banquet speech at the national convention of Sigma Delta Chi Nov. 17, 1938, at the University of Illinois. Regardless of the changes that have occurred in methods of newspaper production and distribution, it is as pertinent today as it was more than four decades ago, and it is likely to continue to be so for another half century.

11

PERSONS AND PERSONALTIES

Everyone likes to see his name or that of a friend or acquaintance in print. This is as true of the city dweller as of anyone who resides in a small town or on a farm. Large newspapers do not refrain from publishing more items concerning births, newcomers to the community, trips, parties, engagements, weddings, illnesses and deaths because they fail to recognize the reader interest in such events but merely because of lack of space. Gossip among urbanites still largely concerns such occurrences as they involve relatives, friends and acquaintances. Community newspapers within the large cities and suburban newspapers are capitalizing increasingly on the metropolitan press' inability any longer to devote much space to such news.

GOSSIP IS NEWS

The Personal Element

In the country weekly, serving a community in which acquaintanceships are proportionately greater, the "personals" column never has ceased to be the chief reader attention-getter. Larger papers are using more and more news briefs after a short period during which there was a feeling that these were "hickish." Today, small- and medium-sized newspapers are ceasing in the attempt to emulate their metropolitan betters and are concerned with how to serve better the needs of their own readers. Reader interest in gossip about "big shots" in the national field having been proved through the popular reception of syndicated columns from New York, Washington and Hollywood, local "It Happened in—," "Heard about—" and similar columns are growing in frequency.

Sources of Brevities

Haunting the waiting rooms of railroad and bus stations, airports, hotel lobbies, clubrooms, floral shops and delicatessen stores and stopping to chat with friends on street corners or at their places of business still are excellent "breaking in" for the cub reporter. Not only does he receive items or tips for the "local happenings" or "news in brief" column but also, while ostensibly in search for such comparatively trivial information he comes across numerous first-rate stories.

Typical of the one-paragraph personals which the small city reporter may obtain just by "hanging around" or by telephone conversations with his friends are the following:

> Mrs. Edwin P. Morrow of Washington, D.C., is visiting at the home of her son, Charles R. Morrow, 636 Sherman avenue. Mrs. Morrow is the widow of the late Edwin P. Morrow, former governor of Kentucky.

> Miss Eva Rathbone entertained her fellow members in the Puella Sunday school class of First Presbyterian church at dinner Friday night at her home, 133 N. Prairie avenue. During the evening, the girls worked on patch quilts to be distributed by the Women's Missionary society of the church.

> Five Milltown students at Augustana college will spend the Thanksgiving weekend with their parents here. They are . . . .

Some papers which do not have a special column for short items of this sort use them as fillers; others restrict their use to the society page or its equivalent. In the country and rural town weeklies such items concern purchases of new farm equipment, planting and harvesting, unusual crops and the like. City dwellers may laugh at such news, but if they have moved to the city from the country or a small place, it is what they look for when the home-town paper arrives each week. And it's what they want to know about their friends in the big city.

The value of such tipsters to large city dailies has diminished somewhat as professional press agents deluge them with tidbits to be used mostly in gossip columns whose conductors no longer have to spend so much time as a generation ago in night clubs, locker rooms, backstage and similar places. Celebrities compete for attention and favorable mention and some column conductors are as famous as those of whom they write.

Faults to Avoid

The three most serious errors to avoid in writing short personals or brevities are (1) underwriting, (2) overwriting, (3) stylistic banality.

Underwriting means writing as a brief what should have been a longer news or feature story, or not getting all the essentials into the brevity itself. The properly written personal really is a news lead. As such, it is good if it fulfills the requirements of a good lead and bad if it doesn't. Note how the following barren brevities might have been made more nearly complete and interesting while still remaining brevities:

Insufficient	Insufficient
A. L. Scobey, 1434 Ellis street, has returned from a two-week trip to San Francisco.	Mr. and Mrs. Edward L. Park-house, 683 Pulliam avenue, entertained 16 guests Monday night at a theater party.

Sufficient	Sufficient
A. L. Scobey, 1434 Ellis street, returned today from San Francisco with the prize given the delegate traveling the farthest distance to attend the annual convention of the Fraternal Order of Leopards there last week. Mr. Scobey represented the local Leopards lodge of which he is commander. The prize was a traveling bag.	To celebrate their 25th wedding anniversary, Mr. and Mrs. Edward L. Parkhouse, 683 Pulliam avenue, entertained 16 guests Monday night at a theater party. Formerly it was believed the Parkhouses had been married only 15 years, but they chose this belated occasion to reveal that they had been secretly wed for ten years before making an announcement.

It easily can be imagined how either of these, especially the second, could have been elaborated into a much longer story with considerable reader interest. Unfortunately, it is not presumptuous to imagine a beginning reporter's getting no more than the original items cited. State or county editors often despair because of the inability of rural correspondents to sense news values. Cub reporters may be able to pick important names out of hotel registers but they may miss the fact that the out-of-town visitor listed inconspicuously among those "in town for the day" is negotiating with the directors of a bank for its purchase, consulting with Chamber of Commerce officials about the establishment of a new industry or applying for a position in the local schools or for the pastorate of a local church. The fault obviously is under-reporting.

Overwriting, on the other hand, means going to the opposite extreme of including irrelevant and unimportant details of little or no interest even to residents of a small community. Such padding may be for the purpose of pleasing a friend or an advertiser, but too much of it alienates more general readers than it attracts. It should be paid for at regular advertising rates.

Employment of an agronomist of high repute by the Ohio Sugar company is an innovation that will meet hearty appreciation by Henry county farmers.

Mr. McLaughlin, an O.S.U. graduate, who has had supervision of the State Experiment station at Holgate for the past six years, and prior to that gained valuable experience at the Wooster experiment station, will have charge of this new department beginning Jan. 1.

Mr. McLaughlin's advice to farmers and beet growers will be of incalculable benefit and every farmer is urged to avail himself of his wise counsel. There are so many perplexing problems that confront the farmer that no doubt this new department will be most heartily welcomed. Adaptability of the different Henry county soils to the various crops is one thing where Mr. McLaughlin's knowledge of agronomy will serve the farmer who seeks his advice most beneficially.

While Mr. McLaughlin may, to a certain degree, specialize in beet culture, he is equally well informed on every phase of agriculture and his advice is free for the asking. The Ohio Sugar company is maintaining this almost solely for the benefit of growers and it hopes every farmer will avail himself of this service which is proffered free.

The most frequent criticism of personals, as used in country weeklies and small-town newspapers, is excessive informality and maudlin rhetoric. A chatty column is one thing; a banal one is another. Too much opinion, the extension of too many good wishes and insipid predictions are sickening to even the uneducated reader, although it is a remarkable fact that many persons who submit unsolicited personal items to large city papers often write them in such a manner. The following illustrative examples of misdirected energy were taken from small-town newspapers:

W. P. Nelson is again on the job at the bank following a seige with chicken pox. Walt had a real mixup with his "kid" disease and he says he was sure sick. Aside from being "well marked" he is okay.

The new band leader, Don Walters, put his Hubbard group through its paces last Saturday and again Tuesday and Wednesday of this week. The youngsters are all eager and ready to go to Iowa City this coming Saturday and do themselves and their community proud. Everything points to a good chance for them to come through with shining colors. The group expects to leave town about 7 o'clock in the morning so as to give the performers time to get some of the kinks from riding out of their system.

So let's cheer them on with three big rahs. All right, here we go— rah! Rah! RAH!

We extend congratulations to Mr. and Mrs. Dave Heden, who were recently united in marriage. We are not acquainted with the groom, but his bride, formerly Agnes Attleson, is well known here as this was her former home though she has been working in Chicago for several years. She has hosts of friends who wish her much joy, for she was a very nice young lady. They expect to make their home in Chicago, where the groom has employment.

TYPES OF PERSONAL NEWS

Births

A generation ago it was considered risque or peephole journalism for Walter Winchell to hint at impending "blessed events" among notables.

Today readers expect their gossip columnists to speculate on whether prominent prospective parents intend to marry. Modern reporters are not handicapped by squeamish taboos, but straight news items of births may be crowded off the page by full-length articles on the merits of this or that birth control pill or contraceptive device, the ethics of abortion or some such subject. Still, babies continue to be created in the same old way and for the routine birth notice, involving ordinary people, the reporter should obtain

1. Names and address of parents.
2. Time and place of birth.
3. Weight of the baby.
4. Sex of the baby.
5. The name, if chosen.

The mother's maiden name may be included if she has not been married more than a few years, if the couple is living in another city and the girl's married name is unfamiliar locally or if she uses her birth name either professionally or generally. If the date of the marriage is mentioned, care must be taken to give it correctly. Libel suits have resulted from mistakes of this sort.

Since all parents supposedly are " proud," that fact is of no news value. And it never has been proved scientifically that newly born babies bounce. A baby's rosy cheeks, lusty lungs and dimpled chin may be taken for granted. " Daughter" or "son" is better than "baby girl" or "baby boy." Do not use "cherub" or "the new arrival to bless the home" or the like.

The name of the attending physician should not be included in a birth notice, or, in fact, in any story of illness or death. This rule is broken in the case of a person of great prominence and in stories in which the physician himself plays a part, as a participant in an accident, etc. Ordinarily, however, the name of the physician is left out, frequently at the request of the local medical society.

Whether the fact that "mother and baby are both doing nicely" is to be included probably is debatable. Ordinarily, however, it seems as though good health should be assumed; if either child or mother is in danger that fact may be included. Likewise, the number, names and ages of other children of the parents of a newly born baby may or may not be mentioned.

> Mr. and Mrs. Ralph Elsasser, 711 Renrose ave., became the parents of a daughter in Swedish-American hospital on Monday. Named Marie Lynette, the infant weighed 5 pounds, 5 ounces at birth. She joins a brother, Terry Lee, 12; and a sister, Vicki Lynn, 8. [Rockford *Star*]

> Mr. and Mrs. Jimmie Collins, Stonington, welcomed their first child, a son, at 4:56 (CST) o'clock Friday night in the St. Vincent Memorial Hospital. He weighed 6 pounds and 6 ounces. The mother is the former Anna Marie Jones. [Taylorville (Ill.) *Breeze-Courier*]

A frequent temptation to a beat reporter is to turn in a story telling of how some new father on his beat acted or announced the event to his coworkers. Such items must be adroitly handled to avoid the common fault of banality.

> It was cigars for everybody today in the office of Mitchell C. Robin, clerk of the Probate court. He explained that his wife, Mrs. Dorothy Robin, had given birth to their first child, a girl, at the Michael Reese hospital.

> Menlo Park, Calif.—(AP)—Sammy Yates showed up in the eighth grade at Central school with a cigar box.
> He opened it and passed out all-day suckers, explaining: "I'm a brother."
> [Chicago *Daily News*]

Medical treatment of sterility has resulted in a considerable increase in multiple births so that the arrival of quintuplets is no longer the story of the year. Nevertheless, they as well as quadruplets, triplets and twins still are newsworthy. Unusual weight or size, physical deformity or the circumstances under which birth took place may elevate the event above the level of the routine birth notice, as was the case in each of the following stories:

> Wenatchee, Wash.—(UP)—Mr. and Mrs. W. E. Robinson of Entiat Valley claim to be parents of the first baby born in an auto trailer in the Pacific northwest. A daugher, Kay, was born to them in March.

> The fire department ambulance crew in charge of Lieut. Irvin Martin aided the stork early Wednesday and a baby was presented to Mrs. Callie Burns, 21, 1216 Freeman avenue. Mother and infant were then taken to the general hospital.

Some newspapers "play" births more prominently than others. One way is to obtain pictures of the newly born, together with short feature stories in which source of the name, brothers and sisters, date of birth or some feature angle may be emphasized. The following is a typical entry from such a column:

> Even if she is a girl, the first child of Mr. and Mrs. William Clifford Richards Jr., 1415 Ashland avenue, was named for her father and is called Billie Mae. Her second name is the first name of her maternal grandmother. Weighing 8 pounds 14 ounces the addition who has made the Richards family a threesome, was born Dec. 2 at St. Paul hospital.

Guests

Whenever a visiting dignitary is entertained at the White House it is news from coast to coast. There is nationwide interest also in the travels of celebrities of all sorts. Just as important are the comings and goings of "ordinary" folk within the circle of one's acquaintance.

> Mr. and Mrs. Ralph J. Peterson and daughter Linda are visiting here from North Hollywood, Calif. They are sharing their stay with Mr. Peterson's brother-in-law and sister in Salt Lake City, Mr. and Mrs. Cleon Anderson, 1851 Harrison Ave., and Mrs. Peterson's mother in Ogden. Mrs. Fred King. The coast matron is the former Phyllis King of Ogden.

Among those entertaining for them during their visit are Mr. and Mrs. Ferdinand Peterson, 1370 E. 9th South; Mr. and Mrs. Jess R. Jensen, 1621 Princeton Ave.; and Mrs. Ray Whitmeyer of Ogden.

The Californians will visit with their son Scott in Army training at Grand Junction, Colo., before returning to Hollywood.   [Salt Lake City *Tribune*]

Newcomers

Even in crowded city apartments, a new family in the building or neighborhood is an event, especially if both households have children through which some of the adults are bound to become acquainted if only for the purpose of discussing discipline. The habit of calling on newcomers virtually has disappeared in the larger cities but is still proper etiquette in the small town. In places of all sizes, curiosity at least must be satisfied. The newspaper is in the best position to appease it.

A one-sentence brevity announcing the change of residence on the real estate page or telling of a newcomer to the community may be all a newspaper feels it can afford. On the other hand, some newspapers subscribe to commercial services which collect data on new residents in the community and are using the information for editorial as well as business purposes.

A newcomers' column serves the purpose both of extending a welcome and of acquainting old-timers with the special interests of the arrivals. Organizations similar to those with which members of the new families were affiliated in their former cities of residence can follow such a column to learn of possible additions to their own rolls.

Newcomer to Phoenix is Ballerina Eileen Colgrove, native of London, England.

She and her husband, Michael Thoday, live at 35 W. Enconto Blvd.

Among Miss Colgrove's diplomas she holds a fellowship, or top degree, from the Imperial Society of Teachers of Dancing in London. This includes degrees in national, ballet, and stage branches. She is a graduate of teachers' course of Sadler's Wells ballet company, and also holds diplomas from the National Association and Midland Association.

Miss Colgrove has done radio and television work on ballet education programs in both England and Canada. She was recently a teacher at the National Ballet Co. summer school session in Toronto. At the summer session she taught children, professional ballerinas, and teachers of ballet.

During her career she has taught some children from the royal family, including the Earl of Uxbridge and Lady Henrietta Paget.

In Phoenix she will instruct at the Ruth Freethy School of Dancing, 16 W. Cypress, beginning Sept. 19.   [Phoenix *Arizona Republic*]

Employment

It is difficult to enforce any rule against "free publicity" connected with new jobs. It is news when a large corporation elects a new president or chairman of its board of directors. Similarly it is news when a friend or acquaintance changes his employment.

Franklin R. Raynor today resigned his position as office manager of the Grayson Real Estate company to accept a similar position with the South Side Realtors. In his new position he succeeds Vincent L. Coke who died recently.

Miss Sylvia Waters, 574 W. Sequoia place, left today for Minocqua, Wis., where she will become director of a Girl Scouts summer camp.

Trips

Friends are interested when anyone takes a trip but may be bored when he returns and insists on relating the commonplace. Nevertheless, a skillful reporter should be able to keep a returned traveler off a textbookish account of the glories of Niagara, the Lincoln Memorial or Yellowstone and find something in the peregrinations of most everyone, regardless of how well-traveled the road taken may have been.

When a person goes away the purpose of his trip may be news, as he may be combining business with pleasure, attending a convention or returning to the scene of an interesting former experience. If the journey is a short one, to be completed in a day, emphasis should not be on the fact that the traveler left but that he is in the other city.

WEAK: Carol Winters left Jefferson City today to visit relatives in Columbia.
BETTER: Carol Winters is spending the weekend with relatives in Columbia.

The shortest type of brevity regarding a trip resembles the following:

Mr. and Mrs. Fred N. Sigman, 1415 N. Cherry street, have returned from a two weeks' visit with their son, Fred Jr., an intern in General hospital, Boston.

Often a returned traveler has experiences to relate or opinions to express which are newsworthy.

By Judy McDermott

By the time Rosemary Brown had lived with the Masai of Tanzania in east Africa for six months, she felt really welcome among the nomadic herdsmen.

"I even received a proposal of marriage," admitted the attractive Reed College coed, who has just returned to the United States.

The proposal was a complete surprise because, Rosemary explained, she had at least two strikes against her.

She owned no cattle—a typical Masai dowry—and she wore her dark blonde hair long, a style considered quite unattractive among the cleanshaven Masai women.

"A Masai friend wanted to know 'how much brides cost in America.' When I said they were free, he thought he'd like to fly right over and select a wife for himself."

STONE CABIN IS HOME

The Portlander lived for six months in a stone cabin on the floor of the Ngorongoro Crater, amidst a wildlife preserve. The government of Tanzania has allowed small villages of Masai, who are chiefly farmers, to live in huts in the crater.

While Rosemary specifically was in Tanzania to study dominance and aggression in baboons with Dr. Carol Creedon, a Reed professor, she welcomed the opportunity to become acquainted with the tribesmen.

[Portland *Oregonian*]

Vacations

Resorts and other vacation places maintain publicity departments to keep faraway newspapers informed of the arrivals and departures of persons from their communities. They also provide articles and pictures of the social notables enjoying themselves (as swimming, tennis, skiing, and so on). Newspapers send their own society page columnists to report the activities of vacationing colonists. The following paragraphs from one such column are typical:

Making the most of their vacation days are Misses Virginia Barrett and Joan Chandler (Carl Walden photo), pictured here at Macfadden-Deauville Cabana club, where they take part in water sports. . . . Tennis also is included in their summer recreation program. . . . Joan, daughter of the Everett W. Chandlers, Miami Shores, is a student at Stephens college, and Virginia's parents are Mr. and Mrs. William Barrett, Miami Shores.

A trip through the Canadian Rockies then on to Alaska is included in the vacation itinerary of Mr. and Mrs. Frank E. Ellis, Miami Beach, who plan to leave next Monday.

They will sail from Vancouver, B.C., and after they return from Alaska they will go to New York. They also plan a sojourn at Hot Springs, Ark., before they return home.

Joining vacation travelers on Monday, Miss Phyllis Brettell left by plane for New York. . . . Phyllis, a daughter of Mr. and Mrs. Clinton Brettell, 1355 Biaritz dr., Normany Isles, will visit her aunt, Mrs. William Hafer, in New York and later will be the guest of Mrs. William N. Guthrie in Woodmont, Conn. . . . Also, she will visit Miss Maeve O'Toole, a Miami Beach winter resident, at her home in Forest Hills, L.I., and will go to Larchmont, N.Y., to visit other friends before she returns home in September.   [Miami *Herald*]

Another typical handling of news of vacations follows:

By Marie McNair

Looking forward to an opportunity to "get away from it all," Mrs. Mitchell Palmer is leaving Sunday for Lake Racquet in the Adirondacks and Mrs. Francis P. Garvan's luxurious camp, open again for the first time since the war.

Train service being what it is to that rather remote section of northern New York, Mrs. Palmer will try a plane from New York to Utica this time and motor the 60 miles from there to camp. It's that or land there by train and arouse the family at 4 A.M.

For almost a score of years Peggy Palmer has been a summer visitor to the Garvan camp. She has known the three boys, Francis, jr., Peter and Anthony, and their sister, Marcia, as enchanting small fry; said goodby to the young Garvans as they went off to war and will be present at Marcia's marriage to Frank Coyle in Spetember.

Wednesday, Francis, jr.—better known as Pat—will celebrate his birthday and a big party's planned. Francis, you may remember, married the lovely Hope Jackson, so well known in Washington. While her husband served in the Air Intelligence, U.S.N., Mrs. Garvan was studying voice, made her debut as an opera singer in the leading role in Tosca in Hartford, Conn., last spring, and according to critics, is definitely slated for greater heights.

[Washington *Post*]

College Students

Directors of publicity at the nation's colleges and universities may not believe it, but to the average newspaper of any size a news item telling of the selection for a homecoming committee of some student from the city has greater news value than the commencement speaker's name, an addition to the curriculum, a solemn pronouncement by the dean of women or even a routine football victory. When the boys and girls return for vacations, win scholastic honors and approach graduation and on many other occasions, the news gets prominent play and pictures are used.

Jack Perry, son of Mr. and Mrs. S. L. Perry, is playing the co-lead part in the Cornell Summer theater's production of "Under Canvas," comedy-drama of tent-show days. The story concerns the hectic lives of a typical tent-show group. "Under Canvas" will be presented to the public on Friday and Saturday nights, July 5 and 6.

Mr. Perry, a freshman at Cornell, is studying journalism and dramatic art.

[Clarion (Iowa) *Wright County Monitor*]

As much a puzzle to Booster college regulars as for four years it was to members of the Suburban Football league is the passing attack of Wayne "Bossy" Wilbur, half-back on the Booster freshman team.

Wilbur, the son of Nellie Wilbur, 148 W. Jackson street, was the mainstay of the Milltown high school football team for three years, two of which he served as captain. . . .

THE SOCIETY PAGE

When New York newspapers near the end of the last century began printing the guest lists of parties attended by members of the so-called 400, they made journalistic history. At first this "invasion of privacy" was resented, but through "leaks" and gate-crashing the news continued to be obtained. Today the problem of most society editors is not how to get news but how to satisfy everyone wanting "nice" notices on the page.

The original and enduring appeal of the society page has been two-fold: (1) to the vanity of those considered important enough to receive mention, (2) to the curiosity of all others regarding the glamorous way of life of their social superiors. In recent years, an increasingly large number of newspapers have come to regard these values as fictitious and to criticize the undemocratic "snob appeal" of the society page. For this and other reasons—including the headaches entailed in arbitrarily deciding who is and who is not socially important—the society page is disappearing. Much of the space formerly devoted to it is being given to news of the activities of clubs and to news of interest to women at all economic levels. Whereas such news formerly was sandwiched in on the society page, the trend now is to squeeze society news in on the club page or woman's page or to leave it for the gossip columnists. The glamour appeal now is provided by movie stars and other entertainers who get full treatment on other pages. They are the modern public heroines or goddesses, not the society matron.

Types of Society News

The typical society page or section consists mainly of the following kinds of news:

Parties: birthday, reunions, anniversary, coming-out, announcement, showers, weekend, house, theater, card and miscellaneous.
Teas, luncheons, dinners, banquets, suppers, cocktail parties and picnics.
Meetings and announcements of meetings of women's organizations, if there is no club page.
Receptions.
Dances and balls.
Benefits, bazaars and the like.
Personal items, if not used in another part of the paper.
Engagements and weddings.

As this list suggests, the society page is written principally for women, although men are interested in many stories of engagements, weddings, parties and personal activities. A majority of society editors are women who have social rank themselves, although many large papers have male society editors. Of whichever sex, the editor should be able to attend major social events on an equal footing with other guests, although only a few occasions require the presence of a reporter. A large majority of society page items are contributed by persons concerned or by social secretaries, either in writing or by telephone. The society editor must be ever on the alert for practical jokers sending or phoning in bogus announcements of engagements, weddings and other social events. Nothing should be used without verification. If the society editor needs pipelines, such people as chefs, florists, hairdressers and delicatessen store operators are among the best to utilize.

Elements in Society News

Most society events of any importance have elements in common which include
Names. Host and hostess; guests of honor; members of the receiving line in order of importance; assistants to hostess in the parlor and dining room;

members of committees; entertainers; musicians and their selections; prominent guests; relation of guest of honor to hostess or of assistants to either.

Decorations. Color scheme, its significance and how it was carried out; flowers, palms and ferns to make room resemble tropical garden, an outdoor scene and so on.

Refreshments. Distinguish between luncheon and tea and between supper, dinner and banquet. At receptions, always learn who poured and who served and ask if these assistants were selected for any particular reason (relatives, sorority sisters, officers of an organization).

Occasion. Is it an anniversary or an annual event? What will be done with any proceeds? Does the place have any significance?

It is difficult to achieve variety in writing similar accounts of social events. Consequently, the society editor welcomes any possible feature.

COVERING SOCIETY NEWS

Policy

In writing routine society news, restraint should be exercised. Every hostess would like to see her party or luncheon mentioned as the "loveliest affair of the season." To avoid offending anyone, such superlatives must be subdued.

There is a tendency, however, toward more informality in longer feature stories concerning important social events. Much of the material on the society or club page is signed. Functions, the proceeds of which go to charity, frequently are given better writeups than private affairs.

The capable writer does not need to use hackneyed adjectives such Ss "gorgeous" and "exquisite." An accurate, impartial description of an object or an event conveys its beauty or importance much better than does an article which makes indiscriminate use of adjectives. Only the writer who is not able to write better descriptions falls back on the old standbys.

A few additional words should be said about some of the more important kinds of stories classifiable as society news.

Receptions

The reception story should emphasize the name of the guest of honor, the occasion for the reception and the receiving line. Likewise, those who assist the hostess, entertainers, musicians and decorations.

Coming-out Parties

A debutante is presented to society by her parents, or, if they are dead, by a near relative. Some biographical data concerning the girl should be included, as well as a description of her dress. A possible feature may be found in the date or place or in the number or names of guests. In some coming-out party stories, the gowns of all the prominent women guests are described.

Engagements

Usually the parents of the bride-to-be announce their daughter's engagement. Sometimes the announcement merely takes the form of a newspaper notice. Often, however, an announcement is made at a social function. If such is the case, the manner of the announcement constitutes the feature. Especially if a girl chooses to announce her own engagement, the attempt is made to invent some novel method. For instance, the intended wife of a bank clerk uses as place cards or favors imitation bank books containing her fiance's picture.

In the announcement story, the names of the bride- and bridegroom-to-be must be mentioned, and also their parents' names and addresses. Also the probable date of the wedding and the city in which the couple will reside. The principals should be identified by their occupations and education. Sometimes the way in which the two met is interesting, as when a war veteran marries the nurse who cared for him in a hospital.

Showers

Female relatives and friends of a bride-to-be are hostesses at showers. Guests are expected to bring gifts. Often the type of gift to be brought is designated. If it is, the shower should be referred to as a kitchen shower, linen shower and so on. Otherwise, it should be called miscellaneous.

Weddings

The backbone of the society page is the wedding story. It is the longest and most difficult to write. Since most weddings are planned, it is possible for the society editor to obtain information about them and even to write them up in advance. In a majority of states a couple contemplating marriage must make application at least three days before the day set for the wedding. The city hall reporter gets the names of couples who apply for marriage licenses and, after including them in a short news item, gives them to the society editor.

The society editor writes an advanced story of the approaching wedding of a young woman who is prominent socially, often using a picture with the story. Many papers do not run such stories or pictures without charge. Ordinarily, the advanced story of a wedding is brief unless the principals are prominent.

After receiving the names of intended brides, the society editor of an average-sized newspaper sends a wedding blank to every bride-to-be about whose marriage she will want a story. This blank contains spaces for the prospective bride to insert answers to the questions suggested. Use of the wedding blank eliminates the necessity of personal reporting and insures accuracy. Seldom does the society editor attend a wedding. Most wedding stories are written from the facts provided by the bride-to-be. A sample wedding blank follows:

WEDDING REPORT

Full name of bride . . . .

Address of bride . . . .

Full names of bride's parents or guardians . . . .

Address of bride's parents . . . .

Full name of bridegroom . . . .

Address of bridegroom . . . .

Full names of bridegroom's parents . . . .

Address of bridegroom's parents . . . .

Date of wedding . . . . Time . . . .

Place of ceremony . . . .

Who will perform ceremony? . . . .

Will bride wear a gown or suit? . . . . Describe . . . .

. . . .

Will she wear a veil? . . . . Is it an heirloom? . . . .

Describe the veil . . . .

Will she carry a prayer book? . . . .

Will she carry or wear flowers? . . . . Describe . . . .

. . . .

Who will give the bride away? (name, address and relationship) . .

. . . .

Name of maid or matron of honor and relationship . . . .

Describe her gown and flowers . . . .

Names and addresses of bridesmaids . . . .

. . . .

Describe their gowns and flowers . . . .

Ribbon, ring or flower bearers . . . .

Describe their gowns and flowers . . . .

Name and address of best man . . . .

Groomsmen . . . .

Ushers . . . .

Will ceremony be formal or informal? . . . .

Musicians . . . .

Musical selections:

  Before ceremony . . . .

  As bridal party enters . . . .

  During ceremony . . . .

  As bridal party leaves . . . .

Order in which bridal party will enter . . . .

. . . .

Decorations (color scheme and how carried out; significance) . . . . .

. . . .

Number of invitations sent out . . . . Probable attendance . . . .

Will a reception follow? . . . . Where? . . . .

How many will attend reception? . . . .

Decorations . . . .

Hostesses:

In parlor ....

In dining room ....

Will breakfast, luncheon or dinner be served? .... Where? ..

Will couple take a trip? ...... Where? .... When? ....

When and where will couple be at home? .....:...............

Bridegroom's occupation and business address.................

Former occupation of the bride.............................

Bridegroom's education and degrees.........................

Bridegroom's fraternal connections.........................

Bride's education and degrees ....

Bride's sorority connections ....

Bridegroom's war record: service, rank, area in which served and
duration, citations, unusual experiences, etc. ....

....

Bride's war record ....

Guests from away, names, initials and addresses ....

....

Other information ....

....

Picking the Feature

The society editor welcomes any possible feature with which to lead off the wedding story. Possible features to give depth to the account include

1. The romance. The manner of meeting or the length of the engagement if unusual. Sometimes childhood sweethearts are united after years of separation. Or there may be an Evangeline or Enoch Arden complication. Ordinarily, unless the bride is a widow, the fact of any previous marriage is omitted. Exceptions to this rule are persons prominent in the news, especially motion picture actors and actresses. In their cases it is common practice to write: "It is her third marriage and his fourth."

2. The place. Perhaps some relative of either party was married in the same church. Maybe an outdoor ceremony is performed on the spot where the betrothal took place. Sometimes a couple selects an unusual site for its nuptials, as an airplane or beneath the water in diving suits. Wedding ceremonies have been performed in hospitals, prisons and by long-distance telephone or radio.

3. The date or hour. It may be the anniversary of the engagement. Perhaps the bride's mother or some other relative was married on the same date. In an effort to make its wedding the first of the year or month, a couple may be married shortly after midnight.

4. Bride's costume. Often a bride wears her mother's dress or veil or some other family heirloom. There is an old superstition that a bride always should wear something old and something new, something borrowed and something blue; many modern brides adhere to this, and some article of a bride's costume may be unusual.

5. *Relationship.* If the scions of two old and prominent families are married, their family connections may constitute the feature. If either is descended from Revolutionary or Colonial ancestry that fact should be played up.

The feature, of course, may be found in any one of a number of other elements. Perhaps the bridegroom wears a military uniform or the bride cuts the wedding cake with her husband's sword. Maybe the minister is a relative. The attendants may be sorority sisters or representatives of some organization. Whatever it is, the society editor tries to find it and to feature it. Anything to drive off the monotony of the stereotyped wedding lead.

Style

The trite and hackneyed style of the "country" wedding story must be avoided. To this end, avoid use of such expressions as "blushing bride," "plighted their troth," "holy wedlock," "linked in matrimony." The word "nuptials" should not be overworked.

The easiest lead sentence is the straightforward: "A and B were married —." For variety, other possibilities include

—exchanged (spoke) nuptial (marriage) vows.
Miss A became the bride of B—
Miss A was married to B.—
First church was the scene of the marriage of —.
A simple ceremony united in marriage Miss A and B—.
The marriage of A and B took place—.
—attended the nuptials of A and B.
Nuptial vows were spoken by A and B—.
The marriage of A and B was solemnized—.
Chaplain C read the service which joined A and B in marriage—.
Chaplain C officiated at —.

Some of these phrases may be appropriate in other parts of the story. When a page includes a half-dozen or more wedding stories, it is desirable to obtain variety. However worded, the lead of the wedding story should contain the feature, if there is one, the names of the principals with the bride's name ordinarily mentioned first and the time and place of the wedding. The principals usually are identified by addresses and parentage.

Writers vary the order of details in the body of the story. Most frequently, perhaps, the bride's costume is described right after the lead, and then the costumes of her attendants. The decorations or order of march, however, may come first. If there is a procession, the order in which it entered the church or home should be described.

The account of any wedding dinner or reception follows the account of the service proper. More nearly complete identification of the principals, the wedding trip and future residence and the list of guests come at the very end. Other elements which enter into the account are included in the sample wedding blank in this chapter.

Note in the following examples of well-written leads to wedding stories how the writers were able to find and play up unusual features. The leads are all from the Forth Wayne *News-Sentinel*:

> The Rev. Val Hennig, minister of St. John's Lutheran Church on the South Whitley Road, read the nuptial service, at which his youngest daughter, Katharine Alice, and Clarence Bade, son of Mrs. Chester Bade, 1721 South Hanna St., were united in marriage at 6 P.M. Saturday, June 29. Edwin Meitzler, organist, accompanied Howard Ropa, vocalist, who gave the musicale before the ceremony.

> Gold vases of white larkspur and Madonna lilies and palms decked the sanctuary of St. John the Baptist Catholic Church where Miss Eileen McGary and Robert John Wiltshire exchanged marriage vows this morning at 10 o'clock. The Rev. Leo Pursley officiated at the double ring ceremony and nuptial mass after a musicale of bridal airs given by Miss Frieda Winegart, organist, and Miss Mary Jo Kohl, who sang "Panis Angelicus" and "On This Day O Beautiful Mother."
> The bride is the daughter of Mr. and Mrs. William James McGary, 117 McKinnie Ave., and her husband the son of Mr. and Mrs. L. Wallace Wiltshire, 4225 South Calhoun St.

> In a quiet ceremony read in the presence of a few intimate friends, Miss Betty Ruth Beard, 2214 Winter St., and Lester Green, of Edgerton, O., were married last Saturday in the rectory of St. Peter's Catholic Church.

Possibly to make it easier to refuse demands for special treatment, the practice is growing of using exactly the same style for similar stories. For example, the Park Forest (Ill.) *Star* uses the following stock lead for engagement announcements:

> Mr. and Mrs. Alexander Miller of Richton Park announce the engagement of their daughter, Clarice, to Edward L. Watson, son of Mr. and Mrs. Herbert Watson of Monroe.

This is how the Cincinnati *Enquirer* handles a wedding story lead:

> The wedding of Miss Wilma Laura Ferber of this city and Clarence C. Hummell of Columbus took place June 12 at New Thought Unity Church. The Rev. Victor Summers officiated and a reception was held at Schueller's Ballroom.

The complete stories in both papers usually run four to six paragraphs.

WOMEN'S OR FAMILY PAGES

Much of the contents of the page commonly called women's or family is syndicated and provides advice to the lovelorn; hints on how to be pregnant, give birth and rear children; advice on how to stay happily married or to live alone and like it; also, advice on how to take care of pets and stay healthy and physically attractive and fit. Experts discuss mental health, how to garden, how to cook (with plentiful recipes provided by advertisers), take care of the hair, be stylish and fashionable. Illustrations often are provided by manufacturers, along with articles which are mostly free publicity. A few lead paragraphs which appeared on a typical up-to-date woman's page follow:

> Fashion is on a big knit-kick this season, and the look comes up fresh and new and full of energy.

> Pants have come a long way from the gardening-housework-car-pool routine. Their fashion potential along with their easy-going manner has cast them in a far more important role.

> At one time if a hostess told a man "casual dress," she could generally predict what he was going to wear. But today, a man might show up in anything from velvet jeans to a suede fringed jacket.

It remains to be proved that this commercialization of the erstwhile society page is preferable and that the contents are of greater interest than the gossip that once prevailed on it. Certainly there is no way to judge which type page is more socially beneficial. One doesn't need to take college journalism courses to prepare himself for this kind of writing. In fact, it would be better for his peace of mind and that of his boss if he didn't.

CONSUMER REPORTING

By contrast, considerable expertise is required for the newly developing field of consumer reporting. According to Francis Pollock, editor of the now defunct *Media & Consumer*, there are already more than 200 persons writing full time about consumer matters. At least a dozen major newspapers and both the Associated Press and United Press International have started consumer beats, and the taboo is beginning to crumble against "naming names," even in product evaluations. To replace traditional puffery in one field, Pollock suggests

> As a start toward better consumer service, the travel sections might open letters-to-the-editor columns to reader give-and-take, as the New York *Times* travel section does. Other consumer features which might be added: periodic reports on the amount of lost baggage, with, of course, the airlines' names (the publicity probably would stimulate better service); features on how to get the most economical travel rates; surveys of reader experiences with travel agents, resorts, and airlines; and any other report that would help the consumer get better value for his travel dollars. . . .
> News organizations could, if they wanted, advise their readers on how one bank's saving plans or mortgage loans compare with those of other area banks. . . . They could, if they wanted, compare rental car rates, or, as the Minneapolis *Star* did, print comparison charts of the octane ratings and prices of gasoline.

Sidney Margoulis, probably the first and certainly the best-known journalistic expert in this field, says:

Consumer journalism is a young profession, the youngest branch of journalism, but already it is making a significant contribution to stemming the many deceptions and diversions that cause the massive waste we have in society today. Without the new interest of the press and often radio and sometimes TV, we probably would not have achieved the useful advances of the past 12 years such as truth-in-lending and other credit reforms on federal and state levels; the new product safety law; advances in regulations governing auto and tire safety; some reforms in food and cosmetic packaging; unit pricing and open dating of foods; the 1962 drug amendments requiring that drugs be proven efficacious as well as safe; the exposure and increasing regulation of multiple distributor investment schemes, and many other money-wasting deceptions whether actually illegal or barely inside the law.

What consumer journalism has accomplished, however, is just a beginning to what really needs to be done, including the massive task of finding ways to curb the present galloping or at least trotting inflation.

GOSSIP COLUMNS

The avidity of readers for "inside dope"—intimate though perhaps inconsequential humorous, pathetic, unusual or anecdotal items—about friends and acquaintances and popular heroes worshipped at a distance has resulted not only in Washington, New York and Hollywood personal columns but also in a recrudescence of local "Around the Town," "On the Square" and similar columns.

The unusual new neon sign in front of a restaurant, the abnormally tall sunflower, the skillfully sculptured snowman, the practical joke played upon a dignified prominent citizen—many of these and other items which give substance to the local gossip column might be developed into separate brevity features. Collected and presented in the individualized style of a particular writer, however, their attention-getting value may be enhanced. Permitted greater stylistic freedom and a bit of friendly editorializing, the gossip columnist also can use a quantity of material which it would be difficult to work up into even an informal news feature.

Anecdotes

After the Chicago *Sun* included in its "Chicago Briefs" column an item telling of the long eyelashes of one of the city's children, mothers actually fought with each other in the newspaper office for the privilege of having their offsprings' lashes measured and photographed. One subsequent item in the series was as follows:

> Move over, Mickey Cribben, Maureen Fitzpatrick, Dolores Wenk, Patricia Capetta and all you other lucky people with those long eyelashes!
> Make room for a newcomer—Patsy Ann Doyle, 5, who lives at 5149 Emerald av. Her mother claims Patsy's blond lashes are a mite over $\frac{5}{8}$ inches long, which is longer than Mickey's, Maureen's, etc. etc.   [Chicago *Sun*]

Columns of anecdotes may be called "Chatter," "It Happened in—," "Evening Chat," "Informing You," "It's News to Me," "Front Row,' "Personally Speaking," or the like. The Wakefield (Mass.) *Daily Item* heads its column "The Item Hears" and begins each paragraph anecdote with "That." Typical items follow:

> That the election of Stephen J. McGrail as the youngest selectman in memory has brought out the reminder that Richard Fazio of 23a Armory st also was one of the youngest men ever to serve on the board. When first elected in 1933, Mr. Fazio was 25 years old.

> That the Board of Public Works has voted to maintain the charges for using the boat ramp at Veterans' Field at the same level. Residents of Wakefield are charged $1 per year for using the ramp to launch their boats, while others must pay $3 per day.

> That visitors to Wakefield from the West ran into what they described as a "gold mine" this week when they were permitted to visit a huge field of corn and select their own, fresh-picked ears for the unusually low price of 50 cents a dozen.

> That a youngster 9 years old and his younger sister of Yale avenue, appeared at the police station Tuesday with a wallet they had found which contained $8. It was discovered at the station that the wallet belonged to a Melrose man.

Night Life

In metropolitan centers the frequenter of night clubs has superseded the social registerite as copy for columnists who make the rounds after dark.

By Elizabeth Rannells

Soft lights, beautiful decor, hors d'oeuvres with the individual touch and solicitous service are the reasons the Town and Country room has become one of the town's quick-clicks. It is the spot for that pre-dinner, pre-show appointment, equally the place for the post-prandial, post-show meeting.

Not for heavy appetites is this addition to the Palmer House. It is just for that lull in the late afternoon, or for that after-the-show session, where every table has its coterie of critics.

And what is almost as important—the feminine guests feel like Powers' models, thanks to the bland and gentle illumination and the flattering colors of the room. They blend with all make-ups, thus putting the distaff customers in the cheerful mood.   [Chicago *Sun*]

Society

To brighten the society page there is the society column—usually signed —which, while newsy, is in keeping with the trend toward interpretative writing to give and explain the news behind the news.

> Effective formals seen recently include Nancy Wilmanns' (Mrs. Fred) strapless kelly green silk faille gown accented with a large pink rose at the waistline . . . Carol Herzfeld in a gown of her own design with a high neckline black lace

bodice atop a bouffant white organdy skirt with inserts of the black lace . . . the strapless white dotted swiss dress of Carolyn Rowe (Mrs. Charles) . . . Nancy Inbusch (Mrs. Ralph) in a crepe black creation featuring a peplum edged with white lace . . . Betty Wright (Mrs. David) in a floral printed crepe gown in a patriotic motif—red, white and blue.

Was Helen Fry's face red when she "gracefully" tripped over the full skirt of her formal at a recent affair and landed in a horizontal position!

[Milwaukee *Journal*]

Plugs

Increasingly local columnists are making the entire world their bailiwick and they mix news of who frequents what local night club with hints regarding new contracts obtained by motion picture, television and other entertainers. Conductors of these columns rely on tipsters, mostly publicity agents for celebrities, to obtain their information. Most of these columns today are nothing but short news items containing commercial value for someone, which in the past would have appeared in the news columns, minus the commercial emphasis, or on an advertising page. Here are typical samples from widely separated parts of the country.

This is definitely Bobby Vinton's year. Bobby's new record, "Wooden Heart," was released Tuesday, the same day Bobby opened in Mill Run. The record sold 200,000 copies that day. Bobby opens in the MGM Grand in Las Vegas Aug. 13. His new CBS show is scheduled for Saturday nights at 6:30 P.M. Bobby sang "The Anniversary Waltz" in Mill Run and asked anyone who had an anniversary to come on stage. The stage was crowded with people, ages 5 to 80, dancing.

Bobby is doing the same show he did 10 years ago when he wasn't a superstar. Bobby said, "I am doing it because that's what my audiences want. My songs are a return to normalcy."

Yul Brunner, star of the musical, "Odyssey," will not allow any whistling backstage in Arie Crown. Mr. B. says whistling detracts actors and the sound can be heard in the audience over the orchestra.

William Colby, chief of the CIA, will probably leave his post at the end of the year. The CIA wants to get more of an administrative-type person to straighten out CIA problems. . . . Jane Fonda is reported to be furious about ex-husband Roger Vadim's autobiography "Memoirs of the Devil." The French filmmaker is said to treat Jane about as unkindly as the CIA did.

[Maggie Daly in Chicago *Tribune*]

Have tongue, will tattle: Dean Borba, former Ch. 11 bossman who recently exited a TV station in Las Vegas is in town looking over job possibilities here—not necessarily in the TV game. His wife Joy is still in Vegas trying to sell their hacienda. . . The former Phyllis York and J. Rich Sports exec Van Liscum have tied the knot and will take a delayed honeymoon in June to the Smokies and to visit her family in Virginia. They'll take their boat and do some fishing along the way. Phyllis, longtime Girl Friday to Energy Center's Jack O'Connell, will remain in that job . . . Cameron Iron prexy Tony Bryan and wife Josephine are planning a jaunt to China later this month . . . Lots of buddies of John Mecom

Sr. and wife Mary Elizabeth are in Harvey, La., today for the christening and launching of their new drill barge. "Liberty." The Mecoms are hosting a big seafood dinner right in Halliburton's Shipyard . . . Virginia Muirhead, wife of Chief Mobile Signs exec Robert M., is home from St. Luke's and doing fine after surgery . . . Photogravity Co. engineer Virgil Whitworth is at the U. of Missouri at Rolla today receiving an honorary professional degree of geological engineering . . .   ["Big City Beat" by Maxine, Houston *Chronicle*]

12

MEETINGS, CONVENTIONS, SPEECHES

A. Meetings
  1. The Preliminary Story
  2. The Follow-up Story
  3. Style
B. Conventions
  1. The Preliminary Notice
  2. The First-Day Story

  3. The Follow-up
  4. Estimating Crowds
C. Speeches
  1. The Preliminary Story
  2. The Follow-up
    a. The Lead
    b. The Body

Meetings, conventions and speeches occupy the attention of the women's organizations mentioned on the society and club pages and of other organizations whose news is printed in other parts of the newspaper. It is impossible for any newspaper to give adequate coverage to any sizable proportion of the total number of groups seeking publicity. Those considered the most newsworthy are of the following types:

1. Those which take an active part in local, state or national political, legal or governmental affairs, as the League of Women Voters, Chamber of Commerce, Daughters of the American Revolution, American Legion.
2. Those that are interested in controversial issues or engaged in extraordinary tactics, as Students for a Democratic Society, Black Panthers, Veterans for Peace, American Civil Liberties Union, National Organization of Women and others.
3. Those which have programs including widely known speakers, musicians, artists and so forth.
4. Those with large, nationwide memberships which hold elaborate conventions annually. Of this type are most fraternal lodges, routine news of which may be ignored but whose yearly meetings are first-rate shows.

In small city dailies and community and suburban newspapers, almost any organization is newsworthy. The initiative may be left to the group to send in its notices voluntarily or the publication may follow a sounder policy of attempting to have complete coverage, especially of such organizations as the P.T.A., church groups, Boy Scouts, Girl Scouts, Y.M.C.A., Y.W.C.A. and so forth.

MEETINGS

The Preliminary Story

Every meeting is held for a purpose and this purpose should be the feature of the preliminary or advanced notice. From the secretary or some other officer of the group which is to meet, the reporter should learn the nature of important business to be discussed, of committees which will report, speakers, entertainment and so on.

Note how the second of the following leads emphasizes purpose:

WEAK: The Cosmos club will hold a meeting at 7:30 o'clock Thursday evening in Swift hall for the purpose of discussing the question of whether or not undergraduate students should own automobiles.

BETTER: Undergraduate ownership of automobiles will be discussed by the Cosmos club at its meeting at 7:30 Thursday evening in Swift hall.

Other vague beginnings to avoid include

There will be a meeting—
The purpose of the meeting—
At 7:30 o'clock—
The first meeting of the year—

The reporter should ask if the meeting is regular or special, business or social. He should inquire if a dinner or refreshments will precede or follow, whether any entertainment—dramatic, musical or otherwise—is planned. The main attraction of the meeting may be some special program. A meeting to elect or install officers, initiate candidates, hear a particular committee report or a speaker or to celebrate an anniversary has an obvious feature from the news standpoint.

The reporter must be sure to obtain the following data:

1. *The organization.* Its exact name, and the name and number of the post or chapter. "Local Odd Fellows" is not enough; instead, write "Keystone Lodge No. 14, I. O. O. F." That is the usual form: name of the local chapter first, then the number and finally the name or usual abbreviation of the national organization.

2. *Time and place.* In the preliminary story this information must be definite and accurate. A meeting scheduled for 8 o'clock should not be mentioned in the news story as to begin at 8:30. "Friday evening" is not enough; the exact hour should be given. Both the building and room should be given in stating the place.

3. *The program.* If there is a program of entertainment, the reporter should obtain it in detail. He must get names of musicians and their selections, names of casts and dramatic coaches, decorations, orchestras, committees in charge. Only the highlights of a program need be mentioned, and in order of importance, rather than in the order included in the program.

Note how purpose is emphasized in the following examples:

The American Legion Auxiliary's 5th District will meet at 8 P.M. Saturday in the Community club rooms, 1600 South Grand avenue, to hear annual reports by district chairmen and to elect delegates to the state and national conventions. Mrs. Martha Watkins, district director, will preside.

A score of California law-enforcement officials gathered here yesterday to discuss ways of living up to the new rule excluding illegally obtained evidence from criminal trials.

It was the first meeting of Attorney General Gerald L. Polk's committee on arrests, searches and seizures.

Polk announced that he will seek an immediate hearing before the State Supreme Court on five Valdavia narcotics cases that were dismissed as a result of the new rule, announced by the high court on April 27.

Sometimes the preliminary notice may be the excuse for a historical sketch of the organization, as

Having enjoyed a vigorous life for 80 years, the United Charities is pausing next week to give itself a birthday party. With a program as impressive as the occasion demands, the celebration will take place at the Palmer House the afternoon of the 16th.

Dr. Vance L. Howland is coming out from Escot to make the principal address of the party, and a pageant and tea will supplement the speeches.

As president of the group, Allan Fort will be chief host. Mrs. Stephen Lorch heads the committee in charge of the event, and is drafting a corps of her young friends who will act as ushers and hostesses in costumes their mothers used to wear as members of the organization.

Since 1897 when 23 Milltown business men founded the organization, it has been run largely by the same families. Victor G. Stoneking, Ernest I. Silsbee, James R. Leary, Austin H. DeZutter and Milo Morgan were some of the founders who named themselves the Milltown Relief and Aid society and obtained a state charter still in use.

They confronted the first big test of their efficiency in 1901 when Mayor William R. Trumbull turned over to them the job of looking after the thousands of Milltownians whose homes were destroyed in the April floods. Until then their chief means of relief had been money, but that spring, with O. A. Thayer as chairman of their shelter committee, they bought timber to build 9,000 homes, one of which still stands on the near southeast side.

Charles W. Riegel, the father of Mrs. Lee Diamond, was president of the society that year and wrote letters of thanks to people in the Hebrides, in Japan and Ecuador, and in more familiar places, for their contributions to Milltown's rebuilding fund.

It was Mr. Thayer's task to distribute building materials, food and clothes that came in from all parts of the country, and files in the present S. Savoy avenue headquarters still contain requests made to the shelter committee.

The Follow-up

In the follow-up or story after the meeting has been held, the outcome, or result, should be featured, and the writer should look to the future. For instance, avoid

Keystone Lodge No. 14, I.O.O.F., last evening voted to build a new million dollar lodge hall.

Rather, emphasize the future, as

Keystone Lodge No. 14, I.O.O.F., will build a million dollar lodge hall, it was decided at last evening's meeting.

Or, better still:

A new lodge hall to cost one million dollars will be erected by Keystone Lodge No. 14, I.O.O.F., as the result of last evening's meeting.

Other beginnings to avoid include

The Cosmos club met last evening—
At a meeting of—
There was a meeting—
The purpose of the meeting was—
One of the most interesting—
The outcome of the meeting—

The reporter should learn the disposition of every item of business. Some matters will be laid on the table or referred to committees. Others will be defeated outright. Some business, of course, will be concluded. If the meeting or business is important, the writer should include in his story, not only the result of balloting, but also the arguments presented by both supporters and opponents of every measure, both those that passed and those that were defeated.

The account of a meeting which has been held never should read as the secretary's minutes. The items of business are mentioned in the order of their importance rather than chronologically as considered at the meeting. So that he can interpret them correctly, the reporter must obtain the exact wordings of resolutions and also the memberships of committees. It is not necessary to mention the presiding officer unless someone other than the president or usual chairman was in charge.

In the follow-up story, the time and place need not be stated so definitely. "Last evening" is sufficient, as the exact moment at which the chairman sounded his gavel is immaterial. The name of the building in which the meeting was held is enough, especially if the organization has a regular meeting place. If the time of the next meeting is not fixed by custom it should be mentioned.

Names of everyone who took part in the program should be obtained if a complete account is desired. If a ladies' auxiliary serves a meal or refreshments, the names of the women who helped should be mentioned.

Note in the following example how the writer caught the spirit or importance of the occasion which he interpreted interestingly:

> The so-called conservative element in the labor union movement was successful in the annual election held Wednesday night by the Milwaukee Federated Trades' council.
>
> Herman Seide was reelected secretary by a vote of 458 to 169 over Al Benson, former sheriff and now organizer for the United Textile Workers of America, a C.I.O. affiliate.
>
> Anton Sterner, nominated to oppose J. F. Friedrick for the post of general organizer, withdrew. Friedrick was reelected by 624 votes.
>
> For secretary-treasurer, Emil Brodde was reelected with 458 to 164 for Severino Pollo. Frank Wietzke, sergeant-at-arms for more than 40 years, was reelected without opposition.
>
> In the contest between conservative and liberal slates for the nine places on the executive board, the same division was apparent. Those elected and their votes are . . . . [Milwaukee *Journal*]

Style

Expressions such as "Members are urged to attend," and "The public is cordially invited" should be avoided. If the purpose of the meeting is stated correctly, the former expression is superfluous. The latter expression is poor because of the "cordially." If an invitation is not cordial, it should not be extended.

Other expressions to avoid include

—was the most important happening.
—was the main business transacted.
—was the topic of discussion.
—featured the meeting.
—was the principal transaction.

CONVENTIONS

Some organizations, such as the American Legion, National Association for the Advancement of Colored People and Americans for Democratic Action, are influential in state and national affairs. Consequently, when one of these organizations meets, what it does is of general interest. Such conventions frequently pass resolutions concerning vital political and business situations and recommend passage of certain laws by state legislatures and Congress. They even send lobbyists to state capitals and to Washington.

Conventions of other organizations which ordinarily are nonpolitical may be of widespread interest because of their large membership. Fraternal orders such as the Masons, Elks and Moose have chapters in all parts of the country, and their conventions attract thousands of delegates from all states. Church groups, businessmen's organizations, scientific and educational bodies consider matters of general interest. Frequently the first announcement of a new scientific discovery or theory is made in a paper presented at a convention of some scientific group.

Aside from the general interest which an important convention creates, there also is local interest, provided the locality is to be represented by delegates. If any local person is an officer or has a part in the program, the local interest is heightened. Many fraternal organizations hold drill team, band, fife and drum corps and other contests at conventions, and the local chapter may compete.

The Preliminary Notice

The first story of a convention usually appears a week or two before the opening session. Almost every important organization has a secretary or official who prepares notices for the press. The advanced notice emphasizes the business of the convention and the important speeches or papers to be given or read. Sometimes the nature of a report which a special committee will make is disclosed in advance.

Note in the following examples of leads of preliminary notices of conventions that the writers emphasize the most important plans from the standpoint of general interest:

> College training for women interested in the field of commerce and business administration will be studied and discussed at the 10th annual convention of Gamma Theta Phi, national professional sorority of commerce and business administration, tomorrow through Sunday in the Windmere hotel.

> The National Federation of Women's Republican Clubs will make congressional campaign issues the principal theme of the organization's third biennial convention in Philadelphia Sept. 26 and 27. Mrs. W. Glen Davis of Akron, president, will direct the sessions at the Bellevue-Stratford hotel. Several hundred delegates from 42 states and the District of Columbia are expected.

In addition to the general story of a convention, or even instead of it, a local newspaper may print a story playing up the "local" angle—the part that local delegates will play, as

> With the hope and expectation of bringing next year's state convention to Milltown, 58 members of Keystone Lodge No. 14, I.O.O.F., accompanied by wives and families, are in Petersburgh today.
> Occasion is the 27th annual convention of the state I.O.O.F. in which several members of the local lodge will play prominent parts.

The First-Day Story

The story which appears just before the convention begins may emphasize the purpose and main business of the meeting, or it may play up the arrival of delegates, the probable attendance and the first day's program. Often a meeting of the officers or executive committee precedes the convention proper.

Some matter related exclusively to the internal organization of the group may be of sufficient general interest to be the feature, as when a rule changing the requirements for membership, or union with another organization, is to be debated. Frequently an internal political fight is anticipated in the election of officers or selection of the next convention city.

> The leaders of the nation's banking fraternity, 8,500 strong, are arriving for the four-day annual American Bankers Association convention.
>
> The meeting, largest since the 1920s, will focus on the perplexing problem of the banker's role in curbing, while not blighting, the boom.
>
> The program at the Conrad Hilton hotel will also include speeches on the farm price problem and the task of building the free world's strength through NATO and the nation's strength through a strong free enterprise economy.
>
> In addition, a wide range of subjects, some of interest chiefly to bankers, others with a general scope, will be discussed.
>
> While thousands of bankers and their wives flock to a private showing of the General Motors Corp. Powerama Sunday, other bankers on 22 special committees—such as those on credit policy and federal legislation—will buckle down to work.
>
> But the committee which may prove to be the most controversial does not meet until Monday. That is the 50-member nominating committee, representing each state.
>
> There's no doubt, short of catastrophe, who the next president will be. He's the vice-president, Fred F. Florence, president, Republic National Bank of Dallas. He'll take over automatically from Homer J. Livingston, president, the First National Bank of Chicago.
>
> The rub will come when a successor vice-president to Florence is named.
>
> Observers think that for the first time in a generation there may be an open fight for control of the ABA, with the issue being state versus national banks.
>
> The "state's righters" argue that they haven't had a president for the last seven years. Because they can't name one directly this year, their strategy is to name the vice-president who will move up to the presidency.
>
> [Chicago *Sun-Times*]

A newspaper printed in the city entertaining a convention joins with the rest of the community in welcoming delegates. Reporters are assigned to gather side features and anecdotes unrelated to the serious business of the convention. Statistics may be included of the oldest delegate, the delegate who has come the longest distance, the delegate who has attended the most conventions, the delegate who flew to the convention by private airplane or arrived in some other unusual manner, the tallest delegate, the shortest and so forth.

The newspaper may take advantage of the opportunity to obtain feature interviews with important or picturesque delegates and speakers. At a gathering of editors of college newspapers, a reporter obtained numerous interviews regarding narcotics on campuses, a subject entirely different from the business of the convention.

The following is a well-written first-day convention story which "catches" the spirit of the occasion:

Cleveland, July 13—(AP)—The Shrine brought its big show to town today and made Cleveland an oriental oasis of parades, concerts, ceremonies and funmaking.

Delegates were arriving by the thousands, by special trains, by automobile by plane and by boat, and tomorrow between 60,000 and 100,000 nobles are expected here for the 57th annual convention of the Ancient and Arabic Order of the Nobles of the Mystic Shrine of North America.

Today was listed on the program as all-Ohio day, with 750 members of the six Ohio temples initiated into the order, but the arrival of delegations from all parts of the country came in for equal attention.

One thousand members of Medinah temple of Chicago, the largest in the order, arrived in spectacular fashion, on the Lake Steamer Seeandbee. The Chicagoans, bedecked in red, green and yellow uniforms and bright red fezzes, paraded from the dock behind Al Koran patrol of Cleveland, and tied up downtown traffic for a half hour.

Medinah sent a brass band, an oriental band, 500 uniformed men, and a headquarters company from its 23,000 members. This year a Chicago man, Thomas J. Houston, is to be elected imperial potentate and the windy city is a contender for next year's convention.

Lulu temple of Philadelphia sent the next largest delegation—900—and presented a quarter-mile long march of sound and color. Moolah temple, St. Louis, with 500 nobles, arrived on the Steamer Eastern States, while Iram temple of Wilkes-Barre, Pa., also came by boat, via Buffalo.

Abu Bekr, Sioux City, attracted attention with its white Arabian mounted patrol of 30 pure white horses. Syria temple, Pittsburgh, was represented by 700 nobles campaigning for the election of J. Milton Ryall for outer guard.

Band concerts, a lake cruise to Put-in Bay, patrol drills and the annual meetings of the recorders and the royal order of jesters, composed of men high in shrinedom, completed the day's program. Tonight was given over to a Mardi Gras and carnival, with Lakeside avenue roped off for the merrymakers.

San Francisco was unexpectedly put forward as a candidate for the next convention of the Shrine of North America. Pacific coast delegates got behind the move at a breakfast given by Leo Youngsworth, Los Angeles, past potentate of Islam temple. Previously Chicago had been the only city mentioned for next year's gathering.

Fourteen nobles of Hella temple, Dallas, came by airplane. Another long distance air delegate was Gerlad Biles, postmaster of the Canal Zone, who flew from Panama to Cleveland.

Lou B. Windsor of Grand Rapids, Mich. is the oldest member of the imperial council present and is attending his 44th annual convention. He was imperial potentate in 1920. Another veteran in attendance is John A. Morrison of Kismet temple, Brooklyn, N.Y., known as the "grand old man of New York Masonry," who says he has attended every convention since "way back when."

Robert B. Kennan of Carnegie, Pa., the tallest delegate attending the Shrine convention, was listed by police today as the first "convention casualty."

Kennan, seven feet tall, was cut on the neck when a bottle of stench fluid was tossed in the lobby of the Hotel Winton. More than 100 persons were routed by the incident, which police blamed on hotel labor troubles.

The Follow-up

After a convention begins, newspapers report its progress. Important speeches and debates are reported, and the outcomes of votes watched. Minor speeches, such as the address of welcome and the response and the humorous after-dinner talks at the banquet, may be ignored by press associations and correspondents, unless someone disregards custom and selects such an occasion for an important statement. Scientific papers and speeches must be written up so as to be understandable to the average reader.

Entertainment provided for delegates and their wives, the convention parade and minor business matters pertaining only to the organization are not given much space. If the organization awards prizes of any sort, the names of the winners are desired by various outside papers whose readers are likely to be interested. Such prizes may be for the best showing in the parade, for the largest delegation, for the delegation coming the longest distance, for drill team, band, or fife and drum corps competition, for the chapter which has increased its membership the most during the year, for the chapter which has contributed most to a certain fund and so on.

The results of the election of officers and selection of the next convention city usually are of general news interest. Papers in cities which bid for the convention or whose chapters have candidates for offices, frequently arrange for prompt coverage of elections, depending upon the importance of the convention.

Estimating Crowds

At athletic contests and other events to which admission is charged, there is no difficulty in obtaining accurate figures on total attendance. When the opposite is the case, especially when the audience or crowd is outdoors, the reporter often must make his own estimate of its size. Police usually estimate the numbers who watch a parade, take part in a demonstration or riot or similar event; but police are no more competent to do so than a trained newsgatherer. Furthermore, their bias is evident, as they underestimate attendance when they are unsympathetic with the purposes of the demonstration and overestimate it when the opposite is the case. So, of course, do newspapers, notoriously so when antiwar demonstrations were popular.

The simple process for audience or crowd estimation is to separate it into sections. That is, count the number of persons occupying a particular area. This is easy when the spectators are seated in a grandstand or auditorium, as all that is needed is to multiply the number of seats in a row by the number of rows, then subtract the apparent number of empty seats. Then cast the eye over the entire assemblage and see how many blocks of similar size there are.

The crowd-counting reporter has it easiest when he has an elevated position as a press box or platform. If he is on the ground he will do well to reach an elevated spot if possible. Otherwise, he will have to move about. He still uses the multiplied bloc system. The beginner can practice by estimating the attendance at athletic contests or the like so as to check his ability when the official attendance announcements are made. A skilled journalist comes very close to the mark.

SPEECHES

The Preliminary Story

In obtaining information for a story about a speech to be given, the reporter must pay special attention to the following:

1. Adequate identification of the speaker.
2. The occasion for the speech.
3. The exact time and place.
4. The exact title of the speech.

Identification of the speaker in the lead may not be lengthy, but the body of the story should contain those facts about the man which indicate that he is qualified to discuss his subject. The opinions of other persons may be obtained and quoted to emphasize the speaker's ability, but the reporter himself should not say that "he is well qualified" or "is an authority on his subject." It is better to give an adequate account of the speaker's experience and let it speak for itself.

The speaker's name usually is more important than his subject and, therefore, should come first in the lead. Sometimes, however, the subject may be more important, but rarely is it advisable to begin with the exact title in quotation marks. Note in the second example below how the writer emphasizes the subject and at the same time the importance of the speaker:

WEAK: "Commercial Aviation" will be the subject of a speech to be given . . . .
BETTER: The causes of several recent commercial airline accidents will be analyzed by . . . .

Sometimes the occasion is more important than either the speaker or his topic, as

The 55th anniversary of the Milltown Salvation Army will be celebrated at 3 P.M. Sunday at the Municipal Opera house with Commander A. K. Asp delivering the principal address, a resume of the Army's rise to second position among local charities.

In addition to a further identification of the speaker, the body of a preliminary speech story should contain the program of the meeting at which the speech will be given and additional details about the occasion.

In the following example of a well-written preliminary speech story, the lead emphasizes the speaker's name, and the body explains his importance and also the occasion on which he is to speak.

State Sen. Charles H. Bradfield, Rushville, will speak on the state parole system at the monthly meeting of the Council of Social Agencies at 12:15 P.M. Thursday at Hotel Wolseley.

A member of the joint legislative committee which recently recommended a complete overhauling of the existent parole system, Senator Bradfield has been a severe critic of Gov. Herbert Crowe for his failure to make a public statement on the committee's report.

"It was Senator Bradfield, more than any other member, who was responsible for the recommendation that a board of alienists be substituted for the present board," declared Maurice S. Honig, president of the council, in announcing Thursday's meeting.

The council's committee on legislation, of which Mrs. Arne Oswald is chairman, will report on the results of its study of the legislative committee's recommendations.

The Follow-up

After the speech has been given, the emphasis should be upon what the speaker said, rather than upon the fact that he spoke. Never write

Bruce Paddock, Prescott city manager, gave a lecture Thursday on "Municipal Government" to the Kiwanis club of Greensboro.

Such a lead is vague and indefinite. It is only a preliminary story lead put into the past tense. It misses the feature entirely.

The feature should be found in something that the speaker said. The reporter must follow the orthodox rule of important details first and must disregard the chronological order of a person's remarks. No good speaker ever makes his most important point in his introduction. The reporter should play up the speaker's most startling or important remark, which may come at the very end of his speech. Such expressions as "The speaker continued" or "In conclusion the speaker said" do not appear in a well-written story.

Every speaker tries to make a point, and the news writer should play up the speaker's attitude toward his subject as a whole. This is not a hard-and-fast rule, however, as frequently it is better to pick for the lead some casual statement or remark that has strong local interest. In playing up an aside or incidental remark, however, care must be taken not to give a wrong impression. It is easy to misrepresent a speaker's attitude by picking a single sentence which, when printed alone, has a very different meaning from that conveyed when the sentence appears in context.

The timeliness of a speaker's remarks may determine selection of the feature. If he refers to some vital public problem of the moment, his opinion regarding it may be more important than anything else he says. This, of course, is contingent upon his prestige as an authority on whatever he may be discussing.

During political campaigns, it is difficult for a reporter who travels with a candidate to write a different story daily, because the aspirant for office gives nearly the same speech day after day, possibly hour after hour. The same difficulty is met with in reporting public lectures by persons who speak frequently on the same subject. If the writeup of the speech is for local consumption only, the feature may be selected on its face value, provided an account of a similar speech by the same person has not been printed recently. The reporter, however, should not play up, as something new and startling, a remark which actually is "old stuff" to both speaker and auditors.

As preparation for speech reporting, there is no substitute for adequate knowledge of both the speaker and his field of interest. A reporter with little or no background in science, for instance, would be completely unable to evaluate the relative importance of points made by a nuclear physicist, some of which might be of great potential general interest. An uninformed reporter in any field might write that a speaker "revealed" or "made known" something that could be found in elementary textbooks on the subject.

To localize the appeal of a speech means to play up any reference which the speaker makes to the immediate locality. Thus, if in the course of a lecture on geology, the speaker declares that the vicinity in which he is visiting is a very fertile field for research, that remark may be the most interesting, from the standpoint of his audience, of any he makes. The same speech, written up for a press association, might have an entirely different lead.

The time and place need not be stated so definitely in the follow-up as in the preliminary story, and the identification of the speaker should be brief.

THE LEAD

Possible rhetorical leads for a follow-up speech story include

1. The speaker's name.
2. The title.
3. A direct quotation.
4. A summary statement of the main point or keynote.
5. The occasion or circumstances.

If there is reason for emphasizing the authority of the speaker, the story may begin with the name, as

Chief of Police Arthur O. Shanesy last night told members of the Chamber of Commerce at their monthly meeting that traffic accidents in the downtown business district are largely the fault of merchants.

Ordinarily, it is weak to begin with the speaker's name, because by so doing the importance of his remarks is minimized. For the same reason, the lead seldom should begin with the exact title unless it is stated in an unusual way or in a way which makes a title lead effective, as

"America's Weakness" is her failure to realize that the frontier has disappeared, according to Prof. Arnold L. Magnus of Booster college's political science department, who spoke on the subject last evening to the Milltown Lions club.

Opinions differ regarding the direct quotation lead. Jackson S. Elliott of the Associated Press once said, "Show me a news story that begins with a direct quotation, no matter how striking it is, and I will show you how it could be improved by taking the quoted statement out of the lead and placing it in the body of the story."

Other editors condone the direct quotation lead when the intention of the writer is to play up some startling statement rather than to epitomize the speaker's general attitude. Obviously, it is seldom that a speaker himself summarizes his entire speech in any one sentence contained in the speech itself.

The following is a fairly good use of the direct quotation lead:

"World War III is inevitable within five years," Harold E. Paulson, professor of political science at Booster college, told the World Affairs club last night in Memorial hall.

The partial-quotation lead is a way to avoid lengthy direct quotations which would lack definiteness, as

Schools, by failing to develop to the full the "creativeness" of all their students, are responsible in large measure for "countless not fully developed humans," Dr. John L. Tildsley, retiring assistant superintendent of schools, told 1,800 art teachers and students yesterday. He spoke at the opening session at the Hotel Pennsylvania of the 28th annual convention of the Eastern Arts association.

The best lead for a speech story is one which summarizes the speaker's general attitude toward his subject or which gives the keynote of the speech.

Kindergarten reading is out of place in high school and college, even if the students are coping with a foreign language.
So a University of Illinois professor told his fellow teachers of French, Friday, in a national meeting in the Palmer House.
"The books we're reading with our students in the first few years of French are far below their intellectual level, and below the seriousness of things, they are reading in other classrooms," declared Prof. Charles A. Knudson, head of romance language at Urbana.
"In short, in French classes we are reading tripe."

[Chicago *Daily News*]

The lead may emphasize the occasion or the ovation given the speaker, the crowd or some unexpected circumstance which occurs during delivery of a speech.

A well-organized group of about 50 hecklers last night failed to persuade State Sen. Roger Parnell to discuss loyalty oaths for public employees.

Instead, the Republican candidate for reelection stuck to his announced topic, "The State's Proposed Highway Program," and police evicted the troublemakers from an audience of about 500 in Masonic hall.

The Vernon County Republican club sponsored the meeting.

If several speech stories are to appear on the same page, as a page in a Monday edition including stories of Sunday's sermons, there should be variety in the use of leads. The average sermon is difficult to report because there seldom is a well-defined feature or keynote. A "title" or "speaker's name" lead may be used for a sermon story.

Beginnings to avoid in writing a speech story include

The feature of the Chemical society meeting last evening in Swift hall was a speech by . . .

Lieut. Amos Andrews spoke to members of the Chemical society in Swift hall on the subject . . .

"Shakespeare" was the topic of an address given last evening in Swift hall by . . .

Speaking at a meeting of the Chemical society last evening in Swift hall, Lieut. Amos Andrews declared that . . .

Pennsylvania limestone was discussed last evening at a Geology society meeting in Swift hall by . . .

All of these leads are vague and indefinite. They do not satisfy the reader's curiosity as to what the speaker thinks about his subject.

THE BODY

Prominent persons, as public officials, usually speak from prepared manuscripts, copies of which often are distributed to newspapermen before actual delivery. This enables a reporter to write part or all of his account in advance. The danger of going to press prematurely is obvious, as the speaker may make last-minute changes or digress from his text.

The safe way is never to publish a speech account until word has been received that delivery actually has begun. Even in such cases, and especially if it is impossible to obey the rule of delay, it is wise to use in the first or second paragraph the identification "in a speech prepared for delivery" on such and such an occasion. This offers protection in case there are unexpected developments. If there is none, the reporter, manuscript in hand, can follow the speaker and make note of any modifications necessary in the story he already has written.

The second paragraph of a speech story ordinarily should explain the occasion on which the speech was given, if the lead does not do so. The rest of the body should consist of paragraphs of alternating direct and indirect quotation. The first paragraph of direction quotation well may be an elaboration of the indirect quotation lead.

If, as often happens, the reporter has an advanced copy of the speech, he has no difficulty in obtaining direct quotations. Otherwise, he must develop facility in taking notes.

The reporter needs to exercise his best judgment in selecting the parts of a speech to quote directly. Ordinarily he should quote directly:

1. Statements representing a strong point of view, especially if related to a newsworthy controversial matter. Often it is more forceful to use the material in indirect quotation first, possibly in the lead, as " Mayor Brinton will not be a candidate for reelection." Readers, however, like to know the exact words which a speaker used and they should be given in the body of the story even though a verbatim account appears elsewhere in the paper.
2. Uniquely worded statements, including ones which might become aphorisms or slogans, as "Lafayette, we are here," "I do not choose to run" and the like.
3. Statements of facts not generally known, perhaps in statistical terms.

Ordinarily, statements which are merely ones of evaluative opinion or which contain old or easily ascertained information can be summarized in a reporter's own words if they are newsworthy at all. It would be foolish, for instance, to quote a labor leader as saying, "Unions are the hope of America." If, however, the president of the National Association of Manufacturers were to say so, it would be a sensational news story lead.

Instead of quoting directly a statement containing an old fact, the reporter can say, "The speaker reminded the audience that white-collar workers are the most difficult to organize" or " He recalled that the governor vetoed the measure two years ago."

How often a "he said" or synonym should be inserted in the body of a speech story depends on the length of the article. In paragraphs of indirect quotation a "he said" should be used as often as needed to make it clear that the ideas expressed are those of the speaker rather than of the writer. Direct quotations should be preceded, broken or followed by a "he said" or its equivalent.

The writer should try to use the most forceful synonym for the verb "to say." Any good dictionary of synonyms or a thesaurus includes many score. Since no two verbs have exactly the same meaning, great care must be exercised in their selection. If a speaker "roared," the interpretative reporter owes it to his readers to say so. If, however, the speaker merely raised his voice normally, grave injustice can be done by a reportorial magnavox.

Substance can be given to the speech story only by the reporter who knows something about the speaker and his subject. Otherwise it is impossible to comprehend the speech as a whole, to digest it with proper emphasis or to convey the proper impression of the occasion on which it was delivered. A speech is an event and the superior reporter comprehends its significance. The factual material of a series of phrases in a sentence or paragraph may come from a half-dozen widely separated portions of the speech as a whole, yet be properly grouped so as to give a complete and accurate summary of the speaker's point of view. Note the knowledge and understanding displayed by the writer of the following story:

By Pat McGuire
News staff writer

Land use planning in Birmingham is still in its infancy, a planning expert told members of the League of Women Voters of Greater Birmingham at a Thursday luncheon meeting.

"Most cities this size have been into planning for 35 or 40 years," said Charles Shirley, deputy executive director, Birmingham Regional Planning Commission. "We probably could have saved some of the more prominent structures around Birmingham if we had gotten started earlier."

Land use will be a major item in the U.S. Congress this year, Shirley said, adding that if the Jackson bill is approved, land planning will be required in every state. There are no federal regulations on land planning at the present time, he said.

Shirley explained the organization of the BRPC and Jim Scott, public information officer for the agency, showed slides detailing the structure of the BRPC.

The Birmingham Regional Planning Commission has no power to enforce, but may only make recommendations to municipalities on land planning, Shirley said. "Our biggest single problem is that by law we are advisors. But in most cases, regional comprehensive planning is required to receive grants."

About 80 to 85 municipalities are now participating in the BRPC program, and a citizen's advisory committee is now in the process of being organized, Shirley said.

Shelby County is the only county in the six-county region served by the commission that employs a planner, Shirley said. A primary land use plan has been developed for the Shelby County area, but has not yet been approved by the citizens, he said.

Current projects the commission hopes to get the go-ahead on include a long range transit study; a strip mining study, to be funded by the Appalachian Regional Council; and a water quality study on the Cahaba and Warrior rivers, under a grant from the Environmental Protection Agency. "The EPA wants the local governments to agree to abide by the results of the study if they are to fund it," Shirley said. "This is where we're having our problem."

Mrs. William Williams is land use study chairman for the league and Mrs. Kenneth Bohannon is league president.   [Birmingham *News*]

13

ILLNESS AND DEATH

A. Illness

B. Mental Health

C. Obituaries
   1. Basic Elements
   2. Circumstances of Death
   3. Reviewing a Life
   4. Morgue Stories
   5. Side Features
   6. The Second-Day Story
   7. The Funeral Story
   8. Follow-ups
   9. The Obituary Blank
   10. Language and Style

D. Suicides
   1. The Motive
   2. The Method
   3. Inquests

E. Accidents, Disasters
   1. Elements of Interest
   2. Picking the Feature
   3. Precautions
   4. Side Features
   5. Perspective

After a three months' strike ended, the Vancouver *Sun* printed a list, in five solid pages of agate type, of all funeral notices it could gather for the period during which publication had been suspended. It did so because that was what readers missed the most, according to Stuart Keate, publisher.

If his friend, or someone with whose name he is familiar because of its prominence in local or world affairs, is ill or dies, the newspaper reader is interested because of the personality involved. If an obscure person has an unusual disease or makes a heroic struggle against affliction, millions of Americans "plug" for him mentally from edition to edition. If a new medical discovery is announced, everyone who may be affected beneficially as a result is pleased to learn of it. If a contagious disease threatens to become an epidemic, readers appreciate being warned of the danger.

ILLNESS

Although the illness story may seem to be routine, it frequently is one of the most difficult to report and write. This is because the medical profession is reluctant to give out information about the condition of patients or about its own discoveries, unusual surgical performances and the like. Physicians hold that they are duty bound to protect the privacy of those under their care, and the ethics of the profession forbids anything suggesting personal publicity. They may feel that knowledge of his condition, gained through a newspaper account, would be detrimental to a patient's recovery, and they do not trust the average reporter to report medical news accurately.

Relatives of a prominent person who is ill usually can be persuaded to authorize the physician in charge to release periodic bulletins regarding the patient's condition, but these may be in scientific language which must be translated. Until newspapers can employ reporters capable of handling medical news with the same understanding that baseball writers have in handling their specialty, the only safe way is to ask the doctors themselves for popular "translations," or to consult a medical dictionary. Because in many cases they have gone to extremes in refusing cooperation with the press, physicians and surgeons must share the blame for inaccuracies which occur in news concerning them. The press also has learned that attending physician may not be entirely truthful in their discussion of the nature of an ailment when a prominent person, say a president of the United States, is involved. If the doctor has written a book, it can be consulted to detect differences between what the man writes and what he says.

Chambers of commerce also are a handicap to adequate coverage of medical news because of the pressure they often exert on editors to play down news of epidemics. Fortunately, few newspapers listen to such requests, holding their social responsibility to be too great and the loss of prestige they would suffer if the contagion reached sizable proportions to be an offsetting consideration. The paper with a sense of responsibility, of course, must take care not to frighten readers unnecessarily.

Most newspapers run a syndicated health column written by an out-standing medical expert who is cautious about diagnosing ailments on the basis of symptoms submitted by readers. Just as they discourage self-medication by patients, so do reputable doctors deplore sensationalism by the press in handling stories of unusual illnesses or treatments, as artificial hearts, organ transplants and the like. Newspapers provide the medium whereby public health officials advise the public on such matters as threats to the purity of the water supply, possible heat prostration and the presence of epidemic diseases.

By Robert S. Kleckner

The misnamed hay fever season with its sneezes and tears—but no fever—is drawing near.

Some hypersensitive individuals already have manifested mild symptoms, although the culprit pollens have not yet appeared here in the atmosphere in measurable numbers.

Melvin Karau, director of all allergenic products at Abbott Laboratories, said that, while normally the season begins in the area in the last week of July, a late spring and lack of rainfall early in the year delayed growth of ragweed and a few other plants whose pollens cause the suffering.

However, he offered the doleful prediction that, come Monday, the pollens might be showing up in amounts to be counted.

The delay, he added, will have nothing to do with possible intensity. The season usually lasts through the second week in September.

Hay fever sufferers, if they cannot get away to pollen-free areas, may get relief by staying in air-conditioned and air-filtered rooms. Certain drugs, doctors say, also are beneficial.

Roughly—and it is rough—some 7,500,000 persons over the nation are victims of the malady.

It also brings symptoms like runny and red eyes, itching, a stuffed nose and a tingle from the palate that climbs right up into the quivering nostrils.

SEE A DOCTOR

The allergy is nothing to be sneezed at. If you have it, you'd better see a doctor to prevent complications like asthma and respiratory ailments that can be serious.

Hay fever got its name in 1819 when Dr. John Bostock, a London physician and a victim of the disease, noted that the time of weeping and sneezing began at the start of the haying season.

It was not until 1831 that pollens were suspected. Twenty years later, Dr. Morrill Wyman of Harvard Medical School came up with proof that dust, train smoke and pollens were involved.

In centuries past, there were some pretty weird treatments. Dr. John Elliotson of Britain in 1831 advocated hypnotism. Also, before the 1800s, leeches were used to bleed patients. Some became so weak they could hardly breathe.

SOME DRASTIC CURES

The archives of Charles Pfizer & Co., a pharmaceutical firm, show that the 1618 edition of the London Pharmacopoeia recommended a diet of fox lungs.

Thomas Sydenham, dubbed the English Hippocrates, recommended "purging of the brain" for strained breathing, although how this was done is still a mystery.

During the 19th Century, nasal surgery also was used. And some doctors suggested strong tobacco smoke and others cold baths.

Once asked by a patient if there was any cure for hay fever, Dr. Oliver Wendell Holmes of Harvard, answered: "Yes. Gravel . . . taken 8 feet deep."

COMMON SENSE RULES

But with modern therapy available, such drastic treatment is not advocated.

There are some common sense rules, medical men say, that help avoid attacks. these include:

No smoking; no swimming in chlorinated pools; no spiced foods; don't garden, cut flowers or use powdered soaps or insecticides; don't drink alcohol —it tends to dilate blood vessels as pollens do; don't get in squabbles with the wife, children or others—emotional upsets can trigger attacks, and don't go for rides in the country.   [Chicago *Sun-Times*]

The following are a few precautions to observe to avoid some of the grossest mistakes which otherwise might occur in medical news:

1. Be cautious about announcing cures for important diseases. The hopes of millions of cancer victims have been raised cruelly through newspaper publicity for discoveries which turned out to be false alarms.
2. Be certain that a newly announced discovery actually is recent. Cases have been reported of some cure or method's being ballyhooed as a startling find when it has been familiar to medical men for years.
3. Go easy on accrediting dogmatic statements to any medical researcher. Few of them ever speak in positive terms. Their efforts may be directed toward a certain goal, but they are extremely cautious about claiming credit for having reached it. Often they report to their scientific brethren on the progress of work they are doing; the newspaper should not credit them with having completed something which they have only begun.
4. Do not use without verification stories of miraculous cures.
5. Do not ascribe a pestilential disease to a person without absolute authority, as such a story, if untrue, is libelous.
6. Do not say a person died "from" instead of "after" an operation, as such a statement may be libelous.
7. Everyone dies of "heart failure." There are diseases of the heart and such a thing as a heart attack.
8. A person does not "entertain" a sickness; and not everyone "suffers" while under a physician's care.
9. Very seldom does a person "have his arm cut off." Rather it is cut off contrary to his plans and wishes.
10. Injuries are not "sustained" but are "received."
11. The nature of a diagnosis ordinarily should be stated unless there is weighty reason for omitting it.
12. Scientific names of diseases may be used provided the popular names also are given.
13. Attach statements of diagnoses and of the seriousness of an epidemic to an authority.
14. Do not mention the name of a physician except in stories of the illness of a prominent individual.
15. Avoid stories of medical freaks unless authorized by a medical association. Expectant mothers can be frightened dangerously by accounts which advance public understanding little or not at all.

MENTAL HEALTH

The fastest growing field of medical knowledge probably is that of mental health. Although the supply of competent psychiatrists still is woefully inadequate, during the past few decades the thinking of many, within and without the medical profession, has been profoundly affected by discoveries and theories regarding the motivations of human behavior.

Among those most influenced by developments in the mental health field have been journalists. They have helped expose bad conditions in many hospitals for the mentally ill and have assisted psychiatrists, social workers, probation and parole officers, educators, judges and others in enlightening the public regarding the many ramifications of the newer knowledge. In its reporting of crime, juvenile delinquency, school problems and similar matters, the press has become much more understanding and consequently more intelligent in its exercise of news judgment.

For "depth" reporting in this field, considerable specialized knowledge is necessary. A typical error of the uninformed is to confuse feeblemindedness with mental illness. The former is lack of intellect, either from birth (amentia) or as a result of brain injury in later life (dementia). The feebleminded today are called "retarded" or "exceptional" and special schools exist for those who are educable—that is, the high-grade morons, not to be confused with lower-grade imbeciles and idiots for whom only custodial care is feasible. Under pressure from mental health authorities, newspapers generally have ceased using "moron" as a synonym for "sex pervert," which it is not.

The trend in mental health work is away from categorizing specific diseases—dementia praecox, schizophrenia, manic depression, catatonia, paranoia and the like—as long study reveals the existence of few pure types. Rather, the psychiatrist recognizes and speaks of symptoms of abnormal behavior. Outstanding book tracing the development of expert thinking is *The Vital Balance* (Viking, 1963) by Dr. Karl Menninger with Martin Mayman and Paul Pruysen, subtitled, "The Life Process in Mental Health and Illness." Long gone, of course, is belief in possession by evil spirits to be exorcised, malicious lunar influence, emotional suffering as a punishment for sin and similar unscientific and superstitious notions.

Although the teachings of Sigmund Freud, stressing the strictly behavioral aspects of mental disease, still influence modern psychiatric thinking more than those of any other scientist in the field, an increasing number of practitioners today are coming to believe that Freudian psychoanalysis is good research to determine the causes of a patient's emotional disturbance but that it falls short as a cure; that, in fact, it may merely provide a patient with a scapegoat, as a parent, for his condition and a rationalization for not making proper effort to correct irresponsible behavior. See *Reality Therapy* (Harper & Row, 1965) by William Glasser.

Experiments continue in the search for ways to cure, or at least alleviate, symptoms through insulin, electric and other types of shock treatments, glandular extracts, tranquilizers and so forth. Newspapermen can do a great disservice by sensationalizing any results of isolated experiments. They also must be careful to distinguish between psychoses (major mental disorders whose victims lose touch with reality) and neuroses, of which most of us may be victims at times. Psychosomatic illnesses are physical disorders which have an emotional base; work toward their understanding and cure progresses but has a long way to go.

Historical examples, notably that of Nazi Germany, give credence to the assumption that large groups, perhaps entire nations even, can act insanely. Certainly there are social psychological causes for the widespread success of fads and fashions, for the popularity, especially if it is sudden, of political and other movements and for crazes of all kinds. Seemingly separate phenomena may be related because of the conditions giving rise to them. For instance, in times of insecurity and fear some people may become strong activists to promote reform or change, whereas others may become escapists. It is not merely coincidental that contemporaneously there are movements of protest and revolt in many fields: on college campuses in almost all parts of the world; among schoolteachers who are unionizing and striking for the first time; within the Roman Catholic Church, where nuns and priests are protesting centuries' old conventions. There are the civil rights, peace and women's liberation movements. Mostly all segments of these groups to date have advocated peaceful tactics, but the patience of many has been strained by the failure of the Establishment to respond and because of the violence, including murder, with which the protestors have been answered.

On the other hand, those who seek solace by some form of escape become beatniks or hippies, exalt their egos by esoteric forms of dress and behavior, by the use of narcotics and by other "cop-out" techniques. Still others, who can no longer find security in the traditional religions, are attracted by revival movements, new cults, astrology, ESP, spiritualism and other forms of superstititon. Many different responses, all to the same motivation.

The mine run reporter cannot be expected to be an expert analyst of public opinion and morality; but some understanding of such matters can enable him to avoid gross error in perpetuating ignorance. This author said his say in his *Understanding Public Opinion*, Sigma Delta Dhi research prize winner, now published by Wm. C. Brown Co., Dubuque, Iowa. Erich Fromm's *Escape From Freedom* (Rinehart, 1941) and *The Sane Society* (Rinehart, 1955) have stood the test of time as outstanding treatises on the nature of collective irresponsibility.

OBITUARIES

Basic Elements

The size obituary a person gets depends upon his importance as news. Even the shortest, however, must include these basic facts:

1. Name of deceased.
2. Identification.
3. Time of death.
4. Place of death.

Two other facts really are essential for even a one- or two-sentence notice:

5. Cause of death.
6. Age of deceased.

Unless death occurs in some unusual way the name (*who*) always is the feature of an obituary. Identification in the brief notice may be by address or occupation only. No authority need be stated unless the dispatch comes from an obscure place or is third- or fourth-hand. Then "it was learned here today" or some similar statement should be used. The paper must be on guard against false rumors of a man's death started by enemies or jokesters.

In giving the age of a dead person some papers permit the form "Henry Baxter, 61, died today," whereas others object to this form on the ground that placing the age after the name indicates the present tense. Papers with this attitude prefer a phrase "at the age of 61 years" or a second sentence, "He was 61 years old."

> Rutherford Regal, 414 Oates street, a City Yards employee, died at 3 A.M. today at his home following a week's illness from pneumonia. He was 43 years old.

A man's importance or the achievement by which he will longest be remembered ordinarily should be used in identifying him, as

By Paul L. Montgomery

Martyn Green, the British actor who set the standard in Gilbert and Sullivan interpretation for half a century, died early yesterday of a blood infection at Presbyterian Hospital in Hollywood, Calif. He was 75 years old.

[New York *Times*]

Sometimes a reporter discovers an interesting circumstance in the life of a relatively unimportant person who has died. Perhaps, for instance, he was present at the assassination of a president, was a pioneer of the locality or a former millionaire or in some other way a romantic figure, as

> William Dickinson, 81, lifelong Milan resident whose grandfather laid out the village and founded and built the Presbyterian church here, died at 6 P.M. yesterday in his home on Dickson street.

> James Mauris, whose restaurant at 1464 E. 57th street has for many years been a rendezvous for faculty members and students of the University of Chicago, died suddenly of a heart attack last night. He was 70 years old.

See Warren J. Brier's "Delicate Art of Writing Obits," in the 1964 *Montana Journalism Review*, for advice on how to write colorful obituaries with dignity.

Circumstances of Death

When a person is known to a large number of readers, the circumstance of his death should be related as that is one of the first things about which a friend inquiries when he hears of another's demise. Circumstances of death include

7. Bedside scene.
8. Last words, messages and so forth.
9. Account of last illness.

In a full-lenth obituary, according to the formula being developed, these facts usually follow the lead.

> Allen E. Schoenlaub, 57, cashier of the First National bank, died suddenly about 8 P.M. yesterday at his home, 1146 Elm street, from a heart attack.
> He was found in the kitchen by his wife after she heard him fall while in quest of a drink of water. About a half hour before the attack, Mr. Schoenlaub complained of feeling queer. He had spent a normal day at the bank and ate dinner with his wife, son, Robert, 22, and daughter, Flora, 18, apparently in excellent health. He had had no previous heart attacks nor any other recent illness.
> A physician whom Mrs. Schoenlaub summoned declared death was due to coronary thrombosis and that Mr. Schoenlaub probably died instantly.
> In addition to his wife and two children, he is survived by a brother, Herbert, Kansas City, Mo., and a sister, Mrs. R. S. Bostrum, Chicago.
> Mr. Schoenlaub was connected with the First National bank for 26 years, the last 18 of which he was cashier. He was born Jan. 30, 1909 at Ann Arbor, Mich., and was graduated from the University of Michigan in 1931. He moved here in 1940 after nine years as teller and cashier of the State Bank & Trust Co., of Dowagiac, Mich.
> Mr. Schoenlaub was an active member of the First Baptist church, having been president of the Men's club from 1966–1973. He also was a member of Keystone Lodge No. 14, B.P.O.E., and of Milltown Lodge No. 150 F. & A.M.
> Funeral arrangements have not yet been made.

Note in the above the presence of three other important elements:

10. Surviving relatives.
11. Funeral plans.
12. Biographical highlights.

Reviewing a Life

Ordinarily the body of an obituary consists mostly of an objective biographical resume of the deceased's career. Eulogies and reminiscences may be included or run as sidebars.

If, however, the death is that of a nationally known or world-famous person, one whom history will remember, the trend is toward interpretative pieces which blend the details of death with attempts to evaluate the person's importance. The purpose is to "place" the subject in history with emphasis upon his lasting contributions. The interpretative obituary is not an editorial, although it is impossible for a writer qualified to pass judgment upon the subject to avoid evaluations.

Leading advocate of this type of obituary writing is Alden Whitman of the New York *Times* who has written:

For openers, let's tell what the deceased was really like in life. If he was a saint, let us by all means say so. Or if he choir-lofted with the comely soprano, let's say that, too. If he was modest and unassuming, let's tell it. Or if he was a braggart and a bore, let's also tell that. If he was a handsome donor to charity, we should make that clear, along with the tax advantages his munificence garnered him. If he was a statesman, let the bells ring out. Or if he was a fixer who put up public buildings for the profit of his friends, let the bells clang too.

Whitman expanded on his views in a book, *The Obituary Story* (Stein & Day). A typical Whitman obituary follows:

By Alden Whitman

Alfred C. Fuller, founder and retired chairman of the Fuller Brush Company and one of the foremost promoters of door-to-door salesmanship, died yesterday in Hartford Hospital of myeloma, a bone-marrow disease. He was 88 years old and lived in nearby West Hartford.

A transplanted Nova Scotia farm boy, Mr. Fuller developed a basement brush-making concern into a giant business, with yearly sales of more than $130 million. In the process he created the Fuller Brush Man as a fixture in American Folklore—the subjects of hundreds of quips and jokes—while elaborating a system of salesmanship that spread throughout the Western world. And Mr. Fuller himself became a storybook success, a man who started out with $375 and amassed many, many millions.

The company's basic product was brushes, but over the years its salesmen's sample cases have grown to include cosmetics and household chemicals. Some products have been phased out by changing life-styles—there is no longer a brush for cleaning derbies, for example—but the concept of bringing wares directly to the consumer, chiefly the housewife, has persisted. There are now about 25,000 salesmen in the United States, Canada and Mexico, each operating as an independent dealer in a fixed territory.

Mr. Fuller owed his success to his grasp of a few key business principles. One was that a few cents worth of bristles and other inexpensive materials, plus hard work, could create a much larger market value. Another was that a politely phrased sales pitch—carefully rehearsed—could almost always break down a buyer's resistance. And a third was that salesmen, if they were sufficiently motivated, could perform wonders.

The ubiquitous Fuller Brush Man (later joined by the Fullerette) paid calls on 85 of 100 American homes. He made deliveries in Alaska by dog team; he sold a doctor who set a dealer's fractured leg; he changed a customer's tire, pulled a tooth, dressed a chicken, hung out the wash. Inevitably, he was also a film subject.

Red Skelton, the comedian, played the title role in "The Fuller Brush Man" and Lucille Ball was the heroine of "The Fuller Brush Girl." In addition, Walt Disney's big bad wolf in "Three Little Pigs" disguised himself as a Fuller Brush Man.

11TH OF 12 CHILDREN

Mr. Fuller, according to his own account, was once almost enticed by a red-haired woman. "Don't lead me into temptation," she remarked invitingly after viewing his brushes. His response, he recalled, was to say, "Madam, I'm not leading you into temptation, but delivering you from evil." The woman purchased three brushes.

In his autobiography, "A Foot in the Door," Alfred Carl Fuller recounted that he had been born on a hardscrabble farm in Berwick, Nova Scotia, Jan. 13, 1885. He was the 11th of 12 children, and grew into a tall, handsome youth. With nothing but a grammar-school education and ambition to live in a more bustling world, he left home for Boston when he was 18.

After a succession of jobs, he went to work in 1905 for the Somerville Brush and Mop Company as a salesman. Having saved $375 in a year, he decided to venture on his own and set up a workshop in the basement of his sister's home. At night he turned out twisted-wire brushes for clothes, the hands, the floor, and sold them house to house by day.

His sales approach then was little different basically from that employed today. Recalling his early experience, Mr. Fuller said:

"I started out by trying to be helpful. I would knock on the door and say, 'Good morning, madam, if there is anything wrong in your house that a good brush could fix, perhaps I could help you.'"

The woman bought a long-handle brush and used it immediately to get at the dust between the flanges of a radiator. "After that," Mr. Fuller went on, "I studied a housewife's needs, and we made a brush for every need."

Later Mr. Fuller perfected ways to get inside the front door. On a rainy day he wore overshoes a size too large so he could get them off quickly. He was polite—"I'll just step in for a moment." And, starting in 1915, he and his dealers gave away a vegetable brush, known as "The Handy." They cost each dealer 3 cents apiece and were presented, of course, inside the door. In a recent year 7.5 million of them were pressed into housewives' hands.

After a selling trip to Hartford early in his career, Mr. Fuller decided to set up a company there in a shed he rented for $11 a month. By 1910 he had 25 salesmen and 6 factory workers. A year later he placed a small advertisement in a national magazine and was swamped with replies from would-be salesmen.

Then and later, those who sold Fuller products were independent dealers buying at wholesale and selling at retail at a profit of about 30 percent. Their incomes varied, depending on their enterprise, but they were (and are) supercharged by company pep talks. At one time, indeed, they were gathered to sing songs, one of which was "Fuller Land; Our Fuller Land," sung to the tune of "Maryland, My Maryland." Even so, dealer turnover was high, running to as much as one-fifth of the total.

PROFITED DURING DEPRESSION

With the proliferation of Fuller Brush Men, the company's sales rose to $5-million yearly by 1920, and to $12-million in 1924. The company did poorly in the Depression year of 1932, but it bounced back to record sales of $10-million in 1937, with a net profit of $208,000. Ten years later the gross was $30-million, and it has been rising since.

Mr. Fuller, who was a kindly and dignified man, even-tempered and agreeable, liked to remind visitors that the word "American terminates in I Can and Dough begins with Do." His own motto, he once said, was:

"With equal opportunity to all and due consideration for each person involved in every transaction, a business must succeed."

In his business life Mr. Fuller joined a score of organizations and clubs. Outside business, his biggest interest was the Christian Science Church, which he joined in 1921. Another concern was education—the University of Hartford, to which he contributed money, and the American School for the Deaf, of which he was a trustee.

Mr. Fuller was president of his company until 1943, when he turned the post over to his older son, Howard, and became chairman of the board, a post he held until 1968. On Howard Fuller's death in 1959, the presidency went to Avard E. Fuller, his younger brother. The company was sold to the Consolidated Foods Corporation in 1968.

Mr. Fuller's first marriage was to Evelyn W. Ellis of Nova Scotia. It lasted from 1908 to 1930, when the couple was divorced. Two years later he married Mary Primose Pelton, who survives, as does his son Avard by his first marriage. Also surviving are two brothers, Harry of Newburg, Ore., and Chester of Kentville, Nova Scotia; five grandchildren, and four great-grandchildren.

Morgue Stories

It is quite likely that Whitman's piece was written before Fuller's death, possibly months or years earlier. Most newspapers have on file biographical sketches of prominent people. It is because they once contained little else except such sketches that newspaper libraries came to be called morgues.

As the Fuller piece illustrates, the morgue story actually is an interpretative biographical sketch in which the writer attempts to evaluate the person and assign him his proper historical importance. In composing it, the reporter has an opportunity to do some of his best writing. The best source of material about the basic facts of a man's life, is, of course, the man himself. Since the morgue sketch is prepared during its subject's lifetime, it usually is written following an interview. Also, the writer consults previously written material about the person and makes his own impartial estimate of the highlights of the career he is reviewing. Most prominent people are willing, even eager, to cooperate in preparing morgue material, and do not consider the experience macabre.

Emphasis in writing should be upon the outstanding characteristics, achievements and activities of the person. The temptation of the young writer is to begin with the fact of a person's birth and to continue with a chronological narrative of his life. In interviewing a person for material about himself it may be convenient to have him tell about himself in such a way but, in writing, the principle to be followed is the same as in all other news writing: most important facts first. The fact of birth seldom is the most important.

When only a short bulletin of an important person's death is received in time for an edition, the morgue part of the printed story may constitute almost the entire printed story.

Side Features

In addition to the obituary proper, a newspaper may print several other related items.

1. It is the habit of newspapers, for instance, to print encomiums of prominent individuals who die. Persons acquainted with the career and reputation of the dead man are solicited for statements which usually are included in a single story with a comprehensive lead. Many of these statements are prepared in writing by the persons quoted; others are written following interviews by reporters who express the interviewee's attitude if not his exact words. Expressions of appreciation of certain persons may be published as separate items. If the president of the United States makes a statement, it usually constitutes a separate item. Dispatches from foreign countries carry separate datelines.
2. Sometimes the death of a prominent person leads to an official proclamation by a public official, ordering flags to be flown at half staff or suggesting the cessation of business on the day or during the hours of the funeral.
3. When messages of condolence are received by members of the dead person's family, a newspaper obtains them for publication, either in place of or in addition to the statements that it gathers itself.
4. Resolutions of sympathy passed by organizations with which the deceased was affiliated usually are given to the press for immediate publication.
5. When a businessman dies, especially in a small community, those who had any dealings with him are interested to know whether the establishment will remain open. Newspapers print notices of how long, if at all, the business will be suspended, and whether other business places will close for any length of time as a gesture of respect.
6. The death of a prominent person is the excuse for a recitation of anecdotes of his life. Persons who were close to the deceased frequently write first-person reminiscences. In smaller communities, newspapers try to find citizens who were acquainted in some way with a prominent person who dies. In after years, on the anniversary of the famous person's death or birth or of some outstanding event in his career, more anecdotes are sought.

The Second-day Story

The second-day story is primarily the preliminary story of the funeral. When more than a day intervenes between death and the funeral, there may be two follow-up stories.

Details to look for in the funeral arrangements include

Time and place.
Who will officiate?
Will services be public or private?
How may will attend?
Arrangements for handling a crowd.

Names of relatives.

Names of notables who will attend.

Will any club, lodge, etc. have a part?

Organizations to attend in a body or to be represented.

Names of musicians and selections.

Who will preach a sermon or deliver a eulogy?

Pallbearers, active and honorary.

Where will burial take place?

What will be the program of the services?

The second-day story also may include additional details of the last illness and death, additional panegyrics, letters of sympathy received by the family, resolutions, memorial services and the floral offerings. If the family requests that friends omit flowers, the newspaper should include the request. If floral offerings are sent, the newspaper should obtain a list and description of the important pieces and the names of the individuals or organizations sending them. Sometimes potential senders of flowers are asked instead to contribute to some worthy cause.

In virtually every case of death, friends of the dead person are given an opportunity to view the body before the time of the funeral or, if the body is not placed on view, to visit with members of the family in a funeral establishment. Newspapers should find out when such visits can be made. Organizations which will not be formally represented at the funeral may pay their respects in a group at any earlier hour.

When a member of Congress dies while in Washington, both houses pass resolutions and appoint committees to accompany the body home. Sometimes they adjourn out of respect. The practice of holding a separate memorial service for every deceased congressman has been dispensed with, and only one memorial service now is held every year at which all members of Congress who have died during the year are eulogized. Many clubs and lodges have a similar custom.

The Funeral Story

When a collection is made of the outstanding newspaper stories of history, it will include more than one account of a funeral. The story of the burial of the unknown soldier by Kirke L. Simpson of the Associated Press has become a classic, as have stories of the funerals of most of the presidents of the United States. The following is a straightforward and dignified account of an important funeral:

By Jack Jones
Times Staff Writer

A celebrity-hungry crowd of perhaps 2,000 persons surrounded a glass-walled chapel at Hillside Memorial Cemetry in Culver City Sunday to stare at the famous who came to say goodby to comedian Jack Benny, 80.

At the conclusion of the short service in which old friend George Burns broke down and in which Bob Hope called Mr. Benny a genius, many of the curious pressed forward to join the line of mourners passing the closed coffin.

The doors to the chapel finally were closed "in respect to the family" and the spectators were asked to leave. But they clung, making it difficult for entertainment stars to reach their limousines.

Comedian Burns, friend of 50 years to the violin-playing Mr. Benny (born Benjamin Kubelsky in Waukegan, Ill.), tried to offer the first tribute, saying, "I don't know whether I'll be able to do this."

Then he murmured some words which were inaudible to those outside depending on loudspeakers. He lapsed into sobs and silence and was helped away from the microphone by Rabbi Edgar F. Magnin.

Comedian Hope was more successful in delivering his prepared eulogy, saying the famed Mr. Benny who died Thusday night of cancer of the pancreas was "a national treasure."

He said of Mr. Benny, "He was stingy to the end. He only gave us 80 years, and that wasn't enough."

Hope said that Mr. Benny was a genius who "didn't just stand on a stage— he owned it."

And his tribute contained a gentle almost lighthearted joke, the salute of one comedian to another. "His first love was the violin, which proves—as Jack used to say—you always hurt the one you love."

But he noted, Mr. Benny raised large amounts of money for various causes with his violin playing.

Hope concluded with, "God keep him; enjoy him. We did—for 80 years."

Among those who reached the service as hard-pressed Culver City police cleared walking space were:

Actors Raymond Massey, Cesar Romero, Frank Sinatra, Gregory Peck, James Stewart, Edgar Bergen, Jack Lemmon, Henry Fonda, Andy Griffith, Walter Matthau . . .

Dinah Shore, Rosalind Russell, Lucy Arnaz, Candice Bergen, and Merle Oberon were there. So were Gov. Reagan, U.S. Sen. John V. Tunney (D-Calif.), and former Sen. (and actor) George Murphy.

His fellow comedians were there: Milton Berle, Hope, Jack Carter, Morey Amsterdam, George Jessel, Groucho Marx, Danny Thomas, Johnny Carson . . .

And, too, the every-Sunday regulars of his old radio (and TV) show gathered: bandleader Phil Harris, singer Dennis Day, Eddie (Rochester) Anderson, announcer Don Wilson and Mel Blanc.

Benny's wife, Mary, who played his girlfriend on the show, arrived with their adopted daughter, Joan, and three grandchildren. But the widow had to sit in the car for a few minutes before the service when the overwhelming scent of lavish floral pieces caused her to feel faint.

At the end of the 20-minute service inside the packed 350-seat seethrough chapel, the crowd pushed in so close that police had to again clear the way so the casket could be moved to the hearse carrying Mr. Benny to private entombment up the hill.

Berle, Peck and Sinatra were among the pallbearers struggling through the onlookers, as were Benny's business manager Irving Fein, Mervyn LeRoy, director Billy Wilder, Leonard Gershe, Fred DeCordova, Hilliard Marks and Armand Deutsch.

"Can you believe this?" one dismayed spectator asked another as some in the crowd ran forward to get close to the casket, pallbearers and the family.

But another woman with a small camera was complaining, "Just as we get up to the chapel, they shut the doors." [Los Angeles *Times*]

Follow-ups

A number of other stories may grow out of that of a death. Virtually everyone who is worthy of an obituary has held some position which will have to be filled. Before a speaker of the house is buried, newspapers print stories speculating as to who will be his successor. Frequently there are changes in business organizations after the death of an executive. A smart editor reads the account of a man's death and notes the organizations, business, fraternal and otherwise, in which he held an office, and assigns reporters to learn how the man's place will be filled in every case.

The courthouse reporter watches for the filing of wills and follows carefully each legal step up to and including the final settlement and discharge.

Memorial services may be held weeks or months after a person's death, schools and clubs may be named for him, monuments and tablets erected to his memory.

The Obituary Blank

The obituary may seem an important assignment, yet it is one of the first that a cub reporter receives. He is as likely to be sent out to gather facts about a death as to frequent a railroad station or hotel in quest of brevities. This is because few obituaries approach in importance those given as examples in this chapter, and because the elements of all stories of death are similar.

Most newspapers have an obituary blank for reporters who gather facts about deaths. These printed forms also are given to undertakers who cooperate in obtaining information for newspapers. A sample blank follows:

OBITUARY REPORT

Full name ....

Residence...

Place of death...........................Time ....

Cause of death...

Duration of illness ....

Present at deathbed......................................

Circumstances of death ....

....

Date of birth............................Place ....

Surviving relatives: Wife or husband ....

Parents .... Address............

Brothers .... Address............

.... Address............

and
Sisters............................. Address.............
.... Address.............
Children........................... Address.............
.... Address.............
.... Address.............
Date of marriage .... Place ....
Came to this country.................. Naturalized..........
Residence here since.................................
Previous residence and duration.............................
Last occupation.......................................
Previous occupations ....
Education, with degrees and dates ....
Fraternal orders, clubs, etc..............................
Distinguished service, fraternal, educational, industrial, political, etc.
....
....
....
Church affiliations ....
War record: Division, war................................
When discharged .... Rank..............
Honors............................ ....
Time of funeral...................... Place ....
Who will officiate ....
Organizations to attend in a body............................
Body will lie in state: When............. Where ....
Active pallbearers.....................................
....
Honorary pallbearers..................................
....
Music...
....
Burial place ....
....
Prominent floral pieces................................
....
Attending from away..................................
....
Additional information ....
....
....

No blank can include every question which a reporter may want answered, and so it is better not to rely entirely upon an undertaker but to interview the nearest living relative.

If he relies upon another to obtain his facts for him, the reporter may miss the feature of his story, especially if death resulted from violence or an accident. Possible features not suggested by the questions on the blank include failure of a close relative to reach the bedside in time; a letter written by the dead person containing instructions for his own funeral; the last words of the deceased; some request made shortly before death; any coincidence in the date, place or manner of death and some other event in the history of the individual or his family.

Language and Style

The language of the obituary should be simple and dignified. The verb "to die" is the safest to use. No religious group can take offense at it but can interpret it to suit its own tenets. "Passed away," "passed on," "called home," "the great beyond," "gone to his reward," "the angel of death," "the grim reaper," "departed this life," and similar expressions should be avoided. Also, let it be repeated, attempts at "fine" writing may be only maudlin. A man does not leave a widow; he leaves a wife.

SUICIDES

In covering a suicide, the reporter seeks the same information about a person's career, funeral arrangements, when the body will lie in state, etc., as in the case of an ordinary obituary. Elements peculiar to the suicide story, however, include

1. The motive.
2. The method.
3. The probable circumstances leading up to the act.
4. The coroner's inquest or medical examiner's report.

The Motive

A person who commits suicide usually is despondent because of financial difficulties, ill health, marital unhappiness, a mental disorder or a philosophic attitude of discouragement toward life in general.

If the person does not leave a letter explaining his motive, the reporter must investigate whichever motives seem most probable. A man's banker or doctor, his business associates and his friends and relatives should be interviewed. The reporter should ask if the person made any previous attempts at suicide, if he ever mentioned suicide, if he appeared to be in good health recently, especially the day before he took his life. How did he take leave of his family and friends? Was there anything at all suspicious about his actions or remarks recently? If he had not consulted a physician recently, others who knew him can pass judgment upon his state of health. His appetite, sleep, recreation or hours of work may have been affected noticeably.

When there is no apparent motive, the news writer should say so and should quote those whom he has interviewed to that effect. He should not attempt to concoct a motive and must be particularly careful not to ascribe a suicidal motive when none was present. Legally, no suicide is a suicide until so called by a coroner's jury or a medical examiner's report, depending on the system in vogue. If there is a doubt, the account of death should be qualified by a statement as "thought to be suicide."

Even when the suicidal motive is present beyond a doubt, some newspapers hesitate to use the word. The editor of a paper in a small community may attempt to protect the feelings of surviving relatives by covering up the suicidal intent. Seldom is such an attempt successful, as an unprejudiced statement of the facts surrounding death indicates either suicide or murder. Only by deliberate fabrication is it possible really to "protect" the widow and other survivors.

It is doubtful, furthermore, whether the paper does as much good as harm in "hushing up" a suicide story. Anyone who knew the dead person will become acquainted with the facts anyway, and if he encounters an effort to deceive him as to what actually happened, he conjectures. The rumors which circulate as to the motive of a suicide usually are much more damaging to a person's reputation than the simple truth would have been. A frank newspaper account puts an end to rumors.

The Method

The method by which suicide was accomplished usually is obvious. A newspaper should not dramatize the means of a suicide or print a story that might encourage another to take his life. A poison used for a suicidal purpose should not be mentioned by name, and if suicide by any other method is prevalent, newspapers should cooperate with authorities by omitting the method.

The coroner or physician summoned to examine the body can estimate the length of time the person has been dead. Members of the family and friends can provide clues as to what actions preceded the accomplishment of the act. The reporter should try to find the person who last saw the deceased alive.

By Fred Ferretti

Robert A. Morse, United States Attorney for the Eastern District of New York, plunged to his death from his fifth-floor Brooklyn Heights apartment yesterday afternoon, hours after he had told the chief judge of the district that he intended to resign.

His death was termed an "apparent suicide" by the police, who said he had told associates and friends that he was "despondent" and "distraught."

Mr. Morse had been United States Attorney since Aug. 3, 1971. He was 45 years old and divorced.

Last night Chief Judge Jacob Mishler and other Eastern District judges met to name an acting United States Attorney for the district, which comprises Brooklyn, Queens, Staten Island and Nassau and Suffolk Counties.

Judge Mishler said last night that Mr. Morse had come to his chambers at

10:30 yesterday morning and told him he intended to resign. "He was agitated, depressed," the judge said. "I asked him why?"

"He mentioned some litigation in Surrogate Court. I didn't want to pry. I tried to comfort him, to tell him things sometimes look worse than they are. But if you've made up your mind, submit your resignation to the President and send me a copy."

The judge said that Mr. Morse had been with him until 11 A.M. "and he only spoke about three or four minutes—the rest of the time he just sat and stared."

His former law partner, Norman Turk, was reported to have told Brooklyn political leaders yesterday that Mr. Morse was "extremely distraught" and had told him he was going to resign.

According to the Brooklyn Republican chairman, George Clark, Mr. Morse was "elated" last Friday when Mr. Clark informed him that his name had been submitted for a Federal judgeship to replace Judge John R. Bartels, whose retirement takes effect Jan. 1.

Mr. Clark said Senator James L. Buckley had told him Mr. Morse would be "very favorably considered" for the judgeship that Mr. Morse, a politically ambitious man, had sought. But a spokesman for Senator Buckley said Mr. Morse's name was but "one of many names dropped into the hopper" of political consideration.

The police said that they did not know the reason for his despondency and that he was not in ill health. Both the police and District Attorney Eugene Gold of Brooklyn said last night that no investigation of Mr. Morse was under way.

According to the police, Mr. Morse leaped to his death at about 2:10 P.M. from a casement window of his fifth-floor, three-and-a-half room apartment at 57 Montague Street.

Two young women saw him fall onto the pavement of Pierrepont Place, on the west side of the apartment house, a 12-story nineteen-fifties vintage white brick building called the Breukelen.

He was shoeless, wearing gray trousers, a blue oxford shirt, dark blue socks, and his glasses, and apparently cracked his skull as he hit the pavement.

He was identified by the superintendent of the building, Luciano Lopez. According to the police, there were no signs of a struggle in Mr. Morse's apartment. A note was found and was turned over to the medical examiner.

One investigator said, "From the looks of the place it had all the marks of a classic suicide."

POLICIES LAID OUT

He said Mr. Morse had apparently taken out his insurance policies and laid them neatly on a table next to the window from which he plunged. Next to them was his United States Attorney's identification card. He had emptied his wallet and laid the contents on the table. He had removed his shoes and taken off his tie. The door was double-locked.

"We've seen the pattern before," the investigator said.

A police source said last night that "some of his fellow workers tell us he was very depressed, he was down at the mouth lately."

Mr. Morse had been on a crash diet, under a doctor's care recently and had lost 35 to 40 pounds, according to the police, and "he was very proud of that." However, others said that Mr. Morse, who was 5 feet 5 inches tall, "had looked terrible" since he dropped from 180 to 140.

Illness and Death 249

Mr. Morse was a Brooklyn-born man who made good on his home ground. President Nixon appointed him United States Attorney in 1971, but Mr. Morse was not averse to telling friends that he longed for either statewide office or a Federal bench appointment.

The police said that Mr. Turk was in the Morse apartment early in the afternoon. According to them, it was shortly after Mr. Turk left that Mr. Morse plunged to his death. Last night Mr. Turk was questioned by the Federal Bureau of Investigation.

In Washington, Robert H. Bork, Acting Attorney General, issued a statement that said in part: "I was shocked to learn of the tragic death of Robert A. Morse. . . . The Department of Justice extends condolences and regrets to his family, friends and associates." [New York *Times*]

Inquests

The coroner, a county official whose duty it is to investigate cases of unusual death, usually orders an inquest into a case believed to be suicide. Sometimes this is delayed until an autopsy is performed on the body and until circumstances of the death are fully determined. The coroner's jury may determine the motive as well as the manner of death. If in doubt, it returns an open verdict.

According to the National Municipal League only nine continental states are still fully covered by the coroner system, 14 others partially covered. In two states which retain the coroner, Ohio and Louisiana, it is required that he be a licensed physician. In 25 states the office of coroner has been replaced by a medical examiner attached to the police department or some other law enforcement agency. It is his obligation to determine the cause of death in cases in which an attending physician cannot sign a death certificate. Neither a coroner's jury verdict nor a medical examiner's report has any more weight in a criminal case than a grand jury chooses to give it.

ACCIDENTS, DISASTERS

Part of the price which modern man pays for the benefits of a highly industrialized society is the danger he runs of sudden, violent injury or death. Automobile accidents result annually in nearly 60,000 deaths and nearly two million injuries. Wrecks of common carriers—railroads, buses, trucks, airplanes, boats—are fewer but are more destructive than in the days of slower speed and less delicate mechanics. Homes, public buildings, industrial plants and mines are better protected against fire and explosions, but an undetected minor flaw may result in a catastrophe without warning. Because of lack of foresight on the part of our grandfathers, we who live in the United States today are facing a national crisis as to how to control floods, dust storms and soil erosion which cause tremendous losses of life and property and, some say, are turning our country into a desert. Other "acts of God," such as hurricanes, tornadoes, earthquakes and cyclones, continue to occur with their same frequency, and man has not yet learned how to protect himself adequately against them. The growing journalistic, as well as general, interest in the problem of protecting the environment against pollution will be considered in Chapter 19.

Elements of Interest

Although they differ from each other by types, and although no two disasters of any kind are alike from the standpoint of news interest, news events pertaining to loss of life and property have in common numerous aspects which a reporter must bear in mind. Among the possible angles which no reporter can overlook are the following:

1. Casualties (dead and injured).
   a. Number killed and injured.
   b. Number who escaped.
   c. Nature of injuries and how received.
   d. Care given injured.
   e. Disposition made of the dead.
   f. Prominence of anyone who was killed or injured or who escaped.
   g. How escape was handicapped or cut off.
2. Property damage.
   a. Estimated loss in value.
   b. Description (kind of building, etc.).
   c. Importance of property (historical significance, etc.).
   d. Other property threatened.
   e. Insurance protection.
   f. Previous disasters in vicinity.
3. Cause of disaster.
   a. Testimony of participants.
   b. Testimony of witnesses.
   c. Testimony of others: fire chief, property owner, relief workers, etc.
   d. How was accident discovered?
   e. Who sounded alarm or summoned aid?
   f. Previous intimation of danger: ship or building condemned, etc.
4. Rescue and relief work.
   a. Number engaged in rescue work, fire fighting, etc.
   b. Are any prominent persons among the relief workers?
   c. Equipment used: number of water lines, chemicals, etc.
   d. Handicaps: wind, inadequate water supply or pressure, etc.
   e. Care of destitute and homeless.
   f. How disaster was prevented from spreading: adjacent buildings soaked, counter forest fire, etc.
   g. How much property was saved? How?
   h. Heroism in rescue work.
5. Description.
   a. Spread of fire, flood, hurricane, etc.

b. Blasts and explosions.
c. Attempts at escape and rescue.
d. Duration.
e. Collapsing walls, etc.
f. Extent and color of flames.
6. Accompanying accidents.
a. Spectators: number and attitude, how controlled, etc.
b. Unusual happenings: room or article untouched, etc.
c. Anxiety of relatives.
7. Legal action as result.
a. Inquests, post mortems, autopsies.
b. Search for arsonist, hit-and-run driver, etc.
c. Protest of insurance company.
d. Negligence of fire fighters, police, etc.
e. Investigation of cause.

In all stories of disaster there is human interest. In most of them, there also are suspense and a recognition of combat between man and the elements. Disaster stories, furthermore, are action stories and contain considerable details as to exactly what happened. If these details are not presented in chronological order, they at least are so arranged as to leave no doubt in the reader's mind regarding the sequence of the most important of them.

Few other types of stories offer the writer greater opportunity for descriptive writing. Although major disaster stories are illustrated, the writer does not rely upon a photograph to do the work of 1,000 or even 100 or 10 words.

Picking the Feature

No formula for writing a disaster story—or any other type of story for that matter—should be accepted as absolute. In general, however, the lead of the disaster story should follow the orthodox rule of playing up the five *w*'s, giving identification and authority and emphasizing the feature. Any one of the elements listed may be the feature of the story at hand. Regardless of what is played up, the occasion must be identified in the lead by the amount of loss, either in lives or property. The reader judges the importance of the disaster by the size of the casualty list or the number of digits after the dollar sign. When the casualty list or inventory of property is long, it is impossible to be specific in the lead. Names, however, must be high in the story. If their number is not prohibitive, they should come immediately after the lead; otherwise, they should be included in a box either within or next to the story proper. If included in the story itself, they should be followed by explanations as to how every casualty or item of damage occurred.

Precautions

The reporter must be careful not to assign blame in an automobile accident, the type of disaster story which he has most frequent occasion to write. Police reports are not adequate protection against libel in such a story as the following:

> Disregarding a traffic signal and a policeman's whistle, Alex Winser, 1421 Talcott street, crashed into an automobile driven by Miss Ruth Hazelhurst, 1191 W. Villas court, at 11 o'clock this morning at Third and Hamilton streets.

The following is a much safer way:

> Two automobiles, one driven by Miss Ruth Hazelhurst, 1191 W. Vilas court, and the other by Alex Winser, 1421 Talcott street, collided at 11 o'clock this morning at Third and Hamilton streets. Neither driver was injured.

Some editors insist on the form "the automobile driven by" or "the automobile in which the couple was riding," instead of "his automobile" or "the couple's machine." This is a precaution against possible libel action when the driver or occupant of a car is not the owner. Other editors consider the precaution unnecessary.

Care must be exercised in using "crashed," "demolished," "destroyed," and other descriptive verbs. The reporter should study the definitions of such words to avoid misapplying them. The makes of automobiles should not be mentioned unless pertinent.

It must be remembered that to collide two bodies must be in motion. Thus, if a moving automobile hits one parked at the curbing, there is no collision; rather, the car in motion strikes the other.

In the attempt to make drivers more careful and thus reduce accidents, some newspapers print daily tables or charts to show the total number of accidents and casualties by comparison with the preceding year. Likewise, since a magazine campaign against automobile accidents a few years ago, newspapers have been more inclined to include frank details of such mishaps to emphasize their horror. Much more gruesome pictures also are being used than formerly.

In the belief that they are performing a public service as well as fostering both reader interest and friendship, some newspapers undisguisedly editorialize in accident stories, as

> The danger of bicycle riding on public streets again was illustrated about 7 P.M. yesterday when Harold, 13-year-old son of Mr. and Mrs. Emil J. Bornstein, 636 Carbany street, was seriously injured in the 1200 block of Chicksaw avenue. He was struck by an automobile driven by O. S. Patrick, 802 Lunt avenue.

Side Features

Any one of the elements which go to make up a complete disaster story conceivably could be played up in a sidebar: acts of heroism, miraculous escapes, rescue and relief work, coincidences, etc. It is customary to use boxes or separate stories for long tabulations of casualties or damages and for lists of previous catastrophes of a similar nature. Eyewitness accounts are provided by victims who had narrow escapes and by bystanders, rescue workers, reporters and others. When the disaster occurs outside the circulation area of the publication, it is customary to use a sidebar or in some other way play up the names of any local persons who were involved.

Perspective

Many disasters can be prevented by such obvious precautions as straightening highways, repairing defective electrical wiring and posting warning signals. Others cannot be controlled without scientific study and analysis and action on a much broader scale. The media of communication can help the public understand why a certain type of disaster is prevalent in a community, area, state or nation by "digging deeper" than the facts related to a specific news event.

> Behind last summer's great natural catastrophe, the devastating floods in Kansas and Missouri, is a simple story. The sweeping tragedy of 44 persons killed, 500,000 persons displaced, 2,000,000 acres flooded, 45,000 houses damaged or destroyed, the teeming Kansas Citys gutted by water and flame, and a $2.5 billion loss is only an effect. Underlying it all is the tale of three dams that became lost in politics in Kansas and the District of Columbia, and never got built.

Sociological phenomena are interrelated. Why flood control projects are not constructed involves consideration of more than selfish political interests. The stories of the depletion of natural resources, chiefly forests and grazing lands, and of soil erosion and other bad consequences of unscientific methods of farming are intricate ones.

Slum area fires usually can be blamed on faulty building codes and/or their improper enforcement. Probing deeper, to obtain perspective, however, the interpretative reporter may discover the origin of overcrowded housing in the heavy migration of Negroes, Puerto Ricans or others into areas where segregation is enforced and programs for integrating newcomers into the economic and social life of the community are inadequate. The machinations of some real estate operators to reap personal profit by playing race against race or nationality group against nationality group may be revealed. Tracing the ownership of tenement property, often concealed by "dummy" titleholders, may be enlightening and a first step toward removal of fire hazards.

At a different level, newspapers can lead the way in educating home owners and tenants in how to preserve and renovate property so as to remove hazards. The famous Baltimore Plan of urban renewal could not have succeeded without the vigorous support of the *Sunpapers*.

Those concerned with safety on the streets and highways still stress the *three E*'s: engineering, education and enforcement. Increasingly, however, researchers are paying more attention to so-called human factors. The psychology of the automobile driver is being studied with remarkable results. The causes of "accident proneness" often are deep-seated within the individual and, for proper understanding, may require study of social factors external to the individual. Only a start has been made toward understanding the interrelationships in this field.

The same is true of most other aspects of the problem as a whole. Too many explanations of why teenagers are more reckless drivers than adults are superficial and contradictory. Simple explanations and answers should be avoided until much more study has been completed. In the meantime, the interpretative journalist can help keep the public informed as to the status of that research.

In 1966 the book *Unsafe at Any Speed* became a best seller and its author, Ralph Nader, was a key witness at congressional hearings which resulted in legislation to compel the automobile industry to pay more attention to the safety of its products. After private detectives hired by the automobile industry failed to uncover anything with which to smear or blackmail him, Nader continued to expose many other shortcomings in the operation of the economic system and encouraged many young journalists to ask why their editors failed to give them more constructive investigative assignments.

14
POLICE, CRIME, CRIMINAL LAW

As the traditional beat system has been superseded or at least supplemented by "subject matter" or "field of interest" beats, and as routine crime has come to be considered comparatively less important by editors whose scope must include the whole world, the stationary police headquarters beat has become comparatively less important. Nevertheless, if for some unimaginable reason a newspaper were compelled to remove all of its beat reporters but one, it would be the man at police headquarters who would remain at his post. This is so, not because crime news is considered so overpoweringly important, but because in addition to learning of homes that have been broken into, checks that have been forged and murders that have been committed, the police reporter usually is the first to turn in tips of accidents, attempted suicides, missing persons, rabid dogs, strikes and many other events about which newspapers carry stories.

Because the police are in close touch with more phases of everyday life than any other news source, the police beat affords excellent training for the beginning reporter and, fortunately, is one which he is likely to get. In the small community, covering police means visiting the police station two or three or more times a day, visiting the scenes of the infrequent important crimes which occur, verifying and amplifying the comparatively meager reports contained on the official police blotter or bulletin and writing all police news worth mention. In a large city, covering police has meant to remain all day at headquarters or at a district station, watching the steadily growing day's report and phoning tips of the most important items (perhaps 25 per cent of the total) to the city desk. When anything happens about which the paper wants more than the beat man can obtain from the police bulletin or by interviewing members of the force or witnesses brought to the station, an assignment man is sent out; the writing is done by rewrite men.

The life of neither the police reporter nor the average police detective resembles very closely that depicted by the continuity strips and magazine short stories. After he has seen one sobbing mother, one hardboiled harlot, one repentant gunman and one of all of the other types who frequent police headquarters, the reporter has seen them all. When this fact dawns upon him, and as he becomes accustomed to the intransigence of all parties concerned in the diurnal police drama, he may have to struggle against both cynicism and discouragement. A good turn at police reporting is the best hazing possible for the callow graduate and aspiring author of the world's greatest novel. There are few newspapermen of importance who did not take the test and pass. An attitude of detached studiousness will enable the beginning reporter to make his police reporting experience what it should be: the most valuable of his entire journalistic career. He must not let his hardboiled attitude blind him to the fact that human beings are not merely statistics and that there is a story about every unfortunate person who runs afoul of the law. It is impossible to obtain any sizable proportion of those stories, but frequent visits of professional novelists and other imaginative writers to police courtrooms show that there is no better place for the writer in search of material.

LEARNING THE ROPES

The Police System

The police reporter has got to know who's who and why at headquarters or at the district station which is his to cover. The setups of police departments differ in details but not fundamentally. At the top is always a chief of police, superintendent of police, police commissioner or some other individual appointed either by the mayor with the approval of the lawmaking body or by a police commission so appointed. Whatever its title, this office is a political one, and its holder may have little or nothing to say about the formation of general policies. If the higher-ups decide that certain "places" are to be allowed to remain open, they remain open until the word comes from above, either as a result of public pressure or for other reasons. The same is true as regards parades, rallies and demonstrations. Under orders from their superiors, police either protect or harass participants. Whenever any change in policy is made it is, of course, the chief who "fronts," making the announcements and receiving the credit; likewise, when something goes wrong he is the scapegoat unless it is possible to "pass the buck" down the line to some underling.

This realistic picture of how the law enforcement system operates may be disturbing to young reporters with an idealistic or reformist nature, but until the public insists on an extension of the civil service system to include heads of police departments and upon strict observance of discipline and honesty throughout the entire system, the situation will not change. The trouble is that the element in the population who might favor an improvement either is unaware of the true state of affairs or is too indolent to do anything about it. The irate citizen who fulminates against the patrolman who looks the other way for a slight consideration or because of orders from above is the same who, when he receives a ticket for parking his automobile overtime, starts on a hunt for someone who knows someone who knows someone. The practice of frightening children into proper behavior by threatening to call a policeman also is not conducive to a helpful attitude on the part of the same children when they become adults.

"Law and order" and "support your police" have been recent political slogans. Usually they mean that their users would like to stifle dissent by groups with views different from theirs. A major problem of honest law enforcement today is to maintain neutrality and not contribute to violent disturbances. Several excellent reports have been made by presidential commissions and it would do the beginning reporter good to take them off the shelves, where they unfortunately rest, neglected, and study them. The best include:

> The Challenge of Crime in a Free Society, a report by the President's Commission on Law Enforcement and Administration of Justice, Nicholas deB. Katzenbach, chairman, February 1967.
>
> The Politics of Protest, by Jerome H. Skolnick, director of Task Force on Violent Aspects of Protest and Confrontation of the National Commission on the Causes and Prevention of Violence, 1969.
>
> Report of the National Advisory Commission on Civil Disorders, Otto Kerner, chairman, March 1968.
>
> Rights in Conflict, the Violent Confrontation of Demonstrators and Police in the Parks and Streets of Chicago During the Week of the Democratic National Convention, a report submitted by Daniel Walker to the National Commission on the Causes and Prevention of Violence, December 1968.
>
> To Establish Justice and to Insure Domestic Tranquility, final report of the National Commission on Causes and Prevention of Violence, Dr. Milton S. Eisenhower, chairman, December 1969.
>
> Violence in America, Historical and Comparative Perspectives, an official

report to the National Commission on the Causes and Prevention of Violence, by Hugh Davis Graham and Ted Robert Gurr, June 1969.

Despite modern training methods, many if not most policemen adhere to the "catch 'em and lock 'em up" school of criminology. Understandably, they want every arrest they make to lead to a conviction in court. They find it difficult to accept the principle of everyone's being considered innocent until proved guilty. They chafe under court restrictions regarding the gathering of evidence which forbid entering a place or searching a suspect without a proper warrant and applaud "no knock" laws which increase their authority. They believe some eavesdropping, wire tapping and even entrapment to be neccessary. They also want more time than the United States Supreme Court says they should have to question or "work over" a suspect before filing charges against him. The police reporter cannot allow himself, while making friendships, to adopt the policeman's psychology. His homework to justify himself psychologically should include Karl Menninger's *The Crime of Punishment* (Viking, 1965), Estes Kefauver's posthumous *Crime in America* (Doubleday, 1951) and Ramsey Clark's *Crime in America* (Simon and Schuster, 1970).

Paid more poorly than would be necessary to attract a higher type of public servant, "coppers" off their assumed dignity are pretty good fellows. Fraternizing with them, the reporter learns to like them. A policeman friend is a real asset and usually can be obtained through mention of his name creditably in connection with some story. Without friends in the department the reporter is worthless, as the formal reports and notations on the police blotter are grossly inadequate in case of an important story. In such instances it is necessary to talk to the policemen assigned to the case or to the principals; to see anyone in custody of the police, of course, requires permission.

A police captain is in executive control of a station which is organized in semimilitary fashion. In small communities, the chief may assume this responsibility or there may be a captain performing the function of chief at night. In large cities, every precinct station is directed by a captain The lieutenants usually head up the different operating divisions, such as traffic, detective and patrol. The sergeant is a "straw boss" who may have charge of a switchboard over which he directs the activities of patrolmen on beats or may take charge of a small squad of patrolmen on some errand or duty. Inspectors may have roving assignments to check up on the operations of district stations or may perform the functions described as usually assigned to lieutenants; it is largely a matter of terminology. Inspectors in the traffic division are an entirely different type, being responsible for investigating the circumstances of traffic accidents.

If there is more than one station in a community, all keep in touch with headquarters by means of a ticker or printer telegraph system, and a central record is kept of all important cases. Police departments even in small cities have two-way radio systems to enable headquarters to talk with cruising patrolmen in police automobiles. Also increasing are bureaus of identification in which photographs, fingerprints and possibly Bertillon records are taken and kept and ballistic and chemical studies made of clues.

To check up on minor occurrences, the police reporter telephones the district stations at intervals throughout the day. For the most part, however, he watches the blotter or bulletin on which appears promptly everything of prime importance; assignment men are sent to district stations when necessary. Most large police departments now have elaborate electronic reporting equipment so the reporter has prompt notice of the occurrence of a crime. It still, however, is necessary for him to use his ingenuity to interview the arresting policemen, the detectives assigned to a case, an assistant district attorney and/ or others. Mechanical recording devices do not do the fact-finding job essential for good coverage of a case.

Entirely separate from the city police is the sheriff who is the law enforcement officer for unincorporated areas within a county. Theoretically, the sherriff can intervene in municipal criminal affairs, but actually he seldom does so except when invited or when local law enforcement breaks down. When such happens, it is extremely newsworthy and someone inevitably charges "politics."

Sheriff's raids are made mostly to break up dope peddling centers and illegal gambling establishments outside city limits. Sheriff traffic police also patrol the highways along with a limited number of state police. In states where the township unit of government persists, the law enforcement officer is the constable and the local judicial officer is the justice of the peace.

County prosecuting attorneys are called circuit or district attorneys or state's attorneys. They are elected locally but are responsible to the state attorney general in the enforcement of state law. Federal prosecutors are district attorneys; federal law enforcement officers are marshals; and preliminary hearings are conducted by commissioners.

What Constitutes Crime

As important to the reporter as knowing police procedure is a knowledge of what constitutes crime. A breach of the law may be either a felony or a misdemeanor. Since the law differs in different states the same offense may be a felony in one state and a misdemeanor in another; and a felony or misdemeanor in one state may not be considered a crime at all in another. A felony always is a serious offense, such as murder, whereas a misdemeanor is a minor offense such as breaking the speed law. Felonies are punishable by death or imprisonment, whereas a misdemeanor usually results in a fine or confinement in a local jail. A *capital* crime is one punishable by death; an *infamous* crime is one punishable by a prison sentence.

Crimes may be classified as follows:

1. Against the person.
   a. Simple assault: threatening, doubling the fist, etc.
   b. Aggravated assault: threat violent enough to cause flight.
   c. Battery: actually striking a person or a rider's horse, spitting on another, etc.
   d. False imprisonment: liberty unlawfully restrained by anyone.

e. Kidnaping: stealing away a person. (May use *abduction* for women or children.)
f. Rape: unlawful carnal knowledge of a woman forcibly detained; statutory rape occurs when girl is minor even though she consents.
g. Maiming (mayhem): disabling or dismembering of the victim by his attacker.
h. Homicide: killing when the victim dies within a year and a day.
   (1) Matricide: killing one's mother.
   (2) Patricide: killing one's father.
   (3) Fratricide: killing one's brother or sister.
   (4) Uxorcide: killing one's wife or husband.
   (5) Justified: in self-defense or in line of duty.
   (6) Felonious: either murder or manslaughter.
i. Manslaughter.
   (1) Voluntary: intentionally in the heat of passion or as the result of extreme provocation.
   (2) Involuntary: unintentional but with criminal negligence.
j. Murder.
   (1) First degree: with expressed malice and premeditation.
   (2) Second degree: with no premeditation but with intent to kill or inflict injury regardless of outcome.
k. Abortion: interfering with pregnancy except as permitted by United States Supreme Court decisions.

2. Against habitation.
   a. Burglary: entering another's dwelling with intent to commit a felony therein; often extended to include any building.
   b. Arson: malicious burning of another's real estate.

3. Against property.
   a. Larceny: taking and converting to use with felonious intent the property of another.
   b. Robbery: larceny with intimidation or violence against the person.
   c. Embezzlement: larceny by means of a breach of confidence.
   d. False pretenses: confidence games, impostures, swindles.
   e. Receiving stolen goods: for sale or concealment; recipient called "fence."
   f. Forgery: altering or falsely marking a piece of writing for private profit or deception of another.
   g. Malicious mischief: killing animals, mutilating or defacing property.
   h. Extortion: blackmail; obtaining illegal compensation to do or not to do any act.

4. Against morality and decency.
   a. Adultery: sexual relations between a married and an unmarried person.
   b. Fornication: sexual relations between unmarried persons.
   c. Bigamy: second marriage without dissolving the first.

    d. Incest: sexual relations between persons so closely related that they are forbidden to marry.

    e. Miscegenation: marriage between races forbidden to intermarry.

    f. Seduction: inducing an unmarried girl to engage in sexual relations by false promises or deception.

    g. Prostitution: promiscuous indulgence in sexual relations by women for profit.

    h. Sodomy: homosexual relations between men.

    i. Obscenity: anything offensive to one's sense of chastity.

    j. Indecency: anything outrageously disgusting.

    k. Contributing to delinquency of a minor: encouraging or permitting any waywardness in youths.

    l. Sabbath laws restricting commercial and other activities on Sundays.

5. Against the public peace.

    a. Breach of the peace. (May cover disorderly conduct and a variety of nuisances.)

    b. Affray: fighting in a public place to the terror of the public.

    c. Unlawful assembly: gathering for purpose of planning or committing illegal act.

    d. Rout: unlawful assembly that begins to move.

    e. Riot: unlawful assembly or rout that becomes tumultuous or violent.

    f. Disturbance of public assembly: interference with legal meeting.

    g. Disorderly conduct. (Statutes stipulate acts forbidden.)

    h. Forcible entry and detainer: illegal seizure or holding of property.

    i. Defamation: libel if written, slander if spoken.

    j. Concealed weapons. (May be listed as disorderly conduct.)

    k. Gaming: playing games for money or games of chance.

    l. Gambling: betting on outcomes of events over which bettors have no control.

6. Against justice and authority.

    a. Treason: breach of allegiance to country; giving enemy aid.

    b. Perjury: false testimony under oath in judicial proceedings.

    c. Bribery: attempt to influence public official in his duties.

    d. Embracery: attempt to influence a juror.

    e. Counterfeiting: making false money which is passed as genuine.

    f. Misconduct in office: extortion, breach of trust, neglect, etc.

    g. Obstructing justice: resisting arrest; refusing to aid arresting officer.

    h. Obstructing punishment: escape; prison breach.

    i. Compounding a felony: agreeing not to prosecute felon or assisting him in evading justice.

    j. Exciting litigation: stirring up lawsuits for profit; barratry; maintenance; champerty.

    k. Election laws: fraud or illegal interference with voting.

l. Conspiracy: planning or plotting to commit crime.

m. Contempt: improper respect for court.

7. Against public safety, health and comfort.

    a. Nuisances: annoyances.

    b. Traffic regulations.

    c. Food and drug acts.

    d. Health regulations.

    e. Safety laws for common carriers; use of explosives, etc.

The police reporter must understand these popular definitions of criminal offenses, the names of which may or may not correspond to the statutory titles which differ somewhat by states.

Criminal Slanguage

Gangster motion pictures have made some underworld slang familiar: "contract," for instance, is "to hire a murderer" and "hit" means "to commit murder." A dictionary of such terms would be thick and under constant revision. What follows is a glossary of terms referred to in the numbers racket operations which originated with the Indianapolis *News.*

Numbers. A form of paper gambling such as baseball tickets, bank and lottery tickets based on a select group of numbers.

Paper gambling. Any form of gambling where the only device needed is paper.

Bank. A form of paper gambling where numbers are written on specially designed slips and the results are based on stock market tallies. The word *bank* is derived from gamblers years ago who used bank clearing house tabulations to pick winning numbers.

Lieutenant. The second-in-command of a numbers racket who picks up numbers and collects money and takes them to a location called a drop.

Pick-up man. He does essentially the same thing as the lieutenant, but usually does not know who is the head man or bank.

Drop. A place where numbers betting is tabulated and winners are decided.

Counthouse. Same as a drop.

Numbers writer. A person who takes numbers bets.

Hit. A winning number.

Flashback. When stock market results are changed by undisclosed business or business late at the stock market which is not immediately recognized, changing the number and sometimes making the house pay two bets.

Cut. Certain numbers are cut in bank gambling. Cut numbers are those either barred or paid one half of their winning value when they hit because they have shown a consistency in hitting. There are good odds of hitting the number.

Bagman. The alleged payoff middleman between police and racketeers.

Baseball tickets. A form of paper gambling based on either current baseball games or last year's games.

Blue book. A book that records last year's baseball run totals for the professional leagues which determines the winner in baseball tickets.

Pea shakes. A way of selecting a winning number for baseball tickets and other gambling.

Layoff. If a certain number is played heavily, one gambler may have his employees bet the same number with other gamblers to absorb part of the loss if the number should hit.

Lid. A limit on amount of a bet.

ELEMENTS OF CRIME NEWS

The Police Blotter

Despite the quantity of news emanating from police headquarters which gets into print, much more that appears on the blotter or bulletin is disregarded by the police reporter. Whereas it is possible to give feature treatment to almost everything that is reported to police, there is so much sameness in most of the routine of law enforcement that such entries on the bulletin as complaints against peddlers, small boys or dogs, notices from the police of other cities to be on the outlook for a certain person or automobile, reports of suspicious characters and lost and found articles go unheeded. What follows is an almost verbatim copy of the entries covering several hours on the police bulletin in an average-sized city, together with the use made of the material by the police reporter:

Bulletin	Newspaper Treatment
The following were injured in auto accident at McCabe and Dunmore and taken to Municipal hospital: Joseph Muenter, 623 Center street, Massillion, Ohio, laceration to hand; Mrs. Ollie Richter, Peru, Ill., age 51, laceration to scalp.	Not used because minor and occurred outside city limits; no local citizens in any way involved. Reporter talked to traffic inspectors who investigated.
L. D. Donaldson, 117 Forest avenue, reports the loss of a male bull dog.	Ignored as trivial.
Grover Mack (c), 1835 Grey avenue, arrested for passing a red light on complaint of Robert A. Kirkhope, 118 N. Park avenue, Waukegan, in connection with accident. Case set for 9/23 and defendant locked up awaiting bond.	Combined with another report, below.
Attempts made to burgalarize Royal Cafe, 1248 Chicago avenue, between 2 A.M. and 6:45 A.M. Used a one-inch drill on rear door. Entrance not gained.	Two-paragraph story, as follows: Burglars early today failed in their attempt to enter and burglarize two Evanston restaurants.
Attempt made to burglarize Helen's Cafe, 523 Dempster street, between 2	A screen over the rear window at the Royal Cafe, 1248 Chicago avenue,

Bulletin	Newspaper Treatment

Bulletin

A.M. and 6 A.M. Used a one-inch drill on rear door. Entrance not gained.

John C. Scale, 826 Sherman avenue, driving a Chevrolet coupe east-bound on Dempster street, at McCormick boulevard, backed into a Studebaker sedan driven by Lawrence G. Briggs, 1238 Oak avenue, and then continued east on Dempster street into city.

John C. Scale, 826 Sherman avenue, was arrested for driving while intoxicated on Dempster street. Locked up and case set for 9/23.

Hugh C. Collins, 809 Washington street, driving a Chevrolet coupe eastbound on Washington street, west of Elmwood avenue, collided with a Ford coupe parked in front of 910 Washington street owned by Richard Steele, 4730¼ Woodlawn avenue, Chicago.

Grover Mark (c), 1835 Grey avenue, driving a Pontiac sedan eastbound on Emerson street, at McCormick boulevard, collided with a Dodge sedan driven north by Robert Kirkhope, 118 S. Park avenie, Waukegan. Dorothy Brush, 1926 Noyes street, received a broken collar bone and was attended at St. Francis hospital.

Stephen Blake, 330 N. Kerr street, picked up around garage at 837 Dale avenue. Held for investigation.

Citizen reported someone in the St. Cloud Hat Shop, 106 Sherwin street No one found. Store locked up.

Newspaper Treatment

was torn but no entrance gained. The burglars also failed to gain entrance at Helen's Cafe, 523 Dempster street, after using a drill on the rear door, police say.

The following are paragraphs near the end of a general accident story, the lead for which was a serious accident, occurring after the reporter left police headquarters:

Two men were arrested on charges of driving under the influence of liquor yesterday after the car in which both of them drove was in two collisions. The men are: Hugh C. Collins, 809 Washington street, and John C. Scale, 826 Sherman avenue.

Scale was driving the car when it was involved in an accident with one driven by Lawrence G. Briggs, 1238 Oak avenue, at Dempster street and McCormick boulevard, police say. He left the scene of the accident, police report, but was arrested a few blocks away.

His companion, Collins, drove the car toward his home, but it hit one owned by Richard Steele, 4730½ Woodlawn avenue, Chicago, parked at the curb in front of 910 Washington street, police say. He continued to his home and was arrested by police on charges of driving while intoxicated and leaving the scene of an accident.

Both drivers in a two-car collision yesterday were arrested by police on charges of passing a red light when police were unable to ascertain which of the drivers passed the light. Grover Mack, 1835 Grey avenue, asserted he had the green light at the intersection at Emerson street and McCormick road. Robert Kirkhope, 118 N. Park avenue Waukegan, driving at right angles to Mack, said he had the green light. The cars collided causing approximately $300 damages.

Dorothy Brush, 1926 Noyes street, was attended at St. Francis hospital for a fractured collar bone.

Ignored as trivial.

Ignored as trivial.

More nearly complete records are turned in on regulation forms in all such cases, and these blanks may be consulted by the police reporter. Usually, however, he prefers to talk to the policemen involved if he can find them, or with the principals. It is not safe practice to rely upon the police bulletin as authentic because policemen are notoriously bad spellers and make numerous mistakes in names and addresses, some of which may be noted in the examples given. If attempts at verification fail, the reporter should accredit his story to the police bulletin. It is presumed, of course, that he knows the law of libel which offers him no protection if he uses the expression, "police say." It is not safe to print news of an arrest until a person has been taken into custody and booked on a certain charge; then the newspaper can relate only what has happened. It is impossible to say without risk that a person is "wanted for having fled the scene of an accident." Rather, the reporter should write that the person is wanted "in connection with the accident . . ." Every item of police news should be verified before being used. As is seen from the examples given, for an adequate account of any item appearing on the police bulletin, more details than given there are needed.

Picking the Feature

All crime stories involve action. They relate to incidents which are potentially exciting when read about, provided the reporter has been resourceful and thorough in his newsgathering. Until a case reaches court, knowledge of law is secondary to ability to observe, describe and imagine all of the angles needing investigation and the sources from which information may be obtainable. The crime reporter, in other words, must possess some of the qualities of a good detective although his purpose is entirely different. He is not out to solve the crime but to learn all that it is possible to find out about it.

Because anything can and constantly does happen, the following list of potential elements of interest in news of crime cannot possibly be complete. It is only suggestive.

1. Casualties.
   a. Lives lost or threatened.
   b. Injuries and how received.
   c. Description of any gun play or fighting.
   d. Disposition of dead and injured.
   e. Prominent names among dead and injured.
2. Property loss.
   a. Value of loss.
   b. Nature of property stolen or destroyed.
   c. Other property threatened.
3. Method of crime.
   a. How entrance was effected.
   b. Weapons or instruments used.
   c. Treatment of victims.

        d. Description of unusual circumstances.
        e. Similarity to previous crimes.
    4. Cause or motive.
        a. Confessions.
        b. Statements of victims.
        c. Statements of police, witnesses and others.
        d. Threats.
    5. Arrests.
        a. Names of persons arrested.
        b. Complaint or policeman making arrest.
        c. Charges entered on police blotter.
        d. Police ingenuity.
        e. Danger incurred by police.
        f. Arraignment.
    6. Clues as to identity of criminals.
        a. Evidence at scene of crime.
        b. Testimony of witnesses.
        c. Statement of police.
        d. Statements of victim and others.
        e. Connection with other crimes.
    7. Search for offender.
        a. Probability of arrest.
        b. Description of missing persons.
        c. Value of clues.
        d. Contact with criminal through ransom notes, etc.

Juveniles

Until fairly recently, most newspapers followed a policy of not using the names of juvenile offenders except in cases of major crimes, such as homicide. Since juvenile delinquency began to increase markedly in the post-World War II years, some modifications in this rule have been made in numerous newsrooms. The Peru (Ind.) *Tribune*, for instance, adopted a new policy after extensive consultations with the chief of police, state police, city police juvenile officers, the county welfare director and Circuit Court judges. The pertinent part of the statement of policy follows:

> The *Tribune* will publish the names, ages, and addresses of all youthful offenders thirteen years of age or older provided:
> 1. in the opinion of the court there is no valid reason for such information to be withheld from publication
> 2. the offenses are not of an extremely minor nature
> 3. the offenders are actually charged with a specific offense.
> These facts will appear, along with all other pertinent facts of the case released by the proper authority.
> The *Tribune* will follow up with stories which tell whether or not the youth charged has been found guilty or not guilty.

No names will be published unless and until charges are actually filed in juvenile court.

The *Tribune* will work closely with all law enforcing officials to make sure a consistent application of policy is adhered to at all times.

Today, Jack E. Howey, managing editor, explains: "Our policy regarding juveniles is to use the names, ages and addresses of all persons 16 and older charged with various offenses. If a juvenile is under 16, we don't publish the name unless the offense is serious enough to be waived into adult court.

"There have been occasions in the past when we have published the names of persons under 16 who have appeared in juvenile court, but such instances have been at the request of the circuit judge who also sits as judge of the juvenile court. Without exception they have involved persons with long arrest records found guilty of crimes or acts of vandalism of a serious nature and the use of the names has come after their appearance in court."

Human Interest

In every community, no matter how small, there occur minor brushes with the law or situations reported to police which, in the hands of a skilled writer, can be made into extremely bright copy. In writing brevities originating on the police beat, the rewrite man is permitted considerable stylistic leeway as the emotional appeal outweighs the news interest.

The dire possibilities of equipping residential structures with an inadequate number of baths was demonstrated here today when two indoor bathers were arrested for causing a riot through the too-prolonged use of the only bathtub in the rooming establishment of which they were tenants.

Unfortunately, the two offenders chose Saturday night for a general over-hauling. The operation consumed so much time that the regular weekly indulgence of the other ten guests, awaiting their turn outside the bathroom door, seemed in jeopardy. After a long wait, during which epithets of an uncomplimentary nature were hissed through the keyhole, disorder broke out among the would-be bathers, and soon took on such proportions that a riot call was sent into police headquarters.

When a sufficient number of patrolmen who were not at the moment taking their Saturday night baths could be corralled and sent to the scene, the two bath monopolists were taken into custody, charged with inciting riot and fined the goodly sum of $3, plus costs.

Leonard Rawlings, 45, of 1968 Winthrop avenue, stepped into a saloon Friday and, between beers, told a fellow he'd sure like to have a new car. And as a result, Leonard's $1,070 poorer.

The fellow, a character in a snappy sports jacket, said that it so happened he had a car to sell. If Leonard would meet him the next day at Division street and Wilmette avenue, he'd accommodate him.

Yesterday, Leonard showed up with his $1,070. The other showed up too, saying, "Let me have the money and I'll be back in a jiffy with the car."

That was 6 P.M. By 10 P.M. Leonard got tired of waiting and trudged to the

Central police station. He reported his loss to Sgt. Michael Thomason, who promptly informed Leonard that he undoubtedly had been swindled by a confidence man.

Other Police News

Not all news originating in police headquarters has to do with law-breaking. Police engage in a variety of noncriminal activities, many of which may be newsworthy. For instance, the missing persons bureau of any large department receives hundreds of calls weekly. Children who leave home in search of adventure, old people who wander off and spouses and parents who desert their families often are news. The first intimation that a crime has been committed also may come from a report that a certain person is missing.

New traffic rules, warnings concerning dangerous intersections, demands that householders make better disposal of their garbage and innumerable similar announcements come from police headquarters. Then there are additions to the staff, retirements, promotions, demotions, citations and social activities within the department itself. Monthly, annual and other reports contain statistics and other information of public interest.

Crime Statistics

Since 1930, the Federal Bureau of Investigation, in cooperation with the International Association of Chiefs of Police, has published *Uniform Crime Reports*. Great caution, however, must be exercised in using the statistics therein contained because they are submitted voluntarily by local police departments. As the FBI itself warns, "In publishing the facts sent in by chiefs of police in different cities, the FBI does not vouch for their accuracy. They are given out as current information which may throw some light on problems of crime and criminal law enforcement."

For several years, the crime figures for New York City were so patently inaccurate that the FBI refused to include them in its reports. After the Chicago police department was reorganized under a new commissioner, its improved reporting system indicated crime had increased 85 per cent in a year. Newspaper investigation, however, previously had supported the Chicago Crime commission's contention that the old department had been officially reporting only about one-third of the crimes it actually handled. Among the devices used to minimize the situation were listing automobiles and other objects as lost instead of stolen, making burglaries seem to be larcenies, making grand larcenies seem to be petty larcenies by "writing down" the amount of loss and so forth.

"With reference to the volume of crime—number of offenses—pressures are always present to keep the figures low," the Chicago Crime commission warns. In addition, the same source declares, numerous known crimes never are reported, including (1) various types of sex offenses because the victims wish to avoid the embarrassment of publicity, (2) those which private citizens fail to report because of lack of confidence in the police, (3) those unreported by citizens who do not wish to become involved in extended court actions and (4) matters which are handled by private police or protective agencies.

Negroes and members of other minority groups are especially reluctant to summon policemen to their neighborhoods. This fact counterbalances, in part at least, the greater avidity with which police often arrest members of minority groups.

All these and numerous other factors contribute to making the best crime statistics of questionable validity. They suggest the caution with which newspapers should handle such news and the opportunity that exists for investigative reporting to uncover the truth.

Whenever there seems to be an increase in crime, especially violent crime, there is likely to be a clamor, to which editors often contribute, that the size of the police force should be increased. It is to conjecture, however, how much good huge forces, even large enough to provide a bodyguard for every citizen, would accomplish inasmuch as approximately three-quarters of all homicides are committed indoors by relatives, friends or acquaintances of the victims, and the really big crime, white-collar corporate crime, is stonewalled until a congressional hearing is held.

Situation Stories

One type of interpretative writing open to the police reporter is that in which he describes, not one or a number of specific crimes, but a situation related to antisocial conduct or law enforcement of continuous public interest.

By Marjean Phillips

A woman's handbag is the sleek complement to a costume, a necessary sack to carry half the paperwork of a household, and an object of convenience, responsible for money, keys, identification and quick aids to beauty. True, it's useful, but this cache is a threat to woman's peace of mind. Why? The thing is always disappearing! Half the trouble, women agree, is due to their own forgetfulness. Also, there is the real danger of a purse thief, particularly now when stores and buses are more crowded with holiday shoppers.

What often happens, according to Miss Betty Lou Martin, retail store buyer, is that women put their purses and coats on a counter and turn away to a mirror to try on a blouse.

"They might not even leave the floor," she said, "but someone sees the temptation, picks up the purse, and is away before anyone notices."

AN EASY MISTAKE

Occasionally, a shopper thinks her purse is lost when it's really on her arm, Miss Martin pointed out.

"With a lot of packages you can't get the feeling of where each item is located," she said. "It's natural to think the purse was left behind. Just like looking for glasses on the forehead!"

Lieut. Ora Gregg of the police department cautions that shoulder-type bags are easy prey for the pickpocket.

"If a woman has that style she should be sure to keep her hand on top," he said. "A pickpocket could bump her and easily flip the purse flag and get the billfold. Bumping is to distract the person. If a thief sees he is failing in an attempt, he is likely to go on and say, 'excuse me.'"

Sometimes a woman takes out her money purse, lays it on the counter, and thinks about something else. Then, it is hard to tell whether this is a lost article or a real purse theft, he pointed out.

"The best thing is to always hold on to the purse, as well as packages," he urged.

LOCK PACKAGES IN CAR

Lieutenant Gregg, who commands the general assignment unit of the detective bureau, also advises women to lock their purchases in the trunk of a car, instead of leaving them out in the back seat or floor. That merely tempts a thief to take out a screw driver and go to work.

The street is the scene of other trouble. A purse thief may approach women walking home alone late at night. Miss Margaret F. Richardson, 3304 Wabash avenue, former policewoman, has this advice: "Scream or throw a fit if someone bothers you."

Miss Richardson recalled an incident when she was surprised by a teenage boy, who worked as a team with another youth. He pulled on her purse (a box type hanging over her arm), and failed to take it because she kept jerking and yelling at him. Then the partner came up and asked to help her pick up a package she dropped in the struggle. Suspicious, she warned, "You get away or I'll scream again!" The two-man system is a common tactic, she explained.

TROUBLES IN OFFICES

Office workers, Miss Richardson says, invite disappointment by leaving pocketbooks out on desks. The purses are safer in a locked drawer. If there is no lock, a secretary can place the handbag in a large manila envelope in the desk farthest from the office entrance. The noise of the drawer opening might alert others.

Women have worked out their own safety rules for homes, such as pulling down window shades before counting money. Also garage doors are closed when the homemaker drives out to go downtown.

It's an achievement for young mothers to get out of a grocery store with a child in one arm, parcels in another and the purse, hopefully, someplace in between.

Mrs. J. M. Bills, 7902 Fairway drive, manages by using a shoulder bag; the safest way is to place its closing side against her body. At home, she doesn't leave her purse in the kitchen where it could be spotted by an intruder.

Mrs. Bills recalled that a friend who frequently lost her purse had the unusual habit of going to the movie and placing her purse on the seat next to her.

Another example of carelessness was cited by Mrs. Ed G. Freed, 5820 the Paseo, who observed that women hang large handbags on the backs of their chairs in restaurants. Mrs. Freed keeps her purse on her lap.

LEFT ON BUSSES

Handbags are numerous in the thousands of articles left on buses and streetcars. Of course, some never reach their owners again. Proof of honesty, however, are the 10,000 to 12,000 items returned by the lost articles department of the

Public Serivce company each year. The clerks at the main office are Mrs. Mary Knight and Mrs. Georgia Ashenfelter.

"Operators turn in lost articles at the car barns each day," Mrs. Knight explained. "A quadruple record is made there and the objects are brought to the general office at Eighth and Delaware for thirty days.

"If there is identification, letters are written asking persons to come in. If unclaimed, after thirty days, the articles are sent back to the finder or the operator," she said.

Even Mrs. Knight has lost her purse . . . on a street car.

"Yes, I lost my purse and it beat me home. The person who found it on the street car took it to my home. I had gone back to look for it," she recalled.

[Kansas City *Star*]

CRIMINAL PROCEDURE

When a person is arrested and charged with a crime, he is taken immediately to a jail or police station where he is held pending arraignment. If the arrest is made upon the complaint of another person, the magistrate or judge already has provided the arresting officer with a *warrant* which commands him to bring the defendant to court. Anyone seeking the arrest of another must affirm under oath that he has reasonable grounds for belief in the guilt of the accused. A *search warrant* permits search of a premise where there is reason to believe evidence of a crime may be found. Unless police on raids have search warrants, their testimony is worthless in court. By a *motion to suppress* the evidence the defense obtains the right to question the arresting officer as to the means by which he gained admittance to the place where the arrest was made. Even though the entrance was legitimate, the case still may be dismissed if *entrapment* (inducing someone to commit a crime) is proved.

Arraignment

A person has a constitutional right to be brought into court promptly to be confronted with the charge against him. When that is done, he gives his legal answer to the charge. If he remains mute, a not guilty plea is entered. Then the court proceeds according to its authority.

> Andrew Konstans, 19, of 5700 Michigan avenue, stood mute on arraignment on a murder charge before Recorder's Judge W. L. Swanson. A plea of not guilty was entered for him and he was remanded without bond for examination Dec. 1.
>
> The murder charge resulted from the death of Policeman Arthur Kendricks, 44, of 156 South Wells street. Kendricks died of three gunshot wounds suffered when he interrupted the holdup of a grocery store Nov. 15.

Preliminary Hearing

If the offense is one over which the inferior court does not have jurisdiction, it holds a hearing to determine whether there is enough presumption of guilt to *bind over* the case for grand jury action in the higher court. If it decides differently, it dismisses the case and frees the suspect. In such a case, either on a coroner's jury verdict or on the initiative of the prosecuting attorney, the case still can be presented to the grand jury. Persons charged with indictable offenses frequently waive preliminary hearing.

Judge John A. Williams, sitting in Felony court, today ordered three women held to the grand jury under bonds of $15,000 each in the theft of checks from hallway mailboxes.

If the court in which the prisoner is arraigned has jurisdiction, it holds, not a preliminary hearing, but a trial. Inferior court trials provide abundant human interest material, more than a paper can use.

Frank Peterson, 30, of 2231 Wells street, was called "the lowest of criminals" today by City Judge Raymond C. Owens who sentenced him to a year in Bridewell for obtaining money under false pretenses.

Peterson was found guilty of taking $10 from Mrs. Sarah Thornton, 619 Clybourn avenue, on the promise that he would go to St. Louis to seek her missing husband.

Pending hearing, the prisoner may be released on *bail*, usually requiring a bond of cash or security. Sometimes a person is released on a *recognizance*, which is merely his written promise to appear when wanted or forfeit a stipulated sum.

The Grand Jury

The grand jury must be distinguished from the petit jury. It does not try a case but merely investigates crimes which have been committed and decides whether there is enough evidence to warrant the expense of bringing the accused persons to trial in the circuit or district court. The grand jury hears the evidence of the prosecution only, and, on the basis of that *ex parte* (one-sided) evidence, it may indict the accused.

An *indictment* may take the form of a *true bill* in case the evidence has been submitted by the prosecuting attorney. If the jury itself gathers evidence of a crime, the indictment is called a *presentment*. A grand jury is supposed to investigate the conduct of government in the territory served by the court and to consider conditions which it thinks should be remedied by law.

In some states, accused persons may be brought to trial upon *informations* submitted by the prosecuting attorney under oath and without a grand jury investigation.

Whenever a crime has been committed and the guilty person has not been ascertained, a *John Doe hearing* is held by the grand jury in the attempt to discover the identity of the person wanted. The prosecuting attorney has the power to summon witnesses to any grand jury hearing.

Grand jury proceedings are secret, but there frequently are leaks from which the reporter benefits. It is contempt of court, however, to publish the results of a grand jury action before it is reported in court. Often, newspapers withhold information even longer so that indicted persons not in custody of police can be arrested on a *bench warrant* (or *capias*) without tipoff.

The reporter should watch (1) the number of indictments naming the same person, (2) the number of counts or charges in the same indictment, (3) the number of persons included in the same indictment. By standing outside the jury room, he can determine who the witnesses were and, on his past knowledge of the case, can speculate as to what their testimony must have been. The law under which indictments are returned and the punishment, in case of ultimate conviction, frequently should be obtained. Some states have immunity laws to permit a witness to testify without incriminating himself. The power of the prosecutor in determining what evidence shall be presented to a grand jury makes him an important political figure, and a trained reporter keeps an eye on his office as a public watchdog. In writing his story, the reporter must use great care to accredit every statement to the true bill.

> Five police officers and six private citizens appeared before the special grand jury investigating police department activities in the jury's second consecutive meeting of the week, Tuesday night at East side court.
> One of the first police officers to be called was Detective Sgt. Thomas Buzalka who remained closeted with the jury for more than an hour. While awaiting call, Buzalka chatted with Robert Hull, head of the police garage, and Patrolman R. L. Lincoln, who also appeared before the jury.
> Emerging from the jury room, Buzalka left the building hurriedly with a brief "good night" thrown over his shoulder to those awaiting their turns.

> Six indictments charging five companies and 14 individuals with illegally obtaining 800,000 gallons of cane syrup were returned by the federal grand jury yesterday before Judge Peter Ennis.
> The indictments followed an investigation by the Agriculture and Justice departments to determine how the companies were complying with a supplement to the federal sugar rationing order.

Pleas and Motions

When someone is arraigned on an indictment, or at any time thereafter up to trial, there are numerous pleas and motions that may be made, chiefly by the defense. Those which merely seek delays are called *pleas in abatement*. One such is a *challenge of the panel* (or *to the array*) which contends that the grand jurors were selected or acted improperly. A motion for a *bill of particulars* asks that the charges be made more specific. A motion for a *continuance* is merely a request for a *postponement*. A *severance* may be asked so that a defendant will not have to stand trial with others named in the same indictment.

A *plea to the jurisdiction* challenges the authority of the court. A motion for a *change of venue* asks that the case be transferred to another court or locale or that a new judge be assigned to it. Motions which would stop all action are *pleas in bar*. One is a *demurrer* which contends that even though true the acts alleged in the indictment do not indicate crime. A *plea of former jeopardy* is an assertion that the accused previously has been tried on the same charge.

The two common pleas, of course, are *guilty* and *not guilty*. A modified form of the former is *nolo contendere* by which the accused says he will not contest the charges. It is frequent after a test case when others awaiting trial realize that they have no chance to "beat the rap." It keeps the defendant's record clear of an admission but otherwise is the equivalent of a guilty plea. If any civil action is brought against the defendant, this plea cannot be used against him.

There is no legal plea of "innocent," but some newspapers use the word instead of "not guilty" as a precautionary measure. They fear that the "not" might get lost in the composing room, thereby committing possible libel.

The one important plea that the prosecution can make is *nolle prosequi* (*nol pros*) which means "do not wish to prosecute." It is made when new evidence convinces the prosecutor of the accused's innocence or when there is insufficient evidence to convict. If it occurs under any other circumstances, an alert newspaper should expose the fact.

> Fifteen to 60 years' imprisonment was in prospect for Frankie Waters, 24-year-old fugitive from a Georgia chain gang, who pleaded guilty yesterday to a charge of robbery in the first degree to cover a 15-count indictment alleging robbery and assaults on women passengers in taxicabs he had stolen.
>
> Waters entered his plea before General Sessions Judge T. L. Bohn. After the plea had been made by Waters' court-assigned counsel, Charles Shueman, Judge Bohn asked:
>
> "Do you realize that if you plead guilty I can give you no less than 15 years and up to 60 years?" . . .

> Circuit Attorney Franklin Moore today dismissed in Circuit Judge Harry Jamieson's court, indictments against six precinct officials in the Fifteenth precinct of the Fourth ward, charged with fraudulent removal and secretion of ballots in the primary election, Aug. 7.
>
> The indictments were returned Nov. 3, but the cases have been continued from time to time by the defendants who said they were not ready for trial. The cases were originally assigned to Judge Charles R. Watson, but transferred to Judge Jamieson on a change of venue.
>
> The last continuance was sought Monday by the state, which said it was not ready for trial, in view of the fact that the State Supreme court had not yet acted on applications for permanent writs of prohibition to prevent the Madison grand jury from examining ballot boxes and other election records of the Fourth ward. Moore told a Journal reporter that the records were needed to prosecute the cases.
>
> Those indicted were . . .

Other Preliminaries

When a fugitive from justice in one state is arrested in another, he may be returned to the jurisdiction where he must answer charges by *extradition*. The procedure is for the governor of the state seeking custody of the fugitive to request the governor of the state in which he is apprehended to return him. It is newsworthy when such a request is denied, as it sometimes is by a northern governor reluctant to send a prisoner back south; or in the case of an ex-convict who has lived an exemplary life for years since a prison break. In federal courts, the equivalent of extradition is *removal* from one jurisdiction to another following hearing before a commissioner.

A description of torture allegedly inflicted upon him in the Georgia State penitentiary was given yesterday by an escaped prisoner as he opened a fight against extradition proceedings to return him to that prison.

He is Leland Brothers, 35, who was released Tuesday from the Stateville penitentiary after serving a one-to-three-year sentence from Brown county for armed robbery.

Yesterday he filed a petition for a writ of habeas corpus in the Wayne County Circuit court.

Wardell Moorison, 31, 5387 N. Culver, has waived extradition proceedings in Seattle and will be returned to Milltown to face charges in connection with separate assault incidents on two Milltown men, according to Pelican County Sheriff Walter Stanchfield.

In both criminal and civil cases, *depositions* may be taken with court permission when there is a likelihood that a witness will be unavailable during trial. A deposition differs from an *affidavit* because it is conducted by a court appointee, both sides are notified and the rules of evidence are followed. In other words, the witness testifies under the same conditions that he would in court; the transcript of his testimony may be introduced as evidence.

Witnesses who do appear in court usually are there as the result of *subpoenas* (court orders) which either side may obtain as a matter of right. A *subpoena duces tecum* orders a witness to produce certain real evidence, usually documents and records.

CRIMINAL TRIALS

Most criminal trials (same is true of civil trials) last only a few hours or minutes. Some, however, take days, weeks or months. The story the day before or on the day of trial may forecast its probable length, based on statements by attorneys for both sides and what the reporter knows of the probable evidence.

First Stories

The reporter should include in his story (1) careful tie-back to the crime itself—time, place, names, events; (2) the charges as stated in the indictment; (3) the possible outcome, meaning the minimum and maximum penalties fixed by law for all of the possible verdicts in the case; (4) the probable evidence with names of witnesses and attorneys' statements, if obtainable, as to what they will attempt to establish; (5) any unusual angles, as possible difficulty in obtaining a jury—for instance, one side may be expected to favor persons of ages, occupations, religion or politics different from those favored by the other side—or maybe this is the first trial of its kind, or the first in a long time, or a new law may be applied to some part of the proceedings. The possibilities are limitless.

Picking the Jury

After the indictment has been read and the plea entered, and after any last-minute motions have been disposed of, selection of the jury begins. The jury of twelve is picked from a panel of *veniremen* prepared by the jury commission or its equivalent. They are questioned by attorneys of both sides and, if found unsatisfactory for reasons which are obvious, may be *challenged for cause*. In addition, each side has a stated number of *peremptory challenges* for which no reasons need be given; usually the defense has twice as many as the prosecution. The questioning of prospective jurors is called the *voir dire* (to speak the truth). Clues to future tactics may be obtained from the types of questions asked veniremen. If, for instance, the prosecutor does not inquire whether they are prejudiced against the death penalty, it is apparent he does not intend to ask for that punishment. If the original panel of veniremen is exhausted without a jury's being completed, additional persons are summoned; they are known as *talesmen* and in inferior courts may be brought in off the street or selected from courtroom spectators.

Opening Statements

The state leads off with a statement of what it intends to prove and the nature of the evidence to be introduced. The prosecutor presents no evidence. The defense may make its reply immediately or may wait until after the prosecution's evidence has been presented.

Evidence

First witnesses for the state are called for the purpose of establishing the *corpus delicti*, or proof that a crime was committed. All testimony is given in answer to questions by attorneys. After *direct examination* by attorneys for the side calling him, a witness is subjected to *cross-examination* by attorneys for the other side. They must restrict their questions to matters about which he already has testified and they often attempt to *impeach a witness* by catching him in contradictory statements. Objections to questions frequently are made by counsel; the judge is the arbiter. Occasionally, the jury is taken from the room while arguments on the admissibility of evidence are heard. A *jury view* is the taking of a jury to the scene of a crime or any other place outside the courtroom for the purpose of observing anything pertinent to the case.

After it has presented all of its evidence, both through the testimony of witnesses and by exhibits, the state *rests*. Then the defense usually automatically makes a motion for a *directed verdict of acquittal* on the ground that the state has failed to prove its case. Most such motions are denied as automatically as they are made; when they are not, there is a news story. A *mistrial* can result in case of gross irregularity as an attempt to bribe a juror.

> The overzealous interest of a juror in a robbery case before County Judge Nova in Brooklyn caused a mistrial yesterday, and brought a reprimand from the court. The juror was William E. Rejall, 54 Tompkins place, Brooklyn, who had sat for two days in the trial of Joseph Fernandez, charged with holding up Felix Orrusti, 173 Washington street, Brooklyn.
>
> When the trial opened yesterday, Rejall stood up and asked if he might question the complainant.
>
> "I took the trouble to visit the scene and I want to ask the complaining witness how he could identify anyone in the dark," the juror explained. Judge Nova appeared surprised.
>
> "You are entitled only to the evidence that is submitted in court in the presence of the defendant," the court said. "You should not have gone to the scene. I must declare a mistrial." [New York *Times*]

All motions having been denied, the defense presents its case, beginning with its opening statement if not already made. Direct and cross-examination proceed as before. There follow *rebuttal* witnesses by the state and frequently the recalling of witnesses by either side for further questioning.

Closing Statements

The prosecuting attorney usually has the right to go first and then to follow the attorney for the defense with a brief rebuttal; frequently he waives his right to speak twice and lets the defense go first. These final statements by attorneys are argumentative. Then the judge *charges* the jury, explaining the law in the case, the possible verdicts it can return and the meaning of each. Often the law stipulates the exact wording a judge must use in at least part of his charge. Judges have little right to comment on the evidence itself but by facial expressions, gestures and verbal emphasis they often can prejudice a jury without the fact being evident in a written transcript.

Reporting Trials

In reporting trials of long duration, the reporter bases every new lead on the most important new development since his last preceding story. Factors to consider are

1. Does some new testimony or other evidence contradict or supplement some preceding evidence?
2. Do the questions asked by defense counsel on cross-examination portend what the constructive defense case will be?

3. Is any of the evidence surprising; that is, has it been unreported in connection with either the crime itself or the trial?
4. How do the versions of what happened as presented by both sides coincide or differ?
5. Is there consistency of purpose in the types of objections raised by counsel and in the judge's rulings on them? Is the defense laying the ground for possible future appeal?

Seeking answers to these and similar questions involves an interpretative approach to the assignment. Much of the reporting "on deadline," however, is likely to be strictly factual. Often testimony can be presented in Q and A (question and answer) form if there is space; otherwise, it can be summarized briefly or the important parts quoted. The courtroom scene, including the attitudes of principals, witnesses, relatives, friends and spectators, is newsworthy, especially if there are any disturbances. In capital cases, the way the defendant acts when the verdict is announced is of interest.

While Vincent Cilenti, 32-year-old ex-convict was in County Jail awaiting trial on a first-degree murder charge, he allegedly attempted to "shakedown" Mrs. Mary Carmigiano a second time in connection with the bombing of Angelo Pappalardo's home.

This was the testimony today of Albert P. Lauerhaus, alleged confederate of Cilenti, who is on trial for blackmail and bombing of the Pappalardo home.

The trial was interrupted shortly before noon when John Draggo of 3861 Montevista Rd., Cleveland Heights, a state witness, repudiated a statement he made to police in 1942 accusing Cilenti of "shaking him down" for $100.

Common Pleas Judge Alva R. Corlett excused the jury, summoned attorneys into his chamber and warned them he would not permit perjury in the courtroom.

TELLS OF BULLDOZING

After the noon recess, Draggo reluctantly told a story of being bulldozed by Cilenti into signing papers which Draggo thought made him cosigner for a loan for purchase of an auto. Later, he said, he learned that he had actually been the one to sign the papers and that Cilenti had placed both car and license in Draggo's name, forcing Draggo to make the payments.

Lauerhaus, 32, said it was in November, 1942, while Cilenti was waiting trial in the murder of Peter Laduca (of which he was acquitted) that he sent for Lauerhaus to visit him at County Jail.

"I want you to see Mrs. Carmigiano," Lauerhaus said Cilenti told him. " She owes me some money. Go out and get it for me."

Q. What did you do then?

A. I went out and she said she didn't owe Cilenti any money. I didn't get any money from her.

Lauerhaus said he couldn't remember the exact amount of money Cilenti said she owed. Mrs. Carmigiano said in testimony yesterday that after paying Cilenti $300 she was approached for $600 more.

Lauerhaus confirmed Mrs. Carmigiano's testimony about how he drove her to see Cilenti in September after the Pappalardo home had been bombed.

Then James P. Hart, assistant county prosecutor, asked him: "Did you ever have any conversation with Cilenti about the bombing?" Lauerhaus said he did, talking to him about how Mrs. Carmigiano had complained that Cilenti had bombed the home without telling her about it or getting her approval.

"What does she think I am, a damn fool?" Lauerhaus said Cilenti told him. "Does she think I'd tell her when I'd be there so she could be in the window waiting for the explosion?"

Mrs. Carmigiano, 1392 SOM Center Rd., Mayfield Heights, yesterday told how Cilenti extorted $300 from her for bombing a neighbor's home without her knowledge or approval.

Mrs. Carmigiano, a real estate agent, said Cilenti first came to see her early in 1942, when she lived on Arrowhead Ave., about renting a house. Later, she related, he returned saying he understood she was having trouble with a neighbor.

Mrs. Carmigiano said she told him of arguments she had with the family of Angelo Pappalardo, 19408 Arrowhead Ave.

A. He said I should punish the people next door.

Q. What did you say?

A. Well, I don't know how to punish them. I'm only a widow. There's nothing I can do about it.

Q. What did Cilenti say to this?

A. He said: "I can take care of it for you." I asked him in what way. He replied: "Just leave it to me. We know how to take care of it for you." I told him I didn't want anybody hurt.

Mrs. Carmigiano moved from Arrowhead Ave. in May, 1942. The Pappalardo home was bombed July 8. She told De Marco she read of the bombing in the newspapers. Then Lauerhaus came to see her several times, she said, telling her: "Cilenti wants to see you."

On the second or third visit he came at night and pushed his way into her house, Mrs. Carmigiano said.

Q. What happened then?

A. He took me in his car to 82d St. and Quincy Ave. He left me in the car awhile. I waited about an hour, so I went into a cafe and asked for Cilenti. They said they didn't know where he was. I went back to the car and someone came out and took me to Cilenti. Cilenti said to me, "The job is done. The boys want their money."

Mrs. Carmigiano said she asked: "What money?"

"They want $300."

"For what?"

"For the Pappalardo job," she said Cilenti replied.

ASKED FOR RECEIPT

The interview, she testified, closed with Cilenti driving her home and telling her to get him the money by 2 P.M. that day. She said she borrowed the money from a friend, took it to Cilenti's home, accompanied by one of her sons. She said she gave the money to Cilenti and when she asked for a receipt she testified he told her:

"Oh, no. We don't do business that way."

Mrs. Carmigiano denied she was operating a still in 1941, but added that Cilenti's purpose in wanting to rent a house from her was to establish a hideout for operation of a still. S. M. Lo Presti, defense attorney, sought to show that the money transaction between Mrs. Carmigiano and Cilenti involved a bootlegging deal rather than a bombing.   [Cleveland *Press*]

Verdicts

The jury leaves the courtroom and deliberates, with the foreman presiding. After the case is over, the reporter may find out, by questioning jurors, how many ballots were taken and how the vote stood every time. The length of time it takes a jury to reach unanimity is newsworthy. If no decision ever is reached, the jury is said to be *hung*, and there is a *mistrial*. Some indication of how a jury is thinking may be obtained if it returns to the jury room to ask further instructions or to have part of the evidence read to it again. The reporter's best tipster as to what goes on in a jury room is the bailiff standing guard at the door.

The defendant must be in court when the verdict is read. If a verdict is reached late at night, it may be written and *sealed* and left with a court official, so that the jurors may leave. All, however, must be present when the envelope is opened and the verdict announced. The losing side may demand a *poll* of the jury, which requires every juror to declare that he concurs. If any juror changes his mind during such a poll it is "hot" copy.

> A Criminal Court jury Wednesday night convicted James Kyler, 22, of the murder of a milkman and set his penalty at 14 years in prison.
>
> The jury of nine men and three women deliberated 8 hours 55 minutes in reaching its verdict. The penalty it recommended is the minimum for murder under state law.
>
> Three boys, 8, 10 and 11 years old, were the chief state witnesses who connected Kyler with the slaying of the milkman, Jerome Giza, 30, of 1740 N. Mason, last Oct. 15. Giza was shot to death during a holdup attempt at 117 S. Rockwell.
>
> Kyler, of 2546 W. Monroe, testified at the trial presided over by Judge Joseph J. Drucker that he was in a friend's home at the time of the slaying. His attorney said he would appeal the verdict.
>
> Lennette Earl Brown, 35, of 2500 W. Warren, accused of participating with Kyler in the hold-up slaying of Giza, will go on trial for murder April 3.
>
> [Chicago *Sun-Times*]

Sentences

Unless it is "not guilty" in a felony case, a jury's verdict is advisory only; the judge accepts or rejects it. He may grant a defense motion to *set aside* the verdict and grant a *new trial* if there have been errors which he knows would cause an appellate court to reverse the verdict and *remand* the case. A motion for *arrest of judgment* accompanies such motions to postpone sentencing.

The leeway permitted a judge in pronouncing sentence is established by statute for every crime. In some cases, he may have no choice at all; convictions on a certain charge may mean an automatic sentence of a certain kind. A *suspended sentence* is one which the convicted person does not have to serve pending good behavior. It is rapidly being replaced by *probation* which gives the convicted person limited freedom of action under the supervision of probation officials; if anyone violates the conditions of his probation, he serves not only the original sentence but an additional one also because of the violation. Probation is most common for minors and first offenders. It should not be confused with *parole* which is the supervised conditional release of prisoners who already have served part of their prison terms.

If someone is convicted on more than one count, he may serve his several sentences *concurrently* or *consecutively*. If the former, he serves only the longest of the several sentences; if the latter, he serves the accumulated total of them all. An *indeterminate* sentence sends a convicted person to the penitentiary for "not less than" a designated number of years, and "not more than" another number of years. The exact time of his release is determined by the state board of paroles. Usually he is not eligible to apply for parole until after at least one-third of his time has been served, so judges often give maximum penalties to run consecutively to make release on parole unlikely.

> Clarence Whittle, 20, of 187 South Water street, was sentenced by Judge John S. Anthony in Criminal court yesterday to serve a term of not less than 10 years to life in the penitentiary for armed robbery.
>
> Judge Anthony overruled a motion for a new trial before pronouncing the sentence. Whittle was convicted by a jury Jan. 10 of holding up a tavern at 1700 Ashland avenue, on Sept. 1 and taking $190.
>
> Whittle faces charges of murdering Michael Storms, 50, a tavern owner of 5800 Market street, on July 15. Four others have pleaded guilty to participating in the shooting of Storms and a fifth is under sentence of 20 years in prison.

Punishments

Despite the trend toward individualized treatment of lawbreakers and the substitution of theories of reformation and protection of society for theories of retaliation and expiation, the criminal law still requires that a convicted person "pay his debt to society." To carry out any sentence is to *execute* it, although the popular connotation of the word limits it to cases in which capital punishment is inflicted. The death penalty was virtually outlawed by the United States Supreme Court but it was being neglected anyway because judges and juries are reluctant to impose it. It is within the power of a governor to *commute* any sentence: that is, to reduce it, as from death to life imprisonment. A governor also can issue a *reprieve* which, however, is merely a postponement of execution. A *pardon* is a granting of freedom. If absolute, it restores civil rights. If conditional, it prescribes limits to the ex-convict's behavior. Few states as yet have adequate systems for recompensing persons proved to have been imprisoned wrongly.

THE ETHICS OF CRIME NEWS

No ethical problem connected with newspaper publishing has been more thoroughly discussed by both newspapermen and laymen than the treatment of crime news. Upon his superiors' attitudes toward the problem depends largely the type of occurrences to which the police reporter pays particular attention and the manner in which he writes his articles. A few papers, notably the *Christian Science Monitor*, generally ignore antisocial behavior; others have experimented with leaving crime news off the front page or of playing it down in the writing. Familiar, on the other hand, is the type of newspaper which considers a sensational crime story as second to few other types in potential reader interest.

It is not so much a question of the amount of crime news but of how it is presented. Contrary to popular opinion, only a small proportion of the total offering of the average newspaper relates to lawlessness. Several sociological studies have revealed that whereas readers guess from 25 to 50 per cent of the contents of the newspaper is crime news the actual proportion is hardly 5 per cent.

A Fair Trial vs. A Free Press

Some newspapers, magazines, and radio and television stations have been accused of inciting to crime by glorifying and making heroes of criminals; of assisting criminals to escape by relating detailed accounts of the activities of police; of interfering with the administration of justice by emphasizing the horrible aspects of brutal crimes, by quoting the prosecuting attorney as to the severe punishment he is going to demand and by editorial comment; of causing unfair suffering on the part of the relatives and friends of principals in a criminal case; and of offending public taste by relating lurid details of crimes and scandals.

The sensational and often inaccurate reporting in the '20s and '30s of several murder trials, especially that of Bruno Richard Hauptmann for the murder of the infant Charles A. Lindbergh Jr., led to the formation of a joint committee from the American Bar Association and the American Newspaper Publishers Association and American Society of Newspaper Editors. As a result there was agreement regarding a long list of rules to prevent recurrence of objectionable behavior by both press and bar. Nevertheless, by far the most important issue today is how much pretrial publicity there should be so as not to interfere with a defendant's right to a fair trial before an impartial jury in an unprejudicial atmosphere. Several later United States Supreme Court decisions and adverse criticism of the press contained in the Warren Commission report on the assassination of President John F. Kennedy have renewed the debate. Although not liking the restrictions placed on them by the court, law enforcement officers have nevertheless become cautious about discussing cases with reporters and scrupulous in obeying the rules imposed upon them as regards questioning of suspects, especially that a suspect must be warned immediately of his right to remain silent and have a lawyer. On the other hand some newspapers toned down quite a bit after the United States Supreme Court ordered a new trial for Dr. Sam Sheppard of Cleveland on the ground that the Cleveland newspapers had made a fair trial for him impossible. Said the court in this case: "The press does not simply publish information about trials, but guards against the miscarriage of justice by subjecting the police, prosecutors and judicial processes to extensive public scrutiny and criticism." At issue, however, is how far the press should go in exercising this function without jeopardizing the rights of the defendant. Neither legal nor journalistic leaders are unanimous in their opinions on the matter or regarding the Warren Commission's statement that "the news media, as well as the police authorities . . . share responsibility for failure of law enforcement in Dallas."

In October 1966 the Advisory Committee on Fair Trial and Free Press of the American Bar Association, of which Massachusetts Judge Paul C. Reardon was chairman, issued a preliminary report which most newspapers felt recommended too-narrow restrictions on the press during a pretrial period. Shortly before the report appeared, the Toledo *Blade* and *Times* adopted a code which other papers have emulated. It includes the following:

Before a trial begins, the Toledo papers pledge to publish only the following data:

¶ The name, age and address of the accused.

¶ How, when and where the arrest was made.

¶ The charge and the identity of the complainant.

¶ The fact that a grand jury has returned an indictment and that a trial date has been set.

The policy will be to provide detailed coverage so that information perhaps held back at the time of the arrest may be published later in the proceeding if and when it will not interfere with the judicial process.

During the progress of the case, unless very special circumstances dictate otherwise, the following types of information will not be published:

¶ Any prior criminal record of the accused.

¶ Any so-called confession the accused may have made other than the fact— if it is one—that he has made a statement to the authorities, but with no indication of the nature of the statement.

¶ Any statements by officials construed as detrimental to the accused.

¶ Any statements by lawyers either detrimental to the accused or concerning any defense that is to be made during trial.

¶ Any names of jurors selected for a particular trial.

¶ Any arguments made in court in the absence of the jury, or evidence excluded from the jury.

Other papers have publicized policy changes. The St. Louis *Post-Dispatch* no longer prints the house number of a burglary victim; nor will it report whether a burglar overlooked other valuables. The Boston *Globe* will print the name of a street on which a crime victim lives but not the house number. In common with most other papers, the New York *Times* will not print the name of a rape victim unless she wants it used in alerting the community. The Peru *Tribune* withholds publicity concerning telephoned bomb threats to businesses, industries and public institutions, believing that most such calls are by publicity seekers.

As related in Chapter 2 (see pages 39–43) the press has reason for alarm because of the increase of judicial gag orders since the Caldwell decision.

Some states have legislated to forbid public officials to release certain information to the press and to punish journalists for publishing it. Many voluntary agreements have been reached among bar, bench and press but the total situation is violative of the original freedom of the press concept.

Newspapers seek to obtain advance notices of judicial gag orders and opportunities to be heard. The judge's defense always is his desire to protect a defendant's rights. In Louisiana a higher court called unconstitutional a judge's gag order prohibiting any editorials, investigative articles or open court testimony related to a pretrial hearing.

Understanding the Criminal

Perhaps the most important adverse criticism of the press in the past has been that it has not taken sufficient cognizance of modern criminological and penological thought. By advocating harshness of treatment as the only corrective, by labeling every sex offender (even before apprehended) as a moron (a scientific term meaning high-grade feeble-minded), by pointing to every paroled prisoner violating his parole as proof of the unsoundness of the parole principle, by ridiculing leading thinkers as maudlin sentimentalists, and in other ways, the media, it is charged, are a sizable obstacle in the movement to replace a barbaric philosophy and methods of curbing antisociability with a scientific approach.

Following a scientific study of the life history of Giuseppe Zangara, the psychopathic immigrant who attempted to assassinate President-elect Franklin D. Roosevelt in 1933, Sidney Kobre said in part regarding the manner in which the American press handled the story:

> Newspapers, in theory, print the news as it occurs, head it according to its significance, and comment on its important aspects. Here, certainly, was an opportunity for them to get at the root of a social evil—to insist, rather than on laws to prevent purchase of guns or enforce deportation of aliens, on the essential nature of the problem. Zangara, had the influences under which he labored been understood (and they might have been discovered when he entered the Italian army, when he passed through the immigration bureau, when he was admitted to citizenship, when he was a patient in a hospital), might have been headed off, his physical and psychological ailments corrected. Suggestions for the isolation and treatment of the class from whom are "recruited the criminal types and cranks" might have been made, along with emphasis on the fact that the class is not composed exclusively of aliens. . . .
>
> The newspapers had opportunity to examine the impulse behind the shooting at its root. . . . For the most part they did not do so. Instead they seized upon the "red" stereotype, or proposed police or legislative methods of dealing with the evil once it had arisen, rather than psychiatric or medical methods of preventing it from arising. . . . Most American editors handling this story chose stereotypes and superficialities rather than the more subtle but certainly more fundamental implications. . . .

Since Kobre wrote this article, later expanded for inclusion in his *Backgrounding the News*, there has been considerable improvement on many newspapers. World War II awakened interest in psychiatry and acquainted millions with the fact that abnormal behavior does not necessarily result from malicious willful choice. Sociological research, furthermore, has proved that what is considered criminal in one environment may be perfectly normal in another, and that, particularly in large cities, there are communities in which the incidence of crime remains virtually constant although the racial or nationality complexion of the population changes many times. Gone is belief in "born" criminals, feeblemindedness as a major cause of criminal behavior, and many other unscientific explanations. Today, psychiatry is throwing light on the peculiarities of the individual offender and sociologists are examining slums, economic status, marital relations and other social factors which breed misbehavior.

In tune with the times, few newspapers any longer consult phrenologists, handwriting experts, fortunetellers and other quacks whenever a major crime occurs. Instead, they interview scientists and they steadily are adding to their own staffs specialists able to do more than invent "cute" headline-fitting nicknames for murderers and their victims.

Indicative of the greater journalistic enlightenment are the first few paragraphs of a full-page article which appeared in the *National Observer* for August 8, 1966.

AUSTIN, TEXAS.

The record will show that Charles Joseph Whitman was not a simple man. But who is?

Whitman was, as the world knows by now, a good student, a conscientious husband, an Eagle Scout, a Marine Corps sharpshooter, a hard worker, handsome, strong, fun to be with, popular.

Then last Monday, in the scorch of a 100-degree Austin day, from near the peak of a 341-foot building, he took a deer rifle and killed 13 people and wounded 31. This was a few hours after he had stabbed to death his pretty wife and shot to death his mother. Then police shot him to death.

Gov. John Connally of Texas has announced that the state will convene in a few weeks a conference of psychiatrists and psychologists who will attempt to piece together the reason for such an action. They may never be able to explain Whitman fully, but perhaps their research will tell something more about the murderous mind.

For never in the annals of mass murder has there been such a clean-cut example of a man run amok. If anything, the lesson of Charley Whitman is to remind us how delicate is the human mind, and how little we know of it.

Reflecting last week on the rampage, a medical authority on mental health said he was not surprised that everyone who knew Whitman described him as such a pleasant person.

"It is a sign of how superficial people are about other people," said the doctor. "We assume we know someone from the way he acts outwardly, but how many people get to know anyone well enough to judge his real being?

"Perhaps a perceptive teacher or minister or friend might have seen the stress he was under. But casual friends did not. More people than we would care to admit have this hostility in them. Fortunately, most can control it.

"The common way of destroying someone [with this hostility] is over a period of 25 or 30 years. This boy just did it suddenly."

It is only now apparent that Whitman's strains and vices were present all the time—suppressed, no doubt, by a fierce will power finally incapable of holding them in check, creating a pressure-pot that erupted beyond civilized understanding.

Unfortunately, says one doctor, the whole story will never be known. The data are forever incomplete. There will be theories, but no one will be certain how valid any of them are.

Before the experts have a crack at it, here are a few of the pieces to the puzzle, some not widely known, which contributed to this deadly state of mind.

15

COURTS, CIVIL LAW, APPEALS

A. Kinds of Law
B. The Court System
  1. Inferior Courts
  2. County and Probate Courts
  3. Courts of First Instance
  4. Appellate Courts
  5. Federal Courts
  6. Officers of the Court
C. Civil Law
  1. Starting an Action
  2. Defending an Action
  3. Civil Trials
  4. Enforcing Civil Law
D. Civil Actions
  1. Damage Suits
  2. Libel
  3. Divorce
  4. Foreclosures
  5. Evictions
  6. Condemnation Suits
  7. Receiverships
  8. Bankruptcy
  9. Injunctions
  10. Contracts

E. Extraordinary Remedies
  1. Prohibition
  2. Certiorari
  3. Mandamus
  4. Quo Warranto
F. Probate Proceedings
  1. Filing a Will
  2. Admitting to Probate
  3. Contesting a Will
G. Rules of Evidence
  1. Nature of Evidence
  2. Burden of Proof
  3. Presumptions
  4. Judicial Notice
  5. Qualifications of Witnesses
  6. Privilege
  7. Leading Questions
  8. Hearsay Evidence
  9. Opinion Evidence
  10. Real Evidence
  11. Circumstantial Evidence
  12. Best Evidence
H. Appeals

Just as it is essential for a sports reporter who covers baseball to understand the rules of the game, so is it necessary for the reporter assigned to the courts to know the basic structure of American law.

KINDS OF LAW

Roughly, all laws can be divided into *public* and *private* (usually called *civil*), the distinction being whether the state (organized society) is a party to the litigation. The dichotomy is not exact because government can be a party to certain types of civil actions. In general, however, the distinction holds. Branches of public law include constitutional, administrative, international and criminal, with the ordinary reporter, of course, being most interested in the last.

The two major divisions of private, or civil, law are *common law* and *equity*. The former is that law which was developed through the centuries in judicial decisions in English courts, and—roughly again—it can be divided into *real* and *personal* law. Real law relates to the possession of and title to property whereas personal law relates to attempts to recover damages for injuries received, to enforce a contract, to bring about the return of property and to settle similar matters. The two major divisions of personal law relate to *contracts* and *torts* (all injuries received other than by violation of contract). Equity law, as developed in the equity (or *chancery*) courts of England, begins where law leaves off. One does not go to equity to recover damages for injuries to himself or his property, but to compel someone to do or to refrain from doing something. Modern equity courts handle such matters as injunctions, foreclosures, receiverships, partitions etc.

The law administered in the courts originates either (1) in the acts of Congress, of a state legislature or of some other lawmaking body, such law being known as *statutory*, or (2) in the accumulated decisions of courts both here and in England, such law being known as *common law*. Courts adhere to the principle of *stare decisis* (let the decision stand), which means that lawyers quote at length from decisions in earlier cases in the attempt to show that the case in hand should be decided similarly. When there has been a pertinent decision by the Supreme Court of the United States or some state appellate court, the issue may seem clearcut. Usually, however, such is not the case. Either the matter at hand differs in some essential from the previously decided case, or the appellate court decision is limited in scope. Also, there may be conflicting decisions in apparently identical cases.

Young reporters should know that, despite the apparent inconsistencies in both the written (*basic*) law itself and common law decisions, and despite their ability to find citations to substantiate both or all sides of almost any argument, lawyers as a whole profess belief in the existence of absolute justice, and hold that the purpose of any court case is to find the abstract principle which applies. Such lawyers are not conscious rogues, whose main interest is to " play a game " and win a judgment for their clients at all costs. They have been trained to think in a precise specialized manner which makes it easy for them to rationalize their actions, even though to the layman the results may not seem tantamount to anything resembling common sense or justice.

THE COURT SYSTEM

A knowledge of the court system of the state in which he works is essential to the reporter assigned to cover the courts. If he moves from one state to another he will discover that even the names of generally similar courts may differ. For instance, what is known as a circuit court in Indiana is called a district court in Nebraska, a superior court in Massachusetts and a supreme court in New York.

The jurisdictions of courts also differ, even between counties of different sizes within the same state. For instance, there may be a separate probate court in one county or state whereas probate matters may be handled by the circuit court or its equivalent in another place. One court may handle both civil and criminal matters or there may be different courts (*common pleas* courts are civil courts; courts of *oyer and terminer* are criminal courts). Similarly, law and equity courts may be separate or combined. The practice is growing of establishing special branches of courts to handle particular kinds of cases, and these branches may be referred to in news stories by their specialized names, such as Renters' Court, Juvenile Court, Traffic Court, Divorce Court. To the reader, it makes little or no difference that such courts really are only branches of a circuit, municipal or county court, but the reporter should know their nature.

It is particularly important that the reporter know which are *courts of record*, that is, ones which keep a permanent record of their proceedings. What happens in *courts not of record* is not privileged and the newspaper which covers them must be careful to avoid committing libel.

Differences in both *substantive law* (defines what is and is not proper behavior) and *adjective law* (defines legal rules and procedures) also provide potential snares for unwary newsmen. For instance, in one state grand larceny may be defined as stealing anything worth more than $15 whereas in another state stealing anything worth less than $100 or .$1,000 may be petty larceny. Since inferior courts generally can handle petty larceny cases but not grand larceny cases, the same offense committed in one jurisdiction will be tried in one type of court whereas if it happens in another jurisdiction it will be tried in a different type court. In one jurisdiction, a civil action may be considered to have begun with the filing of a complaint, whereupon the reporter is safe in reporting it; in another, however, the action is not considered to exist until the other party has been notified. Similar rules may affect all motions by attorneys and court rulings.

Fortunately, the similarities between the 50 court systems are greater than their differences. Roughly, the typical system is as follows:

Inferior Courts

Inferior courts have the least amount of jurisdiction. Generally they can handle criminal cases involving misdemeanors for which the punishment is a fine only. Their jurisdiction in civil matters generally is limited to cases in which the amount of money does not exceed a few hundred dollars. Among the most common of such courts are the following: *justice of the peace* (townships); *police magistrates* (limited to a city or a section of a city); and *city* and *municipal* courts, which, however, in some larger places may have much greater jurisdiction.

County and Probate Courts

The jurisdiction of a county court depends upon what other state courts exist. Thus, it may be an inferior court or a court of first instance, with unlimited jurisdiction in civil and criminal matters. In other cases, it may operate mostly as a probate or juvenile court or as overseer of the election machinery and county institutions and agencies concerned with poor relief, adoptions and similar matters. Probate courts supervise the disposition of the estates of deceased persons and may also handle adoptions, lunacy hearings, commitments of feeble-minded and insane persons and guardianships for minor and incompetents.

Courts of First Instance

The "backbone" courts are the circuit, superior, district, supreme or whatever they are called. In them, all kinds of civil actions may be brought and, unless there are separate criminal courts, criminal matters as well. In some states, there are separate equity, divorce and other courts, but in a large majoirty of states the court of original jurisdiction either has separate calendars or branches for different kinds of civil actions. The criminal court may be set up separately or may be a branch of the circuit court. It may handle all kinds of criminal matters, or there may be separate courts for felonies (as the Court of General Sessions in New York). The number of circuit or district courts in a state is dependent upon the state's size and population. A large city or county may be a circuit in itself and may be permitted a large number of judges, the exact number being established by constitution or statute. Outside of thickly populated areas, a circuit may include two, three, ten or more counties and the judges may hold court at different times in different county seats. The number of terms annually and often their length are established by constitution or statute.

Appellate Courts

Appellate courts do not try cases originally, but only review decisions reached by courts of jurisdiction in the first instance when defeated parties, dissatified with lower court decisions, appeal to the higher courts. In smaller states, there is likely to be only one appellate court, usually called supreme, ranging in size from three to twenty-three judges, either appointed by the governor with the consent of the state legislature or elected (at large or by divisions). In larger states, there are intermediate courts of review, often called circuit courts of appeal, which, however, seldom if ever receive appeals involving constitutional or other important matters. Some of the decisions of the intermediate court may be appealed a second time to the highest appellate court, either as a matter of right or with that court's permission. The three, five, seven or more members of an intermediate appellate court may be appointed or elected, or they may be regularly elected circuit or district court judges assigned to appellate court duty by the supreme court. Appellate courts do not try cases as lower courts do; they merely pass on the arguments of attorneys in the case as presented to them in written form (*briefs*) and orally (at *hearings*). The practice is growing to permit new evidence not introduced in an original trial of a case to be presented to an appellate court, but this is not yet common practice. All appellate court decisions are by majority vote of the judges; there never is anything resembling a jury trial in an appellate court.

Federal Courts

Although it is growing in importance with the passage by Congress of an increasing number of laws defining as federal crimes certain offenses of which formerly only the states took cognizance, and with the establishment of additional federal court districts, the federal judicial system is outside the worries of the average small-city reporter. Anyone arrested in his territory for a federal offense is taken for arraignment to the nearest city in which a federal court is situated.

Despite the activities of the Federal Bureau of Investigation in recent years, kidnaping is not a federal offense because Congress does not believe the Supreme Court would hold constitutional a law declaring it such. The so-called Lindbergh law makes the transportation of a kidnaped person across state lines a federal offense which, together with the federal law against sending ransom notes through the mails, allows the FBI to enter kidnaping cases.

Similar technicalities permit federal agents to participate in other criminal cases. For instance, automobile theft is not a federal crime but transporting stolen automobiles across state lines is prohibited by the Dyer act; seduction is not a federal offense but transporting a female across state lines for immoral purposes is prohibited by the Mann act. The notorious Al Capone was convicted in a federal court not for gangsterism but for failure to make a faithful federal income tax return. Law enforcement officials and others are prosecuted in federal court not for murder but for depriving a dead person of his civil liberties.

In addition to those suggested, cases commonly handled by the federal courts include (1) frauds against the federal government, including embezzlements from national banks; (2) citizenship and denaturalization cases; (3) violations of federal income tax and other revenue laws; (4) violations of post office regulations, including sending threats and other improper material through the mail, rifling mailboxes and other interferences with the mails; (5) violations of federal statutes such as the food and drug acts, antitrust act, Securities and Exchange act, Interstate Commerce act, narcotics act and Railway Labor act; (6) bankruptcy proceedings.

Officers of the Court

Officers of a circuit court or a court with similar jurisdiction are as follows: (1) The *judge* presides during trials, decides points of law, rules on the admissibility of evidence, instructs juries as to the law, pronounces final judgments and sentences, admits criminal defendants to probation. In fact, the judge *is* the court and even his oral orders are authoritative and violations of them constitute contempt of court. (2) The *clerk of court* receives applications and motions made formally to him for the record, preserves pleadings until used in a formal trial, prepares a court docket and trial calendar with the cooperation of the judge, during a trial records all motions and prepares records and orders of the judge, receives moneys paid to the court as fines, damages and judgments. (3) The *prosecuting attorney* prosecutes all civil and criminal actions in which the state is a party, defends actions brought against the county, examines all persons brought before any judge on habeas corpus, gives legal opinions to any county officer or justice of the peace and, in general, represents the constituency electing him in all legal matters. The prosecuting attorney usually is called *district attorney* or *state's attorney*. (4) The *public defender* is paid by the state to defend persons unable to afford private counsel; where no such officer exists the court often appoints a member of the local bar to serve in that capacity. (5) The *bailiff* acts as sergeant-at-arms, announces the opening of court ("Hear ye, hear ye," and so forth), keeps order in the courtroom, calls witnesses, ushers jurors from the jury room and acts as messenger. Many bailiffs really are *sheriff's deputies*, assigned to the courts. In justice of the peace courts the comparable officer is the *constable*, in federal courts it is the *marshal*. (6) The *masters, referees* and *commissioners* act as "assistant judges" in civil matters. They hear protracted testimony and make recommendations to the judge who has final authority. Masters act in *chancery* (equity) matters and referees in *common law* matters. Commissioners in state courts are appointed for particular tasks, mostly investigative; federal commissioners are examining magistrates in criminal matters. (7) The *court reporter* is not an elected official but a licensed stenographer authorized to take verbatim testimony and prepare notes in a transcript of evidence called a record. The court reporter may sell copies of his transcript to parties engaged in a trial; in cases of appeal, several copies of a transcript are necessary. (8) A *friend of the court* is a temporarily appointed adviser to the judge who serves during the particular case for which he is selected. (9) The *jury commissioners* make up a jury list or panel consisting of the names of a certain number of voters in the territory served by the court for each term of court. In smaller counties, the board of supervisors appoints the commissioners; in larger counties, the county judge does so.

CIVIL LAW

Through codification and/or passage of civil practices acts, many states have simplified both substantive and adjective law. Whereas formerly it was necessary to bring parts of the same action in different courts, in the federal courts and many state courts, it now is possible to ask for both legal and equitable relief in the same action. For instance, you can ask for *damages* (legal relief) and for an *injunction* (equitable relief) to prevent continuation of the cause of injury in the same complaint.

The reporter must be warned, however, that such is not universally true. Several Atlantic seaboard states in particular still adhere to old common law and equity definitions and procedures. In those states one would not bring a simple action to set aside a contract or to force compliance with it or to recover damages because of its breach. Rather, one would bring an action in *covenant* (to recover money damages) or *debt* (to recover specific sums) or *assumpsit* (for damages if the contract was not under seal) or *detinue* (to recover specific chattels). Similarly, a damage suit (tort action) would be one in *trespass* (for money damages) or *trespass on the case* (if injuries were not the direct result of the action complained of) or *detinue* (to recover specific chattels) or *replevin* (a statutory right to recover both property and damages), or *trover* (damages in case the property is lost, destroyed or otherwise incapable of return), or *deceit* (damages for a wrong committed deceitfully).

Starting an Action

In noncode states a common law action is an *action at law* whereas a case in equity is a *suit in equity*. In federal courts and states with civil practices acts, there is just one *civil action*. To start it the *plaintiff* (he who brings the action) files a *petition* (also called *declaration* or *complaint* or *statement of claim*) stating clearly the alleged cause for action and the relief which he wishes the court to grant. Every paragraph of the complaint is numbered and is called a *count*. When he files an *answer*, as he must do within a specified period to avoid the plaintiff's winning a *judgment by default*, the *defendant* (often called *respondent*, with any third parties mentioned as equally guilty being *co-respondents*) must admit or deny each count. In the old days, litigants could continue arguing a case on paper almost indefinitely. Under simplified procedures, the *pleadings*—as all such written arguments are called—are limited to two or three by each party.

There follows a typical complaint:

STATE OF ILLINOIS ⎱
                 SS
COUNTY OF COOK ⎰

IN THE SUPERIOR COURT OF COOK COUNTY

IRIS GARDNER,
     Plaintiff
     —vs.—   NO. 42 s 10542
CHARLES W. WRIGLEY,
     Defendant

COMPLAINT AT LAW FOR
BREACH OF CONTRACT
JURY DEMANDED

Now comes IRIS GARDNER, plaintiff in the above entitled cause, and complains of the defendant, CHARLES W. WRIGLEY, as follows:

1. That the plaintiff was, on the 15th day of October A.D. 1937 temporarily sojourning in the City of Chicago, County of Cook and State of Illinois; and, on the date aforesaid, she was about to depart from the said city, county and state, and return to her domiciliary city and state, to-wit: St. Louis, Missouri.

2. That plaintiff had a long social acquaintance and friendship with the defendant, CHARLES W. WRIGLEY, prior to October 15, A.D. 1937, when, on the date, aforesaid, she, the plaintiff, at the special instance and request of the defendant, CHARLES W. WRIGLEY, met the defendant, CHARLES W. WRIGLEY, in his offices, located at 400 North Michigan Avenue, in the City of Chicago, County of Cook and State of Illinois, and that at the place and on the date aforesaid, plaintiff entered into a verbal agreement with the defendant, CHARLES W. WRIGLEY, the substance of which agreement is hereinafter verbatim alleged.

3. That the defendant, CHARLES W. WRIGLEY, was then, and is now, engaged in the advertising business, and was then, and is now, reputed to have considerable material wealth.

4. That the plaintiff was the, and is now, a woman possessed of pulchritude, charm, and numerous other attributes and qualities to enchant, charm, and grace any person; or, in fact, any social circle.

5. That the defendant, CHARLES W. WRIGLEY, met the plaintiff, at the place and on the date aforesaid, at his special instance and request, and then and there the defendant, CHARLES W. WRIGLEY, was expressly charmed and enchanted by the plaintiff, because of plaintiff's charm, graciousness, and other womanly qualities and attributes and thereupon the defendant, CHARLES W. WRIGLEY, informed plaintiff that she was the person for whom he had been searching to assist him, socially and in his business. Whereupon, the parties entered into a verbal agreement, which, in words, figures and substance, is as follows:

a. The defendant, CHALRES W. WRIGLEY, verbally agreed with the plaintiff to pay plaintiff the sum of One Thousand Dollars ($1,000) per month, either in cash, or by letters of credit, or in any other mode or manner the plaintiff might see fit provided the said sum was paid in full to the plaintiff before the expiration of each and every month, commencing on the 1st day of November, A.D. 1937, during the rest of her natural life; and the defendant, CHARLES W. WRIGLEY, further agreed, in order to protect plaintiff, in the event he predeceased plaintiff, to create a trust in the sum of Two Hundred and Fifty Thousand Dollars ($250,000.00), said trust to be evidenced by a trust agreement, the provisions of which trust agreement were to provide that the plaintiff would be entitled to receive the proceeds, rents, profits, and emoluments accruing therefrom, during the plaintiff's natural life.

b. That in consideration of the said verbal agreement, the plaintiff was to cancel her then imminent departure, as aforesaid from the City of Chicago, County of Cook and State of Illinois; and it was further agreed that the plaintiff should reside and domicile continuously in the City of Chicago, County of Cook and State of Illinois, during the natural life of the defendant, CHARLES W. WRIGLEY, in order to assist the defendant, CHARLES W. WRIGLEY, in his social activities, as the defendant might, from time to time, direct, which social activities, according to the defendant, CHARLES W. WRIGLEY, could be efficaciously performed only by the plaintiff, or by some other member of the fair sex with abilities co-equal to those possessed by the plaintiff.

c. That in pursuance of said verbal agreement, the plaintiff remained, resided and domiciled, and continues to remain, reside and domicile, in the City of Chicago, County of Cook and State of Illinois; that the defendant, CHARLES W. WRIGLEY, in pursuance of the terms of said verbal agreement, obtained or rented an apartment on behalf of the plaintiff, at the St. Clair Hotel, and paid plaintiff (in cash or by check, or paid the expenditures of the plaintiff directly to plaintiff's creditors) the stipulated consideration thereof to wit: One Thousand Dollars ($1,000.00) per month, including the rental for said apartment; and that the defendant, CHARLES W. WRIGLEY, continued to comply with the terms of said agreement until on or about the 30th day of May, A.D. 1943, on which date the defendant, CHARLES W. WRIGLEY, expressly repudiated the same, verbally informing and advising plaintiff that he would no longer continue payment thereof, in view of his reduced financial status.

6. That in pursuance of the terms of said verbal agreement, the plaintiff heretofore has exerted much effort, and expended her youth, grace and charm, to the end of ameliorating defendant's social as well as esthetic, well-being.

7. That at the time the aforesaid agreement was entered into defendant was approximately twenty (20) years plaintiff's senior.

8. That the plaintiff has performed each and every condition of her contract with the defendant, CHARLES W. WRIGLEY, whether precedent or subsequent, and she is not in default thereof.

9. That the defendant, CHARLES W. WRIGLEY, has wilfully and maliciously, and without any just cause, but merely whimsically, breached the provisions of said verbal agreement.

10. That the plaintiff has sustained damages, by reason of the breach of said agreement by the defendant, CHARLES W. WRIGLEY, in the sum of Five Hundred Thousand Dollars ($500,000.00).

WHEREFORE, plaintiff brings her suit, and asks that a judgment be entered in her behalf and against the defendant, CHARLES W. WRIGLEY, in the sum of Five Hundred Thousand Dollars ($500,000.00) and costs.

This is how the Chicago *Sun* handled this news:

Suit for $500,000 charging breach of contract, was filed in Superior Court yesterday against Charles W. Wrigley, 71, brother of the late William Wrigley Jr., chewing-gum magnate, by a woman who described herself as possessing "pulchritude, charm, and manner."

She is identified in the bill as Mrs. Iris Gardner, 41, of the St. Clair Hotel.

Her complaint, according to the bill, alleges that Wrigley is not paying her $1,000 a month. He agreed to do this back in 1937, she said, and kept up the payments for six years before quitting.

WRIGLEY INDIGNANT

Wrigley, head of an outdoor advertising firm, with offices at 400 N. Michigan av., indignantly denied the entire alleged transaction. Reached at his home, Canterbury ct., Wilmette, he said:

"It's an outrage to file a suit like that. The lady's husband worked for me 15 years ago.

"She never worked for me. As to the payments of $1,000 a month, why, that's crazy! Where would I get the money? She started after me just after Charlie Chaplin's trouble."

According to the bill, Wrigley, uncle of Philip K. Wrigley, owner of the Chicago Cubs, agreed to pay Mrs. Gardner $1,000 a month for life and, if he died first, leave a $250,000 trust fund to provide the income.

In return, the bill continued, Mrs. Gardner was to "assist him socially and in his business." The agreement, Mrs. Gardner said, was verbal.

Note that (1) the reporter obtained information other than that contained in the complaint, and (2) he exercised great care in ascribing every fact based on the complaint to the complaint itself, by means of such phrases as "according to the bill" and "the bill continued." It is absolutely necessary never to allow any statement in a story based on a legal document to stand by itself, even at the risk of boring repetition of references.

Defending an Action

A defendant who has been properly served by *summons* (law) or *subpoena* (equity) must answer within a prescribed time or at least file an *appearance*, which is an acknowledgment and indication that he will answer later. When the answer is filed the reporter scans it for its contents.

To avoid answering, the defendant may enter a *motion to dismiss* the action, contending that the plaintiff has no legal right to bring it. In such a motion, he may challenge the jurisdiction of the court or the sufficiency of the process by which he was notified of the beginning of the suit; or, most importantly, he may contend that the plaintiff has failed to state a ground for action. Under old procedures, he may enter a *demurrer*, which is a plea that, even if true, the facts alleged do not constitute a cause for action. He also may plead that the *statute of limitations*, which sets the time limit within which such action can be brought, has been violated.

To delay or postpone the case, the defendant may resort to dilatory tactics by a *plea in abatement* which may (1) *challenge the array*—that is, question the procedure by which the panel of veniremen (potential jurors) was selected as the case nears trial; (2) ask a *change of venue*, which is a transfer to another court or branch of the same court on the grounds that judge or jurors are prejudiced; (3) ask a *continuance*, or postponement, for any of a variety of reasons, the merits of which the judge must decide; (4) be a *motion to quash* because the summons was defective.

A special kind of answer is one in *confession and avoidance* wherein the defendant admits the facts but declares he acted within his legal rights. A *counterclaim* is an answer in which the defendant not only denies liability but contends that the plaintiff is obligated to him. Counterclaims are frequent in damage cases involving automobile accidents; each driver blames the other.

When several actions related to the same incident are begun, the court may order that there be a *joinder of parties* or *joinder of causes*. On the other hand, on its own motion or that of one of the parties, the court may grant a *severance* when co-defendants make separate answers. A third party who believes his interests are affected by the action may petition the court for permission to file an *intervening* petition to become either a plaintiff or defendant.

So that he will understand what is going on, the reporter should be familiar with a few other types of motions: (1) a *bill of particulars* may be demanded by the defendant if the complaint is unclear or not sufficiently specific; (2) a *bill of discovery* may be asked if the defendant wishes to examine documents or other material in the plaintiff's possession; (3) either party may ask permission to submit an *interrogatory*, or set of questions, to the other to obtain necessary information; (4) scandalous, redundant, irrelevant or otherwise objectionable portions of any pleading may be eliminated if the court grants a *motion to strike*.

Civil Trials

Unless there is a *default judgment* (or *decree*) because of failure of the defendant to answer or a *summary judgment* because the answer is inadequate or a *judgment by confession* because the defendant admits the plaintiff's charges, the issue becomes joined and, upon motion of either party or the court itself, the case is placed on the trial calendar.

Most civil trials today are heard by a judge alone. In fact, it generally is necessary to make a formal request and pay a court fee at the time of filing a complaint or answer to obtain a civil trial by jury. Except for the preliminary step of selecting the jurors, theoretically the procedure is the same. The steps are as follows:

1. Opening statement by plaintiff, through his attorney, of what he expects to prove.
2. Opening statement by defendant. (Often waived.)
3. Direct examination of plaintiff's witnesses.
4. Cross-examination by defendant of plaintiff's witnesses.
5. Direct and cross-examination of defendant's witnesses.
6. Redirect or rebuttal witnesses for plaintiff.
7. Closing statements by both sides, plaintiff speaking first, then the defendant, and, finally, rebuttal by plaintiff.

In actual practice, a hearing before a judge usually is informal. With all of the principals and their attorneys and witnesses clustered about the bench, the judge may interrupt, change the usual order of procedure and take a hand at questioning. Then he either takes the case under *advisement* (meaning he wants to think it over before deciding) or he enters a *judgment* for either plaintiff or defendant, in a law action, or a *decree* if the case is one at equity. Even if there is a jury, it can only recommend what *damages* are to be assessed against the loser in a law action; the final decision is up to the judge and, upon motion of the losing party or on his own initiative, he can disregard the jury's findings and enter a *judgment notwithstanding the verdict*.

Damages may be (1) *general*, meaning they are the same as might be expected to compensate anyone for the type of loss proved to have been incurred; (2) *special*, those peculiar to the particular case; (3) *nominal*, which are trifling and for the purpose of moral vindicatión only; or (4) *exemplary*, assessed in addition to the general or *compensatory* damages, to punish the other party.

> A judgement for $119,358 against the Global Securities & Holding company as stockholders in the Acorn National bank, was ordered by Federal Judge Frick today in favor of Gerald Swayne, receiver of the bank. The amount of the judgment represented a double assessment against the company as holders of 1001 shares of the bank's stock and $9,358 accrued interest.

A civil action may end in a *nonsuit* if at any time the plaintiff fails to continue; such a judgment naturally is for the defendant. So is a *dismissal*, the difference being, however, that in case of a nonsuit the plaintiff may begin another action whereas a dismissal is a final disposition of a case, unless it is a *dismissal without prejudice* which usually comes upon request of the plaintiff himself. A *consent* judgment is entered when the court approves an out-of-court agreement between the parties. A *declaratory* judgment, obtaininable in federal courts and some state courts, is an informatory opinion in advance of any legal action; by means of it the court declares what its decision would be in the event action were brought. Its use prevents much expensive and useless litigation.

An ordinary judgment or decree is either (1) *final*, or (2) *conditional*, which means certain acts (as exchange of property) must be performed before it becomes final, or (3) *nisi* (unless), which means it becomes final after a certain lapse of time if certain forbidden acts do not occur, or (4) *interlocutory*, in which case restrictions on behavior—as against remarriage —are designated.

Enforcing Civil Law

There is no imprisonment for debt in the United States, so a plaintiff may not be much better off after he receives a judgment against a defendant than before. By applying for a *writ of execution*, the judgment creditor can force sale of the judgment debtor's property to satisfy his claim, but if the debtor does not possess enough assets to meet the obligation it is often better to allow the judgment to stand as a lien against what he does have until the day when it is wise to enforce it. To discover a debtor's assets, a creditor may obtain a court *citation* ordering the debtor to appear in court for questioning by a referee. Failure to comply means that one may be cited for *contempt of court* which, in some cases, may be punished by imprisonment. In such cases, however, the judgment creditor usually has to pay for the debtor's keep. The inmates of "alimony row" in the county jail are contemptuous divorcees.

Either at the beginning of a suit or after a judgment has been obtained, the plaintiff may obtain a *property attachment*, placing the defendant's assets under control of the court to prevent their conversion. A *body attachment* or *execution* is a court order to arrest a principal to prevent his untimely departure from its jurisdiction. A *ne exeat* decree is an order forbidding such departure. *Garnishment* proceedings are for the purpose of attaching a debtor's income, usually his salary, for the benefit of the creditor.

If a court becomes convinced that a supposedly closed case should be reopened, it can entertain a motion to *reinstate* a case which has been dismissed, to *set aside* a verdict, to *vacate* a judgment or to *review* a decree. A *writ of audita querela* stops execution of a judgment when new evidence is presented. A *writ of supersedeas* orders a court officer to stop execution which has not gone too far.

Many damage suits contain a *malice* count which means that the alleged injury was committed intentionally or because of gross negligence. If the court upholds the contention, the guilty defendant may be jailed if he fails to satisfy the judgment.

The following feature story illustrates how an interpretative court reporter can help inform the public regarding legal and judicial matters.

By Leigh Morris

Winning in the courtroom may be the simplest part of a personal injury suit against the city.

Difficulty arises when the victim attempts to collect.

According to City Controler Otto Loser, the city is now 2½ years behind in payment of judgments over $1,000. Those who are to receive less than $1,000 are paid within a few weeks in accordance with state law.

As a result, the individual with a major claim has two options. He may decide to wait out the 2½ years for his money—money that may be needed to pay medical expenses and support a family.

The other option allows the victim to collect his award shortly after the trial, but this may prove expensive. About 60 percent of those with claims choose this method.

Several law firms in the city will purchase judgments, retaining anywhere up to 15 percent for themselves. Thus, a person who has been awarded $10,000, may only get $8,500. Of course, legal expenses must still be paid out of the remaining amount.

"We are actually rendering people a service by buying their claims," said Jonas Wolfberg, a partner in the law firm of Wolfberg & Kroll, 10 N. Clark St.

"We are providing them with money they need and we are entitled to a profit of 15 percent for the time we must wait for the money. I fear we may have to raise the percentage we retain if the tight money market continues."

The source of the problem is the city's tax collection machinery.

For example, in December of 1969 the city appropriated $4.5 million, the maximum allowed under state law, for the city's judgment fund. That money was to cover judgments awarded before December.

However, the city will not receive any of that tax money until May of 1971, and not until September of that year will all tax monies be collected.

The city has moved to ease part of the problem by selling tax anticipation warrants to raise funds to pay judgments.

The city may sell warrants during the same year the taxes are to be collected, but the warrants may only total 75 percent of the tax yield.   [Chicago *Today*]

CIVIL ACTIONS

There are a seemingly interminable number of kinds of actions. Judges and lawyers with years of experience pore over ponderous legal tomes for hours to refresh their memories regarding many of them. The lay reporter cannot be expected to master the intricacies of even an appreciable number of them. If he understands the basic differences between the major types of actions and can translate the most frequently used legal language, he can get along. There are several good law dictionaries which he can consult when he "encounters a new one." What follows are a few suggestions concerning some of the kinds of actions which are most newsworthy.

Damage Suits

The news interest usually is in the incident giving rise to the action: an automobile accident, a surgeon's error and so forth. If so, perhaps the paper carried a story at the time, which means the account of the filing of the complaint should contain a careful tie-back. The reporter should get: names and addresses of principals; the plaintiff's version of exactly what happened, all charges being carefully accredited to the complaint; the comments of the defendant on the charges; the amount of money demanded; is there a malice count?

> Howard Bates filed a $30,000 damage suit in Lanchester District Court Wednesday in connection with a fall he incurred while loading furniture belonging to the defendant, Harold Bride.
> Bates who operates a long-distance moving firm, alleges that on Aug. 3, 1974 while in the process of loading the van to move Bride from Littleton, Colo., to Lincoln, he requested Bride to get him a ladder so he could inspect the load on top of the van.
> He contends that the defendant was negligent in setting up the ladder and, as a result, it collapsed and he suffered a fractured wrist.
> He alleges 20% permanent partial disability.

Strong warning against this type of reporting was included in a letter from Thomas F. Driscoll, assistant managing editor of the Peoria *Journal Star:*

> I have been trying for several years to try to make a dent in the journalistic practice of making a great to-do over damage suits in which the plaintiff seeks sizeable damages. Editors are suckers for a story like this, and lawyers have found that they are virtually certain of getting a story published if they ask for absurdly high dollar damages. You can hardly avoid picking up any paper, any day, in any city without finding a story that so-and-so filed a $9 million damage suit, or a $90 million suit, or $900 million, or $9 billion. Of course, the plaintiff can ask for whatever amount he wants, in punitive damages at least, so the amount sought really is meaningless. But if the lawyer adds enough zeros, even

if the suit makes the most outrageously absurd or trivial allegations, he can be sure that an editor will give it big play. The amount of damages sought has come to be an adjective modifying "damage suit"—as in, "a $5.5 million damage suit"—as though that were the price tag—as in, "a $5,000 Buick." . . . Ridiculous.

When Driscoll complained to the Associated Press for playing up a so-called $3 billion suit, the answer read in part: "All I would have to do is throw the story in the kill drawer and within minutes we'd get 'Need matcher to NY Times special on $3 billion suit filed over bank credit cards'."

Libel

Newspapers are reluctant to give much publicity to libel suits against other publications so as not to encourage similar actions against themselves. Such a policy naturally cannot apply at all times. Here is the way the Denver *Post* handled both the beginning and the end of a libel suit against itself:

> Stanley Furs, Inc., 1600 E. Colfax Ave., and Stanley Calkins, president of the firm, filed libel suits Wednesday morning against the Denver Post and The Rocky Mountain News.
>
> In the complaints filed in Denver District Court, damages are being sought in behalf of Calkins and the firm as a result of articles published April 13 in the two newspapers.
>
> The complaints charge the articles about the firm in a U.S. District Court action was "an unfair, false and malicious account" of the court proceedings.
>
> The stories exposed Calkins and his firm to "public wrath, hatred and ridicule and deprived the business of the benefits of public confidence," the complaints charged.
>
> In the suit against The Post, damages of $550,000 are sought in behalf of the firm and an additional $500,000 is sought in behalf of Calkins.
>
> The suit against the News asks for $1.3 million in damages in behalf of Calkins.
>
> A $1 million libel suit brought against The Denver Post by Stanley Furs, Inc., was dismissed Thursday in Denver District Court.
>
> Judge Zita Weinshienk granted the motion to dismiss at the conclusion of presentation of evidence at a three-day trial. The dismissal motion was made by the newspaper's attorneys, Richard Hall and Thomas Kelley.
>
> The judge held that the evidence had failed to meet the tests needed for proof of libel under Colorado law.
>
> The required standards of evidence, the judge explained, must show the statements were known to be false or printed with reckless disregard as to whether they were true or not.
>
> "There was not sufficient evidence to take the case to the jury on these points," the judge said.
>
> The libel suit was filed by Stanley Calkins, president of the firm, as the result of an April 1973 article. The story discussed a U.S. District Court consent judgment against Calkins and his firm.
>
> A similar lawsuit seeking $2.3 million was filed by Stanley Furs against the Rocky Mountain News as a result of that newspaper's story on the same judgment. A June trial is scheduled in that case.

J. Richard Nathan, the Stanley attorney, said Friday no decision had been made yet on whether the case would be appealed.

Driscoll warns against carelessness in reporting the filing of damage suits, pointing out that the contents of a complaint may not be privileged at the time it is filed and that newspapers thereby publish stories at their own risk. "Some day," he comments, "somebody is going to be sorry for it. Even if not libelous, I think the press ought to be careful about letting people make scurrilous charges against others just because they make them in the form of a lawsuit."

Divorce

Distinguish between *divorce* and *annulment*, and between *separate maintenance* and *alimony*. What are the grounds (desertion, cruelty and so forth)? Watch out for libel when reporting specific incidents cited as grievances (beatings, criminal behavior). The reporter should obtain: names and addresses of both principals; dates of marriage and of separation; names and ages of children and what the bill requests regarding them; suggested disposition of property; whether alimony is requested; whether wife asks court to authorize use of her maiden name. When a case comes to hearing, testimony, of course, can be reported; state whether defendant contests case or allows decree to be obtained by default. States are slowly but steadily passing no-fault divorce laws, making the decree obtainable by mutual agreement without one party's having to state a case against the other.

> Two suits for divorce were filed in circuit court Thursday. Cruelty is charged in both cases.
> Sandra Neisen alleged James Neisen struck her several times. They were married Sept. 30, 1961, and separated Tuesday. She asked the court to order a division of the property in the residence at 26 South Granview, farm machinery and a checking account. She asked for the custody of three children and that a car be given to her.
> Rochelle Williams alleged James N. Williams struck her and ordered her to leave the house and not return. They were married Sept. 13, 1958, and separated in March, 1965. She asked that she be given her equity in real estate in New Jersey.   [Quincy (Ill.) *Herald-Whig*]

Foreclosures

A person who defaults in payments on a mortgage stands to lose the property through foreclosure proceedings. In most states, however, he has an *equity of redemption*—a period of time in which to pay up, even though a court has awarded the property to the mortgage holder.

Evictions

The Renters' Court always is a fertile source for human interest stories. The legal name for actions to evict is *forcible entry and detainer*. During housing shortages, renters' courts are crowded. The reporter does well to examine the statutes of the state for sections pertaining to the rights of landlords to evict or refuse to rent to families with children or pets. He also should read up on statutes and court decisions mostly outlawing restrictive covenants whereby property owners agreed not to sell or lease to Negroes, Jews or members of other minority groups or otherwise restrict the use of property.

Inadequate inspection and inability, under the statutes, of judges to assess heavy penalties mean that large city slumlords consider this court as only a minor nuisance. Reporters are handicapped by protective secrecy laws covering trusts to determine who the real culprits are when outrageous housing conditions are exposed. Urban renewal projects have caused urban center slum areas to increase and worsen as real estate interests use residential land areas for more lucrative purposes and friendly public officials offer little or no interference. Tearjerking, albeit accurate, stories can be written about unfeeling landlords and others who exploit poor and ignorant tenants. One device is to purchase tax delinquent bills so as to make evictions legal. Seldom, however, is the greedy action considered morally commendable.

Despite supposedly protective legislation, blockbusting and redlining persist. The former is the practice of enabling a single Negro family to move into a white neighborhood by making the purchase price extremely low. Then the remaining white property owners are panicked into selling their property at low prices after which it is resold to Negroes at a considerable profit.

Redlining is making geographical boundaries within which banks and other lending institutions do not make loans for building construction or repairs, in the belief that the neighborhood is deteriorating. Residents who continue to deposit money in such institutions complain because their deposits are used for loans outside the area and are a major factor in bringing about deterioration.

Condemnation Suits

When a new street or highway or public building is planned, the proper government agency uses its right of *eminent domain* to purchase—at a fair price—any privately owned land needed for the improvement. Property owners often resist such taking of their property or hold out for higher compensation. Public clamor may cause a change in official plans, as happened when property owners in Connecticut objected to the headquarters of the United Nations being established there. Scandals occur when some public officials use prior knowledge of governmental plans to purchase certain property. They purchase it themselves and consequently reap a profit when its value increases. The insider may not technically be a part of the spending agency but such behavior obviously is not in the public interest.

Receiverships

Creditors or stockholders of a corporation or individuals in financial difficulties may apply to an equity court for appointment of a receiver to conserve assets and rescue the business. A chancery receivership, intended to put a going concern back on its feet, must be distinguished from a receiver in bankruptcy, who is in charge of liquidating a defunct institution. Many banks, hotels, transportation companies and others continue operating under receiverships for years. Often newspapers uncover scandals regarding political favoritism in appointment of receivers or companies with which they do business. Reporters should watch the periodic reports which receivers must make to the courts appointing them.

Bankruptcy

A financial failure may file a *voluntary petition* in bankruptcy, or his creditors may file an *involuntary petition* in his case. The reporter should examine the inventory filed with the petition, to obtain: total assets; total liabilities; nature of the assets (stocks, real estate, controlling interest in other companies, etc.); nature of liabilities; clues as to reasons for failure. Bankruptcy matters are handled by the federal courts. Every petition is referred to a *referee in bankruptcy*, a permanent court officer; the *trustee* is elected by the creditors and, if approved by the court, takes over the task of liquidating the assets and distributing them on a pro rata basis. Instead of dissolving a business, a company may undergo *reorganization* under a court-approved plan. Usually, some creditors are "frozen out" when such happens, and the legal jockeying between them to avoid that happening is newsworthy when the company is important. Since every action of a trustee must be approved by the court, the reporter can keep close to the situation.

Since 1960 there has been a phenomenally steady increase in personal bankruptcy petitions, about 20 times as many as in the '40s. The Consumer Bankruptcy Committee of the American Bar Association blames abuses of credit by both recipients and grantors and would tighten the laws to make such petitions more difficult to file. In this area, as in so many others, the interpretative reporter can find valuable depth situation and trend stories. What follows is about one-third of an excellent explanatory article in this area.

By Richard A. Shaffer
Staff Reporter of The Wall Street Journal

BOGALUSA, La.—Corbett Taylor "just laughed" when Home Finance Service filed suit against him to collect a $568 personal loan. "I had already gone bankrupt on that loan," he says, "and I was sure I was safe."

But Mr. Taylor didn't laugh long. By the time it was all over, Home Finance had collected not only the original $568 but also legal fees, court costs and interest, which brought the total to $939.

A fate similar to Mr. Taylor's appears likely for many of the 178,202 persons who filed for personal bankruptcy in the year ended last June 30. "The plain truth is that for many, many people today bankruptcy just isn't solving their problems," says Royal E. Jackson, chief of the bankruptcy division of the administrative office of U.S. courts. One reason is that, contrary to common beliefs, creditors don't automatically mark off a debt once a person is bankrupt.

Obviously, many who take the bankruptcy route are not innocent victims of misfortune and therefore deserving of creditors' solicitude. Indeed, some creditors say such innocent victims represent a smaller percentage of personal bankruptcies than ever before. Nevertheless, many authorities contend that, despite changes made last year by Congress to rectify the situation, bankruptcy laws still fall far short of their basic aim—to extricate persons hopelessly mired in debt and enable them to get a fresh start.

Consider Corbett Taylor's case:

In 1962 Mr. Taylor, then 30, went through Federal bankruptcy court after a fire destroyed his home and a seven-month strike at Crown Zellerbach cut off his $5,000-a-year income as a boiler-room helper. His debts mounted to $16,350.

But a year after Mr. Taylor was "discharged" from his debts—the term used in such cases—he was sued in Bogalusa city court by Home Finance a subsidiary of CIT Financial Corp. Mr. Taylor says he didn't have the money for a lawyer, and when he failed to show up in court, the judge returned a default judgment against him. This was later upheld by an appeals court. Home Finance then initiated garnishment proceedings and collected the total of $939.

Mr. Taylor concludes that he "didn't gain much, if anything, by bankruptcy. My advice if you're planning to try it is—don't."

Bankruptcy is a Federal process governed by the Bankruptcy Act of 1898, which has been amended several times. A referee in bankruptcy presides over proceedings, which take place in the bankruptcy division of a Federal district court. Although he acts like a judge, the referee is only an employee of the court and is under the supervision of a Federal district judge.

To "take bankruptcy," a person files a schedule of assets and liabilities with the clerk of a district court. Creditors are given a period of time to file claims against the estate, and a trustee for the estate is usually appointed by the court or, less often, elected by creditors. The court may then grant a discharge in bankruptcy—a piece of paper saying the person "hereby is discharged from all debts and claims" besides those "excepted from the operation of a discharge in bankruptcy." And there's the hitch for bankrupt persons. Exceptions include debts created by fraud, alimony, taxes and child support.

In most cases, the key word is "fraud," and the standard procedure has been for the creditor to file suit, generally in a state court. If the debtor shows up, the director will usually allege that the debt was incurred through fraud. The critics contend that the laws allow fraud to be legally proved far too easily.

Many bankrupt persons apparently aren't aware of the exceptions. In at least 20% of bankruptcy cases, creditors file suits to collect debts that the bankrupt individuals believe have been forgiven, according to a study by Prof. Philip Shuchman of the University of Connecticut law school. The practice is so common that in one New York State court not long ago post-bankruptcy lawsuits accounted for 24 of the 57 cases on the calendar.

"These suits are quite successful as collection devices," says Prof. Shuchman, who found that creditors win seven cases out of 10. Many of these are won by default when the debtor, like Mr. Taylor, mistakenly thinks he is free of the obligation or when he lacks funds for a lawyer's fee.

In the Bogalusa city court, such lawsuits can be filed for as little as $10, and unless the bankrupt answers within five days, "we got ourselves a judgment, just like that, for $400 or $500 on the average," says attorney Don Arata, who represents Home Finance and seven other finance companies here.

[*Wall Street Journal*]

Injunctions

Distinguish between a *preliminary restraining order*, which is issued by a judge on ex parte evidence only and without notice, and *temporary* and *permanent injunctions*. The orthodox procedure is for the court to issue a temporary order to the defendant to appear in court and " show cause " why it should not become permanent. In the meantime, the alleged offensive conduct must cease. Injunctions are used to prohibit government agencies and officials from exceeding their authority; to test the constitutionality of a law; to restrain picketing and other activities by labor unions; to restrain corporations from acts injurious to stock- or bond-holders; to compel persons to keep the peace and not interfere with the civil liberties and other rights of others; to stop and prevent nuisances; and for other purposes.

A temporary restraining order halting revocation of the driver's license of Bill J. Alexander and revocation of the auto license and registration of his father, W. Glenn Alexander, has been granted by Lancaster County District Judge Herbert A. Ronin.

The Alexanders requested the restraining order in a suit filed against James Dunlevey, director of the State Motor Vehicles Dept., and Charles P. Kaufman, supervisor of the Financial Responsibility section of the Motor Vehicles Dept.

The suit filed by the two Lincolnites also asks the court to declare the state's financial responsibility act unconstitutional.

Judge Ronin set a hearing for Aug. 3 on a request for a temporary injunction which the Alexanders also requested. [York (Pa.) *Record*]

Contracts

The Asbury Park (N.J.) *Evening Press* summarized a 23-page complaint charging breach of contract as follows:

TRENTON—Patricia H. Endress has filed suit against Brookdale Community College officers and the board of trustees in an effort to regain her $19,000-a-year tenure contract as a professor of journalism.

Ms. Endress was joined in the suit by the Brookdale Community College Faculty Association and the New Jersey Education Association.

The suit, filed by William S. Greenburg, here, also charges breach of contract, libel and slander, and includes a demand for a jury trial on four counts.

Defendants are W. Preston Corderman, chairman of the board of trustees; Donald H. Smith, Brookdale president, and Marvin Clark, Joseph E. Clayton, Mrs. T. Peter Doremus, William O. Fleckenstein, Earl B. Garrison, Ellen

Hannah, Walter S. McAfee, and Leon Zuckerman as members of the board of trustees and individually.

Ms. Endress, who lives at 1204 4th Ave., Asbury Park, said she was given a tenure contract approved by the board of trustees April 25, signed it, and returned it to the college.

However, according to the suit, on June 27 the board of trustees voted to revoke the contract and notified Ms. Endress the following day.

Greenburg said the board acted on the recommendation of Smith.

Smith on June 27 wrote Corderman and board members recommending the services of Professor Endress as a member of the faculty be terminated and that her contract for the period July 1, 1974, to June 30, 1975, be rescinded.

The suit recites that Smith charged:

"In and about the performance of her duties, Miss Endress did violate both the tradition established under board policy, the philosophical platform and goals of the college as the same pertain to freedom of the press and student responsibility for the college newspaper.

"As advisor to the college newspaper, 'The Stall' Miss Endress did violate the editorial prerogatives of the student editor and the student staff.

"Miss Endress did violate her duties and responsibilities as a teacher of journalism and advisor to the college newspaper in that she did order and direct the editor of the college newspaper to publish certain material without his approval and did therefore subvert the function of the editor and her obligation to properly train and advise in accordance with the accepted standards of journalism.

"Miss Endress did not only permit, but actively caused the college newspaper, under her supervisory advice, to make public libelous matter contrary to accepted journalistic standards."

The charges were denied by the plaintiff who also charged she has refused academic appointments elsewhere and sought to preserve her status as a member of the faculty at Brookdale Community College.

The suit charges that the action of Smith in making his recommendation to the board was wrongful and malicious and that the defendants Corderman and Smith conspired to unlawfully breach the contract between Brookdale College and Professor Endress.

The suit charges that the June 27 letter from Smith to the board was libelous and malicious for the purpose of injuring the plaintiff.

The suit contends that Ms. Endress was compelled to spend large sums of money to defend herself against the charges.

The plaintiff seeks a judgment for breach of the contractual relationship.

The suit asks the court to restrain the defendants from enforcing the action of June 27, to order the reinstatement of the plaintiff, to order the board to rescind its action of June 27, and to declare Ms. Endress has the right of tenure.

The suit asks damages, the cost of suit, and reasonable legal fees for the plaintiff. In addition it seeks compensatory and punitive damages from the defendants Corderman and Smith.

A demand for a jury trial on four counts involving the June 27 letter and meeting of the board is included in the 23-page suit.

The same newspaper reported how the three-day trial turned out as follows:

FREEHOLD—Ms. Patricia Endress, 42, has been reinstated at full pay with tenure as a journalism teacher at Brookdale Community College, Middletown Township. A Superior Court judge yesterday also awarded her a total of $104,121 in punitive and compensatory damages and back pay.

Judge Merritt Lane Jr., ruling at the end of a three-day trial, said he took "little stock" in the testimony of several college officials who recommended her job be terminated because of an editorial she wrote for the student newspaper criticizing the chairman of the college board of trustees, W. Preston Corderman.

Ms. Endress, surprised and happy following the ruling, described the charges against her, the trial and the results yesterday as a "profound demonstration" for her students in the rights of a free press under the constitution.

The judge found at least one college official, Dr. John Gallagher, vice president for academic affairs, lied on the witness stand.

He said he "put little stock in any" of the testimony of college President Donald H. Smith, who recommended firing Ms. Endress last June 27, just three days before she was to receive tenure.

Ms. Endress filed her damage suit against the school after the board of trustees voted, on Smith's recommendation, to rescind her 1974–75 contract. Judge Lane ordered the school to give her a 1975–76 contract, starting July 1.

She had charged her 1st and 14th Amendment rights of free speech and free press had been violated because of the termination, and sought damages because she said she was unable to find another teaching job in the area.

Lane agreed, and said Smith apparently decided to seek her ouster almost a month before submitting a written recommendation to the trustees. Meanwhile, said the judge, Smith solicited negative recommendations from his staff to support his decision.

The official reason Ms. Endress was dropped, according to Smith's recommendation, was that she allegedly compelled the student editor to print a "libelous" article and editorial charging Corderman with a conflict of interest and calling for his resignation because his nephew, Allen Corderman, president of Media Systems, Moorestown, got a $25,000 Brookdale contract to supply audio-visual equipment.

Corderman admitted on the witness stand he was an officer in Media Systems when the contract was awarded, but insisted he never voted approval of any contracts or payments to his own firm.

Lane found not only was the editorial "fair comment" on a public official, but that the student editor, William McGee III, had approved and authorized the article and editorial the day before publication.

Gerald Karey, a teacher intern who wrote the article, insisted in court that Corderman denied he was a member of Media Systems when the contract was awarded. Corderman denied he ever said that to Karey.

The judge's hour and 45-minute ruling touched on Ms. Endress' due process rights, her contract rights and whether her firing was for "just cause," in addition to her free press and speech rights.

Ruling on Ms. Endress' argument that her firing violated the 1871 Federal Civil Rights Act, the judge said her editorial was protected under this law as well as under the constitution's 1st Amendment.

The judge said he was "unimpressed" with the school's expert witness, Columbia journalism professor Melvin Mencher, who could find only that Ms. Endress "breached" her professional ethics in participating in preparation of the school newspaper. The Stall. The judge noted the paper was short staffed, and Ms. Endress and Karey often helped out by writing stories.

Lane agreed completely with Ms. Endress' expert witness, Northwestern University journalism professor and author Curtis D. MacDougall, who said the source of information of a news story or editorial made no difference as long as there was no libel in it, and the editorial constituted "fair comment" on a public official.

Corderman, Lane said, is a public official, and the school was required to prove "actual malice" on the part of the editorial writer and reporter in order to refute the claim by Ms. Endress that she was illegally fired. The judge cited the landmark New York Times vs. Sullivan case, which defines fair comment on public officials.

Saying the $25,000 contract covered by The Stall editorial and article was "to put it mildly, questionable," Lane found "nothing imperfect" about the article.

Speaking of the editorial written by Ms. Endress, the judge remarked, "I may disagree with its terms, but that is a far cry from being able to find (actual) malice or reckless disregard (of the facts)."

Punitive damages of $10,000 each were assessed against the following individuals: Smith and board members Marvin A. Clark, Mrs. T. Peter Doremus, William O. Fleckenstein, Earl B. Garrison, Ellen Hannah, and Walter S. McAfee, for a total of $70,000.

There were also assessments of $10,000 compensatory damages and $10,000 for the attorney's fees against Smith and the trustees collectively.

Finally, the judge awarded Ms. Endress $19,121 in pay for the present school year, minus $5,000 she said she earned as a secretary at her adopted daughter's nursery school. Ms. Endress lives in Asbury Park.

There was also another $10,000 punitive and $10,000 compensatory damage judgment against Smith for malicious interference in Ms. Endress' contract rights, but the judge withheld the money amount pending the results of any successful appeals of the other judgment against him. In other words, said the judge, if his ruling against Smith on Ms. Endress' constitutional rights is overturned, Smith still faces the malicious damage judgment.

Charles L. Morgan, school attorney, declined comment on a possible appeal, saying he must "read the decision" and confer with his clients.

EXTRAORDINARY REMEDIES

The equitable relief provided by an injunction originated as an extraordinary remedy, but has become so common it no longer is extraordinary. Almost the same is true of *habeas corpus*, whereby a jailer is required to produce a prisoner in court to answer charges against him. Dating from Magna Charta, it is one of the great Anglo-Saxon democratic protections.

Other so-called extraordinary remedies follow.

Prohibition

Prohibition is a writ issued by a superior court to one of inferior jurisdiction commanding it to desist in handling any matter beyond its authority to consider.

Certiorari

Certiorari also is an inquiry into the behavior of a lower court after it has taken some action. Thus, it usually operates as an appeal, to bring about a review of the lower court's action in the higher court. In granting a writ of certiorari or *writ of review*, as it also is called, however, the higher court merely agrees to look into the matter. It may return the case later.

Mandamus

A *writ of mandamus* is directed by a higher court to administrative officers, corporations or an inferior court ordering some action required by law. It does not specify what the action must be—as in a case where a required appointment is overdue—but it does demand that some action be taken.

Quo Warranto

By a *quo warranto writ*, a higher court inquires into the right of a public official to hold office or of a corporation to exercise a franchise.

PROBATE PROCEEDINGS

When a person dies, the state supervises payment of his debts and distribution of his property. If he dies *testate* (that is, if he leaves a will), unless someone can prove that the contrary should be done, the court sees that its provisions are carried out. It usually appoints the *executor* named in the will to supervise settling the estate; that official, often a relative of the deceased, posts bond for about one-and-a-half times the estimated value of the estate and receives a commission when his work is done. If there is no will (deceased died *intestate*) the court appoints an *administrator*. In many states there now are public administrators. Either executor or administrator receives *letters testamentary* to authorize his work, which includes notification of beneficiaries named in a will or legal heirs if there is no will, advertising for bills against the estate, collecting money due the estate, preparing an inventory of the estate and so forth.

Filing a Will

The first step in probate proceedings is the filing of the will by whoever has it in custody or finds it. Reporters watch for such filings of wills of prominent persons recently deceased. In their case, it is news whether the estate is large or small. As a matter of fact, it usually is difficult or impossible to determine an estate's size from the will itself; it is not known with certainty until an appraisal is made months later. The first public information may come with the filing of an inheritance tax return.

The estate of Henry B. Ritter, Milltown construction contractor, totaled $3,062,182, according to an inheritance tax return filed Thursday with the Vernon County clerk.

Ritter, uncle of former county treasurer Herbert C. Ritter, died Dec. 19, 1976, at the age of 77. He lived at 345 W. Fullerton.

The estate was left in trust to the widow, Lillian, with a provision that upon her death one-half of it go to their children, Mrs. Marjorie O'Neil of 706 S. Sheridan, Barton, and Henry Jr., of 12 E. Scott.

The federal tax on the estate was $358,659 and the state levy, $117,328.

An ingenious reporter in some cases can estimate value by determining the market value of securities or the assessor's valuations of real estate and by similar investigation. Frequently, the nature of an estate is newsworthy as a person may be revealed to be the owner of property which he was not known to possess. From the will, the beneficiaries can be determined, and often a will contains surprises. The first news story should mention when and where the will was drawn and possibly the witnesses. In small places, virtually every will is newsworthy; in larger places, only those of important persons or involving large estates receive mention.

Admitting to Probate

The reporter must not confuse filing a will and admitting a will to probate which is done by court order upon petition of the executor or someone else. Before such a petition is granted it must be "proved" to be genuine and there also must be proof of heirship; usually referees supervise such routine matters. If anything happens to disturb the routine, it probably is newsworthy.

> The will of Richard W. Young, founder and chairman of the board of the Young corporation, who died March 1, at the age of 70, was admitted to probate today by County Judge Thomas Sullivan.
>
> The executors are Thomas B. Young and R. L. Waters. Waters declined to place an estimate on the size of the estate, but it is generally understood to be in the millions.

SETS UP TRUST FUND

> The will sets up a trust fund on behalf of 11 relatives of the industrialist. The division is as follows:
>
> One-sixth of the estate to Thomas B. Young, now president of the Young corporation, a nephew. One-eighth to Frank Young, a nephew. One-eighth to Ruth Young Stoddard, a niece.
>
> One-twelfth to Louise R. White, a niece. One-twelfth to Margaret Rolnick, a niece. One-twelfth to Nancy Young, a niece. One-twelfth to Mary Sheridan, a niece. One-twelfth to Robert Carpenter, a nephew. One-twelfth to Richard Sheridan, a nephew.
>
> One-twenty-fourth to Patricia Young, a grand-niece and one-twenty-fourth to Kent Young, a grand-nephew.

The will provides that the Young Investment company, established by Young, may be liquidated within 12 months of his death and the assets distributed to the stockholders, this with the approval of the executors. It also provides that the entire estate shall be liquidated within 20 years and may be liquidated, if the executors approve, in ten years.

Contesting a Will

By law an interval which varies from three months to two years must elaspse between the time a will is admitted to probate and a *final accounting.* During that period, suit may be brought to break the will, perhaps by a disgruntled relative who was disinherited. Common charges are that the deceased was unduly influenced when he made the will, or was not in full possession of his mental faculties. Sometimes it is charged that the will filed was not the most recent. Such suits usually are filed in courts other than that handling routine probate matters.

> Suit to contest the will of Mrs. Margaret W. Winchester, widow of Charles B. Winchester, an official of Scott & Co., whereby she left most of $100,000 to friends, was filed in Circuit Court yesterday by six relatives, including three sisters and a brother. Mrs. Winchester plunged to her death from a room in the Bacon House last July 27 at the age of 68.
>
> The suit charges she was "eccentric and peculiar" and "susceptible to influence and blandishments," and that undue influence was put upon her in making the will. Attorney G. A. Yates, co-executor under the will, who was left a $20,000 bequest, was her close financial adviser, and Attorney Allan E. Mack, also left $20,000, was his associate, the bill points out.

RULES OF EVIDENCE

To "feel at home," as he should whenever he steps into any courtroom, a reporter must understand the fundamental rules of evidence.

Nature of Evidence

Most evidence is in the form of testimony by witnesses. Other forms of evidence include objects and written material introduced as exhibits. Together they constitute the *proof* whereby it is intended to influence the court's decision. All evidence must be (1) *material*—have a direct relation to the case; (2) *relevant*—pertinent; and (3) *competent*—authoritative. Otherwise, the court will uphold an *objection* to its introduction.

Burden of Proof

In a civil action it is *preponderance of evidence* that counts; in criminal cases, the state must prove guilt *beyond any reasonable doubt.* At all times, the burden of proof rests with the side that must refute evidence which, if allowed to stand, would be injurious to it.

Presumptions

The law presumes that any situation known to exist at one time continues to exist unless proof to the contrary is provided. Thus good character and impeccable behavior on the part of all citizens are presumed until disproved.

Judicial Notice

Common knowledge—such as the organization of government, size and location of cities and countries, business practices and the like—need not be proved in court. Instead, the court "takes notice" of them unless challenged for doing so.

Qualifications of Witnesses

Children, wives, husbands, insane persons, felons, dependents, interested lawyers and other parties once were barred from testifying. Today, the restrictions are much lighter. Almost anyone competent at the time of trial or hearing can be a witness; the credibility to be attached to his testimony is a different matter.

Privilege

The Fifth Amendment to the Constitution of the United States protects anyone from being compelled to testify against himself. In actual practice, refusal to testify because to do so might incriminate oneself often is a "dodge." No lawyer can be compelled to reveal what a client has told him in confidence. Similar protection is afforded physicians and clergymen in many cases and, in several states, newspapermen.

Leading Questions

Witnesses tell their stories in response to questions by attorneys. Those questions cannot be so worded at to suggest the answers desired.

Hearsay Evidence

A witness can testify only to that of which he has firsthand knowledge. He cannot draw inferences from the facts. Exceptions to the rule include dying declarations, spontaneous declarations, confessions and admissions against one's interest.

Opinion Evidence

Anyone is an authority on matters which he has witnessed or which are within the knowledge of an ordinary person. Experts must be qualified before their testimony is considered credible. An expert's opinion often is obtained by means of a *hypothetical question* in which a situation comparable to that at issue is described.

Real Evidence

Clothing, weapons and objects of all sorts are introduced as exhibits. So are models and photographs.

Circumstantial Evidence

Correct inferences often can be drawn from evidence pertaining to a person's behavior both before and after a crime is committed and from his known capacities and predilections. A great deal of the evidence in both civil and criminal cases is circumstantial rather than eyewitness accounts.

Best Evidence

Copies of documents are admissible only when there is proof that originals are unavailable. In every case, the court demands the best possible evidence regarding any point.

APPEALS

Since the trial judge passes on motions for new trials, not many are granted. Only in rare cases, however, does a judge refuse to grant a dissatisfied party the right to take his case to the appellate court. In criminal matters, no appeal is possible by the state in the event of acquittal, but a convicted defendant can appeal; and in civil matters either side can do so.

The distinction between *appeal* (of civil law origin) and *writ of error* (of common law origin) is virtually nonexistent today. Where it exists, it means that in the former instance a case is removed entirely from the lower to the higher court which then can review both the law and the evidence; a writ of error, by contrast, is an original proceeding, not a continuation of that in the lower court.

Appeals are either *as of right* or *by permission* of the upper court as the statutes designate. Common grounds on which an appeal can be made are (1) irregularity of the submission of evidence, (2) new evidence discovered since the trial ended, (3) misconduct of the jury, (4) lack of jurisdiction of the court, (5) an error by the judge in instructing the jury, (6) incompetent witnesses, (7) excessive damages allowed (in civil cases) and (8) influencing or packing of the jury by the adverse party.

A *bill of exceptions* (also called *statement of the case* or *certificate of reasonable doubt*) must set forth clearly and completely the grounds on which appeal is taken. It may be accompanied by a *brief* in which the details are made more elaborate and the case as a whole summarized although the trend is toward simplification of procedure so that only one document is necessary. Certified copies of *transcripts* and *abstracts* of lower court records also are submitted.

The party taking the appeal is known as the *appellant* or *plaintiff in error* and the other party (usually the winner in the lower court) as the *appellee or defendant in error*. It is good practice for a reporter always to ask a defeated party in an important case whether he intends to appeal. Otherwise, he first learns of such action by a *notice of appeal* filed in the appellate court. Today, such notice acts as an automatic *stay of proceedings* or *supersedeas* to hold up execution of any lower court judgment or sentence. In some jurisdictions, however, it is necessary to petition for such writs.

If the higher court's permission is necessary, whatever the court decides regarding a petition is news. If it agrees to review a case, it sets a date for *oral arguments* by attorneys. Then it takes the case *under advisement*. Every justice studies the case independently before the court meets to discuss it. After a vote is taken, the chief justice assigns one justice to prepare the *majority opinion* supporting the court's *decision*. Other members may prepare *concurring opinions* or *dissenting opinions*. Any part of a decision which deals with background not directly pertinent to the case at hand is called *obiter dictum*; it explains the mental processes by which the justices formed their opinions.

By its decision, the appellate court *upholds* or *reverses* or *modifies* the lower court's decision. A *mandate* is an order to a lower court to take any kind of action, and the upper court *remands* the case to the lower so that it can act.

Only an experienced reporter is likely to be assigned to cover appellate court proceedings. By the time he has mastered the art of handling lower court news, he will be thoroughly qualified to do so.

> The United States Circuit Court of Appeals took under review yesterday the criminal conviction of Henry Lustig, millionaire restaurateur, and two others on charges of having defrauded the Federal Government of $2,872,766 in income taxes owed by the Longchamps Restaurant chain.
>
> Decision was reserved after arguments for three and a half hours by former Gov. Nathan L. Miller, attorney for the appellants, and Bruno Schachner, assistant United States Attorney.
>
> Convicted last June 20 on all 23 counts of an indictment were Lustig, who was sentenced to four years in jail, and fined $115,000; E. Allen Lustig, his nephew, secretary of the restaurants, who received a three-year sentence, and Joseph Sobol, an accountant, who was sentenced to two years.
>
> Mr. Miller pursued the argument presented at the trial that the defendants were entitled to immunity from criminal prosecution because of an alleged voluntary disclosure made to William J. Pedrick, collector of internal revenue for the Second District, by Allen Lustig on March 26, 1945.
>
> He told the court that the question to be decided was whether such immunity existed when a disclosure of delinquency had been made prior to the start of a

government investigation and if such a self-incriminating disclosure could be used as a basis for criminal conviction.

Mr. Miller said that at the trial the question of fraud was not contested and that the only question litigated was whether a voluntary disclosure had been made before a Treasury investigation started. He said that a ruling by the lower court judge, Harold Kennedy, that the Treasury Department was not morally bound to keep a promise of immunity from prosecution had the effect of virtually decimating the verdict. . . .   [New York *Times*]

16
POLITICS, ELECTIONS

A. Political Philosophy

B. Political Public Opinion

C. Political Organization
1. Local
2. Precinct and Ward
3. County
4. State, National

D. Precampaign Activities
1. Petitions
2. Registration
3. Primaries
4. Conventions

E. Campaigns
1. Speeches
2. Coverage
3. Roorbacks
4. Issues

F. Elections
1. Predictions
2. Election Day
3. Election Results

G. "Post-mortems"

The American politician is a practical businessman. What he sells is his public service which the public purchases with its ballots. His remuneration is employment by the electorate with all the emoluments that the position entails. As a merchant, the politician is responsive to consumer demand and, in turn, attempts to influence that demand. Independents in other lines of business have plenty of difficulty in withstanding the competition of Big Business with its holding companies, chain stores and conglomerates. The lone wolf in politics is virtually hopeless. Any success he attains is temporary; to get far he must align himself with one of the two large rival organizations which, since the Civil War, have divided the nation's political profits with very little loss to third parties.

Since communism and fascism began to threaten capitalism in Old World countries and since the American New Dealers introduced a new note in our political life, newspaper readers for more than a generation have become increasingly conscious of the broader aspects or philosophic bases of world politics. This awareness, however, still is predominately academic; all that the defeat of candidates standing for principles which formerly were popular means to the practical politician-businessman is that consumer demand has changed. The professor or student of political theory may be aware of national and international social and economic trends which are reflected in overt political events, but few candidates or voters have such breadth of vision. Should an aspirant for office also be a scholar he nevertheless, to be successful (that is, get elected), has to play the game as it is played.

Despite the increase in serious articles—usually Sunday features or those on the editorial page—discussing politics philosophically, the American newspaper remains as practical in its attitude toward the business of getting and staying elected as the politician himself. Because of consolidations, which have left few cities with fewer than 100,000 inhabitants with more than one newspaper, most newspapers today term themselves "independent," whereas formerly they prided themselves on being either Republican or Democratic. This change obviously was made for good business reasons so as not to alienate about 50 per cent of the potential subscribers. Political independence, however, is not tantamount to political indifference as to which party wins a particular election; rather, it means merely that the newspaper reserves the right to decide on which side it will be in each campaign. Theoretically, it is free to be Democratic one year and Republican the next or to support candidates of both parties for different offices in the same election. Once it has made its decision as to whom it will support, the allegedly independent newspaper may be as unfair in his behalf as the frankly aligned paper.

Truly interpretative political writing consists in explaining the immediate phenomenon in terms of long-range trends, national or international. Accepting the fact that practical politicians still do not operate with any appreciable awareness of such trends, pragmatic interpretative political writing consists in identifying leaders with movements and groups—political, economic, religious, ethnic and others—and in "seeing through" motives and actions to discover their probable meaning and effect upon political fortunes.

From whichever angle he regards the political scene, the political reporter, to "keep his feet on the ground," must see beyond the externals which the politician hopes, usually successfully, will be all of which the average voter is aware. What benefits this overcoming of naivete will have for the reporter, outside of the extent to which it furthers his education, are dependent upon the attitude of his superiors. No matter what they profess, newspapers *are* involved in politics and, all the statistical evidence to the contrary, both candidates and voters act as though the press is an important factor. Any aspirant for any office welcomes the support of any newspaper, and any newspaper is glad to have a political friend in public office. As long as a newspaper attacks a politician it advertises him; the most effective journalistic weapon is to ignore a person. Although there have been numerous instances in which exactly that was done, it is not common practice if for no other reason than to avoid "one party press" criticisms which result when a newspaper does not seem to be giving rival candidates for an office equal treatment.

In small cities, the primary interest is local politics inasmuch as the small newspaper has little to gain directly from state or national politics. Local political news is written by staff members whereas material regarding state or national politics is obtained from press associations, syndicates and political headquarters. That all of this news, regardless of how obtained, is presented impartially except in rare instances is obviously absurd to believe. Hence, the reporter seeking to do a meaty objective job is handicapped. In no field of writing is the merely narrative more impotent in serving any public purpose or absence of bias more difficult of attainment. Early in this book, the distinction was made between intentional color and honest interpretation. It should be the responsibility of readers to see that newspapers provide the latter.

In preparing himself to derive the most benefit from his experiences, the newspaper political reporter should (1) know something about political philosophy; (2) be a student of public opinion, its nature and manipulation; (3) understand practical political organization and election machinery; (4) be sufficiently on the "inside" to distinguish the bunkum from the realities of political phenomena.

POLITICAL PHILOSOPHY

Plato, in describing a highly disciplined perfect state in which philosophers would be kings, Aristotle, in advocating a balanced democratic government, and political theorists ever since, expressed points of view which the enlightened political reporter will detect in substance in the arguments of contemporary seekers for public office. Heaven forbid that the college-trained reporter should be a pedantic idealist passing judgment upon twentieth-century practical men of affairs in terms of his favorite thinker of the past. Nevertheless, historical perspective is indispensable in enabling one to "make sense" of modern affairs. Being conversant with the history of political thought, especially with how it has been affected by practical considerations, at least provides the political reporter with the tools for making his work personally instructive.

In the writings of many contemporaries, the aspiring political reporter will find plentiful interpretative analyses of the modern scene. A superabundant amount of material concerning capitalism, communism and fascism, of course, exists. The average person may not be able to tell the difference between these and other political theories, but no political writer can be so ignorant. He should at least know when a demagogue is incorrect in branding an opponent as socialistic or fascistic or the like.

Political writers are a potent force in educating the public regarding the pros and cons of such matters as the two-party versus multiple-party systems, permanent registration, proportionate representation and the direct primary. Nobody, however, can write on such subjects without deep understanding of them.

POLITICAL PUBLIC OPINION

Before formulating an opinion about the nature of public opinion, one must understand what is meant by each word. What is a public? And what is an opinion? Unless one knows the results of scholarly attempts to answer these questions, his own conclusions are invalid. Consequently, a minimum of training in sociology and psychology, or in the dual science social psychology, is essential to the political writer. From a good course or textbook he will learn that few modern thinkers in the field share the faith formerly held in instincts or a group mind as the explanation of why men behave similarly. Instead, inspired by the revelations of the behaviorists, psychoanalysts, anthropologists and other specialists, they are impressed by the importance of cultural conditioning which involves traditions, customs, myths, legends, taboos, superstitions and the like of which most people are dimly conscious if at all. The present author evaluated these factors in *Understanding Public Opinion* (Wm. C. Brown).

The politician as a psychological phenomenon was first effectively treated by Harold D. Lasswell in *Psychopathology and Politics* and by A. B. Wolfe in *Conservatism, Radicalism, and the Scientific Method.* Walter Lippmann's *Public Opinion* and *The Phantom Public* resulted from his observations as a newspaperman. Lincoln Steffens' momentous *Autobiography* was inspired similarly. There is a sizable library on modern propaganda, including political propaganda, and abundant reading material on all other phases of the subject.

Failure of the professional pollsters to predict correctly the outcome of the 1948 presidential election gave impetus to research into the motivations of voting behavior. Paul Lazarsfeld and associates at Columbia University stress the effects of group interrelationships (*The People's Choice, Voting*). Louis Bean emphasizes longtime economic trends (*How to Predict Elections*). Samuel Lubell thinks the effect of nationality and cultural background has been underestimated (*The Future of American Politics, The Revolt of the Moderates*). Angus Campbell and associates demonstrate in *The American Voter* that voting preferences are consistent with a person's total personal and cultural conditioning.

Theodore H. White's quadrennial *The Making of the President* books, beginning with the campaign of 1960, "did more to explain the political process of manipulating the news and the reporter than anything else I've read," according to Patrick Graham, political writer for the Milwaukee *Journal.* No other "behind-the-scenes" book ever got a better response than Joe McGinniss' *The Selling of the President* after 1968. Bob Greene's, *Running* and Timothy Crouse's *The Boys on the Bus* revealed facts about the 1972 campaign which were recalled during the Watergate hearings. The definitive books about the breakup of the Nixon-Agnew administration are *A Heartbeat Away, the Investigation and Resignation of Vice-President Agnew* by Richard M. Cohen and Jules Witcover, *All the President's Men* by Carl Bernstein and Bob Woodward and *The Great Cover-Up* by Barry Sussman.

POLITICAL ORGANIZATION

Local

Municipal political affairs in recent years generally have become dissociated from major party organizations. Candidates for mayor and other city officers run as independents but may be identified in state and national politics as members of established parties which tacitly lend them support. In smaller communities, the rival groups in a municipal campaign are more likely to cross established party lines and to be dissociated from all but strictly local issues.

Because of the nonpartisan character of municipal elections, it should be the newspaper's function properly to identify candidates by the interests of the persons or groups backing them. Local political groups may take names as the People's Party, but these have little or no meaning until party members have held office and given indication of what they represent. A local candidate's backing may be racial, religious, economic, geographic or in some other way classifiable. In preparing slates of candidates, political parties try to have as many of the important elements as possible represented. Furthermore, it is customary to run a Catholic against a Catholic, a Jew against a Jew, someone of Swedish extraction against another with similar ancestry and so on. In this way, awareness of nationality, racial and other backgrounds is kept alive as well as taken advantage of politically.

Precinct and Ward

To assist the party to power in elections involving established political parties, cities are organized by wards and their subdivisions, precincts. The lowest rung on the political organization ladder is that of precinct worker who carries the responsibility of ringing doorbells, talking to voters, handing out campaign literature, watching at the polls and assisting voters to and from polling places. Ambitious workers are conscious of their positions between elections and "talk up" the party or some of its prominent members on all occasions, intensive work, however, is only during the few weeks or months before an election.

Procedure for selecting precinct and ward captains differs, but ordinarily both are elected by registered members of the party in the sections. It may be, however, that only the ward or township captain or chairman is elected and given the responsibility of appointing precinct captains. A precinct, created by the election board, usually contains from 500 to 2,000 voters, and it is the precinct captain's job to carry his precinct in both primary and general elections. Most precinct captains have patronage jobs which depend upon their continued satisfactory performance on election days.

Precinct workers are paid for their work during campaigns by the precinct captain, who gets the money from the ward leader, who gets it from the city or county committee, which raises part of it and gets more from the state or national committee. Original sources of the millions spent annually to assist candidates to get elected are the candidates themselves, public officeholders and others who have obtained employment with the assistance of the party, businessmen who have profited by providing goods and/or services to the party's officeholders, and interested outsiders who believe they have more to gain by a certain candidate's being elected than if his opponent were to win. Some large donors, mostly potential recipients of official largess, bid for the friendship of whoever occupies an important political office and may contribute to the campaign funds of both major parties.

The precinct captain generally is credited with "controlling" at least fifty voters among his friends and relatives, the families of those whom he helps obtain positions on election day as judges and clerks at the polls and others for whom he has done political favors. Unlike the ordinary worker, the precinct captain is active between elections, obtaining minor favors for voters in his precinct, such as assistance when they run afoul of the law, financial help in case of illness or death, advice on how to obtain employment, and any other services which the strength and wealth of the organization permit.

Although the nonpolitically minded person doesn't realize it, if the power of a political party machine is to be broken it must be done in the primary. In the general election, the voter merely has a choice between two or more machine-picked slates. Under any circumstances, bucking the efficiently organized party is virtually impossible; so-called reform slates result from fusions of political cliques or parties out of office at the time and with no hope of victory without each other's cooperation. The history of such fusion movements is one of temporary successes only. The primary laws in many states, furthermore, make starting a third party virtually impossible.

Most candidates for public office at the local level who receive regular party endorsement earned the reward by hard work in the precincts. Not always, however, is this the case. Sometimes, a ward committeeman becomes jealous of the growing popularity of one of his subordinates and maneuvers to get him into a public office where he will be less of a personal power threat. Usually, this means a judgeship or some appointive job whose incumbent is required by the Hatch act or other laws, or by tradition, to minimize his politicking.

County

County chairmen usually are elected by ward and township leaders, some or all of whom constitute the county executive committee. No political leader whose concern is a unit smaller than the county merits the unofficial title of "boss." All bosses, furthermore, are not officeholders or even party officials; they may be influential dictators who prefer to operate in the background. By whatever type of person occupied, the political boss' office is the clearing house for finances and information. Reporters may obtain tips from underlings but seldom get anything official except directly from headquarters.

"Getting next to" a political boss is not impossible, as Lincoln Steffens discovered. How to do it, however, is an individual matter dependent upon the reporter's particular personality. Just as the boss must be cautious about making promises but scrupulous about keeping them once made, so must the political reporter become resigned to learning more "off the record" than on and to not learning anything about a great deal of important party business. It is because newspapers are unable to obtain the information that they do not give more "inside dope." Furthermore, to get what he does, the reporter cannot incur the displeasure of his source. Instead, he often must report seriously what he knows to be the insincere remarks of some demagogue, overlook his personal foibles, correct his bad grammar and in general "cover up" for him. The alternative is openly to defy and fight the party machine; a newspaper finds it difficult to take that attitude against all political groups without discrimination.

The newspaper reporter's task is magnified whenever television cameras are present. In such instances the interviewee, from the president down, usually dominates the occasion. It is his prerogative to designate who his questioners shall be and he can cut off a probing reporter before he has a chance to put all of the questions necessary for a complete story. Political candidates are particularly astute about making the arrangements conducive to their presentation of prepared statements and controlling the entire experience.

State, National

State and national committees nominally exist continuously but are quiescent most of the time, arousing from their lethargy about a year before an election. Most active are potential candidates who are "pulling strings" to obtain machine backing when nominating time comes around. With feigned modesty, the aspirant gets some friend or group of backers to "front" for him so that the suggestion that he run for office may seem to emanate from someone other than himself. To reporters, he is evasive and unambitious and is so quoted by a press which, of course, knows better. Until an official announcement is made, however, it is dangerous to go too far in surmising anyone's intentions.

PRECAMPAIGN ACTIVITIES

Petitions

To have his name placed on the printed ballot as a candidate for office, a person must obtain the signatures of a certain proportion of the voters on nominating petitions which must be filed before a certain date with the proper public official—city clerk, county clerk, secretary of state and so on. Because top positions usually are given to candidates filing their papers first, candidates stand in line waiting for the hour at which it is legal to file them.

It is news both when petitions are taken out and when they are filed. The candidate's name, address, occupation, political experience and general background are included in the first story about his intentions. Sometimes he already has prepared a statement or platform regarding his candidacy although generally that comes later. In city elections, the first petition stories should contain information as to the deadlines for filing, the number of signatures needed and possibly something about the position at stake. The names of prominent signers of a petition are newsworthy.

The next clerk of the Milltown Municipal court will be either the incumbent, Andrew L. Ziegler, or Constable Eustace L. Cohen for whom nominating petitions, containing the required number of signatures, were filed yesterday, the deadline, in the office of City Clerk Jerome Z. Day.

Mr. Ziegler, who has been court clerk since establishment of the municipal court three years ago, filed petitions containing 1,416 names, 11 fewer than the maximum permitted. Cohen's petitions contained 1,043 names. Minimum number of names required was 892, or 5 percent of the vote cast at the last general election.

Graham R. Olson, 146 Arnold avenue, insurance man who took out petition forms last week, failed to file. His name appeared on one of Cohen's petitions. Feature of Ziegler's petitions was one sheet containing only the names of Milltown's 16 aldermen.

Until late yesterday, it was believed petitions would be filed for a candidate backed by the Milltown Democratic organization which took out blanks several days ago.

The election for Municipal court clerk will take place Nov. 3 at the same time as the state and national elections. There will be a separate ballot, however, for the office.

Registration

Eligibility to vote differs by states but some sort of registration usually is required. On certain specified days, all otherwise eligible voters (those who have resided in the state, county and precinct a sufficient length of time, have paid certain taxes, given evidence of literacy, and so forth, as the case may be) appear at their polling places to have their names recorded. Such registration may be quadrennial, annual or permanent; for municipal elections no registration at all may be necessary. Voting by affidavit also may be permitted in case a voter is unable to register on the designated days. If there is permanent registration, the voter merely notifies election officials of a change of address.

The total number of voters registering is news. Knowing that only about 60 per cent of the nation's eligible voters take the trouble to register, crusading editors often investigate abnormally large registrations. Pulitzer prizes have been won by newspapers which checked registration lists to discover "ghost" votes from empty lots, abandoned buildings and transient hotels.

Despite the all-day rain, Saturday's registration of voters for the Nov. 3 election was slightly higher than normal for a first registration day when 21,678 Milltown voters registered, according to City Clerk J. M. Blackburn.

John A. Burgess, Republican township committeeman for Milltown, declared that this total should be 340 greater, to include additional registrants from the Seventh ward: the clerk's office, however, reports that its figure is accurate.

The 21,678 total represents about 70 per cent of the total vote cast in Milltown in 1976. A registration of 65 per cent of voters normally is expected on the first registration day. Final registration day this year will be Tuesday, Oct. 6, when the polling places again will be open from 6 A.M. to 9 P.M. Registration is essential in order to be eligible to vote in November; no affidavits will be accepted.

According to the city clerk's office, Milltown's registration by wards was as follows. . . .

Ghosts also walk in the Eighth ward, at least on municipal election day.

To be specific, Tuesday, April 2, at least three nice spooks materialized in the southernmost ward of Milltown and helped the voters there select their aldermen and other city officials.

One of them called himself Hugh Hillis and gave 130 Elmwood avenue as the apartment building he haunts.

The second and third identified themselves as Thomas Long and Nicholas Reding and claimed to be neighbors in the closets of 333 Howard street, also an apartment building.

Thus it is seen that the ethereal denizens of the Eighth ward differ from those of the Fifth ward, where you will recall from my article of last Friday, the dusky unrealities preferred empty lots as their mundane habitats for the day.

This is not surprising, of course, when it is realized that the Eighth ward is predominately an apartment house section, whereas the Fifth ward is punctuated with wide open spaces.

Here is the dope on Spooks Hillis, Long, and Reding . . . .

Primaries

With the notable exception of the national tickets every four years, most candidates for important office are chosen by party primaries instead of by conventions as formerly. Any citizen may enter a primary election as a candidate for the nomination of any party. A voter, however, can participate in the primary of one party only. The names of only those candidates who have filed nominating petitions appear on the ballot, but the voter can add the name of anyone else. It is seldom, however, that a "write-in "candidate is elected.

In some states, if no candidate receives a majority, runoff primaries are held of the two or three leaders. In most states which have primary laws, a plurality in a single primary is sufficient to nominate.

If there is little contest in his own party, in most states a voter may vote in the primary of another although he intends to vote for his own party candidate in the general election. If too many voters desert it in a general election, however, the party may not receive a large enough proportion of the total vote to receive a place on the ballot at the next election. Likewise, the party voter may forfeit the right to vote in any special primary within the time limit, usually two years, during which it is possible to change party affiliation.

Conventions

Adoption of a direct primary law does not mean the end of state party conventions, but such conventions (or conferences) are held outside the law and for the purpose only of recommending and endorsing candidates to receive the party's nomination at a primary election. Often rival factions within a party hold separate conventions and endorse different slates.

The news writer can estimate the strength of candidates at a state or national convention by comparing the instructions given to delegates. Delegations sometimes support "favorite sons" from their localities and may deadlock a convention by refusing, after the early ballots, to change their votes to one of the leading candidates. Some delegations from states with open primaries are uninstructed.

Knowledgeable political editors suspect deals whenever stubborn delegations suddenly change their positions. Possibly appointment to a cabinet position or judgeship or some other office has been promised someone; or support has been pledged in some future campaign. Maybe the compromise involves stands on issues to be involved in anticipated legislation.

A party convention is called to order by a temporary chairman who gives a prepared keynote speech. Then a permanent chairman is elected and he also gives a speech. Usually the committee's recommendation for permanent chairman is taken, but sometimes rival factions may nominate different candidates. The vote for permanent chairman then may be an indication of how delegates will vote later on other important matters.

The group in control of a state or national committee has the advantage of obtaining a personnel to its liking. Through its committee on credentials it determines which delegates are eligible for seats, if rival delegations from the same locality claim recognition.

Vote on the platform submitted by the committee on resolutions is conducted by a roll call of delegations. After the platform is adopted, with or without amendments, the next procedure is the election of candidates. Often, several ballots are necessary for a choice. When a deadlock continues after several ballots, a "dark horse," someone not among the leaders, may be elected as a compromise candidate.

A party convention frequently is interrupted by the demonstrations of different delegations. When the time to nominate candidates arrives, the roll call begins. Every delegation either nominates someone or passes its turn or permits some other delegation, whose turn normally would come later, to use its opportunity. In addition to the principal nominating speech there may be several other speeches to second a nomination. Every speech is the signal for an outburst of enthusiasm by supporters of the candidate. Unfavorable viewers' reactions to the carnival aspects of the televised proceedings have caused the two major political parties to attempt to streamline their quadrennial conventions somewhat. The stage managers, however, may become overly conscious of what is considered prime viewing time and either slow down or hurry up activities with the nationwide television audience in mind. Thus the conventions tend to become entertainment rather than serious exercises in statesmanship.

In 1972 the networks spent about $8 million to cover the Democratic convention in Miami; the Democratic party and candidates spent less than $3 million. In *The Boys on the Bus*, Timothy Crouse relates the consternation which the Republicans experienced when a British Broadcasting Company reporter obtained a minute-by-minute script of the convention which, Crouse wrote, "simply confirmed what everyone already knew, that the convention was a totally stage-managed coronation of Richard Nixon . . . . The script instructed speakers when to pause, nod and accept 'spontaneous' cheers. It stipulated that at a certain time, a demonstration would interrupt the convention secretary in midsentence." In obedience to the traditional rules of objective reporting, both electronic and print reporters report such incidents straight.

A party *conference* is for the purpose of discussing an important matter. A party *caucus* differs from a conference because all who attend it, by their attendance, pledge themselves to support the decisions of the majority. Insurgent members may stay away from party caucuses because they do not wish to commit themselves to the support of what the majority will favor.

CAMPAIGNS

Speeches

A campaign really gets under way with the first speech of the candidate. In the case of a presidential candidate this is the speech of acceptance of the nomination formerly made at a formal notification ceremony, but in recent years usually at the nominating convention. Although presidential candidates have fresh speeches for every important occasion thereafter, in the case of candidates for less important offices the opening or keynote speech may be the pattern for all others delivered during the campaign. The political reporter traveling with the candidate may be hard put to obtain a fresh angle in reporting the day's forensics, but the local news writers who hear the candidate only once are not so handicapped.

When candidates start calling each other names, hurling challenges, answering each other's arguments and raising new issues, the political reporter's problem is easy. Otherwise, he may be forced to rely upon the press releases of political headquarters. If he travels with a candidate he tells of the crowds, the opinions of local leaders, the reception given the candidate and the like.

In reporting and writing up a political speech the reporter should observe the orthodox rules for such occasions as described in Chapter 12.

Most newspapers try to equalize the space given rival candidates. Often this is difficult to do. William Pride, executive news editor of the Denver *Post*, summarized the difficulty in part as follows:

> Last time around we had a congressional race (suburban) featuring staid, stodgy 3-term incumbent vs. young, sharp, interesting challenger. Problem: how to treat 'em equally. We allotted equal space and traded off reporters following them the last two weeks. The incumbent was a shoo-in from the start, so all he did was stand at factory gates and shopping centers shaking hands. The young guy, full of ideas, uncorked a new major speech about every other day. If we give each half a column, what can we say about the first guy after we say he stood at the entrance to the supermarket all morning? If we give the second guy more space, we get squawks, pickets, etc., so there you are. (I hardly need add that the incumbent was easily re-elected.)

Coverage

A related problem is how to include all of the candidates for all of the offices that will appear on the ballot. Naturally, the most important—president, governor, senator, mayor, etc.—will receive most attention if for no other reason than the fact that the candidates will campaign more vigorously. But despite the trend to making formerly elective offices appointive the voter still is asked to make a multitude of choices. He may stare at a long ballot with scores of unfamiliar names of candidates for public offices about whose duties he knows little or nothing.

A traditional method is to print thumbnail sketches of all candidates shortly before election day. These include the essential facts of family background, education, occupational, civic and political experience. They seldom include statements on issues. In local elections when there is a short ballot, depth interviews can be obtained with all candidates and the written questionnaire method, soliciting answers regarding key issues, can be used effectively. Space is given the candidates' own words in reply.

Still another familiar method is the roundup article of a particular campaign, with emphasis on candidates, issues and campaign tactics.

By Dick Haws

Unlike many political contests in Nebraska, the Second District House race between Republican John McCollister, 48, and Democrat John Hlavacek, 48, has been relatively calm.

In part, this is probably because the two, who are vying for the seat now held by Republican Glenn Cunningham, view each other as "honest, sincere" and deserving of respect.

McCollister says he has "known John for several years. We only live a few blocks apart" in Omaha.

Aside from that, however, another factor which has probably reduced the "fireworks" between the two has been their wide agreement on many issues—especially foreign affairs.

Hlavacek considers foreign affairs "a nonpartisan issue." In line with that, he long ago supported Nixon's Southeast Asian policy, including the intervention in Cambodia.

Describing himself as "probably a conservative on foreign affairs," Hlavacek says he wants the United States "to be a leader" in the world.

McCollister, who calls himself a "Nixon Republican," also endorsed the Nixon course in Southeast Asia some time ago.

The two candidates have disagreed most on selected domestic issues. Both frequently mention the state of the economy.

McCollister blames the overheated economy on the "inability of government over the last 20 years" to provide adequate controls. Hlavacek, however, feels the President should "provide greater leadership" and "apply pressure to the banks" to reduce interest rates.

McCollister, denying he is simply espousing the classical Republican party philosophy, favors "more local involvement in local government."

Hlavecek likes to stress that "it's a brand new world," which makes cooperation and federal involvement imperative. "In our situation today," he said, "where the United States is pretty much an integrated whole, it's pretty difficult for all things to be done locally."

Hlavacek attributes much of his "integrated whole" philosophy to his background. He is a former foreign correspondent who spent 20 years on assignment in India, Cuba, and Jamaica.

He moved to Omaha in 1964 and immediately became one of the most familiar faces on television with his KMTV news analysis show.

In May, 1970, two days before filing for the Second District congressional race Hlavacek registered for the first time as a Democrat. He said he had not registered earlier because "a news analyst must remain independent."

In the primary, Hlavacek narrowly defeated Robert Reilly.

McCollister, on the other hand, has long been associated with Nebraska Republican circles, serving in such positions as 1968 president of Republican Founders Day and as a member of the Republican state executive committee.

McCollister, president of an Omaha oil firm, faced Cunningham in the primary and defeated the seven-term incumbent, receiving about 55% of the more than 45,000 votes cast.

Neither candidate is predicting an easy victory. McCollister feels he has "gained the momentum." Hlavacek, however, thinks "it'll be close, but I'll win."

Biographies of the two candidates, as well as their answers to important questions, will appear in The Sunday Journal and Star-League of Woman Voters Voters Guide, to be published Oct. 25. [Lincoln *Journal*]

Roorbacks

The word "roorback" entered the dictionary as a common noun following the presidential election of 1844 during which a last-minute attempt was made to defeat James K. Polk by newspaper publicity for a fictitious book by a nonexistent author named Roorback supposedly telling of Polk's having bought and branded a number of Negro slaves.

There is a difference between raising false issues and plain lying. The former is for the purpose of misdirecting attention from important to insignificant matters; the latter is sheer falsehood. Roorbacks generally appear as late as possible to be effective and yet permit the opposition insufficient time for an answer. The political reporter always should be wary of a new important issue raised late in a campaign unless it is one which couldn't have been brought up earlier.

May it be said to the credit of newspapermen that they generally have the intelligence to "see through" political humbug, but they are stymied as to what they say, for the reasons which have been enumerated in this chapter. The political reporter who is "taken in" by political bunk is inadequate for the job, which is one for seasoned and not callow persons.

Issues

The interpretative reporter talks not only to candidates and political leaders but also to representatives of civic, business, labor and other groups and with ordinary citizens in the attempt to determine the issues upon which the outcome of an election depends.

Nobody has developed this technique better than Samuel Lubell whose periodic series of articles on the political thinking of "the man in the street" are supplemented by his uncannily correct forecasts of election results. Lubell's methods confound the professional pollsters and academic political analysts who go to elaborate extremes to be certain those whom they interview represent a correct cross-sectional sample of the electorate as a whole.

Lubell studies election results. When he notes similar significant changes in voting behavior, even in precincts thousands of miles apart, he follows his nose for news to the areas to determine the cause. He has "pet" precincts and blocks and even residences in all parts of the country based on past experience of their value as political weather vanes, enabling him to make generalizations. Lubell's main interest is in discovering the reasons for voting behavior rather than merely straw voting. Too much political writing to explain the issues of a campaign derives from the writer's ideas or desires as to what they should be. Neither these pundits nor the politicians determine the issues. Rather, the voters do so, and they favor those candidates who they think hold views closest to their own.

The experienced political reporter who has seen winners and losers come and go for years, perhaps decades, becomes an expert analyst. He notes the distinguishing features of any campaign and creates "total effect" as this example illustrates:

By Laura Foreman
Inquirer Political Writer

Beyond the issues and rhetoric, beyond the out-front hoopla and the behind-the-scenes maneuvering, almost every election has its own ineffable mood, its own individual character.

That's what Democratic City Committee Chairman Peter J. Camiel, who is backing State Sen. Louis G. Hill for mayor, means when he says, "This is not a political campaign—this is a crusade."

That's what State Rep. James J. Tayoun, a partisan of Mayor Frank L. Rizzo, means when he says, "In our wards you can feel an almost religious fervor."

Perhaps because so much is at stake, for Philadelphia and for the politicians who run it, Tuesday's Democratic mayoral primary often seems less a political event, more a holy war.

For Hill, it's a matter of restoring to the city the political and physical "renaissance" of the 1950s that was presided over by his stepfather, the late Mayor Richardson Dilworth, and in the process ridding the city of an administration that Hill considers hopelessly inept and corrupt.

Rizzo, who still holds an almost messianic appeal for his followers, in turn sees the election as a battle to save "the little people" from aristocrats who don't understand or care for them (Hill) as well as from a political machine that exploits them (Camiel).

For Camiel, whose regular Democratic organization is as much a factor in the race as either candidate, the election is a struggle to preserve the party from a man he sees as a dangerous renegade who has betrayed its ideals.

And for the voters, the outcome will certainly determine the governmental direction Philadelphia takes in the near future.

City registration figures show the Democrats with 605,848 registered voters, the Republicans with a meager 227,787. Although it's impossible to say what coalitions might form or dissolve, or what issues and emotions might come to bear on next November's general election, the man who wins the Democratic primary has the strong statistical probability of being mayor for the next four years.

The winner will also determine the future of the Democratic Party, although it is doubtful that changes will be as drastic or immediate as some partisans on both sides anticipate.

For instance, should Rizzo win but fail to obtain a majority of his loyalists on City Council, he would be a lame duck the day he took office, and his opponents could regroup and await his political demise.

Camiel could maintain a power base through control of the row offices—sheriff, clerk of Quarter Sessions Court and register of wills—with the scores of patronage jobs that go with them.

He would probably also retain control of the courts, the Board of Revision of Taxes, numerous state patronage jobs and the county commissioners, who control the city's election machinery.

It is hard to imagine, however, that Camiel would stay on as chairman after failing to topple a man he has called "a Nazi," "a monster" and "a liar," among other things.

Should Hill win, he would probably be content to run the city and not meddle in party affairs.

Should Rizzo lose, his own political career almost surely would be over, and his supporters would face uphill battles to salvage theirs.

Who will win?

A meticulous, division-by-division, in-house analysis by Rizzo supporters concludes that the mayor will be re-elected by 51,730 votes.

A similar analysis from Hill's camp has the challenger winning by 27,000 votes.

Rizzo appeared to be running well ahead as the final month of the campaign began, and his polls and surveys show that he still has a comfortable lead.

Hill, however, has narrowed the gap considerably in the last two to three weeks, largely on the strength of the Camiel organization's efforts.

Rizzo, who had conducted a low-key race for at least six months, seldom discussed the issues and almost never mentioned his opponent, staying instead with the theme of "the man against the machine."

But Hill finally forced the incumbent to take some notice of him with his constant criticism of Rizzo's record on such issues as housing, crime, city planning, the budget and gang control.

But the bottom line on the election remains what it always was: a Rizzo referendum. Voters are divided between those who like the current mayor and those who despise him, and the outcome of the race will be determined by which organization, Camiel's or Rizzo's, can mobilize its ready-made vote.

[Philadelphia *Inquirer*]

ELECTIONS

Predictions

As election day approaches, reporters who have followed the campaign more objectively than candidates or party leaders usually are better able to predict the outcome than they. It is customary for large newspapers which assign reporters to travel with candidates to "switch assignments" at least once as the campaign progresses. That means that one writer will accompany Candidate A for a few weeks and then trade places with the reporter who has been covering Candidate B. Political reporters note the sizes of crowds and especially their composition; they mingle with and talk to voters as well as to professional politicians and local journalists. Straw votes among political writers have shown them better able to forecast election results than publishers, editors or editorial writers.

It is a fast-growing practice for newspapers as well as politicians to employ professional pollsters to note trends, evaluate the effect of issues and incidents and, particularly, predict results. The following two leads on the same page of the New York *Times* a few days before an election are typical as indicating the reliance now placed on polls:

The Washington Star-News

COLUMBUS, Kan., Oct. 29—Six weeks ago Senator Robert Dole was trailing his Democratic opponent, Representative William R. Roy, in his re-election race by 8 to 10 points in the opinion polls.

During October, however, he wiped out Mr. Roy's lead in the same polls and they are now running even.

"I told myself I was too tense, that I needed to relax and smile more," Mr. Dole told an audience in Columbus. "It's easy to smile when you're ahead, so I'm smiling more these days."

Mr. Dole isn't smiling because he's some sort of political Polyanna. The main reasons for his new cheerfulness are (a) an organizational shakeup, (b) a television campaign that appears to have gotten the Watergate demon off his back, and (c) his opponent's errors.

AN ERROR CONCEDED

Mr. Roy concedes he may have been too easygoing in letting Senator Dole wriggle off the Watergate hook in October. . . .

Special to the New York Times

TALLAHASSEE, Fla., Oct. 30—Several Florida political reporters wrote last weekend that they could feel a small shift of voter sentiment toward underdog Republican candidates for both Governor and Senator in Florida.

But public opinion polls have shown Gov. Reubin Askew and Richard Stone, the Democratic candidate for the Senate, so far in front that the election of Jack Eckerd as Senator or Jerry Thomas as Governor would be a dramatic upset.

A victory for Mr. Stone would mean the loss for Florida Republicans of the first Senate seat they have held since the Reconstruction era following the Civil War—a seat now held by Senator Edward J. Gurney, who is not seeking re-election because of criminal charges against him.

Governor Askew had such a big lead that a number of Republicans have endorsed him over Mr. Thomas, a Palm Beach County banker who switched from the Democratic party two years ago. One poll showed the 46-year-old incumbent Governor getting 70 percent of the vote. . . .

When its predictions prove to have been accurate a newspaper may be as jubilant as a winning candidate. A typical "day-after" lead follows:

The Denver Post Poll forecast the 1974 sweep of the Democratic party almost flawlessly.

While actual voting percentages varied in some cases from advance projections, the Post Poll accurately predicted these winners:

—Democrat Gary Hart for U.S. Senate.

—Democrats Dick Lamm and George Brown for governor and lieutenant governor.

—Democrats Pat Schroder, Frank Evans and Tim Wirth for Congress.

—Republican William Armstrong for Congress.

—Democrats Sam Brown for treasurer, J. D. MacFarlane for attorney general and Dick Bernick, Jim Carrigan and Louis Rein for regents of the University of Colorado.

The poll was conducted by Research Services, Inc., of Denver for The Post in the period from Oct. 25 to 30.

There was one miscalculation in a major race—the contest for Congress in the 4th District between GOP incumbent Jim Johnson and Democrat John Carroll.

The poll showed that contest as very close, with Carroll gaining. On that basis, chief pollster John Emery, president of Research Services, projected Carroll as the winner with a 51 per cent vote.

Actually Carroll fell slightly short of Johnson's vote.

Emery correctly called the extremely close race for secretary of state between the appointed Republican incumbent, Nary Estill Buchanan, and Democrat Tony Mullen.

In his last poll report, Emery said Mrs. Buchanan was only about a percentage point ahead of Mullen, but might still win. And she did win, barely, to become the only Republican elected in a statewide vote.

Emery said Tuesday night, as returns were still coming in, that he considered this year's poll remarkably successful.

Another miscalculation in the poll was on Amendment No. 1, the so-called Poundstone amendment, aimed at blocking Denver annexations.

Emery had predicted No. 1 would lose because it was running 8 points behind in the October survey. But the amendment carried.

The poll correctly projected passage of all of the remaining nine ballot proposals.   [Denver *Post*]

The increased amount of emphasis newspapers now give political predictions probably results in large part from the phenomenal success that national television networks have in projecting early returns from a few key precincts to indicate probable winners. The networks almost seem to regard an election as a contest between computers. After every national election there are angry growls from some congressmen who at least would forbid broadcasting the results in Eastern states until after the polls have closed in the West. Critics also contend that the principal function of all journalistic media should be clarification of issues and of candidates' positions rather than bookmaking. In 1956 a team of more than 30 New York *Times* reporters proved it is possible, using traditional reportorial techniques, to forecast accurately. The costly experiment was not repeated and the talents of many who participated in it have since been used more constructively. As for the public, much of it takes as much pleasure from a pollster's error as it does from second-guessing the weatherman.

Election Day

The size of the vote, violence at polling places, amusing anecdotes, the circumstances under which the candidates cast their ballots, last-minute statements and predictions and methods used to get out the vote or persuade voters on their way to the polls provide news on election day before the ballots are counted.

Ordinary newsroom routine is upset on election day as regulars work overtime and extra helpers gather and compile returns. A newspaper may use its news carriers or other employees to wait at polling places until the votes are counted or may receive its returns through campaign headquarters. Often, the police gather returns and release them to reporters. Radio and television have eliminated the newspaper election extra although editions may be set ahead to provide details, background and interpretative material which the electronics media cannot give.

In national elections the three television networks and the two press associations sometimes pool their efforts to gather the returns rapidly. As the results come in by isolated districts they are tabulated, and the political writer prepares a trend story for the first edition. Some outcomes can be predicted comparatively early; often, in a close race, the result is in doubt until the last vote is counted. When the result is apparent, campaign committees and candidates issue statements claiming victory or conceding defeat. Losers send messages of congratulations to winners, and everybody poses for pictures.

If an outcome is close, a loser may demand a recount. Some elections are protested by defeated candidates who charge fraud, stuffing or tampering with ballot boxes and other irregularities. All candidates are required to file statements of campaign expenditures. Investigations of alleged violations of the corrupt practices act during an election are not infrequent.

The mid-election day story should include the number voting and a comparison with previous elections.

Candidates were being nominated in today's statewide primary elections for United States Senator and Representatives in Congress, and for some state and local offices in St. Louis and St. Louis county. In the city and county, balloting was generally light, indicating one of the smallest off-year primary votes in years.

By 4 P.M., it was estimated 61,889 ballots had been cast in the city, following 10 hours of balloting in the 784 precincts. This was 18 percent of the total registration of 343,830.

In the county, an estimated 9,936 ballots were cast by 4 P.M., nine hours after the 7 A.M. opening of the polls. The estimated vote was 7.9 percent of the 125,782 registration.

St. Louis polling places will close at 7 P.M. Those in the county will close at 8:07 P.M. with the exception of those in University City, where the closing time is 8 P.M. The hours given are daylight saving time.

SPECIAL WATCH ON TWO WARDS

Special deputy election commissioners are on duty in all precincts of the Fifth and Sixth Wards, in which a recent recanvass of the registration indicated efforts to pad the lists. Chairman Frank L. Rammacciotti of the Election Board said the deputies were stationed in the two downtown wards to guard against any election irregularities.

Ballots and registration lists for the two wards were not delivered to the polling places until early today. Rammacciotti said this was done because many of the election officials resided outside of the wards and they did not have adequate means to care for them. These were the only two wards where this was done, the ballots and voters' lists having been delivered to election officials in all other wards last night.

The special deputies in the Fifth and Sixth Wards were instructed specifically to guard against ballots being marked openly instead of in the regular voting booth, and to see that all ballots were counted by Republican and Democratic poll officials working together instead of dividing ballots for a separate tabulation by each party's officials.

TWO BALLOTS IN CITY

City voters received two ballots at the polls, a party primary ballot and one for the two amendments to the City Charter and the proposed $4,000,000 bond issue for rubbish collection facilities, each calling for a Yes or No vote.

Proposed amendment No. 1 would permit . . .   [St. Louis *Post-Dispatch*]

Election Results

When all or nearly all returns are in, so that the outcome is known, the news feature naturally is who won. The story also should emphasize (1) by how much—in total votes and proportions; (2) areas in which different candidates were strongest and weakest; (3) upsets—incumbents with long services who were defeated, candidates on a party slate who lost whereas most of the others won; (4) whether results coincide with predictions; (5) what significance the outcome is likely to have both locally and/or nationally, as the case may be; (6) statements by winners, losers and party leaders, and similar matters.

"POST-MORTEMS"

A great deal of postelection interpretative writing is of the "I told you so" or "We should have known it" type. By analyzing the vote in different sections where the electorate is predominantly of one type—workers, members of a particular racial, national or religious group—it is possible to imagine which campaign issues or attitudes antedating the campaign were most effective. The skilled political writer analyzes results in the search for trends. Often, he has to compare local with state and national results to interpret correctly.

When a new officeholder or party takes over a city hall, county building, state or national capitol, the citizenry expects that "there will be some changes made." Party platforms and campaign speeches provide clues as to what they will be, but voters have become suspicious of politicians' promises. Personality sketches and reviews of the past records of successful candidates are valuable.

Compare the following "second thought" analysis with the same writer's preelection piece on pages 331–332.

By Laura Foreman
Inquirer Political Writer

Conventional wisdom has it that primary elections are battles between organizations. But Tuesday's Democratic mayoral primary proved that no machine can win with a candidate who fails to excite popular support.

It also proved that Frank L. Rizzo is a man for his time.

It was an election in which one of the two major candidates, State Sen. Louis G. Hill, was hardly relevant.

The real candidate against Rizzo was Democratic City Committee Chairman Peter J. Camiel, who in one night was transformed from the leader of one of the nation's most powerful big city machines to that saddest of political figures —a boss who failed to produce.

Camiel's hatred of Rizzo was so deep and so personal that the chairman felt, and said, he could beat the incumbent with "any good Democrat."

Lou Hill was a good Democrat, and he had a good Senate record. And he had enough money to finance much of his own campaign.

He viewed himself right to the end as a tough campaigner and could not understand why political observers persisted in characterizing him as dull, drab and lackluster. The reason was that he was dull, drab and lackluster.

He was also a patrician who, by the frequent admission of his own campaign aides, was culturally incapable of understanding the ethnic, blue-collar constituency he sought to represent.

Rizzo was vulnerable on many points of his record, but he was anything but dull. He was also blessed with an instinctive understanding of what mattered to "the little guy"—not ideology, not abstractions and not a return to Hill's liberal renaissance of the 1950s, but rather low taxes, law and order and a man who talked the same street language they did.

Frank Rizzo was one of them, and no one could convince them otherwise. In South Philadelphia alone, they gave him a 33,500 vote lead over Hill—more than the mayor's city-wide margin of victory.

Hill said it himself: "The people who supported me didn't turn out. The people who were frantic for the mayor did."

Here are some other factors in the Rizzo victory:

Camiel didn't think it possible for Rizzo to win any bigger in the seven South Philadelphia wards than he had in 1971. But Rizzo did—by 6,321 more votes.

Camiel expected black animosity against Rizzo to register at the polls. It didn't. He had been a better mayor for them than the blacks expected—he hardly could have been as bad as they expected—and they gave him 3,500 more votes than they had in 1971. More importantly, they did not turn out for Hill. The black turnout was only 37 percent, compared to a citywide turnout of 56 percent of the registered voters.

Hill failed to capitalize on his strength, which was his organizational support. Ward leaders didn't understand him, and most were doubtful they could sell him to their voters. They were right, especially in crucial areas like the Northeast. Camiel expected to cut into Rizzo's 1971 vote heavily in that area. He couldn't.

Rizzo had built an organization of his own. At best, it was roughly equal to Camiel's. So the race was, finally, a popular referendum on Rizzo.

The people spoke:

Rizzo 178,853

Hill 146,847

(With 97 percent of the vote reported.)   [Philadelphia *Inquirer*]

17
GOVERNMENT

As population increases and all phases of life become more complex, "closing the gap" between governed and governors becomes a major problem in a democracy. The journalistic media have a great opportunity and responsibility to stimulate interest and participation on the part of the citizenry in governmental affairs.

Journalism's first obligation is to report fully the activities of public agencies and officials. Since all public issues ultimately are decided by public opinion, the duty includes presentation of the pros and cons of all important matters and expert analysis of them. In other words, interpretative reporting and writing are essential in the field of governmental affairs.

To prepare himself for the role of expert in this field, the aspiring interpretative reporter must be thoroughly grounded in political history and theory. He must understand the nature and purpose of all governmental agencies and the political connections and motivations of public officials and their backers. No matter how public spirited or socially conscious they may be, officeholders are candidates for re-election or reappointment; they do not cease to be politicians and become statesmen suddenly the day they take office.

The interpretative reporter who specializes in governmental news makes use of all of the devices of the interpretative reporter anywhere. To place an immediate occurrence in proper perspective, he may give its historical background. Even before legislators or administrators take action, he may describe the existence of a problem. When a proposal is pending, he explains its nature, the arguments pro and con and the political alignment as regards it. He describes the functions of various offices and officers and reviews the records of the representatives of the people.

CITY GOVERNMENT

Closest to the average newspaper and its readers is city government. The oldest and still most prevalent type of city government is the mayor-council plan. Members of the city council (or board of aldermen) are elected from wards, one or two from a ward, their terms usually staggered so that half of the members always are carryovers. The mayor is elected at large. The trend is toward nonpartisan elections rather than contests between nominees of political parties. When political parties do exist at the city level they usually are not affiliated with the national parties and have names with local significance. Once elected, in some places the mayor has almost unlimited power of appointment of subordinates; in other places the legislative board exercises tight veto power.

If the city has the commission plan, instead of the aldermen there are two, four or six commissioners, usually elected at large, and fewer appointive officers, the duties usually performed by them being assigned to the full-time commissioners. If the city has the city manager plan, the important officer is not the mayor but the city manager who performs the duties, in a small city, of many appointive officers under the mayor-council plan. Under the city manager plan, the office of the mayor, if it is retained at all, may be little more than that of presiding officer at council meetings. A city manager runs a city as a general superintendent operates a business or as a superintendent of schools directs a school system. He is chosen for his expert knowledge of municipal business affairs and is not necessarily a resident of the city at the time of his appointment.

Although city hall still is a beat, large city newspapers, especially, have learned that it is impossible to rely on beat men alone to cover local government. Rather, the trend is toward so-called urban affairs reporters who cover events that overlap governmental levels, as urban renewal, public housing, model cities, etc. Otherwise, the city hall reporter is frustrated when the urban renewal director complains about federal "red tape" and bureaucracy. The "issues" reporter must have a sound background in Housing and Urban Development rules and regulations and other federal and state governmental operational procedures.

Mayor

Under the *mayor-council plan*, which still exists in a majority of American cities, the mayor is chosen as is a governor of a state or a president of the United States, by popular election every two or four years. A significant change has taken place in recent years, however, in that city politics has been divorced from state and national. Except in the larger cities, candidates for mayor generally do not run as Republicans, Democrats or Socialists but as independents, their backing crossing party lines.

Wealthy businessmen and industrialists who live in the suburbs provide financial support for mayors and other city officials who promote measures, as urban renewal and zoning laws, of benefit to their financial interests. Although they cannot vote in the city, these pillars of the Establishment must take an interest in what happens within the city limits because that is where they do business. In recent years staunch diehard suburbanite Republican conservatives have been the financial supporters of strong big-city Democratic political machines, the most notorious example being Chicago under Mayor Daley.

As the executive head of the city, the mayor is the chief news source in the city hall. He should be aware of every important occurrence in all city departments, most of them headed by persons whom he has appointed with the approval of the city council. For details, the reporter should see the department heads themselves, or subordinates in closer touch with the news at hand.

As municipal affairs become more complex and the bureaucracy grows in size, the reporter's access to primary news sources becomes more limited. He has to learn to circumvent press agents alias publicity directors alias public relations counsel alias public affairs vice presidents or directors of information. So he finds it smart to cultivate the good will of telephone operators, receptionists and other potential tipsters, vulgarly known as "leaks."

Because the mayor is called upon to take part in most important non-governmental activities in the city, he is a potent source of miscellaneous tips. He is visited by delegations of all sorts and receives letters of complaint and inquiry; he buys the first Red Cross button, proclaims special days and weeks, welcomes convention delegates, attends meetings and gives speeches.

If he is a strong mayor, he has a program for the city which he reveals in his reports, messages and remarks to the city council. Usually he is close to certain aldermen who introduce motions, resolutions and ordinances embodying his ideas. Unable to speak on legislative matters without leaving the presiding officer's chair, the mayor who is a leader has spokesmen in the council who present his point of view for him.

City Council

Councilmen or *aldermen* usually devote only part time to their official duties, possibly doing little more than attend weekly or semimonthly meetings. Committee meetings are held council night before the general session and may be closed to reporters. Chairmen of important committees, such as finance, streets and welfare are compelled to give some attention to the aldermanic duties throughout the week, at times at least, and may be interviewed in case of important news. A typical order of business for a city council meeting follows:

Roll call by the city clerk.
Minutes of the last meeting.
Communications read by the city clerk.
Standing committees (reports called for in alphabetical order.)
Special committee reports.
Call of wards (each alderman brings up any matter pertaining to his ward which needs council or executive attention.)
Miscellaneous business, including mayoral reports.
Adjournment.

The rules for covering a city council meeting do not differ from those which apply to any other type of meeting. Because of the importance of council meetings, however, it frequently is necessary to write two or more stories adequately to play up different matters affecting the public. It is seldom that a reporter can write his story entirely from the notes he is able to take as motions are made and argued and matters are referred to different committees. Usually he must verify names, the wording of motions and resolutions, the outcome of votes and other matters by consulting the city clerk or his stenographer at the end of a meeting.

In an advance story of a council meeting, the nature of business likely to come up should be emphasized. The experienced reporter usually can anticipate the nature of debate and the lineup of votes. He also should attempt to interpret the significance and possible aftermath of any controversial matter.

The plan to build a $20,000,000 city airport at Pratt and Sumner will be disposed of by formal vote of the common council tonight.

If the lineup of councilmen remains unchanged, the so-called southeast site will go down to defeat by a vote of 5 to 4.

Councilmen Howard, Lane, Otis and Cade favor the northwest airport. Councilmen Moore, Kole, Blede, Masse and Walz are opposed.

MAYOR WANTS ACTION

Mayor McCartney, who also favors the southeast site, has promised that he will try to get a final decision before Jan. 31—the date on which the offer of a gift of 650 acres at the site expires.

Regardless of the outcome, few observers had any hope that tonight's action would be final.

Arthur Schuman, secretary of the Metropolitan Civic Airport Trust, today was on the verge of conceding defeat. He said the would-be donors of the $750,000 for land at the southeast site would have their money returned to them at once.

"Nothing short of a miracle can save it now," Schuman declared.

"They have kicked this around for ten years and now the airlines have moved to St. Martin. I'm all through.

"If the city wants a modern airport now, let the city department heads get one. It's their job from here on. Apparently they don't want the aid of the industrial groups."

WILL SEEK BALLOT

Councilman Otis will attempt to keep the southeast site alive even though voted down tonight. He said he would seek a ballot proposition on the question at the next election, probably in June.

If the northeast site is turned down tonight, St. Martin County Airport will remain as the city's "major interim airport," according to a council resolution already adopted.

Making reliable contacts and keeping friendships while reporting fearlessly is the main problem of the city hall reporter. Clerks and others like to give tips to favorite newsmen but often do so in confidence which must be respected. It frequently requires great reportorial ingenuity to wheedle information out of others while concealing the source of one's knowledge. Often it is best for the city editor to assign a special reporter to a particular story so that the regular man on the beat will not alienate his sources.

Strong papers and state and national press associations have waged vigorous fights in the post-World War II years to end or prevent secret meetings of city councils, village boards and similar groups from which reporters as well as the public are excluded. Some state legislatures have been persuaded to pass laws requiring open sessions. Then the problem becomes one of discovering and exposing the subterfuges which may be used, as informal and unofficial get-togethers, possibly at lunch or in a private home. The newspaper which fights secrecy is acting on the democratic principle that the public's business should not be transacted in private. If it persists it usually wins its campaign because of the public support it generates.

The writer of the following article concentrated on the highlights of the matter under consideration in order to simplify them for readers:

Skokie's village fathers Monday night adopted the largest money bill in the village's 83 year history—a giant $9,959,101.

That's the maximum the trustees can spend between now and next Apr. 30.

It is almost $1.2 million more than was authorized a year ago, and includes these highlights:

—Total salaries to more than 400 employees of $3,299,838, an increase of some $296,000 over 1965–66.

The increases resulted from most employees earning their five per cent merit hikes this year, plus an almost three per cent cost of living increase across the board.

—An overall increase in the corporate (housekeeping) fund of $800,000 (which includes the bulk of the pay hikes).

—A $650,000 decrease in projected spending within the water department.

—The appropriating of $885,800 to cover acquisitions of buses—and land for a terminal—for the projected Intra-Skokie Transit Mass Demonstration Project.

About $550,000 will come in the form of a federal grant.

—A reduction in the library's operating budget of some $250,000, resulting from the voters turndown of the library board's proposal to buy land adjacent to Old Orchard junior high.

—An expected cost of $456,000 to replace or add to the auto-truck fleet.

—An expected $400,000 surplus in the water revenue account which may be transferred to the corporate fund.

—Some $1,226,000 made available to acquire land for bus terminals, fire stations, and water department use.

The entire appropriation ordinance is printed elsewhere in The News today.

However, appropriating money for a given project should not be construed as spending the money, Mayor Smith said.

Mayor Smith said that the ordinance is the legal tool the board must approve before it can spend any money—and then it can spend for only those items included in the ordinance.

"If our revenue projection is correct, this is our program for the use of those funds," he said.   [Skokie (Ill.) *News*]

The same paper did a splendid job of presenting the "news behind the news" of an important local personnel change:

Ben Marsh has accepted the city manager's post in Anchorage, Alaska, effective Sept. 15, and will step down as Skokie's manager Sept. 1.

Mayor Albert J. Smith made the announcement at Monday's meeting to a handful of spectators about two hours after more than 100 residents along and near Crawford ave. had left the council chambers.

Marsh said he was leaving because the Anchorage position:

—Will add to the variety of his professional experience.

—Offers a chance to improve the economic situation for his family, and

—Satisfies his desire for adventure.

He said that only "three or four managerships in the U.S. could meet those specifications and persuade me to leave the association I have found so enjoyable."

He told the board that the Alaskan city has a population of 50,000, the hub of a metropolitan area of nearly three times that size.

"It has 900 municipal employees (more than twice what Skokie employs), an annual budget of $18 million (about 2½ times Skokie's), and operates the telephone, power and water utilities, the port authority, the airport, parks and recreation program and the library."

Marsh, for all practical purposes, has been Skokie's only village manager though historians count him the third.

Arthur Lowther of Denver was hired in early 1958, turned out to be a Milquetoast type, terrified by the political machine then in power.

Lowther lasted eight months then simply left the village hall one evening and returned to Denver as if he had been commuting regularly.

Supt. of Public Works Henry Weber, who retired only three weeks ago, was named acting manager and served until Ben Marsh was hired.

Marsh arrived in Skokie Apr. 1, 1959, exactly seven days before voters "threw the rascals out" and gave the Caucus Party its first opportunity to run the village.

That incoming administration—including trustees Albert J. Smith and William Siegel—were skeptical about Marsh who had been hired by "those guys."

A true pro, Marsh went to work and let the politicians worry about the politics.

In two years time, the voters felt the Caucus Party had lost its sheen, tapped Myron (Mike) Griesdorf to head the new administration, and gave it a four-year lease on the village hall.

One of the subrosa pledges Griesdorf and his supporters made to one another was to unload Marsh at the first opportunity.

That opportunity never came—though there were many times when it sounded like it was knocking on the door.

But Mike Griesdorf learned early in his term that Marsh was an excellent buffer between irate citizens and the administration, that he was more than competent at his job, and that he, like Griesdorf, really wanted "to make a record."

Rather than fire him, Griesdorf came to the realization that he and his chief administrative aide complemented one another.

So he stayed on. . . .   [Skokie (Ill.) *News*].

Disgusted reporters of legislative bodies and governmental agencies at all levels—municipal, county, state and federal—sometimes write in the spirit of the following first half of a Minneapolis *Tribune* news story:

By M. Howard Gelfand
Staff Writer

By 8 P.M., when the show begins, there isn't an empty seat in the house. And no wonder. The most popular repertory company in the suburb of Dayton never does the same show twice.

Not that the cast—the five members of the Dayton City Council—doesn't repeat its favorite lines from time to time: lines like, "Shut up," and "You're out of order," and "What was the motion?"

This week's Monday-night meeting was such a hit that after a five-hour, three-act performance, the Dayton City Council decided to continue the drama next Monday.

When the decision was made it was 1 A.M., and the council hadn't even plowed halfway through its agenda. Still, only a few in the standing-room only audience of 50 had left.

The central issue at the meeting was whether to grant a zoning variance to Dayton developer Erland Maki. Maki wants to build an addition to a development on which he already has constructed 30 houses. The problem is that since he began the development, the council passed a law prohibiting houses on lots of less than 2½ acres. He wants to build 42 more houses on lots of half-an-acre each.

The council never did decide what to do. It seems likely, though, that some sort of compromise will be reached next week.

On one side of the issue is the mayor, Mrs. Gene Nelson. (Mrs. Nelson, 50, is also the police chief, and . . . but that's another story. More of that later.) Mrs. Nelson wanted to grant the variance, and it was partly her refusal to accept a compromise that resulted in the stalemate.

On the other side of the issue—and just about every other issue—is maverick Councilman Gerald Barfuss, a junior-high school art teacher. He contends that granting the variance would be illegal and environmentally unsound. He further says that Maki is guilty of a conflict-of-interest because Maki sits on the city's planning commission.

The scene for the bi-weekly sessions in the northwestern Hennepin County Community is the Dayton City Hall, a blue metal structure that houses two caterpillar trucks but no telephone.

Mrs. Nelson conducts the meetings like a stern schoolmarm, scolding audience members and Barfuss for laughing or talking out of turn.

Barfuss, 33, is her sassy pupil, the incorrigible class wit who accepts the titters of his friends as payment for the admonishments he constantly endures.

Barfuss walked out of a special hearing on the matter held by the council last month, but before he did so he outlined his case against the variance. Mrs. Nelson told him last night:

"You have prematurely presented your opinion at the hearing and unless you've had a change of heart that can stand."

"I'm a council member," he responded, "and I intend to speak."

"I'd like to hear what the other council members have to say," she said.

City Clerk

The *city clerk*, an elective officer, might be termed the city's secretary. He attends council meetings and takes minutes, receives communications addressed to the city, issues licenses (dog, beach and the like), receives nominating petitions, supervises elections and preserves all city records.

Corporation Counsel

A lawyer, the *corporation counsel* is legal adviser to the city and its representative in court in major matters. In smaller communities his duties are performed by the *city attorney*, who, in larger places, is the prosecuting attorney in criminal cases: much of his work relates to minor court cases. His title may be *city solicitor*.

Public Works

The tendency is toward consolidation, under a *commissioner of public works*, of the departments of streets, water, public buildings, local improvements and the like. If the offices are not consolidated, the commissioner of public works has charge of new construction of streets, sewers and so on, whereas the *street commissioner* has the responsibility of seeing that the streets are kept clean and in repair and usually has charge of garbage collection. The *city engineer* works under the commissioner of public works.

The newspaper has it within its power to interpret the activities of these departments for tax-paying readers. One way is by an eyewitness description of their functionings.

By Charles B. Cleveland

A uniformed policeman noted the pile of garbage strewn in the alley; walked around to the apartment with an arrest book in his hand.

This is a frequent scene in Chicago now as every ward has a policeman assigned to arrest garbage violaters who litter alleys and who fail to employ refuse cans.

Let's walk along with Officer Peter Miller, a veteran of nine years at the Fillmore Station, as he enforces laws on refuse in the 29th Ward.

Here's an alley in back of 509 South Keller av., with rubbish and garbage piled alongside the building. There are no refuse cans.

"This alley was cleaned yesterday," Vito Marzullo, ward superintendent said, "now look at it—"

Miller knocked on the apartment door and Mrs. Yolanda Nania, a tenant, answered.

"I think it is a good thing you are doing, trying to keep the alleys clean," she said. "But we have no cans. We had some before but somebody took them."

"Did you dump your garbage in the alley?" she was asked.

She shrugged. "Yes. What else can we do?"

"Notify the owner to get some cans for this building," Officer Miller warned. "I'm going to check here on Saturday and if there are no cans, I'm going to issue a summons and he'll have to go to court."

In back of 4101–03 W. Van Buren st., a pile of rubbish lay alongside a half-filled can. The landlord, Daniel King, was brought down to look at the litter.

"I don't know about it," he said. "That didn't come from our place. Somebody must have come along and dumped it there."

A man came up to the reporter as he watched the scene. "You looking at the alleys?" he asked. The reporter nodded. "How about telling that landlord over there," he pointed across the street, "to get some cans. The people have to dump in the alleys."

A youngster, Barney McCarville, of 4157 W. Van Buren st., also watched the scene. "Our alley doesn't look like that," he said proudly. "We've got cans and we use them and we keep the alley clean."

"We've got seven-day service," Marzullo said, "but if the people won't help—" [Chicago *Daily News*]

The nature of issues that are being debated by public officials can be brought home to the ordinary citizen by emphasizing his stake in the outcome.

By Marion Porter

The man on the street doesn't know and doesn't care whether he is riding on "batch-mix" or "continuous-process" asphalt.

But right now exponents of the two different schools of mixing are having a dignified controversy on the subject.

Because J. W. "Bill" Goose of the Jefferson Construction Company is a continuous-process man, he has not yet been awarded contracts on street jobs on which he was low bidder. City specifications call for the batch-mix method. The contracts are held up pending the arrival of Law Director Gilbert Burnett, now on vacation, who will decide whether the city should, or should not, let contracts to "a nonconforming" bidder, even though he be low bidder.

MAY GET COURT DECISION

"I'm going to get a decision from the Court of Appeals, if necessary, before I do anything," Goose said yesterday. "I'm going to find out if one man can set up specifications as to method of mixing—if specifications of the ingredients are all right, of course."

Works Director James B. Wilson said that the Jefferson Construction Company probably won't get four of the street contracts it bid on, but none of the other recent bidders will get them either, because the City plans to do the work itself.

The company, however, may get two other street contracts on which it was low bidder because they involve street-construction work at property-owners' expense. Burnett will have to rule on this also.

Either method of making asphalt is acceptable to the State Highway Department, said Harry Eads, Anchorage, senior material laboratory aide for the Highway Department. The Jefferson Company now has a State contract for resurfacing sections of Broadway. The Highway Department inspects every carload of the material.

"It's just two different methods of reaching the same conclusion," said Eads. "We don't care how they make it as long as the results are right. If the sprockets and feed gates are set right the continuous-process is just as accurate as the batch-mix; and likewise, if the operators accurately weigh the ingredients in the batch-mix method, it is just as accurate as the continuous-process."

WEIGH INGREDIENTS FIRST

To the layman, the chief difference in the two methods is in the preliminary steps. The batch-mix people weigh the ingredients first. Everything is done by machine in the continuous-process method. One side claims that the machine process is more accurate since it is not subject to the human element of skill, fatigue, and indifference. The batch-mix people lean toward placing trust in man rather than machine.

The Jefferson Construction Company's expensive, gigantic Barber-Green mixing plant on Crittenden Drive is flanked by piles of gravel, rocks and sand. The material is picked up in automatic containers with wickets on them, passed along through a series of conveyor belts; stewed, boiled, stirred, screened and sprayed and comes out as the finished product, untouched by human hands, at the rate of 6 tons in five minutes . . . .   [Louisville *Courier-Journal*]

Finances

The elected officials are usually the mayor, city clerk and city treasurer; other city officers also may be chosen by the voters but usually are appointed by the chief executive with the approval of the council. It is the duty of the *city treasurer*, of course, to collect taxes and other moneys due the city and to pay bills upon executive order. There also may be a *city auditor*, who keeps detailed records of the city's financial setup and acts as financial adviser. Also there may be a *city collector*, who is chiefly a desk clerk to take in money, and a *purchasing agent*, in charge of buying material authorized by the city council.

The financial setup of a city requires study to be understood. The reporter struggling to comprehend it has the consolation of knowing that many city officials don't know what it's all about. State law limits the taxing power of a municipality, usually by restricting the rate at which each $100 of assessed valuation of real and personal property can be taxed for each of several different purposes. The city's budget cannot call for expenditures beyond the total tax collection possible for a given purpose, such as streets, parks and libraries. The financial operations of a city furthermore are limited by state laws, restricting the city's bonding power. A city, for instance, may be allowed to issue tax anticipation warrants to only 50 or 75 per cent of the total amount which would be realized from the collection of taxes if all were paid. Financial houses which purchase these warrants, however, may not be willing to approve the issuance of as many as the law would permit. In Illinois, a city's bonding power is limited to 2½ per cent of assessed valuation.

The reporter with a good grounding in economics and commerce courses has an advantage in comprehending municipal finance. Any reasonably intelligent reporter, however, can grasp it if it is explained clearly to him. He should not feel embarrassed to ask some city official qualified to do so—the city treasurer, auditor or chairman of the council finance committee perhaps—to give him an hour's time to outline the basic principles of the system. Once he has mastered the essentials himself he will be in a position to perform a valuable public service by making every story related to city finance a lesson in an important phase of government for tax-paying readers. With training, he may even be an authority on the finances of his own city at least.

At least three financial stories annually are of "sure fire" interest. They are (1) announcement by the assessor of the assessed valuations of real property, (2) announcement of tax rates and (3) passage of the city budget.

The assessment story may not be an annual one, as many places have new assessments biennially or quadrennially. There invariably follow interminable appeals to the board of tax appeals by property owners seeking reductions, and there always is at least one additional news story regarding the quantity of such suits. It is in the public interest that those who pay taxes understand the procedure by which they are levied.

The interpretative reporter's function is to translate proposals and actions into terms that the ordinary taxpayer can understand, usually to point out how the reader will be affected personally.

> Operating on the theory that the Ewing school district and Lane County's government won't certify a need for any more property tax money to operate in the coming fiscal year than they did in 1976, State Tax Commissioner Herbert Dilweg proposed a 42% increase in Gopher City real estate values

which should cost the average homeowner between $3.50 and $4.25 next year.

It wouldn't even be that much, had not the 1976 Legislature seen fit to continue a series of fixed special property-tax mill levies, rather than appropriate set dollar amounts to operations financed from those levies.

The Fairview Tribune asked real estate men to point out three typical Fairview properties—two homes and a vacant lot—and supply their current market price.

With that as a start, The Tribune researched these properties' county and city tax valuations and applied mill levies against the valuations for 1976 and 1977.

INEQUITIES IN FAIRVIEW

A by-product of the brief study was documentation of real estate valuation inequities in Fairview.

A house now on the market for $17,750 is valued by the county assessor's office at $9,985, while another house with a sale price of $13,950 is on the assessor's tax books for $10,756.

A vacant lot on the market now for $4,500 has an actual value on the county assessor's records of $1,345.

Assessed value—the value on which property tax mill levies are computed—is 25% of actual value.

The state tax commissioner's office says it is aware of many inequities within Lane County real estate valuations—one compared to another.

But the state's position is that it is the sole responsibility of county officials to guarantee intracounty equalization.

Theoretically, as valuations rise and governmental tax needs remain the same, mill levies go down proportionately.

This, of course, is theory.

It doesn't always work out that way.

For example, of the current 11.73 mills of the state property tax levy, 4.3 mills make up the total of special, fixed levies.

GENERAL FUND CHANGES

These 4.3 mills will remain the same whether the State Board of Equalization accepts the tax commissioner's recommendation, increases it, lowers it or rejects it completely.

Only the general fund portion of the state levy—7.43 mills last year—is subject to any rise and fall, based upon valuation adjustments.

When he knows the valuation placed on his property and the legally adopted tax rate (the amount he will have to pay for each $100 worth of assessed valuation), the taxpayer can figure out his own tax bill. Taxpayers' suits to set aside a tax rate in whole or part on the basis that some item in the city budget is improper are frequent. Usual practice in such cases, and when appeals are pending from the assessor's valuations, is to pay the tax under protest. If the protest is allowed, often after an appellate court decision, refunds are made. To postpone tax collections until after all appeals are decided would be to deprive the city of revenue.

The newspaper which takes seriously the watchdog function should keep a constant eye on the assessor's office. It should insist on learning, so as to inform the public, what rules the assessor follows in so-called special cases.

Too often it seems that political friends of the administration are the chief beneficiaries. In large places the Establishment is more concerned over who controls the assessor's office than it is over most other offices. This is especially true now that the old central business districts are fighting to maintain their financial supremacy over the suburban and outlying shopping centers. Provided that property is not assessed too high, urban renewal projects may make it possible for older people, potentially good spenders, to live near the old central shopping areas. Expensive high rise apartments often replace slums where the purchasing power of the residents was negligible. Public buildings and recreational centers also attract upper and middle class people.

Other Offices and Boards

The police and fire departments and the courts already have been discussed and schools will be the subject of the next section. There remain the offices of the building commissioner, commissioner of health, superintendent of playgrounds and recreation, other minor officers (sealer, purchasing agent and so forth) and the numerous official and semiofficial boards and commissions.

The first requisite of the city hall reporter is to be aware of the existence of these offices and boards and of their functions. In no two communities is the setup exactly alike, although generally to be found are the following: civil service commission, zoning board, park board, board of tax appeals, liquor control, library board and planning commission. The number of land clearance commissions, urban renewal and housing authorities is increasing. So also are various types of pollution control agencies. There may be any of the following boards or commissions: traffic safety, local improvements, recreation, health and quite a few more.

In some cities, these groups are active and newsworthy; in others they are dormant, their existence seeming to serve little purpose other than to provide the mayor with the opportunity to appoint minor political followers to prestige positions. A live chairman, however, can make any one of the groups a vital factor in municipal affairs. The civil service commission, for instance, can cease being the rubber stamp for political appointments that it is in many places and can become a real watchdog of the merit system by insisting that all jobs which should be filled by civil service examinations be so filled, that the spirit of civil service not be defeated through repeated temporary appointments in lieu of holding examinations to fill vacancies, that too much weight not be given in the final ratings of candidates to the "intangible" qualifications as contained in the recommendations of political friends, that dismissals from city employment be for valid reasons rather than as a result of trumped-up charges and that the conduct of examinations be absolutely honest.

Most large city newspapers now have welfare beats which take reporters to a multitude of local, state and national offices engaged in operating a variety of programs. According to Lois Wille of the Chicago *Daily News*, in the past several years the welfare field has become an important offshoot of political reporting. The fact that government agencies, rather than privately supported agencies, are the biggest supplier of welfare services puts welfare in the political arena and makes it a key function of governments. Says Mrs. Wille: "Groups struggling to compete with an established machine have learned to use welfare services as a means of gaining political power. For example, the movement to give free medical care to the poor through 'people's health clinics' has a dual purpose: to mobilize physicians and nurses and other volunteers to give genuine service to the poor, and to organize viable political action groups in poor communities that often have no 'clout' in city hall. And, as a result, City Hall may react by trying to sabotage the clinics. Thus, we have a good political story going as well as a welfare story."

Advises Mrs. Wille: "Treat welfare reporting as the big story it is. An occasional and feature story about a child whose brain has been damaged because he nibbled lead-poisoned paint crumbling from tenement walls is not enough. You have to find out who owns the building, whether city officials have enforced housing codes to repair the broken walls, who, if anyone, will treat and cure the child, and who, if anyone, will fix the house so he won't get sick again."

Increasingly since New Deal days federal funds have become available for local projects. With the largess have come standards which states and municipalities must observe. Perhaps the most newsworthy situations resulting from conflicts over whether federal rules are being obeyed relate to charges of discrimination against minority groups regarding employment compensated for in part by money from Washington.

Urban Renewal

No aspect of local governmental operations in the large cities has grown more in importance in recent years than slum clearance and urban renewal. Federal, state and local funds are involved and many metropolitan centers are undergoing wholesale renovations costing into the millions or billions of dollars. Whereas a generation ago the strength of a political machine was its ability to act as a welfare and relief organization—the Tammany Hall method—today municipal political leaders feel that their strength comes mostly from their ability to remake the appearance of their bailiwicks by tearing down and rebuilding. Mayors and their planning, housing and land clearance boards trot to Washington to seek approval of "workable plans" the first step in obtaining federal funds for any program. There follow an interminable number of steps, including legislative and administrative action at three levels of government, condemnation proceedings, letting of contracts, demolition, housing of dispossessed tenants, haggling over plans for buildings, streets, the location of parks, schools and the like. Civil libertarians and human relations groups often are apprehensive over the futures of Negroes and members of other minority groups who are most frequently affected by slum clearance projects dubbed "people removal."

The movement of whites to the suburbs means that the proportion of non-whites within the big city limits is becoming greater. Political as well as social and economic upheavals result. Inevitably, despite the fear of racists, little revolutionary fervor has developed among the underdog groups. Negroes and other minorities don't want to overthrow the system; they just want to become a part of it and benefit fairly therefrom. Most so-called liberated blacks unfortunately act just like white people. They haven't reformed much of anything any more than did the women a half century ago when they obtained the suffrage or than did the 18-year-old new voters more recently.

So intricate and important has this field of activity become that large newspapers increasingly are hiring or training reportorial specialists to keep up with developments.

Some critics, notably Jane Jacobs in *The Death and Life of Great American Cities*, contend that federally supported urban renewal programs are destructive of small independent businesses and are a weapon used by large commercial interests in central business districts to combat the growth of suburbs and outlying shopping centers and to preserve their economic power. A new gimmick to attempt to bolster the traditional central business district is the mall, a closed-off street where vehicular traffic is forbidden and there is plenty of shrubbery.

Journalistic watchdogs should probe to determine the extent to which uprooting people from old neighborhoods has created new social and economic problems. Martin Anderson wrote in *The Federal Bulldozer* that during the 1950–60 period 126,000 dwelling units in good condition were destroyed to make way for urban renewal projects which resulted in public or private commercial construction. Only 28,000 new housing units were built in the same areas.

What is the quality of the new housing to which displaced persons go? Consider health, educational and other facilities. Do dislodged families merely form new slums in other localities? Is there any hope for the small businessman? What leadership is being provided and with what success by church, political, community and other groups, including aggressive self-help councils?

SCHOOLS AND EDUCATION

Routine coverage of school news is not too difficult. It consists of watching such items as enrollment figures, bond issues, faculty and curriculum changes, new buildings and equipment, commencement and other programs, student activities and the like. What follows is a routine story of a board of education meeting.

> Stephen Construction company of Glenwood was named last week to construct a new addition to Brookwood junior high school, school district No. 167.
> The board of education awarded the contract to the company in the amount of $520,918. Base bids had been received from 13 firms on the addition.

Stephen Construction company built the original school building at Longwood, board president Weldon Nygren noted.

At the board's continued meeting on Wednesday, Superintendent Louis M. Prevost announced that 1,662 pupils presently are enrolled in the district, an increase to date of 122 students. He also reported Brookwood elementary school enrollment at 630 and pointed out that grade three had class sizes of 34 and 35 students.

Anticipated additional enrollments during the course of the present school year, due to construction of 62 more homes in the district, will require an additional mobile unit to house the students, Prevost said. He was authorized by the board to obtain bids for the additional unit to alleviate crowded conditions in the third grades.

The board discussed participation in the building program for trainable mentally handicapped of the South Cook County Special Education cooperative (SPEED), and endorsed the joint-agreement program. A resolution was adopted specifying that District 167 shall bear a share of the program's cost not to exceed the yield of a tax levy of two percent for five years.

Board president Nygren selected the board professional negotiations committee and named Gene Kappel as chairman. Robert Brady and Kathleen Huck were appointed to serve for the 1970–71 school year.

In other actions, the board directed Prevost to obtain a bid from Horace Mann before deciding an award of insurance coverage for all school district employes, awarded a contract for $425 to Lustig Construction company to install a window in the Longwood school kitchen and authorized purchase of 18 desks from Lowrey-McDonnell company for Brookwood junior high school.

Raymond Brejcha reported that life safety construction work at Brookwood elementary school was "essentially complete."

The board also approved the hiring of personnel. Approval was granted for the employment of Mrs. Karolyn Margerum as an elementary librarian at $7,800 per year, for the hiring of a full time library clerk at Brookwood elementary school to assist the librarian and for the payment of $400 to Mrs. Janet Dart to supervise girls' extra-curricular physical education activities.

The board approved a motion to support a memorial fund drive by the PTA to be conducted in tribute to Mrs. Lucile Barron. Mrs. Barron, who taught in District 167 for more than 17 years, died September 5.

In final action, the board appointed Kappel, Barton Herr and John Dougherty to represent the school district at a meeting of the Chicago Heights planning commission. [Park Forest (Ill.) *Star*]

Helping citizens—over 50 per cent of whose local tax dollars go to maintain the public schools—understand what's going on educationally is a different matter. When the children of World War II veterans began reaching school age in the early '50s, there was hardly a school district in the United States which did not find it necessary to expand its educational facilities. Nevertheless, in many places there persisted grave shortages in buildings, classrooms, equipment and teachers. By the mid '70s the war babies were graduated and many communities faced with financial problems considered closing some schools and firing some teachers. Protests by parents and others made many school board meetings much livelier than ever before.

As the total tax burden—federal, state and local—grew during the cold war period and the Vietnam War, taxpayers became reluctant to approve school bond issues and little progress was made toward obtaining financial aid from the federal government. Whereas formerly school elections aroused only meager interest, by the mid '60s exactly the opposite was coming to be the case in many places. Many voters, furthermore, voted against proposed bond issues or proposals to raise the tax rate as a protest against heavy taxation, most of it federal income tax about which ordinary people lack the opportunity to express themselves directly at the polls. So they vote against any and all taxes presented to them, regardless of their own immediate best interests.

In addition to the basic problem of finances, other educational issues have become controversial and, consequently, newsworthy.

Integration

In the '50s the entire world knew, from news reports and pictures, of the violence connected with attempts to implement the United States Supreme Court decision that racial segregation must end in schools. In the '70s the nation's image as the citadel of democracy suffered again when violence flared in the aftermath of court orders that school children be bussed to foster integration.

In the interim there were incessant court battles and incidents to make the international headlines, as the goals of equality still eluded millions. School segregation exists in many places as a result of housing segregation. Some bond issues for the construction of new schools were defeated in the suburbs to discourage the migration of Negroes and other minorities.

Most newspapers are moderate or liberal in their attitude toward the school integration issue and generally strive for strict objectivity in reporting news of the controversy. Most agree that the quality of education in ghetto schools must be vastly improved. Aroused black parents have brought pressure resulting in benefits to all students as a result of the abolition of so-called tracking systems whereby children are assigned to classes on the basis of intelligence and other tests now generally discredited.

Religion

Public taxpayers' assistance to parochial schools became a political issue in the '70s as the schools, mostly Roman Catholic, pleaded inability to continue to exist without it and exerted pressure on Congress, state legislatures and delegates to constitutional conventions to find ways to circumvent the constitutional separation of church and state.

The parochial school crisis followed a considerable increase in their number and enrollment in the '50s and early '60s, the period of the war babies. As the need for public assistance grew, traditional Catholic opposition to bond issues to support public schools diminished, and promotion of shared-time plans—whereby parochial school students take some studies in public schools—grew. Catholics also became candidates for public school boards, causing bitter campaigns in some places.

The Catholic argument is that their children should benefit from free bus transportation and similar services and that such assistance is "child aid" and not "church aid." Catholics have traditionally fought federal aid to education programs in Congress because their schools were not included on an equal basis. The Catholic church is very secretive about its finances and wealth.

In opposition, the crying need of public schools for more funds, especially in the ghettoes and rural areas, is argued; the contention is advanced that two school systems, both financed by public funds, obviously cost more than a single system and are likely to be inferior. Furthermore, it is argued that the religious education presumably provided parochial school students is outdated and the existence of the dual system is divisive and undemocratic.

Leading the opposition to parochiaid is Americans United for Separation of Church and State, which publishes the magazine *Church and State*, and lobbies. It applauded the United States Supreme Court decisions which forbade use of school property for released-time religious instruction and outlawed prescribed prayers and bible readings in the public schools. Bound to become an increasingly crucial issue are the tax exemptions for church-owned real estate not used for religious purposes. Not only the parochial schools but municipalities are in a financial bind, and more than 50 per cent of the potentially taxable land in many of them is tax exempt.

Delinquency

From one standpoint, the history of public school education in America could be written to show how, step by step, the schools have assumed responsibilities formerly considered the prerogative of the home, factory or other institutions. Most broadening of the curriculum has resulted from outside pressure, including statutes requiring that this or that—American history, the dangers of dope addiction, automobile driving and the like—be taught. As a consequence, the student's free choice is limited, especially if he is among the increasing number who seek to meet college entrance requirements. Were it not for compulsory attendance laws, the already serious "dropout" problem would be greater. Problem children are generally ones in revolt against regimentation, real or imagined. In the huge high schools of today, potentially disturbed adolescents develop intense feelings of frustration. Despite physical education and intramural athletic programs, participation in varsity sports is limited to an increasingly smaller proportion of the student body. The same is true of other school activities, with opportunities to become officers or star performers restricted to the minority. In several large cities, post-athletic contest riots between fans representing rival schools have become serious. The emphasis which rooting alumni insist colleges and universities place on sports, especially football, sets a nationwide pattern. Exposures of widespread professional gambling activities, which include attempts, successful and otherwise, to bribe players, occur frequently.

Maintaining discipline has become a major problem at all levels. Teachers and pupils alike are the frequent victims of violence and police and security guards are necessary to preserve order and protect property. Teachers often blame indifferent parents who in turn say the schools are too permissive and should straighten out any disturbed youngsters.

Even if the schools solved all the problems suggested in this section, of course, the problem of juvenile delinquency would continue to exist because its social and economic causes are mostly outside, not inside, the school walls.

Student Unrest

It would be a grave error also to conclude that widespread unrest among college and high school students is instigated or led by delinquents or those academically deficient. Exactly the contrary is the case. The picket lines, sit downs and other manifestations of discontent have attracted the best, not the poorest, students throughout the United States and the rest of the world, in many parts of which there have been disturbances much more serious than any in this country, as, for example, Tokyo, Mexico, Paris and Rome. After all, foreign students and teachers traditionally have been much more alert to social injustices and much more active in attempting to correct them than have their American counterparts.

The revolt of the students is matched by that of public school teachers, who have finally overcome their prejudice against labor unions and are organizing and joining them to bargain collectively and to strike in all parts of the country. It is foolhardy to limit coverage of such incidents to the immediate overt incidents as unrelated to other forms of protest: the civil rights movement, the peace movement, the women's liberation movement, uprisings of American Indians, Mexican-Americans (Chicanos) and other minority ethnic groups, unionization of priests and nuns, unionization of policemen, nurses and many others. Economic and social unrest is worldwide. The newspaper reporter does not have the perspective of a historian or a cultural anthropologist of a century from now, but he can avoid overemphasis of minor incidents and help his readers to be aware of the fact that many apparently isolated events actually are related.

Many high school dropouts charge that the curricula are not "relevant" to contemporary life. Now that 18-year-olds are eligible to vote, the question arises as to how well the public schools have acquainted them with even the existence of the issues regarding which they will be expected to have opinions as voters in a democracy. Pressure groups, mostly conservative, in the past have influenced school authorities to softpedal the so-called controversial and, as a result, curricula have continued to stress rote learning, nonfunctional English theme writing, foreign languages, mathematics and pre-World War II history. This corrupts the original concept of the free public school system which was to prepare citizens for participation in a democracy. Teachers colleges have gone in for so much theory and methodological experimentation that students in many places are little more than human guinea pigs for pedagogical game playing. Character education, personality development, vocational training, sensitivity experiences and similar programs may possess some value but they contribute little to producing perceptive voters.

Exceptional Children

Counselors, psychologists, psychiatrists and other advisers deal with individual problems of disturbed and other children. Special classes or instructions exist for physically handicapped children—the deaf, dumb, blind, crippled and mentally retarded—and the gifted child is attracting more and more attention. Opinions differ as to whether children should be grouped according to potential ability, usually determined by intelligence or other tests, or achievement. On the one hand, the consciousness of being labeled superior, medium or inferior is considered disturbing to some children who will have to compete in a world of unequals. On the other hand, it is contended that fast learners are held back if instruction has to be kept at the level of the slowest. The pros and cons of this matter have been debated by educators and parents for a number of years in many parts of the country.

Automation

Related to this issue is the controversy over the extent to which instruction should be standardized in the interest of reducing teaching burdens. Under the influence of teachers colleges during the past generation, testing of many kinds—intelligence, aptitude, achievement and so forth—has developed considerably. The results are used for placement of students in classes in the grades and high schools and by colleges and universities to determine admissions. Criticism is growing that if improperly used these tests result in "giving a student a number" at an early age and prejudice teachers' attitudes toward actual classroom work. Also, and more seriously, it is contended that the tests do not measure a student's ability to organize his thoughts, his total understanding of a topic, imagination, ingenuity or originality. Devised for fast grading by machines, the tests require the student merely to put an x after which of three of four answers to a question is correct. University professors, especially in the professional schools such as law and medicine, complain that students are coming to lack the ability to express themselves and that automatized teaching makes for conformist robots. Teaching machines, airborne television programs and the like ease the teacher problem, it is admitted, but stultify initiative and creativeness.

Protest against excess testing and tracking has grown with the increase in the proportion of black students in the big city schools. Black parents say they are tired of having their children labeled inferior because they score lower on tests prepared for children with different cultural backgrounds.

Academic Freedom

There is hardly an American community which has not had a "case" involving a teacher with allegedly heretical ideas, a reading list which someone does not like or a textbook or magazine under attack by a patriotic or other pressure group. The best way to keep abreast of developments is by reading the *Newsletter on Intellectual Freedom* of the American Library Association. The situation unquestionably has made teaching less attractive to many young men and women and has contributed to the development of the strong administrator type of school superintendent. As in all other aspects of contemporary complex society, rules and regulations and forms and reports have multiplied in the school system. Teachers often complain that they are left too little time to teach and that they have increasingly less to say about the determination of educational policy. In huge school systems, not only pupils but teachers as well run the risk of becoming merely numbers.

Lengthy as it may seem, the foregoing discussion has by no means exhausted the subject. Educational news by contrast with school news requires the attention of journalists with specialized knowledge and understanding. It is a great field for the interpretative reporter.

COUNTY GOVERNMENT

The county building is what ordinarily is known as the courthouse because the county court is the most important room in it. The same building probably also contains the circuit court and possibly the municipal court, if there is one, and the court of a police magistrate or justice of the peace. There also are other offices of county officials.

County Board

Corresponding to the city council (or *board of aldermen*) of a city is the *county board*, sometimes called *board of commissioners* or *board of supervisors*, which is the governing body of a county. Its president (or chairman) may either be elected by the voters or be selected by the board members who are elected by townships or at large. In smaller places, the board may meet infrequently, as bimonthly or semiannually; in large places it meets almost as frequently as the city council. Its powers are limited because the county is primarily an agent of the state in collecting taxes, enforcing laws, recording documents, constructing and maintaining highways, providing poor relief, administering rural schools, supervising nominations and elections, guarding public health and performing other similar functions. These duties are the responsibility of the elective county officers.

County Clerk

Secretary of the county board, the *county clerk* also issues licenses (wedding, hunting and the like), accepts nominating papers, supervises the printing of ballots, receives election returns and keeps county records. If there is not a separate elective officer, *a register of deeds*, he also records articles of incorporation, receives applications for corporation charters and keeps all other records and documents of private transactions. It is to him one writes for a copy of his birth certificate or to prove ownership of a piece of property.

Duties of the *sheriff*, *prosecuting attorney* and *coroner* and the operation of the county court already have been explained. The sheriff usually has his office in the county jail and the coroner may be a practicing physician or undertaker with a private office.

The *county treasurer* is an agent of the state, collecting taxes which he forwards to the state capital. He pays county employees out of funds reallocated to the county from the state and meets other obligations in similar fashion. The *county assessor* assesses the value of property in the county, prepares maps to show real estate ownership and reports his findings to the state.

The *county highway commissioner*, *county engineer*, *county surveyor*, *county superintendent of schools*, *county health officer*, *county agricultural agent* and other county officials perform duties suggested by their titles.

With the "population explosion" into the suburbs, county government has had to pay more attention to unincorporated areas because they inevitably are involved in problems related to water supply, transportation, recreation, policing and the like. Counties also operate poor farms, homes for the aged, jails, general hospitals, special hospitals for the tubercular, mentally ill and others, nursing homes and other institutions which cities and states also maintain. The awarding of contracts must be watched carefully as well as the quality of service performed. Illegal operations, as gambling, banned from the cities, may flourish in nearby areas.

An authoritative interpretative reporter may goad public officials to take action at the same time he enlightens readers regarding a governmental function.

By Len Kholos

Erie County commissioners' refusal to enter into regional planning with the city is not only hampering efforts to attract new industry, it is actually costing Erie taxpayers extra thousands of dollars.

In an interview with The Erie Dispatch last week, J. Cal Callahan, of Morris Knowles Inc., disclosed that the federal government is willing to pay half the cost of developing a workable program when more than one community is involved.

"The federal government feels that regional planning is the only sensible vehicle for progress, not only to promote orderly growth of an area but to prevent mistakes that will be costly in future years," Callahan said.

How is refusal of the county leaders to cooperate costing Erie taxpayers money?

Before the government will forward funds for redevelopment, whether it be for industrial or residential purposes, the communities involved must prepare a workable program.

Erie has already spent $5,000 and has contracted to spend $25,000 more to prepare this program in order to become eligible for federal planning money.

Assuming that the cost of work within the city would cost the same amount in a regional planning setup, the federal government would then have paid $15,000 plus half the costs incurred outside the city limits.

* * *

Can the individual communities in the county do anything to protect their own futures?

County Solicitor Jacob Held has told county commissioners that they cannot spend any money for planning. This came as a surprise to local government observers.

Held may also claim that the boroughs and townships are not allowed to spend money to plan for themselves.

On the other hand, the government will pay half the costs of preparing a workable program for communities of less than 25,000 population or, if they join in the city's planning efforts, half of the cost of the joint project.

* * *

We have explained why the federal government wants communities to have a workable program before it will forward funds for redevelopment. Now, here is what a workable program includes:

1. Sound local housing and health codes, enforced; an end to tolerating illegal, degrading, unhealthy substandard structures and areas.

2. A general master plan for community development, an end to haphazard planning and growth, a road map for the future.

3. Basic analysis of neighborhoods and the kind of treatment needed, an inventory of blighted and threatened areas upon which a plan of treatment to stop blight in its tracks can be developed.

4. An effective administrative organization to run the program, coordinated activity toward a common purpose by all offices and arms of the local government.

5. Financial capacity to carry out the program, utilizing local revenues and resources to build a better community for the future instead of continuing to pay heavily for past mistakes.

6. Rehousing of displaced families; expanding the supply of good housing for all income groups, through new construction and rehabilitation, so that families paying premium prices for slums can be rehoused.

7. Full-fledged, community-wide citizen participation and support, public demand for a better community and public backing for the steps needed to get it. [Erie *Dispatch*]

STATE GOVERNMENT

Unless he works in one of the 50 state capitals, the beginning reporter has little contact with state governmental offices. If he is ambitious to become the state capital correspondent for a metropolitan newspaper as a possible step toward a similar position in Washington D.C., covering the city hall and local politics provides excellent training.

Although he does not attend legislative sessions or visit the offices of state officers, some member of the editorial staff of the small city newspaper follows what is happening at the state capital as the local community is certain to be affected. City officials, civic organizations and other individuals and groups discuss state governmental matters and make known their opinions to their representatives in the legislature. Often it is necessary to obtain passage of a state law before it is possible for the city council to take some desired action; the corporation counsel may write such laws which members of the legislature from the district introduce and push to adoption.

The following are examples of how to localize what is happening at the state capital so as to emphasize its importance and the role played by local persons:

> Mayor Walter E. Lewis today urged State Rep. Oscar R. Fall and State Sen. James L. Born to support the bill pending in the state legislature which would permit Milltown and other cities in the state between 25,000 and 100,000 population to establish a municipal court.

> All doubt as to the legality of Milltown's compulsory automobile testing station was removed today when Gov. Dale O. Hart signed the enabling act prepared by Corporation Counsel V. K. Kenwood and passed unanimously last week by both houses of the legislature.

> Representatives of The Crib, Milltown's foundling home, will go to the state capital tomorrow to join the lobby fighting passage of a bill which would establish a state department of public welfare. The bill is considered a threat to the local institution because it is believed a state department with power to direct all such establishments would insist upon regulations which The Crib could not meet and continue to exist.

> Killing of the remaining state library appropriation in Springfield last night in the term-end jam by a legislature anxious to adjourn late tonight, will deprive Milltown of the purchase of books and periodicals to the amount of $6,000 during the next two years, Miss Edith Delancey, city librarian, revealed today.

Local newspapers use, often by rewriting to play up the local angle, press releases from state offices. State representatives may write weekly newsletters to summarize legislative activities. Press associations in state capitals handle special queries from newspaper clients regarding matters of special interest. Only the largest papers, however, can afford to maintain bureaus in the capitals, either while the legislatures are in session or at any other time. Such assignments almost invariably go to reporters with experience covering local politics and government.

FEDERAL GOVERNMENT

Of the major divisions of the federal government only one has a peacetime representative in the small city or town. That is the Postal Service which in 1970 replaced the Post Office Department which had existed since colonial days. In moderate-sized cities, at least for a few days before April 15, representatives of the Internal Revenue Service of the Department of the Treasury may be there to assist taxpayers in making the filing deadline.

A record high in the number of federal income tax returns filed and payments received was reported yesterday at the office of the collector of internal revenue here.

The approach of the midnight deadline brought thousands of persons to the office and there was sufficient extra help to take care of taxpayers who needed assistance in filling out the forms. Extra cashiers were on hand to accept payments. Because taxpayers had familiarized themselves with their problems, comparatively few had to wait long in line.

The peak in the day's business came in the early afternoon, but there were long lines in the early evening. Early closing of offices and manufacturing establishments, as well as the complete shut-down for some for the entire day, also helped make easier the trips of the last-minute visitors to the tax offices.

Payments in cash, money orders and checks totaling $150,000,000 were received yesterday. One check was for $1,000,000. In the two previous weeks $50,000,000 had been paid in person and through the mail.

In the internal revenue offices there were hundreds of bags of mail waiting to be opened. The opening of this mail, containing millions of dollars in checks and money orders, will begin tomorrow and will be finished by the end of the week.

With the exceptions noted, the federal government as a local news source in a small city hardly exists. As its power increases and that of the states declines, however, the lives of American citizens are more and more affected by it. Whereas the press associations and special column writers from Washington must be relied on for interpretations of major current events in the national capital, intelligent handling of much local news requires an understanding of national political issues and events.

Work for the unemployed, for instance, in depression years was provided through funds supplied by the federal government. In wartime there was the Office of Price Administration. Financial assistance also has been obtained through such federal agencies as the Home Owners Loan corporation and the Federal Housing administration, and the bank deposits of most everyone today are insured through the Federal Deposit Insurance corporation. Most far-reaching, perhaps, is the federal Social Security act, which provides for old age pensions, Medicare, unemployment insurance, aid for dependent children, widows, the blind and other needy persons, and the Fair Labor Standards (wage and hour) act.

To write about how the local community is affected by these and other federal governmental activities without understanding them is not conducive to effectiveness.

It was the suburbs' turn today to absorb some criticism from the United States Public Health Service.

Milk sanitation conditions in several of them were found to be below a high standard set by Milltown, the federal agency said in a report released by the Advisory Committee of the Milltown-Wayne County Health survey.

Richmond had a rating of only 75.01 per cent for raw milk from 40 dairy farms under control of its health department and 73.15 per cent for three pasteurization plants, the report showed.

This compared with Milltown's rating of 91 per cent compliance with conditions set up in the recommended USPHS ordinance and code.

"The weighted rating for all milk sold in Richmond was 86.74 per cent," the surveyors declared, "the increase being due to the fact that 80 per cent of the milk sold in the city was being produced under the control of other agencies maintaining a more efficient control.

"It is advisable that Richmond adopt the standard ordinance and limit sale of milk to Grade A pasteurized in order to be in line with the state, Milltown, and other communities in the county."

Sanitation control of milk also was found to be "less than satisfactory" in Bluffs, Blytheville and Lakeside.

Milltown's milk control was praised by the surveyors, and the report commented, "there has been no communicable disease epidemic traced to the Milltown milk supply since 1936."

Nevertheless, the USPHS declared improvement in inspection services is needed immediately "if these high standards are to be protected."

The report also criticized an ordinance recently adopted by the county commissioners requiring all milk and milk products to be pasteurized, but not specifying grading.

18

BUSINESS, FINANCE, LABOR, AGRICULTURE

A. Business
  1. Routine News
  2. Localization
  3. Trends

B. Finance
  1. Stock Exchanges
  2. Seeking Explanations
  3. Definitions

C. Problems and Policies
  1. Secrecy
  2. "Puffery"
  3. "Payola"
  4. Codes

D. Labor
  1. Labor Laws
  2. Covering Labor
  3. Labor Problems
  4. Stressing the Public Interest
    a. Union Affairs
    b. Policy Statements
    c. Management Agreements
    d. Union Demands
    e. Strikes

E. Agriculture
  1. Political Power
  2. The Urbanite's Stake

Since the end of World War II, the number of shareholders of publicly owned corporations in the United States has more than tripled to a total of more than 30 million. This does not mean that control of the management policies of American businesses and industries has passed into the hands of housewives, widows, factory workers and middle-class shopkeepers. In fact, in monetary terms, the total ownership of stocks and bonds by small investors still is but a minute fraction of the invested wealth of the nation. It does mean, however, that millions of newspaper readers who formerly ignored the financial and business pages now have a vested interest in them. As a result, such pages are being expanded and their contents geared to appeal to the average reader and not just to the broker or banker. The phenomenal increase in general readership of the *Wall Street Journal* and the popularity of some syndicated columns in this field have helped inspire many newspapers to give greater attention to business and financial news, and specializing in this kind of journalism has become much more attractive to active newspapermen, especially beginners.

Whereas a generation ago ability to read a financial ticker tape, bank statement and annual report of a corporation was about all that was required of him, today's business or financial page reporter must be able to explain as well as report what goes on in his field of activity. Several developments have made almost nonexistent the strictly local business news story. Among these have been the growth of retail chain stores which are parts of nationwide operations or conglomerates, the mushrooming of shopping centers serving more than one community, the specialization of factory production so that few products any more are manufactured all in one plant, the growth of dependency of small industries upon large ones for subcontracts and of large industries upon the federal government for orders, the increase in foreign trade and investments, multinational corporations, government aid to underdeveloped countries and other similar trends which add up to this: what happens almost anywhere else in the world today can affect the prosperity of the small town, which is no longer self-sufficient economically as it may have been in grandfather's day.

BUSINESS

Despite the trend toward localization of as much as possible of what appears on the business-financial pages, there is no business beat as such. That is, the reporter's day is not spent making regular "stops" comparable to those which other newsgatherers make at police headquarters, city hall and so on. Rather, covering a story for the business page means mostly investigating a tip or following up an idea, and every assignment may require making contacts with an entirely different set of news sources. Thus, the business page reporter must be fully conversant with the public and private agencies from which information of all kinds can be obtained.

Routine News

Publicity departments of businesses, industries, trade organizations and governmental agencies voluntarily supply the bulk of the routine news in this field: new advertising campaigns; new products; stock sales; production figures; expansion programs; comments on pending legislation, court decisions or other events affecting business; big orders received; reports on dollar sales; new models; personnel changes in partnerships, corporation officials, managerial appointments, promotions and the like; new building or other expansion plans; moves to new locations; public shows and exhibits.

Trade associations and institutes make reports covering entire industries monthly, quarterly, semiannually and annually. The weekly reports on department store sales have been taken over by the Commerce Department from the Federal Reserve banks and are regarded as a "holy index" even though they do not include suburban stores or discount houses. Federal Reserve bank monthly reports are an index to the state of the overall economy and usually include profiles of particular industries. Some university business schools issue composite weekly reports on department store sales using percentages instead of dollars. For instance, the University of Pittsburgh School of Business issues a composite weekly report on sales of three major department stores. Sales are listed for the preceding week, for the preceding four weeks, for Jan. 1 to date and for how they compare with similar periods of the previous years. There is a breakdown of downtown and suburban sales along with the total metropolitan percentages.

The monthly Federal Reserve index of industrial production gives information regarding the outputs of mines, mills and so on. Even more up-to-date are the reports put out by some state agencies—for example, the *Illinois Business Review*, a monthly summary published by the Bureau of Economic and Business Research of the College of Commerce of the University of Illinois. Its summaries are made public from two to six weeks after the data are gathered whereas government figures may be two or three months old. Similar first-rate reports are put out in Indiana and Texas, among other states.

Other good overall business and economic indicators are monthly and weekly reports on carloadings; reports of shipments of folding paper cartons; reports on shipments of collapsible metal tubes; weekly Edison Electric Institute reports on electrical production and percentage changes. Gross national product reports (dollar values of all goods and services produced) are widely used but price increases and inflation will affect this index and possibly give a false picture of the nation's real output.

Monthly employment reports from state bureaus are economic indicators. The Pittsburgh bureau covers the four-county metropolitan area. Although the figures are a month to six weeks late, they suggest how the local economy is doing. Included is the unemployment rate, the number of people looking for work, new filings for benefits, size of the local work force and a breakdown of employment in industries with a comparison to the same month in earlier years.

Since so much of this news originates or at least is announced in New York or Washington, it first reaches local newspaper offices throughout the country via press association financial wires. The business page editor must be highly selective and naturally considers the particular interests of the readers in his circulation area. It is easy to clutter a page with indiscriminate use of commodity market reports—livestock market prices, dairy, poultry, produce, grains, prices of various futures, dividends and earning tables and the like.

Typical examples of how the business reporter obtains information would be the following: a railroad shipping clerk knew that a company which was close-mouthed was on the decline because its shippings had fallen off; a city assessor provided information on plans for a major shopping center with which the reporter confronted the developer who persuaded him to postpone publication in exchange for a promise of an exclusive story eventually; a department store official had an informed guess on the sales volume of a statewide chain which did not disclose sales or earnings; a paragraph in a routine quarterly report of a company indicated a major change in marketing plans; a union official confirmed rumors of a reduction in a plant's production as indicated by the laying off of a large number of employees. Frequently, a business reporter can persuade a company to talk even though it at first declares, "We don't want to say anything for competitive reasons," by pointing out that he can dig out the information he wants from Dun & Bradstreet reports or from other sources available to competitors as well as everyone else.

Even in the case of a routine story, the explanation may be the feature. For example, businesses have been known to move to avoid the disturbance caused by jet airplanes. A concern once changed location because the vibrations from trucks on nearby highways interrupted the manufacture of delicate parts. More significantly, a major appliance store pulled out of a shopping center, saying that shopping habits had changed and customers did not care to hunt for major durable goods in the midst of other commodities.

A routine story could be written:

XYZ Cola reported lower earnings, etc.

More significant would be

The coldest weather in 79 years cut XYZ Cola sales to the lowest in 20 years, etc.

If stories are written in this way, one leading business and financial editor commented, "Aunt Jane with her $1\frac{1}{2}$ shares of XYZ Cola stock won't be so prone to seek to oust the dumb bunny management."

The following is a typical *Wall Street Journal* lead which offers explanation as well as facts:

Prices for most major commodity futures declined yesterday. July and October copper, "M" coffee, and all deliveries of corn, lard, and July oats at Chicago fell to new season lows.

Continued selling of cash corn by the government was responsible for the decline in corn prices. It was the fifth session in the last six that prices dropped to new season lows. The government is selling corn to keep market prices low and penalize farmers who did not participate in the crop reduction program.

The market price for corn declined despite news that a large export business is pending. Egypt yesterday was in the U.S. market for one million bushels of corn. From one million to two million bushels of corn are expected to be sold this week to European nations. The United Kingdom is also scheduled to buy U.S. corn.

The price for scrap copper was reduced $\frac{1}{4}$ cent a pound yesterday. The London copper market also was down. Last week the smelters reduced their buying price for scrap copper $\frac{1}{2}$ cent a pound.

A lack of export buying and slow domestic consumer demand for lard brought active selling into the futures market. Declines ranged to $\frac{1}{2}$ cent a pound.

Livestock prices generally weakened because of a seasonal increase in marketings.

The reporter must not be so naive as to accept uncritically whatever he is told. An electric plant once moved out of the state saying that the "labor climate" was unfavorable. Several months later it advertised its plant for sale, citing as an advantage, "skilled, stable labor." One Wisconsin business editor has this warning note:

> Business executives pressed for "why?" usually tell reporters that it's all due to high taxes, unreasonable wage demands by labor, too much government interference, not enough tariff protection and spiraling costs of goods and services. Never mentioned in public (it's been called the "conspiracy of silence") is the fact that other factors may have had a more important part in lower profits, salary cuts, layoffs, production cutbacks, plant moves and shutdowns, etc. The other factors include bad guesses by management on product acceptance, excessive production costs, poor scheduling, bad design, insufficient market research, lack of quality control and/or generally poor management.

Localization

Famine in India, an earthquake in Japan, revolution in Venezuela or the peaceful overthrow of a government anywhere can affect local business conditions. This it may do directly if an industry sells or buys abroad, or indirectly if anyone with whom it does business is directly affected.

Local opinion should be sought whenever important new legislation is proposed, introduced, passed or tested in the courts. Always the desideratum should be "How will this affect us locally?" The same is true of work stoppages from strikes or for other reasons. If the commodity is coal, oil, steel or some other basic which is used locally by manufacturers or the public, estimates of stockpiles should be obtained.

The direct relationship between the politics of a foreign nation and an American business was stressed by Donald K. White in the following column in the San Francisco *Chronicle*:

> Gillette Co. looks sharp, feels sharp and is sharp as a result of the Tory victory in the British elections last month.
>
> The company's stock was down to $66.37½ a share the day before the election and the prognosis was for a rough go if the voting went against the Tories.
>
> But it didn't and investors took heart and brought the stock back up to $72.50 a share last week.
>
> On the surface there doesn't seem to be much connection between elections in Britain and razor blades, the Friday night fights, VIV lipstick, Pamper shampoo and Toni home permanents. The last three items are also Gillette products.
>
> The connection becomes clear when you realize Gillette got 43 per cent of its net profit from overseas sources last year. And the bulk of that profit came from the clean-shaven British, who voted back into office the party Gillette investors felt was better for their interests.

Trends

Any old-timer knows that methods of doing business have changed considerably during his lifetime. It requires journalistic perception, however, to become aware of a new development when it is still new. In the early '60s it was apparent that speedier transportation, including "piggy backing" by trucks and railroads, had made it expedient for local businessmen to maintain smaller inventories than formerly. Both the Chicago stockyards and railroad passenger service were in decline, much more foodstuffs of all kinds were being rushed in refrigerator cars from place of origin to place of consumption, one-industry towns were disappearing, chambers of commerce were more intent on attracting diversification and other changes were occurring which affected the entire social as well as the economic life of communities.

Two of the most significant new businesses were retail discount houses and leasing companies. The former originated shortly after the end of World War II in New England in abandoned factory towns, most of them depleted as industries moved south, often as a result of strong state governmental inducement, to obtain cheaper, usually nonunion labor. Some smart operators bought the distress merchandise of retailers who faced bankruptcy and made fortunes. Through their operations it was learned that customers take to self-service in department stores as well as in groceries and this type of merchandising spread, mostly in the suburbs where automobile parking was made available. The Chicago *Daily News* ran a "roundup" piece to highlight the increasing importance of leasing:

By Dale Morrison

A growing Chicago firm counts among its assets a fleet of airplanes, ocean-going vessels, a pickle washer, a fortune cookie machine and a hog farrower.

It will soon add a strudel dough machine to its holdings.

What's more, as its name indicates, Nationwide Leasing Co. doesn't use any of the diverse items it carries on its books—it leases them to people who do.

"Long-term leasing isn't new in itself," said Robert Sheridan, Nationwide's youthful president. "What's new is leasing as a business in its own right."

Sheridan's 4-year-old company was the first general leasing firm headquartered in Chicago. The first in the nation—U.S. Leasing Co.—was founded in San Francisco only nine years ago.

Nationwide now has offices at 11 S. LaSalle and in New York, Boston, Houston, Wichita, Kan., St. Louis and Dallas.

In essence, what Nationwide and similar firms do is put up money for expanding enterprises.

Take the case of a cooky cutter manufacturer who wants to set up a new plant. The company has land and buildings, but lacks equipment and capital.

The company doesn't want to tie up its commercial bank credit with a long-term loan for fixed assets.

By turning to a leasing company, the firm can order cooky cutters of the type it wants from the manufacturer it chooses. The leasing company foots the bill, then collects rent from the cooky firm for use of the equipment.

A variation of the standard leasing arrangement is sometimes useful to companies that have all the equipment they need, but are hungry for working capital.

They can sell some of their equipment to the leasing company, pay rent on it and use the ready cash from the sale.

Nationwide currently leases about $25,000,000 in equipment to more than 2,000 firms.

"The big companies have seen the advantages in leasing," Sheridan said. "And the smaller companies sometimes haven't had anywhere else to turn.

"The middle-sized firms that we feel could really benefit from out service are just beginning to come around."

Among Nationwide's biggest lessees is RCA, which rents about $3,000,000 in defense and other equipment.

Most of Nationwide's leases run from five to 10 years, during which the equipment is amortized and Nationwide collects its markup (about 6 per cent a year), Sheridan said.

When the original lease is up, it can be extended on a year to year basis at reduced rentals.

Besides being a financing tool, Sheridan said leasing has become a potent aid to selling. About half Nationwide's business comes to it through manufacturers' representatives who direct their sales prospects to the firm.

How big will leasing get?

"It's growing at 40 per cent a year now, and we're just getting started," Sheridan said.

FINANCE

Until they broadened their scope to include business news, most newspaper financial pages contained little more than listings of transactions on the New York and/or other stock exchanges. Such charts still are used and every editor must exercise judgment as to what items to include in the limited amount of space at his disposal. He does so by editing the listings transmitted by the press associations or obtained from local brokerage houses to include those securities in which his readers have the greatest interest, because they are those of outstanding nationally known companies or of companies which have plants or do business in the community.

Stock Exchanges

Elementary is ability to read stock quotations. A typical line as follows:

High	Low	Stocks Div.	Sales in 100's	High	Low	Close	Net Change
26⅞	18⅝	Jeff. 1	278	20¾	19⅛	20	−1¼

This means that the highest price for which one share of Jefferson company stock sold during the current year was $26⅞ and the lowest price was $18⅝ per share. The "1" means that the stock paid $1 per share in dividends last year. This day, 27,800 shares were sold on the exchange, at prices which ranged from \$20¾ to \$19⅛ per share. The last day's sale was for \$20 which was \$1¼ less than the closing sale the preceding day.

This is the raw material on the basis of which the financial reporter describes the "ups" and "downs" of the market. Since perhaps 90 per cent of all stock trading takes place in New York, what happens on the New York Stock Exchange is, of course, of primary importance. There are also, however, the American Stock Exchange, with about one-third the amount of trading as the New York Stock Exchange, the Midwest Stock Exchange in Chicago and numerous small exchanges in different cities throughout the country. Before its securities can be listed on an exchange, the corporation must register under the Securities and Exchange act of 1934 which means it must meet minimum standards of financial soundness. Then its application must be approved by the exchange's board of governors. This act does not guarantee the value of the stock but, because of the double scrutiny by federal government and exchange, listed stocks generally are considered more secure. Over-the-counter sales, however, more than double the accumulated total of sales on all the exchanges combined. They are sales made by their issuers either directly to the public or through some agents other than an exchange. The securities are mostly those of companies with less than \$300,000 annual gross sales which means they are not registered with the SEC. The salesmen are supervised by their own self-regulatory agency, the National Association of Securities Dealers, which provides information to the press, as does the National Quotation bureau. The NASDAQ has a computerized network of traders dealing in about 1,800 OTC companies, to provide an "instant market" for any issue on a list. There are more than 50,000 OTC stocks and they remain a risky investment, but NASDAQ has added credibility, at least to companies on the list, which include Budweiser, American Express and some other giants.

The advantages of a stock exchange are said to be (1) to provide financial facilities for the convenient transaction of business, (2) to maintain high standards of commercial honor and integrity and (3) to promote just and equitable principles of trade and business. This is decidedly not to say, however, that most other trading is unethical, dangerous or otherwise undesirable. As a matter of fact, the extent to which what happens on the large exchanges actually reflects the state of the nation's financial health is a matter of considerable dispute. Certain it is that the exchanges respond emotionally to political and other news and the prices of particular securities may fluctuate wildly within a matter of hours or minutes. Some skeptics say that a great deal of what goes on is just dignified or aristocratic gambling.

Seeking Explanations

Whatever the truth may be, the financial reporter has the responsibility to seek reasons for important fluctuations. He is aided in the first instance by the Dow Jones & Co. ticker-tape news service which continuously transmits selected stock quotations, late news on the grain, meat and foreign markets, sometimes baseball scores and top national and international news. Its most important function is reporting business news of all kinds and its averages of what stocks are doing in accumulated major categories—industrials, railroads, utilities are widely accepted as indices of the financial market as a whole. How the averages operate was described for lay readers by the Chicago *Daily News* as follows:

By Joe Beckman

Ask a broker, "How's the market?" and you'll usually hear him say something like, "The Dow Jones industrial average was up about 3 points the last hour."

Everyone connected with the securities market discusses the Dow Jones averages, but just what are they and how are they computed?

Dow Jones & Co., operator of the news service known to LaSalle Streeters as "the broad tape," compiles averages on several different types of investments.

Those watched by most market followers are the industrial, rail, utility and composite stock averages, reported each hour and at the close.

But while the averages have many followers, they also have many critics.

The critics charge that using an average of 30 or 65 stocks hardly can tell you what the more than 1,100 common stocks on the New York Exchange are doing.

Their criticism is well taken from one point of view, because occasionally the average will move in one direction while the bulk of stocks in the market will go the other way.

Even so, as Dow Jones itself says:

"The purpose of the averages is to give a general rather than precise idea of the fluctuations in the securities markets and to provide a basis of historical continuity of security price movements."

In a sense, the investor should use the averages as a doctor uses a thermometer. It is an important diagnostic tool, but certainly it is not the only one.

Of the stock averages compiled by Dow Jones, the industrial average is the one investors most carefully scrutinize.

The industrial average is made up of the stock prices of 30 industrial corporations, generally regarded as "blue chips."

These are: Allied Chemical, Aluminum Co., American Can, American Telephone, American Tobacco, Anaconda, Bethlehem Steel, Chrysler, Du Pont, Eastman Kodak, General Electric, General Foods, General Motors, Goodyear, International Harvester and International Nickel.

Also included are International Paper, Johns-Manville, Owens-Illinois Glass, Procter & Gamble, Sears, Roebuck, Standard Oil of Calif., Standard Oil of N.J., Swift, Texaco, Union Carbide, United Aircraft, U.S. Steel, Westinghouse Electric and Woolworth.

The average goes back to Jan. 2, 1897, when Dow Jones began publication of the daily average closing prices of 12 active stocks. This continued until 1916 when the list was increased to 20. This list was increased to 30 on Oct. 1, 1928.

The stocks in the average now and then are changed to stay modern. Otherwise, the average today might have a buggy whip manufacturer among its components. Substitutions also are made when a stock becomes too inactive or its price is too low.

To compute the average, you would think that Dow Jones would simply take the 30 stocks' prices, add them up and divide by 30.

Not so, though this is the way it was done in the beginning. When stocks were split or a stock dividend was declared, the divisor had to be changed.

Dow Jones at first multiplied the price of each split share by the amount of the split to get away from the distortion that would otherwise have been caused.

In 1928, it adopted the method still used. The night before a split is to take effect, the average is worked out in the usual way.

Then the stocks' prices are added up again, but with the stock that is about to be split included as if the split were already a fact. This total is divided by the average already calculated.

The result is the new divisor, which today is 3.09 for the industrial average. It won't be changed again until a component is split or a stock dividend is declared.

The history of the railroad average also dates back to Jan. 2, 1897. Originally it was comprised of 12 railroads, but this was increased to 20 on March 7, 1928.

The roads in the list now are the Santa Fe, Atlantic Coast Line, Baltimore & Ohio, Canadian Pacific, Chesapeake & Ohio, Chicago & North Western, Rock Island, Delaware & Hudson, Erie-Lackawanna, Great Northern, Illinois Central, Kansas City Southern, Louisville & Nashville, New York Central, Nickel Plate, Norfolk & Western, Pennsylvania, Southern Ry. and Union Pacific.

The rail divisor now is 5.34 and it is not changed if the stock split, stock dividend, or substitution causes a distortion of less than 2 points in the railroad average.

The Dow Jones utility average was started in late 1929 and was made up of 20 stocks, but five stocks were dropped from the list June 2, 1938.

It is comprised of American Electric Power, Cleveland Electric Illuminating, Columbia Gas System, Commonwealth Edison, Consolidated Natural Gas, Detroit Edison, Houston Light & Power, Niagara Mohawk Power, Pacific Gas & Electric, Panhandle Eastern Pipe Line, Peoples Gas, Philadelphia Electric, Public Service Electric & Gas and Southern California Edison.

The utility average divisor currently is 7.91.

The composite average is an average of the 65 stocks making up the other three stock averages and its divisor is now 16.47. The average was begun Nov. 9, 1933.

Many people, both in and out of the market, err when they report an average "up $3." Correct terminology is in points, not dollars, since the changing divisors ruin direct dollar-point relations.

Since January 1968 Dow Jones has had competition from the Reuter Financial Report which is oriented to the information needs of the financial community—banks, insurance companies, mutual funds and other "institutional investors" as well as brokerage houses—with few newspaper clients. The Reuter General News wire, however, carries a considerable amount of economic news under the Business Beat tagline so Reuter press clients can pick up the major business news and exclusive feature stories written for the financial wire. The result has been to "sharpen" the Dow Jones service. The new financial service is only one aspect of the British news agency's increased coverage of American news since dissolution of its exchange agreement with the Associated Press, so the competition may be expected to become keener.

Tax selling occurs near the end of the year when investors get rid of securities to establish a loss for income tax purposes, which suggests the importance to the financial reporter of understanding the effect tax laws have on market operations. The layman often is mystified by sales of what from all indications are profitable businesses, for instance. Often they occur so that the seller can pay a capital gains tax of 25 per cent on the difference between the value of the property when he purchased it and its value at the time of his own sale. This, his financial advisers have figured out, means a greater long-run return on his investment than staying in business and paying the graduated corporation income tax. Put in laymen's language this means it sometimes is bad business to be too successful provided one wants to stay in the same line of work.

Many in the financial world consider the Standard & Poor ratings and analyses a better clue to the economy as a whole than the Dow Jones averages. The latter are based on a formula devised a long time ago and do not include electronics, airlines and some other more recently developed industries. Standard & Poor uses a list of 500 stocks which is more modern.

The American Stock Exchange and the New York Stock Exchange use rapid computers to transmit indexes based on all stock transactions, not just those of selected stocks. The American Index reflects the average price changes of more than 1,000 common stocks and the New York Exchange Index does the same for approximately 1,550 common stocks and it also has special common stock indexes for transportation, utility, finance and industrial.

Another valuable source of business and financial news is Dun & Bradstreet which, among other things, issues a monthly report on business failures based on data from 25 large cities. The emphasis is on explanation as is also true of the Dun & Bradstreet annual and other reports.

The possible assignments for the business-financial page are interminable. The alert interpretative reporter constantly asks "why?" especially when any form of behavior seems to become widespread, as investing capital abroad, establishing branch banks, splitting stock, purchasing government bonds or shares of an investment club or mutual fund rather than investing directly in common stocks, and so forth.

Called major yardsticks for determining the success or failure of government policies are the consumer price index and wholesale price index disclosed every month by the United States Bureau of Labor Statistics. Often erroneously called a cost of living index, the CPI is a report on the prices of 400 goods and services, from butter and beef to bowling balls. It is compiled after checking 15,000 retail stores and outlets throughout the country every month. Vital to understanding the index is its use of weights for every commodity or service. Food, for example, is calculated to be 24.8 per cent of a consumer's budget, housing 33.3 per cent and transportation 12.6 per cent.

Chicago *Tribune* expert Alvin Nagelberg describes the indexes:

> The CPI is a handy way to assess the erosion of the dollar's purchasing power. And for some people it also is a defensive tool to protect their income against advancing prices.

Today, more than 5.1 million workers are covered by labor contracts providing for wage increases when the CPI affects the income of:

Some 29 million Social Security beneficiaries.

Two million retired military and federal civil service employes and survivors.

About 13 million food stamp recipients.

It guides the national school lunch program, sets the poverty threshold level for health and welfare programs, has been used as an escalator for rental payments, and has played a role in divorce settlements.

It is estimated that the income and benefits of one-half of the population is affected by the CPI.

A one per cent change in the index triggers at least a $1 billion increase in income under escalation provisions. An error of only 0.1 per cent can lead to a misallocation of more than $100 million.

The CPI and WPI reports have often sent the stock market off in one direction or another. . . .

The Bureau of Labor Statistics first developed a CPI after World War I as a way of arriving at a fair pay scale. Quarterly indexes were started in 1935 and monthly indices in 1940. The CPI was revised in 1940, 1946, 1953, and 1964 and is due for another change in 1977 when two indices are scheduled to be published.

The problem today is that the population has grown so fast and the buying tastes and patterns have changed so much that some features of the CPI are obsolete. Also, there is a drive to get a more comprehensive and thus more accurate CPI. . . .

On the other hand, the WPI is basically a collection of prices solicited by mailed questionnaires to firms and trade associations. It's a compilation of 2,000 individual prices at the primary market level. That means the price of an item—whether a raw material product or finished product—the first time it is sold into the marketplace.

The CPI is not a true cost of living index because it does not take substitutions into account. If the price of beef goes sky high, the consumer may switch to buying more chicken. If the cost of repair services soars, the consumer may postpone repairs. Yet the CPI continues to reflect the same purchases, in the same proportions, each month. . . .

Definitions

Because of the injury that might otherwise result, the business-financial page reporter must be deadly accurate. Among other precautions he must observe is not to use business or financial terms unless he thoroughly understands their meaning. He should not hesitate to ask a news source to define and explain unfamiliar words and expressions. Among the fundamentals in his lexicon are the following:

Arbitration. Submitting a dispute to a third party to decide and agreeing to abide by his decision.

Articles of incorporation. The charter granted by the state permitting the organization of a corporation. It usually contains details relating to such matters as the purpose or purposes for which the corporation is formed, its principal place of business, the number of its directors and the amount of its capitalization.

Audit. Verification of records and accounts.

Balance sheet. The report of a company's assets and liabilities, profits and losses.

Bankruptcy. Abandonment of one's business and assignment of his assets to his creditors which discharges the debtor from future liability, enables the creditors to secure title to all the debtor's assets and provides a pro rata distribution of the assets among all creditors. A petition in bankruptcy may be voluntary if initiated by the debtor, or involuntary if initiated by the creditors.

Bear. (Stock or produce exchange.) One who believes the market will decline and contracts to sell securities or commodities at some future date at a certain price in the belief he will be able to buy them for resale at a lower one. In a bear market, the average price of all stocks drops because of widespread selling.

Big board. New York Stock Exchange.

Blue chip stock. Well-established stock, leading and essential industries stock.

Bond. A formal promise, always under seal, by the maker, usually a corporation, to pay a principal sum of money at a specified time and interest at a fixed rate at regular intervals. *Registered bonds* are paid only to the party named in the instrument and recorded on the corporation's books. A *coupon bond* is payable to bearer and may be transferred by mere delivery.

Broker. A financial agent who buys and sells securities for others, usually on a commission basis.

Bucket shop. A phony securities exchange which really engages in speculation or gambling on the ups and downs of the market.

Bull. (Stock or produce exchange.) One who expects, or tries to effect, a rise in prices. Sometimes a great number of people decide more or less at the same time to buy stocks. Such general buying action raises the average price of all stocks. If the price rise is big enough and lasts long enough, it is a bull market.

Call loans. Subject to payment upon demand.

Cats and dogs. Highly speculative and usually low-priced stocks which do not pay dividends.

Check off. Reduction from employee's pay checks of union dues which the employer then transmits to union officials.

Clearing house. A device to simplify and facilitate the daily exchange of checks and drafts and the settlement of balances among associated banks.

Collateral. Stocks, bonds and other evidences of property deposited by a borrower to secure a loan, as a pledge or guarantee that the loan will be repaid at maturity.

Collective bargaining. Bargaining between an organized group of workers and an employer instead of between each individual worker and an employer.

Conciliation. The attempt to settle a dispute by consultation with rival parties who do not pledge themselves to abide by any third person's decisions.

Controlling ownership. A controlling owner is one who owns sufficient shares to give him stockholder voting control which may sometimes be less than 50 per cent of the total stock.

Corporation. Any body consisting of one or more individuals treated by the law as a unit. The rights and liabilities of a business corporation are distinct from those of the individuals which comprise it.

Craft union. A labor organization of skilled workers doing similar work. Called a horizontal union because no one craft union would include all workers in any one large industry.

Credit. Postponed money payment; a promise to pay money or its equivalent at some future time.

Curb. A market for securities not listed on any regular exchange.

Debenture. Similar to a bond except that the security is the company's earnings only.

Deficit financing, debt management. Financial arrangements by United States treasury, companies operating at a loss to borrow new cash, consolidate debts, shift from short to long term loans, refinance and so forth. The objective generally is to reduce interest charges, put loan repayments on regular basis, assure enough funds to meet payroll costs and bills for raw materials.

Depletion. Exhaustion or using up of assets, such as raw materials used for production.

Depreciation. Loss of value through use or disuse.

Discount. Receiving payment on an acceptance or note from bank for a consideration. The indorser still is responsible in case the maker of the note or acceptance defaults.

Discount rate. The interest charged for discounting a note.

Dividend. The share of the surplus distributed to a stockholder.

Dumping. The sale of products abroad at prices lower than those charged at home.

Escalator clause. A provision in a union contract whereby wages fluctuate with the cost of living.

Feather bedding. Union rules to slow up or reduce work and to prevent speed-up so as to protect jobs and avoid unemployment.

Federal Reserve banks. Banker's banks dealing only with member banks and the government, the purpose of which as set forth in the preamble of the act creating them is "to furnish an elastic currency, to afford means of rediscounting commercial paper, to establish a more effective supervision of banking in the United States, and for other purposes."

Foreign exchange. A clearing house to adjust balances between countries.

Futures. A contract for future delivery.

Hedging. Selling or purchasing a security or commodity to offset the purchase or sale of another security or commodity.

Holding company. A corporation which produces nothing for the market but merely invests in the securities of other corporations.

Hot issue. A security which meets a heavy demand on being sold publicly for the first time. Price rises sharply and original buyers, if they sell, make a quick profit.

Hung up. The plight of an investor who has capital tied up in a stock which has slumped below his purchase price. He can't sell without taking a loss.

Income, earnings or profit. Must be used with modifiers: net, gross, operating, nonoperating, etc. Net profit is figure most people are interested in. Gross profit is sales less cost of selling the goods. Operating profit is gross profit less operating expenses (overhead). Net profit is operating profit less income taxes, any other charges or extraordinary expenses.

Index numbers. An index number represents the price of a group of commodities, or the average price during a given period, which is used as a basis or standard with which to compare the prices of these commodities at other dates.

Industrial union. A labor organization in which membership is open to all workers, skilled or unskilled, within any industry. Called vertical instead of horizontal because of its inclusiveness.

Insolvent. Unable to pay one's debts.

Insurance. A contract whereby one party, for a consideration, promises to indemnify another party in the event a specified loss occurs.

Interest. The price paid for the use of capital.

Interlocking directors. Individuals who are on the boards of two or more corporations which do business with each other.

Investment club or house. Small investors pool their resources, usually by monthly payments, for the purpose of purchasing securities. They profit in proportion to their investment.

Jurisdictional strike. Members of one union refuse to work if those of another union are employed.

Lamb. A beginner at speculation. He follows the flock, blindly.

Liquidation. Conversion of available assets into cash.

Lockout. The wholesale exclusion of workers from a plant by an employer.

Long or short. A customer is "long" in securities which he owns, or "short" in securities he has sold but does not own.

Maintenance of membership. Workers must remain union members during life of contract with employer.

Majority owner. One who owns 50.1 per cent or more of the stock of a company.

Margin. To buy securities on margin means to do so without putting up the full purchase price in cash, with a broker lending the rest.

Mediation. Third party attempts to end a dispute by persuasion.

Monopoly. That substantial unit of action on the part of one or more persons engaged in some kind of business which gives exclusive control, more particularly, though not solely, with respect to price.

Mutual fund. A corporation which invests members' capital in securities and pays dividends on the earnings.

Net income. See *Income.*

Nonprofit. Yielding no dividends or financial advantage to owners.

Odd-lot investor. A broker who combines small requests for sales or purchases by several customers to be able to make an adequately sized bid on the exchange.

Open and closed shop. An open shop is one in which both union and nonunion workers are employed. A closed shop is one in which either nonunion or union workers only are employed.

Option. The right to have first chance, as in the purchase of property, usually obtained by a money payment which is not returnable if the deal falls through.

Overhead. Expense of equipment, stock and maintenance which is relatively constant regardless of production.

Premium income. In insurance, the income of an insurance company from premiums paid by policy holders. Interest and dividends from investments are the other major source of revenue.

Prime rate. The interest rate charged by banks to customers—business firms and individuals—who have the best credit ratings and solid collateral. Prime rate generally is one percentage point higher than the discount rate —the interest rate which federal reserve banks charge on loans made by commercial banks from the reserve bank.

Profit and loss statement. It summarizes income and expenses of an organization or business, to show net profit or loss for the fiscal period covered.

Profit sharing. Sharing with workers the profits of good years; in effect, a bonus based on profits.

Proxy statement. A signed document to give another authority to act for the signer. Proxy fights develop at stockholders' meetings when rival groups solicit proxies from absent stockholders.

Receiver. A temporary court-appointed officer to conduct a bankrupt business in the interest of the creditors.

Receivership. Operation of a business by the creditors when the debtor otherwise would be bankrupt or in danger of bankruptcy.

Rediscounting. The purchasing by one bank of a note or bill of exchange held by another.

Rent. The price paid for the use of land or anything else.

Reserve. Lawful money or other liquid assets which a bank must keep on hand to insure prompt payment of its deposits and liabilities.

Revenue. Generally, the cash received in any fiscal period. It may include cash from sales of goods or services (operating revenue) and cash from investments, sale of property or from other sources such as patent rights, royalties and license agreements (nonoperating revenue).

Right-to-work laws. Open shop laws.

Sabotage. A conscious or willful act on the part of workers intended to reduce the output of production or to restrict trade and reduce profits by the withdrawal of efficiency from work and by putting machinery out of order and producing as little as possible without getting dismissed from the job.

Scab. A strikebreaker.

Sell short. To contract to sell securities one does not own in the expectation of being able to buy them later more cheaply.

Speculation. Taking a risk when making a purchase in the hope that future developments will make the deal profitable.

Stock certificate. A stock certificate represents one or more shares of the corporation's capital. Its price is determined by the market, usually a stock exchange, where securities are bought and sold. *Preferred stock* holders have a prior claim on the company's assets before the *common stock* holders in the event of bankruptcy. *Cumulative stock* arrears are paid before the common stock receives a dividend in case dividends are omitted at certain periods. *Participating preferred stock* entitles the holder to a share in the profits, in addition to the stated dividend.

Stock split. Increasing the total number of shares of stock, usually by doubling the number and dividing the par value of each share. This has the same effect as a stock dividend but is treated differently for taxation purposes. It enables small investors to buy more easily.

Surplus. The equity of stockholders in a corporation above the par value of the capital stock.

Sweetheart contract. One between management and a labor leader which benefits them at the expense of the rank and file.

Trust. A company which deals in capital and handles funds that are principally inactive, thus conserving existing wealth.

Trustee in bankruptcy. Court-appointed officer who converts a bankrupt's assets into cash and pays the creditors.

Underwriting. Insuring against loss, to guarantee to meet an obligation if the original party fails to do so.

Wildcat strike. One not authorized by union officials.

Yellow dog contract. A contract for labor in which the worker is required to promise not to join any labor union during the term of his employment.

PROBLEMS AND POLICIES

As the scope and consequently the readership of the business-financial page increase, so do the problems of the editor and the need for a strong sense of social responsibility. Tips are received from many sources—brokers, lawyers, union leaders, competitors, shipping agents, trade associations and the like—and some of the tipsters may be motivated by other than pure public-spiritedness. Misinformation or injudicious handling of news may be injurious to innocent persons. Premature disclosure regarding a pending real estate transaction, for example, may ruin a potential deal. And then there is the little old lady who reads a story about the profits being made by raisers of soybeans and wants to cash in her small savings to speculate on the grain market. She calls the editor for further information and advice.

Secrecy

Increasingly, the business reporter is likely to be stymied because of federal government security regulations which make it impossible for even the most cooperative official or public relations counsel to provide information. Often the editor suspects that there is too much "hush-hush" about what happens to be common knowledge in his community, so he may contact the Freedom of Information Committee of the American Society of Newspaper Editors or some such group to see what can be done about "knocking some sense" into the heads of some Washington bureaucrats. Seldom, however, does he dare defy requests from officials with proper credentials.

"Puffery"

Biggest perpetual problem is how to distinguish between legitimate news and free publicity. "Business Office Musts" from the advertising department are distasteful to any editor who wants to use only the yardstick of legitimate public interest. This means that he wishes to keep no blacklist of nonadvertisers whose news is to be ignored or played down and he resents any successful attempt to persuade him to use a spurious story whose only effect is to increase someone's sales.

Especially in the sections devoted to real estate and main business district news, the business-financial page may seem to be a booster page and its editor to be interested in promoting the best interests of the community—much as the sports editor usually promotes the success of the home-town team. Emphasis on innovation and progress, however, does not mean excessive "puffery" provided there is plenty of legitimate news available which almost always is the case. How to teach this lesson to business executives and their public relations representatives, however, is not often easy.

Special real estate and similar sections are a thing apart. The copy between the advertisements may be unashamedly free publicity. Most of it is handout material, although some papers strive valiantly to localize and legitimatize it. Advertisers generally believe that such "good will" material enhances the value of their advertisements. Many skeptical newspapermen believe that a good obituary or other legitimate story would serve their purposes better; but they are still to be convinced. One doesn't need to attend a school of journalism or even go to college to learn to produce that kind of tripe. In fact, he would be well advised not to do so.

Some businessmen who employ expensive public relations men want to be relieved of responsibility. They expect the highly paid help to maintain relations with the press and both boss and public relations men resent it when a journalist attempts to circumvent this line of authority. Often, however, it is imperative to do so. One of the best places is the cocktail party. This is a genteel type of "payola" to which many business enterprises are addicted. The business reporter may be as bored as the society reporter who attends a tea party a day, but he might otherwise not get the opportunity to rub elbows with top executives. More naive than their public relations men, these officials often provide tips and information of importance, and possibly exclusive as far as the imbibing newsman is concerned. It is a constant source of amazement to newspapermen how ignorant those who make the news usually are as regards its reporting and editing. They do, however, understand that any business enterprise must operate in accordance with rules and, although not understanding, are often prone to accept the explanation "That is not done," when a reporter diplomatically rejects a suggestion.

"Payola"

How far the reporter should go in accepting favors from news sources is a stickler. Many of them can afford expensive gifts at Christmas or on other occasions and may be offended if a friendly newspaperman refuses to accept their largess. Most editors wish there were an easy rule applicable to all occasions. Some forbid their staff members to accept any presents, even passes to public entertainments and certainly not expensive junkets by airplane to be present at the dedication of a new plant or on some similar occasion. Others are willing to accept anything which does not cost more than a fifth of whisky. Still others will take whatever a news source is handing out to other friends. Whatever rule is adopted, difficulty arises in enforcing it without making exceptions.

There have been a few cases of financial writers who used their inside knowledge of the market for personal profit. The Securities and Exchange Commission has taken action against writers who purchased stock just prior to boosting it in their columns after which they sold at considerable profit. The practice is growing for newspapers to require financial writers to reveal their holdings, to their editors at least. The St. Petersburg *Times* issued regulations which state: "It is a violation of company rules for any staff member to make or hold any investment which in any way might pose a conflict of interest." Richard J. Haiman, managing editor, explained: "In practice it means that no staff member holds any stock in any local companies or in any national companies about which a St. Petersburg *Times* reporter ever would have occasion to write."

Codes

What follows are extracts from a memorandum on "Business News Policy," issued to the staff by Creed C. Black, then executive editor of the Wilmington (Del.) *News-Journal.*

> One of the traditional and thorny problems of newspapers is distinguishing between legitimate news of the business world and free advertising. Wilmington has its share of both legitimate business news stories and space-grabbers. The aim of our newspapers is to get the legitimate news in and keep the puffs out.
> Our policy is based on the premise that the decision on whether an item will be published will rest with the news departments.
> Advertising salesmen have been instructed to explain that they have no connection with the news departments, and advertisers are being requested to deal directly with our city desks when they have stories they consider newsworthy.
> Our decisions will be based solely on news value. If it's news, no amount of advertising will keep it out of the paper; if it isn't news, no amount of advertising will get it in.

To follow such a policy successfully, consistency is absolutely essential. If we slip up in one instance, we're putting ourselves in a position that's hard to explain the next time somebody wants similar treatment and wants to know why we won't do thus-and-so for him when we did it for so-and-so . . . .

There will be no attempt here to set down a comprehensive list of hard-and-fast rules, for that's obviously impractical. But here are some general guidelines on various types of items we encounter:

Personnel Changes. Appointments, promotions, resignations, etc., are news up—or down—to a point, depending on how important the job is. Obviously we can't cover all personnel changes in the business and industrial community, so we must be selective.

Probably the biggest problem here, just because of the sheer weight of numbers, is with the Du Pont Company. I am told that the public relations department there does a good bit of screening in its releases. But if you are in doubt about the importance of a Du Pont position, consult the PR people. Ditto for Hercules, Atlas, etc.

New Businesses. A new business or a change in ownership is news. So is a major expansion of an established firm, or a major remodeling project. Let's not get sucked in, however, by somebody who's just added another showcase or finally put a badly needed coat of paint on the walls.

And when pictures are justified, let's strive for something besides ground-breakings and ribbon-cuttings.

Giveaways. Everybody who's giving something away seems to think we should provide full coverage, including photos of the jubilant winners. We shouldn't and we won't.

Our first consideration here is the lottery laws. If anything must be bought to make one eligible for the prize, the drawing is legally a lottery and we can't touch the story.

Beyond that, our general policy is that we aren't interested in giveaways unless there's something unusual enough to give the story an angle that will enable it to stand on its own as a readable human interest feature. And even when a story is justified, the name of the firm giving away the prize should be only an incidental part of the story.

Business Anniversaries. The fact that a firm has been in business for *x* number of years hardly excites our readers, even though some businessmen have the idea this qualifies as big news every 12 months. We will not report such anniversaries except on special occasions—such as a 50th, 75th, or 100th anniversary.

Dealerships. It is not news when a men's clothing store adds a new line of shirts; it is news when an auto dealer takes on a new car. The distinction (and it can be applied generally) depends on both the nature of the product and the type of business. A clothing store, for example, handles scores of products; an auto dealer handles only one or two lines, and usually he is the exclusive dealer for these.

Company Awards. If a company could get newspaper coverage of awards it makes or prizes it gives its own employees, there would be no limit on the number of plaques, scrolls, certificates and gold keys gathering dust in Wilmington households. So let's help fight the dust menace by covering only very special awards within a company—a recognition of 50 years of service, for example—or genuine honors bestowed by professional organizations embracing more than a single company.

Special Sections.   Special sections are somewhat of a case apart, since their aim is frankly promotional. Even so, no editorial content will be devoted to a special section event unless participation in it is broad enough to give it general interest. And in *all* special sections, remember, the editorial content is as good —or as bad—as *we* make it. If it sounds like advertising, that's our fault.

Trade News.   Strictly apart from the question of what is and what is not a legitimate business news story, there's the problem of whether to use commercial names of businesses or products in other news stories.

No pat rule is possible here. A good general guide is to use commercial names only when the story would be incomplete without them. You don't have to say, for instance, that thieves looted a Buick parked in front of the Wilmington Dry Goods; a car parked on Market Street would do. But if an elevator falls in a store, name the store; if a man jumped out of a hotel window, name the hotel.

There has been a tendency in our papers to go out of the way not only to describe a car as a compact car but to name the make as well. Only if the size of the car is an important element of the story is it necessary to designate it as a compact, and the make is almost never relevant. . . .

We will not use stories on the sale of individual homes unless historic interest or something similar makes them especially newsworthy. The sale of such a home or of commercial property should be reported immediately and not saved for the real estate pages. Prices are permissible if known.

Stories and photos on the real estate pages should be confined to developments or general trends instead of to individual homes for sale. That is, a picture of one home in a new development would be permissible, but we would want to avoid using a single home that's come on the market in an established neighborhood. Price ranges of homes in a development are permissible.

Let's be sure we don't use repeated pictures or stories on the same development and let's also avoid follow-up stories on crowd turnouts at individual developments and stick to general roundups on the state of the real estate market.

Several years ago, the Atlanta newspapers got together to draw up a statement as to how to reduce the "puff" evil to a minimum. In part, the agreement read as follows:

The following items are specific types of publicity which we will NOT carry in the future:
a. Fashion shows, cooking schools, garden schools or any similar promotion of any kind originated by or which has any commercial connection with any business.
b. Beauty specialists.
c. Pictures of salesmen or managers who change jobs or pictures of new members of organizations.
d. Pictures of buyers.
e. Pictures of either the exterior or interior of stores except in those cases which might be considered in the light of real estate news.
f. Interiors of buildings.
g. Special promotions such as the "Bell Ringers," "Hour Glass" teasers, etc.

h. Luncheons or store promotions.
i. Entertainment of prominent people by stores.
j. Receptions for authors in book departments.
k. Pictures of merchandise. It is understood that this not only includes retail but distributors' publicity; as, for example, pictures of distributors holding a can of beer, etc.
l. Pictures of grocery chain new members.
m. Santa Claus promotions.
n. Robots and trick automobiles disguised as locomotives, etc.
o. All promotions on the part of stores which feature the Junior League, the debutantes or other social celebrities.
p. All commercial promotions such as state fairs, carnivals, auto races, flower shows, etc. This does not apply to civic enterprises or those enterprises which are operated strictly for charity, as for example, Scottish Rite hospital, but it is understood that where publicity is given these promotions the names of no retail or commercial organizations are to be used.
q. Photograph contests, dancing schools, insurance stories, stories and pictures of used car lots.
r. Elimination of travel, resort publicity.
s. Any paid local ads simulating news matter must take the word "Advertisement" spelled out in 8-point black.
t. No automobile publicity will be carried in daily paper. All must go Sundays.
u. All special sections for advertisers cannot carry over 30 per cent publicity.

Special: Photographs of meetings of business organizations, which hold conventions in Atlanta; pictures will be used of men of prominence who attend. These will be run in one column cuts only.

Publicity on wrestling matches will be limited to 3 inches on week days and 3 inches on Sunday before the match, but story after the match will be based on news value as determined by sports department.

Advertisers should not be given preference over any other teams in soft ball leagues. No requests will come from business office on soft ball stories.

In addition, according to *Editor & Publisher*, unwritten understandings between news executives on the papers included, in substance, the following:

Mention of meeting places (such as restaurants and department stores) is to be considered part of the story in advance material, but not to be used in stories appearing following the event.

Stories about airlines, railroads, bus lines and other transportation services are "out," except in cases of change of regular schedules, when brief stories are permitted, or of revolutionary changes in services offered the public. (Airconditioning not included in the latter category.)

No definite rule promulgated on bowling. The commercial angle, however, should be subordinated as much as possible and individuals rather than commercial teams played up.

In stories of skeet shooting events, names of powder companies, cartridge and shot gun manufacturers, and hardware stores eliminated.

Stories about lectures, concerts, recitals, football and baseball games and other musical, educational and sports events shall not contain location of the place where tickets may be purchased, nor the price of tickets.

No publicity shall be given music or dancing teachers, except, perhaps, in the case of annual concerts.

Stories having to do with the arrival of athletic teams or so-called notables shall not mention the hotel at which they are stopping.

In stories about benefit dances by organizations, the name of the orchestra shall not be used, except in the rare cases when nationally known orchestras are brought to the city.

Identification of persons in stories of all types to be eliminated as far as possible where identification mentions name of some commercial organization.

Brief stories about merchants' associations and similar business-promoting organizations accepted, provided commercial affiliation of members is eliminated.

In stories about changes in price of gasoline, names of all companies must be eliminated.

Stories about changes in law firms and changes of location are "out." Changes which affect the titles of prominent firms are approved, however.

Names of undertakers shall not be used in connection with ambulance calls to accident or crime scenes. Use of undertakers' names in death stories left to the individual editors, but the consensus is that names of funeral directors should be used prior to the funeral and not after it has been held.

LABOR

The history of the American labor movement is as much that of a struggle of different ideologies for supremacy within the ranks of labor itself as it is that of a fight between capital and labor for a share of the national wealth and income. In its early stages, organized labor was handicapped because of its control by leaders of foreign birth or influence and by native-born intellectuals who lacked experience as workers and were discredited further because of their known unorthodoxy in other fields.

In the middle half of the nineteenth century, labor was too prone to espouse every new economic or political theory that offered a possible step upward on the economic scale. Agrarianism, idealistic cooperative plans, greenbackism, the single tax, free silver and syndicalism were among the ideologies with sizable followings within the ranks of labor. Until the American Federation of Labor emerged as powerful under the leadership of Samuel Gompers late in the nineteenth century, organized labor hardly was an important permanent factor in American economic and political life.

The AFL's triumph over the Knights of Labor represented a victory for the craft union as opposed to industrial unionism, of the "aristocracy of labor" idea over the "one big union" idea. Gompers and his followers believed in working within the existent capitalistic system, seeking through unions of craftsmen organized horizontally throughout industry as a whole to obtain the maximum benefits for the workers. The Knights of Labor had admitted unskilled as well as skilled workers.

Craft unionism remained dominant until 1936, when, under the leadership of John L. Lewis, the Committee (later called Congress) for Industrial Organization began to organize many large basic industries, such as the mining, motor and steel industries, in which large masses of unskilled workers were not eligible for membership in craft unions. CIO unions were industrial or vertical unions because membership in them was all-inclusive within a given plant in which there might conceivably be numerous craft unions.

In December 1955, the two big organizations reunited as the AFL–CIO, but today many old units of each, at all levels from international to local, still operate with virtually unchanged autonomy. Also, still independent are the railway brotherhoods and a number of other large groups, as the miners and teamsters and several mavericks which were expelled as left-wing by the CIO in 1949.

Despite the comparative contemporary strength of the labor movement as a whole, not more than one-fourth of the entire labor force belong to unions. Little progress ever has been made among white-collar (professional) workers whose proportion of the total labor force continues to grow with the expanding service industries and as mechanical automation reduces the ranks of the blue-collar workers.

In the United States, with its rugged individualistic frontier tradition and its democratic open class social system, there never has developed strong class consciousness at any social or economic level. Despite considerable demagoguery to the contrary, socialistic and communistic ideas never have attracted any appreciable number of rank-and-file working people. There is no political labor party as in many other parts of the world, and organized political activity by labor always has been condemned by the rest of the populace. Because of the absence of class consciousness as a welding force, there has developed a strong type of labor leader in the United States. Whoever happens to be the leading labor figure at any time is bound to be considered a "public enemy" by antilaborites. Regardless of the justice involved, this has been true of such widely different labor leaders as Samuel Gompers, Eugene V. Debs, John L. Lewis, Sidney Hillman, Walter Reuther, James Petrillo, Harry Bridges and James Hoffa.

Because it never has enjoyed the confidence of an appreciable proportion of the American people, organized labor has been faced with the problem of avoiding mistakes which are more costly to it than similar ones are to any other segment of the population.

Labor Laws

The National Labor Relations (Wagner) act of 1935 was called labor's magna charta because it gave federal protection to the right to organize and bargain collectively and to maintain closed shops. It was mostly under its protection that the CIO became established in the mass production industries, using the Gandhi-inspired sit-down strike strategy. The Taft-Hartley act of 1947 and the Landrum-Griffin act of 1959 considerably weakened the basic law from the standpoint of labor. Among other things the former outlawed jurisdictional strikes (one union against another), secondary boycotts, strikes for union recognition and the closed shop except by majority vote of eligible employees. It also stipulated penalties for breaches of contract and boycotts by unions, forbade union contributions and expenditures for political purposes, forbade the services of the National Labor Relations board to unions which had not registered financial information and filed anticommunist affidavits for all its officers, allowed employers greater freedom to campaign against unionization of workers and gave the federal government the power to use injunctions to compel an eighty-day "cooling-off" period before a strike could be called.

The Labor-Management Reporting and Disclosures act (Landrum-Griffin) of 1959 was aimed at racketeering labor officials. Among other things it required annual reports from all unions, gave the FBI power to enter cases of suspected violations, forbade "hot cargo" pacts in which a trucker, for example, refused to handle cargo from another trucker if the union labeled it forbidden, outlawed extortion or blackmail publicity, outlawed "sweet-heart" contracts between unscrupulous employers and labor leaders and provided for secret ballots in union elections, machinery for ousting crooked union officials and a ban against arbitrary raising of union dues or assessments without a secret ballot vote of the members.

In the 1950s, several states adopted "right-to-work" laws. These were a misnomer for open shop as they guaranteed nobody a job and were intended to forbid closed union shops under any circumstance. In its behalf, organized labor increased agitation for the guaranteed annual wage, shorter work week and strengthening or recovery of old protections as maintenance of membership clauses, seniority rights, check-off systems for the collection of dues, pensions, longer vacations, profit sharing plans and the like.

Covering Labor

Important as all these other factors indisputably are, the basic issue involved in most contract disputes is wages. As in the case of business, there is no regular labor beat. The smart labor reporter notes in his futures book the dates of expirations of contracts between important unions and industries and, weeks or months in advance, starts interviewing both management and labor officials to determine what exactly will be at stake when the new contracts are up for negotiation.

Newspaper headlines naturally emphasize conflict, especially when it leads to strikes and lockouts. It is easy to overlook the fact that the overwhelming majority of labor-management affairs are conducted harmoniously and that there are numerous companies and even entire industries in which there has been little or no trouble for decades or longer. Labor leaders have traditionally charged that when matters do come to a point of conflict, the press underplays its side of the story. During the day-by-day account of a strike, the issues causing it often become lost because of the emphasis given incidents of violence, hotheaded statements by leaders and human intertes accounts.

Labor Problems

Understandable today is the contention that any major or protracted shutdown in any part of the American economy would be catastrophic throughout the entire economy, so interrelated have all parts of it become. How to preserve the dignity and freedom to work or not to work guaranteed all Americans in the Thirteenth amendment to the Constitution and at the same time protect the innocent masses from the repercussions of a strike or lockout is a major social and political issue. Through its Mediation and Conciliation service, the federal government investigates and provides leadership in bringing about peaceful settlements of most disputes. During periods of comparatively full production and high prosperity, as during a cold war with huge government expenditures to keep industry going, its successes far outnumber its failures. Organized labor has been a leading supporter of American foreign policy and local unions prod employers to be diligent in seeking good government contracts to maintain full employment. If such a condition continues, organized labor may be expected to devote more of its energy to worker education programs and to plans to assist workers to participate in community affairs.

Greatest obstacle to such activities continues to be the matter of racial integration. AFL unions were discriminatory against Negroes and the unskilled foreign born. The CIO forbade such discrimination, but unions must share with management the blame for the slowness with which Negroes and members of other minority groups obtain equal job opportunities, are upgraded and are given seniority rights, not to mention managerial positions.

Stressing the Public Interest

In covering many aspects of labor news, the reporter should consider the public interest as paramount.

UNION AFFAIRS

Aside from the same reader interest that exists regarding the activities of any large organization, in the cases of unions there is the additional public interest as regards their control and policies.

POLICY STATEMENTS

Organized labor is a political force. Consequently, it is significant news when a large union or prominent labor leaders comment upon some current matter of widespread interest.

MANAGEMENT AGREEMENTS

In the field of labor, as in all others, it is conflict that attracts attention although, as in other fields, such as marital relations and law observance, strife is the exception rather than the rule. Nevertheless, changes in wages and hours and working conditions of thousands of employees affect a whole community.

With increases of $15,000 in appropriations ($10,000 from the city and $5,000 from the county), the Chattanooga Public Library has prepared a schedule of salary increases for its overworked staff.

In an administrative committee report to the board of trustees yesterday, Mrs. Griffin Martin, chairman, said, "The completion of a salary scale and scheme of service by the staff association (members of the library staff) and the adoption of this by the board of trustees is an outstanding accomplishment of the year."

The increases will leave the public library here below other comparable libraries in salaries, but the new scale is expected to help the library fill several vacancies for which competent librarians could not be secured at the salaries previously within the scope of the library budget. . . .   [Chattanooga *Times*]

Higher retail meat prices faced housewives today as butcher shops prepared to hike pay for their workmen $10 a week.

The agreement providing for the pay increase, which is retroactive to Oct. 1, was accepted last night at a meeting of 4,000 members of the AFL Amalgamated Meat Cutters and Butcher Workmen in Carmen's Hall.

The session was called by Emmet Kelly, international vice-president of the union and secretary-treasurer of the Chicago local. . . .

[Chicago *Daily News*]

UNION DEMANDS

When management balks at union demands, a strike is always a potential threat. State and federal conciliators may step in to attempt mediation; one side may offer to arbitrate. In all such cases, the reporter should seek the versions of both union and management as to the issues: what the union asks and what management offers. This involves comparing the new conditions sought with existing ones. A resume of the past history of relations between the particular company and the union may suggest the possibility of peaceful settlement in the current situation.

STRIKES

Unless it is a "wildcat," a strike is preceded by a strike vote of the membership. Maybe this vote may be taken long in advance of the actual walkout and may consist in authorizing the officers to use their own discretion. In states with "cooling off" periods it may be necessary to file notices of intention to strike weeks or months in advance. One result of such laws may be that a union keeps an industry under almost perpetual notice, as was the case frequently under the wartime Smith-Connally act.

After a strike begins, the reporter describes factually what happens: (1) how many members of what unions walk out, when and where; (2) what is the status of picketing—number engaged, location and activities; (3) police handling of the situation and comment by both union and management on the handling; (4) violence or threats of violence; (5) the effect upon the public because of curtailed production or services; (6) efforts to settle the strike. A fair treatment of labor disputes requires constant contact with both sides and equal space to comments. Also, good reporting consists in frequent reminders as to the issues involved; that is, the union's demands and the company's counterproposals. Too often tempers become so inflamed that by the time a strike ends nobody remembers what it was all about in the first place. The newspaper which never forgets that no one, including the participants, really wants a strike contributes toward peaceful settlement by not contributing to the incipient ill will.

What follows is an excellent example of clarifying issues and presenting both sides in a labor dispute:

A wildcat strike yesterday at Peoria Malleable Foundry over the dismissal of a union employe is now a strike to "eliminate racism" from the operation of the plant, officials of Local 140 of the United Electrical, Radio and Machine Workers of America said last night.

A company spokesman denied the racism charge, and called the strike a violation of the contract.

Fired on the grounds that he struck a foreman was Local 140 President Robert Reddick, 1115 Warren St., a Negro. He has been president of the local for six years.

The incident occurred Monday, union spokesmen reported. They said that Reddick was fired Tuesday, and meetings between the union and management were held on the matter Wednesday and at noon yesterday.

The strike began after the company declined to either reinstate Reddick or deal the same disciplinary measures to the foreman, who is white, union officials said.

All of the union members, about 185, who make up the work force outside the non-supervisory and office personnel, walked off their jobs, both union and company spokesmen said.

The union membership is about 85 or 90 per cent black, and all other plant employes except one foreman are white, union officials said.

"The company has foremen who are downright racists," said Florence Criley, a union international representative from the Chicago regional office. "There isn't a black face in the front office (which has about 15 employes), and racist remarks are made by the foremen about the black men in the shop."

Will Jones of Chicago, a union field representative, said the matter has "gone too far" for the union to accept anything other than full reinstatement of Reddick.

Jones and Miss Criley said Reddick had worked at the plant 19 years without any previous trouble.

Jones and Miss Criley said that if Reddick is held to be solely to blame, "no worker will be safe from the foremen in the future."

"There has never been any (racial) trouble in the past," asserted Plant Supt. John Kauzlarich last night. "We've got real good relations. This is really unusual."

He said Reddick had hit the foreman "several times."

The work stoppage is in violation of the contract grievance procedure, Kauzlarich said.

Peoria Malleable is a division of the Woodward Co., which is a division of the Mead Corporation. It is at the foot of Alexander street.

[Peoria *Journal-Star*]

William Eaton, who handled labor news for the United Press International in Washington for many years, gives the following advice:

The reporter starting on the labor beat needs a certain persistence to over-come (1) the mild paranoia of most labor leaders toward the commercial press, and (2) the timidity of most management spokesmen in dealing with the nosey newspaperman. A new labor reporter also should:

Walk a picket line—and listen.

Find a friend on each side of the bargaining table and not neglect the mediators, either.

Be cautious about predictions on the length of strikes and the imminence of settlements.

Learn to wait for hours outside a bargaining room and eat cold hamburgers at 3 o'clock in the morning.

Keep the faith with the rank-and-file.

Never violate a trust.

AGRICULTURE

An area of potential news which is generally neglected by city daily news-papers is the rural, farm or agricultural sector. Generally such papers rely on the press associations to cover Washington and state capital developments regarding farm legislation. Some press releases from agricultural organizations are rewritten to stress local angles and, especially in smaller places, columns written by local county agents are sometimes run. By comparison with the treatment given business and/or labor, this coverage is meager. As a result the press is accused of neglecting its responsibility by ignoring changes that have occurred in farming. "Too many daily papers run farm news as if it were a running battle between farmers and the secretary of agriculture or between farmers and town people—or between farmers themselves," accord-ing to former Secretary of Agriculture Orville Freeman.

Most newspapers which formerly gave greater coverage to farm news have long since ceased the attempt to instruct farmers in how to farm, leaving that area to the farm magazines. Commenting on Freeman's criticism, B. B. Watson, farm editor of the Hannibal (Mo.) *Courier-Post*, emphasized a "con-flict of objectives" as follows: "Farm news as such is primarily local or at least regional in character, is pedantic, repetitious, highly compartmentalized and is seldom productive of advertising revenues in proportion to other elements in the news."

Other editors explain that agricultural news is slanted to interest the public as a whole. As Stanley Lantz, farm editor of the Bloomington (Ill.) *Pantagraph*, puts it, it is "not written in 'farmer talk' to the mythical man in the overalls and straw hat."

That such a man is mythical is seen in the statistics regarding changes in rural America since the country's origin. Whereas in colonial days 90 per cent of the population was rural, today about 5 per cent is, down from 18 per cent at the end of World War II. American farm units reached their all-time peak of 6,500,000 in 1935. A quarter century later there were only 2,500,000 units, approximately half of them marginal and not needed to supply the nation's food supply. The small independent farmer is almost nonexistent today. Agriculture has become very Big Business. The top 20 so-called farmers get more income than the bottom 350,000.

Political Power

Several United States Supreme Court decisions in the '60s led to considerable changes in the rural-urban balance of political power. States have had to reapportion congressional and legislative districts in accordance with the equal representation rule: one voter, one vote. Previously, through gerrymandering and refusal of the rural-dominated legislatures to reapportion, the farm areas were represented way out of proportion to their population strength. For instance, a Georgia farmer's vote was 62 times more effective than that of a Georgia city man. A typical situation existed in Michigan where an upper peninsula congressman represented 177,431 persons whereas a Detroit congressman spoke for 802,994.

Logrolling by members of the Farm Bloc, representative of noncompetitive agricultural interests as cotton and cattle, wheat and vegetables, no longer is so effective with total rural representation reduced. No drastic changes have occurred yet, but as the power structure is altered by deaths and elections cities should find it easier to obtain needed laws from state legislatures and possibly be able to rely less heavily on Washington. The effort of the farm lobbies should diminish. The Big Three of such lobbies are the American Farm Bureau of over two million members, generally sympathetic to the larger and wealthier farm owners; the National Farmers Union with about 250,000 members, a gadfly New Deal-born organization of small and independent farmers; and the National Grange, whose 700,000 members regard it mostly as a social group instead of as a militant political force as it was when it began shortly after the Civil War. There is also the National Farmers Organization with almost 200,000 members which, however, engages mostly in marketing bargaining activities.

Today's federal agricultural policy is still substantially the same as that established in early New Deal days by Henry A. Wallace and associates. The essential feature is to keep farm income high by payments to farmers for participation in the Soil Conservation program whereby part of their acreage is kept idle and by loans through the Commodity Credit Corporation secured by products which can be forfeited in case the market price stays low.

These and similar efforts are geared to what is called parity, the relationship between the well-being of the farmer and nonfarm population using the period 1910–14 as the base. Devised years ago by the American Farm Bureau, it has been called a statistical monstrosity, and the Bureau in recent years has favored reduction or elimination of federal farm supports. The small independent farmers, however, insist that the present policy is necessary for their continued existence, even through the large corporate farms admittedly benefit more from it and do not need it to survive. Ceilings on federal governmental subsidies to big producers are favored increasingly by urban-suburban members of Congress, who now outnumber their rural area colleagues.

Critics of the present policy correctly point out that it is handicapped in achieving its aims because it still is based on acreage rather than productivity. Today an hour of farm labor produces five times as much as was true a generation ago and crop production by acres is up about 75 per cent. All of this has been accomplished by the technological revolution which began in the late nineteenth century with the threshing machine, reaper and similar machines and by the experimental work of the land grant agricultural colleges which have made higher education an essential for farming today. Contemporary farming is Big Business and expensive. The family farm is becoming obsolete.

The Urbanite's Stake

Today more workers are engaged in transporting, processing and selling food than are engaged in producing it, and the farmer receives only about 35 cents of every dollar that the housewife spends in the grocery store. Her interest is many-sided. She wants the best for the least cost. William Longgood of the New York *Times* with his *The Poisons in Your Food* (Simon and Schuster, 1960), Rachel Carson in *Silent Spring* (Houghton Mifflin, 1962) and many others since them have made the housewife aware of the health hazards resulting from many current agricultural practices. Nutritionists have made her conscious of vitamins, calories and balanced diets. Recipes are an indispensable part of most publications today. The developing field of consumer reporting was described in Chapter 11. What follows is an attempt to interpret a matter of concern to "city slickers" so they can understand it.

By Roger Croft

If beleaguered housewives are hoping for an early relief in the soaring price of sugar they are in for a bitter disappointment. And if any would-be economic sleuth is searching for sinister, speculating gnomes in Zurich his mission is likely to be unsuccessful.

Sugar prices, to be sure, are running rampant. Today, housewives are paying about 70 cents a pound compared with 13 cents a pound at the beginning of this year.

The refining companies are similarly having to fork out about six times the money they pay for raw sugar—now about $1,300 a ton against $328 a ton last January. Such a 600 per cent take-off in the price of sugar for the housewife makes current inflationary trends of 10 per cent to 12 per cent a year in food costs look puny indeed.

What is really behind this phenomenal rise in the price of one of our basic foodstuffs?

First and foremost it's a question of supply and demand. Crop failures, rapidly rising demand from developing countries and the inability or reluctance of producers to react quickly to changes in demand are the major causes of today's sugar shortages.

GLIMMER OF HOPE

Prospects for an early fall in sugar prices are therefore slim. But there is one glimmer of hope on the horizon.

Sugar brokers report that sugar "futures" (contracts to buy sugar several months from now) are beginning to drop a little. For example, in London spot sugar (today's price) is 570 pounds sterling a ton. Next month's price is a discouraging 581 pounds sterling. But by August, 1975 the price drops to 519 pounds a ton and for October of next year the slide continues to 490 pounds a ton.

The slight weakening in the futures prices reflects the prospect of a better sugar crop next year—the beet crop is harvested in the early fall. The European and the Soviet Union's beet crop this year was hit by early frost and a wet spring. The sugar cane producers, which account for roughly 60 per cent of world supplies and are mainly the tropical countries like Cuba, Mauritius and the Philippines were physically unable to boost their production to make up for the short-fall in beet supplies.

One reason producers find it difficult to boost the supplies of sugar in one part of the world to make up for a shortage elsewhere is that a sugar-making plant costs around $50 million—and that's a lot of money to invest to produce a commodity whose price, given a good crop, could spiral downwards as fast as it has rocketed skywards this year.

Apart from such hefty capital costs, production costs have climbed sharply for the sugar growers this year. Fertilizer prices have increased sharply, partly because of the quadrupling in the price of crude oil—and labor costs, even in the developing, tropical nations, are on a steep upward trajectory.

On the heels of the OPEC nations' collective price-fixing for crude oil, the question in many people's minds is still whether there has not been some conspiratorial cartelization moves by the producer countries.

"No way," says Leslie Palmer, president of Czarnikow Montreal Ltd., world-wide sugar brokers.

"Why would anyone want to hoard sugar now that the price is up five or sixfold? They would be unloading, taking their profits. But there is no sign of this whatsoever.

"As to cartels, they fix prices. The price of sugar has been rising inexorably all year."

There has been heavy buying from the Middle East and this has given rise to guesses about Arab sugar speculations. . . .   [Montreal *Star*]

19
RELIGION, SCIENCE

A. Religion
 1. Promoting Understanding
 2. Church and Politics
 3. Religious Group Pressure
 4. Church News
 5. Reporters' Qualifications
 6. Correct Nomenclature

B. Science
 1. Science News Today
 2. The Newspaper's Responsibility
 3. Major Fields of Interest
  a. Atomic Energy
  b. Space Exploration
  c. Energy and the Environment
 4. The Weather
 5. Reporters' Qualifications

RELIGION

Less than a generation ago a standard Friday or Saturday feature in almost any daily newspaper was a column or page of church notices, listing the times of Sunday services and possibly sermon subjects and announcements of meetings of church organizations throughout the week to come. Today, this Saturday ghetto, as it came to be called by church editors, has disappeared from all except some small dailies and community and suburban weeklies. Newsworthy events involving churches and churchmen, such as appointment or installation of a new pastor, dedication of a new building, a public concert or lecture or the like, are reported throughout the regular news sections on any day of the week.

This desegregation of church news is a consequence of one of the most important changes in journalistic news practices in recent or perhaps all times. It involves a shift of interest from church news to news of religion, including religious ideologies and controversies. Abandoned is the traditional hush-hush policy as regards religious conflict and supercaution to avoid giving the slightest offense to anyone, the longtime policy which had as its commendable purpose the avoidance of ill will and conflict. As Gustavus W. Myers detailed in *A History of Bigotry in the United States* (Random House, 1943), religious intolerance has been severe throughout American history, with virtually every one of the 300 or so denominations which exist in this country having suffered from some sort of discrimination at one time or another. On the whole, however, freedom of religion and separation of church and state, as guaranteed by the Constitution, have worked well for two centuries and nobody, least of all the press, has wanted to stir up trouble.

Promoting Understanding

The abandoning of taboos against anything but gingerly handling of matters involving religious differences does not mean journalistic incitement to bitter divisiveness. Quite the contrary, for the first time normal reporting techniques are being applied to religious news with the intent of transmitting information "across the closed borders of denominational differences and thus making for better mutual understanding," in the words of George Cornell, Associated Press religion editor. To quote him further,

> Since religious education is denominationally segregated for the average person, and since prevailing practice in this country has kept the subject out of the public school classroom, most people have been left largely uninformed or misinformed about each other's religion, and dependent mostly on hearsay or backfence supposition. This has caused one of the deep social sores in America's religiously heterogeneous makeup, and informative reporting across the compartmentalized lines has helped and is helping to make for fuller all-around understanding. And this is one of the values in the information business. Now that the ecumenical movement has exploded all over the map, it is extending the process.

The single event which, more than any other, caused the revolution in the journalistic treatment of religious news was the Second Vatican Council, from 1962 to 1965. The 2,300 Roman Catholic bishops were revealed to have sharp differences on a multitude of matters, both theological and social, thus dispelling forever the myth of unanimity among the leaders of a supposedly monolithic medieval institution. Although Pope John XXIII died in 1963, the liberal reformist spirit which he espoused grew and among the revered ancient practices that were modified was secrecy of deliberations. Perspicacious newsmen explained that most of the supposed new positions, as collegiality, had been debated for decades in scholarly journals, largely in Latin, and the council merely affirmed a consensus that had developed and in some cases, as the role of bishops, represented the unfinished agenda of Vatican Council I in 1870. Commenting on the continued debates, Edward B. "Ted" Fiske of the New York *Times*, declared

> Some future council will have to ratify a new consensus. The difference is that while the last debate was carried on in private, the current one is going on under the glare of publicity and the media in fact become factors in the consensus that will emerge. Many Catholic bishops, among others, will not accept this and still cling to the idea that responsible deliberations can be carried on in secret. This, however, will have to change and already is. Witness the new policies of financial disclosures, semiopen bishops' meetings, news conferences, etc.

Journalistic media now give routine coverage to such news as modernization of the habits of nuns, ending the restriction against eating meat on Fridays, removal from the official liturgical calendar of St. Valentine, St. Christopher and about 200 other erstwhile saints, the unionization of priests and their demands, including an end to celibacy, on their bishops and other matters which formerly were played down or ignored so as not to risk offending anyone. In recent years many nuns and priests have been active in civic affairs, visibly in the streets with civil rights and antiwar protesters. They also have been candidates for public office, often successfully, and have participated in ecumenical movements with Protestants, Jews and other non-Catholics. Priests are organizing, sometimes in labor unions, to advocate reforms, and the complacency of the hierarchy is being shaken by such books as *Infallible? An Inquiry* (Doubleday, 1971), by Hans Kung, eminent Catholic theologian. These and similar developments cause the furor over Paul Blanshard's several books, chiefly *Catholic Power and American Freedom*, which appeared in 1949, to be forgotten. Nevertheless, the long past history of fear, suspicion and conflict cannot be ignored by the journalist in this field. In recent years several denominations, especially the Episcopalians, have become badly split on the issue of ordaining women.

Church and Politics

The timid role of the Roman Catholic church in Mussolini's Italy and Hitler's Germany has been criticized by several recent historians who correctly point out that the wartime and post-wartime power of the Vatican was a matter of widespread alarm, assuaged only by the Vatican's strong anticommunist policies, and disregardful of the ironic fact that outside the Soviet Union—in such nations as Italy, Hungary, Poland and others—the majority of Communists are also Catholics. Postwar fears grew as the American Catholic church became the principal financial support of the worldwide Catholic missionary efforts and contributed heavily to other causes operated from headquarters in Rome. So great was the Protestant protest that President Truman had to abandon plans to name an ambassador to the Vatican. The first Catholic president, John F. Kennedy, helped diminish anti-Catholic fears, especially because of his disagreement with church leaders regarding federal aid to parochial schools and other measures that might infringe upon the traditional principle of separation of church and state.

Nevertheless, it is a historical fact that religious peace up to the immediate past was more apparent than real. For more than a century, religious controversy was at a minimum because the United States was predominantly a Protestant nation. Split into almost 300 sects, Protestants could proselyte each other but, except for the Know Nothings just before the Civil War and the Ku Klux Klan immediately afterward, few felt great alarm over Roman Catholicism. In the late 20th century, however, there is visible evidence of the extent to which the two major divisions of Christianity are pulling even. Church statistics of all sorts are extremely unreliable, because of different methods of counting communicants. The best available indicate that between the two campaigns, 1928 and 1960, in which Catholics were nominees for the presidency, the American Roman Catholic population increased from 19,000,000 to 40,000,000. According to the 1974 *Yearbook of American Churches*, it then grew to 49,000,000. Total church membership for all denominations is given as 131,429,575. Gallup polls showed church attendance was down in 1973 to 40 per cent from a 49 per cent high in 1958. By contrast, the percentages for church attendance in some foreign countries were as follows: Canada, 44; Netherlands, 36; Greece, 26; Australia, 25; Great Britain, 20; Uruguay, 18. Still, total church attendance in the United States during 1973 was 4.4 billion whereas only 290 million attended sports events. Contributions to churches and synagogues totaled $11 billion compared to $221 million in gate receipts at sports events.

All statistics regarding church membership are unreliable because of widely different methods of counting members—some from birth, others from adolescence, etc.—and of dropping nonparticipants from the roles (once a member, always a member is the rule for some but not all). Nevertheless, the best evidence seems to indicate that organized religion is not the factor in the everyday lives of people that it was up to a generation ago. In January 1975 Gallup pollsters reported 62 per cent of all Americans believe religion can answer most of the problems of the day. In 1957 the proportion was 81 per cent. Lip service still is paid to oath taking, prayers and other acts involving faith; but there is not the constant fear of hellfire or of offending unseen deities, nor the desire to placate them by ritual, sacrifice, penance or ordeal. There is less attention to dogma, creed and ceremony, less superstition and mythology and consequently less fanaticism, possibly less or at least a different type of intolerance and/or bigotry. And few if any inquisitions or pogroms. As pot (drugs) lost popularity with youth, esoteric gurus, faith healers, prophets, Satan cultists and lots of hallelujah increased to rival the established churches.

Because the Republicans were entrenched among the upper economic classes, during the second half of the nineteenth century the Democrats made strong appeals to the immigrants who came in waves and settled in the large urban centers to do the most menial work. The social welfare services, developed by Tammany Hall in New York and by other urban Democratic organizations, resulted in the recruitment of most of these new citizens into the Democratic party. They were predominantly from southern Europe and were Roman Catholics. Today, their grandchildren run the city governments of virtually every large city in the United States, although the exodus of the older white elements to the suburbs is increasing the importance of the urban Negro voter and has resulted in the election of several black mayors. The relationship which exists between parishioners and their church is suggested by the appellation usually given the local Catholic archdiocese office. It is Powerhouse, and its opposition to any important public issue jeopardizes its success. Public health commissioners do well to clear promotional matter related to venereal diseases, birth control and some other matters so as not to risk public chastisement. The hierarchy is concerned over assignment of judges to such courts as Juvenile, Divorce, Domestic Relations and Family, and with the attitudes of social welfare workers, hospital administrators and the like.

Religious Group Pressure

At all levels of government, the activities of religious groups interested in censoring motion pictures, plays, magazines, books and the like are opposed by civil libertarians, most strongly represented by the American Civil Liberties Union. A generation ago it was Protestant groups which were most active, censoring books in Boston and fostering laws forbidding the teaching of Darwinism in the South. More recently Catholic groups, as the Legion of Decency and the National Organization for Decent Literature, brought pressure on motion picture theaters, libraries and bookstores and advocated the establishment of official censorship boards. Today, in a period of unparalleled freedom in the arts, religious groups concentrate on encouraging good works rather than condemning poor productions. The Broadcasting and Film Commission of the National Council of Churches (Protestant) and the National Catholic Office of Motion Pictures still comment on films but motion picture critics are not intimidated by them as once was the case. Instead, they pay attention to the Motion Picture Association of America reviews and ratings. The revival of Sunday blue laws, forbidding certain commercial operations, as the sale of used automobiles, is more economic than religious in origin. Such groups as the Jews and Seventh Day Adventists, however, are in opposition for religious reasons. Differences in religious viewpoints certainly are paramount in legislative and public discussion of many matters, as dissemination of birth control information, abolition of anti-abortion laws, easier divorce laws, elimination of restrictions on adoptions by parents with religious backgrounds different from those of the children involved and many more. Growing journalistic practice is to cover such news on its merits, identifying adversaries but emphasizing issues.

The schools probably are the battleground for more religious controversies than any other institution. In the late '40s the United States Supreme Court ruled that school properties cannot be used for religious instruction but that so-called released-time programs, whereby children are excused from school to go elsewhere for religious instruction, are legal. Originally supported by Protestants who feared the effect of the decline in Sunday School attendance, released-time programs now are also approved by Catholics especially in areas where there are no parochial schools. Jews are unalterably opposed. Still to be tested in the United States Supreme Court are shared-time programs whereby parochial school students take some of their work in public schools.

Although the state and federal governments already contribute considerable sums to local boards of education, through such programs as those which provide hot lunches and through the National Defense act and similar legislation, "federal aid to education" is a controversial phrase whenever a bill is before Congress to provide large-scale federal expenditures for school building construction, teachers' salaries or other services. Many Catholics oppose such federal aid unless it is provided parochial as well as public schools and have succeeded in blocking several proposals, even when they were endorsed by the nation's first Roman Catholic president. Catholics argue that free transportation for parochial school students and similar benefits are proper governmental expenditures as they are made to benefit children rather than churches. Under President Johnson's War on Poverty programs such grants multiplied but not without protest from such organizations as Americans United for Separation of Church and State. That group also is attacking sales or gifts of public property to religious instutitions and much tax exemption of church-owned property, especially that not used for strictly religious purposes.

United States Supreme Court decisions outlawing a New York Regents Prayer and compulsory Bible reading in public schools have been followed by attempts, so far unsuccessful, to amend the United States Constitution to permit such practices.

Other controversial matters which may have local angles include compulsory flag salutes or other patriotic exercises to which Jehovah's Witnesses and others may object; compulsory blood transfusions for Jehovah's Witnesses and some others; vaccination and other health requirements repulsive to Christian Scientists; what religious emphasis can be given to Christmas programs without offending Jews; the propriety of Catholics' serving on public school boards; inspection of the quality of education in parochial schools and, most importantly perhaps, legalization of abortion. The lobbying activities of some religious groups may make important journalistic copy, as in the following example:

By James H. Bowman

When the Quakers go to Washington, they go as registered lobbyists—the only church in the country to do so.

Only the 120,000-member Society of Friends has taken the legislative bull by the horns and set up an out-and-out legislative pressure group.

Conservative critics within much larger denominations insist that their own leaders have been doing this without admitting it.

Not so the spiritual descendants of William Penn, who as the son of a British admiral did his own share of hanging around a legislative body (Parliament) to achieve secular ends.

The goal Penn gained was a slice of the New World, then opening for colonists such as he who were looking for a home away from home.

The goals sought by contemporary Quakers in the United States are nothing like that.

The Friends Committee on National Legislation levels its brotherly love guns at the Indochina war, increased military spending and the draft.

They shoot for "a meaningful family assistance program" and a "reordering of national priorities."

In pursuit of the latter, they zero in, without apology to anybody because their committee is not tax-exempt, on electing candidates they think will help these goals.

How do they do it? In an age when denominations are splitting at the seams over issues of social involvement, how do the Quakers get away with this kind of partisanship?

Largely by staying in close contact with the "constituency" that supports the committee, said the director of its Illinois-Wisconsin office this week, Richard Weston.

The committee staff spends roughly half its time going to "meetings" (Quaker language for local churches) explaining themselves and checking out local opinion.

Not all support for the committee comes from Quakers, Weston said, but far more (80 per cent) comes from them than for the American Friends Service Committee, a separate organization that has done such things as deliver medical supplies to North Vietnam.

The legislation committee seeks "to win the assent of reasonable minds," according to a brochure, and so they have to sit and talk with people.

Recent testimony by the legislative committee (a registered lobbyist, recall) before the Senate Finance Committee supported a guaranteed annual income.

"Three years ago, we couldn't have done that," Weston said. "We presented a position paper that was 2½ years in the making, involving constant consultation with Friends. What was presented was the eighth draft of that paper."

Weston thinks the Friends' positions have greater force with congressmen and senators because, unlike veterans' groups seeking pension increases, for instance, they are not out for things that directly benefit themselves.

Some may accuse them of grinding a pacifistic ax. But the thrust of their argument remains "largely moral," he said.

One prominent Washingtonian has proven inaccessible to the Friends, however—a man raised as one, Richard M. Nixon.

When he was vice president, they got to him, Weston said. But Mr. Nixon the President has been unavailable on five different occasions.

The Washington Friends Meeting (hastily formed when Quaker Herbert Hoover came to town in 1929) has been contacted by the White House, however, to see which of them can be cleared for security purposes.

Once cleared, they would be ready to attend one of the celebrated Sunday-morning services when it came time for a Quaker minister to lead it, Weston said.

You couldn't have a Quaker preacher up there, and only one Quaker in the audience, he reasons.   [Chicago *Daily News*]

Offensive to some churchmen, as it is to many others, is the newspaper practice of running daily horoscopes despite the protest of those who say astrology, in addition to being made obsolete by astronomy, involves fatalistic concepts inimical to religious ideas of free will and individual responsibility. Some papers also like to play up claims of visions, revelations and apparently miraculous escapes. Journalistic critics assert that when someone says that the "Man Upstairs" heard his prayers and was responsible for his escape from death, the implication is that others who prayed in vain deserved the fate

that befell them and is a blasphemous assumption. Nevertheless, some newspapers feature such claims and may be prone to inquire of anyone who con-
fronts disaster or experiences sorrow whether he or others involved had
premonitions. Superstition may be perpetuated by the attention paid ESP
(extrasensory perception), spiritualistic seances, flying saucers, astrology,
Loch Ness and other nonexistent monsters, haunted houses and on the
treatment given Friday the 13th, Ground Hog day and similar occasions.
A frequent problem is how to handle the remarks of a public speaker who
insists that God is on his side and condemns others as irreligious, sacrilegious
or atheistic. So many prominent men of affairs take this line that it is difficult
to edit their remarks to delete all such unfounded, unfair and unprovable
expressions. In all probability they speak carelessly rather than from belief in
predestination, which is contrary to the teachings of most churches.

Church News

Although they have disappeared from most large and many small daily
newspapers, church pages still are to be found in small dailies and weeklies.
They usually specialize in announcements of Sunday observances to come
but also publicize special events and meetings of church organizations.

Handling all of this routine church news is time consuming and easy
to the extent that church authorities cooperate in preparing material adequately and on time. Personal acquaintanceships between reporter and
news sources are important so that ill will does not result from mistaken
ideas regarding deadlines and space limitations.

Covering all of the sermons delivered any Sunday in any place of any
size is impossible. Some papers ignore them all. Others "take turns," reporting a minimum but different sample each week. Still others run "A
Reporter Goes to Church" piece written by a staff member who attends a
different church each week. Sometimes these pieces are more than accounts
of particular services and include historical background regarding the church
and possibly an explanation of the major tenets of the denomination. Always,
however, great care is taken not to offend, to explain dogma and ritual
sympathetically from the standpoint of the believer.

Most people know little about religions other than their own. Helping
them understand the faith of others, however, never has been considered
to be a function of periodical journalism. About the only occasion on which
this rule is broken is on a religious holiday.

> The Fall season symbolizes the dwindling of the old year for most people,
> but for those of the Jewish faith, October is the beginning of the new year 5731.
> The solemn new year rites for Jews are known as the High Holy Days and
> begin this year the first day of the new year, Oct. 1, ending Oct. 10.
> The High Holy Days are especially rich in tradition and symbolism, not only
> for those who are Jewish, but for all religions. Described as a period of con-
> fession by Rabbi Bernard Gold of the Parkway Jewish Center, the High Holy
> Days are a "time of individual personal stock-taking." They are 10 days of
> repentance, he said.

The High Holy Days differ from other Jewish holidays because of their personal relevancy. Holidays such as Passover, which marks the exodus of the Jews from Egypt, and the Tabernacles, a special day for the people of Israel, are historical and agricultural. But the High Holy Days may really be observed by all those of all faiths who desire forgiveness from sins against God and man.

"The Jewish religion concentrates on the sins against man," explained Rabbi Gold, "because we feel these are the hardest to forgive and be forgiven."

The High Holy Days begin with the Jewish New Year, Rosh Hashanah. Rosh Hashanah, according to the Bible, is the first day of the seventh month of the year. Because the Jewish calendar is partially lunar and partially solar, it differs from the standard Gregorian calendar. And so the seventh month falls sometime during September or October.

"Tradition," explained Rabbi Gold, "says that the world was created on the first day of the seventh month, which would be Rosh Hashanah."

Beginning with Rosh Hashanah, the Jewish petition to be inscribed in the Book of Life, a legendary book in Jewish religious life. Ten days later, on the Day of Atonement, Yom Kippur, worshippers petition to be sealed in the Book of Life. The Jewish religion has three ways of securing this petition—prayer repentance, and charity.

Yom Kippur is observed by a complete day of services in the synagogue. When it falls on the Sabbath day it is often called the Sabbath of Sabbaths to signify the importance of the Sabbath.

The service on the eve of Yom Kippur is often called the Kol Nidre service, named after the prayer that begins the service.

A fast is observed beginning at Sundown on the eve of Yom Kippur and continuing until sundown of the next day. The purpose is "to put the mind completely on prayer," explained Rabbi Gold.

Yom Kippur also marks the handing down of the second set of Ten Commandments to the Jews. Moses broke the first set given at Pentecost when he discovered the people worshipping a golden calf at the foot of Mt. Sinai. Moses received the second set at Yom Kippur.

The symbol of the zodiac sign of Libra (Sept.-Oct.) the scales, also plays an important role in the Jewish rites. The scales symbolize justice and mercy, which are the emphasis of the High Holy Days.

"The High Holy Days are universal," says Rabbi Gold, "Because anyone may take this time to evaluate his life, whether Jewish or not."

[Penn Hills (Pa.) *Progress*]

An important consequence of the broadened journalistic interest in this field is consideration of theological issues even when there is no specific news peg. Outstanding recent example was the space given in the feature as well as news sections and on the editorial page to the God Is Dead movement. Similarly, it is no longer uncommon to read pros and cons regarding the virginity of Mary, the divinity of Jesus, the probability of miracles and immortality. Even seminarians today debate the necessity of a belief in God. Such issues are quite different from those which engaged the theologians in the past: the proper form of baptism, the reality of transubstantiation, of angels and the like.

Church news is put to the same test as all other news: the extent of its appeal. Thus, an item of interest to only one congregation seldom is used unless it involves something innovative. Comings and goings of pastors and rabbis are news in the same way that changes in business and industry leadership are news. Churches long have been involved in social and welfare work, operating charities, hospitals and other institutions which often are newsworthy. Even such news is more valuable if related to outside issues and interests. The leadership provided civil rights, antiwar and other groups by church leaders such as Martin Luther King in Alabama, Father James Groppi in Milwaukee, the Berrigan brothers and others made plenty of front page news.

Reporters' Qualifications

According to the late Richard Cardinal Cushing of Boston, "It is not too much to suppose that the time is coming when we will expect the religious news reporter to have attended, for some time at least, a school of theology or divinity or religion; that he is in simple terms an expert in his own work."

Quite obviously Cardinal Cushing believed that a journalist with training in any religion would be able to report fairly news of other denominations. Editors are coming to be of the same opinion. Edward B. "Ted" Fiske of the New York *Times* is a Presbyterian minister, William B. MacKaye of the Washington *Post* had a year at General Theological Seminary and other religion news writers similarly have had specialized training. All leading publications are represented among the 108 members of the Religious Newswriters' Association, formed in 1945. The object of its Newsletters is to advance professional standards in the secular press.

The Religious News Service was established in 1933 as an independently managed agency of the National Conference of Christians and Jews. It has both a daily and a weekly service for more than 800 news outlets. "Its objective reporting promotes understanding among diverse groups of issues which may be divisive, and thus contributes to national unity," RNS contends, Served by a global network of nearly 1,000 professional journalists who search out and develop stories of interest to the religious constituency, RNS also provides a daily photo service.

There are also the Catholic Press Association, which operates the National Catholic News Service, and the Associated Church Press for Protestants. Since 1953 there has existed the James Supple award given annually for excellence in reporting religious news in the secular press, named in honor of James Supple of the Chicago *Sun*, who was killed in an air crash in 1950 while en route to Korea. Since 1970 there also has been an award memorializing the late Harold Schachern, religion editor of the Detroit *News*. It is given for editing a church page or religion section in the secular press. In 1974 the Louis Cassels award was created in honour of the late UPI religion writer. It is for papers with circulations under 50,000.

The expertise needed by a religious journalist was stressed by Sanche de Gramont in an article, "Covering the Ecumenical Council," in the September 1965 *Nieman Reports*:

The reporter must penetrate the mechanisms of the council, learn its vocabulary, be alive to the significance of an apparently trivial event such as a change in the order of seating (at first, the patriarchs were seated after the cardinals, then, across from the cardinals, to make it clear that in rank they were not less than the cardinals, a clarification of Vatican policy), and build up sources who can fill in the omissions in the daily communique. The historian must consider the day's story in terms of church evolution. A vote allowing married men to become deacons seems pointless unless one knows what the Catholic position on ecclesiastical celibacy has been over the centuries. The much abused term "collegiality" is meaningless outside the context of papal infallibility voted at the First Vatican Council in 1870. The theologian must consider collegiality in terms of the apostolic succession, that is Christ's passing on the succession of his church to Peter and the apostles. He must also reconcile the Pope's supreme and total authority with the powers handed down to the bishops. The prophet must evaluate the impact of collegiality on the church, and show how the existing institutions will be modified when the bishops' share in the government of the church is defined.

George Cornell, religion editor of the Associated Press, believes that modern readers are much better educated and informed so that they recognize words related to science and technology—as radiation, astronaut, genealogy and electrocardiograph—but are stumped when it comes to such elementary religious terms as atonement, apostolic succession, mystical body, presbyter and justification of faith. It is the responsibility of the specialist religion writer to promote public enlightenment.

A *Christianity Today* survey in March 1971 resulted in replies from 180 religion news reporters for the secular media out of 460 who were queried. Of them 146 said they hold church or synagogue membership; 107 said they are active in local congregations and 25 are active in a larger unit of their denomination.

Correct Nomenclature

When he was religious news editor of the Nashville *Tennessean*, the Rev. James W. Carty Jr., professor of journalism at Bethany (W. Va.) College, prepared the following warning:

> Incorrect use of titles in the reporting of church news discourages reader interest, but correct use helps build confidence in the reliability of the news, feature and interpretative articles.
> In fact, the wrong designations can draw some hot protests. The appropriate bring grateful letters or phone calls.
> A reporter has to be cautious lest he use the wrong synonym for the sake of variety.
> An example concerns the different designations for the spiritual heads of the church. Many terms are available. They include the Reverend, Rabbi, priest, minister, pastor, evangelist clergyman, father, brother. Actually, these concepts have different meanings. Some are interchangeable with different denominations; others are not.

A Catholic priest would be called the Reverend or Father and lives in the rectory. A Monsignor is the Rt. Rev.; a bishop, the Most Reverend; a nun, Sister.

Christian Science has practitioners, lecturers, readers. A title would be Reader John Jones.

The words reverend, pastor, doctor, or clergyman would not be used for the Church of Christ minister or evangelist. Two other correct terms for addressing them are preacher or brother.

An Episcopal clergyman, a deacon or priest, would be called the Reverend, and lives in the rectory. A dean is the Very Reverend. A bishop is the Right Reverend; an archbishop, of which there are none in the United States, would be called the Most Reverend.

A Jewish clergyman would be called Rabbi or Doctor if he holds that degree.

The Lutheran designation would be Pastor John Jones or the Reverend.

A Methodist pastor, minister or preacher also would be called the Reverend. The Episcopal head is Bishop John Jones, never the Right or Most Reverend.

Seventh-day Adventist pastors are addressed as Elder.

Presbyterian ministers also are called the Reverend Mister. Their residence is the manse.

Groups also are concerned about their title. Most resent being called a sect.

America's two largest indigenous groups, the Christian Church (Disciples of Christ) and Church of Christ, do not want to be called denominations. They prefer brotherhood or religious movement.

Other groups are careful about stating the power of conventions. For example, Southern Baptists and Christian churches (Disciples of Christ) are careful to point out that the convention resolutions are not binding on congregations, which are autonomous. Both groups use the title the Reverend for pastors, preachers, ministers.

And editors, remember also not to displease women. Don't call their presbyterial a presbytery.

SCIENCE

After 400 years of virtually incessant scientific discoveries disastrous to ignorance and superstition, there remain sizable minorities who are apparently unaffected by or antagonistic to such iconoclasts as Galileo Galilei, Sir Isaac Newton, Charles Darwin and Albert Einstein. Symbolically, astronauts recite the mythological Story of Creation from Genesis while circling the moon and newspapers feature daily horoscopes and give serious treatment to astrology, spiritualism, clairvoyance, extrasensory perception, sea monsters, poltergeists, haunted houses, fortune telling, faith healing, miraculous escapes, premonitions, flying saucers, reincarnation, good and bad luck charms, professional soothsayers' prophecies and the like.

Not so easily disregarded as the philosophical and ethical implications of scientific knowledge are the tangible evidences of applied science. Since World War II, no matter what the effect on their preconceptions, few have been able to ignore (1) the release of atomic energy, (2) space exploration and (3) the critical state of pollution of air and water and the depletion of natural resources in an overpopulated world. It is called an Age of Science. In view of man's stubborn refusal or inability to accept the deeper implications of reality, as it has been revealed, the present would more properly be called an Age of Technology. Today the average man tinkers with his television set, automobile and household electrical appliances, takes motion pictures, dreams of owning his own airplane and uses scientific or technical language unknown just a few years ago. The Jules Verne science fiction novels of his great-grandfather's day and the Tom Swift and Boy Aviators yarns that commanded his grandfather's attention are old stuff to modern youth. So, in fact, are the science fiction magazines of his own boyhood, so rapidly has fact caught up with imaginative fiction.

Actually there is no such thing as Science. Rather, there are sciences, scores of them, man-made categorizations for convenience in studying and utilizing knowledge. A generation ago high schools offered courses in physics, chemistry and biology and that was presumed to about cover the field. Today it takes three solid pages just for the table of contents of *A Guide to Science Reading* (Signet Science Library), compiled and edited by Hilary T. Deason of the American Association for the Advancement of Science. Take one of the shortest main sections, "Earth Sciences." Listed are History of Geology, Geophysics, Oceanography-Physical, Meteorology and Paleontology. So specialized is knowledge becoming that the experts, who know more and more about less and less, find it difficult to converse with each other, even in closely related fields.

Science News Today

As the awful power of science to make the planet uninhabitable became apparent, the absolute necessity for everyone's understanding something of the implications of scientific progress (?) became recognized.

Even before the atom bomb and sputniks, newspapers had awakened to their social responsibility as regards science. The remarkable improvement, in completeness of coverage, in accuracy and clarity of writing and, in general, in social purpose, followed years of misunderstanding and consequent inadequate cooperation between scientific writers and scientists. Out of the name-calling came a mutual decision to "get together" in a common program to protect the public against false science and to assist it in obtaining the maximum benefit from what the experimental laboratories and the scholars' studies are revealing daily, almost hourly.

By assigning to scientific news, men with sufficient training to talk the language of those whom they must interview, newspapers have broken down much of the reluctance of inventors, medical men and theoretical scientists to give information to the press. Whatever hesitancy to cooperate remains results from several factors: fear of being considered a publicity seeker, fear of revealing the nature of an experiment before absolute proof has been obtained, a feeling that one's fellow scientists deserve to hear of a new scientific fact or theory for the first time at a learned gathering, fear of being misquoted, doubt of the reporter's ability to translate a technical matter into popular terms, fear that improper emphasis will be given to sensational, unimportant aspects of a news item.

On the other hand, partly through the pressure of well-intentioned journalists, many leading scientists have come to realize the value to them of sharing their findings with the public, of their social obligation to do so and of the sincerity of a vast majority of present-day newspapermen in attempting to do a completely honest and creditable job. Scientists and writers cooperate to combat "quacks."

Dr. Irvine H. Page described the lingering doubts of many medical men in an article in *Modern Medicine* which *Saturday Review* reprinted Feb. 3, 1968. After expressing shock because of a television offer of $50,000 to a patient for exclusive rights to broadcast his heart transplant operation, Dr. Page wrote,

> There are two aspects of reporting. The one concerns publicity after a discovery is reasonably established and reported in a scientific publication; the other concerns the precipitate announcement to the press of the discovery of a new procedure, especially one of magnitude, before it has been adequately tested. An example of the first was the discovery of insulin and its use in diabetes. The most recent example of the other is the artificial heart.

Only by adherence to the highest ethical principles can editors and reporters retain the confidence of public-spirited scientists in all fields. It is unrealistic to condemn the press for sensationalizing science when so much scientific news cannot be described by any word other than sensational. To be guarded against is the faker or publicity seeker. A century and a half ago the New York *Sun* could get away with its hoax concerning life on the moon because of public ignorance. Today such a hoax would succeed for exactly the opposite reason: because the "impossible" has happened so many times there is nobody willing to doubt anything. If the astronauts had declared the dark side of the moon, never visible to earthlings, is inhabited, they would have been believed. The same is true of virtually any item of science fiction posing as fact. In some regards science has made man more, not less, gullible and credulous.

On the other hand, there must be caution so as not to uphold orthodox scientists who are as adamant as religious fundamentalists in resisting new ideas destructive to some of their own pet theories and systems of thought. Scientists can be as fanatical and narrow-minded as defenders of the faith, no matter what. A classic example was provided by the threat of several of America's leading astronomers to boycott all Macmillan textbooks unless the company discontinued publication of *Worlds in Collision* by Immanuel Velikovsky. Similar violent opposition also was shown the same author's other books, all published by Doubleday, which has no textbook department. They are *Ages in Chaos*, *Earth in Upheaval* and *Oedipus and Akhnaton*. More than a decade later many of Velikovsky's theories were validated by Mariner and other space flights.

Journalists also must be mindful of the depth and breadth of the revolt within the organized ranks of scientists by peace-minded and socially conscious, mostly younger, persons who object to the extent to which their older colleagues have cooperated with the military-industrial establishment in promoting the war effort, mainly by the development of weapons inimical to the continuation of life on this planet. Newsgatherers must realize that in most part they are dealing with businessmen, that few pure scientists have kept their purity. Rather, they seek to make discoveries of value to their commercial or military employers. Student recognition of this situation is a strong contributing factor to widespread campus unrest.

In view of the attention now given atomic energy, other energy sources, space exploration, pollution control and other recent scientific topics, it is difficult to recall that newspapers of the past virtually ignored Robert Fulton, Charles Darwin, Samuel F. B. Morse and the Wright brothers.

The Newspaper's Responsibility

In the stories of sufferers from virulent diseases who have been given pathetic false hope because of premature announcements of new cures, of lives and fortunes which have been lost because of misplaced confidence in inventions, and of persecution and injustice resulting from unscientific superstition is implied the social responsibility of the newspaper as regards scientific news. Likewise, for that matter, is implied the duty that the reputable scientist has not only to maintain proper caution himself but to discipline his fellows as well.

The rise of science, since primitive man thought the sun was alive, moving across the sky each day, and attempted to cajole the unseen forces to his own gain, has been one of overcoming the obstacles which ignorance and tradition have put in the way of knowledge. The present, however, truly is a scientific age and a major theory or discovery in any branch of science may have tremendous effect upon man's way of living and his manner of thinking.

What scientists deplore is reporting which they consider "shallow, inept and totally lacking in scope and understanding," to use the phraseology which Dr. Jonathan Karas of the Lowell Technological Institute applied to the radio and television handling of the first manned Soviet orbital space flight. Dr. Karas said,

> Apparently, most networks and local stations had done little background scientific research in preparing for an event that was inevitable and sent anyone available to interview local scientists. Consequently, the public, eager to learn the details of what had happened, was subjected to answers to shop-worn questions such as: "Is this significant?" "When will the Russians land on Mars?" "Does this mean that the United States is behind in space travel?" Such questions, to which obvious answers are apparent, left some of the scientists being interviewed staring in amazement.
>
> The reason was obvious. Newscasters well qualified to report on fires or con-

duct man-on-the-street interviews were suddenly asked by their stations to interview scientists about a scientific feat—they found themselves good reporters caught in the wrong language so they pulled out the standard questions—nondefinitive and lackluster. . . .

Since 1957, radio and television stations have been informing the public about lack of a definitive educational plan, lack of American understanding, and other changes which must be made. Yet these same stations have made no moves to obtain scientific counsel in preparing to report scientific news to the public. They should learn a lesson from the progressive newspapers and periodicals who recognize the value of science writers and editors to cover and report on scientific news.

Scientists are appalled when some journalist refers indiscriminately to a new scientific announcement as a "major breakthrough" or "major advance" or "a key to life." They deplore journalistic playing up and exaggerating the significance of a medical or scientific contribution.

A point the scientists have conceded, in the face of evidence, is that dramatizing an item of scientific news does not destroy its educational value. Austin H. Clark, eminent biologist, for instance, once confessed that he would not object to a newspaper article beginning

Those unfeeling mothers who leave their babies on the doorsteps of prosperous people's houses have their counterparts among the birds. . . .

as a popular translation of a scientific paper in which he might declare

Most cuckoos, the honey-guides of Africa, the weaver finches, some hangnests, our cow birds, the rice-grackle, a south American duck, and, according to recent information, one of the paradise birds, lay their eggs in nests of the other birds which hatch these eggs and raise the young.

Journalism professors Michael Ryan of Temple University and James W. Tankard Jr. of the University of Texas studied "Problem Areas in Science News Reporting, Writing and Editing" and made these recommendations:

1. Science reporters, like reporters in other areas (such as government), should dig for information beyond the publicity handout.

2. Science reporters should use journal articles and published reports to verify and improve the accuracy of their stories. They should not rely solely on interviews with scientists.

3. Science reporters should resist the temptation to exaggerate or oversimplify in a lead sentence for the purpose of attracting reader interest; many scientists report that "catchy" leads distort their findings.

4. Science reporters should pay particular attention to quoting sources accurately and in context. This may be more important in science than in other areas of news because of the care with which scientists use language.

5. Science reporters should be cautious in introducing lay terminology that the scientist himself did not actually use. Scientists often object to such terminology and find it inaccurate.

6. Science reporters should be wary of interpreting a scientist's technical conclusions, as scientists often think such interpretations are misleading.

7. Science reporters should avoid the temptation to sensationalize information about science. As one responding scientist pointed out, progress in science is slow and often does not make "good copy."

8. Science reporters should avoid using the words "cure" and "breakthrough" unless the scientist himself approves the use of the words in describing his work.

9. Science reporters should consider giving information sources an opportunity to review articles or parts of articles for accuracy before publication. Such a review can be done with the reporter still making the final editorial decision, and it might help prevent serious inaccuracies.

10. Headline writers should resist the temptation to put simplistic, cute, or "scare" headlines on science stories.

11. Make-up editors should be aware that the practice of cutting news stories from the bottom to fit available space may not apply very well to science stories, as science articles often need to be reported completely to make sense.

12. Finally, scientists themselves should accept their share of the responsibility for accurate communication of science information to the public. In the words of one of the responding scientists, they should learn to "think about their work [in] a simple and adequate manner that the layman can understand."

Dr. Dael Wolfle, executive officer of the American Association for the Advancement of Science, has lamented: "The chief thing wrong with science news writing is the audience. The average reader does not know enough about science to let the reporter do his best job."

That is the challenge. That is the opportunity.

Major Fields of Interest

ATOMIC ENERGY

William Laurence, New York *Times* science editor, was in the air over Nagasaki when the second atomic bomb was dropped on Japan in August 1945. He had been privy to the secret experimentations at Oak Ridge, Tenn., Los Alamos, N.M., and other places and had the confidence of both the military and scientific authorities. By now it is known to every schoolboy that there is no secret regarding how nuclear energy is released. The atomic armaments race was over the technological details of the destructive weapon, and the speed with which the Soviet Union produced its own bomb proved that the scientists who opposed secrecy were correct.

From the start the tremendous scientific breakthrough, for which basic credit goes to Albert Einstein, has served the purposes of politicians and militarists more than it has private industry or the common man. It was a shocker when the Nobel prize-winning Englishman P. M. R. Blackett published his *Fear, War and the Bomb* in 1948 and revealed that the strategic purpose of bombing Hiroshima was to try to keep the Russians from honoring their Yalta Conference pledge to enter the war; the bomb's use was unnecessary in order to defeat the Japanese. Since then many others, including former Secretary of State James F. Byrnes, have confirmed the Blackett revelation. A foreign journalist, Robert Jungk, wrote two books to depict the awfulness that the atomic age already had produced. They are *Brighter than 10,000 Stars* and *The Future Is Already Here.*

The United States Atomic Energy Commission has an 80-page book, *Nuclear Terms, a Brief Glossary*, whose original compiler was James D. Lyman of the AEC Division of Public Information.

SPACE EXPLORATION

The debate over how much and what next in the space exploration program also has been more political and financial than scientific, much to the disgust of many journalists as well as scientists. Too often it has seemed that the launchings at Cape Canaveral were conducted in a circus atmosphere. Hundreds of journalists seated in bleachers had less opportunity to observe details than television watchers. The reporter has had to be alert to distinguish between a publicity or political propaganda stunt and a genuinely important event; and the science writer's task has been made difficult by extravagant announcements of innovations in several governmental programs, space and missiles prominently. The idea altogether too often has been to beat the Russians regardless of need or value of the venture. Government-imposed secrecy has, of course, been the biggest handicap of all to adequate coverage.

No further proof of the extent to which journalistic science writing has developed exists than the book *We Are Not Alone* (McGraw-Hill, 1964) by Walter Sullivan, science editor of the New York *Times*. It is a masterful job of collating the evidence for conscious life somewhere else in outer space. It made predictions which Mariner flights verified. No amateur scientist Sullivan, and he is not alone. Another masterly job by Sullivan is *Continents in Motion, the New Earth Debate* (McGraw-Hill, 1974).

The basic authority for writers in the space exploration field is the *Dictionary of Technical Terms for Aerospace Use*, National Aeronautics and Space Administration SP-7, 1965. What follows is a condensed version of the glossary attached to the press kit for Apollo X.

Ablating materials. Special heat-dissipating materials on the surface of a spacecraft that vaporize during reentry.

Accelerometer. An instrument to sense accelerative forces and convert them into corresponding electrical quantities usually for controlling, measuring, indicating or recording purposes.

Adapter skirt. A flange or extension of a stage or section that provides a ready means of fitting another stage or section to it.

Antipode. Point on surface of planet exactly 180 degrees opposite from reciprocal point on a line projected through center of body. In Apollo usage, antipode refers to a line from the center of the Moon through the center of the Earth and projected to the Earth surface on the opposite side. The antipode crosses the mid-Pacific recovery line along the 165th meridian of longitude once each 24 hours.

Apocynthion. Point at which object in lunar orbit is farthest from the lunar surface—object having been launched from body other than Moon. (*Cynthia*, Roman goddess of Moon.)

Apogee. The point at which a moon or artificial satellite in its orbit is farthest from Earth.

Apolune. Point at which object launched from the Moon into lunar orbit is farthest from lunar surface, e.g.: ascent stage of lunar module after staging into lunar orbit following lunar landing.

Attitude. The position of an aerospace vehicle as determined by the inclination of its axes to some frame of reference; for Apollo, and inertial, space-fixed reference is used.

Burnout. The point when combustion ceases in a rocket engine.

Canard. A short, stubby winglike element affixed to the launch escape tower to provide CM blunt end forward aerodynamic capture during an abort.

Celestial guidance. The guidance of a vehicle by reference to celestial bodies.

Cislunar. Adjective referring to space between Earth and the Moon, or between Earth and Moon's orbit.

Closed loop. Automatic control units linked together with a process to form an endless chain.

Deboost. A retrograde maneuver which lowers either perigree or apogee of an orbiting spacecraft. Not to be confused with deorbit.

Declination. Angular measurement of a body above or below celestial equator, measured north or south along the body's hour circle. Corresponds to Earth surface latitude.

Delta V. Velocity change.

Down-link. The part of a communication system that receives, processes and displays data from a spacecraft.

Entry corridor. The final flight path of the spacecraft before and during Earth reentry.

Ephemeris. Orbital measurements (apogee, perigee, inclination, period, etc.) of one celestial body in relation to another at given times. In spaceflight, the orbital measurements of a spacecraft relative to the celestial body about which it orbited.

Escape velocity. The speed a body must attain to overcome a gravitational field, such as that of Earth; the velocity of escape at the Earth's surface is 36,700 feet-per-second.

Fairing. A piece, part of structure having a smooth, streamlined outline, used to cover a nonstreamlined object or to smooth a junction.

Fuel cell. An electrochemical generator in which the chemical energy from the reaction of oxygen and a fuel is converted directly into electricity.

g or g force. Force exerted upon an object by gravity or by reaction to acceleration or deceleration, as in a change of direction: one g is the measure of force required to accelerate a body at the rate of 32.16 feet-per-second.

Inertial guidance. Guidance by means of the measurement and integration of acceleration from on board the spacecraft. A sophisticated automatic navigation system using gyroscopic devices, accelerometers, etc., for high-speed vehicles. It absorbs and interprets such data as speed, position, etc., and automatically adjusts the vehicle to a predetermined flight path. Essentially, it knows where it's going and where it is by knowing where it came from and how it got there. It does not give out any radio frequency signal so it cannot be detected by radar or jammed.

Injection. The process of boosting a spacecraft into a calculated trajectory.

Insertion. The process of boosting a spacecraft into an orbit around the Earth or other celestial body.

Multiplexing. The simultaneous transmission of two or more signals within a single channel. The three basic methods of multiplexing involve the separation of signals by time division, frequency division and phase division.

Optical navigation. Navigation by sight, as opposed to inertial methods, using stars or other visible objects as reference.

Oxidizer. In a rocket propellant, a substance such as liquid oxygen or nitrogen tetroxide which supports combustion of the fuel.

Penumbra. Semi-dark portion of a shadow in which light is partly cut off, e.g.: surface of Moon or Earth away from Sun where the disc of the Sun is only partly obscured.

Pericynthion. Point nearest Moon of object in lunar orbit—object having been launched from body other than Moon.

Perigee. Point at which a Moon or an artificial satellite in its orbit is closest to the Earth.

Perilune. The point at which a satellite (e.g.: a spacecraft) in its orbit is closest to the Moon. Differs from pericynthion in that the orbit is Moon-originated.

Reentry. The return of a spacecraft that reenters the atmosphere after flight above it.

Retrorocket. A rocket that gives thrust in a direction opposite to the direction of the object's motion.

S-band. A radiofrequency band of 1,550 to 5,200 megahertz.

Selenographic. Adjective relating to physical geography of Moon. Specifically, positions on lunar surface as measured in latitude from lunar equator and in longitude from a reference lunar meridian.

Sidereal. Adjective relating to measurement of time, position or angle in relation to the celestial sphere and the vernal equinox.

State vector. Ground-generated spacecraft position, velocity and timing information uplinked to the spacecraft computer for crew use as a navigational reference.

Terminator. Separation line between lighted and dark portions of celestial body which is not self luminous.

Umbra. Darkest part of a shadow in which light is completely absent, e.g.: surface of Moon or Earth away from Sun where the disc of the Sun is completely obscured.

Up-link data. Information fed by radio signal from the ground to a spacecraft.

Yaw. Angular displacement of a space vehicle about its vertical (Z) axis.

For the rest of this century the most significant journalistic assignment probably increasingly will be what already is known as the Survival Story— how to provide enough energy for the ever-growing human race without degrading the planet to the point where it is uninhabitable. There will be incidents: oil slicks, leakages of radioactive and other dangerous material, controversial oil and gas pipelines, community protests against construction of energy power production plants, air pollution including degradation of the ozone layer, forest fire prevention, legislation to regulate strip mining, rules for fishing and hunting to protect endangered species—mammal, marine, bird and plant. Such stories are covered objectively as spot news. However, editors rapidly are realizing that the total picture is broader than any single event and one of the most demanding and challenging journalistic specialties of the immediate future is bound to be this.

Perspective is important as in all areas. The conservation movement began early in the century under Theodore Roosevelt and Gifford Pinchot. It attracted mostly hunters who were interested in all natural resources but recognized that if the earth became unfit for wildlife to inhabit it soon wouldn't be habitable for men. They saw nature as a giant mosaic; if you remove one piece (wildlife, or even a single species), you may destroy the whole. Alda Leopold, "father of the conservation ethic," perceived that the key to wildlife survival was the protection of the wildlife habitat. Licensed and regulated hunting which protects threatened or endangered species and takes only surplus animals is not a threat to wildlife; in fact, it prevents overpopulation of predators, starvation, overgrazing and destruction of habitat. Destruction of habitat by bulldozers, pesticides, pollutants, etc. is the threat not only to wildlife but also to the quality of human life.

Most of the old line conservation organizations still have a special interest in wildlife. Among the most important of them are the Audubon Society and the Izaak Walton League. The National Wildlife Federation, representing 53 state and territorial groups, with a membership of about 3.5 million, was an outgrowth of a 1936 conference called by President Franklin D. Roosevelt "to bring together all interested organizations, agencies and individuals in behalf of restoration of land, water, forests and wildlife resources."

The publication in 1962 of Rachel Carson's *Silent Spring* awakened many to the enormity of the problem of the delicate ecological interrelationships of wildlife and man and to the perils of pollution. Among the resulting new groups are the Sierra Club, Wilderness Society, Friends of the Earth, Environmental Policy Center, Environmental Action, Zero Population Growth, Center for Science in the Public Interest, Citizens Committee on Natural Resources and scores of others listed in the *Conservation Directory* published by the National Wildlife Federation, 1412 Sixteenth St. NW, Washington, D.C. 20036, an essential reference. Ralph Nader's Public Interest Research Group also has ongoing projects in water pollution and nuclear power. It is engaged mostly in litigation whereas some of the other groups lobby or engage in public educational activities.

The obstacles to success for environmental programs are moneyed interests—oil companies, gun manufacturers, lumbermen and innumerable others. They plead the needs of the public for their services and insist they must not be hampered in their search for raw materials, even when they are exploitive. There is no denying that the demand for more power and gadgets has increased and that today's luxuries usually become tomorrow's necessities.

Foremost among newspapermen in stressing the importance of this field is Gladwin Hill of the New York *Times*. What follows are quotations from his article "Are We Booting the Big Story Again?" in the December 1969 *Bulletin* of the American Society of Newspaper Editors:

> There seems to be a widespread lack of recognition that environmental deterioration is not just a random series of occurrences and conditions, but a revolutionary development—the world's most pervasive epidemic, if you will; one integrated, continuing story, transcending in importance and duration the Vietnam War, WW 2 or any other story you could name, not excluding the day-to-day *saga* from the nation's capital; and an unawareness that the story must be conveyed to the public in its true dimension. . . .
>
> Air pollution, water pollution, refuse disposal are not detached phenomena; they are all facets of the one suddenly pressing problem of disposing of our wastes, on the surface of a spherical spaceship of very limited capacity. National parks, wild rivers, freeways, vanishing species and even excess population can be viewed as another aspect of the environmental problem: the critical question of land use.
>
> It's later than most people think. Meteorologists are pointing out that the permanent contamination of the atmosphere by combustion products is lowering worldwide temperatures measurably—and that the Ice Age represented only a general four degree temperature difference from what obtains now. . . .
>
> It is not altogether surprising that there is journalist laggardness in this area. The environmental story is probably the toughest story newspapers have ever had to come to grips with. They are inherently oriented to the status quo, to the established order—governmental, economic and social. Their forte has always been reporting deviations from this norm.
>
> But the environmental story peculiarly involves the rejection of much of the status quo—rejection of prevailing physical condition, rejection of economic mores and governmental mechanisms that have permitted these conditions to come about, rejection of the shibboleth of bigness, rejection even of the hallowed function of endlessly reproducing the human species.
>
> Much air pollution comes from local industry, a sacred cow. Water pollution comes either from industry or from inadequate sewage treatment that local officials haven't had the gumption or the public support to improve. . . .
>
> The biggest environmental problem is the global population explosion.

The following glossary was prepared by Robert F. Kunz, executive vice president of the Connecticut Conservation Association which has approved its reproduction here after its original appearance in the Jan. 2, 1971, *Saturday Review*.

The following glossary is intended as a guide to some of the more common terms appearing in our news media, related to the current crisis concerning the quality of our environment.

Airshed.   A common air supply demarcated by arbitrary or convenient borders, such as an urban area.

Allowable release levels.   Levels of nuclear radiation that are officially accepted as harmless to humans. Some scientists claim there is no radiation level below which genetic damage, cancer, or shortening of life does not occur.

Aquifers.   Underground water-bearing rock strata that supply most of our well water.

Biodegradable.   Organic susbstance that is quickly broken down by normal environmental processes.

Biological magnification.   The process whereby an organism can build up and store quantities of a substance vastly in excess of the average concentration in its environment. For example, oysters can extract pesticides to 80,000 times the amount in the water around them.

Biosphere.   That envelope made up of the Earth's waters, land crust, and atmosphere where all organisms, including man, live.

Biota.   All living organisms, both plant and animal, of a region or period.

BOD.   The biological oxygen demand of aquatic organisms for survival.

Carcinogen.   A substance capable of provoking cancer.

Chlorinated hydrocarbons.   Insecticides that last for years or decades, travel around the globe in the air and water, and accumulate in hazardous concentrations in the tissues of non-target animals. Examples are: DDT, DDD, Endrin, TDE, Aldrin, Dieldrin, Toxaphene, Heptachlor, and Lindane (BHC).

Coliform bacteria.   Microscopic one-celled organisms that are always but not exclusively present in human intestines.

Compost.   A mixing of garbage and degradable trash with soil in a pile. Bacteria in the soil cause decomposition and thereby return desirable organic material back to nature.

Decibel.   The unit of measuring the intensity of sound. Zero on the decibel scale is the slightest sound that can be heard by humans—rustling leaves, breathing. The scale: EARDRUM RUPTURES (140 decibels—jet taking off), DEAFENING (100 decibles—thunder, car horn at three feet, loud motorcycle, loud power lawn mower), VERY LOUD (eighty decibels—portable sander, food blender; continued exposure brings about loss of hearing, impossible to use phone); LOUD (sixty decibels—city playground, average restaurant or living room); FAINT (twenty decibels—courtroom or classroom, private office, a whisper at five feet).

Decomposers.   Living plants and animals, chiefly fungi and bacteria, that live by extracting energy from the tissues of dead plants and animals.

Demography.   The study of populations—births, deaths, marriages, etc.—by means of statistics.

Ecocide.   A substance which enters, permeates, and kills an entire system, be that system an insect pest, a lake, or a man-environment community.

Ecosystem.   An integrated unit or "system" in nature, sufficient unto itself, to be studied as a separate entity—e.g., a rotting log in the forest, a coral atoll, a continent, or the Earth with all its biota.

Effluent.   A discharge from an exit that is relatively self-contained, such as an industrial smokestack, nuclear power plant thermal plume, or a sewage treatment plant; generally carrying pollutants.

Energy cycle. The process by which the energy of the sun is passed from one living organism to another or is stored, as in coal or oil.

Environment. All that surrounds a designated ecosystem.

Estuary. A coastal area of high marine productivity where fresh and salt waters mingle, including the associated tidal rivers, marshes, flats, lagoons, bays, and shallow sounds.

Eutrophication. An aging process that occurs to aquatic ecosystems naturally over a long period of time. Nutrients entering the water support an increasingly dense growth of aquatic life, which depletes the oxygen supply. In time, the body of water progresses from lake or pond to swamp, marsh, and meadow. Eutrophication can be accelerated by excessive nutrient enrichment resulting from man-made fertilizers, detergents, and human and animal wastes.

Green revolution. The hoped-for arithmetical increase in agricultural production that would provide food for the geometrically increasing human population.

Greenhouse effect. The effect of pollutants in the air that absorb infrared or heat rays and so prevent the radiation back into space of a certain fraction of the energy Earth receives from the sun.

Herbicide. A kind of chemical that injures or kills plant life by interfering with normal growth.

Hydrology. The study of water in all its forms and manifestations in the biosphere.

Inversion. An atmospheric condition occurring when a layer of cool air sits on a layer of hot air and prevents the warmer air from rising. If the stagnant hot air is heavily polluted, it becomes increasingly harmful to life.

Nitrogen fixation. The process whereby bacteria and other soil microorganisms convert atmospheric nitrogen into nitrates, which become available to growing plants.

Non-renewable resources. Resources that once used (or misused) cannot renew themselves. For example: coal, oil.

Particulates. Dust and soot in the air.

Phosphates. Salts and esters of phosphoric acid, containing phosphorus.

Photosynthesis. The photochemical process by which the energy in light, acting in presence of a catalyst—such as the pigment chlorophyll—converts atmospheric carbon dioxide, water, and inorganic salts into tissue. The fundamental food-making process in green plants on which all life on Earth directly or indirectly depends.

Plankton. The microscopic floating plant and animal organisms of lakes, rivers, and oceans. Basic organisms in the food chains leading to the large fishes and aquatic mammals. A critical source of oxygen for the entire world.

Pollution. The condition of any system unable to recleanse itself.

Producers. Green plants upon which all other living things ultimately depend.

Pumped storage power plant. A technological device designed to supply extra electric power during peak-load periods. At those hours (late evening, early morning) when extra power is available, water is pumped from a lower to an upper reservoir. During the periods of peak-load demand (beginning and end of the workday), the stored water is dropped through turbines to produce the needed power.

Recycling.   The reutilization of natural resources and man-made products.
Renewable resources.   Those biological resources which renew themselves by
  growth and reproduction.
Smog.   As originally defined in England, smoke plus fog equals smog. It has
  come to mean air that is heavily contaminated with particulates, nitrogen
  oxides, and waste hydrocarbons.
Sonic boom.   Shock wave produced by movement of objects through the
  atmosphere at speeds faster than the speed of sound.
Symbiosis.   The association of two or more organisms for mutual benefit.
Thermal pollution.   The ejection of heated water into the environment, usually
  aquatic ecosystems, raising the temperature above normal limits.
Trophic level.   The energy level at which an organism sustains itself.
Wetland.   Inland—any area that is more or less regularly wet or flooded, where
  the water table stands at or above the land surface for at least part of the
  year. Coastal—land types such as salt marshes, tidal marshes, and brackish
  marshes subject to saline and/or tidal influences.

THE WEATHER

With maps, charts, illustrations and other devices, serious and "happy
talk" television announcers often calling themselves expert meteorologists
have made the weather into a major journalistic interest. Newspapers continue soberly to correct the record but all journalistic soothsayers get their
information from the same source, the National Weather Service of the
National Oceanic and Atmosphere Administration, a part of the Department of Commerce. That agency was long known simply as the Weather
Bureau. If, as is often the case in small places, there is no local representative
of the Service to provide official information, the newspaper obtains the most
reliable data available from other sources. Possibly a college or high school
can provide it; if compelled to rely upon its own resources, the newspaper
at least can make certain that its thermometer is properly set up. As any
conversationalist knows, the weather is interesting even when there are
no hurricanes, floods or droughts. Since man lived in caves his everyday life
has been dependent to a large extent upon the behavior of the elements:
the machine or power age has not reduced man's dependency in this respect.
In fact, in many aspects of life, it has increased the dependency, as delicate
machines may require certain atmospheric conditions for proper operation.

ELEMENTS OF INTEREST

It is not necessary to read a newspaper to know that it is abnormally hot
or cold or that there has been a thunderstorm, but the reader does expect
his newspaper to supply authentic statistics about the weather, the widespread consequences of any unusual climatic condition and predictions as
to a change in the situation.

To meet this reader demand, newspapers print weather reports and forecasts daily. The maximum and minimum temperatures for the preceding
twenty-four hours and the next day's forecast frequently are printed on the
first page with detailed hourly readings, reports from other cities, wind

velocity, rainfall and other details on an inside page. If the weather becomes unusual in any way, a full-length news story is written.

When the weather becomes extreme, the reporter should seek information including the following:

1. Statistics and explanation.
   a. Maximum and minimum for day.
   b. Hourly readings.
   c. Comparison with other days during the season.
   d. Comparison with all-time records for the same date, month and season.
   e. Comparison with situations in other localities.
   f. Humidity, wind velocity, etc.
   g. Predictions: when relief expected.
   h. Official description of nature of phenomenon.
2. Casualties.
   a. Illness and death directly caused by the weather.
      (1) Heat prostrations.
      (2) Freezing.
      (3) Lightning.
      (4) Tornadoes, cyclones and hurricanes.
      (5) Floods.
      (6) Sleet and hail.
   b. Injuries and deaths of which the weather was a contributing cause.
      (1) Drownings.
      (2) Spoiled food.
      (3) Accidents from slippery pavements, snow, wind, etc.
      (4) Fires.
      (5) Heart disease from heat exhaustion.
3. Property damage.
   a. Telephone and telegraph wires.
   b. Water craft sunk.
   c. Bridges and highways, pavements buckling.
   d. Farm buildings and animals.
   e. Automobiles, buses and other public conveyances.
4. Interference with ordinary life.
   a. Transportation.
      (1) Railroads.
      (2) Buslines and streetcars.
      (3) Airlines.
      (4) Highways and bridges.
      (5) Private automobiles.
   b. Communication.
      (1) Mail service.
      (2) Telephone.
      (3) Telegraph.

     (4) Cable.
     (5) Radio.
     (6) Stoppage of food and other supplies.
  c. Public utilities.
     (1) Electric lights.
     (2) Gas pressure.
     (3) Water supply.
     (4) Fuel shortage.
5. Methods of seeking relief.
  a. Increased demands on water supply.
  b. Bathing beaches and parks.
  c. Trips.
  d. Sale of fans.
  e. Children cooled by hydrants, hoses, etc.
6. Methods of handling situation.
  a. Police activity.
  b. Volunteer groups: Boy Scouts, Legionnaires, etc.
  c. Red Cross, Civil Defense and other relief agencies.
  d. Use of ashes and other materials.
  e. Public warnings on driving, diet, etc.
7. Freaks.
  a. Narrow escapes.
  b. Undamaged property surrounded by desolation.
  c. Unusual accidents.

WRITING THE STORY

Because the weather affects every reader in his daily activities, no matter what unusual features are included or how the story is written the reporter must include in his account as many of the preceding elements as are pertinent. Emphasis should be on the effects of an unusual weather condition—casualties, damage, disrupted service—and on the basic statistics such as temperature, inches of rain or snowfall and wind velocity.

By Dick Main

A mass of tropical air brought muggy heat and scattered drizzles to much of Southern California Thursday on heels of the Los Angeles Basin's worst early season smog siege.

The clouds and moisture moved into Southern California from Arizona and Mexico but were expected to disappear by today.

U.S. Weather Bureau forecasters stuck by their original forecast for a warm and sunny July 4 holiday weekend throughout Southern California.

But the Air Pollution Control District called for moderate to heavy smog today and apparently anticipated little change in conditions through the weekend.

A smog alert was called at 12:15 P.M. Thursday and remained in effect until 3:26 P.M. It was the fourth alert of the year, making this the smoggiest year on record so far.

No other year has had four alerts so early in the season. In 1956, there were three alerts by July 2 and the year ended with a total of 10, the most in any year since the Air Pollution Control District started calling alerts in 1955.

Thursday's alert was called when the ozone count passed .50 parts per million at the APCD's West San Gabriel Valley Station. The count reached a peak of .57 ppm.

Other top ozone readings included: East San Gabriel Valley, .54; Pomona-Walnut, .44; Southeast area between the Pomona and Artesia freeways, .39; Orange County, .38; East San Fernando Valley, .36, and Civic Center, .27.

High temperatures added to the general discomfort in Southern California inland areas.

Peak readings included: Needles, 111 degrees—the highest reported in the nation; Blythe, 109; El Centro, 105; Palm Springs and Northridge, 104; Palmdale and San Bernardino, 102; Burbank, 101; Pasadena, 100, and Civic Center, 95.

Relative humidity ranged from 33 % to 78 % in the Civic Center but the figures varied widely in coastal valleys as the tropical air mass moved in.

Drizzles fell in southern Orange County and parts of Los Angeles County.

Residual clouds could cause some thundershowers in mountain and desert areas today, forecasters said.

At 3:41 P.M., a SigAlert was issued warning of heavy traffic on outbound lanes of all Los Angeles freeways—apparently caused by motorists getting an early start on the holiday weekend. The SigAlert was lifted at 9 P.M.

Meanwhile, more brush fires were reported in hot, dry interior areas. Eighteen brush or grass fires broke out in Riverside and San Bernardino counties, including a 124-acre grass blaze in Soquel Canyon near Chino. It reportedly was started from an ordnance fuse experiment at an Aerojet General test facility.   [Los Angeles *Times*]

The effects of weather on people often best can be explained by roundup descriptive accounts.

By Jim McVicar

A half-million people, some who live here and some who don't, went places and did things under sunny San Diego skies yesterday.

An estimated 100,000 persons enjoyed balmy air and water temperatures at the seashore from San Clemente to Imperial Beach.

Between 50,000 and 75,000 persons crowded North Island Naval Air Station to help celebrate its 50th birthday anniversary.

The San Diego Zoo counted 13,301 through its turnstiles and Sea World's attendance was 11,000 for the day. Some folks went to the horse races—12,570 to Caliente in Mexico and 13,662 to Del Mar.

Campers overflowed sites along the coast. All 397 spots were filled at South Carlsbad and San Elijo State Beach parks and rangers said they'd turned away 150 cars by late afternoon. At San Clemente State Beach, there's a five-day waiting period, a ranger said.

Mountain picnic and camping areas—state and county facilities—did brisk business. At the Laguna resorts an overflow camping area was pressed into service and auto traffic was fairly heavy.

The weather was ideal for sailing and water skiing and there was a lot of both in San Diego and Mission bays and out to sea.

Police said traffic was quite heavy at the international border and congestion on Avenida Revolucion in downtown Tijuana was a little worse than usual for a Saturday afternoon.

Law enforcement agencies and people who deal with San Diego's recreational activities figured that at least 500,000 persons were on the move.

A lot of them came to town Friday night from the north, as they do each weekend to escape the Los Angeles smog. Motels and hotels generally were full, but that isn't news anymore. Some rooms were available in scattered locations.

"This is as typical a weekend weatherwise as you'll have," said meteorologist Kurt Muerdter, who forecast nice weather again today.

The high temperature at Lindbergh Field was 77, one degree below normal for an Aug. 26. The high today should be 76.

It was much warmer inland, with temperatures in the 80s recorded in the foothills and 90s in the inland valleys. It was 94 at Gillespie Field in El Cajon.

"This reduces the fire danger in one respect and makes it worse in another," said Ira Pearman, dispatcher with the U.S. Division of Forestry "We've been troubled with lightning fires for several days. Now we have the problem of lower humidity and dry brush."

He explained that the electrical storms sometimes would bring some rain, which at least kept the mountain growth damp part of the time. With that condition gone, campers, and picnickers will have to be particularly careful with their fires and matches, he said.

The fire danger seemed to be the only negative thing about the weekend.

There were few rescues at the beach. Rip currents, which plagued bathers and surfers last week, were not causing swimmers or lifeguards too much grief yesterday.   [San Diego *Union*]

INTERPRETATIONS

Public curiosity concerning unusual weather conditions is a form of scientific interest. To satisfy it, the media communication cannot be expected to define every meteorological term as it appears in a news account, as many of the most common must be used almost daily. When occasion seems to demand, however, parenthetical inserts, sidebars and longer feature articles can be used, mostly for the benefit of middle-aged readers who went to junior high school before its curriculum was enriched by elementary instruction in this field.

After many decades of stubborn refusal to popularize its vocabulary, the National Weather Service has relented in recent years. It takes cognizance of popular usage now by permitting such phrases as "unusually fine weather" and "clear and bright" in its forecasts.

Explanations of natural phenomena can be given in scientifically accurate but easily understood language.

Washington—(UP)—A Weather Bureau spokesman said Wednesday that the mid-continent's scourge of tornadoes was "unusual" in scope but otherwise "typical."

He said the conditions that produced the wind barrage were "a classical arrangement" of warm and cold air masses. This occurs frequently in April and May.

Cold air masses from the Pacific and Canada tangled with masses of warm and moist air from the Gulf of Mexico. Tongues of cold air pushed out on top of lighter warm air.

Result: tornado-breeding turbulence along a line or "front" where the conflicting air masses ran afoul of each other.

*　　*　　*

Except for the great extent of the tornado area, the weather conditions were "typical for April and May."

When the turbulence is not too great, the result is thunderstorms. When it becomes "extraordinarily severe" tornadoes develop.

Radar observation of some of Tuesday's storm areas showed violent updrafts surging as high as 40,000 to 50,000 feet. When only thunderstorms develop, the updrafts usually go no higher than 20,000 or 30,000 feet.

*　　*　　*

Reports received here, the Bureau spokesman said, indicate the tornado warning system worked well except for a few storms.

The bureau's "severe local storm warning service" is headquartered at Kansas City.

It gets storm reports from thousands of volunteer and professional observers. When tornado conditions appear, the service issues warnings that may cover as many as four or five states.

It cannot pinpoint communities where tornadoes actually may appear. Tornado conditions may blanket an area of 10,000 square miles or larger.

*　　*　　*　　*

The bureau pins its hope of perfecting tornado warning on radar. Radar can spot storm conditions for 150 miles in all directions.

Radar warning systems are operating in several Texas communities and a few others elsewhere, including Kansas City, Oklahoma City and Wichita, Kan. . . .

[Chicago *Daily News*]

DEFINITIONS

To write understandable weather accounts, the reporter must know the meaning of the most important meteorological terms. The following list was prepared especially for this chapter by J. R. Fulks who retired recently after many years in the Chicago office of the United States National Weather Service:

Barometer. An instrument for measuring atmospheric pressure. There are two types. In one, the mercurial barometer, pressure is measured as the height (commonly expressed in the United States in inches) to which the atmosphere will lift mercury in a vacuum. An average height of the barometer at sea level is about 29.9 inches, and in the lowest several thousand feet one inch less for each thousand feet above sea level. The other type of barometer is the aneroid which measures air pressure by the expansion or contraction of one of more metal vacuum cells. Pressure is also measured in millimeters of mercury, but the international unit used by meteorological services is the millibar (1 millibar equals 1000 dynes; 30 inches of mercury equals 1015.92 millibars). An airplane altimeter is a high-precision aneroid barometer. Ordinarily, when the barometer is above 30.25 there will be good weather for 24 hours or more. When the barometer goes below 27.90 wind and rain are likely.

Blizzard. Strong wind and low temperature accompanied by blowing snow. The National Weather Service uses this term for winds greater than 35 mph, temperatures below 20°F, and visibilities less than ¼ mile. The snow may be either falling or may be picked up from the ground by the wind.

Ceiling. An aviation term used in the United States to designate the height above ground of the lowest opaque cloud layer which covers more than half the sky.

Cold wave. A sudden drop of temperature. Defined by the United States National Weather Service for each region and season. A typical wintertime cold wave in the central United States is a drop of 20 degrees (from the temperature 24 hours earlier) to below 10°F.

Contrail. The name of a cloud which forms behind high-flying aircraft.

Cyclone. Same as a *low.* The term *cyclone* refers to its system of rotating winds. It is a moving storm, usually accompanied by rain or snow.

Degree days. The number of degrees that the day's mean temperature is below 65°F. These are totaled monthly and seasonally to obtain a measure of heating needs. Cooling degree days are the number of degrees the day's mean temperature is above 65°; they indicate air conditioning needs.

Dew point. The temperature to which air must be cooled for fog to form. It is an index of the amount of moisture in the air.

Fog. A condition of lowered visibility caused by minute water droplets suspended in the air. It is a cloud resting on the ground.

Forecasts, weather. Statements of expected weather, prepared by specially trained professional meteorologists. They are based on weather data collected rapidly over a large portion of the world. To obtain the most probable expected weather, the forecaster uses prognostic computations made by the electronic computer, considers other physical and statistical factors and applies judgment based on long experience. Specific forecasts are generally for periods of one to three days at the most, but the National Weather Service issues both five-day and monthly forecasts of *average* conditions. Weather forecasts are of many types, such as public, aviation, marine, agricultural and forest-fire weather. The National Weather Service also prepares and issues flood forecasts, watches and warnings.

Front. A boundary between two different air masses, one colder than the other. A *cold front* moves toward the warmer air, a *warm front* toward the colder air. When a cold front overtakes a warm front, they form an *occluded* front.

Frost. A deposit of ice crystals on outside objects caused by condensation of moisture from the atmosphere on clear cold nights. Killing frost is defined as the first frost of autumn sufficient to kill essentially all vegetation in the area.

High. An area of high barometric pressure, usually several hundred to a thousand miles or more in diameter. In the Northern Hemisphere, winds blow clockwise about a high center. The approach of a high generally means improving weather—the ending of rain or snow, then clearing, colder and finally somewhat warmer as a result of sunshine. The weather in highs, like lows, varies from one high to another and will differ depending on where the center passes. A slow-moving high may cause fog, and often accumulation of air pollution, in and near its center.

Humidity. A general term applying to any of various measures of the amount of moisture in the atmosphere. See *Relative humidity*.

Hurricane. The name applied in the Caribbean Region, Gulf of Mexico, North Atlantic and eastern North Pacific (off Mexico) to a tropical cyclone in which the strongest winds are 75 miles per hour or greater. The same type of storm in the western Pacific is called a typhoon.

Inversion. An increase of temperature with height, in contrast to a normal decrease with height. Inversions at or near the ground trap pollutants by preventing their upward dispersion.

Jet stream. A line or band of maximum wind speeds high in the atmosphere, generally somewhere between 30,000 and 40,000 feet. The speeds are often in excess of 100 mph.

Lake breeze. A relatively cool breeze which frequently blows, on warm afternoons, from a cool lake onto adjacent warmer land. It may extend less than a mile or as much as several miles inland.

Lake effect. A general term which applies to any effect to a lake on weather. Near the shores of the Great Lakes a sometimes spectacular effect is that of heavy snowfall over a small area (perhaps a county). It is caused by moisture-laden air in winter moving from the lake onto the land, the air having been originally very cold, probably much below 0°F, before it moved onto the lake.

Local storm. Any storm of small scale, such as a thunderstorm. *Severe local storms* are those likely to cause damage, including severe thunderstorms, damaging hail and tornadoes.

Low. An area of low barometric pressure usually a few hundred miles in diameter. In the Northern Hemisphere, winds blow counterclockwise around a low center. Typically, the approach of a low means worsening weather—increasing cloudiness and finally rain or snow, but the pattern of weather varies for different lows and will be different depending on how far away the center actually passes. The low may affect weather up to several hundred miles from its center. Usually, as a low approaches, the weather becomes warmer, then colder as the low passes; this is typical of a low that passes to the north, but there may be little or no warmer weather if the low passes to the south.

Mean temperature. The average temperature over any specified period of time, such as a day, month or year. The United States National Weather Service uses the average of the lowest and highest temperature of each day as the mean temperature—an approximation that is very close to the true mean.

Mist. A condition intermediate between fog and haze—a thin fog. Also, in the United States, often applied to drizzle (fine rain).

Precipitation. Water droplets or frozen water particles falling to the ground. It includes rain, drizzle, freezing rain, freezing drizzle, snow, snow pellets, snow grains, hail, ice pellets (in the United States, sleet) and ice needles. The term *precipitation* is applied also to total measured depth of precipitation for which purpose any frozen form is first melted.

Precipitation probability. In the United States National Weather Service forecasts, the probability that .01 inch or more of precipitation will fall at any one point in the forecast area during the specified time period, usually 12 hours.

Relative humidity. A commonly used measure of atmospheric humidity. It is the percentage of moisture actually in the air compared to the amount it would hold if completely saturated at the given temperature. High humidity contributes to human discomfort at high temperatures but only slightly so if at all at low temperatures. Indoor relative humidity is sometimes applied to the relative humidity which outside air will have when heated to indoor temperature (usually taken as 72°F).

Shower. A rain of short duration, such as with a thunderstorm. Typically, showers begin abruptly and the intensity of precipitation varies considerably. There may be many separate showers on a day of showery weather. The term is also used with other than rain, for example, *snow shower* or *sleet shower*.

Sleet. In the United States frozen rain drops, but in Great Britain a mixture of rain and snow.

Smog. A contraction of the words "smoke" and "fog." It is, however, applied commonly in large cities or industrial areas when the pollutants may include other types in addition to smoke and fog.

Squall. A strong wind which begins suddenly and lasts a matter of minutes—somewhat longer than a gust. Also, especially in nautical usage, a sudden strong wind and an accompanying cloud mass that may produce precipitation, thunder and lightning. A *squall line* is a line or band of active thunderstorms.

Storm. A general term that may mean a cyclone, thunderstorm, wind storm, dust storm, snow storm, hail storm, tornado, hurricane or the like.

Storm warning. Can be a warning of any type of storm, but is applied more specifically to warnings for mariners. Marine storm warnings are of four types. *Small Craft* (less than 39 mph), *Gale* (39–54 mph), *Storm* (55–73 mph) and *Hurricane* (74 mph and greater). On the Great Lakes, the term *Small Craft Advisory* is used instead of *Small Craft Warning*, and *Storm* is used for any speed above 54 mph (*Hurricane* is not used). The figures refer to wind speeds.

Temperature-humidity index. A measure of human discomfort in warm weather. It takes into account the effect of both temperature and humidity. Exactly, THI equals 0.4 times air temperature plus wet bulb temperature, plus 15, all in degrees Fahrenheit. With a THI of 70, nearly everyone feels comfortable; at 75, at least half the people become uncomfortable; at 79 or higher, nearly everyone is uncomfortable. Fewer people, however, are uncomfortable if there is a good breeze.

Thundershower. A thunderstorm accompanied by rain.

Tornado. A small, violently rotating storm, commonly a few hundred yards in diameter. It accompanies a thunderstorm, but only a very few thunderstorms have tornadoes. Direction of rotation is usually the same as that of a Low, and the strongest winds range generally 100 to 300 mph. In addition to wind effect, some damage to structures is caused by low atmospheric pressure in the tornado center which causes buildings to collapse outward.

Water vapor. Water in gaseous form. The atmosphere always contains some water vapor, but the amount varies greatly. In hot humid conditions, it sometimes constitutes as much as 2 per cent (by weight) of the air. At low temperatures, the amount is much less. Water vapor is invisible, but when it condenses it forms water droplets that become visible as clouds or fog.

Watch. A bulletin issued by the United States National Weather Service to alert the public to conditions which may require issuance of later warnings. The warnings, when issued, are generally for smaller areas and give more specific locations and times.

Wind direction. The direction *from* which wind blows.

Reporters' Qualifications

It would be utterly impossible for anyone, including both journalists and scientists themselves, to be expert in more than one or a few of the multitudinous branches into which scientific knowledge is separated. What scientists of all kinds have in common is a belief in the importance of science and the scientific spirit of open-minded inquiry which survives despite any prostitution to business or military interests by many scientists.

The science reporter must know enough about the fundamental sciences, physical and organic, to be able to converse with professional scientists. If he is well grounded in any scientific field, he will find it easier to grasp meanings in other fields. He must win the respect and confidence of the scholars he interviews by his knowledge and attitude. He must overcome the risk of acting as apologist for scientists.

The public interest is the prime consideration of the science reporter as it should be of any responsible journalist. This means critical analysis of scientific proporals and it may mean warning and shocking readers.

In 1934 the National Association of Science Writers was founded under the leadership of David Dietz who in 1921 had become the nation's first science writer employed by Scripps-Howard. At present the association, with a membership of about 950, publishes a bimonthly *Newsletter* which provides a forum for the discussion of problems of scientific newsgathering. There also exists the Council for the Advancement of Science Writing in Journalism

Schools. Leading journalism educator to promote the training of science writers is Prof. Hillier Krieghbaum of New York University.

Already there is accelerating realization of the high moral sense which both scientists and science writers must develop. Today it is not what next but to what end shall we use what we already know or are on the verge of finding out. In *Harper's* for March 1975 Horace Freeland Judson, writing mostly on molecular biology, asks, "What are we afraid of?" The opportunity and/or obligation of the science writer is clear as Judson becomes specific:

> We are now into the third or fourth cycle of alarms about all this; the subject is intrinsically sensational, as can be seen from the examples that recur. What do you think, then, of choosing the sex of your children-to-be? Of growing human embryos outside the body and experimenting with them? Of genetic screening, to skim the trash out of the gene pool by determining who shall be permitted to breed? Of cloning, or the multiplication of large numbers of genetically identical individuals—what one entirely serious writer has described as the "asexual reproduction of 10,000 Mao Tse-tungs?" Of genetic engineering, or the creation of posthuman creatures with new or magnified bodily or mental strengths—what another serious writer has called "parahumans, or 'modified men' . . . chimeras (part animal) or cyborg-androids (part prosthetes)"?

Arthur Snider, science editor of the Chicago *Daily News*, notes that "the content of newspaper science writing has shifted to ethical and social science stories. Questions such as: When is a patient dead? Shall genetics be used to make a super race? Shall a substitute mother carry the fertilized egg of another woman to term? Who shall get the kidney?"

The following are extracts from a statement directed to potential science writers by Casey Bukro, environment editor of the Chicago *Tribune*:

> Look at what they did to Lake Erie.
> Look at what they did to the air in Los Angeles.
> Look at what they did to the American bison.
> If you're not moved by these classic examples of America's indifference to the destruction of the earth and life upon it, then you're not cut out to be an environmental writer. . . .
> Resist. Ask why these things happen. Don't settle for fuzzy answers. Don't shrug and say you can't fight city hall. Don't let them snow you. There are answers somewhere. Find them.
> The cornerstone of the environmental beat is questioning and testing so-called conventional wisdom: That growth is good, that more is better, that biggest is best, for example.
> The environmental beat had a part in exploring national policies that put economic values above human values. The need for this kind of exploration will go on. But you've got to be ready for it. . . .
> Environmental reporting needs a modern generation of Renaissance men and women without tunnel vision who can understand complexities, who can see how many subtle forces move gargantuan issues like strings on a puppet. . . .
> Accuracy is not served by publishing raw lists of facts and figures and two

opposing viewpoints. Environmental reporters will be asked to explain "what it means." In doing this, environmental reporters—whatever their label—have a chance to forge a link between our ancient natural world and our modern technological society.

Some experts believe we'll avoid environmental blunders in the future by getting doctors, lawyers, sociologists, engineers, city planners, and others to rule on the consequences and benefits of urban development projects.

Prepare for that day so you'll know what they're all talking about and pull it all together.

20

SPORTS, REVIEWING AND CRITICISM, FEATURES

A. Sports
  1. The Sports Reporter
    a. Remaining Cool
    b. Following Plays
    c. Knowing the Rules
    d. Knowing the Records
    e. Talking the Language
  2. Writing Sports News
B. Reviewing and Criticism
  1. The Reporter-Critic
    a. Essayists
    b. Formulas
    c. Reviewing
    d. Criticism
  2. Handling the Assignment
    a. Motion Pictures
    b. The Stage
    c. Entertainment Places
    d. Radio and Television
    e. Books
    f. Music
    g. The Dance
    h. The Fine Arts
C. Features
  1. Featurized News
    a. Oddities
    b. Converted Assignment
    c. Situations
    d. Events
  2. Straight Features
    a. Familiar Places
    b. Obscure Places
    c. Familiar Persons·
    d. Obscure Persons
    e. Occupational Types
    f. Historical
    g. Stunts
    h. Situations

The country clubs with their golf courses, tennis courts, swimming pools and other athletic facilities have proved to be fascinating places. Churches, boys' clubs and other organizations engaged in social service work have discovered the value of sports in character building. Schools have responded to criticism and pressure and are developing intramural as well as interscholastic or intercollegiate sports programs. Inspired by the widespread alarm over ecology, there is increased public interest in the outdoors. Not just hunting, fishing, camping, boating and hiking, but full utilization of nature's facilities for such activities as campouts, nature walks, study of soil, water, forest and wildlife, organized through amateur efforts to fight all forms of pollution and extinction of wildlife, to prevent forest fires, preserve scenic wonders and wild rivers and streams, and so forth.

As a result of these and other trends, Americans—men, women and children—are playing games much more than they did a decade ago, and even metropolitan newspapers are devoting more space to the outdoors and to amateur athletics than formerly. At the same time attendance records at professional contests of all sorts—baseball, football, basketball, hockey, golf, tennis and the like—keep being broken. Attendance is bound to skyrocket as the result of court orders that schools and colleges provide equal opportunities for girls and women.

SPORTS

Knowledge of the fine points of a game which comes from having played it oneself increases a person's interest in the skill of experts at the sport. Baseball became established as the national sport at a time when it was the most common sandlot pastime; in later years, the boys who played it relived vicariously the thrills of their adolescence through the achievements of Christy Mathewson, Babe Ruth, Ted Williams and others. Today, with young and old enjoying golf, tennis, bowling, swimming and other sports, interest in professional experts in these fields is growing.

With all professional sports and many amateur sports, such as college football, conducted for profit, the miles and miles of space devoted annually to sports news in the nation's newspapers is actually unpaid-for advertising. It is free publicity, however, which newspapers are not reluctant to give, because, for a large number of readers, the sports page is the most interesting in the paper. A few editors have experimented in reducing the space devoted to sports news but have been forced, by reader pressure, to abandon the attempt to make those who profit from sports pay for their advertising.

The Sports Reporter

High value is put upon the experience gained in writing sports, generally for two reasons: (1) only the critics and reviewers have anywhere near comparable freedom as to both what they say and the manner of saying it, and (2) there is no audience more critical than that consisting of sports fans who demand of a writer absolute accuracy and soundness of critical judgment.

REMAINING COOL

Everyone who attends an athletic event does so in quest of pleasure— that is, everyone except the sports reporters. This does not mean that sports reporters do not enjoy their work; it does mean that they cannot permit their enthusiasm to approach that which the fan displays. The press box is not a cheering section because its inhabitants have all they can do to follow closely what is happening so as to explain the difficult plays and decisions for fans who were too busy spurring on alma mater to notice exactly what happened. It is pleasant for the reporter to view sports events from the best seats and without paying admission, but he never is able to assume the carefree attitude of the casual fan.

FOLLOWING PLAYS

From his superior vantage point, the sports reporter should be expected to observe accurately. In many sports, the action is so fast that spectators cannot always follow it. The news story should let the bleacherite know what kind of pitch went for a home run or should tell the fans who sat in the cheap seats how the knockout blow was struck. At major sports events, the work of newspapermen is facilitated by the assistance of an official scorer who decides whether a hit or an error is to be scored. There also will be statisticians to prepare details in addition to those going into the official score book. At minor events, however, the reporter usually has to compile most of his own statistics. If, in addition to a general story of an event, a play-by-play account is desired, customary practice is to assign two reporters. An indispensable part of any featured sports story is a summary or box score, as the particular sport requires, which is run separately or at the end of the story proper. To the fan, the summary or box score is a complete account in itself.

KNOWING THE RULES

The sports fan not only attends contests but also receives considerable pleasure from discussing the past performances and future chances of players and teams. A favorite pastime is to second-guess the coach or manager and to pass judgment upon the abilities of referees and umpires. Just as popular among fans is criticism of the writeups of sports reporters. In other words, the sports writer has to "know his stuff" just as much as do players and officials. It is inconceivable that a reporter not understand the rules of the game he is covering. Writers of business news can make mistakes which only economists recognize; sports writers produce copy for readers who think they know as much as they.

KNOWING THE RECORDS

To keep up with what is expected of him, the sports reporter not only must understand the rule book but also must know the record book containing the statistics of what players and teams have done in the past. Otherwise, he will not know whether a particular achievement is unusual. The reporter whose mind is a storehouse of information regarding the history of sports is in a position to enrich his copy considerably. He can compare players of today with those of yesterday and frequently may remember "way back when" something, recalled by an immediate event, occurred. At his disposal, in case his memory is weak, are numerous sports record books in the newspaper's morgue.

A New York sports writer of a generation ago, Charles Dryden, is given credit for having been first to introduce on the sports page an informality and originality of language which would scandalize readers if found in the regular news sections. The credit for genius due Dryden has been dimmed because of the banal depths to which thousands of imitators, consciously or unconsciously, have sunk since then. Stanley Walker, longtime New York *Herald Tribune* city editor, wrote: "If it is true, and it appears to be, that Dryden was the father of whimsical baseball reporting, then the man has a great deal to answer for. He may have freed some reporters and afforded them the chance to do their gorgeous word-painting with a bold and lavish hand, but for every one he liberated he set demons to work in the brains of a dozen others—demons which made American sports writing the most horrendous mess of gibberish ever set before the eyes of a reader."

Today the desideratum in effective sports writing is informality and originality without triteness. Expressions which fans use in discussing a game cannot be considered hackneyed, but overuse of any word weakens any news story, sports or otherwise. For every sport there is a vernacular used by players and fans, familiar examples being "love" in tennis and "fore" in golf, with which the sports writer must be thoroughly familiar. It is in his use of shopworn synonyms to describe typical plays that he must be cautious.

Writing Sports News

One advantage the sports writer has over the reporter who specializes in political, governmental, business, scientific or any other type of news: the rules are definite and, despite occasional minor changes, remain the same year after year in all parts of the country. This situation, which contributes to the case of sports reporting, also may lead to monotony. It is the belief of many successful writers that the opportunity to develop an individual writing style, which sports reporting affords more than any other kind of newspaper work, exists up to a certain point only, after which the sports reporter should do the more serious writing for which his work has trained him. On the other hand, however, there are scores of first-rate sports writers whose copy seems just as fresh as ever after years of writing. Outstanding is Walter (Red) Smith, whose syndicated column originated with the New York *Herald Tribune* and survived the paper. In late 1971 he became a regular New York *Times* columnist.

In reporting amateur or local sports, the sports reporter almost invariably supports the home team. Any criticism of local heroes is constructive and usually is consistent with what a large number of fans believe. The tendency to "build up" local players may be overdone to the detriment of both the players and writer when performances do not square with predictions. The sports writer has a friendly attitude and makes it clear that he, as well as his readers, wants the home team to win. On the other hand, he must not act as a virtual public relations man for a coach or manager who may wish to use him to send up deceptive trial balloons to confuse opponents, or to promote his own interests.

Although all contests of a particular sport are played according to the same rules, the major news interest of an individual game might be any one of a number of potential elements. In determining the feature of a game, the sports reporter considers the following:

1. Significance.
   a. Is a championship at stake?
   b. Effect of the result on the all-time records of the contestants.
   c. Effect of the result on the season's records of the contestants.
   d. Are the contestants old rivals?
   e. Are they resuming relations after a long period?
   f. Will the outcome suggest either contestant's probable strength against future opponents?
2. Probable outcome.
   a. Relative weight and experience of contestants.
   b. Ability as demonstrated against other opponents, especially common ones.
   c. Improvement during the season.
   d. New plays, tactics, etc.
   e. New players, return of injured players, strength of substitutes, etc.
   f. Former contests between the two contestants.
   g. Weather conditions favorable to either contestant.
   h. Lack of practice, injuries and other handicaps.
   i. Tradition of not being able to win away from home.
   j. Recent record, slumps, etc.
3. How victory was won.
   a. The winning play, if score was close.
   b. The style of play of both winner and loser.
   c. Costly errors and mistakes of judgment.
   d. Spurts which overcame opponent's lead.
4. Important plays.
   a. How each score was made.
   b. Spectacular catches, strokes, etc.
   c. The result of "hunches."
   d. Penalties, fouls, etc.
   e. Disputed decisions of umpire or referee.
5. Individual records, stars, etc.
   a. Records broken.
   b. High scores.
   c. Players who "delivered" in pinches.
   d. Teamwork.
   e. Players not up to usual form.
6. Injuries.

7. The occasion or crowd.
    a. Size of crowd; a record?
    b. An annual event?
    c. Enthusiasm, riots, demonstrations, etc.
8. The weather.
    a. Condition of track or playing field.
    b. Effect of heat or cold.
    c. Effect of sun on fielders, etc.
    d. Which side was more handicapped? Why?
    e. Delays because of rain, etc.
9. Box score, summary and statistics.

REVIEWING AND CRITICISM

If he is not ambitious to become a foreign correspondent or a sports columnist, the college-trained cub reporter is likely to want to be a critic—motion picture, dramatic, musical, literary or art. Unfortunately for the youngster with talent which might lead to success in such writing, the average small newspaper offers him inadequate opportunities for either experience or editorial guidance. As a result, many—including some of the best that the schools of journalism turn out—redirect their energies into other channels.

This section is intended both for the few who create opportunities for themselves, perhaps by developing a column of motion picture or book criticism in addition to their other work, and for the regular staff members who draw the assignments to cover the annual high school play, the local art club's exhibits, the occasional Broadway cast which makes a one-night stop and the home talent Gilbert and Sullivan light opera.

The Reporter-Critic

ESSAYISTS

The lure of critical reviewing, in addition to free tickets, probably is the opportunity it seems to offer for self-expression. The great critics, including Matthew Arnold, Stuart Sherman and George Bernard Shaw, also have been creative artists and social philosophers. In addition to explaining to their readers how some muralist, playwright or composer regarded life, they have chronicled their own reactions.

To prevent his "spouting off" too much on the basis of only textbook knowledge and classroom discussions, it is perhaps fortunate that the beginning reporter is hampered in his critical writing. Before he can be a competent critic he must first serve an apprenticeship as a reviewer. When he covers a dramatic, musical or any other kind of aesthetic event, he does well to accept the assignment as one in straight news reporting. That is, while he is learning.

The purpose of the average member of a small town audience at a motion picture, play or concert is pleasure seeking. A safe guide for the tyro in reviewing, therefore, is the reaction of audiences; no matter how high he rises in critical writing, it supplies an element of news interest of which he always must take cognizance. What got applause? What evoked laughs? Regardless of what the reporter thinks of the audience's taste, to make a fair report of the occasion he must mention what indisputably were its high points from the standpoint of those for whom it was presented.

This advice is not tantamount to condoning the practice of building a review upon fatuous sentences or short paragraphs lauding every performer, but it is intended as a brake for those who might be tempted to use a night at the opera merely as an inspiration for an essay upon the fallacies of hedonism as demonstrated by "Faust" or a dissertation on the evidence regarding Hamlet's insanity.

The following is an example of a straightforward, objective report:

By Elaine Markoutsas

Christmas trees and lights. Candy canes. Sleigh bells. Angels. Reindeer. Santa Claus.

It wouldn't be Christmas without them. And it wouldn't be Christmas without "The Nutcracker," which opened Thursday night for 24 performances [thru Jan. 4] at the Arie Crown Theater.

The classic late 19th century ballet, set to the superb Tchaikovsky score and updated by Ruth Page, has become a tradition in Chicago, juxtaposed with other important works of art. Some make it an annual addition to their holiday fare. Others, present company included, are dazzled by the event as first-time-first-nighters. It's for everybody, and you don't have to know a thing about ballet or music to enjoy it. [Chicago *Tribune*]

FORMULAS

The critic with a bias is as dangerous as the political or labor reporter whose prejudices forbid his interpreting fairly the activities or viewpoints of more than one side in a controversy. In criticism, application of a formula as to what an artistic form should be often results in conclusions as grotesque as condemning a cow for not being a horse.

An example of a critic with a formula is one who believes art should exist for art's sake only and that no artistic form ever should be utilized for propagandistic purposes. As a result, if the hero of a motion picture or play happens to be identified with a particular racial, nationality, economic or other type or group, the critic is likely stupidly to condemn the entire production as propaganda, even though it be an honest and perhaps brilliant attempt to describe sympathetically a certain segment of life.

Even worse than the opponent of propaganda is the exponent of it who is sympathetic only when a certain theory is promulgated by the particular art form under review. Such critics dismiss books, plays or other artistic creations with (to them) derisive adjectives, as "romantic" or "too realistic," with a condescension which, in the small community at least, cannot but brand them as supercilious or, as the critics' critics may put it, "half-baked highbrows."

The critic with a formula is bound to be mostly a negative, carping, constantly dissatisfied one. Because a Hollywood production does not square with his conception of what the Old Globe players would have done, he sees no good in the result. Regretting that some artistic hero of his did not execute the idea, he is likely to make absurd comparisions between what is and what might have been.

The essence of competent reviewing of any kind is understanding an artist's purpose so as to interpret it to others. Any art form—painting, drama, the novel, music—is a medium of communication. No artistic creation should be condemned merely because of inability to understand its language, although those who hold that the artist should use a vocabulary which it is possible for others to learn have a valid point.

The duty of the reviewer or critic, in addition to that of describing a piece of art or an artistic event, should be to assist his readers in an understanding of the artist's motives to enhance their enjoyment of it. This obligation is prerequisite to that of passing expert judgment upon the artist's success in his undertaking; the role of evaluator is one which the critic-reporter should postpone until he has reached maturity himself in objective understanding, and not even then if his public consists largely of laymen. The greatest service the newspaper which gives space to artistic news can perform for both artists and spectators or auditors is to interpret the former to the latter. The educational background that such service requires easily may be imagined.

The writer of the following example attempted to explain motives without passing judgment:

By Bob Rohrer

The political side of America's struggle for independence receives engrossing and frequently amusing treatment in the Broadway musical play "1776," now being performed with patriotic gusto by the road show company at the Atlanta Civic Center.

The plot covers the last months of the second Continental Congress in Philadelphia, which—after considerable political maneuvering—approved the Declaration of Independence as war raged between Colonial and British troops.

Authors Peter Stone and Sherman Edwards have skillfully blended a wealth of historical detail—much of it humorous—with imaginative dialogue and warm-blooded, affectionate parodies of the men who supported and opposed independence.

The production itself moves vigorously; the staccato pacing of the deftly-handled ensemble scenes alternates effectively with strategically placed slower interludes, and the surging action never backs over itself.

There are quite a few fine individual performances. Particularly outstanding are the efforts of Don Perkins, who is convincingly choleric as the irascible John Adams; Paul Tripp, who turns in a wry performance of an earthy Benjamin Franklin; Reid Shelton, who livens the production with an explosively uninhibited portrayal of the unabashedly egotistical Richard Henry Lee of the Virginia Lees, and Larry Small, who is effective in a small part as a courier who sings a moving anti-war ballad—just about the only memorable musical number in the show.   [Atlanta *Constitution*]

The difference between reviewing and criticism has been implied in the discussions under both previous headings. No matter how critical he may become with experience and expert judgment, no writer of the arts can overlook his duty to supply the answer to the question "What is it like?" to the reader who has not read the book, attended the play or viewed the exhibit in question.

Is it a book about Russia or about how to raise puppies? A farce or a tragedy? A painting in imitation of Cezanne or one suggestive of Paul Cadmus? The reader who must select the books he reads, the motion pictures, plays and musical events he attends, expects the newspaper to tell him the answers. He wants, furthermore, an honest, fair statement, not an advertiser's blurb; and he doesn't want his pleasure spoiled by being told too much. That is, if the success of the playwright or novelist depends upon an unusual plot incident, it is unfair to both the artist and his audience for the writer to reveal its nature. How to convey an adequate impression of the nature of an artistic creation without spoiling one's fun demands only that quality known as common sense.

WOMAN OF VIOLENCE. By Geula Cohen. Translated by Hillel Halkin. 275 pp. New York: Holt, Rinehart and Winston, $5.95.

Reviewed by
Emily C. McDonald

"Woman of Violence" is the story of Geula Cohen and the life she led as a member of the notorious Stern Gang—which fought for the liberation of Palestine from the British. The gang—also known as the Lechi—was composed not only of terrorists, but also of idealists.

Geula Cohen was no exception.

She left her comfortable family life while still a student to join the freedom fight. First she tried the sanctioned organization—Betar. Then she turned to the more revolutionary Estel. Still not satisfied, she finally let herself be "recruited" into the Lechi.

From that day on her life changed completely. She went underground and rarely emerged from hiding except under cover of night. Geula learned to fight, to hide, to recruit, and—perhaps most important of all—to put dreams and ideals into action.

Finally, Geula became one of the "voices" on the Hebrew underground radio. Her voice brought news and inspiration to thousands of Jews eagerly awaiting news of the freedom fighters.

Although her work was dangerous, she never feared the danger. Her family was under surveillance, her friends were captured and put to death—still she went on with her broadcasts.

Then she too was captured. Through the Lechi underground, however, her escape was planned and finally brought about. She immediately returned to work.

Geula's memoirs end on the eve of Independence Day, 1948. Her active work in the Lechi ended then, too. She watched the celebrating but couldn't take part in it. The independence gained was not the Lechi ideal. As she put it:

"But I would remain outside. An ancient, heady melody that had started long ago would continue to resound far beyond these voices and frontiers."

[Nashville *Banner*]

CRITICISM

To pass judgment on the merits of a book, play, painting, musical number, motion picture or any other attempt at art demands expert judgment. To be an expert, one must have a specialist's education and training. This does not mean necessarily that the newspaper critic must be able to produce masterpieces himself to be qualified to pass judgment on the efforts of another, but it does mean that he must have a thoroughgoing understanding of the field about which he writes.

It is not peculiar that supposedly expert critics often do not agree. Neither do political theorists, economists or scientists. A difference of opinion among specialists, however, is based upon sound principles whereas philistines have as their premises only stereotypes.

The critic who wins the respect of readers usually is one who has proved his ability to report correctly an artistic event and to review fairly the nature of a piece of art. If he can observe correctly and interpret with understanding, he also may be trusted as an artistic "tipster." If he lacks either of the other qualities, however, his starred selections will be ignored.

These, then, are the three responsibilities of the finished critic, which the ambitious beginner would do well to master one at a time in order (1) to describe objectively an artistic object or event, (2) to explain what the artist intends it to convey and (3) to pass expert judgment on the artist's success in achieving his purpose.

Note in the following example how the writer, although passing critical judgments, remained aware of his role as reporter:

By Albert Goldberg
Times Staff Writer

The differences in technique among dancers qualified to be principals in such an organization as the Bolshoi Ballet are generally so minute as to defy anything except pedantic expert analysis.

But the differences in personalities can be enormous and readily apparent, and it was this factor, with six changes of cast in the leading roles, that made the Bolshoi's second performance of "Don Quixote" in Shrine Auditorium Thursday night a much livelier and more convincing affair than the one of the previous evening.

Type casting is not ordinarily one of the basic principles of ballet, but it was utilized to maximum advantage by placing Ekaterina Maximova and Vladimir Vasiliev in the roles of Kitri and Basil the Barber. Seldom has a couple—they are Mr. and Mrs. in private life—been better matched in every respect than this irresistible pair of handsome youngsters.

THEIR YOUTH

Naturally they capitalize on their youth and beauty, but their skills go far beyond the physical aspects. Though quite different in other respects, Miss Maximova has something of the radiance of Margot Fonteyn. She lights up the stage with her petite, mischievous sparkle, and she dances with a buoyancy that completely reflects her personality. . . .

It is characteristic of the ensemble principle on which the Bolshoi operates that Natalia Bessmertnova, the troupe's third-ranking ballerina, should turn up unannounced in the comparatively minor part of the Queen of the Driads. Though brief, she made its opportunities count with a serene elegance of style and technique that aroused anticipation of more extended roles.

Alexander Lavreniuk took over the Toreador with a welcome addition of refinement and aloofness, and Rimma Kerelskaya, the Queen of the Driads on opening night, injected more variety and less routine into the street dancer. Maya Samokhalova, the previous street dancer, did the first variation in the last act, but we'll have to take that on faith.   [Los Angeles *Times*]

Handling the Assignment

Two factors which the reviewer-critic must bear in mind are the following: (1) Are those upon whose work he is to pass judgment professionals or amateurs? (2) Is the performance (dramatic or musical), production, presentation or object of art an original creation or a copy or imitation?

It is unfair to judge an amateur by professional standards. The home talent cast usually gets as much fun out of rehearsing and acting as do the relatives and friends who witness the result. Generally, amateur events should be reported objectively with the audience's reactions as the guide.

Whereas Broadway first-nighters are as interested in the work of a play-wright as in the excellence of actors, when the local dramatic club puts on something by Oscar Wilde or Somerset Maugham, it is stupid to place the emphasis in the review upon the familiar plot or problem with which the dramatist was concerned. Rather, it is the acting and staging which should command attention.

The broader the critic's background, the better able he is to make comparisons between immediate and past events. If he has seen several actresses play the same part, he can explain the differences in interpretations. When a motion picture is adapted from a novel, short story or stage play, he can point out the changes made in plot and artistic emphasis. The same orchestra under different conductors behaves differently in rendering the same musical masterpiece; two authors handling the same subject may have little in common as to either method or conclusions.

MOTION PICTURES

There are few places large enough to support a newspaper which do not also have a motion picture theater. For the assistance of small-town editors, motion picture producers issue publicity material descriptive of their films and performers. Obviously, however, much to be preferred is the locally written review or criticism composed from the standpoint of the audience rather than that of the advertiser; fearlessness is a quality without which motion picture reviewing is likely to be jejune.

The film "Janis," which opens today at the King's Court, Oakland, is a disappointing work that sheds little light on the late singer's life.

In addition to several shallow interviews with her, there are scenes of her in concert, including outtakes from the film "Woodstock." But they are repetitious and she sings some songs as many as three times, with little variance in style. Also, they show her in a bad light and she comes across not as an emotion-laden blues singer but a frenzied screamer whose greatest strength is cast-iron vocal cords.

The only nonboring parts are an interview on the Dick Cavett show and scenes of her returning to Port Arthur, Texas, for her 10th class reunion. Both of these segments show a bit of the person behind the mystique, but in no way get to the heart of the singer.

The biggest gap in the film is the lack of interviews with Joplin relatives, associates and friends, which could give viewers more of an insight into her character than the superficial interviews with her contained in the film.

Much of the film is grainy, and some scenes seem to have been shot by a cameraman who paid his dues filming bar mitzvahs (the studio segment, for example).

Also, the editing could have been tighter and several sequences could have been eliminated altogether.

For those who go to see "Janis" in order to find out what made her tick or what led to her untimely death in late 1970 from a heroin overdose, the film will disappoint.

But it may satisfy Joplin fans who are interested in nothing more than seeing her perform. [Mike Kalina in Pittsburgh *Post-Gazette*]

THE STAGE

What has been said about the motion picture applies also to the legitimate stage. If the play is a much-acted one, the reviewer should not devote any appreciable amount of space to relating the story of the plot or to describing the general motive. Rather, he should perform the difficult task of distinguishing between the acting and the actor's role and should consider stage management and direction. Obviously, to criticize effectively he must have some acquaintance with the technique of play production.

If the play is a production, the critic rightfully evaluates the playwright's success in achieving his purpose. Is there proper congruity in settings, costumes, language and plot? Is the action logical or is the happy ending arrived at by a series of unnatural coincidences? Are exits and entrances merely artificial devices to get characters on and off the stage?

If the production deals with a problem, is it met squarely or is it falsely simplified? Are the characters truly representative of the types they portray or are they superficial or caricatures? Is the play propaganda? If it points a moral, is the playwright sincere or naive or bigoted? Is anything risque just smut for smut's sake or is it essential for dramatic completeness?

These are just a few of the questions the critic must ask himself. For whatever conclusions he reaches he must give sound reasons.

Truly great dramatic critics have been students of life as well as of the drama. "Ideally," according to Norman Nadel, critic for the old New York

World-Telegram, "the theater critic should be a Renaissance man." As explained in *Editor & Publisher* for April 23, 1966, his idea of such a man is one "with a knowledge of architecture, sculpture, painting, music, government, history, philosophy and other liberal arts subjects." Nadel suggests that college students finish their four-year course with a good classical and historical background so as "to have perspective and to understand the art form in relation to the world as it exists." He urges a knowledge of philosophy because "people turn to a play to express a philosophical question," and a knowledge of history of the theater and playwriting "to recognize a play's originality and importance and to acquire an intellectual appreciation of the play form."

Walter Kerr, long with the New York *Herald Tribune* and now drama critic for the New York *Times*, believes a drama critic must have an extensive background in dramatic literature on a broad humanistic base. John Mason Brown feels that critics should be able to "feel, touch and have sight of the world." He advises students aspiring to be drama critics to get a thorough knowledge of history. Richard Watts of the New York *Post* emphasizes the value of studying the English language as well.

By John Neville

Witches wrought havoc in Salem, Mass., in 1792 and some of their devilment carried over to Wednesday night's Community Theaters of Greater Dallas production of "The Crucible."

However, the happenings at the Rotunda Theater in the First Methodist Church are more deserving of a short session on the ducking stool than the ultimate noose or burning stake.

In fine, CTGD's first cooperative effort which united talents gleaned from the seven "little theater" groups that comprise the organization is better than amateur, yet far from professional. This is to be understood, yet there were too many things that smacked of the "let's get some of the gang together and put on a play" about the production.

Again to elucidate, lines were blown, scene changes were slow and, considering the sparcity of properties, too much scenery was chewed.

Dr. Burnet M. Hobgood, chairman of the SMU drama department, who directed "The Crucible," was confronted with the problem of welding a large number of part-time players from seven companies into a cohesive whole. This he did admirably. But he is no miracle worker, so there were many loose ends. For one thing, none of the players and seemingly few of the technical people were conversant with the intricacies of theater-in-the-round. Also, the Miller drama, which deals with the hysteria generated by the claims that witches (and warlocks) were destroying the children of Salem, can reach such heights of excitement that the actors can be caught up in the maelstrom and lose their stage discipline. Both of these factors were present in the CTGD production.

This is not to say that Dallas' most recent attempt at community theater was not successful. It was. . . . [Dallas *Morning News*]

ENTERTAINMENT PLACES

Today the form of entertainment closest to the old-time vaudeville program is found in night clubs, cabarets, hotels, summer resorts and similar places. Performers appear solo, delivering monologues, making music, dancing, engaging in pantomime or even acrobatic and other circus-type acts. The skill of the performer is what's at stake and that occupies the attention of the critic-reviewer more than perhaps anywhere else in the entertainment or artistic world today.

Marty Allen has the body of a Japanese wrestler gone to seed, the face of a troll and a hairdo inspired by a Brillo pad.

But he comes across beautifully in his act at the Holiday House, where he is substituting for Joan Rivers, whose week-long engagement was canceled at the Monroeville supper club.

Allen mixes up his fast-paced act well. One moment he bombards the audience with one-liners (his delivery is so good that you laugh even at jokes you've heard before); at another moment he might be doing a character sketch, like "Johnny Money," a hilarious spoof on Johnny Cash. He also does an interesting pantomime routine about an aging clown and hoofs it up in a finale about the sights and sounds of New York City.

Assisting Allen is Colleen Kincaid, who sings while he takes costume breaks, and she comes across well.

A fine singer, she also is an excellent dancer (she's a former member of the Golddiggers) and has not only an engaging stage presence but also an engaging physical presence.

Allen does one number with Kincaid called "Hey Big Spender" from "Sweet Charity." In this bit Allen is in drag, wearing platinum blonde wig, red silk shift and rhinestone earrings. He camps it up heavily looking like an aging hooker who would have trouble turning on a lightbulb.

Allen, a Pittsburgher, localizes some of his jokes and each area reference is met with guffaws. Also drawing a big response is a segment in which a bewigged and bejeweled Allen does a bewitching satire of Elvis Presley.

[Mike Kalina in Pittsburgh *Post-Gazette*]

RADIO AND TELEVISION

Newspaper criticism of television still is experimental. No orthodox formula has become widespread. Much of the columnar material is anecdotal or program announcements. The job of critically commenting on any appreciable amount of what is presented viewers is staggering. Celebrity interviews regularly make news for the news pages. The critic generally concentrates on dramatic performances as in the following first-rate example:

By Ann Hodges
TV-Radio Editor

Two fine actors made the most of a whimsical account of the biblical battle for a man's soul Friday night on NBC, as stars of "Hallmark Hall of Fame's" traditional pre-Easter presentation.

The play was "Gideon," Paddy Chayefsky's perceptive rewrite of Old Testament history, and it was a delightful, intellectual exercise performed nobly by the principal protagonists.

The essence of the drama was a two character play on words, with Chayefsky's dialogue a challenging collection of wit and wisdom.

And both Peter Ustinov and Jose Ferrer were equal to the challenge.

Ustinov was perfect as the bumbling herdsman, astounded to find himself chosen by the Lord to lead Israel to victory over the Midianites.

And Ferrer was equally good as the Lord, for once faced with an impossible task—that of transforming an average, everyday human being into a man of God.

Ustinov's Gideon was a sly and doubting disciple, at first not at all sure that "lamps, horns, and an army of 300 uncompromising cowards" could turn the tide of battle—even with the Lord leading the way.

And once the war was won, Gideon found himself too much the mortal man to deny his own vanity. He expected to be a hero, maybe even a king, and when the Lord denied him such fruits of victory, he denied his Lord.

There were no great scenes of battle or multitudes of worshippers in this production.

The only crowd scene was one brief belly dance performed by Little Egypt, a Brooklyn-born Lebanese practitioner of that ancient art. She was Orpah, the role she created in the original Broadway version of the play.

On TV the play was an intimate picture of a man's relationship to his God. It was well suited to the small screen. [Houston *Chronicle*]

BOOKS

The first task of the editor of a book review page is one of selection of those few of the 25,000 or more new titles published annually which are to receive mention. Harry Hanson, veteran newspaper and magazine book reviewer, told an *Editor & Publisher* interviewer,

> The daily book review lifts a book from an overtowering mass of printed material and makes it an integral part of life. It often becomes news of the first order. Between the covers of all these volumes there may be an authoritative voice touching on our vital problems, and if this is true, that voice certainly deserves a hearing. The book reviewer's job, it seems to me, is to sort this flood of titles, find the one that fits in the day's news, and then write about it as news.

That the first duty of the writer about books is to assist readers to select those they wish to read also was the viewpoint of another leading reviewer, Joseph Wood Krutch, who said,

> The best review is not the one which is trying to be something else. It is not an independent essay on the subject of the book in hand and not an aesthetic discourse upon one of the literary genres. The best book review is the best review of the book in question, and the better it is the closer it sticks to its ostensible subject. . . . However penetrating a piece of writing may be, it is not a good review if it leaves the reader wondering what the book itself is like as a whole or it is concerned with only some aspects of the book's quality.

As to the style of book reviewing or criticizing there is no formula. The writer is free to use virtually any method he chooses, the only test being the effectiveness of the style used. Somewhere in the review or criticism the writer should be expected to classify the book as to type—fiction, philosophy, biography—to describe its contents, communicate something of its quality and pass judgment upon it.

A temptation which even seasoned reviewers sometimes do not resist is to use the writing as opportunity for personal therapy, with the result that seems sophomorically sophisticated or pseudo-intellectual. Take, for instance, the first paragraphs of Godfrey Hodgson's review of *The Glory and the Dream* by William Manchester in the Washington *Post*:

> When this Brobdingnagian work first thumped on my desk for review, I took note of its bulk and of the inflated rhetoric of the title, and my first impulse was to dismiss it as the ultimate *Guiness Book of Records* champion nonbook.
>
> I would count its pages, I said to myself, and I did. There are 1302 of them. That is not counting end pages, forematter, acknowledgments, bibliography, copyright, acknowledgments, and index.
>
> All of which it is provided with so lavishly that one might suppose that it is as scholarly as the *Monumenta Germaniae Historica*, which it is not. At something over 500 words to the page, that is more than two-thirds of a million words.
>
> Next I thought I would weigh it on the kitchen scales. And that, too, I did, though it proved harder than I imagined since the chic little brass weights that I gave my wife for Christmas a few years ago only go up to two pounds avoirdupois, and Manchester is out of that division. As far as I was able to determine with the help of a pound of beans and a can of grapefruit segments, however, *The Glory and the Dream* tips the scales at around three pounds, eight ounces.
>
> And then, I supposed, I would write a savage little review, commenting on the economics of book publishing, and ending, perhaps, "A book, however, this is not."
>
> And yet I was wrong. It is even rather a good book of its kind, so long as one does not expect too much from it.

Another standard method is to relate the current volume to earlier works by the same author, as John Brooks did when he reviewed the Manchester book in the Chicago *Tribune*:

> William Manchester is famous for *The Death of a President*, the "Kennedy book" of the 1966 headlines remembered less for its hair-raising account of the assassination of John F. Kennedy than for the prepublication objections to it by the fallen President's relatives and friends. Among his other books are *The Arms of Krupp* and a novel of much merit, *The City of Anger*.
>
> Now he has written an enormous (1,300 page) popular history of the United States over four recent decades. Thru the sheer nerve of his undertaking and the dogged persistence of his execution of it, he almost batters the reader's critical faculties into submission and brings him to a helpless nod of assent. Almost, but not quite.
>
> Prominent among the pitfalls of popular history-writing are the following:
>   (1) Drawing instant mood-pictures of past years with the help of phrases like "It was a time of . . ." and "It was that kind of year."
>   (2) Evoking instant nostalgia by writing down old song titles.
>   (3) Sounding like *Time* magazine.
>   (4) Sounding like Dos Passos in "*U.S.A.*"
>   (5) Contriving corny melodrama by withholding a famous name until the end of an anecdote ("And that man's name was. . . .")

(6) Trying to convey a sense of destiny by faking detailed knowledge of the playpen days of people later to be famous ("Fifteen-year-old John F. Kennedy heard the long, plaintive wail of the steam whistle at the Choate School in Wallingford, Conn.").

A more scholarly approach is to compare a new book to others dealing with the same subject, as illustrated by the following from what John P. Roche wrote for *Saturday Review*:

Historical chronicles come in different styles, perspectives, and sizes. Federick Lewis Allen, for example, utilized the principle of parsimony in his *Only Yesterday*. He made no effort to cover everything, but he did write a book. Cabell Phillips, in his *1929–1939: From the Crash to the Blitz*, drew extensively on *The New York Times* (the volume is one in a series called *The New York Times* Chronicle of American Life), but the result is far more than a scissors-and-paste job; reading it, one gets the distinct impression of a mind at work, of priorities established and maintained. Then, of course, there are the specialized works, such as Irving Bernstein's *The Lean Years*, which view American life through the prism of the working class.

Now comes William Manchester with an immense narrative history of the United States from 1932 to 1972. I began reading it with great interest, because the time frame is precisely the span of my political consciousness. This could be the story of my generation. Unfortunately it is not. By the time I emerged from the seemingly interminable 1,300 pages, I was convinced that Manchester had simply taken a vacuum cleaner to his task and swept up every bit of information, meaningful and trivial, and had never sat down to sort out the wheat from the chaff.

How different experts can react differently is illustrated by the following examples. The first is by Alfred Kazin, author of *Bright Book of Life: American Novelists and Storytellers from Hemingway to Mailer*:

This fluent, likeable, can't-put-it-down narrative history of America from the Bonus Army to Watergate is popular history in our special tradition of literary merchandising. It is all about the audience that will read it. Mr. Manchester is a steadier and more reliable source on American vicissitudes than photograph books, Theodore H. White, Time and Life, Frederick Lewis Allen, The New York Times Op-Ed page, Norman Mailer, Betty Friedan, Peanuts, et al. But his real virtue is not just that he is a dependable fact man with an eye for the unexpected fact and that he tells his story with all the ease of a practiced rewrite man who has been inspired by Dos Passos. He is really obsessed by the American audience, the great American consensus, the mass, the popular mind itself. He is confident that there is an all-present character called the American people and that he can describe 40 years of simultaneous experience. He identifies with this character and makes you believe that your whole life has been lived inside it. Reading Manchester, you run with the Bonus Army, lift up your chin like Roosevelt, put up the flag at Iwo Jima, and nervously dismiss MacArthur. You are against Communism *and* the Cold War. You participate!

Manchester is always thinking about *you*, you who are reading him, you who read history and can afford 20 dollars for a book. This book is your life.

By contrast, the author of this book—who also wrote *Hoaxes* and *Gideon's Army, the Story of the Progressive Party of 1948*—wrote the following for syndication by Field Enterprises:

> Just about everything that happened for 30 years—in politics, diplomacy, education, science, labor-management relations, public health, the arts, entertainment, fads and fashions, civil rights, civil liberties, law, sports and all else— receives at least brief mention in this 1,397 page narrative.
>
> There are some editorial jibes, such as that Elvis Presley was lewd and vulgar, Lyndon Johnson "characteristically said one thing while believing the exact opposite," the Prince Rainier-Grace Kelly wedding was an M-G-M press agent's dream. Typical of longer evaluative comments are:
>
> "He (Eisenhower) was a backslapper; Nixon was a brooder. In economics and political ethics the general was a fundamentalist. The senator was a relativist, an opportunist, and a fatalist," and "by 1961 the space race no longer had any bearing on national security . . . or on the pursuit of knowledge."
>
> Mostly, the tome is objective reporting of what appeared on the front pages. William Manchester has no inside dope, no behind-the-scenes facts, no skeletons dragged out of closets. He makes no sociological interpretation of the era as a whole, notes no trends nor relationships between the multitudinous events he summarizes. Without historical perspective, he merely records the "what" and leaves the "why" to abler scholars.

MUSIC

The reporter who is timid about covering a musical event because he lacks technical training in music at least has the consolation that by far a majority of his readers, both those who attended the event under review and those who didn't, know no more than he. The superior musical review, of course, is written for both the professor of music and the music-lover. The qualities demanded of the music critic were summarized as follows by the late Lawrence Gilman, long music critic for the New York *Herald Tribune*:

> The best music critic is a good newspaperman. Of course, he must know music, deeply and thoroughly and exactly; he must know what he is talking about. But the first and indispensable requirement of any article written for a newspaper, no matter on what subject is that it must be readable—it must be interesting as well as clearly intelligible to the lay reader of average education. A professional musician might be able to write a competent, technical account of a composition or a musical performance. But his review would probably be interesting only to other musicians.
>
> The chief aim of a newspaper critic must be to interest the general reader. And if he can interest those readers who have not heard the performance, as well as those who have, he is entitled to call it a day. Quite apart from its value as a report and estimate of a musical performance, his criticism must be able to stand alone as an interesting, readable story.

It is the musician in whom the musical critic primarily is interested, because only occasionally, even in the large cities, is he required to pass judgment upon a new symphony, opera or other musical creation. Thus, if the audience includes musically trained auditors, he may well take his cue from their reactions as to the merits of the performance. If he is woefully lacking in musical training, he can make his entire story descriptive of the audience or the personalities of the musicians.

By John H. Harvey
Staff Writer

Elisabeth Schwarzkopf, making what is billed as her farwell American tour, gave the University Artists Course something to remember her by Tuesday night in Northrop Auditorium.

It was a souvenir of her interpretive art rather than of the full greatness of her voice, which has suffered the inevitable erosion of time. Her program, all German lieder except for two songs by Grieg, was shrewdly chosen for attractive exploitation of her present vocal estate. It was, therefore, on the lighter side, with few items probing darker moods or making heavy vocal demands.

But within these limits, the German soprano's voice had the old gleam and flexibility, and her control, her many felicitous turns of phrase, and her range and subtlety of expression made for an absorbing recital. Her excellent rhythmic sense was an important element in giving wings to a melodic line.

By no means a major number on her program, but a prime example of her art, was her finely wrought performance of Grieg's "Ich liebe dich," which had a cameo-like quality, fresh in spite of the song's overfamiliarity.

Most affectingly expressed of the more substantial works was Hugo Wolf's "Kennst du das Land?" In fact, all of the Wolf songs on the program showed Miss Schwarzkopf a masterly interpreter of that composer. These also included "Schlafendes Jesukind," "Die Zigeunerin" and those delightful, light-hearted charmers, "Trau nicht der Liebe," "In der Schatten meiner Locken," "Nein, junger Herr" and "Ich hab' in Penna."

Story-telling songs, like Mahler's "Um schlimme Kinder artig zu machen," Brahms' "Salamander" and Liszt's "Die drei Zigeuner" and those calling for characterization found her a mistress of those media. Among the latter were Schumann's "Die Kartenlegerin," in which the young girl tells her fortune while her mother dozes; and several of the Wolf songs.

Schubert's "Gretchen am Spinnrade" which opened the program was a bit cautious and restrained; the soprano seemed feeling her way into the program at that point. But "Der Lindenbaum" and "Fruehlingssehnsucht" were beautifully interpreted.

Characterization again was the strong point in Richard Strauss' setting of Ophelia's mad songs from "Hamlet."

Martin Isepp, who was Janet Baker's keyboard collaborator in her recital here in January, performed equally valuable services for Miss Schwarzkopf.

[St. Paul *Pioneer Press*]

THE DANCE

Whereas music is written with complete directions by the composer to guide the virtuoso, and whereas rules for the playwright, novelist, painter and sculptor may be found in textbooks, no way as yet has been devised to score the movements which characterize what, historical evidence proves, was one of the first if not the original form of art. Motion picture recording may prove the way out for future teachers of the dance who wish to convey the qualities of the work of a Rudolph Nureyev or a Martha Graham.

The medium of the dance is motion, but motion may be either abstract or pantomimic, rhythmic or natural. Folk dancing, being pantomimic, reflects the customs of the people participating in it. Natural dancing consists in such normal movements as running, walking, skipping and leaping without studied posing. What is called the German school of dancing emphasizes strength, endurance and precision of movement. The ballet is rhythmic and repetitious. Greek or classical dancing, revived after World War I by the late Isadora Duncan, is symbolic and involves the entire body, not just the head, arms and legs. Miss Duncan considered her art interpretative of poetry, music, the movements of nature and of moods and emotions; as such, it defied analysis.

To review a dancing entertainment with any intelligence, the reporter must understand the principles superficially sketched in the preceding two paragraphs. A sympathetic attitude perhaps is more essential than in reviewing any other form of art, if for no other reason than that it is the form with which the average person has the least everyday contact.

By Linda Winer

New London, Conn.—A slice of American dance life from the '40s was revived here when the Martha Graham Company took over the Connecticut College American Dance Festival. Somehow, when talking about Miss Graham, the word "slice" seems just right.

Her dances cut their way almost rudely thru superfluous movement and nonessential illusions while she lands with blade right on the nerve endings that lead to the pulse of emotion. That kind of black tension hit like a sustained muscle spasm from the opening dissonant chords of "Cave of the Heart" and continued without much relief thru "Diversion of Angels" and "Deaths and Entrances." Kind of makes you feel gored.

"Cave of the Heart," based on Medea's vengence upon Jason, dates back to 1947, when Miss Graham danced the role of the wronged sorceress. Saturday, Helen McGehee, a company veteran of more than 20 years, did the vamping.

Past the immediate visceral command of Samuel Barber's heavy rhythmic music and past the convulsive gesture comes the essence of meaning thru movement. Jason, danced by Richard Gain, and his new princess, Takako Asakawa, comprise one raised vertex of the dramatic triangle. She's like a doll, or better a perfect trophy, and he, a Greek athlete who can carry his prize proudly on his huge shoulders and whose extended firm arms open his chest for the world to admire. You just can't hate them.

Back a bit, and in the center of Isamu Noguchi's three point set, is the one woman Greek chorus, Matt Turney—all angles of long bones, folds and drapes, unable to look upon the horror of the situation, long palms facing the sky in bewilderment.

*   *   *

And then Medea, with a minimum of motion, skulking in long black slinky dress [Flash Gordon evil eyebrows], her awkward advances rebuffed, jerking in neurotic knots, arms making wide stiff arcs, hands almost like claws, caressing and hating the hatred within her, releases the poison for an oily triumph over them, defeat against herself.

Well, about then we were ready for what the program described as a "lyrical ballet about the pleasure and playfulness, quick joy and quick sadness of being in love." A revival of "Diversion of Angels," for 11 dancers, first introduced at Connecticut College in 1948. Done in Chicago in '49. . . .

[Chicago *Sunday Tribune*]

THE FINE ARTS

The camera was to a large extent the cause of the contemporary "war" in the field of painting which has repercussions among the sculptors and architects as well. Dadaism, futurism, surrealism and other recent "schools" of art are revolts against the formal, and a popular explanation given laymen is that the day of the portrait painter is gone and with it a theory as to the purpose of art. It is argued that the role of the 20th-century artist is to communicate an idea or an emotion; the extremes to which some go in up-setting tradition is dumfounding to laymen. In the works of such painters as Grant Wood and Thomas Benton, so-called regional artists, is found an abandonment of the photographic purpose, but the models still are recogniz-able. Some abstract art has as many interpretations as there are interpreters.

Peter Schjeldahl epitomized recent trends in the New York *Times* for Sept. 20, 1970, in an article, "From Creative Plumbing to Lyrical Abstrac-tion?" which began as follows:

The 1960's in American abstract painting was a period of conscientious esthetic and technical pure research, remarkable for its tireless experimentation with hard-edged stripes, disks and polygons of solid color. The avant-garde of a decade ago, having thrived during the Abstract Expressionist 50's on seem-ingly slapdash procedures followed in an intellectual climate of romantic asser-tiveness and big ideas, took with a sort of cool, evangelical passion to the new use of T-squares and masking tape, and began to couch its self-advertisement in impeccably dry, quasi-scientific language.

How to combine reporting and expert critical analysis is demonstrated in the following from the New York *Times* for Sept. 26, 1970.

By Hilton Kramer

The rose is a venerable subject in the history of painting but there are no roses to be found in this history quite like those that appear in the paintings of Bert Carpenter, whose one-man show is now installed at the Zabriskie Gallery, 699 Madison Avenue at 63d Street.

For Mr. Carpenter, while lavishing a familiar lyricism on the realization of this conventional subject, manages to transform it into something quite different—the materials of "heroic" painting.

•

Mr. Carpenter projects his imagery of roses on a monumental scale, making of each petal, leaf and stem a weighty architectural member. The roses in his paintings are giant roses, monument roses—roses that carry the humble di-mensions of nature into the realm of pictorial fantasy. And yet, he effects this magical change in scale without sacrificing anything of the "realism" of his depictions. These roses, as large as the head of man, retain all their tender luminosity.

Sports, Reviewing and Criticism, Features 453

As a sheer technical feat, the exhibition is remarkable. But it is also extremely interesting as virtuoso painting. Mr. Carpenter has adopted something of Alex Katz's pictorial strategy in enlarging his subjects to more than life-size, and the particular "cropping" he employs seems to owe something to Philip Pearlstein's painting—Mr. Carpenter often cuts off the tops and bottoms of his roses the way Mr. Pearlstein crops his views of naked models. But whatever he may have borrowed in the realm of formal ideas, Mr. Carpenter's pictures establish a presence all his own. He is an interesting and powerful painter.

Current tendencies in painting, sculpture and architecture are not new. The history of art reveals that throughout the centuries every conceivable theory has been tried out. Likewise, the search for a definition of art is as old as artistic criticism; upon his answer to the question depends largely the nature of what an artist produces.

Through reading and fraternizing with artistic people the reporter can become educated in the meaning of art to the different "schools," the work of whose representatives he is called upon to review. In no other field is the responsibility for interpreting the artist to his public greater than in that of the manual arts. In fact, such interpretation is about all there is to this kind of criticism.

The opportunity and responsibility of the newspaper today were explained by Herbert Kupferberg, then editor for the arts of the late New York *Herald Tribune*, in an article, "The Art of Covering the Arts," in *Nieman Reports* for March 1965. His final paragraph was as follows:

> For better or for worse, the world of the arts today is wider than it has ever been. It encompasses not only the patron of the art galleries on New York's Fifty-seventh Street, but the housewife who finds Van Gogh and Renoir reproductions amid the breakfast foods and beauty aids at her local supermarket. It includes the teen-ager buying his first Beethoven symphony at the discount record counter no less than the dowager with a subscription to the Metropolitan Opera. It even touches the millions of visitors who rode the moving platform past Michelangelo's Pieta at the New York World's Fair without being fully aware of whether they were undergoing an artistic or touristic or religious experience, but recognizing that for a brief moment they had entered a realm of beauty. Today a newspaper that makes any pretense at reflecting the life around it, or at appealing to the broad interests of an alert readership, no longer has any real option as to whether it will cover the arts. Its only choice is whether it will cover them badly or well.

FEATURES

The difference between news and feature stories is largely one of intention. Numerous examples in preceding chapters have illustrated how unorthodox journalistic rhetorical methods, customarily associated with feature writing, may be used to improve ordinary news stories in which the writer's purpose is to be informative about overt happenings. On the other hand, a feature article emphasizing human interest may be composed according to the standard rules for formal news writing.

In addition to designating those stories of events which might have been written up in straight news style, the term "feature" also is used to include human interest stories related to or suggested by news events, a quantity of different types of articles only slightly or not at all connected with any news item, and a growing number of special informative articles and regular columns of advice and instructions.

Featurized News

"Make it into a feature," the reporter says to himself or is told by the city editor when he has a schedule of facts about something which actually has happened of little public importance but of considerable potential reader interest.

ODDITIES

One of the milestones in the evolution of the modern newspaper occurred when the James Gordon Bennetts began printing accounts of happenings which previously had been considered too trivial to merit attention. Today, without consciousness of the loss of any dignity, the average newspaper balances its offering of serious matter by a liberal sprinkling of "brighteners," usually brief, cleverly written feature items of relatively unimportant happenings. Some papers group a number of such shorts each day in a column headed "Oddities in the News," "Strange as It May Seem" or some similar title.

Columbus, Ohio—(UP)—Exasperated by the endless questions of 3-year-old Harold Thompson, a neighbor who was painting his house painted the child red "from head to foot" and sent him home.

The child's mother, Mrs. Lester Thompson, scrubbed him clean—except for a few red splotches—and sent him out to play again.

A few minutes later, she charged in a police complaint, the child returned. This time he was painted a battleship gray.

It was her last day in Williamsville, and Mrs. Mary McLain, who has lived 50 years there, was saddened at the thought.

But she was willing to leave. Her husband, James, 75-year-old city employee retired, wanted to go back to St. Louis, the home town he had left more than 50 years before.

He had retired a year ago, and his old home had been in his thoughts ever since.

And so they were leaving. The house at 678 Thorn ave., had been sold a week ago. The moving van, loaded with their furniture, was in front, ready to take their goods and their life to St. Louis.

Only one piece of furniture—Mrs. McLain's old worn rocking chair—had been left out.

It remained on the porch, where she had rocked contentedly in it ever since a stroke five years earlier had paralyzed her legs. There, on the porch, she would rock quietly, exchanging greetings with her neighbors. But now she was leaving.

"I'm going to sit down in my good old chair for the last time," Mrs. McLain told her husband, and her voice was sad.

"We've been very happy, haven't we, James?" she murmured as she closed her eyes to fix forever in her mind the sight of the street she was leaving.

After a few moments her husband shook her gently.

"It's time to be going, dear," he warned.

Mrs. McLain did not answer. She had gone already.

The doctor who examined her said that Mrs. McLain had died of a heart attack.

CONVERTED ASSIGNMENT

Often a reporter goes out on what he believes to be a serious assignment and encounters a situation lending itself much more readily to feature than straight news treatment. Or he may be instructed, "If it isn't worth a news story, write a feature about it," such an order implying what every city editor believes—that a competent reporter should be able to write a feature story about anything. Decision to give feature treatment to what otherwise might be a regular news story may be influenced by another newspaper's having published an earlier account in orthodox style. This happens frequently when the article is of an evening event for an afternoon newspaper and a morning newspaper already has had a story about it.

This is the story of the conversion of a newspaper reporter.

Traditionally, he's a hard nut to crack anyway, but when religion is concerned, he's doubly so. Last night he entered the Salvation Army building at Sherman avenue and Greenwood street with a cuss word in his eye and leering sarcasm on his face.

Inside was a big tent, staked out in the regular canvas oval camp-meeting style. The reporter could hear the evangelistic exordium coming from the female in the pulpit.

Pushing back the tent flap, he trod down the sawdust aisle. The female was leading a hymn. He snorted in contempt and looked disdainfully at the weaklings all around him who had religion. The girl in the pulpit attracted his eye— he wasn't an old reporter. She was dressed in the Army's trim uniform and wore the black-ribboned bonnet. There was an aura of something almost celestial around her. It quieted the reporter's disbelief.

LOOKS AROUND HIM

He looked around him. A carnival procession of lights was stretched over a bar nailed across the tent pole in the rude semblance of a cross. Overhead the canvas top was billowing in a draft, almost as though a prairie wind had struck it. Late visitors came in, like shades of Gypsy Smith and Billy Sunday. They shuffled down the sawdust aisle, stirring up a smell of fresh pine shavings.

The varnished seats down in front that resembled the dismantled rows of some ancient nickelodeon were filling with other shades. There were Adam Goa and his congregation from the holy thinking plains of Kansas. From somewhere came the dulcimer tones of a piano and the muffled percussion of a drum. The reporter wanted to join in the inspired hymn. The tent was billowing above again, and down in front Adam Goa's shades had risen and were whooping up an old chantey. . . .

The reporter, with a bursting chest, seized the hymn book. It was titled "Fralsnings—Armens Sangbok." It wasn't enough to erase the vision of Adam Goa down there in front. Then came the sounds of creaking wagon wheels and grandfather Jewel lived again. He was straight and stalwart and was handing down Miss Mary Ann, with an arm around her waist.

Other late-arriving rustics were gathering outside making noises, and the prairie wind was blowing over groves of trees wherein the young folk paid homage to Eros.

The reporter strove to shut out all this. It was religion, that of his old home state, and it wasn't becoming to his profession. Uncle Jimmy, another famed Kansas exhorter, was stumping up to the pulpit preparatory to the revival meetin' rogations. And there was the shade of Beulah Woolson, the soul who had been inside the gates of heaven. Oh Lord!

The reporter, half blinded, broke suddenly up the sawdust aisle. They were singing a hymn behind him.

O neighbors have you seen old Rummy,
With a scowl upon his face?
I saw him on the street this morning,
And he's going to leave the place!
He's going to leave the place!
Old Rummy's going to pack his baggage,
For it's getting mighty warm!

The reporter dashed past the poster advertising the Army's sunshine brigade. In the street again, he shook his head clear.

"Cripes," he muttered, "that old-time religion in Evanston, and it almost got me, too!"   [Evanston (Ill.) *News-Index*]

SITUATIONS

Not a single event but a series of them may suggest a featurized situation story to a reporter or editor. Such articles have a strong element of news interest, as they summarize and possibly explain what "everybody" is doing or talking about. They are not concocted features but are based upon recent events. In their *Pathways to Print* the late Harry F. Harrington and Lawrence Martin explained the difference between the situation feature and the interpretative article as follows:

> The situation feature differs from the strictly interpretative story mainly in that it is content to assemble the evidence pro and con—or at most to offer a symposium of opinion, leaving the interpretation largely to the individual reader. This type of feature article creates nothing essentially new; it simply analyzes and coordinates, smoothing out difficulties and hazy impressions which waylay a reader who is not in a position to understand all of the hidden implications of a series of events, In its fullest expression, the situation story is a fusion of the past, present and future.

A situation story explains the "atmosphere" in which an immediate incident or series of incidents must be understood. It may be known as a "roundup" story.

By Kathy Gosnell
Staff Writer

Motorcycles are here to stay.

They come in all shapes and sizes and so do the people who buy them.

Teenagers buy them because they are cheaper than cars. Business men buy them because they outmaneuver cars.

Some people buy them for the feeling of "the wind in your hair," says Jack Koske of Koske Import Motors in Palatine.

The growing popularity of cycles had brought growing concern about safety problems.

Sen. Vance Hartke (D-Ind.) two weeks ago told the United States Senate of an "epidemic of motorcycle accidents."

The National Safety Council figures show 1,580 cyclists killed in 1965, as compared to 1,118 in 1964 and 882 in 1963.

On both state and national levels there is talk of safety regulations ranging from mandatory wearing of crash helmets to special tests and licensing for cycle drivers.

But increased publicity noting climbing death tolls and the possibility of regulation are apparently not daunting the spirit of the cyclists.

Two million cycles and scooters are registered in the United States and some five million people are driving them, according to the Motorcycle, Scooter, and Allied Trades Association.

In Illinois 56,753 cycles were registered last year.

One possible form government action might take is the establishment of special tests and licensing for motorcycle drivers in addition to the present requirements for a driver's license.

Such action would probably make special instruction mandatory. Some dealers do instruct buyers now; others don't care.

Koske said he refuses to sell a cycle to anyone until he is sure of the buyer's ability to handle the machine.

This training has paid off. "As far as we know there has never been an accident involving a bike we've sold," he said.

Koske said he would be "100 per cent behind" regulation of licensing and testing for cyclists, saying dealers who are not concerned with safety are committing a "severe injustice." . . .

John Lemme, 23, has been driving a cycle for nine years and racing for seven. He is in his fourth year of professional racing and will participate in the national short track championship race at Sante Fe track in Hinsdale this month.

Cyclists should wear heavy clothing, preferably leather, to prevent minor cuts and wounds in case of a fall, Lemme said.

Crash helmets and face masks should also be worn, he said.

When driving on the road, cyclists should keep their headlights on to help other drivers to notice them. Too often people driving cars do not see cycles, Lemme said.

The most important thing to remember, he advised, is to stay alert at all times.

Lemme attributes the increase in accidents in part to the "different kind of people who are riding motorcycles." . . .   [Arlington Heights (Ill.) *Herald*]

EVENTS

"Go out and see what is going on at—" the city editor may say. His purpose is not investigation, certainly not expose; rather, he wants a news feature on an organization or activity not lending itself to straight news treatment but of public interest or importance.

By Emery Hutchison

Forty children who know prejudice only as a big word were frolicking in the spray arching from a fire hose.

The sight, a typical one at Camp Reinberg, near Palatine, is a recommended antidote to anyone who has been reading the lynch news from Georgia.

The skins of half the children were dark.

The experiment in inter-racial summer camping is one of the first of its kind.

Ninety-six youngsters, 48 of them Negroes, are enjoying a 10-day outing at the camp under the auspices of two Chicago community houses.

They are the fifth of seven groups from low income families who are taking turns in sharing the fun of outdoor life at the camp.

Watching the bathing youngsters from the shade of a tree was William Brueckner, 47, the outing supervisor and head resident of Emerson House, 645 N. Wood st.

"The children mix well," he said with satisfaction. "Even the smallest, and we have them as young as 5, discuss their differences in color, but that's all it is to them.

"And we hope that's all it ever will be."

A barefoot Negro boy about 10, stepping as gingerly as a tight-rope walker on the rough grass, headed for his cottage, then stopped with a grimace.

"Mr. Brueckner!" he cried, "How'm I gonna walk in these old sickleburrs?"

Brueckner lifted the boy to one shoulder and carried him on his way.

A 5-year-old Negro boy, slightly envious, decided he also wanted to play "horsie," and an 8-year-old white youngster obliged.

"I got lost today—twice," the "horsie" boasted to his rider.

Henry Cameron, 26, one of the counselors from Parkway Community House, 5120 South Park Way, looked on with a grin.

Cameron, a Negro, is a visiting student from Georgetown, British Guiana.

"They play like brothers," said the lanky youth. "Whatever we cultivate in them here," he added, his face becoming serious, "will be to their advantage later in life."　　　　　　　　　　　　　　　　　　　[Chicago *Daily News*]

Straight Features

Not related to any current news event, the straight newspaper feature article originates as an idea with a reporter or editor. In gathering material for it, the feature writer may stumble upon newsworthy information which lends weight to his story; the origin of his quest, however, was a desire to supplement rather than expand upon the day's regular news budget.

FAMILIAR PLACES

To make the commonplace attractive is a popular feature assignment. Although the average citizen uses the public parks and beaches, knows the names of the city's leading industries and the locations of important buildings, monuments and other landmarks, he may not be acquainted with the "inside" regarding them—their origin, history, laborious upkeep. The skilled feature writer should be able to find a new interesting angle about the city's most widely known institutions.

By Ed Reynolds

Geary Street slices through San Francisco like one of those split mockups that shows the interior workings.

It isn't a particularly good mock-up because Geary St., although known as one of San Francisco's better streets, is not exactly "definite."

In fact, it has the reputation of being "not quite."

It is not quite the "Main Stem" of San Francisco in the way that Mission St. is by cutting right through the city from the waterfront into Daly City and along Old Mission Road toward the Peninsula. Or like Market St. is by footing the downtown triangle and being the location of the city's major stores such as The Emporium.

GOOD RESTAURANTS

The truth is that Geary St. is a nice, respectable street that is lifted out of mediocrity by having a park at each end, by being the site of San Francisco's theatrical district, and by having some better than average restaurants on the upper end along the Avenues.

The theatrical district is on the swingingest block of the whole street between Mason and Taylor. Not only does the theatrical crowd gather at the Geary and Curran, which are side by side, but the lonely inhabitants of the honeycomb apartment houses collect in the bars for companionship.

There is no danger of any of them running dry as there are eight taverns in this single block. Here are to be found the Geary Cellar, Between Acts, On Q Lounge, Curtain Call, Stage Lounge, Sazerac and the Clift Hotel.

Despite the number of taverns there is an unusual rapport among the owners indicating that there is business enough for all.

When Jack Pryle ended his regime in the Show Club (now the Stage Lounge) on Feb. 21, 1962, the whole block turned out to give him a going away party. They held a sidewalk parade with bagpipes and a cornet for music.

Probably the greatest excitement on the block occurred on April 28, 1954, when Leo "Yammo" Walk was shot in the entrance to the Show Club....

[San Francisco *Examiner*]

OBSCURE PLACES

Straying off the beaten path, the roving reporter finds sections of his own community which neither he nor the "other half" realized exist. Such a reporter is able to make the "ole home town" much more interesting than heretofore.

We visited two nudists camps in New Jersey recently to see just what happens there and what kind of people nudists are.

Both camps—Goodland, a mile and a half from Hackettstown, and Sunshine Park, three miles from Mays Landing on the main road from Philadelphia to Ocean City—are affiliated with the American Sunbathing Association, the leading nudist organization in the country with 35 clubs in 15 states. Two states, New York and Ohio, have anti-nudism laws, though there are some nudists camps in upstate New York.

Both camps are strict about admitting visitors. Starers are thrown out on their ears, and single men are allowed at Sunshine Park only if accompanied by a woman member of their families, or by their fiancees.

No liquor or beer is permitted at either of the two camps.

Both Goodland and Sunshine Park are small resort communities where members may own or rent small cottages. Accommodations are also available for transients. As at ordinary resorts, the main activities at nudist camps are outdoor sports: swimming, volleyball, boating, sunbathing, etc.—and in the evening games like bridge or ping-pong. The only difference is that at nudist camps you do most or all these things naked.

Going without clothes is not required, but at Sunshine Park almost everyone wears nothing at all, or at most shoes and a sunhat, from getting up time in the morning until retiring at night. At Goodland, clothes are worn at meals.

Before visiting a nudist camp, we were worried about what our reactions might be. We needn't have been. After a few minutes, going without clothes seems the most natural thing in the world. Our experience, and one of the old hands said it had been his too, was that at first we were conscious only that everyone else was not wearing clothes. Later we remembered we didn't have any on either. . . .   [PM]

FAMILIAR PERSONS

When a person enters the public limelight for the first time he is worthy of a write-up to satisfy curiosity regarding him. Thereafter, as long as he continues successful or interesting, he is the potential subject of innumerable articles. What is he like? How did he do it? To what does he accredit his success? If he had it to do over again, how would he behave differently? These questions suggest only a few of the many angles from which a widely known citizen may be reintroduced to readers. Frequent practice is to run a series of "who's who" articles on the community's leading figures.

By John H. Corcoran, Jr.
From New York City

The situation is so typically Phyllis. Cloris Leachman is locked out of her suite at the Plaza and she has to *go*. "I've been drinking tea all morning, and I'm all water from the waist down," she announces as we meet in the lobby. She is here to promote her appearance April 10 in the Hollywood Television Theatre production of *Ladies of the Corridor*, by Dorothy Parker and Arnaud d'Usseau, on public television. But that, if I will excuse her, will have to wait a moment.

We are inside the suite now, a startled chambermaid having been accosted by a pleading Cloris Leachman with a request for a passkey. (Ms. Leachman has lost her own key, and I understand how Phyllis failed to pick up Rhoda for her wedding.) Here I'm presented with a second surprise: Ms. Leachman, her publicist informs me, will be interviewed in bed; she has been moving at a sandstorm pace for three days and must have her rest. I sit on the bed's edge, and moments later the star appears in a full slip, demurely covered by an enormous black boa.

She crawls under the covers and tells me to ask questions, "but first take off your shoes and make yourself comfortable." She then turns over, closes her eyes, and clutches a pillow. I'm struck with a sudden fear: I will soon be interviewing a sleeping woman.

KEEPING A BALANCE

It's a wasted worry; in the next hour Ms. Leachman imparts more information than some people do in a lifetime. She rambles through a jazz riff of verbal improvisations, self-interrupts in mid-thought, questions herself and her interviewer, pounces upon great philosophic conclusions, then quickly erases them with more questions. She slips easily into characters she has portrayed. Now she is Phyllis, speaking in the carefully clipped word monuments that leave Mary Tyler Moore speechless and Rhoda fuming. Then she is Lulu Ames, her role in *Ladies of the Corridor*, trying to balance two disparate life-styles. This is a great imponderable to Cloris Leachman, I learn—the balance between family life (she has five children) and developing oneself as a person.

In the play Ms. Leachman is a recently widowed woman who moves from her Akron, Ohio, home to begin a new life in New York City. She feels a strong bond with the character; she too, fled from the Midwest. "They hired Edna Best to play Lulu," she says. "She's a fine English actress, but Lulu is from Akron. An English actress cannot know, in her pores, the experiences of a Midwestern woman. Having been from the Midwest, no one can play Lulu as I can." . . .

"SOMETHING LACKING"

Very much the women's liberationist, Ms. Leachman sees *Ladies* as an object lesson for women seeking to avoid unfulfilled existences. "There is something lacking in women," Lulu Ames says. "We're told you grow up and get married —and we did. Our husbands were busy; we weren't part of their lives; and as we got older, we weren't part of anybody's lives."

"The worst thing that ever happened to women," adds Ms. Leachman, "is for them to get married and be put in a pumpkin shell of a beautiful house with the green Ticonderoga lawn, and then be left there. What's the worst punishment in a prison? Solitary confinement. It's a culture shock I don't think women recover from, sometimes ever."

But a career ("I hate that word, it sounds like you're pursuing something!") and family life do not easily mix, she admits.

A SON HAVING FUN

"I pay a price working. I really do. My little girl is young enough that I can let her take a day off from school when I'm home and we can just rattle around together. But my 11-year-old son is more difficult now. So my husband and I have to be more careful. The boy's having a great time, but he knows I'm not there, so why come home? We decided we are going to have to spend more time with him. Let him know we are there."

But what seems to be an answer becomes another question. "I don't know: How much time *should* you spend with the kids? Maybe it's just out of guilt, and they're as bored as we are. Maybe it's just misusing each other's energies."

She clutches the pillow and turns dreamy, her thoughts perhaps at her home in Los Angeles. "I wish, for instance, that when I got home, we could all "—she hesitates, checking the interviewer's face for reaction—"read poetry together. But everyone's so busy. One son's getting a rock group together. One's practicing piano. Another's doing homework . . . They're all good things, but . . . I miss a sort of mini-salon idea, where there could be a sharing of, of poetry, of something that is richer and slower." . . .   [*National Observer*]

Likewise in every community are scores or hundreds of persons, not so much in the limelight, who nevertheless have had picturesque lives or unique experiences. In fact, there probably is nobody about whom an interesting feature article could not be written by a skillful interviewer.

By Cal Turner
Evening News Staff Writer

Bessie and Carrie Bonawitz rolled up their sleeves this morning and, over a bowl of cereal, watched the new day break. The calendar on the wall still said some nice things about molasses and the clouds with big muscles whispered of rain.

With or without it, Bessie, 44, and Carrie, 42, would cut the day in half and tidy up the crumbs.

Operating a 115-acre farm off of Red Top Rd. in South Hanover Twp., by themselves, the sisters have known no other world than the farm.

"It's been in family for 85 years now," said Bessie, lean and tanned as Carrie, slightly taller, but with the same brown eyes and a smile that tries to back up. "We share the work and it's up every morning at 5 and in bed about 9:30."

Sitting at the small kitchen table while the spotless pale green linoleum on the floor caught a handful of daylight, Bessie admitted each day was "work" and when it came time to sit down "and turn on the teevee" there just wasn't "much to talk about."

The sisters began operating the farm by themselves when their father died in 1959 at the age of 79. There had been four boys and seven girls.

"But everybody moved away," said Bessie, smiling slightly. "Found better paying jobs."

Corn, wheat, barley and grass for hay are the principal crops on the farm, which tags the eye like a bright child's toy tucked in the green and brown dip of the hills.

The house, barn and milking room are white as a sheet, trimmed in green. In the shadows of the bean trees, two large, old dogs growl at a mad fly that springs from the heavy, pungent odor of the barn. Near a dilapidated corn crib, the blade of a plow is polished by the sunlight.

"I'm plowing now for barley," said Carrie, grinning . . . .

[Harrisburg (Pa.) *Evening News*]

In addition to whatever news interest he may have as an individual, everyone is the potential source of a feature article because of the way in which he earns a living. When hard put to it to find a personality easily worked up into a story, the reporter can seek out someone engaged in a job about which what he has to say can be used effectively.

By David Warner

"Where," the voice on the phone asked a City Hall worker, "can I get a license for my lion?"

Another fellow wanted the city to come pick up his mother-in-law, who, he believed, was cleverly disguised as a cat cavorting about his backyard.

Which is not to forget the lady who threatened to call the President of the United States as part of a crusade to get her street salted one snowy day.

Effie Mousadis, the 29-year-old supervisor of the Mayor's Service Center at City Hall has heard those and many more gripes, complaints, inquiries and requests during her four years on the job.

As a matter of fact, she figures she, and her staff of four, get about 110 calls, visits or letters a day from Pittsburghers.

In 1974, Mrs. Mousadis figures they were contacted about 30,000 times by city residents looking for help and information.

(Memo to you lion lovers: The city doesn't have licenses for your charming little pets.)

However, Mrs. Mousadis figures 70 per cent of the complaints her department gets are cleared up satisfactorily.

She and her staff occupy space in the lobby of the city treasurer's office on the ground floor of the City-County Building.

While many residents walk in to complain in person, most call the special number, 261-7410.

After the staff finds out what the problem is, the complaint is forwarded to one of the other city departments for action.

The problem is usually cleared up within two weeks, she said.

Mrs. Mousadis didn't hesitate when asked what her most frequent complaints are.

In the winter, it's salt on the streets and garbage collection, she indicated, and in the summer it's the cleaning of vacant lots and tree pruning.

That's not to say, however, the service center doesn't get other types of complaints too.

For instance, there were 549 complaints about rats last year.

And there's apparently an entire brigade of citizens who want to talk about potholes. . . . [Pittsburgh *Press*]

HISTORICAL

The familiar or unusual place or person feature quite frequently is historical, as there is no community without a building or citizen associated with some important event of the past. Old-timers like to recall events of yesterday. If possible, the historical feature should be illustrated with pictures taken at the time of the event being recalled.

The mystery of an old sign painted on the upper portion of the west wall of a four-story building at 414–18 Market street, was partly solved today by two St. Louisans who are keenly interested in the history and architecture of the city's oldest buildings. They are John A. Bryan, research architect at the Jefferson National Expansion Memorial, and Dr. William G. Swekosky, a dentist whose hobby is the history of old buildings.

The sign which caused them to delve into old city directories advertises "Crow & Farrell, Dry Goods." Who Crow and Farrell were and the years when they did business have perplexed many persons. Recently, however, Bryan and Swekosky, working independently, decided to find out for themselves.

Bryan, using an old city directory, said he found that the dry goods establishment occupied the ground floor at 418 Market about 1864, but he was unable to identify either Mr. Farrell or Mr. Crow. The latter, he says, is not the Wayman Crow who was a former member of the legislature and a leader in the establishment of Elliott Seminary, now Washington University. Wayman Crow's dry goods firm was on Main (now First) street, Bryan said.

Dr. Swekosky said the firm of Crow and Farrell was in the wholesale and retail dry goods business and rented space at the Market street address from 1868 to 1876. The firm was headed by William F. Crow and John Farrell, he said, and later was at the northwest corner of Fourth street and Washington avenue, but he was unable to identify the two men any further.

The sign is in black letters on a white background painted on the rough brick wall. It was uncovered when the adjoining five-story commercial structure, on the southeast corner of Market street and Broadway, was torn down last year. The site today is a parking lot. . . .   [St. Louis *Post-Dispatch*]

STUNTS

The stunt reporter courts adventure and finds it in submarines, airplanes, ambulances, breadlines, slums, morgues, police patrols and all sorts of out-of-the-way places. Reporters impersonate beggars, unemployed persons, street-corner Santa Clauses and criminals to obtain feature stories about the reactions of others and an insight into how certain types of individuals exist.

By Joseph Fisher

I parlayed the weightiest assignment in town into a series of small fortunes with a handful of pennies.

Amazing? Well, I would say it is all in the weigh you look at it. I did it from a vantage point atop of several scales in the downtown area.

It all began as part of an experiment to test the accuracy of penny weight scales in Rockford. Here are the facts. The discrepancies are subject to weighing.

"WEIGHED IN" OFFICIALLY

Needing a base for my calculations, I weighed in on the city health department scale.

My weight established at 182½ pounds, I set out with my handful of pennies in pursuit of accuracy and fortune.

My first stop was an E. State st. drug store. "Your weight and fortune," the sign on the scale read.

Stepping up, I turned the fortune knob to the query: "Shall I be boss in my family?" For a penny, I got the answer: "Yes, by fighting." The scale recorded my fighting weight at 182¼.

On W. State st., I spotted an intriguing challenge extended by a scale in front of a 5 and 10-cent store. "Free, if you guess your weight," was the proffered invitation.

"WHAT A GAMBLER!"

Gambler that I am, I decided to risk it. Turning the weight estimator to 182½, I recklessly deposited a penny and watched the needle stop at 183½. I was on the verge of yelling "fake" when my penny was refunded despite the one-pound variance.

Next I moved over to the Rockford Potato company on Elm st. It specializes in handling sacks. I weighed in at an even 181.

In quick succession, I tested scales in a W. State st. restaurant, the Illinois National Bank, and a S. Main st. restaurant. I got three different answers: 184, 183, and 182.

At the bus station, my "exact" weight, according to the scale, was 182. In a S. Main st. drug store I ballooned to 183¾.

I resumed my fortune quest on a scale in another W. State 5 and 10-cent store. For a penny, I was informed I "have tact, personality, and great magnetism. You usually attain your aim without very much difficulty," the fortune card concluded.

The last prophecy seemed contradictory since the space reserved for my weight came out blank. I was in complete agreement with the first part of my fortune.

FINDS DOUBLE FEATURE

In a N. Main st. theater, I was treated to a double feature—one scale in the lounge, and another on the mezzanine.

The lounge scale recorded my weight at 184¾. Its fortune apparatus failed to answer my question: "What shall I eat?" I weighed 182½ on the mezzanine scale, but I was unable to find out if "my friends like my singing."

At another N. Main st. theater, I learned I would prosper "through hard work." My weight was back to 183½.

I shed a half a pound and slumped to 183 in a N. Main st. drug store.

Back on E. State st., I returned to the drug store where I weighed 182½. Now, I concentrated on finding out about the future.

Successive turns on the fortune knob, at a penny a turn revealed that I "will have no great sorrow," "prosper, if I work," but still end up with an inheritance that "will be a legacy of debts."

DISILLUSIONED, TRIES NAVY

Disillusioned, I headed for the naval recruiter's office in the post office building.

"Your fortune's with the navy son," Chief Recruiter E. F. Brannin assured me.

Land lover that I am, I explained I was willing to face the rigors of civilian life. The disappointed chief put me on the scale and said I weighed 182½.

I headed back to the office. I weigh 182½—I guess.

[Rockford (Ill.) *Register-Republic*]

SITUATIONS

Differing from the roundup story of a series of current news events, the straight situation feature article is "trumped up" by an investigating reporter. What happens to discarded automobiles? What name appears most frequently in the city directory? How do college students earn their tuitions? What pets are most popular in the community? Do men and women differ in what they look for in apartments? These questions suggest the types of assignment which originate as "hunches." Factual, even statistical in content, the written stories nevertheless were "manufactured."

By Dale Morrison

As you mull over your income tax forms this weekend in a last minute rush to meet the April 17 deadline, you may wonder where it all goes.

Not the money, everybody knows where that goes.

But what about Form 1040 or 1040A or 1040W or Schedule G, or the other monuments to documented confusion that Americans use to keep their government in the green?

When John Q. Taxpayer drops his tax return in the corner mailbox he launches it on a seven-year trip to oblivion with a few interesting way points.

Before it's forgotten, it's processed, probed and purged by a small army of experts.

The government's first processing step, naturally enough, is to remove returns from their envelopes.

It may not sound like much but it's a big job.

This week the Chicago office of the Internal Revenue Service has 140 employees doing nothing but opening envelopes, taking out forms, and noting on the return the amount of money sent in.

Harold R. All, district director of the I.R.S. here, said his office is expected to receive about 600,000 pieces of mail a day early next week.

From Jan. 1 to the week of the tax deadline it receives an average of 80,000 returns a day.

Once the envelope is opened, returns and money—in the form of checks, currency or money order—part company.

At the end of each working day the receipts from the 26 northern Illinois counties served by the Chicago office are deposited in the I.R.S. account of the Federal Reserve Bank of Chicago.

Deposits from personal income tax payments average $11,000,000 a day during the height of the season and total about $2 billion a year.

Uncle Sam can tap the I.R.S. account to meet current expenses the minute the money is in the bank.

Meanwhile, the incoming returns are broken down into more than 20 categories.

Mailing lists are made up from each category—wage earner, small businessman, farmer, etc.—so that next year each taxpayer receives the same series of forms he filed this year.

At this stage, raw material for statistical surveys is drawn from the forms.

In the next processing step, the arithmetic in each return is checked.

I.R.S. auditors say that of the 2,800,000 taxpayers who file in the Chicago area, many have divergent views on the sum of 2 and 2.

About two-thirds of the returns are checked by hand and eye.

A skilled Comptometer operator can work through 35 returns an hour.

The other third—returns filed on punched card (Form 1040A)—are shipped to the I.R.S.'s service center in Kansas City, Mo.

There, electronics data processing machines check addition hundreds of times faster than flesh and blood processors.

Next comes the check for what revenue men delicately call "irregularities."

Highly trained agents scan each return, looking for those little apparent inconsistencies that frequently send poor John Q. scurrying for his records and sometimes send tax cheats to jail.

More often an agent's curiosity is aroused by what appear to be exorbitant business or medical expenses. The taxpayer is then asked to come in and give documentary proof of his claims.

Occasionally agents pick a return at random and ask the taxpayer to justify it.

Once over the checking hurdles returns are divided into two classes: those that will cost the government money and those that need a bill for the taxpayer.

Of late, the I.R.S. has gone to some pains to get out refunds before it sends out bills.

If a refund is due, the government must pay before June 1 or face 6 per cent interest charges. Interest from taxpayers who owe money starts the day the return is due.

Once accounts are squared the returns are confined to filing cabinets covering some 25,000 square feet of the main Chicago I.R.S. office.

After three years of dust-gathering there, they are moved to the two-square block federal records building at 78th St. and Deamington, where they gather more dust for another four years.

With the expiration of the statute of limitations at the end of seven years, the returns are just so much scrap to the government, just as well forgotten.

The forms are bundled and either sold to scrap dealers or burned.

[Chicago *Daily News*]

Becoming proficient as a feature writer is excellent preparation for interpretative reporting and writing of more significant happenings in city, state, nation and the world.

APPENDIX

STYLE

One important effect of technological change on the newsroom has been the standardization of the stylebook. Traditionally newspaper style was arbitrary and inconsistent, differing from paper to paper. Now, with an increasing amount of copy reaching the editorial desks from electronic sources, both within and without the office, the task of copy reading has been simplified by adoption of uniform style rules. They are those devised by the Associated Press and United Press International. Warning is given that a considerably revised edition of the *Newswire Stylebook* will be completed within a year. As of now, however, Chapters 1, 2, 3 and 4 of the book's 11 chapters are as follows:

Capitalization I

1.1 CAPITALIZE titles preceding a name: Secretary of State John Foster Dulles. LOWER CASE title standing alone or following a name: John Foster Dulles, secretary of state. EXCEPTION: Incumbent president of the United States is always capitalized. Do not capitalize candidate for president, no president may seize, etc.

1.2 CAPITALIZE government officials when used with name as title: Queen Elizabeth II, Premier Debre, etc. LOWER CASE when standing alone or following a name: Debre, premier of France.

1.3 CAPITALIZE Pope in all usage; pontiff is lower case.

1.4 CAPITALIZE foreign religious leader titles Imam, Patriarch, etc., but LOWER CASE standing alone or following a name. EXCEPTION: Pope and Dalai Lama, capitalized in all usage. (See Section VIII)

1.5 CAPITALIZE titles of authority before name but LOWER CASE standing alone or following a name: Ambassador John Jones; Jones, ambassador; the ambassador. (See 1.12, 3.31)

1.6 Long titles should follow a name: John Jones, executive director of the commercial department of Blank & Co. Richard Roe, secretary-treasurer, Blank & Co. (See 6.5)

1.7 LOWER CASE occupational or "false" titles such as day laborer John Jones, rookie left-handed pitcher Bill Wills, defense attorney John Jones. (See 2.14)

1.8 CAPITALIZE Union, Republic, Colonies referring to the United States; Republic of Korea, French Fifth Republic. (See 2.12)

1.9 CAPITALIZE U.S. Congress, Senate, House, Cabinet; Legislature when preceded by name of state; City Council; Security Council. LOWER CASE when standing alone: The legislature passed 300 bills.
The building is the Capitol, the city is capital.
Do not capitalize "congress" when it is used as a synonym for convention. (See 1.20)

1.10 CAPITALIZE committee in full names: Senate Judiciary Committee, House Ways and Means Committee, etc. LOWER CASE "subcommittee" in titles and standing alone, also "committee" standing alone.
In some shortened versions of long committee names, do not capitalize: Special Senate Select Committee to Investigate Improper Labor-Management Practices often is rackets committee, not capitalized.

1.11 CAPITALIZE full titles: Interstate Commerce Commission, New York State Thruway Authority, International Atomic Energy Authority, etc., LOWER CASE authority, commission, etc., standing alone. (See 2.1)

1.12 CAPITALIZE Supreme Court, Juvenile Court, 6th U.S. Circuit Court of Appeals, etc. (See 4.2) Specify which U.S. Court such as district, patent, tax, etc. It is Juvenile Court Judge John Jones and not Juvenile Judge John Jones.

1.13 CAPITALIZE Social Security (Administration, Act) when referring to U.S. system: He was receiving Social Security payments. LOWER CASE use in general sense: He was an advocate of social security for old age.

1.14 CAPITALIZE U.S. armed forces: Army (USA), Air Force (USAF), Navy (USN), Marines (USMC), Coast Guard, National Guard but LOWER CASE all foreign except Royal Air Force (RAF) and Royal Canadian Air Force (RCAF); French Foreign Legion, no abbreviation.
CAPITALIZE Marine, Coast Guardman, Swiss Guard, Evzone, Bengal Lancer, etc. LOWER CASE solider, sailor, etc. NOTE: It is Coast Guardman (no "s") if member of U.S. Coast Guard.
CAPITALIZE Irish Republican Army (political). (See 1.20)

1.15 CAPITALIZE Joint Chiefs of Staff but LOWER CASE chiefs of staff.

1.16 CAPITALIZE holidays, historic events, ecclesiastical feasts, fast days, special events, hurricanes, typhoons, etc. Mothers Day, Labor Day, Battle of the Bulge, Good Friday, Passover, Christmas, Halloween, National Safety Week, Hurricane Hazel, Typhoon Tilda, New Year's (Day, Eve) but LOWER CASE: What will the new year bring? At the start of the new year, etc.

1.17 CAPITALIZE Antarctica, Arctic Circle but not antarctic or arctic.

1.18 CAPITALIZE specific regions: Middle East, Mideast, Middle West, Midwest, Upper Peninsula (Michigan), Southern (Illinois, California) Texas (Oklahoma) Panhandle, Orient, Chicago's near South Side, Loop, etc.

1.19 CAPITALIZE ideological or political areas: East-West, East Germany, West Germany. LOWER CASE mere direction: Snow fell in western North Dakota.

1.20 CAPITALIZE political parties and members but not "party." Democrat, Democratic, Republican, Socialist, Independent, Nationalist, Communist, Congress (India) etc. LOWER CASE democratic form of government, republican system, socialism, communism, etc.

CAPITALIZE Red when used as political, geographic, military, etc., descriptive.

LOWER CASE nationalist in referring to a partisan of a country.

CAPITALIZE Algerian Liberation Front (FLN) and Irish Republican Army (IRA). (See 1.14).

1.21 CAPITALIZE names of fraternal organizations: B'nai B'rith (no abbreviation), Ancient Free & Accepted Masons (AF&AM), Knights of Columbus (K. of C. as departure from 2.1). (See 2.5)

1.22 CAPITALIZE Deity and He, His, Him denoting Deity but not who, whose, whom. CAPITALIZE Talmud, Koran, Bible and all names of the Bible, confessions of faith and their adherents. (See Section VIII)

CAPITALIZE Satan and Hades but not devil and hell.

1.23 CAPITALIZE Civil War, War Between the States, Korean War, Revolution (U.S. and Bolshevik), World War I, World War II, etc.

1.24 CAPITALIZE names of races: Caucasian, Chinese, Negro, Indian, etc. LOWER CASE black, white, red (See 2.20), yellow. Do NOT use "colored" for Negro except in National Association for the Advancement of Colored People. Colored is correct in African usage.

Identification by race should be made when it is pertinent.

1.25 CAPITALIZE common noun as part of formal name: Hoover Dam, Missouri River, Barr County Courthouse. LOWER CASE dam, river, courthouse, etc., standing alone. CAPITALIZE Empire State Building, Blue Room, Carlton House (hotel), Carlton house (home), Wall Street, Hollywood Boulevard. (See 4.1)

Plurals would be: Broad and Main streets.

1.26 CAPITALIZE species of livestock, animals, fowl, etc., but LOWER CASE noun: Airedale, terrier, Percheron, horse; Hereford, white-face, etc.

1.27 CAPITALIZE names of flowers: Peace rose, etc. If Latin generic names are used CAPITALIZE the genus (camellia, Thea japonica).

1.28 CAPITALIZE trade names and trademark names: Super Sabre Jet, Thunderjet, but Boeing 707 jet (jet descriptive, not part of name), Pan Am Clipper.

"Coke" is a registered trademark of Coca-Cola and is not a synonym for soft drinks. "Thermos" is a registered trademark. Use vacuum bottle (flask, jug) instead.

Use generic, or broad, term preferably in all trademark names.

1.29 Some proper names have acquired independent common meaning and are not capitalized. They include paris green, dutch door, brussels sprouts, etc. Check dictionary.

1.30 CAPITALIZE titles of books, plays, hymns, poems, songs, etc., and place in quotation marks: "The Courtship of Miles Standish." (See 3.26)

The words a, in, of, etc., are capitalized only at the start or end of a title: "Of Thee I Sing" and "All Returns Are In" as examples.

1.31 CAPITALIZE first word of a quotation making a complete sentence after a comma or colon: Franklin said, "A penny saved is a penny earned." (See 3.16)

1.32 CAPITALIZE names of organizations, expositions, etc., Boy Scouts, Red Cross, World's Fair, Iowa State Fair but LOWER CASE scout, fair standing alone.

1.33 CAPITALIZATION of names should follow the use of preference of the person. In general, foreign particles are lower case when used with a forename, initials or title: Charles de Gaulle, Gen. de Gaulle, but De Gaulle without forename or title. (See 3.5, 6.4)

In anglicized versions the article usually is capitalized: Fiorello La Guardia.

It is E. I. du Pont de Nemours and Du Pont; Irenee du Pont but Samuel F. Du Pont (his usage).

1.34 CAPITALIZE fanciful appellations: Buckeye State, Leatherneck, Project Mercury, Operation Deep Freeze (Deepfreeze, one word, is trademark.)

1.35 CAPITALIZE decorations, awards, etc. Medal of Honor, Nobel Peace Prize.

Abbreviations II

2.1 First mention of organizations, firms, agencies, groups, etc., should be spelled out. Exception: AFL-CIO. In names that do not have commonly known abbreviations, the abbreviation should be bracketed after the spelled name. Thereafter in the story the abbreviation may be used. Example:

The desire was expressed in the Inter-American Economic and Social Council (IA-ECOSOC) of the Organization of American States (OAS) in considering the European Economic Cooperation Organization (ECCO).

Distant Early Warning line (DEW line).

General Agreement of Tariffs and Trade (GATT).

2.2 ABBREVIATE time zones, airplane designations, ships, distress call, military terms, etc. EDT, CST, MIG17, B60, Military Police (MP), absent without official leave (AWOL), SOS (but May Day), USS Iowa, SS Brasil. (See 3.3, 10.12, 6.15)

2.3 ABBREVIATE business firms: Warner Bros.; Brown Implement Co.; Amalgamated Leather, Ltd.; Smith & Co., Inc. (See 3.40)

2.4 ABBREVIATE St., Ave., Blvd., Ter., in addresses but not Point, Port, Circle, Plaza, Place, Drive, Oval, Road, Lane. Examples:

16 E. 72nd St. (single "E" with period); 16 Gregory Ave. NW (no periods in "NW"); Sunset Boulevard, Main Street, Fifth Avenue (no addresses). (See 1.25, 4.1)

2.5 Lower case abbreviations usually take periods. The rule of thumb is if the letters without periods spell words, periods are needed. Examples: c.o.d., f.o.b., etc. However, m.p.h., a.m., p.m.

Periods are not needed in 35mm (film), 105mm (armament), ips (tape recording).

In news stories first mention of speed should be "miles an hour" or "miles per hour" and thereafter in story use m.p.h.

ABBREVIATE versus as vs. (with period).

2.6 ABBREVIATE states which follow cities (towns, villages, etc.), airbases, Indian agencies, national parks, etc. (See 3.23)

2.7 Standard abbreviations for states (rule of thumb is abbreviate none of six letters or less except Texas):

Ala.	Ill.	Miss.	N.M.	Tenn.
Ariz.	Ind.	Mo.	N.Y.	Tex.
Ark.	Kan.	Mont.	Okla.	Vt.
Calif.	Ky.	Neb.	Ore.	Va.
Colo.	La.	Nev.	Pa.	Wash.
Conn.	Md.	N.C.	R.I.	Wis.
Del.	Mass.	N.D.	S.C.	W.Va.
Fla.	Mich.	N.H.	S.D.	Wyo.
Ga.	Minn.	N.J.		

Do not abbreviate Alaska, Hawaii, Idaho, Iowa, Ohio, Maine or Utah.

All states are spelled standing alone: He went to Minnesota at the turn of the century.

2.8 ABBREVIATIONS:

C.Z.	P.R.	V.I.	Atla.	B.C.	Man.	N.S.
Que.	Ont.	Sask.	Nfld.	N.B.	B.W.I.	P.E.I.

but obscure ones should be spelled in story, such as Prince Edward Island, etc.

2.9 B.C. as abbreviation of Canadian province must be preceded by town name; B.C., the era, must be preceded by a date.

2.10 ABBREVIATE U.S.S.R. and U.A.R. in datelines.

2.11 ABBREVIATE United Nations and United States in titles: U.S. Junior Chamber of Commerce (Jaycees as exception in abbreviation by letters), U.N. Educational, Scientific and Cultural Organization (UNESCO). (See 2.1, 3.3)

2.12 Spell United States and United Nations when used as a noun. U.S.A. and U.N. as nouns may be used in texts or direct quotations.

2.13 ABBREVIATE and capitalize religious, fraternal, scholastic or honorary degrees, etc., but lower case when spelled: B.A., bachelor of arts. (See 8.4)

2.14 ABBREVIATE titles and capitalize: Mr., Mrs., M., Mlle., Dr., Prof., Sen., Rep., Asst., Lt. Gov., Gov. Gen., Supt., Atty. Gen., Dist. Atty., in titles before names but not after names. Do not abbreviate attorney in: The statement by defense attorney John Jones, etc. (See 1.7)

2.15 Mr. is used only with Mrs., or with clerical titles (except in texts or verbatim quotes). (See 8.4, 8.9, 8.10)

2.16 Do NOT abbreviate port, association, point, detective, department, deputy, commandant, commodore, field marshal, general manager, secretary-general, secretary, treasurer, fleet admiral or general of the armies (but Adm. Nimitz or Gen. Pershing is correct). (See 2.21)
Do NOT abbreviate " guaranteed annual wage " and do NOT abbreviate Christmas.

2.17 ABBREVIATE months when used with dates: Oct. 12, 1492; but spell out otherwise as October 1492. Abbreviations for months are Jan., Feb., Aug., Sept., Oct., Nov., Dec. Do not abbreviate March, April, May, June or July except in tabular or financial routine where the abbreviations are Mar, Apr, Jun, Jly and spell May.

2.18 Days of the week are abbreviated only in tabular matter or financial routine where they are Mon, Tue, Wed, Thu, Fri, Sat, Sun. The proper word division for Wednesday is: Wednes-day.

2.19 ABBREVIATE St. and Ste. as in Sault Ste. Marie, St. Louis, St. Lawrence, etc. (except Saint John, N.B.). Abbreviate the mountain but spell the city: Mt. Everest, Mount Vernon; Abbreviate army post but spell city: Ft. Sill, Fort Meyer.

2.20 Do not abbreviate Alexander, Benjamin, Charles, Frederick, William, etc., as Alec, Alex, Ben., Benj., Chas., etc., unless person does so himself. Follow person's preference.

2.21 Military abbreviations:

ARMY

General	Gen.	First Sergeant	1st. Sgt.
Lieutenant General	Lt. Gen.	Specialist Eight	Spec. 8
Major General	Maj. Gen.	Platoon Sergeant	Platoon Sgt.
Brigadier General	Brig. Gen.	Sergeant First Class	Sgt. 1.C.
Colonel	Col.	Specialist Seven	Spec. 7
Lieutenant Colonel	Lt. Col.	Staff Sergeant	S. Sgt.
Major	Maj.	Specialist Six	Spec. 6
Captain	Capt.	Sergeant	Sgt.
Lieutenant	Lt.	Specialist Five	Spec. 5
Chief Warrant Officer	CWO	Corporal	Cpl.
Warrant Officer	WO	Specialist Four	Spec. 4
Sergeant Major	Sgt. Maj.	Private First Class	Pfc.
Specialist Nine	Spec. 9	Private	Pvt.
Master Sergeant	M. Sgt.	Recruit	Rct.

NAVY, COAST GUARD

Admiral	Adm.
Vice Admiral	Vice Adm.
Rear Admiral	Rear Adm.
Commodore	Commodore
Captain	Capt.
Commander	Cmdr.
Lieutenant Commander	Lt. Cmdr.
Lieutenant	Lt.
Lieutenant Junior Grade	Lt. (j.g.)
Ensign	Ens.
Commissioned Warrant Officer	CWO
Warrant Officer	WO
Master Chief Petty Officer	M.CPO
Senior Chief Petty Officer	S.CPO
Chief Petty Officer	CPO
Petty Officer 1st Class	PO 1.C.
Petty Officer Second Class	PO 2.C.
Petty Officer Third Class	PO 3.C.
Seaman	Seaman
Seaman Apprentice	Seaman Appren.
Seaman Recruit	Seaman Rct.

MARINE CORPS

Commissioned officers are abbreviated the same as Army, warrant officers the same as Navy. Noncommissioned designations are the same as Army except specialist and:

Master Gunnery Sergeant	Mgy. Sgt.
Gunnery Sergeant	Gunnery Sgt.
Lance Corporal	Lance Cpl.

AIR FORCE

Air Force commissioned officers are abbreviated the same as Army. Noncommissioned designations include:

Chief Master Sergeant	CM. Sgt.
Senior Master Sergeant	SM. Sgt.
Master Sergeant	M. Sgt.
Technical Sergeant	T. Sgt.
Staff Sergeant	S. Sgt.
Airman 1st Class	Airman 1.C.
Airman 2nd Class	Airman 2.C.
Airman 3rd Class	Airman 3.C.
Airman Basic	Airman

The Air Force also may designate certain other descriptions as radarman, navigator, etc., but such designations are not abbreviated.

The Navy has numerous ratings such as machinist, torpedoman, etc., and they are not abbreviated.

The Army, Coast Guard and Marine Corps also may describe personnel by specific duty in addition to rank.

Note: The period is used in several abbreviations, such as Spec. 1.C., in Teletypesetter in the absence of the diagonal or slash mark.

Punctuation III

Punctuation in printing serves the same purpose as voice inflection in speaking. Proper phrasing avoids ambiguity, insures clarity and lessens need for punctuation.

THE PERIOD

3.1 The period is used after a declarative or imperative sentence: The facing is Vermont marble. Shut the door.

The period is used after a question intended as a suggestion: Tell how it was done.

The period is used in summary form:

1. Korean War. 2. Domestic policy. A. Punctuate properly. B. Write simply.

3.2 The period is used for ellipsis and in some columnist material.
Ellipsis: The combine ... was secure.
Column: Esther Williams gets the role. ... John Hay signed a new contract.
Rephrasing to avoid ellipses is preferable.

3.3 The period is used in abbreviations: U.S., U.N., c.o.d., etc. (See
Section II for variations)

3.4 The period separates integer and decimal: 3.75 per cent; $8.25; 1.25
meters. (See 7.1, 7.2, 7.5, 7.7)

3.5 The period is omitted after a letter casually used as a name, and
where a person omits the period in his name:
A said to B that he was not watching.
Herman B Wells (his usage). (See 1.33)

THE COMMA

3.6 The comma separates words or figures:
What the solution is, is a question.
Aug. 1, 1960.   1,234,567
The comma serves in a series:
The woman was short, slender, blonde, well-dressed and old.
x, y and z.   1, 2 and 3.
The Selma, Ala., group saw the governor.

3.7 Do not use comma before " of ": Brown of Arkadelphia.

3.8 Newspaper usage has, in most cases, eliminated the comma before
" and " and " or " but this practice does not lessen the need for the mark in:
Fish abounded in the lake, and the shore was lined with deer.

3.9 The comma is used to set off attribution: The work, he said, is
exacting. It is used in scores: Milwaukee 6, St. Louis 5.

3.10 The comma is used to separate in apposition or contrast:
Smithwick, the favorite, won handily.
But: The car that failed had been ahead.

3.11 The comma is omitted before Roman numerals, Jr., Sr., the am-
persand, dash, in street addresses, telephone numbers and serial numbers:
Louis XVI, John Jones Jr., Smith & Co., ORegon 3-3617, 12345 Oak St.,
A1234567. (See 4.4)

THE SEMICOLON

3.12 The semicolon separates phrases containing commas to avoid confusion, and separates statements of contrast and statements too closely
related:

The draperies, which were ornate, displeased me; the walls, light blue, were pleasing.

The party consisted of B. M. Jordan; R. J. Kelly, his secretary; Mrs. Jordan; Martha Brown, her nurse; and three servants. (Without the semicolons, that could be read as nine persons.)

THE APOSTROPHE

3.13 The apostrophe indicates the possessive case of nouns, omission of figures, and contractions.

Usually the possessive of a singular noun not ending in " s " is formed by adding the apostrophe and " s "; the plural noun by adding the " s " and then the apostrophe: boys' wear, men's wear.

The apostrophe also is used in the plural possessive " es "; Joneses' house.

The " s " is dropped and only the apostrophe used in " for conscience' sake " or in a sibilant double or triple " s " as " Moses' tablet."

In single letters: A's.

3.14 The apostrophe is used in contractions: I've, isn't; in omission of figures: '90, '90s, class of '22. (See 4.3)

3.15 The apostrophe use or lack of should follow the official name of group, institution, locality, etc.: Johns Hopkins University, Actors Equity Association, Court of St. James's (variation of possessive ending).

THE COLON

3.16 The colon precedes the final clause summarizing prior matter; introduces listings, statements and texts; marks discontinuity, and takes the place of an implied " for instance ":

The question came up: What does he want to do? (See 1.31)

States and funds allotted were: Alabama $6,000; Arizona $4,000, etc.

3.17 The colon is used in clock time: 8:15 p.m. (See 4.9)

3.18 The colon is used in Bible and legal citations:

Matt 2:14. Missouri Statutes 3: 245–260.

THE EXCLAMATION POINT

3.19 The exclamation point is used to indicate surprise, appeal, incredulity or other strong emotion:

How wonderful! What! He yelled, " Come here!"

THE QUESTION MARK

3.20 The question mark follows a direct question, marks a gap or uncertainty and in the latter use is enclosed in parentheses:

What happened to Jones?

It was April 13 (?) that I saw him.

The mark also is used in public proceedings, interviews, etc.:

Q. Were you there? A. I don't recall.

Exception: Where, in interviews, the question or answer is of some length, it is preferable to paragraph both Q. and A.

PARENTHESES

3.21 Parentheses set off material, or an element of a sentence.

It is not the custom (at least in the areas mentioned) to stand at attention.

3.22 Where location identification is needed but is not part of the official name: The Springfield (Ohio) Historical Society edition, etc. It is not necessary to bracket: The Springfield, Ohio, area population, etc.

3.23 Parentheses are not used around political-geographical designation: Sen. Theodore Francis Green, D-R.I., and Rep. Charles A. Halleck, R-Ind., were invited. (See 2.6)

3.24 Parentheses set off letters or figures in a series: The order of importance will be (a) general acceptance, (b) costs, and (c) opposition.

3.25 Where part of a sentence is parenthetical and the punctuation mark comes at the end of the sentence it goes outside:

He habitually uses two words incorrectly (practical and practicable).

Ordinarily the mark goes inside: (The foregoing was taken from an essay.)

Several paragraphs of parenthetical matter start with the opening mark on each paragraph and the final paragraph is ended with a closing parenthesis with the punctuation inside.

QUOTATION MARKS

3.26 Quotation marks enclose direct quotations; are used around phrases in ironical uses; around slang expressions; misnomers; titles of books, plays, poems, songs, lectures or speeches when the full title is used; hymns; movies; TV programs, etc. (See 1.30, 10.14)

3.27 Use quotation marks instead of parentheses around nicknames apart from the name: Smith, who weighed 280, was called "Slim."

Harold "Red" Grange.

The comma and period are placed inside the quotation marks. Other punctuation is placed according to construction:

Why call it a "gentlemen's agreement"?

The sequence in multiple quotations:

"The question is 'Does his position violate the "gentlemen's 'post-haste' agreement" so eloquently described by my colleague as "tommyrot"?'"

THE DASH

3.28 The dash indicates a sudden change. Examples:

He claimed—no one denied it—that he had priority.

It can be used instead of parentheses in many cases: 10 pounds—$28—paid.

If that man should gain control—God forbid!—our troubles will have only begun.

The monarch—shall we call him a knave or a fool?—approved it.

3.29 The dash is used after the logotype and before the first word of a story:

NEW YORK (logotype)—Mayor, etc.

3.30 The dash also is used as the minus sign in temperatures to indicate below-zero temperature: Duluth —12.

THE HYPHEN

3.31 The hyphen is one of the least correctly used, and most abused, marks. It is used properly to form compound words, to divide words in composition, in figures, in some abbreviations, and to separate double vowels in some cases.

The general rule for hyphens is that "like" characters take the hyphen, "unlike" characters do not.

A-bomb, U-boat, 20-20 vision, 3D, B60, MIG17, 3-2 (odds and scores), secretary-treasurer, south-southwest, north-central.

Exception: 4-H Club.

3.32 Adjectival use must be clear. (See 5.6)

The 6-foot man eating shark was killed (the man was).

The 6-foot man-eating shark was killed (the shark was).

3.33 Suspensive hyphenation:

The A- and H-bombs were exploded.

The 5- and 6-year-olds attend morning classes.

3.34 Ordinarily in prefixes ending in vowels and followed by the same vowel, the hyphen is used: pre-empt, re-elect. (Check dictionary for exceptions such as cooperate, coed, coordinates, etc.)

3.35 NEVER use the hyphen with adverb ending in "ly" such as badly damaged, fully informed, newly chosen, etc.

3.36 The hyphen also serves to distinguish meaning of similarly spelled words: recover, re-cover; resent, re-sent.

3.37 The hyphen also separates a prefix from a proper noun: pre-Raphaelite, un-American, etc.

3.38 The prefix "ex" is hyphened: ex-champion.

3.39 The hyphen has been abandoned in newspaper usage in weekend, worldwide, nationwide, etc.

THE AMPERSAND

3.40 The ampersand is used in abbreviations and firm names: Jones & Co., AT&T, etc. (See 2.3)

Numerals IV

In general, spell below 10, use numerals for 10 and above.

4.1 Numerals are used exclusively in tabular and statistical matter, records, election returns, times, speeds, latitude and longitude, temperatures, highways, distances, dimensions, heights, ages, ratios, proportions, military units, political divisions, orchestra instruments, court districts or divisions, handicaps, betting odds and dates (Fourth of July and July Fourth acceptable).

Use figures in all man or animal ages. Spell under 10 for inanimates: four-mile-trip, four miles from the center, etc.

Exceptions Fifth Avenue, Fifth Republic of France (See 1.25, 2.4), Big Ten, Dartmouth eleven.

The forms: 3-year-old girl, the girl is 3, 5 feet 2, 5-foot-2 trench, Washington won, 6-3; $10 shirt, seven-cent stamp, eight-hour day, five-day week, 60 cents (See 4.6), .38-caliber pistol.

6:30 p.m. or 6:30 o'clock Monday night (never 6:30 p.m. Monday night, or 6:30 p.m. o'clock). (See 6.15)

The vote was 1,345 for and 1,300 against.

The ratio was 6 to 4, but the 6-4 ratio.

It is 20th century but Twentieth Century Limited (train).

In series, keep the simplest related forms:

There are 3 ten-room houses, 1 fourteen-room house, 25 five-room houses and 40 four-room houses in the development.

$4 million but four million persons—the $ is equivalent of second numeral.

4.2 Numerals: 6th Fleet, 1st Army, 2nd Division, 10th Ward, 22nd District, 8th U.S. Circuit Court of Appeals.

Arabic numerals for spacecraft, missiles, etc.

4.3 Casual numbers are spelled:

A thousand times no! Gay Nineties. (See 3.14)

Wouldn't touch it with a ten-foot pole (but: The flag hung from a 10-foot pole—an exact measure).

4.4 Roman numerals are used for personal sequence, Pope, war, royalty, act, yacht and horse: John Jones III (some may prefer and use 3rd),

Pope John XXIII, World War I, King George V, Act II, Shamrock IX, Hanover II. (See 3.11)

4.5   Highways: U.S. 301, Interstate 90, Illinois 34.

4.6   In amounts of more than a million, round numbers take the dollar sign and million, billion, etc., are spelled. Decimalization is carried to two places: $4.35 million.

Exact amounts would be: $4,351,242.

Less than a million the form: $500, $1,000, $650,000, etc.

The same decimalization form is used for figures other than money such as population, automobile registration, etc. (See 4.1)

Spell "cents" in amounts less than a dollar. (See 4.1, 7.5)

See Section VII for exceptions in market routine.

In ranges: $12 million to $14 million (or billion) not $12 to $14 million (or billion).

4.7   The English pound sign is not used. Spell "pounds" after figures and convert to dollars. (See 3.28)

4.8   Fractions in Teletypesetter are confined to matrices of 8ths: $\frac{1}{8}$, $\frac{1}{4}$, $\frac{3}{8}$, $\frac{1}{2}$, $\frac{5}{8}$, $\frac{3}{4}$, $\frac{7}{8}$. Other fractions require the hyphen 3-16, 9-10, 1-3, etc.

Fractions used alone are spelled: three-fourths of a mile.

If the diagonal or slash (/) is incorporated in Teletypesetter operation, that symbol will replace the hyphen in fractions other than 8ths. The "plus" sign now occupies that casting-machine channel in the agate font and the hyphen will continue to be used in the agate font for fractions other than 8ths.

Stories dealing with percentages use figures; an isolated one-time reference under 10 is spelled as: four per cent of the population is illiterate.

4.9   Time sequences are given in figures: 2:30:21.6 (hours, minutes, seconds, tenths). (See 3.17)

4.10   Metric measurements use the comma in three-figure sequences except that kilocycles and meters in electronics are printed solid unless 10ths are included and the 10ths are set off by a period.

4.11   Serial numbers are printed solid: A1234567.

4.12   Write it No. 1 boy. No. 2 candidate, etc.

INDEX